Big Data Analytics Using Artificial Intelligence

Big Data Analytics Using Artificial Intelligence

Editors

Amir H. Gandomi
Fang Chen
Laith Abualigah

 Basel • Beijing • Wuhan • Barcelona • Belgrade • Novi Sad • Cluj • Manchester

Editors

Amir H. Gandomi
University of Technology Sydney
Ultimo, Australia

Fang Chen
University of Technology Sydney
Ultimo, Australia

Laith Abualigah
Middle East University
Amman, Jordan

Editorial Office
MDPI
St. Alban-Anlage 66
4052 Basel, Switzerland

This is a reprint of articles from the Special Issue published online in the open access journal *Electronics* (ISSN 2079-9292) (available at: https://www.mdpi.com/journal/electronics/special_issues/BDA_AI).

For citation purposes, cite each article independently as indicated on the article page online and as indicated below:

Lastname, A.A.; Lastname, B.B. Article Title. *Journal Name* **Year**, *Volume Number*, Page Range.

ISBN 978-3-0365-8766-0 (Hbk)
ISBN 978-3-0365-8767-7 (PDF)
doi.org/10.3390/books978-3-0365-8767-7

Contents

About the Editors . . . . **vii**

Abdelazim G. Hussien, Laith Abualigah, Raed Abu Zitar, Fatma A. Hashim, Mohamed Amin, Abeer Saber, et al.
Recent Advances in Harris Hawks Optimization: A Comparative Study and Applications
Reprinted from: *Electronics* **2022**, *11*, 1919, doi:10.3390/electronics11121919 . . . . **1**

Manisha Singh, Gurubasavaraj Veeranna Pujar, Sethu Arun Kumar, Meduri Bhagyalalitha, Handattu Shankaranarayana Akshatha, Belal Abuhaija, et al.
Evolution of Machine Learning in Tuberculosis Diagnosis: A Review of Deep Learning-Based Medical Applications
Reprinted from: *Electronics* **2022**, *11*, 2634, doi:10.3390/electronics11172634 . . . . **51**

Mohammad H. Nadimi-Shahraki, Shokooh Taghian, Seyedali Mirjalili, Laith Abualigah, Mohamed Abd Elaziz and Diego Oliva
EWOA-OPF: Effective Whale Optimization Algorithm to Solve Optimal Power Flow Problem
Reprinted from: *Electronics* **2021**, *10*, 2975, doi:10.3390/electronics10232975 . . . . **75**

Mohammad H. Nadimi-Shahraki, Saeed Mohammadi, Hoda Zamani, Mostafa Gandomi and Amir H. Gandomi
A Hybrid Imputation Method for Multi-Pattern Missing Data: A Case Study on Type II Diabetes Diagnosis
Reprinted from: *Electronics* **2021**, *10*, 3167, doi:10.3390/electronics10243167 . . . . **99**

Mohammad Kamel Daradkeh
A Hybrid Data Analytics Framework with Sentiment Convergence and Multi-Feature Fusion for Stock Trend Prediction
Reprinted from: *Electronics* **2022**, *11*, 250, doi:10.3390/electronics11020250 . . . . **119**

Noor Saleh Alfaiz and Suliman Mohamed Fati
Enhanced Credit Card Fraud Detection Model Using Machine Learning
Reprinted from: *Electronics* **2022**, *11*, 662, doi:10.3390/electronics11040662 . . . . **139**

Mona A. S. Ali, Kishore Balasubramanian, Gayathri Devi Krishnamoorthy, Suresh Muthusamy, Santhiya Pandiyan, Hitesh Panchal, et al.
Classification of Glaucoma Based on Elephant-Herding Optimization Algorithm and Deep Belief Network
Reprinted from: *Electronics* **2022**, *11*, 1763, doi:10.3390/electronics11111763 . . . . **155**

Fathimathul Rajeena P. P., Rasha Orban, Kogilavani Shanmuga Vadivel, Malliga Subramanian, Suresh Muthusamy, Diaa Salam Abd Elminaam, et al.
A Novel Method for the Classification of Butterfly Species Using Pre-Trained CNN Models
Reprinted from: *Electronics* **2022**, *11*, 2016, doi:10.3390/electronics11132016 . . . . **173**

Mohammad Daradkeh, Laith Abualigah, Shadi Atalla and Wathiq Mansoor
Scientometric Analysis and Classification of Research Using Convolutional Neural Networks: A Case Study in Data Science and Analytics
Reprinted from: *Electronics* **2022**, *11*, 2066, doi:10.3390/electronics11132066 . . . . **193**

Mona A. S. Ai, Anitha Shanmugam, Suresh Muthusamy, Chandrasekaran Viswanathan, Hitesh Panchal, Mahendran Krishnamoorthy
Real-Time Facemask Detection for Preventing COVID-19 Spread Using Transfer Learning Based Deep Neural Network
Reprinted from: *Electronics* **2022**, *11*, 2250, doi:10.3390/electronics11142250 . . . . **215**

Imran Mir, Faiza Gul, Suleman Mir, Mansoor Ahmed Khan, Nasir Saeed, Laith Abualigah, et al.
A Survey of Trajectory Planning Techniques for Autonomous Systems
Reprinted from: *Electronics* **2022**, *11*, 2801, doi:10.3390/electronics11182801 237

Shadi AlZu'bi, Raed Abu Zitar, Bilal Hawashin, Samia Abu Shanab, Amjed Zraiqat, Ala Mughaid, et al.
A Novel Deep Learning Technique for Detecting Emotional Impact in Online Education
Reprinted from: *Electronics* **2022**, *11*, 2964, doi:10.3390/electronics11182964 263

Muneer Nusir, Ali Louati, Hassen Louati, Usman Tariq, Raed Abu Zitar, Laith Abualigah and Amir H. Gandomi
Design Research Insights on Text Mining Analysis: Establishing the Most Used and Trends in Keywords of Design Research Journals
Reprinted from: *Electronics* **2022**, *11*, 3930, doi:10.3390/electronics11233930 287

Debabrata Swain, Utsav Mehta, Ayush Bhatt, Hardeep Patel, Kevin Patel, Devanshu Mehta, et al.
A Robust Chronic Kidney Disease Classifier Using Machine Learning
Reprinted from: *Electronics* **2023**, *12*, 212, doi:10.3390/electronics12010212 309

Amir H. Gandomi, Fang Chen and Laith Abualigah
Big Data Analytics Using Artificial Intelligence
Reprinted from: *Electronics* **2023**, *12*, 957, doi:10.3390/electronics12040957 323

About the Editors

Amir H. Gandomi

Amir H. Gandomi is a Professor of Data Science and an ARC DECRA Fellow at the Faculty of Engineering & Information Technology, University of Technology Sydney. He is also affiliated with Obuda University, Budapest, as a Distinguished Professor. Prior to joining UTS, Prof. Gandomi was an Assistant Professor at Stevens Institute of Technology, and a distinguished research fellow at BEACON center, Michigan State University. Prof. Gandomi has published 350+ journal papers and 12 books, which collectively have been cited 44,000+ times (H-index = 94). He has been named as one of the most influential scientific minds and received the Highly Cited Researcher award (top 1% publications and 0.1% researchers) from Web of Science for six consecutive years, from 2017 to 2022. In the recent most impactful researcher list, done by Stanford University and released by Elsevier, Prof Amir H Gandomi is ranked among the top 1,000 researchers (top 0.01%) and top 50 researchers in AI and Image Processing subfield in 2021! He also ranked 17th in GP bibliography among more than 15,000 researchers. He has received multiple prestigious awards for his research excellence and impact, such as the 2023 Achenbach Medal and the 2022 Walter L. Huber Prize, the highest-level mid-career research award in all areas of civil engineering. He has served as associate editor, editor, and guest editor in several prestigious journals, such as AE of IEEE Networks and IEEE IoTJ. His research interests are global optimisation and (big) data analytics using machine learning and evolutionary computations in particular.

Fang Chen

Distinguished Professor Fang Chen is an award-winning, internationally recognised leader in artificial intelligence (AI) and data science. She is passionately innovative in her work, architecting and implementing data-driven solutions to problems met in industry and governments. Her experience in solving these complex real-life problems in large-scale networks spans transport, water, energy, health, agriculture and many more sectors. She is also actively promoting ethical, human-centred AI. Fang won the "Oscar" of Australian science – the Australian Museum Eureka Prize 2018 for Excellence in Data Science. She is the "Water Professional of the Year", awarded by the Australian Water Association in 2016. In 2021, she won the Australia and New Zealand "Women in AI" Award in Infrastructure and the NSW Premier's Prize of Science and Engineering. Fang leads multidisciplinary teams of experts, with whom she has won major scientific and industry awards on the national level. These include the Intelligent Transport Systems Australia National Award 2014, 2015 and 2018; the NSW iAwards 2017; the VIC iAwards 2019 and 2020; and the National Award and NSW "Research and Innovation Award" 2018 and 2022 from the Australian Water Association. She has built up a career in achieving innovation, developing digital transformation strategies, and executing them with leadership and passion. Her vast experience in many segments of industry, governments, and academic environments allows her to formulate strategies for innovation, development, products and business growth. Distinguished Professor Chen also has extensive global experience with more than 100 different entities across North America, Europe and many parts of Asia, under extremely varied circumstances from early-stage R&D to product development and deployment.

Laith Abualigah

Laith Abualigah is an Associate Professor at Prince Hussein Bin Abdullah College for Information Technology, Al Al-Bayt University, Jordan. He is also a distinguished researcher at the

School of Computer Science, Universiti Sains Malaysia, Malaysia. He received his first degree from Al-Albayt University, Computer Information System, Jordan, in 2011. He earned a Master's degree in Computer Science from Al-Albayt University, Jordan, in 2014. He received a Ph.D. degree from the School of Computer Science at Universiti Sains Malaysia (USM), Malaysia, in 2018. According to the report published by Clarivate, he was a highly cited researcher in 2021 and 2022 and among the 1% influential researchers, which depicts the 6,938 top scientists in the world. He was also the first researcher in the domain of Computer Science in Jordan in 2021. According to the report published by Stanford University in 2020, Abualigah is one of the top 2% most influential scholars, which depicts the 100,000 top scientists in the world. Abualigah has published more than 400 journal papers and books, which collectively have been cited more than 15100 times (H-index = 58). His main research interests focus on Arithmetic Optimization Algorithm (AOA), Bio-inspired Computing, Nature-inspired Computing, Swarm Intelligence, Artificial Intelligence, Meta-heuristic Modeling, and Optimization Algorithms, Evolutionary Computations, Information Retrieval, Text clustering, Feature Selection, Combinatorial Problems, Optimization, Advanced Machine Learning, Big data, and Natural Language Processing.

Review

Recent Advances in Harris Hawks Optimization: A Comparative Study and Applications

Abdelazim G. Hussien [1,2,*], **Laith Abualigah** [3], **Raed Abu Zitar** [4], **Fatma A. Hashim** [5], **Mohamed Amin** [6], **Abeer Saber** [7], **Khaled H. Almotairi** [8] and **Amir H. Gandomi** [9,*]

[1] Department of Computer and Information Science, Linköping University, 581 83 Linköping, Sweden
[2] Faculty of Science, Fayoum University, Fayoum 2933110, Egypt
[3] Faculty of Computer Sciences and Informatics, Amman Arab University, Amman 11953, Jordan; aligah.2020@gmail.com
[4] Sorbonne Center of Artificial Intelligence, Sorbonne University-Abu Dhabi, Abu Dhabi 38044, United Arab Emirates; raed.zitar@sorbonne.ae
[5] Faculty of Engineering, Helwan University, Cairo 4034572, Egypt; fatma_hashim@h-eng.helwan.edu.eg
[6] Faculty of Science, Menoufia University, Menoufia 6131567, Egypt; mohamed_amin110@yahoo.com
[7] Department of Computer Science, Faculty of Computers and Information, Kafr El-Sheikh University, Kafr El-Sheikh 6860404, Egypt; abeersaber@gmail.com
[8] Computer Engineering Department, Computer and Information Systems College, Umm Al-Qura University, Makkah 21955, Saudi Arabia; khmotairi@uqu.edu.sa
[9] Faculty of Engineering and Information Technology, University of Technology Sydney, Ultimo, NSW 2007, Australia
[*] Correspondence: abdelazim.hussien@liu.se (A.G.H.); gandomi@uts.edu.au (A.H.G.)

Citation: Hussien, A.G.; Abualigah, L.; Abu Zitar, R.; Hashim, F.A.; Amin, M.; Saber, A.; Almotairi, K.H.; Gandomi, A.H. Recent Advances in Harris Hawks Optimization: A Comparative Study and Applications. *Electronics* **2022**, *11*, 1919. https://doi.org/10.3390/electronics11121919

Academic Editor: Esteban Tlelo-Cuautle

Received: 3 May 2022
Accepted: 10 June 2022
Published: 20 June 2022

Publisher's Note: MDPI stays neutral with regard to jurisdictional claims in published maps and institutional affiliations.

Abstract: The Harris hawk optimizer is a recent population-based metaheuristics algorithm that simulates the hunting behavior of hawks. This swarm-based optimizer performs the optimization procedure using a novel way of exploration and exploitation and the multiphases of search. In this review research, we focused on the applications and developments of the recent well-established robust optimizer Harris hawk optimizer (HHO) as one of the most popular swarm-based techniques of 2020. Moreover, several experiments were carried out to prove the powerfulness and effectivness of HHO compared with nine other state-of-art algorithms using Congress on Evolutionary Computation (CEC2005) and CEC2017. The literature review paper includes deep insight about possible future directions and possible ideas worth investigations regarding the new variants of the HHO algorithm and its widespread applications.

Keywords: Harris hawks optimization; metaheuristics; optimization problems; variants; applications

1. Introduction

The optimization area has witnessed a wide range of applications in understanding the solutions of many new problems due to the fast progress of industrial technologies and artificial intelligence [1–5]. Such rapid progress requires the development of new technologies for tackling hard and challenging problems in a reasonable time. Many proposals and research attempts have been introduced by researchers with years of experience based on two classes of deterministic methods and stochastic-based methods [6–9]. In the first-class, there is a need for gradient info and details of the search space. The later class does not need such info and can handle black-box optimization without knowing mathematics details of the objective function, based on sensing and touching the surface of the problems. One of the popular classes of these stochastic optimizers is a swarm and evolutionary method [10–13]. Table 1 shows a list of metaheuristic algorithms belonging to this class and their algorithmic behavior.

Table 1. A list of some optimization algorithms based on their components.

Class	Algorithmic Behavior	Algorithms	Ref.	Year
Evolutionary	Breeding-based Evolution	Genetic Algorithm (GA)	[14]	1992
	Breeding-based Evolution	Genetic programming (GP)	[15]	1992
	Influenced by representative solutions	Differential Evolution (DE)	[16]	1997
	Breeding-based Evolution	Evolution Strategies	[17]	2002
	Mathematical Arithmetic operators	Arithmetic Optimization Algorithm	[18]	2021
Swarm intelligence	Influenced by representative solutions	Particle Swarm Optimization (PSO)	[19]	1995
	Creation and Stimergy	Ant Colony optimization (ACO)	[20]	1999
	Creation–Combination	Harmony Search Algorithm (HS)	[21]	2001
	Influenced by representative solutions	Artificial Bee Colony (ABC)	[22]	2007
	Influenced by the entire population	Central Force Optimization (CFO)	[23]	2007
	Creation–Combination	Biogeography-based optimization (BBO)	[24]	2008
	Influenced by representative solutions	Cuckoo Search (CS)	[25]	2009
	Influenced by neighborhoods	Bacterial Foraging Optimization (BFO)	[26]	2009
	Influenced by the entire population	Gravitational Search Algorithm (GSA)	[27]	2009
	Influenced by the entire population	Firefly Optimizer (FFO)	[28]	2010
	Influenced by representative solutions	Teaching–Learning-Based Optimizer (TLBO)	[29]	2011
	Influenced by representative solutions	Fruit Fly Optimization (FFO)	[30]	2012
	Influenced by representative solutions	Krill Herd (KH)	[31]	2012
	Influenced by representative solutions	Grey Wolf Optimizer (GWO)	[32]	2014
	Influenced by representative solutions	Harris Hawks Optimizer (HHO)	[33]	2019
	Influenced by representative solutions	Henry Gas Solubility Optimization (HGSO)	[34]	2019
	Influenced by representative solutions	Slime mold algorithm (SMA)	[35]	2020
	Influenced by mating behavior of snakes	Snake Optimizer	[36]	2022

These swarm-based and evolutionary methods seed a random set of solutions as initial guesses, and then they evolve and improve the initial solutions until convergence to a high-quality suboptimal or optimal solution [37–41]. The core operators of evolutionary techniques are crossovers and mutations to generate new gens from parent solutions based on some ideas inspired by the evolution of nature. The swarm-based solvers may also use such operations, but they organize initial swarms based on the interaction of two fundamental cores for scattering them and then intensifying them into specific high-potential areas [42–44]. Swarm-based approaches are developed and utilized in many areas of machine learning and artificial intelligence according to the cooperative intellect life of self-organized and reorganized coordination, e.g., artificial clusters of randomly generated agents. This way of problem solving is well-known among the swarm-intelligence community; due to such a delicate balance between the exploration and exploitation steps, it is a hard target to achieve [45–47].

There are many ways to classify these methods as well, but generally, some researchers, who benefit from a source of inspiration, classify these methods based on their source of inspiration [48–50]. More scientific classification has been conducted based on the algorithmic behavior of these methods by [51–53]. However, this field has some diseases that still have not healed. First, many population-based methods cannot show a high performance or novelty in their mathematical rationalities but have a new source of inspiration, and they are well-known as questioned metaphor-based methods. For instance, the well-known gray wolf optimizer (GWO) has a structural defect, and it shows uncertain performance for problems whose optimal solutions are not zero but near-zero points such as epsilon, as discovered by [54,55]. Moreover, the core equations of many new optimizers can be constructed using the particle swarm optimizer (PSO) and differential evolution (DE) methods or other popular swarm-based methods [56]. This means the inspiration and metaphor-based language made it easy to develop unoriginal or "pseudonovel" solvers that show "pseudoefficient" efficacy. More and more, the wisdom of new researchers grows, they understand and reach the conclusion that "performance matters", not the source of inspiration. The Harris hawk optimizer (HHO) was an attempt to reach not only better performance but also low-cost and efficient operators within a new stochastic optimizer.

Another way that exists in the literature is a method that distinguishes each method based on the source of inspiration. Based on this system of classification, metaheuristic algorithms (MAs) can be classified into five different categories: Evolutionary Algorithms, Swarm Intelligence, Physics-based algorithms, Human-based algorithms, and Sport-based algorithms [57]. The first category, Evolutionary Algorithms (EAs), refers to algorithms which are inspired by nature and simulate natural creatures' behaviors such as mutations, crossover, selection, elitism, and reproduction. Examples of these algorithms are the Genetic Algorithm (GA) by [14], Genetic Programming (GP) by [58], Differential Evolution (DE) by [16], Evolutionary Programming (EP) by [59], Evolution Strategy (ES) by [60], Biogeography-Based Optimizer (BBO) by [24], and Backtracking Search Algorithm (BSA) by [61]. The second category is Swarm-Intelligence (SI)-based algorithms, which are inspired from the social behavior of swarms, birds, insects, fish, and animals. The top three most popular examples of SI algorithms are Particle Swarm Optimization (PSO) by [19], Ant Colony Optimization (ACO) by [20], and Artificial Bee Colony (ABC) Algorithm by [62]. Some other SI-based algorithms that have their place in the literature regardless of their performance and originality include the Cuckoo Search Algorithm (CS) by [25], Firefly Algorithm (FA) by [63], COOT bird [64], Krill Herd (KH) by [31], Cat Swarm Optimization (CSO) by [65], Bat Algorithm (BA) by [66], Symbiotic Organisms Search (SOS) [67], Grey Wolf Optimizer (GWO) by [32], Moth–Flame Optimization (MFO) Algorithm checked by [68,69], Virus Colony Search (VCS) [70], Whale Optimization Algorithm (WOA)checked by [71,72], Grasshopper Optimization Algorithm (GOA) by [73], Salp Swarm Algorithm by [74,75], Crow Search Algorithm (CSA) reviewed by [76], Symbiotic Organisms Search (SOS) by [77], Reptile Search Algorithm (RSA) by [78], Butterfly Optimization Algorithm (BOA) by [79], Remora Optimization Algorithm (ROA) [80], Wild Horse Optimizer (WHO) [81], Seagull Optimization Algorithm (SOA) by [82], and Ant Lion Optimizer (ALO) reviewed by [83]. The third category is the Physics-based algorithms, which refers to the algorithms inspired from chemical rules or physical phenomena. Some examples of this class are Simulated Annealing (SA) by [84], Gravitational Search Algorithm (GSA) by [27], Big-Bang Big-Crunch (BBBC) by [85], Lightning Search Algorithm (LSA) by [86], Electromagnetic Field Optimization (EFO) by [87], Thermal Exchange Optimization (TEO) by [88], Vortex Search Algorithm (VSA) by [89], Electrosearch Algorithm (ESA) by [90], Atom Search Optimization (ASO) by [91], Chemical Reaction Optimization by [92], and Henry Gas Solubility Optimization (HGSO) by [34]. The fourth class is Human-based algorithms (HA), which refers to the algorithms inspired from human behaviors such as Harmony Search (HS) by [21], Teaching–Learning-Based Algorithm (TLBO) by [29], the ideology algorithm by [93], human mental search (HMS) by [94], Brain storm optimization (BSO) by [95], Social Emotional Optimization Algorithm (ESOA) by [96], Socio-Evolution and Learning Optimization (SELO) by [97], and Human Group Formation (HGF) by [98]. The last category is Sport-based algorithms that simulate sport activities and games. Some interesting examples include League Championship Algorithm by [99], Golden Ball Algorithm by [100], World Cup Optimization by [101], Arithmetic Optimization Algorithm (AOA) by [18], and others [81,102,103].

The Harris hawks optimization is a recently developed algorithm that simulates Harris hawks' special hunting behavior known as "seven kills". The HHO algorithm [33] has some unique features compared with other popular swarm-based optimization methods. The first is that this optimizer utilizes a time-varying rule which evolves by more iterations of the method during exploration and exploitation. Such a way of shifting from exploration to exploitation propensities can make it subsequently flexible when the optimizer is in front of an undesirable difficulty in the feature space. Another advantage is that the algorithm has a progressive trend during the convergence process and when shifting from the first diversification/exploration phase to the intensification/exploitation core. The quality of results in HHO is relatively higher compared with other popular methods, and this feature also supported the widespread applications of this solver. Moreover, the exploitation phase of this method is compelling based on a greedy manner in picking the best solutions explored so far and ignoring low-quality solutions obtained until that iteration. We review different applications of this optimizer in the next parts of this survey to see how its features make it a fitting choice for real-world cases.

HHO is similar to all metaheurstics algorithms. HHO has many benefits (advantages) and a smaller number of disadvantages. HHO advantages can be listed as follows:

- Good convergence speed.
- Powerful neighborhood search characteristic.
- Good balance between exploration and exploitation.
- Suitable for many kinds of problems.
- Easy to implement.
- Adaptability, scalability, flexibility, and robustness.

The disadvantages of HHO, as with all other algorithms, is that it may stick in local optima, and there is no theatrical converging study frame.

This paper is organized as follows. Section 2 presents the original procedure of the studied HHO. Section 3 presents the variants of the HHO. Section 4 presents the application of the HHO. Section 5 presents a brief discussion about the HHO with its advantages. Finally, the conclusion and future works are given in Section 6.

2. Review Methodology

The aims of this study are to present a comprehensive review of all HHO aspects and how the researchers and scholars are encouraged and motivated to use it in various disciplines. Since the suggestion of this algorithm, it has received huge attention from scholars all over the world. According to Google Scholar (https://scholar.google.com/scholar?cites=16912266037349375725&as_sdt=2005&sciodt=0,5&hl=en (accessed on 31 December 2021)), it has been cited more than "1231" times. Moreover, the original study is also selected as a hot paper and one of the most ranked studies in both Scopus (https://www.scopus.com/record/pubmetrics.uri?eid=2-s2.0-85063421586&origin=recordpage (accessed on 31 December 2021)) and Web of Science (https://www.webofscience.com/wos/woscc/full-record/WOS:000469154500064 (accessed on 31 December 2021)). Firstly, a preliminary study was conducted, after that, we performed a search on studies that referred to the HHO original study to make a list of keywords we must use to perform the search. Secondly, skimming and scanning methods were used to select relevant studies. Thirdly, a checking and screening process was performed to extract data. Finally, we sorted the data and classified ideas (papers).

3. Harris Hawks Optimization (HHO)

The Harris hawks optimization is a recently introduced population-based optimization method suggested by Heidari et al. [33] in which the authors tried to simulate the Harris hawk's cooperative behavior in nature. Some hawks try to surprise prey using some techniques (tracing and encircling–approaching and attacking). The HHO pseudocode can be founded in Algorithm 1. The authors simulated hawks' behavior in 3 steps.

The logical diagram of the HHO can be given in Figure 1.

(i) The first step (exploration phase) can be formulated as follows:

$$X(t+1) = \begin{cases} X_{rand}(t) - r_1|X_{rand}(t) - 2r_2X(t)| & q \geq 0.5 \\ X_{rabbit}(t) - X_m(t) - r_3(LB + r_4(UB - LB)) & if \ r_4 < 0.5 \end{cases} \tag{1}$$

where $X(t)$ and $X(t+1)$ refer to hawk location in the current iteration and next iteration, respectively, $r_1, r_2, r_3, r_4,$ and q are stochastic numbers in the interval $[0,1]$, X_{rabbit} and $X_{rand}(t)$ refer to rabbit location (best position) and randomly selected hawk location, respectively, and $X_m(t)$ can be calculated from the following Equation (2).

$$X_m(t) = \frac{1}{N}\sum_{i=1}^{N} X_i(t) \tag{2}$$

where $X_i(t)$ refers to each hawk position and N is the maximum iteration number.

(ii) Transition from exploration to exploitation

$$E = 2E_o(1 - \frac{t}{T})$$ (3)

where E_o and E are the initial energy and the escaping energy, respectively. If $E_o \geq 1$, then exploration occurs. Otherwise, exploitation happens. This step can be identified in 4 scenarios:

Soft besiege: occurs if $r \geq 0.5$ and $|E| \geq 0.5$, which can be obtained from the following equation:

$$X(t+1) = \Delta X(t) - E|JX_{rabbit}(t) - X(t)|$$ (4)

$$\Delta X(t) = X_{rabbit} - X(t)$$ (5)

$\Delta X(t)$ refers to the difference between location of current hawk and location of prey. $J = 2(1 - r_5)$ where $r_5 \in [0, 1]$.

Hard besiege occurs if $r \geq 0$ and $|E| < 0$. This scenario is formulated as:

$$X(t+1) = X_{rabbit} - E|\Delta X(t)|$$ (6)

Advanced rapid dives while soft surround: if $r < 0$ and $|E| \geq 0$. The next hawk move is obtained by Equation (7).

$$Y = X_{rabbit}(t) - E|JX_{rabbit(t)-X(t)}|$$ (7)

$$Z = Y + S \times LF(D)$$ (8)

where S is a random vector and D refers to dimension. LF is levy flight, which can be obtained from the following equation:

$$LF(x) = \frac{u \times \sigma}{|v|^{\frac{1}{\beta}}}, \sigma = (\frac{\Gamma(1+\beta) \times sin(\frac{\pi\beta}{2})}{\Gamma(\frac{1+\beta}{2} \times \beta \times 2^{\frac{\beta-1}{2}})})^{\frac{1}{\beta}}$$ (9)

where β is fixed and equal to 1.5, u and v refer to random numbers $\in (0, 1)$. The final equation can be given as

$$X(t+1) = \begin{cases} Y & F(Y) < F(X(t)) \\ Z & F(Z) < F(X(t)) \end{cases}$$ (10)

Advanced rapid dives while hard surround: occurs if $r < 0.5$ and $|E| < 0.5$. This behavior can be shown as follows:

$$X(t+1) = \begin{cases} Y' & F(Y') < F(X(t)) \\ Z' & F(Z') < F(X(t)) \end{cases}$$ (11)

where Y' and Z' are calculated from the following equations:

$$Y' = X_{rabbit}(t) - E|JX_{rabbit} - X_m|$$ (12)

$$Z' = Y + S \times LF(D)$$ (13)

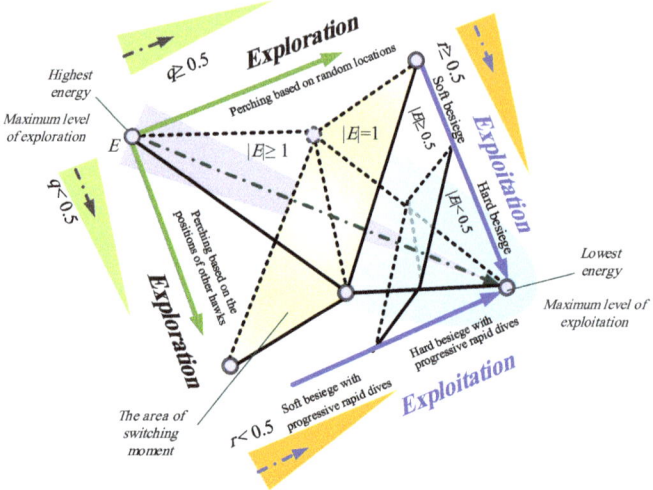

Figure 1. The logical diagram of HHO.

Algorithm 1 Harris Hawks Optimization Algorithm.

Initialize the parameters (Popsize (N), MaxIter (T), LB, UB, and Dim
Initialize a population x_i i = 1, 2, …, n.
while (*iter* $\leq$ *MaxIter*) **do**
    Compute the fitness function for each hawk x_i
    X_{rabbit} = the best search agent
    for each hawk (x_i) **do**
        Update initial energy E_o, Jump Strength J Equation (3)
        if ($|E| \geq 1$) **then**
            Update hawk position using Equation (1)
        end if
        if ($|E| < 1$) **then**
            if ($r \geq 0.5$ and $|E| \geq 0.5$) **then**
                Update hawk position by Equation (4)
            else if ($r \geq 0.5$ and $|E| < 0.5$) **then**
                Update hawk position by Equation (6)
            else if ($r < 0.5$ and $|E| \geq 0.5$) **then**
                Update hawk position by Equation (8)
            else if
                then Update hawk using Equation (9)
            end if
        end if
    end for
end while
Return X_{rabbit}.

---

4. Experimental Results

4.1. Parameter Setting

In all these experiments, we used the same parameter setting, which is given in Table 2, which gives the number of dimensions, number of individuals, and maximum number of iterations. These experiments were carried out using Matlab 2021b on Intel(R) Core(TM) i5-5200 machine with 6 GBs of RAM. The setting of compared algorithms in both CEC2005 and CEC2017 can be found in Table 3.

Table 2. Experiments parameters settings.

No.	Parameter Name	Value
1	Population Size	30
2	Dim	30
3	Max number of iteration	500

Table 3. Metaheuristic algorithms parameters settings.

Alg.	Parameter	Value
GOA	GMaX	1
	GMin	0.004
	fl	2
TEO	u	1
	v	0.001
SCA	a	2
EHO	Elephants number	50
	Clans number	5
	Kept elephants number	2
	The scale factor α	0.5
	The scale factor β	0.1
SSA	c_1, c_2, c_3	*rand*
WOA	a	2
HHO	β	1.5
AEO	r_1, r_2, and r	*rand*
	h	$2 \times \text{rand} - 1$
L-SHADE	Pbest	0.1
	Arc rate	2
LSHADE-EpSin	Pbest	0.1
	Arc rate	2
CMAES	α	2

4.2. Experimental Results of CEC 2005

CEC 2005 is a classical benchmark mathematical functions that contains many mathematical function types (Unimodal, multimodal, hybrid, and composite). Here, we compared HHO with the Genetic Algorithm (GA) [104], Covariance Matrix adaptation Evolution Strategy (CMAES) [105], Linear population size reduction-Success-History Adaptation for Differential Evolution (L-SHADE) [106], Ensemble Sinusoidal incorporated with L-SHADE (LSHADE-EpSin) [107], Sine Cosine Algorithm (SCA) [108], Grasshopper Optimization Algorithm (GOA) [73], Whale Optimization Algorithm (WOA) [48], Thermal Exchange Optimization (TEO) [88], and Artificial Ecosystem Optimization (AEO) [109].

Table 4 shows the results of these algorithms. It is easy to notice that the HHO has a good performance compared with the others. Moreover, Figures 2 and 3 show the convergence curves of these algorithms, whereas Figures 4 and 5 show their boxplot. The Wilcoxon Rank Sum (WRS) test was carried out with a 5% percentage between the HHO and the other algorithms to prove its superiority. The results of the Wilcoxon test can be found in Table 5.

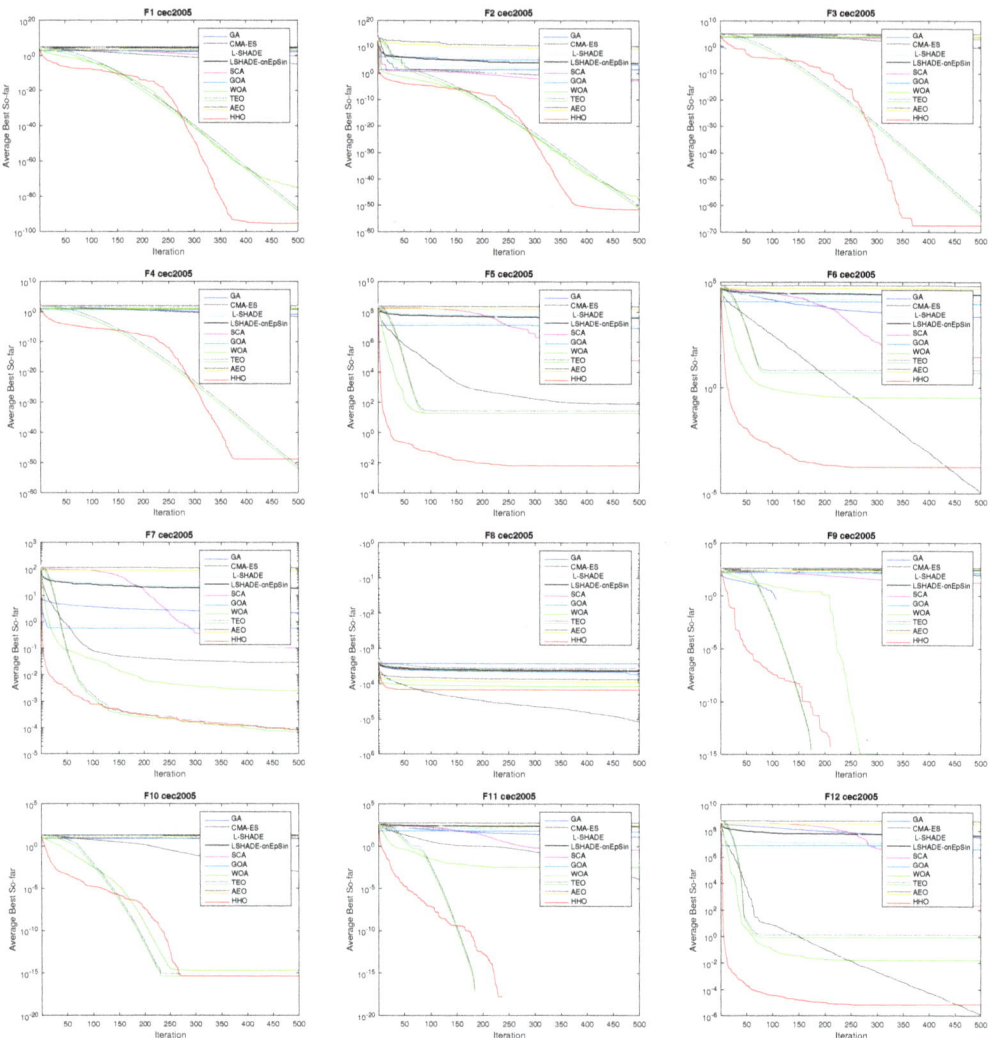

Figure 2. Convergence curve for HHO against other competitors from F1–F12 CEC2005.

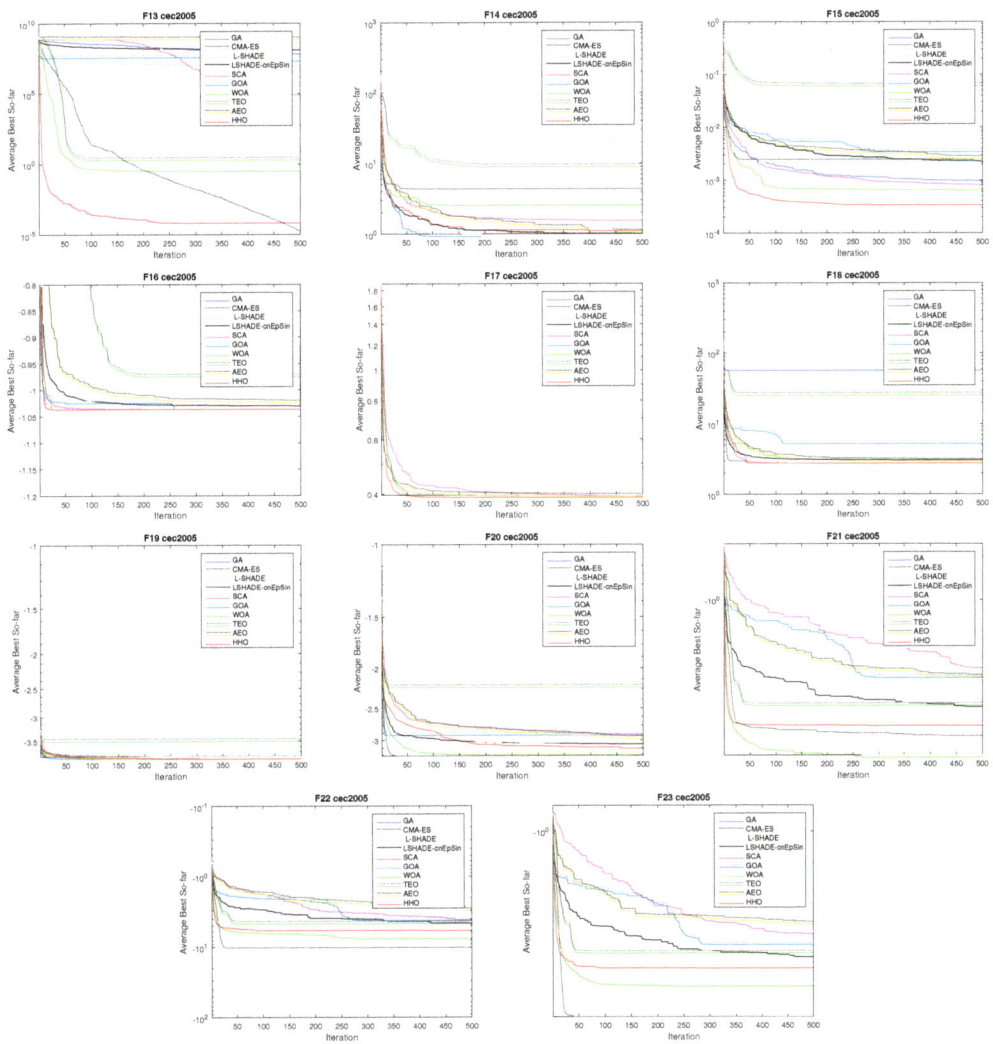

Figure 3. Convergence curve for HHO against other competitors from F13–F23 CEC2005.

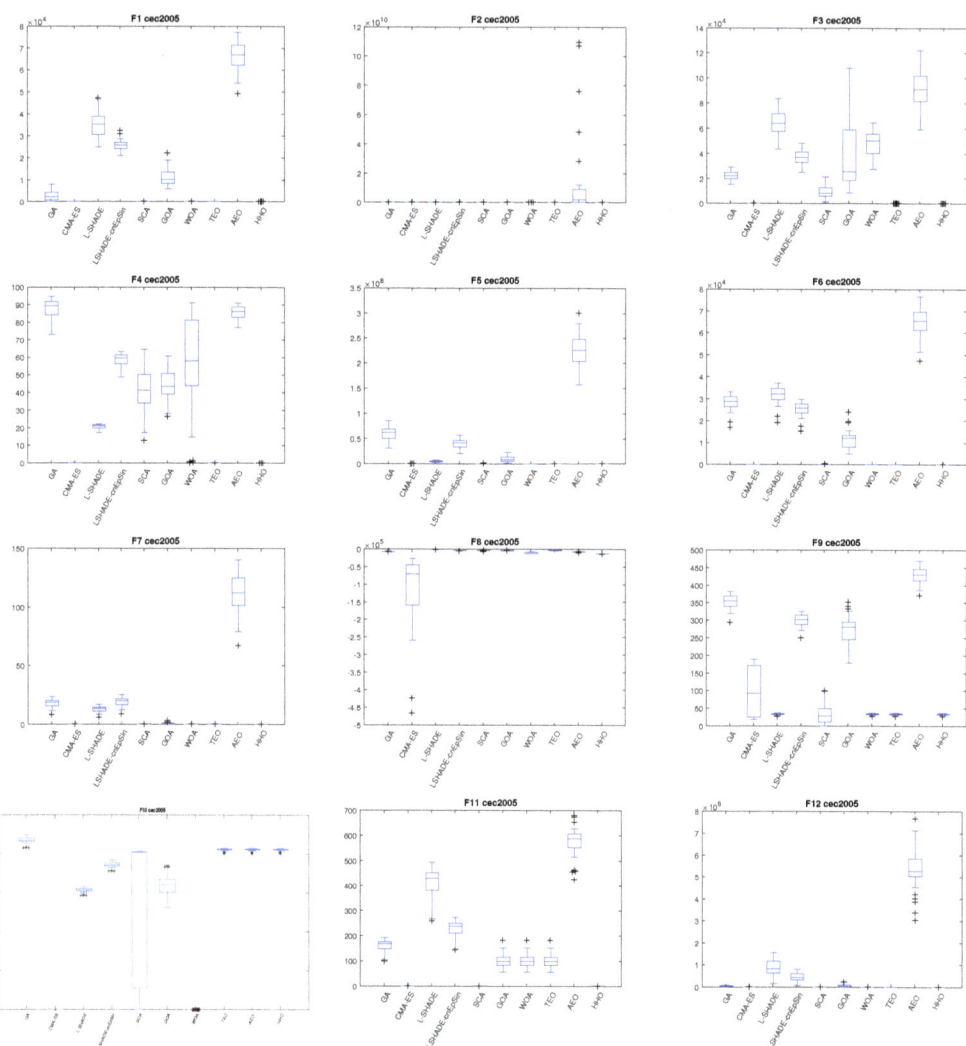

Figure 4. Boxplot of some functions from F1–F12 for all algorithms.

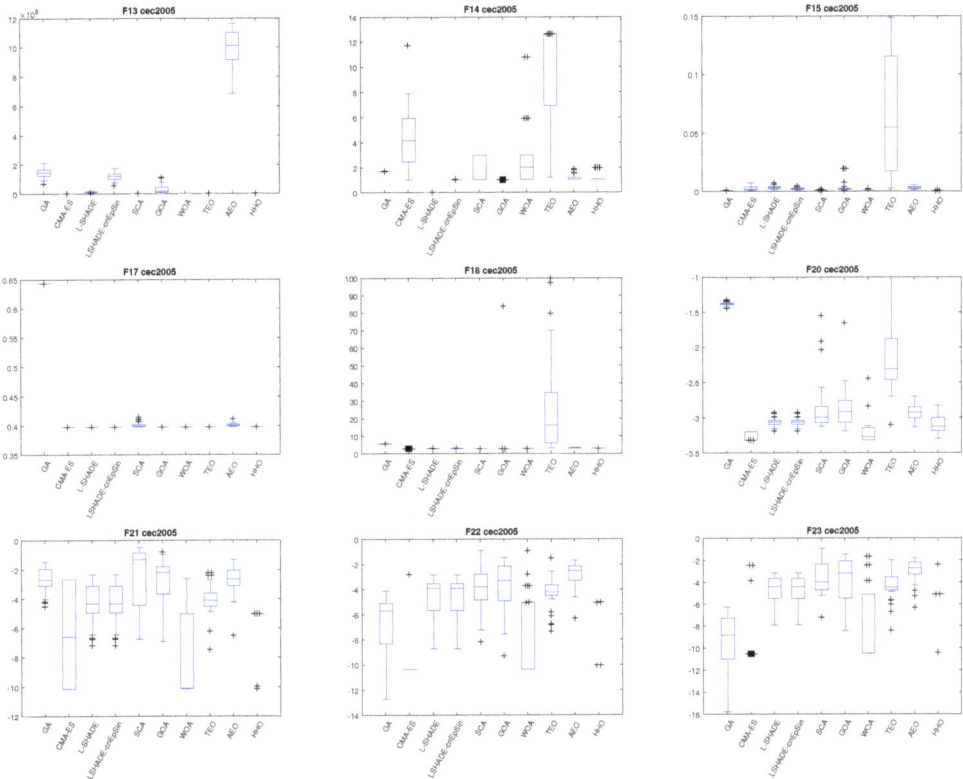

Figure 5. Boxplot of some functions from F13–F23 for all algorithms.

4.3. Experimental Results of CEC 2017

To prove the powerfulness and effectiveness of the HHO, we performed a comparison between HHO and the number of metaheurstic algorithms using CEC 2017. These algorithms are the Genetic Algorithm (GA) [104], Linear population size reduction-Success-History Adaptation for Differential Evolution (L-SHADE) [106], Ensemble Sinusoidal incorporated with L-SHADE (LSHADE-EpSin) [107], Sine Cosine Algorithm (SCA) [108], Grasshopper Optimization Algorithm (GOA) [73], Whale Optimization Algorithm (WOA) [48], Thermal Exchange Optimization (TEO) [88], Artificial Ecosystem Optimization (AEO) [109], and Henry Gas solubility optimization (HGSO) [34].

The results of such a comparison are shown in Table 6 in terms of average and standard deviation for fitness value. From this table, it is clear that the HHO has a good performance. Moreover, Figures 6–8 show convergence curves of the HHO compared with the above-mentioned algorithms, where we conclude that the HHO has a good speed convergence. Moreover, Figures 9–11 show the boxplot of the HHO compared with the other algorithms.

Table 4. The comparison results of all algorithms over 23 functions.

F		GA	CMAES	L-SHADE	LSHADE-EpSin	SCA	GOA	WOA	TEO	AEO	HHO
F1	Avg	2.79×10^3	9.74×10^{-6}	3.52×10^4	2.57×10^4	8.87	1.10×10^4	4.38×10^{-74}	1.58×10^{-87}	6.64×10^4	8.61×10^{-95}
	STD	2.20×10^3	4.55×10^{-6}	6.18×10^3	2.62×10^3	1.24×10^1	4.15×10^3	1.56×10^{-73}	7.38×10^{-88}	6.18×10^3	4.50×10^{-94}
F2	Avg	1.53×10^2	4.98×10^{-3}	6.03×10^3	4.50×10^3	1.24×10^{-2}	8.48×10^2	1.06×10^{-74}	6.57×10^{-51}	1.44×10^{10}	2.24×10^{-51}
	STD	8.70	2.28×10^{-3}	1.68×10^4	1.26×10^4	1.56×10^{-2}	3.53×10^3	5.82×10^{-74}	1.27×10^{-50}	3.03×10^{10}	8.46×10^{-51}
F3	Avg	5.66×10^{-1}	4.60×10^{-1}	6.45×10^4	3.70×10^4	8.80×10^3	3.91×10^4	4.79×10^4	1.08×10^{-63}	9.11×10^4	3.26×10^{-67}
	STD	3.55×10^{-1}	2.38×10^{-1}	9.94×10^3	5.70×10^3	5.10×10^3	2.81×10^4	1.06×10^4	5.89×10^{-63}	1.44×10^4	1.78×10^{-66}
F4	Avg	1.02	2.34×10^{-2}	2.05×10^1	5.83×10^1	4.01×10^1	4.40×10^1	5.57×10^1	8.53×10^{-52}	8.58×10^1	1.22×10^{-48}
	STD	1.22×10^{-1}	5.16×10^{-3}	1.37	3.89	1.36×10^1	8.62	2.94×10^1	3.09×10^{-52}	3.59	4.49×10^{-48}
F5	Avg	9.04×10^1	8.08×10^1	5.03×10^6	4.02×10^7	8.70×10^4	1.01×10^7	2.79×10^1	2.90×10^1	2.24×10^8	9.37×10^{-3}
	STD	1.16×10^2	1.88×10^2	1.19×10^6	9.55×10^6	2.50×10^5	6.05×10^6	5.39×10^{-1}	3.36×10^{-2}	3.71×10^7	1.36×10^{-2}
F6	Avg	2.91×10^3	1.13×10^{-5}	3.15×10^4	2.51×10^4	3.63×10^1	1.15×10^4	4.53×10^{-1}	6.71	6.49×10^4	2.28×10^{-4}
	STD	2.03×10^3	4.74×10^{-6}	4.19×10^3	3.34×10^3	7.15×10^1	4.43×10^3	2.31×10^{-1}	7.18×10^{-1}	6.69×10^3	2.94×10^{-4}
F7	Avg	2.65	2.88×10^{-2}	1.25×10^1	1.87×10^1	1.21×10^{-1}	6.26×10^{-1}	3.15×10^{-3}	8.50×10^{-5}	1.11×10^2	1.05×10^{-4}
	STD	7.81×10^{-1}	9.43×10^{-3}	2.61	3.91	1.20×10^{-1}	6.74×10^{-1}	3.83×10^{-3}	6.77×10^{-5}	1.85×10^1	9.05×10^{-5}
F8	Avg	-2.29×10^3	-1.19×10^5	-9.60×10^2	-4.28×10^3	-3.79×10^3	-4.52×10^3	-9.99×10^3	-3.63×10^3	-7.46×10^3	-1.26×10^4
	STD	5.31×10^2	1.10×10^5	5.71×10^1	2.55×10^2	4.11×10^2	5.50×10^2	1.76×10^3	9.25×10^2	5.94×10^2	1.40
F9	Avg	5.68×10^1	9.64×10^1	3.34×10^1	2.98×10^2	3.39×10^1	2.74×10^2	0.00	0.00	4.29×10^2	0.00
	STD	2.45×10^1	7.02×10^1	1.94	1.74×10^1	3.07×10^1	4.03×10^1	0.00	0.00	2.48×10^1	0.00
F10	Avg	8.22×10^1	9.78×10^{-4}	1.53×10^1	1.85×10^1	1.43×10^1	1.59×10^1	4.09×10^{-15}	8.88×10^{-16}	2.05×10^1	8.88×10^{-16}
	STD	3.65×10^1	2.01×10^{-4}	3.11×10^{-1}	3.77×10^{-1}	8.79	1.45	2.70×10^{-16}	0.00	1.64×10^{-1}	0.00
F11	Avg	2.47×10^1	1.31×10^{-4}	4.06×10^2	2.24×10^2	7.81×10^{-1}	1.01×10^2	6.97×10^{-3}	0.00	5.73×10^2	0.00
	STD	2.07×10^1	5.06×10^{-5}	6.57×10^1	3.63×10^1	3.78×10^{-1}	2.85×10^1	2.69×10^{-2}	0.00	6.20×10^1	0.00
F12	Avg	4.89×10^7	1.23×10^{-6}	8.70×10^7	4.46×10^7	3.38×10^2	6.18×10^6	2.58×10^{-2}	1.33	5.33×10^8	1.10×10^{-5}
	STD	4.40×10^7	5.97×10^{-7}	3.63×10^7	1.86×10^7	9.13×10^2	7.74×10^6	1.49×10^{-2}	2.64×10^{-1}	9.99×10^7	1.64×10^{-5}
F13	Avg	9.06×10^7	1.89×10^{-5}	1.21×10^7	1.18×10^8	1.24×10^5	2.87×10^7	4.75×10^{-1}	3.00	9.85×10^8	1.00×10^{-4}
	STD	7.53×10^7	6.95×10^{-6}	2.91×10^6	2.84×10^7	4.31×10^5	3.03×10^7	3.02×10^{-1}	2.79×10^{-3}	1.35×10^8	2.29×10^{-4}

Table 4. *Cont.*

F		GA	CMAES	L-SHADE	LSHADE-EpSin	SCA	GOA	WOA	TEO	AEO	HHO
F14	Avg	4.02×10^{-1}	4.33	9.07×10^{-1}	1.00	1.66	9.9×10^{-1}	2.77	9.78	1.15	1.20
	STD	3.75×10^{-3}	2.45	8.47×10^{-3}	9.36×10^{-3}	9.48×10^{-1}	4.30×10^{-16}	2.65	3.73	2.47×10^{-1}	4.04×10^{-1}
F15	Avg	3.19×10^{-3}	2.49×10^{-3}	3.38×10^{-3}	2.17×10^{-3}	9.25×10^{-4}	3.80×10^{-3}	7.30×10^{-4}	6.71×10^{-2}	2.86×10^{-3}	3.75×10^{-4}
	STD	1.38×10^{-3}	1.65×10^{-3}	1.47×10^{-3}	9.40×10^{-4}	3.53×10^{-4}	5.57×10^{-3}	5.05×10^{-4}	5.22×10^{-2}	1.16×10^{-3}	1.67×10^{-4}
F16	Avg	-1.03	-1.03	-1.03	-1.03	-1.03	-1.03	-1.03	-9.70×10^{-1}	-1.02	-1.03
	STD	1.43×10^{-3}	6.78×10^{-16}	1.43×10^{-1}	1.43×10^{-3}	4.76×10^{-5}	3.21×10^{-13}	2.53×10^{-9}	1.20×10^{-1}	1.08×10^{-2}	5.55×10^{-9}
F17	Avg	3.98×10^{-1}	3.98×10^{-1}	3.98×10^{-1}	3.98×10^{-1}	4.01×10^{-1}	3.98×10^{-1}	3.98×10^{-1}	3.98×10^{-1}	4.01×10^{-1}	3.98×10^{-1}
	STD	8.87×10^{-6}	8.87×10^{-6}	8.87×10^{-6}	8.87×10^{-6}	4.24×10^{-6}	8.87×10^{-6}	8.87×10^{-6}	8.87×10^{-6}	2.86×10^{-3}	3.88×10^{-5}
F18	Avg	6.21×10^1	3.00	3.04	3.04	3.00	5.70	3.00	2.75×10^1	3.18	3.00
	STD	6.18×10^1	1.13×10^{-15}	4.38×10^{-2}	4.38×10^{-2}	1.00×10^{-4}	1.48×10^1	1.46×10^{-4}	2.91×10^1	1.68×10^{-1}	5.56×10^{-7}
F19	Avg	-3.86	-3.86	-3.86	-3.86	-3.85	-3.86	-3.86	-3.44	-3.85	-3.86
	STD	2.83×10^{-3}	2.71×10^{-15}	2.83×10^{-3}	2.83×10^{-3}	3.63×10^{-3}	2.83×10^{-3}	1.00×10^{-2}	2.87×10^{-1}	5.09×10^{-3}	3.78×10^{-3}
F20	Avg	-3.07	-3.27	-3.07	-3.07	-2.86	-2.87	-3.21	-2.19	-2.93	-3.10
	STD	5.62×10^{-2}	5.99×10^{-2}	5.62×10^{-2}	5.62×10^{-2}	3.83×10^{-1}	3.00×10^{-1}	1.80×10^{-1}	4.42×10^{-1}	1.12×10^{-1}	1.31×10^{-1}
F21	Avg	-4.30	-6.39	-4.30	-4.30	-2.46	-2.81	-8.36	-4.08	-2.78	-5.38
	STD	1.41	3.65	1.41	1.41	1.96	1.73	2.59	1.12	9.83×10^{-1}	1.27
F22	Avg	-4.71	-1.01×10^1	-4.71	-4.71	-3.79	-3.88	-7.03	-4.29	-2.84	-5.4137
	STD	1.69	1.39	1.69	1.69	1.72	1.94	3.11	1.29	1.01	1.261067
F23	Avg	-4.70	-9.77	-4.70	-4.70	-3.44	-3.91	-6.51	-4.33	-3.04	-5.21
	STD	1.30	2.34	1.30	1.30	1.70	2.32	3.12	1.31	1.07	1.10

Table 5. Wilcoxon rank sum test results for HHO against other algorithms CEC2020 Dim = 20.

F	GA	L-SHADE	LSHADE-EpSin	SCA	GOA	WOA	TEO	HGSO	AEO
F1	3.01986×10^{-11}	3.01986×10^{-11}	3.01986×10^{-11}	3.01986×10^{-11}	3.01986×10^{-11}	3.01986×10^{-11}	3.01986×10^{-11}	3.01986×10^{-11}	3.01986×10^{-11}
F2	3.01986×10^{-11}	3.01986×10^{-11}	3.01986×10^{-11}	3.01986×10^{-11}	3.01986×10^{-11}	3.01986×10^{-11}	0.673495053	9.53321×10^{-11}	3.01986×10^{-11}
F3	1.21178×10^{-12}	3.01986×10^{-11}	3.01986×10^{-11}	3.01986×10^{-11}	3.01986×10^{-11}	3.01986×10^{-11}	3.01986×10^{-11}	5.57265×10^{-11}	3.01986×10^{-11}
F4	1.72025×10^{-12}	3.01986×10^{-12}	3.01986×10^{-11}	3.01986×10^{-11}	3.01986×10^{-11}	3.01986×10^{-11}	3.01986×10^{-11}	0.853381737	3.01986×10^{-11}
F5	1.21178×10^{-12}	3.01986×10^{-11}	3.01986×10^{-11}	3.01986×10^{-11}	3.01986×10^{-11}	3.01986×10^{-11}	3.01986×10^{-11}	3.01986×10^{-11}	3.01986×10^{-11}
F6	3.019×10^{-11}	6.356×10^{-5}	3.019×10^{-11}	3.019×10^{-11}	3.019×10^{-11}	3.019×10^{-11}	3.019×10^{-11}	3.019×10^{-11}	3.019×10^{-11}
F7	3.019×10^{-11}	3.019×10^{-11}	3.019×10^{-11}	3.019×10^{-11}	3.019×10^{-11}	3.019×10^{-11}	2.921×10^{-11}	0.559230536	3.019×10^{-11}
F8	3.019×10^{-11}	3.019×10^{-11}	3.019×10^{-11}	3.019×10^{-11}	3.019×10^{-11}	3.019×10^{-11}	1.776×10^{-10}	3.019×10^{-11}	3.019×10^{-11}
F9	1.211×10^{-12}	1.211×10^{-12}	1.211×10^{-12}	1.211×10^{-12}	1.211×10^{-12}	1.211×10^{-12}	NaN	NaN	1.211×10^{-12}
F10	1.193×10^{-12}	1.211×10^{-12}	1.211×10^{-12}	1.211×10^{-12}	1.211×10^{-12}	1.211×10^{-12}	1.024×10^{-7}	NaN	1.211×10^{-12}
F11	1.211×10^{-12}	1.211×10^{-12}	1.211×10^{-12}	1.211×10^{-12}	1.211×10^{-12}	1.211×10^{-12}	0.160802121	1.211×10^{-12}	1.211×10^{-12}
F12	3.017×10^{-11}	0.005322078	3.019×10^{-11}	3.019×10^{-11}	3.019×10^{-11}	3.019×10^{-11}	3.019×10^{-11}	3.019×10^{-11}	3.019×10^{-11}
F13	8.480×10^{-9}	0.818745653	3.019×10^{-11}	3.019×10^{-11}	3.017×10^{-11}	3.017×10^{-11}	3.017×10^{-11}	3.017×10^{-11}	3.019×10^{-11}
F14	3.019×10^{-11}	9.755×10^{-10}	3.019×10^{-11}	6.76501×10^{-5}	1.107×10^{-6}	2.110×10^{-11}	0.000556111	5.494×10^{-11}	6.765×10^{-5}
F15	3.019×10^{-11}	6.695×10^{-11}	3.019×10^{-11}	4.504×10^{-11}	5.072×10^{-10}	4.077×10^{-11}	3.157×10^{-5}	3.019×10^{-11}	3.338×10^{-11}
F16	3.019×10^{-11}	1.211×10^{-12}	3.019×10^{-11}	3.019×10^{-11}	3.019×10^{-11}	1.697×10^{-8}	0.773119942	2.389×10^{-8}	3.019×10^{-11}
F17	0.311053163	0.311053163	0.311053163	0.311053163	5.427×10^{-11}	0.311053163	0.311053163	0.311053163	5.427×10^{-11}
F18	3.019×10^{-11}	4.107×10^{-12}	3.019×10^{-11}	3.019×10^{-11}	8.993×10^{-11}	2.002×10^{-6}	1.956×10^{-10}	3.019×10^{-11}	3.019×10^{-11}
F19	0.000268057	1.211×10^{-12}	0.000268057	0.000268057	2.601×10^{-8}	0.000268057	0.157975689	8.152×10^{-11}	9.832×10^{-8}
F20	0.045146208	8.885×10^{-9}	0.045146208	0.045146208	0.000158461	0.000149316	0.00033679	9.918×10^{-11}	6.282×10^{-10}
F21	0.000178356	0.725538189	0.000178356	0.000178356	5.967×10^{-9}	6.045×10^{-7}	3.081×10^{-8}	5.967×10^{-9}	4.615×10^{-10}
F22	0.006097142	1.943×10^{-10}	0.006097142	0.006097142	5.967×10^{-9}	0.000178356	0.003182959	4.744×10^{-6}	4.615×10^{-10}
F23	0.003848068	2.251×10^{-8}	0.003848068	0.003848068	3.964×10^{-8}	0.002052334	0.000356384	3.157×10^{-5}	3.351×10^{-8}

Table 6. The comparison results of all algorithms over 30 functions.

F		GA	L-SHADE	LSHADE-EpSin	SCA	GOA	WOA	TEO	HGSO	AEO	HHO
F1	Avg	4.83×10^{10}	1.11×10^{10}	5.36×10^{10}	2.10×10^{10}	6.68×10^{10}	5.29×10^{9}	6.32×10^{10}	2.31×10^{10}	1.13×10^{11}	5.13×10^{8}
	STD	9.34×10^{8}	4.83×10^{9}	8.13×10^{9}	3.75×10^{10}	1.16×10^{10}	1.56×10^{9}	8.36×10^{9}	4.77×10^{8}	1.37×10^{10}	3.09×10^{8}
F2	Avg	NA	NA	NA	NA	NA	NA	NA	NA	NA	NA
	STD	NA	NA	NA	NA	NA	NA	NA	NA	NA	NA
F3	Avg	6.28×10^{9}	1.77×10^{5}	1.28×10^{5}	7.87×10^{4}	3.29×10^{5}	2.85×10^{5}	9.12×10^{4}	7.15×10^{4}	2.50×10^{5}	5.57×10^{4}
	STD	2.66×10^{10}	5.49×10^{4}	1.88×10^{4}	1.29×10^{4}	1.51×10^{5}	7.90×10^{4}	7.33×10^{3}	6.75×10^{3}	4.56×10^{4}	6.11×10^{3}
F4	Avg	2.54×10^{4}	1.94×10^{3}	1.33×10^{4}	3.29×10^{3}	1.61×10^{4}	1.32×10^{3}	2.37×10^{4}	4.54×10^{3}	3.53×10^{4}	7.31×10^{2}
	STD	8.39×10^{3}	6.54×10^{2}	2.63×10^{3}	8.81×10^{2}	6.18×10^{3}	4.43×10^{2}	4.20×10^{3}	1.34×10^{3}	5.98×10^{3}	1.43×10^{2}
F5	Avg	8.34×10^{2}	8.19×10^{2}	9.42×10^{2}	8.30×10^{2}	1.00×10^{3}	8.61×10^{2}	9.38×10^{2}	8.60×10^{2}	1.14×10^{3}	7.57×10^{2}
	STD	2.91×10^{1}	2.16×10^{1}	1.89×10^{1}	2.40×10^{1}	5.82×10^{1}	5.06×10^{1}	3.59×10^{1}	2.00×10^{1}	5.19×10^{1}	3.45×10^{1}
F6	Avg	6.60×10^{2}	6.53×10^{2}	6.91×10^{2}	6.65×10^{2}	7.07×10^{2}	6.84×10^{2}	6.97×10^{2}	6.79×10^{2}	7.27×10^{2}	6.69×10^{2}
	STD	9.87	8.04	7.11	6.21	1.64×10^{1}	1.30×10^{1}	6.63	6.38	7.30	6.94
F7	Avg	1.36×10^{3}	1.24×10^{3}	2.07×10^{3}	1.23×10^{3}	1.78×10^{3}	1.32×10^{3}	1.45×10^{3}	1.26×10^{3}	3.40×10^{3}	1.32×10^{3}
	STD	6.94×10^{1}	6.71×10^{1}	9.70×10^{1}	5.82×10^{1}	1.67×10^{2}	7.93×10^{1}	5.77×10^{1}	5.13×10^{1}	2.64×10^{2}	6.23×10^{1}
F8	Avg	1.08×10^{3}	1.10×10^{3}	1.20×10^{3}	1.10×10^{3}	1.24×10^{3}	1.07×10^{3}	1.16×10^{3}	1.10×10^{3}	1.36×10^{3}	9.85×10^{2}
	STD	3.58×10^{1}	3.45×10^{1}	2.60×10^{1}	1.98×10^{1}	4.93×10^{1}	6.39×10^{1}	2.48×10^{1}	1.99×10^{1}	4.66×10^{1}	1.96×10^{1}
F9	Avg	1.63×10^{4}	8.37×10^{3}	1.68×10^{4}	8.52×10^{3}	2.13×10^{4}	1.06×10^{4}	1.08×10^{4}	9.02×10^{3}	3.32×10^{4}	8.94×10^{3}
	STD	3.73×10^{3}	2.57×10^{3}	1.86×10^{3}	1.91×10^{3}	6.80×10^{3}	3.48×10^{3}	1.27×10^{3}	9.62×10^{2}	4.37×10^{3}	7.75×10^{2}
F10	Avg	7.91×10^{3}	9.39×10^{3}	8.83×10^{3}	8.88×10^{3}	8.99×10^{3}	7.51×10^{3}	9.22×10^{3}	7.71×10^{3}	9.02×10^{3}	5.93×10^{3}
	STD	5.12×10^{2}	6.82×10^{2}	3.02×10^{2}	4.0×10^{2}	6.72×10^{2}	7.13×10^{2}	4.89×10^{2}	4.55×10^{2}	2.99×10^{2}	7.74×10^{2}
F11	Avg	2.19×10^{5}	7.38×10^{3}	9.12×10^{3}	3.58×10^{3}	2.87×10^{4}	1.05×10^{4}	4.02×10^{4}	6.01×10^{3}	2.29×10^{4}	1.65×10^{3}
	STD	3.42×10^{5}	3.92×10^{3}	1.85×10^{3}	1.11×10^{3}	1.16×10^{4}	4.64×10^{3}	7.88×10^{4}	7.81×10^{2}	5.70×10^{3}	1.58×10^{2}
F12	Avg	1.37×10^{10}	8.41×10^{8}	8.03×10^{9}	2.90×10^{9}	9.36×10^{9}	5.23×10^{8}	1.94×10^{9}	3.77×10^{9}	1.64×10^{10}	9.86×10^{7}
	STD	3.05×10^{9}	3.82×10^{8}	1.53×10^{9}	7.99×10^{8}	3.60×10^{8}	3.82×10^{8}	3.20×10^{8}	1.13×10^{8}	3.09×10^{8}	6.97×10^{7}

Table 6. *Cont.*

F		GA	L-SHADE	LSHADE-EpSin	SCA	GOA	WOA	TEO	HGSO	AEO	HHO
F13	Avg	1.99×10^{10}	2.56×10^{8}	3.64×10^{9}	1.15×10^{8}	5.93×10^{8}	1.47×10^{7}	2.17×10^{10}	1.70×10^{9}	9.16×10^{9}	1.07×10^{6}
	STD	6.87×10^{9}	2.73×10^{8}	9.23×10^{8}	5.04×10^{8}	3.28×10^{9}	1.93×10^{7}	7.87×10^{9}	8.10×10^{8}	2.62×10^{9}	6.62×10^{5}
F14	Avg	8.26×10^{7}	1.00×10^{6}	1.66×10^{6}	7.71×10^{5}	6.71×10^{6}	2.26×10^{6}	3.47×10^{7}	$1.46v$	3.61×10^{6}	1.70×10^{6}
	STD	5.40×10^{7}	1.13×10^{6}	7.57×10^{5}	8.49×10^{5}	$5.18v$	2.55×10^{6}	3.77×10^{7}	6.04×10^{5}	1.61×10^{6}	1.69×10^{6}
F15	Avg	4.01×10^{9}	1.96×10^{7}	4.42×10^{8}	6.70×10^{7}	7.82×10^{8}	6.64×10^{6}	1.99×10^{8}	1.15×10^{7}	1.15×10^{9}	1.27×10^{5}
	STD	1.67×10^{9}	2.10×10^{7}	1.74×10^{8}	5.54×10^{7}	4.90×10^{8}	7.77×10^{6}	9.49×10^{8}	6.46×10^{6}	4.44×10^{8}	8.11×10^{4}
F16	Avg	7.76×10^{3}	4.17×10^{3}	4.97×10^{3}	4.07×10^{3}	5.07×10^{3}	4.52×10^{3}	8.20×10^{3}	4.30×10^{3}	5.98×10^{3}	3.71×10^{3}
	STD	1.37×10^{3}	3.11×10^{2}	2.42×10^{2}	3.05×10^{2}	5.74×10^{2}	6.95×10^{2}	2.17×10^{3}	2.58×10^{2}	3.87×10^{2}	5.04×10^{2}
F17	Avg	5.87×10^{4}	2.97×10^{3}	3.29×10^{3}	2.82×10^{3}	3.79×10^{3}	2.78×10^{3}	1.56×10^{4}	2.97×10^{3}	4.28×10^{3}	2.75×10^{3}
	STD	5.39×10^{4}	2.23×10^{2}	1.38×10^{2}	1.76×10^{2}	4.24×10^{2}	3.41×10^{2}	1.54×10^{4}	1.79×10^{2}	4.47×10^{2}	2.49×10^{2}
F18	Avg	6.24×10^{8}	1.12×10^{7}	2.39×10^{7}	1.43×10^{7}	8.22×10^{7}	1.34×10^{7}	3.95×10^{8}	1.18×10^{7}	5.33×10^{7}	3.37×10^{6}
	STD	4.07×10^{8}	9.78×10^{6}	1.08×10^{7}	9.37×10^{6}	7.69×10^{7}	1.53×10^{7}	3.66×10^{8}	5.69×10^{6}	3.47×10^{7}	3.79×10^{6}
F19	Avg	4.48×10^{9}	2.26×10^{7}	6.65×10^{8}	8.85×10^{7}	1.08×10^{9}	2.17×10^{7}	2.65×10^{9}	5.60×10^{7}	2.58×10^{9}	1.58×10^{6}
	STD	2.27×10^{9}	2.25×10^{7}	2.89×10^{8}	3.94×10^{7}	6.25×10^{8}	3.15×10^{7}	1.59×10^{9}	3.52×10^{7}	8.11×10^{8}	1.44×10^{6}
F20	Avg	3.24×10^{3}	3.23×10^{3}	2.97×10^{3}	2.96×10^{3}	3.25×10^{3}	2.93×10^{3}	3.28×10^{3}	2.84×10^{3}	3.20×10^{3}	2.83×10^{3}
	STD	1.53×10^{2}	1.70×10^{2}	1.24×10^{2}	1.53×10^{2}	1.15×10^{2}	2.31×10^{2}	2.28×10^{2}	1.27×10^{2}	1.15×10^{2}	1.92×10^{2}
F21	Avg	2.66×10^{3}	2.59×10^{3}	2.71×10^{3}	2.60×10^{3}	2.77×10^{3}	2.62×10^{3}	2.81×10^{3}	2.64×10^{3}	2.87×10^{3}	2.61×10^{3}
	STD	7.17×10^{1}	3.12×10^{1}	2.28×10^{1}	2.38×10^{1}	6.02×10^{1}	6.05×10^{1}	5.82×10^{1}	3.05×10^{1}	3.13×10^{1}	6.02×10^{1}
F22	Avg	8.87×10^{3}	6.67×10^{3}	8.68×10^{3}	1.01×10^{4}	9.70×10^{3}	8.19×10^{3}	1.00×10^{4}	5.02×10^{3}	1.02×10^{4}	$7.05v$
	STD	1.54×10^{3}	2.62×10^{3}	6.30×10^{2}	1.02×10^{3}	1.28×10^{3}	1.73×10^{3}	7.17×10^{2}	8.07×10^{2}	4.15×10^{2}	2.03×10^{3}
F23	Avg	3.42×10^{3}	3.00×10^{3}	3.34×10^{3}	3.08×10^{3}	3.23×10^{3}	3.15×10^{3}	4.03×10^{3}	3.23×10^{3}	3.41×10^{3}	3.32×10^{3}
	STD	1.25×10^{2}	4.88×10^{1}	4.35×10^{1}	3.41×10^{1}	1.08×10^{2}	7.73×10^{1}	2.33×10^{2}	6.06×10^{1}	5.20×10^{1}	1.92×10^{2}

Table 6. *Cont.*

F		GA	L-SHADE	LSHADE-EpSin	SCA	GOA	WOA	TEO	HGSO	AEO	HHO
F24	Avg	3.59×10^3	3.15υ	3.55×10^3	3.25×10^3	3.28×10^3	3.23×10^3	4.48×10^3	3.44×10^3	3.51×10^3	3.46×10^3
	STD	1.37×10^2	4.37×10^1	5.89×10^1	4.67×10^1	5.97×10^1	9.13×10^1	2.27×10^2	6.22×10^1	4.62×10^1	1.68×10^2
F25	Avg	1.15×10^4	3.54×10^3	6.81×10^3	3.62×10^3	6.89×10^3	3.26×10^3	6.78×10^3	3.68×10^3	1.56×10^4	3.01×10^3
	STD	3.54×10^3	1.96×10^2	8.53×10^2	2.44×10^2	1.71×10^3	8.79×10^1	9.49×10^2	2.18×10^2	2.27×10^3	3.43×10^1
F26	Avg	1.30×10^4	7.34×10^3	1.04×10^4	8.03×10^3	1.02×10^4	8.41×10^3	1.31×10^4	8.40×10^3	1.25×10^4	8.10×10^3
	STD	1.78×10^3	4.72×10^2	5.16×10^2	3.66×10^2	1.19×10^3	1.31×10^3	1.16×10^3	6.20×10^2	7.50×10^2	1.23×10^3
F27	Avg	4.47×10^3	3.38×10^3	3.97×10^3	3.56×10^3	3.66×10^3	3.48×10^3	5.66×10^3	3.20×10^3	3.70×10^3	3.61×10^3
	STD	3.75×10^2	4.85×10^1	1.25×10^2	7.56×10^1	2.39×10^2	1.37×10^2	5.72×10^2	8.63×10^{-5}	9.64×10^1	1.96×10^2
F28	Avg	9.66×10^3	4.22×10^3	6.96×10^3	4.52×10^3	7.55×10^3	3.89×10^3	8.33×10^3	4.65×10^3	8.82×10^3	3.50×10^3
	STD	1.75×10^3	3.56×10^2	5.10×10^2	4.34×10^2	1.24×10^3	2.27×10^2	8.61×10^2	6.86×10^2	8.00×10^2	1.34×10^2
F29	Avg	1.09×10^5	5.23×10^3	5.98×10^3	5.35×10^3	6.57×10^3	5.66×10^3	1.71×10^4	5.28×10^3	6.76×10^3	5.06×10^3
	STD	1.15×10^5	3.13×10^2	3.76×10^2	3.78×10^2	8.11×10^2	6.46×10^2	9.77×10^3	4.97×10^2	6.18×10^2	4.11×10^2
F30	Avg	3.25×10^9	3.64×10^7	4.81×10^9	2.03×10^8	7.21×10^8	6.96×10^7	3.63×10^8	2.07×10^8	9.92×10^8	1.52×10^7
	STD	1.25×10^9	2.41×10^7	1.29×10^8	8.22×10^7	5.21×10^8	6.95×10^7	1.79×10^9	6.29×10^7	2.79×10^8	1.32×10^7

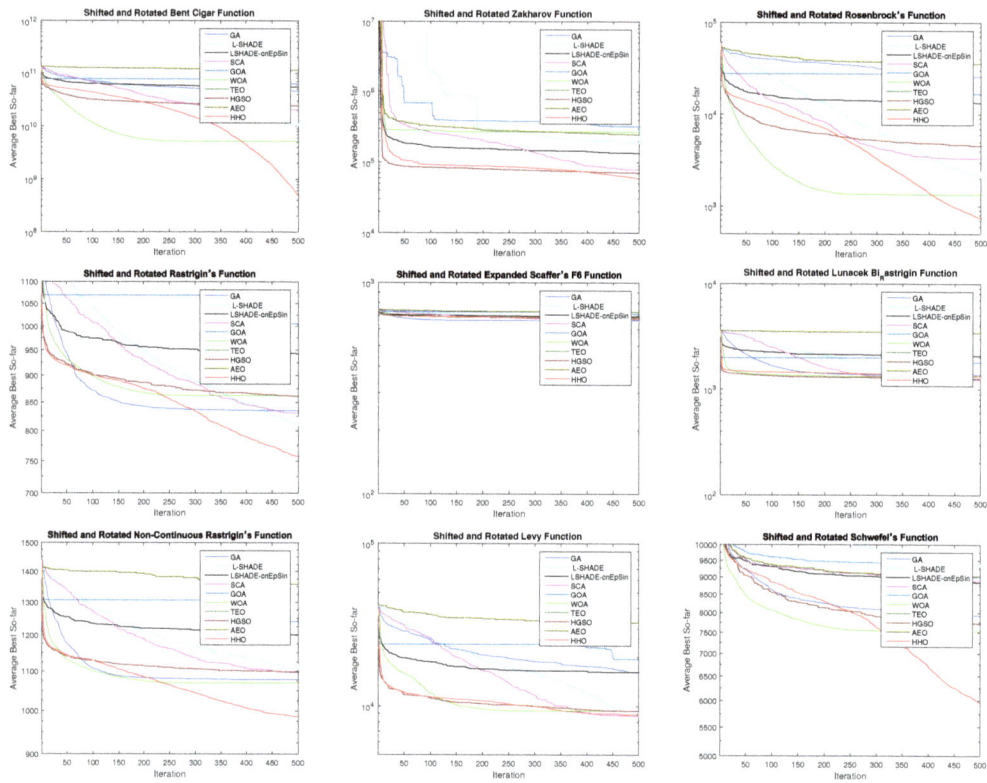

Figure 6. Convergence curve for HHO against other competitors from F1–F10 CEC2017.

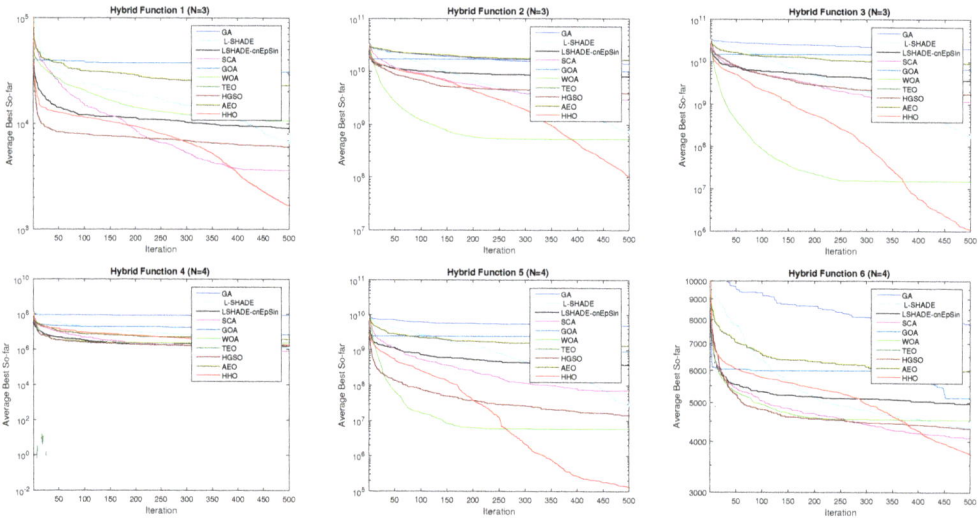

Figure 7. *Cont.*

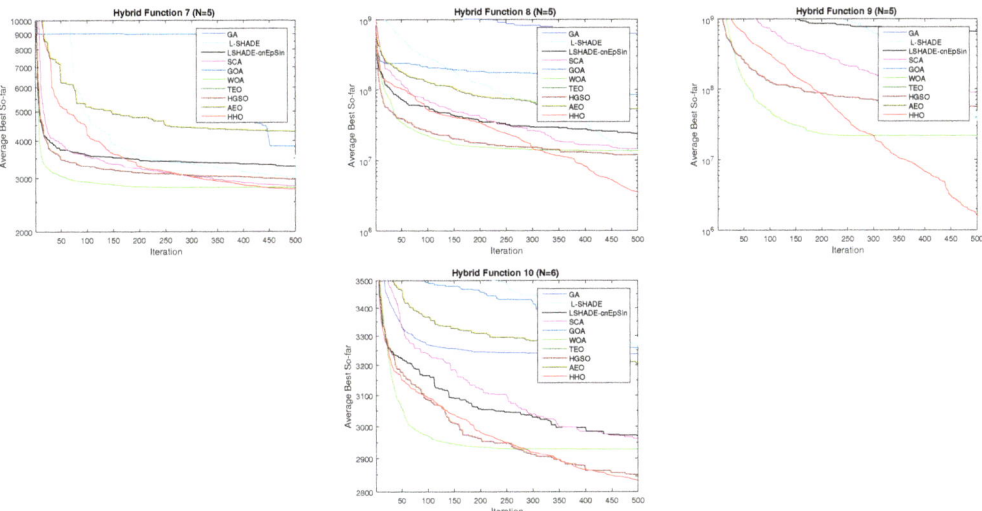

Figure 7. Convergence curve for HHO against other competitors from F11–F20 CEC2017.

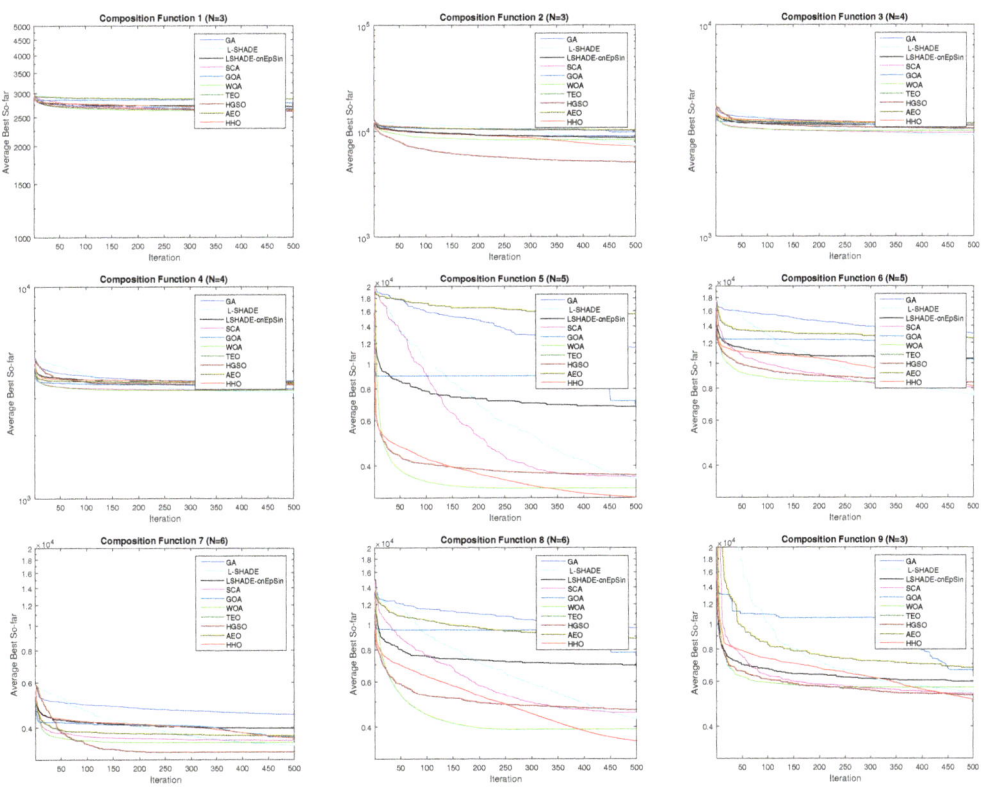

Figure 8. *Cont.*

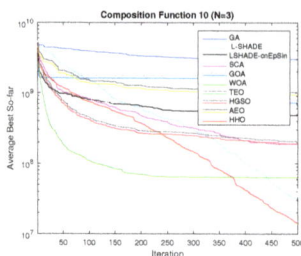

Figure 8. Convergence curve for HHO against other competitors from F21—F30 CEC2017.

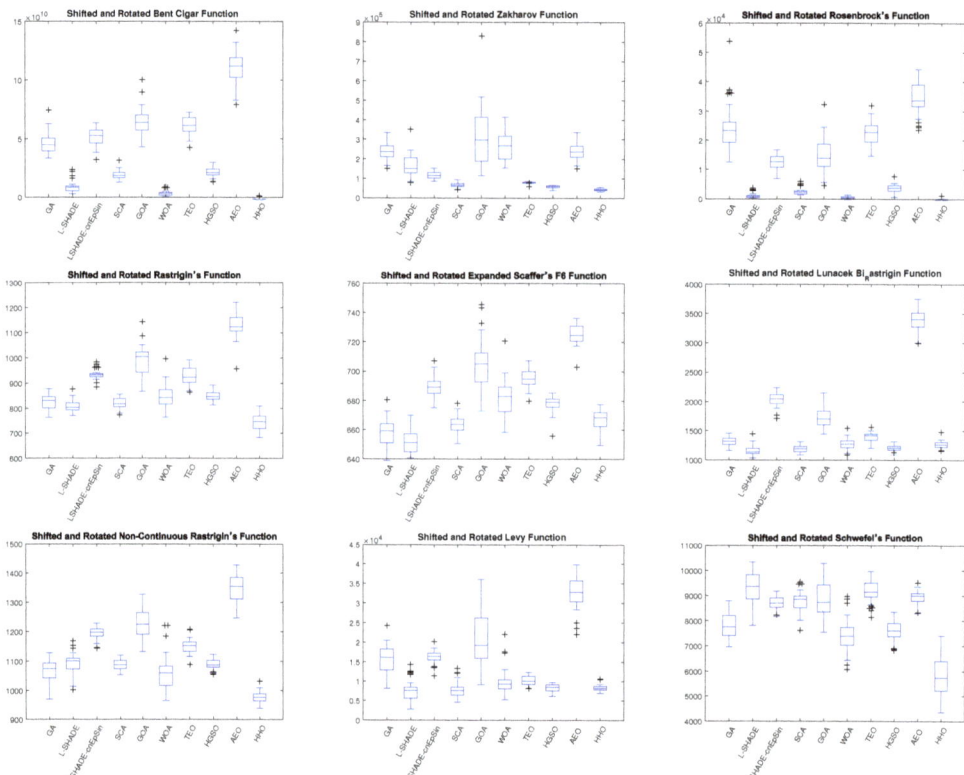

Figure 9. Boxplot of some functions from F1–F10 for all algorithms.

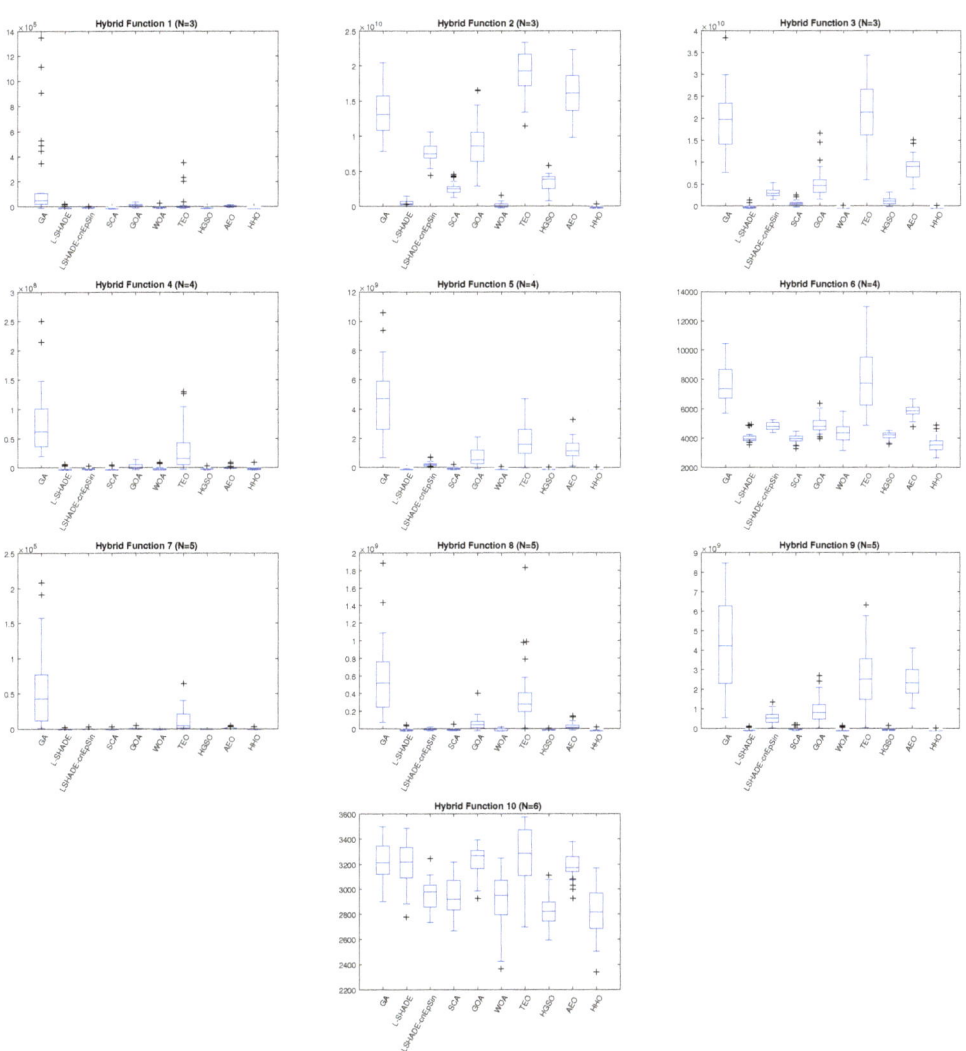

Figure 10. Boxplot of some functions from F11–F20 for all algorithms.

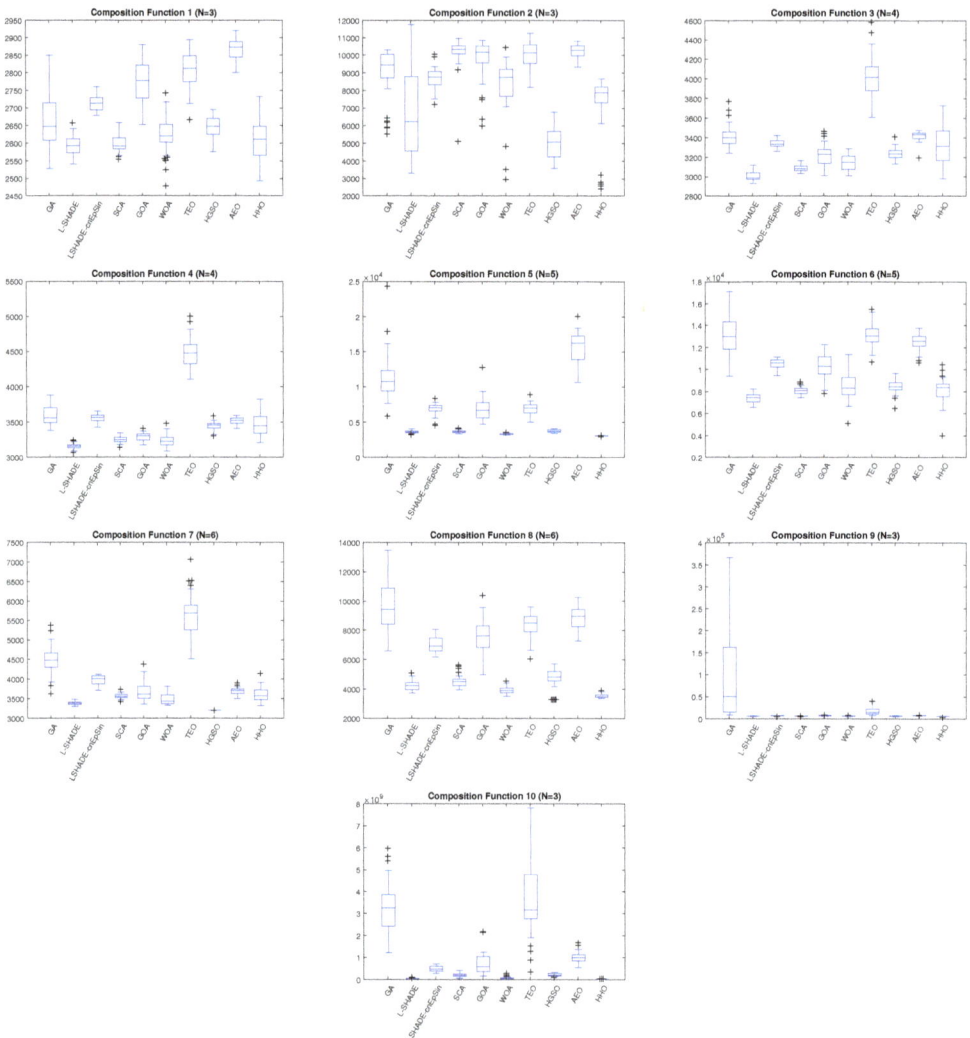

Figure 11. Boxplot of some functions from F21–F30 for all algorithms.

5. HHO Variants

5.1. Enhancement to HHO

In the literature, there exist many studies which enhanced the HHO using many mathematical operators. These studies can be summarized, as shown in Table 7.

Table 7. Summary of literature review on variants and modified HHO algorithms.

SN.	Modification Name	Ref.	Authors	Journal/Conf.	Year	Remarks
1	Binary HHO (BHHO)	[110]	Too et al.	Electronics	2019	Authors introduced two binary versions of HHO called (BHHO) and Quadratic Binary HHO (QBHHO).
2	Opposite HHO (OHHO)	[111]	Hans et al.	Journal of Interdisciplinary Mathematics	2020	Authors applied OHHO in feature selection in breast cancer classification.
3	EHHO	[112]	Jiao et al.	Energy	2020	Authors combined OBL and (OL) in HHO.
4	NCOHHO	[113]	Fan et al.	Evolutionary Intelligence	2020	Authors improved HHO by two mechanisms: neighborhood centroid and opposite-based learning.
5	IHHO	[114]	Song et al.	Energy Sources	2020	Two techniques were employed: Quasi-Oppositional and Chaos theory.
6	LMHHO	[115]	Hussain et al.	IEEE Access	2019	Long-term HHO algorithm (LMHHO) in which information share of multiple promising areas is shared.
7	CMDHHO	[116]	Golilarz et al.	IEEE Access	2020	3 techniques are used with HHO, namely: Chaos theory, Multipopulation topological structure, and DE operators: mutation and crossover.
8	GCHHO	[117]	Song et al.	Knowledge-based Systems	2020	Gaussian mutation and Cuckoo Search were employed in HHO.
9	AHHO	[117]	Wunnava et al.	Applied Soft Computing	2020	Authors used mutation strategy to force the escape energy in the interval [0, 2].
10	(DHHO/M)	[118]	Jia et al.	Remote Sensing	2019	A dynamic HHO algorithm with mutation strategy is proposed.
11	vibrational HHO (VHHO)	[119]	Shao et al.	Measurement	2020	VHHO is proposed by embedding SVM into HHO and using a periodic mutation.
12	GBHHO	[120]	Wei et al.	IEEE ACCESS	2020	Authors developed an improved HHO approach by using Gaussian barebone (GB)

5.1.1. Enhanced HHO

Li et al. [121] tried to speed the HHO convergence by introducing an enhanced the HHO version using two strategies: (1) enhancing the HHO exploration by using opposite-based learning and logarithmic spiral and (2) the Modify Rosenbrock Method (RM) to fuse HHO in order to improve convergence accuracy and enhance the HHO local search capability. The authors tested their algorithm, which is called (RLHHO), using 30 IEEE CEC 2014 and 23 traditional benchmark functions. They compared their results with eight standard metaheurstic algorithms and six advanced ones. In [122], Ariui et al. developed an enhanced version of the HHO by hybridizing the JOS operator with the HHO. JOS consists of two other operators: Dynamic Opposite (DO) and Selective Leading Opposition (SLO). The authors assumed that JOS increases the HHO exploration capabilities, whereas DO increases HHO exploration capabilities.

5.1.2. Binary HHO

Many binary variants of the HHO have been introduced. For example, Too et al. [110] introduced a binary version of the HHO called (BHHO) using two transfer functions: S-shaped and V-shaped. Furthermore, they proposed another version called Quadratic Binary HHO (QBHHO). They compared their versions with five different MAs, namely binary differential evolution, binary flower pollination algorithm, genetic algorithm, and binary salp swarm algorithm. The same work was conducted by Thaher et al. [123] in which the authors applied their algorithm to feature selection. Moreover, Thaher and Arman [124] developed another version of the HHO called enhanced binary HHO (EBHHO) by using the multiswarm technique, in which the population is divided into three groups. Each group has a leader, and the fittest leader is able to guide more agents. Furthermore, they used three classifiers: K-nearest neighbors (KNN), Linear Discriminant Analysis (LDA), and Decision Tree (DT). Likewise, in [125], Chellal and Benmessahed developed a binary version of the HHO in order to be able to have an accurate detection of a protein complex.

Dokeroglu et al. [126] developed a binary version of multiobjective HHO to be able to solve a classification problem. They introduced novel discrete besiege (exploitation) and perching (exploration) operators. They used four machine learning techniques: Support Vector Machines (SVM), Decision Trees, Logistic regression, and Extreme Learning Machines. They used a COVID-19 dataset. Moreover, Chantar et al. [127] developed a binary HHO version using the Time-Varying Scheme. The new version, which is called BHHO-TVS, is used to solve classification problems. They used 18 different datasets to prove the significant performance of BHHO-TVS.

5.1.3. Opposite HHO

Hans et al. [111] proposed a new version of the HHO called (OHHO), based on the opposition-based learning (OBL) strategy. They applied the OHHO in feature selection in breast cancer classification. Fan et al. [113] proposed a novel HHO version called NCOHHO, which improves the HHO by two mechanisms: neighborhood centroid and opposite-based learning. In NCOHHO, neighborhood centroid is considered a reference point in generating the opposite particle. Likewise, Gupta et al. [128] used four strategies on the HHO namely: proposing a new nonlinear parameter for the prey energy, greedy selection, different rapid dives, and OBL. Other studies that used optimization methods to solve the parameter extraction problems refer to [129–131].

Jiao et al. [112] introduced a novel HHO called EHHO which employed OBL and Orthogonal Learning (OL).

Likewise, another improved approach of HHO was made by Song et al. [114] called IHHO, in which two techniques were employed: (1) Quasi-Oppositional and (2) Chaos theory.

Amer et al. [132] developed another version of the HHO called Elite Learning HHO (ELHHO). They used elite opposition-based learning to improve exploration phase quality.

5.1.4. Modified HHO

Akdag et al. [133] developed a modified HHO version by using seven different random distribution functions in order to show how stochastic search affects HHO performance. Moreover, Zhang et al. [134] tried to balance the exploration and exploitation phases by focusing on prey escaping energy (E). They introduced six different strategies to update E.

Yousri et al. [135] proposed an improved version of the HHO by modifying exploration strategies by using levy flight instead of depending on prey position. Moreover, they updated the hawks' position based on three randomly chosen hawks instead of the random update technique. Likewise, Zhao et al. [136] developed another modified version of the HHO by using a chaotic method called the Singer mechanism. They also used the levy flight mechanism in order to enhance HHO convergence.

Hussain et al. [115] developed a long-term HHO algorithm (LMHHO) which shares multiple promising areas of information. With such information, more exploration capability is given to the HHO. The authors used CEC 2017 and classical functions to validate their algorithm.

Liu et al. [137] proposed an improved HHO algorithm that combined the Nelder–Mead Simplex algorithm and the crisscrossed algorithm crossover technique which is called the horizontal and vertical crossover mechanism. The authors applied their algorithm, which is called CCNMHHO, in photovoltaic parameter estimation.

Rizk-Allah and Hassanien [138] developed a hybrid HHO algorithm which combined Nelder–Mead with the Harris algorithm. They validated their algorithm using six differential equations and four engineering differential equations.

Youssri et al. [139] developed a modified version of the HHO, called Fractional-Order modified HHO (FMHHO), which used the fractional calculus (FOC) memory concept. They tested the FMHHO using 23 benchmark functions in addition to the IEEE CEC 2017 ones. They applied it for proton exchange membrane for modeling of fuel cells. Moreover, Irfan et al. [140] proposed a modified HHO (MHHO) by using crowding distance and roulette wheel selection. They tested it using the IEEE 8 and 15 bus systems.

Ge et al. [141] suggested another improved HHO version using the predator–rabbit distributance method.

Singh et al. [142] used opposition-based learning (OBL) to enahnce the HHO. They applied the novel algorithm which is called OHHO to data clustering and tested it using 10 benchmark datasets.

5.1.5. Improved HHO

Kardani et al. [143] introduced another improved version of the HHO and extreme learning machine (ELM). Their novel algorithm, which is called ELM-IHHO, tried to overcome the limitations of the HHO by using a mutation mechanism. The authors applied ELM-IHHO in the prediction of light carbon permeability. They compared their results with ELM-based algorithms such as PSO, GA, and SMA. Moreoever, Guo et al. [144] used the random unscented sigma mutation strategy to improve the HHO. Their novel HHO version used quasi-reflection learning and quasi-opposite learning strategies in order to enhance generation diversity. They also implemented logarithmic nonlinear convergence factor to have a good balance between local and global searches.

Liu [145] developed an improved version of the HHO (IHHO). In the IHHO, a new search process is added to improve candidate solution quality. They applied it in the Job-Shop Scheduling problem. Duan and Liu [146] introduced the golden sine strategy to improve the HHO. The novel algorithm can enhance the diversity of population and improve its performance.

Hu et al. [147] developed another variant of the HHO called IHHO using two techniques: (1) adding velocity to the HHO from the Particle Swarm Optimization Algorithm and (2) using the crossover scheme from the artificial Tree algorithm [148]. They used 23 functions to test the IHHO and compared the results with 11 metaheuristics algorithms. They applied it in stock market prediction.

Moreover, Selim et al. [149] tried to enhance the HHO by returning hawks to rabbit position instead of returning them to the maximum and minimum variables' limits. They also developed a multiobjective version. Moreover, a novel search mechanism was proposed by Sihwail et al. [150] to improve HHO performance by mutation neighborhood search and rollback techniques.

Another enhanced HHO version was proposed in [116], in which the authors tried to enhance the HHO by using three techniques: (1) Chaos theory, (2) Multipopulation topological structure, and (3) Differential evolution operators: mutation and crossover. The authors applied their algorithm, which is known as the CMDHHO, in image applications.

In order to have the right balance between exploitation and exploration search in the HHO, Song et al. [151] developed an enhanced HHO version called GCHHO, where two techniques were employed, namely the Gaussian mutation and Cuckoo Search dimension decision techniques. To test GCHHO, CEC 2017 functions were used in addition to three engineering problems. The authors compared GCHHO with classical HHO, WOA, MFO, BA, SCA, FA, and PSO.

Moreover, Yin et al. [152] tried to prevent the HHO from falling in the local optimum region by developing an improved version of the HHO called NOL-HHO, in which there are Nonlinear Control Parameter and Random Opposition-based Learning strategies.

Ridha et al. [153] developed a boosted HHO (BHHO) algorithm which employed the random exploration strategy from the Flower Pollination Algorithm (FPA) and the mutation strategy from differential evolution. Wei et al. [120] developed another improved HHO approach that uses Gaussian barebone (GB). They tested their algorithm, which is called GBHHO, using the CEC 2014 problems. Zhang et al. [154] used the adaptive cooperative foraging technique and dispersed foraging strategy to improve the HHO. Their algorithm, which known as ADHHO, was tested using a CEC 2014 benchmark function.

A vibrational HHO (VHHO) was proposed by Shao et al. [119] to prevent the HHO particles from converging around local optima by embedding SVM into HHO and using a frequent mutation. VHHO was compared with SCA, PSO, and classical HHO.

5.1.6. Chaotic HHO

Many chaotic HHO variants have been proposed. Menesy et al. [155] proposed a chaotic HHO algorithm (CHHO) using ten chaotic functions. They compared their algorithm with conventional HHO, GWO, CS-EO, and SSO. The authors claimed that the experimental results show the superiority of CHHO over other algorithms. Likewise, Chen et al. [156] developed a new version termed EHHO, in which the chaotic local search method is used in addition to OBL techniques. Statistical results show that the EHHO achieved better results than other competitors. The authors applied EHHO in identifying photovoltaic cells parameters. Moreover, Gao et al. [157] used tent map with HHO.

Dhawale et al. [158] developed an improved chaotic HHO (CHHO). They tested their algorithm using 23 benchmark functions and compared it with SSA, DE, PSO, GWO, MVO, MFO, SCA, CS, TSA, GA, MMA, ACO, and HS. They argued that the CHHO outperformed all mentioned algorithms.

Basha et al. [159] developed a variant chaotic HHO using quasi-reflection learning. They applied it in order to enhance CNN design for classifying different brain tumor grades using magnetic resonance imaging. The authors tested their model using 10 benchmark functions, and after that they used two datasets. Likewise, Hussien and Amin in [160] developed a novel HHO version based on the chaotic local search, opposition-based learning, and self adaption mechanism. They evaluated their model using IEEE CEC 2017 and applied the novel algorithm, which is called m-HHO, in feature selection.

Dehkordi et al. [161] introduced a nonlinear-based chaotic HHO algorithm. The new algorithm, which known as (NCHHO), is applied to solve the Internet of Vehicles (IoV) optimization problem.

5.1.7. Dynamic HHO with Mutation Mechanism

Jia et al. [118] developed a dynamic HHO algorithm with mutation strategy. Instead of decreasing the energy escaping parameter E from 2 to 0, they introduced a dynamic control parameter to be able to avoid local optimum solutions. The authors claimed that this dynamic control would prevent the solution from getting stacked in local optimum as E in the original cannot take values greater than 1 in the second half of iterations.

5.1.8. Other HHO Variants

An adaptive HHO technique has been proposed by Wunnava et al. [117], which is called AHHO. The authors used mutation strategy to force the escape energy in the interval [0, 2]. The AHHO was tested using 23 classical functions and 30 functions obtained from CEC 2014.

To strengthen HHO performance, two strategies from Cuckoo Search were introduced to the HHO by Song et al. [151]. They used the dimension decided strategy and Gaussian mutation. They tested their algorithm, GCHHO, using 30 functions from IEEE CEC 2017.

Jiao et al. [162] proposed a multistrategy search HHO using the Least Squares Support Vector Machine (LSSVM). They used the Gauss chaotic method as the initialization method. They also employed the neighborhood perturbation mechanism, variable spiral search strategy, and adaptive weight. They used 23 functions in addition to CEC 2017 suit test functions to prove the effectiveness of their algorithm.

Zhong and Li [163] developed a hybrid algorithm called the Comprehensive Learning Harris Hawks Equilibrium Optimizer (CLHHEO) algorithm. The authors used three operators: the equilibrium optimizer operator, comprehensive learning, and terminal replacement mechanism. They used EO operators to enhance the HHO exploration capacity. Comprehensive Learning was employed in the CLHHEO to share agent knowledge in order to enhance the convergence capacity. They used the terminal replacement technique to prevent the CLHHEO from falling in local stagnation. The authors compared the CLHHEO with CLPSO, PSO, GWO, BBBC, WOA, DA, SSA, AOA, SOA, and classical HHO using 15 benchmark functions and 10 constrained problems.

Abd Elaziz et al. [164] developed an algorithm called multilayer HHO based on the algorithm called multileader HHO, which is based on Differential Evolution (MLHHDE). They introduced a memory structure that makes hawks learn from the global best positions and the best historical ones. DE is employed in order to increase the exploration phase. They used CEC 2017 benchmark functions.

Bujok [165] developed an advanced HHO algorithm that archive each old solution. He compared his algorithm using 22 real-world problems from CEC 2011.

Al-Batar et al. [166] enhanced the exploration phase of the original HHO by introducing the survival-of-the-fittest evolutionary principle that helps smooth transitions from exploration to exploitation. The authors used three, strategies namely proportional, linear ranked-based, and tournament methods. They tested their algorithms using 23 mathematical functions and 3 constrained problems.

Qu et al. [167] tried to improve the HHO by employing Variable Neighborhood Learning (VNL) which is used to balance between exploration and exploitation. They also used F-score to narrow down selection range and used mutation to increase diversity.

Nandi and Kamboj [168] combined canis lupus and the Grey wolf optimizer to improve the HHO. The novel algorithm, which is called hHHO-GWO, was tested on CEC 2005, CEC-BC-2017, and 11 different engineering problems.

Gölcük and Ozsoydan [169] developed a hybrid algorithm which combines both the Teaching–Learning-based Optimization (TLBO) with the HHO. The new algorithm (ITL-HHO) is design to give a proper balance between exploitation and exploration. The authors tested theirs using 33 benchmark function (CEC 2006 and CEC 2009) and 10 multidisciplinary engineering problems.

Yu et al. [170] proposed a modified HHO called compact HHO (cHHO) in which only one hawk is used to search for the optimal solution instead of many hawks.

5.2. Hybrid HHO

The HHO has been hybridized with many other algorithms as shown in Table 8. Wang et al. [171,172] presented a hybrid algorithm called the Improved Hybrid AO-HHO (IHAOHHO) that combines the HHO and Aquila Optimizer [173]. They used the opposition-based learning strategy and Representative-based Hunting (RH) to improve both the exploitation and exploration phases. They tested their algorithm using 23 benchmark functions. They compared their results with classical HHO and AO and five other state-of-art algorithms.

In order to improve HHO performance, the authors in [174] used SSA as a local search in HHO. They argued that their algorithm, which is called MHHO, has better performance than the conventional HHO. Attiya et al. [175] tried to enhance HHO convergence and solutions by employing Simulated Annealing (SA) as a local search strategy. Their algorithm, which is called HHOSA, was compared with PSO, FA, SSA, MFO, and HHO. The authors applied HHOSA in a job scheduling problem.

HHO has been integrated with Differential Evolution by Fu et al. [176]. They developed an algorithm called Improved Differential evolution, and the HHO was termed as IHDEHHO. They applied it to forecast wind speed using kernel extreme learning and phase space reconstruction.

Abd Elaziz et al. [177] proposed a hybrid algorithm, which is called HHOSSA, that combined the HHO with SSA. In HHOSSA, the population is divided into two halves in which HHO is used to update the first half of solutions and SSA is used to update the other half. To evaluate their algorithm, they used thirty-six functions from IEEE CEC 2005.

Moreover, a hybrid HHO algorithm called CHHO-CS, which refers to chaotic HHO cuckoo search algorithm, has been developed by Houssein et al. [178]. The CHHO-CS is used to control the HHO's main position vectors, and the chaotic map is employed for updating the parameters of control energy. Another hybrid algorithm is presented by Barshandeh et al. [179], called the hybrid multipopulation algorithm. Firstly, the population is divided into many subpopulations. Then, a hybrid algorithm between HHO and the Artificial Ecosystem Optimization (AEO) is used. Furthermore, the authors used chaos theory, levy flight, local search algorithm, and quasi-oppositional learning.

Xie et al. [180] tried to solve the HHO's shortcomings by proposing a hybrid algorithm that combined the HHO and Henary Gas Solubility Optimization (HGSO) algorithm. The authors used two benchmark functions to verify their algorithm: CEC 2005 and CEC2017. The authors compared HHO-HGSO with Marine Predator Algorithm (MPA), WOA, LSA, HHO, WCA, and HGSO.

Likewise, in [181], Fu et al. integrated GWO in the HHO by using two layers for population activity. In the first layer (bottom layer), solutions are updated using mutation-based GWO. On the other hand, the solutions in the upper layer are updated by employing the HHO.

Qu et al. [182] introduced an improved HHO approach that used information exchange. In the novel algorithm, which is termed as IEHHO, hawks can share and realize sufficient information when exploring preys. They also used a dynamic disturbance term that depends on sine and cosine in order to enhance the escaping energy.

In [183], an intensified HHO is proposed by Kamboj et al., where a hybrid HHO is combined with SCA (hHHO-SCA). They verified their model using CEC 2017 and CEC 2018 and compared it with SCA, HHO, ALO, MFO, GWO, GSA, BA, CS, and GOA.

Moreover, an algorithm called hHHO-IGWO was proposed by Dhawale and Kamboj [184] which improved GWO with the HHO. Another hybrid algorithm between SCA and HHO was developed [185] in which a mutation strategy was used.

Suresh et al. [186] developed a hybrid chaotic multiverse HHO (CMVHHO). The authors used chaotic MV in the first generation and after that the HHO was used to update positions.

Table 8. Summary of the literature review on hybrid HHO algorithms.

SN.	Modification Name	Ref.	Authors	Journal /Conf.	Year	Remarks
1	MHHO	[174]	Jouhari et al.	Symmetry	2020	SSA has been used as a local search in HHO.
2	HHOSA	[175]	Attiya et al.	Computational Intelligence and Neuroscience	2020	SA is used as a local search strategy. The authors applied HHOSA in a job scheduling problem.
3	IHDEHHO	[176]	Fu et al.	Renewable Energy	2020	Improved Differential evolution version is hybridized with HHO.
4	HHOSSA	[177]	Abd Elaziz et al.	Applied Soft Computing	2020	Population is divided into 2 halves, the first half using HHO and other half using SSA.
5	CHHO-CS	[178]	Houssein et al.	Scientific Reports	2020	HHO is hybridized with cuckoo search and chaotic theory.
6	HMPA	[179]	Barshandeh et al.	Engineering with Computers	2020	Population is divided to many subpopulations. Then, HHO and AEO are used.
7	HHO-HGSO	[180]	Xie et al.	IEEE Access	2020	HHO is combined with HGSO algorithm.
8	IEHHO	[181]	Fu et al.	Energy Conversion and Management	2020	2 layers for population activity were developed. In the first layer a mutation-based GWO was used, and in the second one HHO was used.
9	hHHO-SCA	[183]	Kamboj et al.	Applied Soft Computing	2020	HHO is combined with SCA (hHHO-SCA).

ElSayed and Elattar [187] developed a hybrid algorithm which combines HHO with Sequential Quadratic Programming (HHO-SQP) in order to obtain the optimal overcurrent relay coordination that relays incorporating distributed generation.

Kaveh et al. [188] developed a hybrid algorithm called Imperialist Competitive HHO (ICHHO) that used the Imperialist Competitive Algorithm (ICA) [189] to improve the HHO's exploration performance. They tested their model using 23 mathematical functions and many common engineering problems.

Sihwail et al. [190] developed a hybrid algorithm called the Netwon-Harris Hawks Optimization (NHHO) in which Netwon's technique second-order is used to correct digits in order to solve nonlinear equation systems.

Another hybrid algorithm combines Differential Evolution (DE) with HHO and Gaining-Sharing Knowledge algorithm (GSK) [191]. The new algorithm is abbreviated as DEGH and was developed using the "rand/1" DE operator and GSK two-phase strategy. They also used self-adaption crossover probability to strengthen the relationship between selection, mutation, and crossover. They used 32 benchmark functions and compared DEGH with 8 state-of-the-art algorithms.

Another hybrid version between DE and HHO has been proposed by Abualigah et al. [192], where DE is used to enhance the HHO exploitation experience. The novel hybrid algorithm, known as H-HHO, was used to obtain cluster optimal numbers to each dataset.

Azar et al. [193] developed a prediction model using the Least Square Support Vector Machine (LS-SVM) and Adaptive Neuro-Fuzzy Inference System (ANFIS). ANFIS was optimized by the HHO (ANFIS-HHO). The authors argued that the HHO increases the ANFIS prediction performance.

Firouzi et al. [194] developed a hybrid algorithm which combines both the HHO and Nelder–Mead Optimization. They used it to determine the depth and location of a microsystem crack. They compared their algorithm with classical HHO, GOA, WOA, and DA. Lie et al. [195] developed a hybrid algorithm that combines the Fireworks Algorithm (FWA) [98] with the HHO based on the mechanism of dynamic competition. The authors used CEC 2005 to verify the powerfulness of their algorithm, which is called (DCFW-HHO). They compared it with MPA, WOA, WCA, LSA, FWA, and HHO.

Li et al. [196] developed an enhanced hybrid algorithm called Elite Evolutionary Strategy HHO (EESHHO). They tested their algorithm using 29 functions (6 hybrid functions from CEC2017 + 23 basic functions).

Ahmed [197] developed a hybrid algorithm between the HHO and homotopy analytical method (HAM) to solve partial differential equations.

Yuan et al. [198] developed a hybrid HHO algorithm that combines Harris hawks with instinctive reaction Strategy (IRS). The novel algorithm (IRSHHO) is tested using five mathematical functions.

Setiawan et al. [199] developed a hybrid algorithm called (HHO-SVR) in which SVR is optimized using the HHO.

5.3. Multiobject HHO

Hossain et al. [200] introduced a multiobjective version of HHO based on the 2-hop routing mechanism. The novel algorithm is applied for the cognitive Radio-Vehicular Ad Hoc Network. Dabba et al. [201] introduced another multiobjective binary algorithm based on the HHO. The novel algorithm, MOBHHO, was applied on microarray data gene selection by using two fitness functions: SVM and KNN. Another binary multiobjective version was proposed in [126].

Jangir et al. [202] developed a nondominated sorting multiobjective HHO (NSHHO). They tested their algorithm using 46 multiobjective real-world problems.

Du et al. [203] proposed a multiobjective HHO called (MOHHO) in order to tune extreme learning machine (ELM) parameters and applied it in air pollution prediction and forecasting. The authors evaluated their model, MOHHO-ELM, using 12 air pollutant concentrations recorded from 3 cities. Moreover, Islam et al. [204] tried to solve multiobjective optimal power flow. Likewise, an improved multiobjective version of the HHO was introduced by Selim et al. [149], which is termed as MOIHHHO. The authors applied it to find the optimal DG size and location.

Fu and Lu [205] developed an improved version of the HHO called (HMOHHO), in which hybrid techniques are integrated with the HHO, including Latin hypercube sampling initialization, mutation technique, and a modified differential evolution operator. The authors used UF and ZDT to validate their algorithm.

Piri and Mohapatra [206] presented a multiobjective Quadratic Binary (MOQBHHO) approach using KNN. The authors used Crowding Distance (CD) to pick the best solution from nondominated ones. They compared MOQBHHO with MOBHHO-S, MOGA, MOALO, and NSGA-II.

6. HHO Applications

HHO has been successfully applied to many applications, as shown in Figure 12 and Table 9.

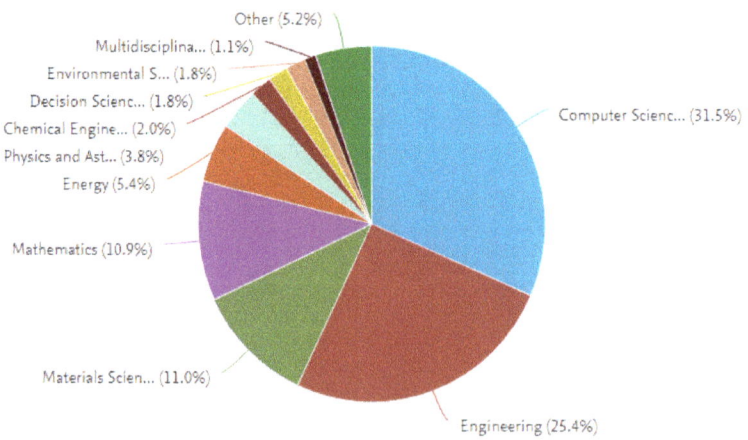

Figure 12. Distribution of HHO-related papers in many applications, as reported by Scopus.

Table 9. The applications of HHO algorithm.

Proposed	Application	Description	Results and Conclusion	Year and Authors	(Ref.)
HHOPSO	reactive power planning problem	HHo with PSO	HHOPSO has better results than HHO	Shekarappa et al.	[207]
CMBHHO	distribution generator (DG)	crossover and mutation is used in HHO	CMBHHO outperforms HHO, LSA, GA, and TLBO	Mohandas and Devanathan	[208]
WHHO	PV solar	Whippy HHO	WHHO achieves better results	Naeijian et al.	[209]
NCOHHO	ANN	training multilayer feed-forward ANN	NCOHHO tested using 5 different datasets	Fan et al.	[113]
HHO-DE	multilevel thresholding image	Ostu's and Kapur's entropy method used	outperforms all other algorithms	Bao et al.	[210]
HHO	flow shop scheduling	hybrid algorithm based on HHO is designed	HHO achieved good results compared with others	Utama and Widodo	[211]
MEHHO1 and MEHHO2	Feature selection	saving memory mechanism and adopting a learning strategy are used	MEHHO1 achieved good results compared with HHO	Too et al.	[212]
DHGHHD	drug discovery	HGSO enhanced HHO	2 real-world datasets were used	Abd Elaziz and Yousri	[213]
CovH2SD	COVID-19	HHO was used to optimize CNN	transfer learning techniques using 9 convolutional NN	Balaha et al.	[214]

6.1. Power

6.1.1. Optimal Power Flow

Recently, electrical energy utilities are increasing rapidly with wide demand [215,216]. To face such a problem, interconnected networks have emerged with differential power systems [217].

Optimal Power Flow (OPF) can be considered as an optimization problem. Hussain et al. [115] applied their algorithm to solve the OPF problem. They claimed that their algorithm, which is called LMHHO, achieved better results than classical HHO. Another attempt to solve OPF was made by Islam et al. [218], in which the HHO was compared with ALO, WOA, SSA, MFO, and the Glow Warm algorithm. The same authors solved the same problem in [204] with consideration to environmental emission. Likewise, a modified HHO introduced in [133] has been applied to solve OPF.

Akdag et al. [133] developed a modified HHO version using seven random distribution functions, namely normal distribution, F distribution, Rayleigh distribution, chi-square distribution, exponential distribution, Student's distribution, and lognormal distribution. The authors applied their algorithm to Optimal Power Flow (OPF) and applied it to the IEEE 30-bus test system.

Paital et al. [219] tuned interval fuzzy type-2 lead-lag using the HHO. The novel algorithm (Dual-IT2FL) was applied to find the enhancement of stability in unified power flow controllers (UPFC).

Shekarappa et al. [207] used a hybrid algorithm between HHO and PSO called (HHOPSO) to solvea reactive power planning problem. The HHOPSO was tested using IEEE 57-bus. Mohanty and Panda [220] adapted the HHO using the Sine and Cosine Algorithm. Their developed algorithm, which is called (ScaHHO), was utilized in order to tune an adaptive fuzzy proportional integrated (AFPID) for hybrid power system frequency controller.

6.1.2. Distributed Generation

Abdel Aleem et al. [221] tried to solve the optimal design of C-type resonance-free harmonic filter in a distributed system using the HHO. The authors claimed that the HHO has better results than the other compared algorithm.

Moreover, Diaaeldin et al. [222] used the HHO to obtain the optimal reconfiguration of the network in distributed systems. Abdelsalam et al. [223] presented a smart unit model for multisource operation and cost management based on the HHO algorithm. Mohandas and Devanathan [208] used crossover and mutation with the HHO. The novel algorithm, which is called (CMBHHO), is applied to configure the network by distribution generator (DG) size and optimal location. They compared it with GSA, ALO, LSA, HSA, GA, FWA, RGA, GA, TLBO, and HHO.

Mossa et al. [224] developed a model to estimate proton exchange membrane fuel cell (PEMFC) parameters based on the HHO.

Chakraborty et al. [225] tried to use the HHO to select the optimum capacity, site, and number of solar DG. They used two benchmark functions: IEEE 33 and IEEE 69 bus radial.

6.1.3. Photovoltaic Models

Due to continuous and huge increases in energy demand, solar photovoltaic (PV), which is based on solar cells systems, has gained huge momentum. The HHO has been successfully applied to solve PV problems. Liu et al. [137] used their algorithm, called CCNMHHO, in finding the optimal PV model parameters. The authors state that CCN-MHHO has competitive results when compared with other well-known and state-of-the-art algorithms. Likewise, Jiao et al. [112] used their developed algorithm (EHHO) in finding PV parameters and for the construction of its model with high precision. Moreover, in [135], the authors used their novel approach to find the optimal array reconfiguration PV in alleviation the influence of partial shading. Likewise, Qias et al. [226] tried to extract the parameters of 3-diode PV (TDPV).

Chen et al. [156] tried to identify PV cell parameters by an enhanced HHO version termed EHHO. They compared their algorithm with CLPSO, IJAYA, and GOTLBO. Sahoo has conducted similar work, as has Sahoo and Panda [227], in which they control solar PV frequency.

Naeijian et al. [209] used their developed HHO version, which called Whippy HHO (WHHO), in estimating PV solar cell parameters.

6.1.4. Wind Applications

In [228], Fang et al. developed a multiobject mutation operator (HMOHHO) which is used to acquire kernel identification voltera parameters. They applied it to forecast wind speed.

Roy et al. [229] used the HHO to reduce the interconnected wind turbines. They compared it with PSO, FPA, GWO, MVO, WOA, MFO, and BOA.

6.1.5. Economic Load Dispatch Problem

The Economic Load Dispatch Problem can be considered as one of the most common and important problems in power systems [230,231].

Pham et al. [232] employed multirestart strategy and OBL to enhance the HHO. The novel algorithm is applied to solve ELD with nonsmooth cost functions. They argued that results are superior when compared with previous studies.

6.1.6. Unit Commitment Problem

Nandi and Kamboj [233] tried to hybridize the Sine Cosine Algorithm and Memetic Algorithm using the HHO. They applied it to solve a unit commitment problem with photovoltaic applications. SCA is used in power provision, whereas ELD is performed by HHO.

6.2. Computer Science

6.2.1. Artificial Neural Network

Sammen et al. [234] used the HHO in order to enhance Artificial Neural Network (ANN) performance and proposed a hybrid model called ANN-HHO. the authors compared their novel model with ANN-GA, ANN-PSO, and classical ANN. They argued that the ANN-HHO outperformed other compared algorithms. The same work was conducted by Essa et al. [235], in which their model is compared against the Support Vector Machine (SVM) and the traditional ANN. They applied the novel model to improve active solar productivity prediction.

Fan et al. [113] used their novel algorithm, NCOHHO, in training a multilayer feed-forward neural network using five different datasets. A similar work which combined the HHO with ANN was conducted by Moayedi et al. [236] and applied to predict the compression coefficient of soil. The authors argued that the HHO is better than GOA in training ANN.

Moreover, in [237] Kolli and Tatavarth developed the Harris Water Optimization (HWO) based on a deep recurrent neural network (RNN) to detect fraud in a bank transaction.

Artificial Neural Networks (ANNs) are one of the most famous and popular learning methods that simulate the biological nervous system. The HHO has been used by many authors to train ANNs. Bacanin et al. [238] tried to adapt the HHO algorithm to train ANNs. They used two popular classification datasets to test their proposed approach. Moreover, Atta et al. [239] applied their enhanced version of the HHO in order to train a feed-forward neural network. They compared their method with eight metaheurstic algorithms using five classification datasets. A hybrid algorithm between the HHO and Whale Optimization Algorithm was developed to enhance ANN by Agarwal et al. [240].

Bac et al. [241] developed a hybrid model based on the HHO and Multiple Layers Perceptron (MLP). They used their developed system, which is called HHO-MLP, to estimate the efficiency of heavy metal absorption using nanotube-type halloysite.

Alamir in [242] proposed an enhanced ANN using the HHO to predict food liking in different masking background presence noise levels and types. Simsek and Alagoz [243] used an ANN learning model and the HHO in order to develop analysis schemes for optimal engine behavior. Likewise, Zhang et al. [244] estimated clay's friction angle using deep NN and the HHO to evaluate slope stability. Murugadoss used Deep Convolution ANN (DCANN) with the HHO to have an early diabetes prediction.

6.2.2. Image Processing

In [210], Bao et al. applied their hybrid algorithm that combined the HHO with differential evolution (HHO-DE) in the segmentation of color multilevel thresholding images by using two techniques: Ostu's method and Kapur's entropy. They compared their results with seven other algorithms using ten images. They argued that HHO-DE outperforms all other algorithms in terms of structure, similarity index, peak signal-to-noise ratio, and feature similarity index. Similar work has been conducted by Wunnava et al. [245]. In addition to using DE, they modified the exploration phase by limiting the escape energy in the interval $\in [2, 3]$.

Moreover, Golilarz et al. [246] utilized the HHO for obtaining the optimal thresholding function parameters for satellite images. Jia et al. [118] employed their algorithm, which is called dynamic HHO, with mutation (DHHO/M) in order to segment satellite images by using three criteria: Kanpur's entropy, Tsallis entropy, and Otsu. Similar work has been conducted by Shahid et al. [247], in which denoising of the image was presented in the wavelet domain.

In [248], an efficient HHO variant was introduced by Esparza et al. in which they used minimum cross-entropy as a fitness function since they applied it to image segmentation. To validate their method, they compared it with K-means and fuzzy iterAg.

Naik et al. [249] proposed a leader HHO (LHHO) in order to enhance the exploration of algorithm. They applied it for 2-D Masi entropy multilevel image thresholding. They used segmentation metrics such as PSNR, FSIM, and SSIM [250].

6.2.3. Scheduling Problem

Machine scheduling can be considered as a decision-making optimization process that has a vital role in transport, manufacturing, etc.

Jouhari et al. [174] used SSA with the HHO in solving a machine scheduling problem. Moreover, Attiya et al. [175] used a modified version of the HHO called HHOSA in order to solve a scheduling job in the cloud environment.

Utama and Widodo [211] developed a hybrid algorithm based on the HHO to solve a flow shop scheduling problem (FSSP).

6.2.4. Feature Selection

Feature Selection (FS) is one of the most important preprocessing techniques which aims to reduce features which may influence machine learning performance [251–253]. The HHO has been used in solving FS problems. For example, Thaher et al. [123] used a binary version of the HHO in solving the FS problem. They used nine high-dimensional datasets.

Moreover, the authors in [254] used the HHO with Simulated Annealing and Bitwise operators (AND and OR). They used 19 datasets of all sizes. They claimed that HHOBSA has good results when compared with others.

A similar work was conducted by Thaher and Arman [124], where they used five different datasets. They used the ADASYN technique. Moreover, Sihwail et al. [150] used IHHO in order to solve the FS problem. They used 20 datasets with different feature dimensionality levels (low, moderate, and high). They compared IHHHO with seven other algorithms. Thaher et al. [255] detected Arabic tweets' false information using the hybrid HHO algorithm based on ML models and feature selection. Their algorithm, which is called Binary HHO Logistic Regression (LR), has better results compared with other previous work on the same dataset. In [254], Abdel-Basset et al. tried to hybridize the HHO with Simulated Annealing based on a bitwise operator. They applied the novel algorithm, which is called (HHOBSA), in a feature selection problem using 24 datasets and 19 artificial ones.

Moreover, in [256] Turabieh et al. proposed an enhanced version of the HHO and applied it to a feature selection problem using K-Nearest Neighbor (KNN). They applied it in order to predict the performance of students. They evaluated their prediction system using many machine learning classifiers such as kNN, Naïve Bayes, Layered recurrent neural network (LRNN), and Artificial Neural Network.

Al-Wajih et al. [257] introduced a hybrid algorithm which combined the HHO with the Grey Wolf Optimizer. The new algorithm, which is called HBGWOHHO, used sigmoid function to transfer from the continuous to binary domain. They compared it with Binary Particle Swarm Optimization (BPSO), Binary Genetic Algorithm (BGA), Binary Grey Wolf Optimizer (BGWO), Binary Harris Hawks Optimizer (BHHO), and Binary Hybrid BWOPSO. They assumed that their algorithm had better accuracy and a smaller size of selected features.

Khurma et al. [258] developed two binary HHO versions based on filter approach for feature selection. The first one applies mutual information with the HHO for any two features. The second version applies the HHO with each feature's group entropy. The authors assumed that the first approach selects fewer feature subsets, whereas the second one achieves higher classification accuracy.

Too et al. [212] enhanced the HHO algorithm by saving the memory mechanism and adopting a learning strategy. The novel algorithms, which are called MEHHO1 and MEHHO2, were employed to solve a feature selection problem. These approaches were evaluated using thirteen benchmark datasets with low-dimensional and eight others with high-dimensional ones.

6.2.5. Traveling Salesman Problem

Yaser and Ku-Mahamud [259] applied their hybrid algorithm called the Harris Hawk Optimizer Ant Colony System (HHO-ACS) in solving the Traveling Salesman Problem (TSP). They used many symmetric TSP instances such as bayg29, att48, berlin52, bays29, eil51, st70, eil76, and eil101. They compared the novel algorithm with Black hole [260], PSO, DA, GA, and ACO. They argued that the HHO-ACS has a good performance compared with them.

Ismael et al. [261] developed a new version of the HHO to solve an FS problem using V-support regression.

6.3. Wireless Sensor Network

The wireless sensor network (WSN) has recently been used in many fields, such as smart homes, health care, and environment detection, due to its features such as self-organizing and being environment friendly [262,263]. Sriniv and Amgoth in [264] used the HHO with SSA in proposing an energy-efficient WSN.

Likewise, Bhat and Venkata [265] used the HHO in classifying node coverage ranges to an incoming neighbor and outgoing neighbor. This technique is based on area minimization. the authors tested the HHO-MA in a 2D square, 2D C-shape, 3D G-shape, 3D cube, and 3D mountain. In [266], Singh and Prakash used the HHO to find the optimal place of multiple optical networks. Xu et al. [267] used the HHO in the intelligent reflecting surface by trying to maximize signal power by optimizing access point beamforming.

Sharma and Prakash [268] developed a model called HHO-LPWSN which used the HHO to localize sensors nodes in a wireless sensor network.

6.4. Medical Applications

A pulse-coupled neural network (PCNN) based on the HHO called HHO-PCNN has been developed by Jia et al. [269]. They applied it in image segmentation using many performance indicators (UM, CM, Recall, Dice, and Precision). The results were compared with WOA-PCNN, SCA-PCNN, PSO-PCNN, SSA-PCNN, MVO-PCNN, and GWO-PCNN. They claimed that their method has the best results.

Moreover, In [270], Rammurthy and Mahesh used their hybrid algorithm Whale HHO (WHHO) with deep learning classifier in detecting brain tumors using MRI images from two datasets: BRATS and SimBRATS.

Moreover, Abd Elaziz et al. [177] employed their method, called competitive chain HHO, in multilevel image thresholding using eleven natural gray scales. An adaptive HHO, which was proposed by Wunnava et al. [117], has been applied in D gray gradient multilevel image thresholding. They proved that their algorithm using I2DGG outperforms all other methods.

Moreover, Golilarz et al. [116] used their algorithm (CMDHHO), which is based on multipopulation differential evolution, in denoising satellite images.

Suresh et al. [186] used their chaotic hybrid algorithm, which is based on the deep kernel machine learning classifier CMVHHO-DKMLC, to classify medical diagnoses.

In [271], Kaur et al. employed Dimension Learning-based Hunting (DLH) with the original HHO. The novel algorithm, known as DLHO, was developed for biomedical datasets. The authors applied it to detect breast cancer.

Likewise, Chacko and Chacko [272] used the HHO to integrate watermarks on various strengths. The bits of watermarking were merged with Deep Learning Convolution NN (DLCNN). DLCNN used the HHO to identify watermarks.

Bandyopadhyay et al. [273] used the altruism concept and chaotic initialization to improve the HHO. Their novel algorithm was applied to segment brain Magnetic Resonance Images (MRI) using 18 benchmark images taken from the brainweb and WBE databases.

Iswisi et al. [274] used HHO in order to select the optimal cluster centers in fuzzy C-means (FCM) and segmentation. They tested their model using many brain MRIs.

Balamurugan et al. [275] tried to classify heart disease using adaptive HHO and deep GA. Their classified features were clustered using adaptive HHO, whereas enhanced deep GA was used to process classification processes. They used the UCI dataset to test their novel algorithm.

Abd Elaziz et al. [164] used their developed algorithm, called multilayer HHO, which based on DE (MLHHDE), to predict H1N1 viruses.

Qu et al. [167] used their algorithm, called VNLHHO, to be able enhance the classification of gene expression by improving the performance of feature selection. They used the Bayesian Classifier as a fitness function. They tested their model using profile data of the gene expression of different eight tumor types.

6.5. Chemical Engineering and Drug Discovery

Cheminformatics or chemical engineering is a field which is interested in discovering, analyzing, and predicting the properties of molecules by combining processes from mathematics and information science [276].

Houssein et al. [277] used the HHO with two classification techniques: SVM and kNN. By using two datasets: MonoAmine Oxidase and QSAR Biodegradation, they proved that the HHO-SVM achieved better results than the HHO-KNN. Moreover, in [178], the same authors hybridized the HHO with Cuckoo Search (CS) and chaotic maps and used SVM as an objective function. They proved that CHHO-CS is better than PSO, MFO, GWO, SSA, and SCA.

Abd Elaziz and Yousri [213] used the Henary Gas Solubility Optimization (HGSO) to enhance the HHO. They applied their algorithm (DHGHHD) to predict drug discovery and design using two real-world datasets.

Houssien et al. [278] used genetic algorithm operators (crossover and mutation) in addition to OBL and random OBL strategies in classical HHO to select chemical descriptors/features and compound activities.

6.6. Electronic and Control Engineering

Proportional–Integral Derivative (PID) controllers are used in order to improve Automatic Voltage Regulator (AVR) performance. Ekinic et al. [279] used the HHO to tune the PID parameters in AVR systems. Moreover, the same authors used the same algorithm [280] in tuning a DC motor PID controller by minimizing multiplied absolute error (ITAE) time. They compared their approach with the Grey Wolf Optimizer, Atom Search Algorithm, and Sine Cosine Algorithm. Moreover, the same authors [281] applied the HHO to tune the Fractional Order PID (FOPID) controller. They used it in a DC–DC buck. They compared their algorithm, which is called HHO-FOPID, with WOA-PID and GA-PID.

Likewise, Fu and Lu [205] developed a multiobjective PID controller based on the HHO with hybrid strategies (HMOHHO) for Hydraulic Turbine Governing Systems (HTGS).

Yousri et al. [282] used the HHO to evaluate PI parameter controllers which simulate load frequency control in the multi-interconnected system by using two systems: (1) two interconnected thermal areas and comprised PV and (2) four PV plants, two thermal plants, and a wind turbine. They compared the HHO against SCA, MVO, ALO, and GWO.

Barakat et al. [283] developed an interconnected power system LFC using PD-PI cascade control.

Munagala and Jatoth [284] tried to design a Fractional-order PID (FOPID) using the HHO for speed control.

6.7. Geological Engineering

The gravity-triggered mass downward movements can be used to define landslides. Bui et al. [285] applied the HHO to landslide susceptibility analysis. The authors used 208 historical landslides to build a predictive tool using ANN.

Moreover, Moayedi et al. applied the HHO to train multilayer perceptron (MLP). They used it in the footings bearing capacity assessments over two-layer foundation soils.

Murlidhar et al. [286] introduced a novel version of the HHO based on the multilayer perceptron neural network to predict flyrock distance induced by mine blasting.

Yu et al. [287] developed an ELM model based on the HHO in order to forecast mine blasting peak particle velocity.

Payani et al. [288] used the HHO and Bat Algorithm with machine learning tools (ANFIS/SVR) in order to improve modeling of a landslide spatial.

6.8. Building and Construction or Civil Engineering

Golafshani et al. [289] used the Radial Basis Function neural network (RBFNN) and multilayer neural network (MLNN) with the HHO in order to measure concrete Compressive Strength (CS). Parsa and Naderpour [290] tried to estimate the strength of shear of reinforced concrete walls using the HHO with support vector regression.

Kardani et al. [143] applied ICHHO to structural optimization using five truss structures.

6.9. Coronavirus COVID-19

The new coronavirus, also known as COVID-19, was termed as an infectious disease by the World Health Organization (WHO). This virus began in China (Wuhan city) and has affected billions of people's lives [291,292]. Computer science researchers tried to use the HHO to analyze and detect this virus.

Balaha et al. [214] tried to propose an approach, called CovH2SD, in order to detect COVID-19 from chest Computed Tomography (CT) images. They applied transfer learning techniques using nine convolutional NNs, namely: ResNet101, ResNet50, VGG16, VGG19, MobileNetV1, MobileNetV2,Xception, DenseNet121, and DenseNet169.

Another work was conducted by Houssein et al. [293] to classify COVID-19 genes using SVM. They used a big gene expression cancer (RNA-Seq) dataset with 20531 features to test their model. Hu et al. [294] employed the HHO with the Extreme Learning Machine (ELM) to detect COVID-19 severity using blood gas analysis. They used Specular Reflection Learning and named the new HHO algorithm HHOSRL.

Ye et al. [295] developed the fuzzy KNN HHO method to predict and diagnose COVID-19. They compared their algorithm, which is called HHO-FKNN, with several machine learning algorithms and argued that it has a higher classification and better stability. Moreover, Bandyopadhyay et al. [296] used their hybrid algorithm, which combined chaotic HHO with SA, to screen COVID-19 CT scans.

6.10. Other Applications

6.10.1. Microchannel Heat Sinks Design

Electronic devices' thermal management has become very important in product designs that require more efficiency and power. Abbasi et al. [297] tried to used the HHO in the microchannel heat sinks design. The authors compared their results with the Newton–Raphson method, PSO, GOA, WOA, DA, and the bees Optimization Algorithm.

6.10.2. Chart Patterns Recognition

Golilarz et al. [298] proposed a novel automatic approach based on the HHO and deep learning (ConvNet) for nine control chat patterns (CCP). In this approach, the CPP recognition method, the unprocessed data are passed and processed using more than one hidden layer in order to extract all representation features.

6.10.3. Water Distribution

Khalifeh et al. [299] developed a model based on the HHO in order to optimize the distribution network of water in a city named Homashahr in Iran from September 2018 to October 2019. the authors stated that the HHO proved efficiency in finding the optimal water network design.

6.10.4. Internet of Things

The Internet of Things (IoT) gives the ability to different entities to access the environment, monitor it, and communicate with other entities [300]. Seyfollahi and Ghaffari [301] developed a scheme for handling Reliable Data Dissemination in IoT (RDDI) based on the HHO. The authors evaluated their schemes using three comparative approaches using five different metrics: reliability, energy consumption, end-to-end delay, packet forwarding distance, and computational overhead. Moreover, Saravanan et al. [302] proposed a PI controller based on the HHO. They tuned BLDC motor parameters in the globe with IoT establishment.

6.10.5. Short-Term Load Forecasting

Tayab et al. [303] proposed a novel hybrid algorithm called HHO-FNN by training feed-forward neural network (FNN) using the HHO. They applied it in predicting load demand in the electric market in Queensland. They compared HHO-FNN with PSO, ANN, and PSO based on a support vector machine and a back-propagation neural network.

6.10.6. Cardiomyopathy

Ding et al. [304] developed a fuzzy HHO algorithm (FHHO) to monitor cardiomyopathy patients using wearable devices and sensors. They introduced Wearable Sensing Data Optimization (WSDO) to have accurate cardiomyopathy data.

6.10.7. Qos-Aware Service Composition

Li et al. [305] tried to solve QoS-aware Web Service (QWSC) problems and drawbacks using a metaheuristic algorithm by developing a method to construct fuzzy neighborhood relations and combining the HHO with logical chaotic function.

6.10.8. PEMFC Parameter Estimation

Mossa et al. [224] employed the HHO in order to evaluate the Proton Exchange Membrane Fuel Cell (PEMFC) unknown parameters. They tested it using three PEMFC stacks: 500W SR-12 PEM, BCS 500-W PEM, and 250 W. They claimed that based on the HHO it surpassed other algorithms in convergence speed and accuracy.

6.10.9. DVR Control System

ElKady et al. [306] employed the HHO to develop an optimized, enhanced, and less complex Dynamic Voltage Restorer (DVR). The results are compared with PSO and WOA. The authors used MATLAB/Simulink to simulate a system via Typhoon HIL402 real-time emulator validation.

7. A Brief Discussion

In this paper, we reviewed the most contemporary works and developments in the improvement and verification of the HHO. As collected works show, there are several points to be considered for both the conventional HHO and the enhanced variants of HHO. First, the performance matter. The different studies verified that one of the reasons for interest in the HHO over other competitors is its performance. Due to several reasons such as dynamic components, greedy selection, and multiphase searching rules, the HHO can show high-quality results in the same conditions that other methods are applied. This is one of the main whys and wherefores that the HHO is utilized in tracked papers. The second reason is the need for performance optimization. In most of the variants, the authors mention that the stability of the optimizer needs to be improved to reach higher levels of the convergence and lower stagnation problems. This requirement is a need in all population-based methods to make a more stable balance among the local and global search inclinations.

Second, most of the studies have enhanced the sense of balance among the exploratory and exploitative propensities of the HHO. The accuracy of results an convergence speed are the most frequent features enhanced in the literature until now. Hence, we observed in the studied papers that the authors applied the HHO and its variants to many new problems and datasets. As per the no free lunch (NFL) [307] theorem, the authors more and more understood, compared with before 2019, that for tackling new problems, how to adapt algorithm features and how some of their enhanced operations of each method contribute to the efficacy of the final results. Hence, they could investigate different performance aspects of the HHO in dealing with many real-world problems. The last but not least is to further enhance the quality of the results of the HHO with more deep evolutionary basis, such as coevolutionary technology, multipopulation approaches, memetic methods, and parallel computing. Such bases can further assist in harmonizing global and local trends, which will result in better variants of the HHO. Another aspect we want to suggest is that if the literature also attaches the source codes of their enhanced variants, it will be more productive for future research on the HHO, and they can also compare their variants with previous ideas.

8. Conclusions and Future Work

In this survey paper, we reviewed the recent applications and variants of the recently well-established robust optimizer, Harris hawk optimizer (HHO), as blueone of the most popular swarm-based techniques in recent years. The original HHO includes a set of random solutions, as a population-based method, which can perform two phases of global searches and four phases of local searches. The HHO can show high flexibility in the transition of phases and has several dynamic components that assist it in more efficient exploratory and exploitative trends. The literature review also contained an in-depth review of enhanced versions, the way they enhanced, and application domains.

There are several possible future directions and possible ideas worth investigations regarding the new variants of the HHO algorithm and its widespread applications. First, the HHO is still one year old and several problems in the machine learning domain, mainly feature selection, are still not resolved. Moreover, it is expected that authors provide more balance measures into their analysis and provide more about what resulted in the computational complexity of variants after modifications. Although the HHO is a relatively fast method, such analysis can help the literature to be more open regarding the time of computations.

Author Contributions: A.G.H.: conceptualization, supervision, methodology, formal analysis, resources, data curation, and writing—original draft preparation. L.A. and K.H.A.: conceptualization, supervision, writing—review and editing, project administration, and funding acquisition. R.A.Z., F.A.H., M.A. and A.S.: conceptualization, writing—review and editing, and supervision. A.H.G.: conceptualization and writing—review and editing. All authors have read and agreed to the published version of the manuscript.

Funding: This research received no external funding.

Acknowledgments: The authors would like to thank the Deanship of Scientific Research at Umm Al-Qura University for supporting this work by Grant Code: (22UQU4320277DSR07).

Conflicts of Interest: The authors declare no conflict of interest.

References

1. Abualigah, L. Group search optimizer: A nature-inspired meta-heuristic optimization algorithm with its results, variants, and applications. *Neural Comput. Appl.* **2020**, *33*, 2949–2972. [CrossRef]
2. Zitar, R.A.; Abualigah, L.; Al-Dmour, N.A. Review and analysis for the Red Deer Algorithm. *J. Ambient. Intell. Humaniz. Comput.* **2021**, 1–11. [CrossRef] [PubMed]
3. Hashim, F.A.; Salem, N.M.; Seddik, A.F. Automatic segmentation of optic disc from color fundus images. *Jokull J.* **2013**, *63*, 142–153.
4. Fathi, H.; AlSalman, H.; Gumaei, A.; Manhrawy, I.I.; Hussien, A.G.; El-Kafrawy, P. An Efficient Cancer Classification Model Using Microarray and High-Dimensional Data. *Comput. Intell. Neurosci.* **2021**, *2021*. [CrossRef] [PubMed]
5. Nadimi-Shahraki, M.H.; Taghian, S.; Mirjalili, S.; Zamani, H.; Bahreininejad, A. GGWO: Gaze cues learning-based grey wolf optimizer and its applications for solving engineering problems. *J. Comput. Sci.* **2022**, *61*, 101636. [CrossRef]
6. Almotairi, K.H.; Abualigah, L. Hybrid reptile search algorithm and remora optimization algorithm for optimization tasks and data clustering. *Symmetry* **2022**, *14*, 458. [CrossRef]
7. Shah, A.; Azam, N.; Alanazi, E.; Yao, J. Image blurring and sharpening inspired three-way clustering approach. *Appl. Intell.* **2022**, 1–25. [CrossRef]
8. Alotaibi, Y. A New Meta-Heuristics Data Clustering Algorithm Based on Tabu Search and Adaptive Search Memory. *Symmetry* **2022**, *14*, 623. [CrossRef]
9. Tejani, G.G.; Kumar, S.; Gandomi, A.H. Multi-objective heat transfer search algorithm for truss optimization. *Eng. Comput.* **2021**, *37*, 641–662. [CrossRef]
10. Shehab, M.; Abualigah, L.; Al Hamad, H.; Alabool, H.; Alshinwan, M.; Khasawneh, A.M. Moth–flame optimization algorithm: Variants and applications. *Neural Comput. Appl.* **2020**, *32*, 9859–9884. [CrossRef]

11. Abualigah, L. Multi-verse optimizer algorithm: A comprehensive survey of its results, variants, and applications. *Neural Comput. Appl.* **2020**, *32*, 12381–12401. [CrossRef]
12. Islam, M.J.; Basalamah, S.; Ahmadi, M.; Sid-Ahmed, M.A. Capsule image segmentation in pharmaceutical applications using edge-based techniques. In Proceedings of the 2011 IEEE International Conference on Electro/Information Technology, Mankato, MN, USA, 15–17 May 2011; pp. 1–5.
13. Kumar, S.; Tejani, G.G.; Pholdee, N.; Bureerat, S. Multi-objective passing vehicle search algorithm for structure optimization. *Expert Syst. Appl.* **2021**, *169*, 114511. [CrossRef]
14. Holland, J.H. Genetic algorithms. *Sci. Am.* **1992**, *267*, 66–73. [CrossRef]
15. Koza, J.R. *Genetic Programming II, Automatic Discovery of Reusable Subprograms*; MIT Press: Cambridge, MA, USA, 1992.
16. Storn, R.; Price, K. Differential evolution–a simple and efficient heuristic for global optimization over continuous spaces. *J. Glob. Optim.* **1997**, *11*, 341–359. [CrossRef]
17. Beyer, H.G.; Schwefel, H.P. Evolution strategies—A comprehensive introduction. *Nat. Comput.* **2002**, *1*, 3–52. [CrossRef]
18. Abualigah, L.; Diabat, A.; Mirjalili, S.; Abd Elaziz, M.; Gandomi, A.H. The Arithmetic Optimization Algorithm. *Comput. Methods Appl. Mech. Eng.* **2021**, *376*, 113609. [CrossRef]
19. Eberhart, R.; Kennedy, J. A new optimizer using particle swarm theory. In Proceedings of the MHS'95. Proceedings of the Sixth International Symposium on Micro Machine and Human Science, Nagoya, Japan, 4–6 October 1995; pp. 39–43.
20. Dorigo, M.; Di Caro, G. Ant colony optimization: A new meta-heuristic. In Proceedings of the 1999 Congress on Evolutionary Computation-CEC99 (Cat. No. 99TH8406), Washington, DC, USA, 6–9 July 1999; Volume 2, pp. 1470–1477.
21. Geem, Z.W.; Kim, J.H.; Loganathan, G.V. A new heuristic optimization algorithm: Harmony search. *Simulation* **2001**, *76*, 60–68. [CrossRef]
22. Karaboga, D.; Basturk, B. A powerful and efficient algorithm for numerical function optimization: Artificial bee colony (ABC) algorithm. *J. Glob. Optim.* **2007**, *39*, 459–471. [CrossRef]
23. Formato, R.A. Central Force Optimization. *Prog. Electromagn. Res.* **2007**, *77*, 425–491. [CrossRef]
24. Simon, D. Biogeography-based optimization. *IEEE Trans. Evol. Comput.* **2008**, *12*, 702–713. [CrossRef]
25. Yang, X.S.; Deb, S. Cuckoo search via Lévy flights. In Proceedings of the 2009 World Congress on Nature & Biologically Inspired Computing (NaBIC), Coimbatore, India, 9–11 December 2009; pp. 210–214.
26. Das, S.; Biswas, A.; Dasgupta, S.; Abraham, A. Bacterial foraging optimization algorithm: Theoretical foundations, analysis, and applications. In *Foundations of Computational Intelligence*; Springer: Berlin/Heidelberg, Germany, 2009; Volume 3, pp. 23–55.
27. Rashedi, E.; Nezamabadi-Pour, H.; Saryazdi, S. GSA: A gravitational search algorithm. *Inf. Sci.* **2009**, *179*, 2232–2248. [CrossRef]
28. Yang, X.S. Firefly algorithm, stochastic test functions and design optimisation. *Int. J. Bio-Inspired Comput.* **2010**, *2*, 78–84. [CrossRef]
29. Rao, R.V.; Savsani, V.J.; Vakharia, D. Teaching–learning-based optimization: A novel method for constrained mechanical design optimization problems. *Comput.-Aided Des.* **2011**, *43*, 303–315. [CrossRef]
30. Pan, W.T. A new fruit fly optimization algorithm: Taking the financial distress model as an example. *Knowl.-Based Syst.* **2012**, *26*, 69–74. [CrossRef]
31. Gandomi, A.H.; Alavi, A.H. Krill herd: A new bio-inspired optimization algorithm. *Commun. Nonlinear Sci. Numer. Simul.* **2012**, *17*, 4831–4845. [CrossRef]
32. Mirjalili, S.; Mirjalili, S.M.; Lewis, A. Grey wolf optimizer. *Adv. Eng. Softw.* **2014**, *69*, 46–61. [CrossRef]
33. Heidari, A.A.; Mirjalili, S.; Faris, H.; Aljarah, I.; Mafarja, M.; Chen, H. Harris hawks optimization: Algorithm and applications. *Future Gener. Comput. Syst.* **2019**, *97*, 849–872. [CrossRef]
34. Hashim, F.A.; Houssein, E.H.; Mabrouk, M.S.; Al-Atabany, W.; Mirjalili, S. Henry gas solubility optimization: A novel physics-based algorithm. *Future Gener. Comput. Syst.* **2019**, *101*, 646–667. [CrossRef]
35. Li, S.; Chen, H.; Wang, M.; Heidari, A.A.; Mirjalili, S. Slime mould algorithm: A new method for stochastic optimization. *Future Gener. Comput. Syst.* **2020**, *111*, 300–323. [CrossRef]
36. Hashim, F.A.; Hussien, A.G. Snake Optimizer: A novel meta-heuristic optimization Algorithm. *Knowl.-Based Syst.* **2022**, *242*, 108320. [CrossRef]
37. Abualigah, L.; Shehab, M.; Alshinwan, M.; Mirjalili, S.; Abd Elaziz, M. Ant Lion Optimizer: A Comprehensive Survey of Its Variants and Applications. *Arch. Comput. Methods Eng* **2020**, *242*, 108320. [CrossRef]
38. Alsalibi, B.; Mirjalili, S.; Abualigah, L.; Gandomi, A.H. A Comprehensive Survey on the Recent Variants and Applications of Membrane-Inspired Evolutionary Algorithms. *Arch. Comput. Methods Eng.* **2022**, 1–17. [CrossRef]
39. Hashim, F.; Salem, N.; Seddik, A. Optic disc boundary detection from digital fundus images. *J. Med. Imaging Health Inform.* **2015**, *5*, 50–56. [CrossRef]
40. Abualigah, L.; Almotairi, K.H.; Abd Elaziz, M.; Shehab, M.; Altalhi, M. Enhanced Flow Direction Arithmetic Optimization Algorithm for mathematical optimization problems with applications of data clustering. *Eng. Anal. Bound. Elem.* **2022**, *138*, 13–29. [CrossRef]
41. Kumar, S.; Tejani, G.G.; Pholdee, N.; Bureerat, S.; Mehta, P. Hybrid heat transfer search and passing vehicle search optimizer for multi-objective structural optimization. *Knowl.-Based Syst.* **2021**, *212*, 106556. [CrossRef]
42. Abualigah, L.; Shehab, M.; Alshinwan, M.; Alabool, H. Salp swarm algorithm: A comprehensive survey. *Neural Comput. Appl.* **2019**, *32*, 11195–11215. [CrossRef]

43. Nadimi-Shahraki, M.H.; Zamani, H. DMDE: Diversity-maintained multi-trial vector differential evolution algorithm for non-decomposition large-scale global optimization. *Expert Syst. Appl.* **2022**, *198*, 116895. [CrossRef]

44. Zamani, H.; Nadimi-Shahraki, M.H.; Gandomi, A.H. Starling murmuration optimizer: A novel bio-inspired algorithm for global and engineering optimization. *Comput. Methods Appl. Mech. Eng.* **2022**, *392*, 114616. [CrossRef]

45. Abualigah, L.; Diabat, A.; Geem, Z.W. A Comprehensive Survey of the Harmony Search Algorithm in Clustering Applications. *Appl. Sci.* **2020**, *10*, 3827. [CrossRef]

46. Abualigah, L.; Gandomi, A.H.; Elaziz, M.A.; Hussien, A.G.; Khasawneh, A.M.; Alshinwan, M.; Houssein, E.H. Nature-inspired optimization algorithms for text document clustering—A comprehensive analysis. *Algorithms* **2020**, *13*, 345. [CrossRef]

47. Nadimi-Shahraki, M.H.; Fatahi, A.; Zamani, H.; Mirjalili, S.; Abualigah, L.; Abd Elaziz, M. Migration-based moth-flame optimization algorithm. *Processes* **2021**, *9*, 2276. [CrossRef]

48. Mirjalili, S.; Lewis, A. The whale optimization algorithm. *Adv. Eng. Softw.* **2016**, *95*, 51–67. [CrossRef]

49. Nadimi-Shahraki, M.H.; Taghian, S.; Mirjalili, S.; Ewees, A.A.; Abualigah, L.; Abd Elaziz, M. MTV-MFO: Multi-Trial Vector-Based Moth-Flame Optimization Algorithm. *Symmetry* **2021**, *13*, 2388. [CrossRef]

50. Fatani, A.; Dahou, A.; Al-Qaness, M.A.; Lu, S.; Elaziz, M.A. Advanced feature extraction and selection approach using deep learning and Aquila optimizer for IoT intrusion detection system. *Sensors* **2021**, *22*, 140. [CrossRef] [PubMed]

51. Molina, D.; Poyatos, J.; Del Ser, J.; García, S.; Hussain, A.; Herrera, F. Comprehensive Taxonomies of Nature-and Bio-inspired Optimization: Inspiration versus Algorithmic Behavior, Critical Analysis and Recommendations. *arXiv* **2020**, arXiv:2002.08136.

52. Nadimi-Shahraki, M.H.; Taghian, S.; Mirjalili, S.; Abualigah, L.; Abd Elaziz, M.; Oliva, D. EWOA-OPF: Effective Whale Optimization Algorithm to Solve Optimal Power Flow Problem. *Electronics* **2021**, *10*, 2975. [CrossRef]

53. Kharrich, M.; Abualigah, L.; Kamel, S.; AbdEl-Sattar, H.; Tostado-Véliz, M. An Improved Arithmetic Optimization Algorithm for design of a microgrid with energy storage system: Case study of El Kharga Oasis, Egypt. *J. Energy Storage* **2022**, *51*, 104343. [CrossRef]

54. Niu, P.; Niu, S.; Chang, L. The defect of the Grey Wolf optimization algorithm and its verification method. *Knowl.-Based Syst.* **2019**, *171*, 37–43. [CrossRef]

55. Hashim, F.; Mabrouk, M.S.; Al-Atabany, W. GWOMF: Grey Wolf Optimization for Motif Finding. In Proceedings of the 2017 13th International Computer Engineering Conference (ICENCO), Cairo, Egypt, 27–28 December 2017; pp. 141–146.

56. Sörensen, K. Metaheuristics—The metaphor exposed. *Int. Trans. Oper. Res.* **2015**, *22*, 3–18. [CrossRef]

57. Hassanien, A.E.; Emary, E. *Swarm Intelligence: Principles, Advances, and Applications*; CRC Press: Boca Raton, FL, USA, 2018.

58. Koza, J.R. *Genetic Programming II*; MIT Press: Cambridge, UK, 1994; Volume 17.

59. Yao, X.; Liu, Y.; Lin, G. Evolutionary programming made faster. *IEEE Trans. Evol. Comput.* **1999**, *3*, 82–102.

60. Andrew, A.M. Evolution and optimum seeking. *Kybernetes* **1998**, *27*, 975–978. [CrossRef]

61. Civicioglu, P. Backtracking search optimization algorithm for numerical optimization problems. *Appl. Math. Comput.* **2013**, *219*, 8121–8144. [CrossRef]

62. Karaboga, D.; Basturk, B. Artificial bee colony (ABC) optimization algorithm for solving constrained optimization problems. In *International Fuzzy Systems Association World Congress*; Springer: Berlin/Heidelberg, Germany, 2007; pp. 789–798.

63. Yang, X.S. Firefly algorithms for multimodal optimization. In *International Symposium on Stochastic Algorithms*; Springer: Berlin/Heidelberg, Germany, 2009; pp. 169–178.

64. Mostafa, R.R.; Hussien, A.G.; Khan, M.A.; Kadry, S.; Hashim, F. Enhanced COOT optimization algorithm for Dimensionality Reduction. In Proceedings of the 2022 Fifth International Conference of Women in Data Science at Prince Sultan University (WiDS PSU), Riyadh, Saudi Arabia, 28–29 March 2022. [CrossRef]

65. Chu, S.C.; Tsai, P.W.; Pan, J.S. Cat swarm optimization. In *Pacific Rim International Conference on Artificial Intelligence*; Springer: Berlin/Heidelberg, Germany, 2006; pp. 854–858.

66. Yang, X.S. A new metaheuristic bat-inspired algorithm. In *Nature Inspired Cooperative Strategies for Optimization (NICSO 2010)*; Springer: Berlin/Heidelberg, Germany, 2010; pp. 65–74.

67. Kumar, S.; Tejani, G.G.; Mirjalili, S. Modified symbiotic organisms search for structural optimization. *Eng. Comput.* **2019**, *35*, 1269–1296. [CrossRef]

68. Nadimi-Shahraki, M.H.; Fatahi, A.; Zamani, H.; Mirjalili, S.; Abualigah, L. An Improved Moth-Flame Optimization Algorithm with Adaptation Mechanism to Solve Numerical and Mechanical Engineering Problems. *Entropy* **2021**, *23*, 1637. [CrossRef] [PubMed]

69. Hussien, A.G.; Amin, M.; Abd El Aziz, M. A comprehensive review of moth-flame optimisation: Variants, hybrids, and applications. *J. Exp. Theor. Artif. Intell.* **2020**, *32*, 705–725. [CrossRef]

70. Hussien, A.G.; Heidari, A.A.; Ye, X.; Liang, G.; Chen, H.; Pan, Z. Boosting whale optimization with evolution strategy and Gaussian random walks: An image segmentation method. *Eng. Comput.* **2022**, 1–45. [CrossRef]

71. Hussien, A.G.; Hassanien, A.E.; Houssein, E.H.; Amin, M.; Azar, A.T. New binary whale optimization algorithm for discrete optimization problems. *Eng. Optim.* **2020**, *52*, 945–959. [CrossRef]

72. Hussien, A.G.; Oliva, D.; Houssein, E.H.; Juan, A.A.; Yu, X. Binary whale optimization algorithm for dimensionality reduction. *Mathematics* **2020**, *8*, 1821. [CrossRef]

73. Saremi, S.; Mirjalili, S.; Lewis, A. Grasshopper optimisation algorithm: Theory and application. *Adv. Eng. Softw.* **2017**, *105*, 30–47. [CrossRef]

74. Mirjalili, S.; Gandomi, A.H.; Mirjalili, S.Z.; Saremi, S.; Faris, H.; Mirjalili, S.M. Salp Swarm Algorithm: A bio-inspired optimizer for engineering design problems. *Adv. Eng. Softw.* **2017**, *114*, 163–191. [CrossRef]
75. Hussien, A.G. An enhanced opposition-based Salp Swarm Algorithm for global optimization and engineering problems. *J. Ambient. Intell. Humaniz. Comput.* **2021**, *13*, 129–150. [CrossRef]
76. Hussien, A.G.; Amin, M.; Wang, M.; Liang, G.; Alsanad, A.; Gumaei, A.; Chen, H. Crow Search Algorithm: Theory, Recent Advances, and Applications. *IEEE Access* **2020**, *8*, 173548–173565. [CrossRef]
77. Cheng, M.Y.; Prayogo, D. Symbiotic organisms search: A new metaheuristic optimization algorithm. *Comput. Struct.* **2014**, *139*, 98–112. [CrossRef]
78. Abualigah, L.; Abd Elaziz, M.; Sumari, P.; Geem, Z.W.; Gandomi, A.H. Reptile Search Algorithm (RSA): A nature-inspired meta-heuristic optimizer. *Expert Syst. Appl.* **2022**, *191*, 116158. [CrossRef]
79. Arora, S.; Singh, S. Butterfly optimization algorithm: A novel approach for global optimization. *Soft Comput.* **2019**, *23*, 715–734. [CrossRef]
80. Wang, S.; Hussien, A.G.; Jia, H.; Abualigah, L.; Zheng, R. Enhanced Remora Optimization Algorithm for Solving Constrained Engineering Optimization Problems. *Mathematics* **2022**, *10*, 1696. [CrossRef]
81. Zheng, R.; Jia, H.; Abualigah, L.; Liu, Q.; Wang, S. An improved arithmetic optimization algorithm with forced switching mechanism for global optimization problems. *Math. Biosci. Eng.* **2022**, *19*, 473–512. [CrossRef]
82. Dhiman, G.; Kumar, V. Seagull optimization algorithm: Theory and its applications for large-scale industrial engineering problems. *Knowl.-Based Syst.* **2019**, *165*, 169–196. [CrossRef]
83. Assiri, A.S.; Hussien, A.G.; Amin, M. Ant Lion Optimization: Variants, hybrids, and applications. *IEEE Access* **2020**, *8*, 77746–77764. [CrossRef]
84. Kirkpatrick, S.; Gelatt, C.D.; Vecchi, M.P. Optimization by simulated annealing. *Science* **1983**, *220*, 671–680. [CrossRef]
85. Erol, O.K.; Eksin, I. A new optimization method: Big bang–big crunch. *Adv. Eng. Softw.* **2006**, *37*, 106–111. [CrossRef]
86. Shareef, H.; Ibrahim, A.A.; Mutlag, A.H. Lightning search algorithm. *Appl. Soft Comput.* **2015**, *36*, 315–333. [CrossRef]
87. Abedinpourshotorban, H.; Shamsuddin, S.M.; Beheshti, Z.; Jawawi, D.N. Electromagnetic field optimization: A physics-inspired metaheuristic optimization algorithm. *Swarm Evol. Comput.* **2016**, *26*, 8–22. [CrossRef]
88. Kaveh, A.; Dadras, A. A novel meta-heuristic optimization algorithm: Thermal exchange optimization. *Adv. Eng. Softw.* **2017**, *110*, 69–84. [CrossRef]
89. Doğan, B.; Ölmez, T. A new metaheuristic for numerical function optimization: Vortex Search algorithm. *Inf. Sci.* **2015**, *293*, 125–145. [CrossRef]
90. Tabari, A.; Ahmad, A. A new optimization method: Electro-Search algorithm. *Comput. Chem. Eng.* **2017**, *103*, 1–11. [CrossRef]
91. Zhao, W.; Wang, L.; Zhang, Z. A novel atom search optimization for dispersion coefficient estimation in groundwater. *Future Gener. Comput. Syst.* **2019**, *91*, 601–610. [CrossRef]
92. Lam, A.Y.; Li, V.O. Chemical-reaction-inspired metaheuristic for optimization. *IEEE Trans. Evol. Comput.* **2009**, *14*, 381–399. [CrossRef]
93. Huan, T.T.; Kulkarni, A.J.; Kanesan, J.; Huang, C.J.; Abraham, A. Ideology algorithm: A socio-inspired optimization methodology. *Neural Comput. Appl.* **2017**, *28*, 845–876. [CrossRef]
94. Mousavirad, S.J.; Ebrahimpour-Komleh, H. Human mental search: A new population-based metaheuristic optimization algorithm. *Appl. Intell.* **2017**, *47*, 850–887. [CrossRef]
95. Shi, Y. Brain storm optimization algorithm. In *International Conference in Swarm Intelligence*; Springer: Berlin/Heidelberg, Germany, 2011; pp. 303–309.
96. Xu, Y.; Cui, Z.; Zeng, J. Social emotional optimization algorithm for nonlinear constrained optimization problems. In *International Conference on Swarm, Evolutionary, and Memetic Computing*; Springer: Berlin/Heidelberg, Germany, 2010; pp. 583–590.
97. Kumar, M.; Kulkarni, A.J.; Satapathy, S.C. Socio evolution & learning optimization algorithm: A socio-inspired optimization methodology. *Future Gener. Comput. Syst.* **2018**, *81*, 252–272.
98. Tan, Y.; Zhu, Y. Fireworks algorithm for optimization. In *International Conference in Swarm Intelligence*; Springer: Berlin/Heidelberg, Germany, 2010; pp. 355–364.
99. Kashan, A.H. League championship algorithm: A new algorithm for numerical function optimization. In Proceedings of the 2009 International Conference of Soft Computing and Pattern Recognition, Malacca, Malaysia, 4–7 December 2009; pp. 43–48.
100. Osaba, E.; Diaz, F.; Onieva, E. Golden ball: A novel meta-heuristic to solve combinatorial optimization problems based on soccer concepts. *Appl. Intell.* **2014**, *41*, 145–166. [CrossRef]
101. Razmjooy, N.; Khalilpour, M.; Ramezani, M. A new meta-heuristic optimization algorithm inspired by FIFA world cup competitions: Theory and its application in PID designing for AVR system. *J. Control Autom. Electr. Syst.* **2016**, *27*, 419–440. [CrossRef]
102. Zheng, R.; Jia, H.; Abualigah, L.; Liu, Q.; Wang, S. Deep ensemble of slime mold algorithm and arithmetic optimization algorithm for global optimization. *Processes* **2021**, *9*, 1774. [CrossRef]
103. Wang, S.; Liu, Q.; Liu, Y.; Jia, H.; Abualigah, L.; Zheng, R.; Wu, D. A Hybrid SSA and SMA with mutation opposition-based learning for constrained engineering problems. *Comput. Intell. Neurosci.* **2021**, *2021*. [CrossRef] [PubMed]
104. Goldberg, D.E.; Holland, J.H. Genetic algorithms and machine learning. In Proceedings of the Sixth Annual Conference on Computational Learning Theory, Santa Cruz, CA, USA, 26–28 July 1993.

105. Hansen, N.; Müller, S.D.; Koumoutsakos, P. Reducing the time complexity of the derandomized evolution strategy with covariance matrix adaptation (CMA-ES). *Evol. Comput.* **2003**, *11*, 1–18. [CrossRef]
106. Tanabe, R.; Fukunaga, A.S. Improving the search performance of SHADE using linear population size reduction. In Proceedings of the 2014 IEEE Congress on Evolutionary Computation (CEC), Beijing, China, 6–11 July 2014; pp. 1658–1665.
107. Awad, N.H.; Ali, M.Z.; Suganthan, P.N.; Reynolds, R.G. An ensemble sinusoidal parameter adaptation incorporated with L-SHADE for solving CEC2014 benchmark problems. In Proceedings of the 2016 IEEE Congress on Evolutionary Computation (CEC), Vancouver, BC, Canada, 24–29 July 2016; pp. 2958–2965.
108. Mirjalili, S. SCA: A sine cosine algorithm for solving optimization problems. *Knowl.-Based Syst.* **2016**, *96*, 120–133. [CrossRef]
109. Zhao, W.; Wang, L.; Zhang, Z. Artificial ecosystem-based optimization: A novel nature-inspired meta-heuristic algorithm. *Neural Comput. Appl.* **2020**, *32*, 9383–9425. [CrossRef]
110. Too, J.; Abdullah, A.R.; Mohd Saad, N. A new quadratic binary harris hawk optimization for feature selection. *Electronics* **2019**, *8*, 1130. [CrossRef]
111. Hans, R.; Kaur, H.; Kaur, N. Opposition-based Harris Hawks optimization algorithm for feature selection in breast mass classification. *J. Interdiscip. Math.* **2020**, *23*, 97–106.
112. Jiao, S.; Chong, G.; Huang, C.; Hu, H.; Wang, M.; Heidari, A.A.; Chen, H.; Zhao, X. Orthogonally adapted Harris Hawk Optimization for parameter estimation of photovoltaic models. *Energy* **2020**, *203*, 117804. [CrossRef]
113. Fan, C.; Zhou, Y.; Tang, Z. Neighborhood centroid opposite-based learning Harris Hawks optimization for training neural networks. *Evol. Intell.* **2020**, *14*, 1847–1867. [CrossRef]
114. Song, Y.; Tan, X.; Mizzi, S. Optimal parameter extraction of the proton exchange membrane fuel cells based on a new Harris Hawks Optimization algorithm. *Energy Sources Part A Recover. Util. Environ. Eff.* **2020**, 1–18. [CrossRef]
115. Hussain, K.; Zhu, W.; Salleh, M.N.M. Long-term memory Harris' hawk optimization for high dimensional and optimal power flow problems. *IEEE Access* **2019**, *7*, 147596–147616. [CrossRef]
116. Golilarz, N.A.; Mirmozaffari, M.; Gashteroodkhani, T.A.; Ali, L.; Dolatsara, H.A.; Boskabadi, A.; Yazdi, M. Optimized wavelet-based satellite image de-noising with multi-population differential evolution-assisted harris hawks optimization algorithm. *IEEE Access* **2020**, *8*, 133076–133085. [CrossRef]
117. Wunnava, A.; Naik, M.K.; Panda, R.; Jena, B.; Abraham, A. An adaptive Harris hawks optimization technique for two dimensional grey gradient based multilevel image thresholding. *Appl. Soft Comput.* **2020**, *95*, 106526. [CrossRef]
118. Jia, H.; Lang, C.; Oliva, D.; Song, W.; Peng, X. Dynamic harris hawks optimization with mutation mechanism for satellite image segmentation. *Remote Sens.* **2019**, *11*, 1421. [CrossRef]
119. Shao, K.; Fu, W.; Tan, J.; Wang, K. Coordinated Approach Fusing Time-shift Multiscale Dispersion Entropy and Vibrational Harris Hawks Optimization-based SVM for Fault Diagnosis of Rolling Bearing. *Measurement* **2020**, *173*, 108580. [CrossRef]
120. Wei, Y.; Lv, H.; Chen, M.; Wang, M.; Heidari, A.A.; Chen, H.; Li, C. Predicting Entrepreneurial Intention of Students: An Extreme Learning Machine With Gaussian Barebone Harris Hawks Optimizer. *IEEE Access* **2020**, *8*, 76841–76855. [CrossRef]
121. Li, C.; Li, J.; Chen, H.; Jin, M.; Ren, H. Enhanced Harris hawks optimization with multi-strategy for global optimization tasks. *Expert Syst. Appl.* **2021**, *185*, 115499. [CrossRef]
122. Arini, F.Y.; Chiewchanwattana, S.; Soomlek, C.; Sunat, K. Joint Opposite Selection (JOS): A premiere joint of selective leading opposition and dynamic opposite enhanced Harris' hawks optimization for solving single-objective problems. *Expert Syst. Appl.* **2022**, *188*, 116001. [CrossRef]
123. Thaher, T.; Heidari, A.A.; Mafarja, M.; Dong, J.S.; Mirjalili, S. Binary Harris Hawks optimizer for high-dimensional, low sample size feature selection. In *Evolutionary Machine Learning Techniques*; Springer: Berlin/Heidelberg, Germany, 2020; pp. 251–272.
124. Thaher, T.; Arman, N. Efficient Multi-Swarm Binary Harris Hawks Optimization as a Feature Selection Approach for Software Fault Prediction. In Proceedings of the 2020 11th International Conference on Information and Communication Systems (ICICS), Irbid, Jordan, 7–9 April 2020; pp. 249–254.
125. Chellal, M.; Benmessahel, I. Dynamic Complex Protein Detection using Binary Harris Hawks Optimization. In *Journal of Physics: Conference Series*; IOP Publishing: Bristol, UK, 2020; Volume 1642, p. 012019.
126. Dokeroglu, T.; Deniz, A.; Kiziloz, H.E. A robust multiobjective Harris' Hawks Optimization algorithm for the binary classification problem. *Knowl.-Based Syst.* **2021**, *227*, 107219. [CrossRef]
127. Chantar, H.; Thaher, T.; Turabieh, H.; Mafarja, M.; Sheta, A. BHHO-TVS: A binary harris hawks optimizer with time-varying scheme for solving data classification problems. *Appl. Sci.* **2021**, *11*, 6516. [CrossRef]
128. Gupta, S.; Deep, K.; Heidari, A.A.; Moayedi, H.; Wang, M. Opposition-based Learning Harris Hawks Optimization with Advanced Transition Rules: Principles and Analysis. *Expert Syst. Appl.* **2020**, *158*, 113510. [CrossRef]
129. Ridha, H.M.; Hizam, H.; Mirjalili, S.; Othman, M.L.; Ya'acob, M.E.; Abualigah, L. A Novel Theoretical and Practical Methodology for Extracting the Parameters of the Single and Double Diode Photovoltaic Models (December 2021). *IEEE Access* **2022**, *10*, 11110–11137. [CrossRef]
130. Abbassi, A.; Mehrez, R.B.; Touaiti, B.; Abualigah, L.; Touti, E. Parameterization of Photovoltaic Solar Cell Double-Diode Model based on Improved Arithmetic Optimization Algorithm. *Optik* **2022**, *253*, 168600. [CrossRef]
131. Jamei, M.; Karbasi, M.; Mosharaf-Dehkordi, M.; Olumegbon, I.A.; Abualigah, L.; Said, Z.; Asadi, A. Estimating the density of hybrid nanofluids for thermal energy application: Application of non-parametric and evolutionary polynomial regression data-intelligent techniques. *Measurement* **2021**, *189*, 110524. [CrossRef]

132. Amer, D.A.; Attiya, G.; Zeidan, I.; Nasr, A.A. Elite learning Harris hawks optimizer for multi-objective task scheduling in cloud computing. *J. Supercomput.* **2021**, *78*, 2793–2818. [CrossRef]

133. Akdag, O.; Ates, A.; Yeroglu, C. Modification of Harris hawks optimization algorithm with random distribution functions for optimum power flow problem. *Neural Comput. Appl.* **2021**, *33*, 1959–1985. [CrossRef]

134. Zhang, Y.; Zhou, X.; Shih, P.C. Modified Harris Hawks Optimization Algorithm for Global Optimization Problems. *Arab. J. Sci. Eng.* **2020**, *45*, 10949–10974. [CrossRef]

135. Yousri, D.; Allam, D.; Eteiba, M.B. Optimal photovoltaic array reconfiguration for alleviating the partial shading influence based on a modified harris hawks optimizer. *Energy Convers. Manag.* **2020**, *206*, 112470. [CrossRef]

136. Zhao, L.; Li, Z.; Chen, H.; Li, J.; Xiao, J.; Yousefi, N. A multi-criteria optimization for a CCHP with the fuel cell as primary mover using modified Harris Hawks optimization. *Energy Sources Part A Recover. Util. Environ. Eff.* **2020**, 1–16. [CrossRef]

137. Liu, Y.; Chong, G.; Heidari, A.A.; Chen, H.; Liang, G.; Ye, X.; Cai, Z.; Wang, M. Horizontal and vertical crossover of Harris hawk optimizer with Nelder-Mead simplex for parameter estimation of photovoltaic models. *Energy Convers. Manag.* **2020**, *223*, 113211. [CrossRef]

138. Rizk-Allah, R.M.; Hassanien, A.E. A hybrid Harris hawks-Nelder-Mead optimization for practical nonlinear ordinary differential equations. *Evol. Intell.* **2020**, *15*, 141–165. [CrossRef]

139. Yousri, D.; Mirjalili, S.; Machado, J.T.; Thanikanti, S.B.; Fathy, A. Efficient fractional-order modified Harris hawks optimizer for proton exchange membrane fuel cell modeling. *Eng. Appl. Artif. Intell.* **2021**, *100*, 104193. [CrossRef]

140. Irfan, M.; Oh, S.R.; Rhee, S.B. An Effective Coordination Setting for Directional Overcurrent Relays Using Modified Harris Hawk Optimization. *Electronics* **2021**, *10*, 3007. [CrossRef]

141. Ge, L.; Liu, J.; Yan, J.; Rafiq, M.U. Improved Harris Hawks Optimization for Configuration of PV Intelligent Edge Terminals. *IEEE Trans. Sustain. Comput.* **2021**. [CrossRef]

142. Singh, T.; Panda, S.S.; Mohanty, S.R.; Dwibedy, A. Opposition learning based Harris hawks optimizer for data clustering. *J. Ambient. Intell. Humaniz. Comput.* **2021**, 1–16. [CrossRef]

143. Kardani, N.; Bardhan, A.; Roy, B.; Samui, P.; Nazem, M.; Armaghani, D.J.; Zhou, A. A novel improved Harris Hawks optimization algorithm coupled with ELM for predicting permeability of tight carbonates. *Eng. Comput.* **2021**, 1–24. [CrossRef]

144. Guo, W.; Xu, P.; Dai, F.; Zhao, F.; Wu, M. Improved Harris hawks optimization algorithm based on random unscented sigma point mutation strategy. *Appl. Soft Comput.* **2021**, *113*, 108012. [CrossRef]

145. Liu, C. An improved Harris hawks optimizer for job-shop scheduling problem. *J. Supercomput.* **2021**, *77*, 14090–14129. [CrossRef]

146. Duan, Y.X.; Liu, C.Y. An improved Harris Hawk algorithm based on Golden Sine mechanism. In Proceedings of the 2021 4th International Conference on Advanced Electronic Materials, Computers and Software Engineering (AEMCSE), Changsha, China, 26–28 March 2021; pp. 493–497.

147. Hu, H.; Ao, Y.; Bai, Y.; Cheng, R.; Xu, T. An Improved Harris's Hawks Optimization for SAR Target Recognition and Stock Market Index Prediction. *IEEE Access* **2020**, *8*, 65891–65910. [CrossRef]

148. Li, Q.; Song, K.; He, Z.; Li, E.; Cheng, A.; Chen, T. The artificial tree (AT) algorithm. *Eng. Appl. Artif. Intell.* **2017**, *65*, 99–110. [CrossRef]

149. Selim, A.; Kamel, S.; Alghamdi, A.S.; Jurado, F. Optimal Placement of DGs in Distribution System Using an Improved Harris Hawks Optimizer Based on Single-and Multi-Objective Approaches. *IEEE Access* **2020**, *8*, 52815–52829. [CrossRef]

150. Sihwail, R.; Omar, K.; Ariffin, K.A.Z.; Tubishat, M. Improved Harris Hawks Optimization Using Elite Opposition-Based Learning and Novel Search Mechanism for Feature Selection. *IEEE Access* **2020**, *8*, 121127–121145. [CrossRef]

151. Song, S.; Wang, P.; Heidari, A.A.; Wang, M.; Zhao, X.; Chen, H.; He, W.; Xu, S. Dimension decided Harris hawks optimization with Gaussian mutation: Balance analysis and diversity patterns. *Knowl.-Based Syst.* **2021**, *215*, 106425. [CrossRef]

152. Yin, Q.; Cao, B.; Li, X.; Wang, B.; Zhang, Q.; Wei, X. An Intelligent Optimization Algorithm for Constructing a DNA Storage Code: NOL-HHO. *Int. J. Mol. Sci.* **2020**, *21*, 2191. [CrossRef]

153. Ridha, H.M.; Heidari, A.A.; Wang, M.; Chen, H. Boosted mutation-based Harris hawks optimizer for parameters identification of single-diode solar cell models. *Energy Convers. Manag.* **2020**, *209*, 112660. [CrossRef]

154. Zhang, X.; Zhao, K.; Niu, Y. Improved Harris Hawks Optimization Based on Adaptive Cooperative Foraging and Dispersed Foraging Strategies. *IEEE Access* **2020**, *8*, 160297–160314. [CrossRef]

155. Menesy, A.S.; Sultan, H.M.; Selim, A.; Ashmawy, M.G.; Kamel, S. Developing and applying chaotic harris hawks optimization technique for extracting parameters of several proton exchange membrane fuel cell stacks. *IEEE Access* **2019**, *8*, 1146–1159. [CrossRef]

156. Chen, H.; Jiao, S.; Wang, M.; Heidari, A.A.; Zhao, X. Parameters identification of photovoltaic cells and modules using diversification-enriched Harris hawks optimization with chaotic drifts. *J. Clean. Prod.* **2020**, *244*, 118778. [CrossRef]

157. Gao, Z.-M.; Zhao, J.; Hu, Y.-R.; Chen, H.-F. The improved Harris hawk optimization algorithm with the Tent map. In Proceedings of the 2019 3rd International Conference on Electronic Information Technology and Computer Engineering (EITCE), Xiamen, China, 18–20 October 2019; pp. 336–339.

158. Dhawale, D.; Kamboj, V.K.; Anand, P. An improved Chaotic Harris Hawks Optimizer for solving numerical and engineering optimization problems. *Eng. Comput.* **2021**, 1–46. [CrossRef]

159. Basha, J.; Bacanin, N.; Vukobrat, N.; Zivkovic, M.; Venkatachalam, K.; Hubálovský, S.; Trojovský, P. Chaotic Harris Hawks Optimization with Quasi-Reflection-Based Learning: An Application to Enhance CNN Design. *Sensors* **2021**, *21*, 6654. [CrossRef]

160. Hussien, A.G.; Amin, M. A self-adaptive Harris Hawks optimization algorithm with opposition-based learning and chaotic local search strategy for global optimization and feature selection. *Int. J. Mach. Learn. Cybern.* **2021**, *13*, 309–336. [CrossRef]

161. Dehkordi, A.A.; Sadiq, A.S.; Mirjalili, S.; Ghafoor, K.Z. Nonlinear-based Chaotic Harris Hawks Optimizer: Algorithm and Internet of Vehicles application. *Appl. Soft Comput.* **2021**, *109*, 107574. [CrossRef]

162. Jiao, S.; Wang, C.; Gao, R.; Li, Y.; Zhang, Q. Harris Hawks Optimization with Multi-Strategy Search and Application. *Symmetry* **2021**, *13*, 2364. [CrossRef]

163. Zhong, C.; Li, G. Comprehensive learning Harris hawks-equilibrium optimization with terminal replacement mechanism for constrained optimization problems. *Expert Syst. Appl.* **2021**, *192*, 116432. [CrossRef]

164. Abd Elaziz, M.; Yang, H.; Lu, S. A multi-leader Harris hawk optimization based on differential evolution for feature selection and prediction influenza viruses H1N1. *Artif. Intell. Rev.* **2022**, 55, 2675–2732. [CrossRef]

165. Bujok, P. Harris Hawks Optimisation: Using of an Archive. In *International Conference on Artificial Intelligence and Soft Computing*; Springer: Berlin/Heidelberg, Germany, 2021; pp. 415–423.

166. Al-Betar, M.A.; Awadallah, M.A.; Heidari, A.A.; Chen, H.; Al-Khraisat, H.; Li, C. Survival exploration strategies for harris hawks optimizer. *Expert Syst. Appl.* **2021**, *168*, 114243. [CrossRef]

167. Qu, C.; Zhang, L.; Li, J.; Deng, F.; Tang, Y.; Zeng, X.; Peng, X. Improving feature selection performance for classification of gene expression data using Harris Hawks optimizer with variable neighborhood learning. *Briefings Bioinform.* **2021**, *22*, bbab097. [CrossRef]

168. Nandi, A.; Kamboj, V.K. A Canis lupus inspired upgraded Harris hawks optimizer for nonlinear, constrained, continuous, and discrete engineering design problem. *Int. J. Numer. Methods Eng.* **2021**, *122*, 1051–1088. [CrossRef]

169. Gölcük, İ.; Ozsoydan, F.B. Quantum particles-enhanced multiple Harris Hawks swarms for dynamic optimization problems. *Expert Syst. Appl.* **2021**, *167*, 114202. [CrossRef]

170. Yu, Z.; Du, J.; Li, G. Compact Harris Hawks Optimization Algorithm. In Proceedings of the 2021 40th Chinese Control Conference (CCC), Shanghai, China, 26–28 July 2021; pp. 1925–1930.

171. Wang, S.; Jia, H.; Liu, Q.; Zheng, R. An improved hybrid Aquila Optimizer and Harris Hawks Optimization for global optimization. *Math. Biosci. Eng* **2021**, *18*, 7076–7109. [CrossRef] [PubMed]

172. Wang, S.; Jia, H.; Abualigah, L.; Liu, Q.; Zheng, R. An improved hybrid aquila optimizer and harris hawks algorithm for solving industrial engineering optimization problems. *Processes* **2021**, *9*, 1551. [CrossRef]

173. Abualigah, L.; Yousri, D.; Abd Elaziz, M.; Ewees, A.A.; Al-qaness, M.A.; Gandomi, A.H. Aquila Optimizer: A novel meta-heuristic optimization Algorithm. *Comput. Ind. Eng.* **2021**, *157*, 107250. [CrossRef]

174. Jouhari, H.; Lei, D.; Al-qaness, M.A.; Elaziz, M.A.; Damaševičius, R.; Korytkowski, M.; Ewees, A.A. Modified Harris Hawks Optimizer for Solving Machine Scheduling Problems. *Symmetry* **2020**, *12*, 1460. [CrossRef]

175. Attiya, I.; Abd Elaziz, M.; Xiong, S. Job scheduling in cloud computing using a modified harris hawks optimization and simulated annealing algorithm. *Comput. Intell. Neurosci.* **2020**, *2020*. [CrossRef]

176. Fu, W.; Zhang, K.; Wang, K.; Wen, B.; Fang, P.; Zou, F. A hybrid approach for multi-step wind speed forecasting based on two-layer decomposition, improved hybrid DE-HHO optimization and KELM. *Renew. Energy* **2021**, *164*, 211–229. [CrossRef]

177. Abd Elaziz, M.; Heidari, A.A.; Fujita, H.; Moayedi, H. A competitive chain-based Harris Hawks Optimizer for global optimization and multi-level image thresholding problems. *Appl. Soft Comput.* **2020**, *95*, 106347. [CrossRef]

178. Houssein, E.H.; Hosney, M.E.; Elhoseny, M.; Oliva, D.; Mohamed, W.M.; Hassaballah, M. Hybrid Harris hawks optimization with cuckoo search for drug design and discovery in chemoinformatics. *Sci. Rep.* **2020**, *10*, 14439. [CrossRef]

179. Barshandeh, S.; Piri, F.; Sangani, S.R. HMPA: An innovative hybrid multi-population algorithm based on artificial ecosystem-based and Harris Hawks optimization algorithms for engineering problems. *Eng. Comput.* **2022**, *38*, 1581–1625. [CrossRef]

180. Xie, W.; Xing, C.; Wang, J.; Guo, S.; Guo, M.W.; Zhu, L.F. Hybrid Henry Gas Solubility Optimization Algorithm Based on the Harris Hawk Optimization. *IEEE Access* **2020**, *8*, 144665–144692. [CrossRef]

181. Fu, W.; Wang, K.; Tan, J.; Zhang, K. A composite framework coupling multiple feature selection, compound prediction models and novel hybrid swarm optimizer-based synchronization optimization strategy for multi-step ahead short-term wind speed forecasting. *Energy Convers. Manag.* **2020**, *205*, 112461. [CrossRef]

182. Qu, C.; He, W.; Peng, X.; Peng, X. Harris Hawks Optimization with Information Exchange. *Appl. Math. Model.* **2020**, *84*, 52–75. [CrossRef]

183. Kamboj, V.K.; Nandi, A.; Bhadoria, A.; Sehgal, S. An intensify Harris Hawks optimizer for numerical and engineering optimization problems. *Appl. Soft Comput.* **2020**, *89*, 106018. [CrossRef]

184. Dhawale, D.; Kamboj, V.K. hHHO-IGWO: A New Hybrid Harris Hawks Optimizer for Solving Global Optimization Problems. In Proceedings of the 2020 International Conference on Computation, Automation and Knowledge Management (ICCAKM), Dubai, United Arab Emirates, 9–10 January 2020; pp. 52–57.

185. Fu, W.; Shao, K.; Tan, J.; Wang, K. Fault diagnosis for rolling bearings based on composite multiscale fine-sorted dispersion entropy and SVM with hybrid mutation SCA-HHO algorithm optimization. *IEEE Access* **2020**, *8*, 13086–13104. [CrossRef]

186. Suresh, T.; Brijet, Z.; Sheeba, T.B. CMVHHO-DKMLC: A Chaotic Multi Verse Harris Hawks optimization (CMV-HHO) algorithm based deep kernel optimized machine learning classifier for medical diagnosis. *Biomed. Signal Process. Control* **2021**, *70*, 103034. [CrossRef]

187. ElSayed, S.K.; Elattar, E.E. Hybrid Harris hawks optimization with sequential quadratic programming for optimal coordination of directional overcurrent relays incorporating distributed generation. *Alex. Eng. J.* **2021**, *60*, 2421–2433. [CrossRef]

188. Kaveh, A.; Rahmani, P.; Eslamlou, A.D. An efficient hybrid approach based on Harris Hawks optimization and imperialist competitive algorithm for structural optimization. *Eng. Comput.* **2021**, 1–29. [CrossRef]

189. Atashpaz-Gargari, E.; Lucas, C. Imperialist competitive algorithm: An algorithm for optimization inspired by imperialistic competition. In Proceedings of the 2007 IEEE Congress on Evolutionary Computation, Singapore, 25–28 September 2007; pp. 4661–4667.

190. Sihwail, R.; Solaiman, O.S.; Omar, K.; Ariffin, K.A.Z.; Alswaitti, M.; Hashim, I. A Hybrid Approach for Solving Systems of Nonlinear Equations Using Harris Hawks Optimization and Newton's Method. *IEEE Access* **2021**, *9*, 95791–95807. [CrossRef]

191. Mohamed, A.W.; Hadi, A.A.; Mohamed, A.K. Gaining-sharing knowledge based algorithm for solving optimization problems: A novel nature-inspired algorithm. *Int. J. Mach. Learn. Cybern.* **2020**, *11*, 1501–1529. [CrossRef]

192. Abualigah, L.; Abd Elaziz, M.; Shehab, M.; Ahmad Alomari, O.; Alshinwan, M.; Alabool, H.; Al-Arabiat, D.A. Hybrid Harris Hawks Optimization with Differential Evolution for Data Clustering. In *Metaheuristics in Machine Learning: Theory and Applications*; Springer: Berlin/Heidelberg, Germany, 2021; pp. 267–299.

193. Azar, N.A.; Milan, S.G.; Kayhomayoon, Z. The prediction of longitudinal dispersion coefficient in natural streams using LS-SVM and ANFIS optimized by Harris hawk optimization algorithm. *J. Contam. Hydrol.* **2021**, *240*, 103781. [CrossRef] [PubMed]

194. Firouzi, B.; Abbasi, A.; Sendur, P. Identification and evaluation of cracks in electrostatically actuated resonant gas sensors using Harris Hawk/Nelder Mead and perturbation methods. *Smart Struct. Syst.* **2021**, *28*, 121–142.

195. Li, W.; Shi, R.; Zou, H.; Dong, J. Fireworks Harris Hawk Algorithm Based on Dynamic Competition Mechanism for Numerical Optimization. In *International Conference on Swarm Intelligence*; Springer: Berlin/Heidelberg, Germany, 2021; pp. 441–450.

196. Li, C.; Li, J.; Chen, H.; Heidari, A.A. Memetic Harris Hawks Optimization: Developments and perspectives on project scheduling and QoS-aware web service composition. *Expert Syst. Appl.* **2021**, *171*, 114529. [CrossRef]

197. Ahmad, A.A. Solving partial differential equations via a hybrid method between homotopy analytical method and Harris hawks optimization algorithm. *Int. J. Nonlinear Anal. Appl.* **2022**, *13*, 663–671.

198. Yuan, Y.; Ren, J.; Zu, J.; Mu, X. An adaptive instinctive reaction strategy based on Harris hawks optimization algorithm for numerical optimization problems. *AIP Adv.* **2021**, *11*, 025012. [CrossRef]

199. Setiawan, I.N.; Kurniawan, R.; Yuniarto, B.; Caraka, R.E.; Pardamean, B. Parameter Optimization of Support Vector Regression Using Harris Hawks Optimization. *Procedia Comput. Sci.* **2021**, *179*, 17–24. [CrossRef]

200. Hossain, M.A.; Noor, R.M.; Yau, K.L.A.; Azzuhri, S.R.; Z'Abar, M.R.; Ahmedy, I.; Jabbarpour, M.R. Multi-Objective Harris Hawks Optimization Algorithm Based 2-Hop Routing Algorithm for CR-VANET. *IEEE Access* **2021**, *9*, 58230–58242. [CrossRef]

201. Dabba, A.; Tari, A.; Meftali, S. A new multi-objective binary Harris Hawks optimization for gene selection in microarray data. *J. Ambient. Intell. Humaniz. Comput.* **2021**, 1–20. [CrossRef]

202. Jangir, P.; Heidari, A.A.; Chen, H. Elitist non-dominated sorting Harris hawks optimization: Framework and developments for multi-objective problems. *Expert Syst. Appl.* **2021**, *186*, 115747. [CrossRef]

203. Du, P.; Wang, J.; Hao, Y.; Niu, T.; Yang, W. A novel hybrid model based on multi-objective Harris hawks optimization algorithm for daily PM2.5 and PM10 forecasting. *Appl. Soft Comput.* **2020**, *96*, 106620. [CrossRef]

204. Islam, M.Z.; Wahab, N.I.A.; Veerasamy, V.; Hizam, H.; Mailah, N.F.; Guerrero, J.M.; Mohd Nasir, M.N. A Harris Hawks Optimization Based Single-and Multi-Objective Optimal Power Flow Considering Environmental Emission. *Sustainability* **2020**, *12*, 5248. [CrossRef]

205. Fu, W.; Lu, Q. Multiobjective Optimal Control of FOPID Controller for Hydraulic Turbine Governing Systems Based on Reinforced Multiobjective Harris Hawks Optimization Coupling with Hybrid Strategies. *Complexity* **2020**, *2020*. [CrossRef]

206. Piri, J.; Mohapatra, P. An Analytical Study of Modified Multi-objective Harris Hawk Optimizer Towards Medical Data Feature Selection. *Comput. Biol. Med.* **2021**, *135*, 104558. [CrossRef]

207. Shekarappa G, S.; Mahapatra, S.; Raj, S. Voltage constrained reactive power planning problem for reactive loading variation using hybrid harris hawk particle swarm optimizer. *Electr. Power Components Syst.* **2021**, *49*, 421–435. [CrossRef]

208. Mohandas, P.; Devanathan, S.T. Reconfiguration with DG location and capacity optimization using crossover mutation based Harris Hawk Optimization algorithm (CMBHHO). *Appl. Soft Comput.* **2021**, *113*, 107982. [CrossRef]

209. Naeijian, M.; Rahimnejad, A.; Ebrahimi, S.M.; Pourmousa, N.; Gadsden, S.A. Parameter estimation of PV solar cells and modules using Whippy Harris Hawks Optimization Algorithm. *Energy Rep.* **2021**, *7*, 4047–4063. [CrossRef]

210. Bao, X.; Jia, H.; Lang, C. A novel hybrid harris hawks optimization for color image multilevel thresholding segmentation. *IEEE Access* **2019**, *7*, 76529–76546. [CrossRef]

211. Utama, D.M.; Widodo, D.S. An energy-efficient flow shop scheduling using hybrid Harris hawks optimization. *Bull. Electr. Eng. Inform.* **2021**, *10*, 1154–1163. [CrossRef]

212. Too, J.; Liang, G.; Chen, H. Memory-based Harris hawk optimization with learning agents: A feature selection approach. *Eng. Comput.* **2021**, 1–22. [CrossRef]

213. Abd Elaziz, M.; Yousri, D. Automatic selection of heavy-tailed distributions-based synergy Henry gas solubility and Harris hawk optimizer for feature selection: Case study drug design and discovery. *Artif. Intell. Rev.* **2021**, *54*, 4685–4730. [CrossRef]

214. Balaha, H.M.; El-Gendy, E.M.; Saafan, M.M. CovH2SD: A COVID-19 detection approach based on Harris Hawks Optimization and stacked deep learning. *Expert Syst. Appl.* **2021**, *186*, 115805. [CrossRef] [PubMed]

215. Abualigah, L.; Abd Elaziz, M.; Hussien, A.G.; Alsalibi, B.; Jalali, S.M.J.; Gandomi, A.H. Lightning search algorithm: A comprehensive survey. *Appl. Intell.* **2021**, *51*, 2353–2376. [CrossRef] [PubMed]

216. Abualigah, L.; Zitar, R.A.; Almotairi, K.H.; Hussein, A.M.; Abd Elaziz, M.; Nikoo, M.R.; Gandomi, A.H. Wind, Solar, and Photovoltaic Renewable Energy Systems with and without Energy Storage Optimization: A Survey of Advanced Machine Learning and Deep Learning Techniques. *Energies* **2022**, *15*, 578. [CrossRef]

217. Al Shinwan, M.; Abualigah, L.; Huy, T.D.; Younes Shdefat, A.; Altalhi, M.; Kim, C.; El-Sappagh, S.; Abd Elaziz, M.; Kwak, K.S. An Efficient 5G Data Plan Approach Based on Partially Distributed Mobility Architecture. *Sensors* **2022**, *22*, 349. [CrossRef] [PubMed]

218. Islam, M.Z.; Wahab, N.I.A.; Veerasamy, V.; Hizam, H.; Mailah, N.F.; Khan, A.; Sabo, A. Optimal Power Flow using a Novel Harris Hawk Optimization Algorithm to Minimize Fuel Cost and Power loss. In Proceedings of the 2019 IEEE Conference on Sustainable Utilization and Development in Engineering and Technologies (CSUDET), Penang, Malaysia, 7–9 November 2019; pp. 246–250.

219. Paital, S.R.; Ray, P.K.; Mohanty, S.R. A robust dual interval type-2 fuzzy lead-lag based UPFC for stability enhancement using Harris Hawks Optimization. *ISA Trans.* **2022**, *123*, 425–442. [CrossRef]

220. Mohanty, D.; Panda, S. Sine cosine adopted Harris' hawks optimization for function optimization and power system frequency controller design. *Int. Trans. Electr. Energy Syst.* **2021**, *31*, e12915. [CrossRef]

221. Abdel Aleem, S.H.E.; Zobaa, A.F.; Balci, M.E.; Ismael, S.M. Harmonic overloading minimization of frequency-dependent components in harmonics polluted distribution systems using harris hawks optimization algorithm. *IEEE Access* **2019**, *7*, 100824–100837. [CrossRef]

222. Diaaeldin, I.M.; Aleem, S.H.A.; El-Rafei, A.; Abdelaziz, A.Y.; Ćalasan, M. Optimal Network Reconfiguration and Distributed Generation Allocation using Harris Hawks Optimization. In Proceedings of the 2020 24th International Conference on Information Technology (IT), Zabljak, Montenegro, 18–22 February 2020; pp. 1–6.

223. Abdelsalam, M.; Diab, H.Y.; El-Bary, A. A Metaheuristic Harris Hawk Optimization Approach for Coordinated Control of Energy Management in Distributed Generation Based Microgrids. *Appl. Sci.* **2021**, *11*, 4085. [CrossRef]

224. Mossa, M.A.; Kamel, O.M.; Sultan, H.M.; Diab, A.A.Z. Parameter estimation of PEMFC model based on Harris Hawks' optimization and atom search optimization algorithms. *Neural Comput. Appl.* **2020**, *33*, 5555–5570. [CrossRef]

225. Chakraborty, S.; Verma, S.; Salgotra, A.; Elavarasan, R.M.; Elangovan, D.; Mihet-Popa, L. Solar-Based DG Allocation Using Harris Hawks Optimization While Considering Practical Aspects. *Energies* **2021**, *14*, 5206. [CrossRef]

226. Qais, M.H.; Hasanien, H.M.; Alghuwainem, S. Parameters extraction of three-diode photovoltaic model using computation and Harris Hawks optimization. *Energy* **2020**, *195*, 117040. [CrossRef]

227. Sahoo, B.P.; Panda, S. Load Frequency Control of Solar Photovoltaic/Wind/Biogas/Biodiesel Generator Based Isolated Microgrid Using Harris Hawks Optimization. In Proceedings of the 2020 First International Conference on Power, Control and Computing Technologies (ICPC2T), Raipur, India, 3–5 January 2020; pp. 188–193.

228. Fang, P.; Fu, W.; Wang, K.; Xiong, D.; Zhang, K. A compositive architecture coupling outlier correction, EWT, nonlinear Volterra multi-model fusion with multi-objective optimization for short-term wind speed forecasting. *Appl. Energy* **2021**, *307*, 118191. [CrossRef]

229. Roy, R.; Mukherjee, V.; Singh, R.P. Harris hawks optimization algorithm for model order reduction of interconnected wind turbines. *ISA Trans.* **2021**. [CrossRef]

230. Hassan, M.H.; Kamel, S.; Abualigah, L.; Eid, A. Development and application of slime mould algorithm for optimal economic emission dispatch. *Expert Syst. Appl.* **2021**, *182*, 115205. [CrossRef]

231. Houssein, E.H.; Dirar, M.; Abualigah, L.; Mohamed, W.M. An efficient equilibrium optimizer with support vector regression for stock market prediction. *Neural Comput. Appl.* **2021**, *34*, 3165–3200. [CrossRef]

232. Pham, T.N.; Van Tran, L.; Dao, S.V.T. A Multi-Restart Dynamic Harris Hawk Optimization Algorithm for the Economic Load Dispatch Problem. *IEEE Access* **2021**, *9*, 122180–122206. [CrossRef]

233. Nandi, A.; Kamboj, V.K. A meliorated Harris Hawks optimizer for combinatorial unit commitment problem with photovoltaic applications. *J. Electr. Syst. Inf. Technol.* **2021**, *8*, 1–73. [CrossRef]

234. Sammen, S.S.; Ghorbani, M.A.; Malik, A.; Tikhamarine, Y.; AmirRahmani, M.; Al-Ansari, N.; Chau, K.W. Enhanced Artificial Neural Network with Harris Hawks Optimization for Predicting Scour Depth Downstream of Ski-Jump Spillway. *Appl. Sci.* **2020**, *10*, 5160. [CrossRef]

235. Essa, F.; Abd Elaziz, M.; Elsheikh, A.H. An enhanced productivity prediction model of active solar still using artificial neural network and Harris Hawks optimizer. *Appl. Therm. Eng.* **2020**, *170*, 115020. [CrossRef]

236. Moayedi, H.; Gör, M.; Lyu, Z.; Bui, D.T. Herding Behaviors of grasshopper and Harris hawk for hybridizing the neural network in predicting the soil compression coefficient. *Measurement* **2020**, *152*, 107389. [CrossRef]

237. Kolli, C.S.; Tatavarthi, U.D. Fraud detection in bank transaction with wrapper model and Harris water optimization-based deep recurrent neural network. *Kybernetes* **2021**, *50*, 1731–1750. [CrossRef]

238. Bacanin, N.; Vukobrat, N.; Zivkovic, M.; Bezdan, T.; Strumberger, I. Improved Harris Hawks Optimization Adapted for Artificial Neural Network Training. In *International Conference on Intelligent and Fuzzy Systems*; Springer: Berlin/Heidelberg, Germany, 2021; pp. 281–289.

239. Atta, E.A.; Ali, A.F.; Elshamy, A.A. Chaotic Harris Hawk Optimization Algorithm for Training Feed-Forward Neural Network. In *International Conference on Advanced Intelligent Systems and Informatics*; Springer: Berlin/Heidelberg, Germany, 2021; pp. 382–391.

240. Agarwal, P.; Farooqi, N.; Gupta, A.; Mehta, S.; Khandelwal, S. A New Harris Hawk Whale Optimization Algorithm for Enhancing Neural Networks. In Proceedings of the 2021 Thirteenth International Conference on Contemporary Computing (IC3-2021), Noida, India, 5–7 August 2021; pp. 179–186.

241. Bac, B.H.; Nguyen, H.; Thao, N.T.T.; Hanh, V.T.; Duyen, L.T.; Dung, N.T.; Du, N.K.; Hiep, N.H. Estimating heavy metals absorption efficiency in an aqueous solution using nanotube-type halloysite from weathered pegmatites and a novel Harris hawks optimization-based multiple layers perceptron neural network. *Eng. Comput.* **2021**, 1–16. [CrossRef]

242. Alamir, M.A. An enhanced artificial neural network model using the Harris Hawks optimiser for predicting food liking in the presence of background noise. *Appl. Acoust.* **2021**, *178*, 108022. [CrossRef]

243. Simsek, O.I.; Alagoz, B.B. A Computational Intelligent Analysis Scheme for Optimal Engine Behavior by Using Artificial Neural Network Learning Models and Harris Hawk Optimization. In Proceedings of the 2021 International Conference on Information Technology (ICIT), Amman, Jordan, 14–15 July 2021; pp. 361–365.

244. Zhang, H.; Nguyen, H.; Bui, X.N.; Pradhan, B.; Asteris, P.G.; Costache, R.; Aryal, J. A generalized artificial intelligence model for estimating the friction angle of clays in evaluating slope stability using a deep neural network and Harris Hawks optimization algorithm. *Eng. Comput.* **2021**, 1–14. [CrossRef]

245. Wunnava, A.; Naik, M.K.; Panda, R.; Jena, B.; Abraham, A. A differential evolutionary adaptive Harris hawks optimization for two dimensional practical Masi entropy-based multilevel image thresholding. *J. King Saud-Univ.-Comput. Inf. Sci.* **2020**. [CrossRef]

246. Golilarz, N.A.; Gao, H.; Demirel, H. Satellite image de-noising with harris hawks meta heuristic optimization algorithm and improved adaptive generalized gaussian distribution threshold function. *IEEE Access* **2019**, *7*, 57459–57468. [CrossRef]

247. Shahid, M.; Li, J.P.; Golilarz, N.A.; Addeh, A.; Khan, J.; Haq, A.U. Wavelet Based Image DE-Noising with Optimized Thresholding Using HHO Algorithm. In Proceedings of the 2019 16th International Computer Conference on Wavelet Active Media Technology and Information Processing, Chengdu, China, 14–15 December 2019; pp. 6–12.

248. Rodríguez-Esparza, E.; Zanella-Calzada, L.A.; Oliva, D.; Heidari, A.A.; Zaldivar, D.; Pérez-Cisneros, M.; Foong, L.K. An Efficient Harris Hawks-inspired Image Segmentation Method. *Expert Syst. Appl.* **2020**, *155*, 113428. [CrossRef]

249. Naik, M.K.; Panda, R.; Wunnava, A.; Jena, B.; Abraham, A. A leader Harris hawks optimization for 2-D Masi entropy-based multilevel image thresholding. *Multimed. Tools Appl.* **2021**, *80*, 35543–35583. [CrossRef]

250. Lin, S.; Jia, H.; Abualigah, L.; Altalhi, M. Enhanced Slime Mould Algorithm for Multilevel Thresholding Image Segmentation Using Entropy Measures. *Entropy* **2021**, *23*, 1700. [CrossRef]

251. Hussien, A.G.; Hassanien, A.E.; Houssein, E.H.; Bhattacharyya, S.; Amin, M. S-shaped Binary Whale Optimization Algorithm for Feature Selection. In *Recent Trends in Signal and Image Processing*; Springer: Berlin/Heidelberg, Germany, 2019; pp. 79–87.

252. Hussien, A.G.; Houssein, E.H.; Hassanien, A.E. A binary whale optimization algorithm with hyperbolic tangent fitness function for feature selection. In Proceedings of the 2017 Eighth International Conference on Intelligent Computing and Information Systems (ICICIS), Cairo, Egypt, 5–7 December 2017; pp. 166–172.

253. Abualigah, L.M.Q. *Feature Selection and Enhanced Krill Herd Algorithm for Text Document Clustering*; Springer: Berlin/Heidelberg, Germany, 2019.

254. Abdel-Basset, M.; Ding, W.; El-Shahat, D. A hybrid Harris Hawks optimization algorithm with simulated annealing for feature selection. *Artif. Intell. Rev.* **2021**, *54*, 593–637. [CrossRef]

255. Thaher, T.; Saheb, M.; Turabieh, H.; Chantar, H. Intelligent Detection of False Information in Arabic Tweets Utilizing Hybrid Harris Hawks Based Feature Selection and Machine Learning Models. *Symmetry* **2021**, *13*, 556. [CrossRef]

256. Turabieh, H.; Al Azwari, S.; Rokaya, M.; Alosaimi, W.; Alharbi, A.; Alhakami, W.; Alnfiai, M. Enhanced harris hawks optimization as a feature selection for the prediction of student performance. *Computing* **2021**, *103*, 1417–1438. [CrossRef]

257. Al-Wajih, R.; Abdulkadir, S.J.; Aziz, N.; Al-Tashi, Q.; Talpur, N. Hybrid Binary Grey Wolf With Harris Hawks Optimizer for Feature Selection. *IEEE Access* **2021**, *9*, 31662–31677. [CrossRef]

258. Khurma, R.A.; Awadallah, M.A.; Aljarah, I. Binary Harris Hawks Optimisation Filter Based Approach for Feature Selection. In Proceedings of the 2021 Palestinian International Conference on Information and Communication Technology (PICICT), Gaza, Palestine, 28–29 September 2021; pp. 59–64.

259. Yasear, S.A.; Ku-Mahamud, K.R. Fine-Tuning the Ant Colony System Algorithm Through Harris's Hawk Optimizer for Travelling Salesman Problem. *Int. J. Intell. Eng. Syst.* **2021**, *14*, 136–145. [CrossRef]

260. Hatamlou, A. Black hole: A new heuristic optimization approach for data clustering. *Inf. Sci.* **2013**, *222*, 175–184. [CrossRef]

261. Ismael, O.M.; Qasim, O.S.; Algamal, Z.Y. A new adaptive algorithm for v-support vector regression with feature selection using Harris hawks optimization algorithm. In *Journal of Physics: Conference Series*; IOP Publishing: Bristol, UK, 2021; Volume 1897, p. 012057.

262. Safaldin, M.; Otair, M.; Abualigah, L. Improved binary gray wolf optimizer and SVM for intrusion detection system in wireless sensor networks. *J. Ambient. Intell. Humaniz. Comput.* **2021**, *12*, 1559–1576. [CrossRef]

263. Khasawneh, A.M.; Kaiwartya, O.; Abualigah, L.M.; Lloret, J. Green computing in underwater wireless sensor networks pressure centric energy modeling. *IEEE Syst. J.* **2020**, *14*, 4735–4745. [CrossRef]

264. Srinivas, M.; Amgoth, T. EE-hHHSS: Energy-efficient wireless sensor network with mobile sink strategy using hybrid Harris hawk-salp swarm optimization algorithm. *Int. J. Commun. Syst.* **2020**, *33*, e4569. [CrossRef]

265. Bhat, S.J.; Venkata, S.K. An optimization based localization with area minimization for heterogeneous wireless sensor networks in anisotropic fields. *Comput. Netw.* **2020**, *179*, 107371. [CrossRef]
266. Singh, P.; Prakash, S. Optimizing multiple ONUs placement in Fiber-Wireless (FiWi) access network using Grasshopper and Harris Hawks Optimization Algorithms. *Opt. Fiber Technol.* **2020**, *60*, 102357. [CrossRef]
267. Xu, H.; Zhang, G.; Zhao, J.; Pham, Q.-V. Intelligent reflecting surface aided wireless networks-Harris Hawks optimization for beamforming design. *arXiv* **2020**, arXiv:2010.01900.
268. Sharma, R.; Prakash, S. HHO-LPWSN: Harris Hawks Optimization Algorithm for Sensor Nodes Localization Problem in Wireless Sensor Networks. *EAI Endorsed Trans. Scalable Inf. Syst.* **2021**, *8*, e5. [CrossRef]
269. Jia, H.; Peng, X.; Kang, L.; Li, Y.; Jiang, Z.; Sun, K. Pulse coupled neural network based on Harris hawks optimization algorithm for image segmentation. *Multimed. Tools Appl.* **2020**, *79*, 28369–28392. [CrossRef]
270. Rammurthy, D.; Mahesh, P. Whale Harris hawks optimization based deep learning classifier for brain tumor detection using MRI images. *J. King Saud-Univ.-Comput. Inf. Sci.* **2020**. [CrossRef]
271. Kaur, N.; Kaur, L.; Cheema, S.S. An enhanced version of Harris Hawks Optimization by dimension learning-based hunting for Breast Cancer Detection. *Sci. Rep.* **2021**, *11*, 21933. [CrossRef]
272. Chacko, A.; Chacko, S. Deep learning-based robust medical image watermarking exploiting DCT and Harris hawks optimization. *Int. J. Intell. Syst.* **2021**. [CrossRef]
273. Bandyopadhyay, R.; Kundu, R.; Oliva, D.; Sarkar, R. Segmentation of brain MRI using an altruistic Harris Hawks' Optimization algorithm. *Knowl.-Based Syst.* **2021**, *232*, 107468. [CrossRef]
274. Iswisi, A.F.; Karan, O.; Rahebi, J. Diagnosis of Multiple Sclerosis Disease in Brain Magnetic Resonance Imaging Based on the Harris Hawks Optimization Algorithm. *BioMed Res. Int.* **2021**, *2021*. [CrossRef]
275. Balamurugan, R.; Ratheesh, S.; Venila, Y.M. Classification of heart disease using adaptive Harris hawk optimization-based clustering algorithm and enhanced deep genetic algorithm. *Soft Comput.* **2021**, *26*, 2357–2373. [CrossRef]
276. Hussien, A.G.; Hassanien, A.E.; Houssein, E.H. Swarming behaviour of salps algorithm for predicting chemical compound activities. In Proceedings of the 2017 Eighth International Conference on Intelligent Computing and Information Systems (ICICIS), Cairo, Egypt, 5–7 December 2017; pp. 315–320.
277. Houssein, E.H.; Hosney, M.E.; Oliva, D.; Mohamed, W.M.; Hassaballah, M. A novel hybrid Harris hawks optimization and support vector machines for drug design and discovery. *Comput. Chem. Eng.* **2020**, *133*, 106656. [CrossRef]
278. Houssein, E.H.; Neggaz, N.; Hosney, M.E.; Mohamed, W.M.; Hassaballah, M. Enhanced harris hawks optimization with genetic operators for selection chemical descriptors and compounds activities. *Neural Comput. Appl.* **2021**, *33*, 13601–13618. [CrossRef]
279. Ekinci, S.; Hekimoğlu, B.; Eker, E. Optimum Design of PID Controller in AVR System Using Harris Hawks Optimization. In Proceedings of the 2019 3rd International Symposium on Multidisciplinary Studies and Innovative Technologies (ISMSIT), Ankara, Turkey, 11–13 October 2019; pp. 1–6.
280. Ekinci, S.; Izci, D.; Hekimoğlu, B. PID Speed Control of DC Motor Using Harris Hawks Optimization Algorithm. In Proceedings of the 2020 International Conference on Electrical, Communication, and Computer Engineering (ICECCE), Istanbul, Turkey, 12–13 June 2020; pp. 1–6.
281. Ekinci, S.; Hekimoğlu, B.; Demirören, A.; Kaya, S. Harris Hawks Optimization Approach for Tuning of FOPID Controller in DC-DC Buck Converter. In Proceedings of the 2019 International Artificial Intelligence and Data Processing Symposium (IDAP), Malatya, Turkey, 21–22 September 2019; pp. 1–9.
282. Yousri, D.; Babu, T.S.; Fathy, A. Recent methodology based Harris Hawks optimizer for designing load frequency control incorporated in multi-interconnected renewable energy plants. *Sustain. Energy, Grids Netw.* **2020**, *22*, 100352. [CrossRef]
283. Barakat, M.; Donkol, A.; Hamed, H.F.; Salama, G.M. Harris hawks-based optimization algorithm for automatic LFC of the interconnected power system using PD-PI cascade control. *J. Electr. Eng. Technol.* **2021**, *16*, 1845–1865. [CrossRef]
284. Munagala, V.K.; Jatoth, R.K. Design of Fractional-Order PID/PID Controller for Speed Control of DC Motor Using Harris Hawks Optimization. In *Intelligent Algorithms for Analysis and Control of Dynamical Systems*; Springer: Berlin/Heidelberg, Germany, 2021; pp. 103–113.
285. Bui, D.T.; Moayedi, H.; Kalantar, B.; Osouli, A.; Gör, M.; Pradhan, B.; Nguyen, H.; Rashid, A.S.A. Harris hawks optimization: A novel swarm intelligence technique for spatial assessment of landslide susceptibility. *Sensors* **2019**, *19*, 3590. [CrossRef] [PubMed]
286. Murlidhar, B.R.; Nguyen, H.; Rostami, J.; Bui, X.; Armaghani, D.J.; Ragam, P.; Mohamad, E.T. Prediction of flyrock distance induced by mine blasting using a novel Harris Hawks optimization-based multi-layer perceptron neural network. *J. Rock Mech. Geotech. Eng.* **2021**, *13*, 1413–1427. [CrossRef]
287. Yu, C.; Koopialipoor, M.; Murlidhar, B.R.; Mohammed, A.S.; Armaghani, D.J.; Mohamad, E.T.; Wang, Z. Optimal ELM–Harris Hawks optimization and ELM–Grasshopper optimization models to forecast peak particle velocity resulting from mine blasting. *Nat. Resour. Res.* **2021**, *30*, 2647–2662. [CrossRef]
288. Paryani, S.; Neshat, A.; Pradhan, B. Improvement of landslide spatial modeling using machine learning methods and two Harris hawks and bat algorithms. *Egypt. J. Remote Sens. Space Sci.* **2021**, *24*, 845–855. [CrossRef]
289. Golafshani, E.M.; Arashpour, M.; Behnood, A. Predicting the compressive strength of green concretes using Harris hawks optimization-based data-driven methods. *Constr. Build. Mater.* **2022**, *318*, 125944. [CrossRef]

290. Parsa, P.; Naderpour, H. Shear strength estimation of reinforced concrete walls using support vector regression improved by Teaching–learning-based optimization, Particle Swarm optimization, and Harris Hawks Optimization algorithms. *J. Build. Eng.* **2021**, *44*, 102593. [CrossRef]
291. Zaim, S.; Chong, J.H.; Sankaranarayanan, V.; Harky, A. COVID-19 and multiorgan response. *Curr. Probl. Cardiol.* **2020**, *45*, 100618. [CrossRef]
292. Xu, S.; Li, Y. Beware of the second wave of COVID-19. *Lancet* **2020**, *395*, 1321–1322. [CrossRef]
293. Houssein, E.H.; Ahmad, M.; Hosney, M.E.; Mazzara, M. Classification Approach for COVID-19 Gene Based on Harris Hawks Optimization. In *Artificial Intelligence for COVID-19*; Springer: Berlin/Heidelberg, Germany, 2021; pp. 575–594.
294. Hu, J.; Heidari, A.A.; Shou, Y.; Ye, H.; Wang, L.; Huang, X.; Chen, H.; Chen, Y.; Wu, P. Detection of COVID-19 severity using blood gas analysis parameters and Harris hawks optimized extreme learning machine. *Comput. Biol. Med.* **2021**, *142*, 105166. [CrossRef]
295. Ye, H.; Wu, P.; Zhu, T.; Xiao, Z.; Zhang, X.; Zheng, L.; Zheng, R.; Sun, Y.; Zhou, W.; Fu, Q.; et al. Diagnosing coronavirus disease 2019 (COVID-19): Efficient Harris Hawks-inspired fuzzy K-nearest neighbor prediction methods. *IEEE Access* **2021**, *9*, 17787–17802. [CrossRef]
296. Bandyopadhyay, R.; Basu, A.; Cuevas, E.; Sarkar, R. Harris Hawks optimisation with Simulated Annealing as a deep feature selection method for screening of COVID-19 CT-scans. *Appl. Soft Comput.* **2021**, *111*, 107698. [CrossRef]
297. Abbasi, A.; Firouzi, B.; Sendur, P. On the application of Harris hawks optimization (HHO) algorithm to the design of microchannel heat sinks. *Eng. Comput.* **2019**, *37*, 1409–1428. [CrossRef]
298. Golilarz, N.A.; Addeh, A.; Gao, H.; Ali, L.; Roshandeh, A.M.; Munir, H.M.; Khan, R.U. A new automatic method for control chart patterns recognition based on ConvNet and Harris Hawks meta heuristic optimization algorithm. *IEEE Access* **2019**, *7*, 149398–149405. [CrossRef]
299. Khalifeh, S.; Akbarifard, S.; Khalifeh, V.; Zallaghi, E. Optimization of Water Distribution of Network Systems Using the Harris Hawks Optimization Algorithm (Case study: Homashahr City). *MethodsX* **2020**, *7*, 100948. [CrossRef]
300. Abd Elaziz, M.; Abualigah, L.; Ibrahim, R.A.; Attiya, I. IoT Workflow Scheduling Using Intelligent Arithmetic Optimization Algorithm in Fog Computing. *Comput. Intell. Neurosci.* **2021**, *2021*. [CrossRef]
301. Seyfollahi, A.; Ghaffari, A. Reliable data dissemination for the Internet of Things using Harris hawks optimization. *Peer-to-Peer Netw. Appl.* **2020**, *13*, 1886–1902. [CrossRef]
302. Saravanan, G.; Ibrahim, A.M.; Kumar, D.S.; Vanitha, U.; Chandrika, V. Iot Based Speed Control Of BLDC Motor With Harris Hawks Optimization Controller. *Int. J. Grid Distrib. Comput.* **2020**, *13*, 1902–1915.
303. Tayab, U.B.; Zia, A.; Yang, F.; Lu, J.; Kashif, M. Short-term load forecasting for microgrid energy management system using hybrid HHO-FNN model with best-basis stationary wavelet packet transform. *Energy* **2020**, *203*, 117857. [CrossRef]
304. Ding, W.; Abdel-Basset, M.; Eldrandaly, K.A.; Abdel-Fatah, L.; de Albuquerque, V.H.C. Smart Supervision of Cardiomyopathy Based on Fuzzy Harris Hawks Optimizer and Wearable Sensing Data Optimization: A New Model. *IEEE Trans. Cybern.* **2020**, *51*, 4944–4958. [CrossRef]
305. Li, C.; Li, J.; Chen, H. A Meta-Heuristic-Based Approach for Qos-Aware Service Composition. *IEEE Access* **2020**, *8*, 69579–69592. [CrossRef]
306. Elkady, Z.; Abdel-Rahim, N.; Mansour, A.A.; Bendary, F.M. Enhanced DVR Control System based on the Harris Hawks Optimization Algorithm. *IEEE Access* **2020**, *8*, 177721–177733. [CrossRef]
307. Wolpert, D.H.; Macready, W.G. No free lunch theorems for optimization. *IEEE Trans. Evol. Comput.* **1997**, *1*, 67–82. [CrossRef]

 *electronics*

Review

Evolution of Machine Learning in Tuberculosis Diagnosis: A Review of Deep Learning-Based Medical Applications

Manisha Singh [1], Gurubasavaraj Veeranna Pujar [1,*], Sethu Arun Kumar [1], Meduri Bhagyalalitha [1], Handattu Shankaranarayana Akshatha [1], Belal Abuhaija [2,*], Anas Ratib Alsoud [3], Laith Abualigah [3,4], Narasimha M. Beeraka [5,6] and Amir H. Gandomi [7,*]

[1] Department of Pharmaceutical Chemistry, JSS College of Pharmacy, JSS Academy of Higher Education and Research, Sri Shivarathreeshwara Nagara, Mysuru 570015, India
[2] Department of Computer Science, Wenzhou—Kean University, Wenzhou 325015, China
[3] Hourani Center for Applied Scientific Research, Al-Ahliyya Amman University, Amman 19328, Jordan
[4] Faculty of Information Technology, Middle East University, Amman 11831, Jordan
[5] Department of Human Anatomy, I.M. Sechenov First Moscow State Medical University (Sechenov University), 8/2 Trubetskaya Street, 119991 Moscow, Russia
[6] Center of Excellence in Molecular Biology and Regenerative Medicine (CEMR), Department of Biochemistry, JSS Academy of Higher Education and Research (JSS AHER), Mysuru 570015, India
[7] Faculty of Engineering and Information Technology, University of Technology Sydney, Ultimo, NSW 2007, Australia
* Correspondence: gvpujar@jssuni.edu.in (G.V.P.); babuhaij@kean.edu (B.A.); gandomi@uts.edu.au (A.H.G.)

Citation: Singh, M.; Pujar, G.V.; Kumar, S.A.; Bhagyalalitha, M.; Akshatha, H.S.; Abuhaija, B.; Alsoud, A.R.; Abualigah, L.; Beeraka, N.M.; Gandomi, A.H. Evolution of Machine Learning in Tuberculosis Diagnosis: A Review of Deep Learning-Based Medical Applications. *Electronics* **2022**, *11*, 2634. https://doi.org/10.3390/electronics11172634

Academic Editor: Rashid Mehmood

Received: 7 July 2022
Accepted: 12 August 2022
Published: 23 August 2022

Abstract: Tuberculosis (TB) is an infectious disease that has been a major menace to human health globally, causing millions of deaths yearly. Well-timed diagnosis and treatment are an arch to full recovery of the patient. Computer-aided diagnosis (CAD) has been a hopeful choice for TB diagnosis. Many CAD approaches using machine learning have been applied for TB diagnosis, specific to the artificial intelligence (AI) domain, which has led to the resurgence of AI in the medical field. Deep learning (DL), a major branch of AI, provides bigger room for diagnosing deadly TB disease. This review is focused on the limitations of conventional TB diagnostics and a broad description of various machine learning algorithms and their applications in TB diagnosis. Furthermore, various deep learning methods integrated with other systems such as neuro-fuzzy logic, genetic algorithm, and artificial immune systems are discussed. Finally, multiple state-of-the-art tools such as CAD4TB, Lunit INSIGHT, qXR, and InferRead DR Chest are summarized to view AI-assisted future aspects in TB diagnosis.

Keywords: tuberculosis; deep learning; neural networks; TB diagnosis

1. Introduction

Tuberculosis is a complex and chronic disease caused by a widely spread microbe, *Mycobacterium tuberculosis* (MTB). It is a slow-growing microbe that can ride out in extracellular and intracellular conditions [1]. It can also go into the latency phase and reverts to the exponential growth phase when the host gets into an immune-compromised condition [2]. In 2019, Word Health Organization (WHO) reported that around 10.0 million people had been infected, and 1.4 million individuals died from TB infection [1]. Furthermore, tuberculosis is a leading cause of death globally, forming a worldwide health crisis, particularly for HIV and immune-deficient patients [3]. TB also disproportionately affects developing countries, which suffer from a high TB burden due to a lack of expert radiologists and medical equipment [4].

Further, multi- and extensively drug-resistant mycobacterium strains have made it challenging to control tuberculosis [5]. In many cases, it is suspected to worsen by turning into totally drug-resistant TB, making it even more challenging for treatment [2]. Identifying such resistant strains of MTB and early diagnosis of patients will be a significant challenge in the coming decades. Artificial intelligence has been a stowed solution for fighting against TB.

Computer-aided diagnostics (CAD) tools have been a boon in interpreting medical imaging and promising assistance to radiologists in TB diagnosis. Many recent works have been conducted to build a high-performance diagnostic system. For example, a CAD model was built to diagnose the TB cavity, which could identify areas of interest in the chest X-ray image. It overcame the drawbacks of the existing CAD systems that failed to identify the TB cavities due to superimposed anatomic parts in the lung field [6]. Similarly, a CAD algorithm was developed that could directly detect TB. The features of this algorithm could identify and extract the images of ribs from the chest radiograph. This development led to a clear picture of the lung surface for detecting lesions or opaque mass, leading to a more focused TB diagnosis [7]. Recent advancements in AI programming have led to the development of algorithms that could detect more TB features. A TB detecting channel was built on similar grounds that sequentially combined techniques such as texture analysis, masking, and chest radiograph analysis. The algorithm focused on lesions and cavitary features and enveloped the diverse presentation of TB [8].

A more advanced CAD system was built in which the model applied image pre-processing to the chest X-ray images, thereby enhancing the image quality. The developed algorithm also firstly segmented the lung field and extracted the required features that were analyzed using a classifier to predict the presence of TB. The algorithm used the Shenzhen and the Montgomery databases [9] (which have additionally been used in various deep learning algorithms) and achieved an accuracy of 95.6% [10]. The development of more advanced algorithms, i.e., deep learning models, has helped clinicians to deliver high precision in their work. Deep learning in integration with fuzzy logic, genetic algorithms, and the artificial immune system has come up with several simple processes, leading to an increased scope in TB diagnosis specificity and efficiency. A mobile health technology was developed using deep learning to improve TB diagnosis in marginalized and developing countries. The work aimed to reduce the diagnosis delay of the deadly disease by developing a tech-socio system that could classify chest X-ray images into different types of TB manifestation [11]. Similarly, a novel method for TB screening was built using deep learning, which used a lesion-specific filtering system. In this method, automated features were extracted by the model depending on the target from the provided data.

The model was pre-trained using a transfer learning process, which helped to overcome the problem of handling high-resolution X-ray images and training many parameters using limited images, which led to the model's high performance [12]. Furthermore, deep learning has also been used to develop state-of-the-art tools such as CAD4TB, Lunit INSIGHT, qXR, etc., for early and efficient TB diagnosis. This review focused on aspects that have already successfully demonstrated its usefulness as a promising sub-field and will reflect refinement and promise for the new AI phase in TB diagnosis.

2. Tuberculosis (TB) and Its Occurrence

TB is an airborne bacterial infection caused by *Mycobacterium tuberculosis* (MTB), which mainly attacks the lungs [13]. However, the microbe may also spread to other body parts, such as the guts, skeleton, brain, and gland, from the lungs via different routes. When an infected TB person sneezes, spits, or coughs, the bacteria are expelled from the body. If inhaled by a healthy person, even in minimal quantities, these bacteria can cause TB [14]. People who exhibit symptoms are called active TB (ATB) patients [15], whereas TB patients without any signs are called latent TB (LTB) patients [16]. LTB patients cannot spread the disease to other people but have a high risk of developing TB if they do not maintain a healthy lifestyle (Figure 1). Moreover, people with weak immune systems due to infections such as diabetes and HIV; undernourishment; or people prone to using tobacco products are at high risk of catching TB if they come into contact with a TB-infected person [17]. When the bacteria can invade other body organs such as the bone, spine, and brain, it is called extrapulmonary tuberculosis (EPT). Miliary tuberculosis is a rare type of active

TB in which the mycobacterium enters the other body organs via blood vessels. It infects various organs at once, including the lungs, spinal cord, and heart, making this kind of TB disease highly deadly [18]. Active TB is further classified into multidrug-resistant TB (MDR-TB) and extensively drug-resistant TB (XDR-TB). MDR-TB shows resistance to first-line antitubercular drugs due to the patient's irregular treatment or insufficient and inadequate quality supply of drugs for the treatment. XDR-TB is resistant to both first-line and second-line antitubercular drugs (capreomycin, kanamycin, and amikacin) [19].

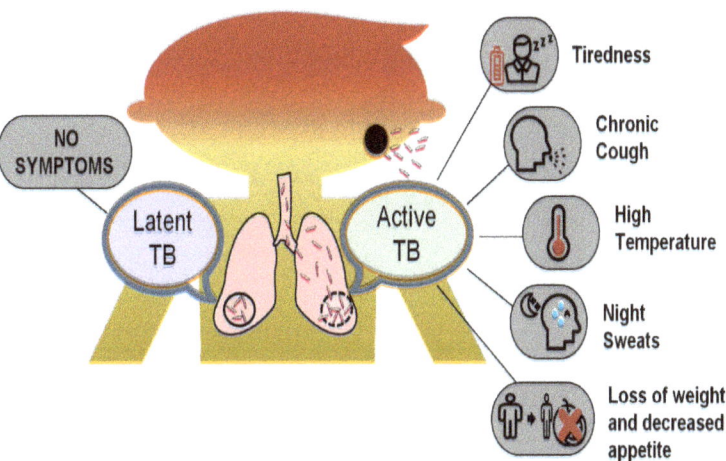

Figure 1. Diagrammatic representation of symptoms of active and latent TB.

3. Conventional Diagnostic Techniques for Pulmonary TB

Early diagnosis of pulmonary tuberculosis is a preference for disease management. It is beneficial for both the patient and the public well-being, reducing the chances of further disease transmission in the community [20]. The diagnosis of TB disease is a combination of related symptoms and an investigation of the patient's history for important information. The problem involved with early TB diagnosis is the slow bacterial reproduction inside the patient's lungs that takes quite some time before showing the disease symptoms [21]. Presently several tests exist for the TB diagnosis and a few of which are chest X-ray [22], conventional light microscopy [23], light-emitting diode (LED) fluorescence smear microscopy [23], [24], liquid culture with drug susceptibility testing (DST) [25], lipoarabinomannan (LAM) lateral flow assay [26], Xpert MTB/RIF [27], first-line (FL) line probe assay (LPA) [28], second-line (SL) line probe assay (LPA) [29] and Loopamp *Mycobacterium tuberculosis* complex assay [30]. Early evaluation of pulmonary TB is performed by microscopic examination, sputum cultures, and chest X-rays. In contrast, the diagnosis of drug-resistant strains is made via a drug susceptibility test (DST) [21]. The traditional methods are tedious to perform, time-consuming, and require more time to interpret reports for diagnosing disease and drug resistance.

Moreover, this process gets delayed in detecting the disease early, leading to the patient's suffering and further transmission of the disease to the surrounding healthy human [31]. Therefore, many immunoassay techniques have also been developed for the rapid diagnosis of TB, which have high sensitivity and require less time [32]. However, these tests' major disadvantage is their cost in laboratory establishments, and the requirement of highly skilled staff is given in Table 1 [33].

Table 1. Limitations of conventional methods used in TB diagnosis.

S.No	Test	Principle	Detects	Drawbacks	Refs.
1	Chest X-ray	Imaging of inflammations in the lungs	Active tuberculosis	• Low sensitivity and specificity. • Cannot examine EPT.	[22]
2	Conventional light microscopy	Light microscopy is used to visualize the *Mycobacterium* in the sputum smear	Active tuberculosis	• Low sensitivity in cases of HIV/TB co-infection.	[23]
3	Fluorescent LED microscopy	Fluorescence microscopy is used to visualize the *Mycobacterium* in the sputum sample	Active tuberculosis	• Tedious and time-consuming. • High cost.	[23,24]
4	Liquid culturing with drug susceptibility testing	Liquid media is used to culture *Mycobacterium*	Active tuberculosis and drug resistance	• Tedious and time-consuming.	[25]
5	Lipoarabinomannan lateral flow assay	Detects antigen	Active tuberculosis in HIV-positive patients	• High cost of laboratory establishment. • Requires skilled staff.	[26]
6	Xpert MTB/RIF	Nucleic acid amplification test using quantitative PCR	Active tuberculosis and drug resistance mainly for rifampicin	• High cost of laboratory establishment. • Requires skilled staff.	[27]
7	Line probe assay for drug resistance to first-line anti-TB drugs (FL-LPA)	Nucleic acid amplification test using the line probe assay	Active tuberculosis and drug resistance to first-line anti-TB drugs	• High cost of laboratory establishment. • Requires skilled staff.	[28]
8	Line probe assay for drug resistance to second-line anti-TB drugs (SL-LPA)	Nucleic acid amplification test using the line probe assay	Active tuberculosis and drug resistance to second-line anti-TB drugs including injectable	• High cost of laboratory establishment. • Requires skilled staff.	[29]
9	Loopamp *M. tuberculosis* complex assay	Nucleic acid amplification test using loop-mediated isothermal amplification	Active tuberculosis	• High cost of laboratory establishment. • Requires skilled staff. • Not able to detect drug resistance.	[30]

4. History of AI Applications in TB Diagnosis

Many researchers have applied AI to TB diagnosis, contending the challenge of predicting and evaluating tuberculosis. The introduction of neural networks (Perceptron's [34] and their improved versions) bought the idea of the pattern recognition method, which could recognize the structural patterns [35,36] in chest X-ray images and help in diagnosis. Artificial neural networks (ANN) started to impact TB diagnosis around early 1990 due to programs for pattern recognition. In 1990, a neural network was built to distinguish between the different kinds of interstitial lung diseases, including tuberculosis. The training dataset was prepared using ten cases for each of the nine types of lung disease. The model showed good performance and results, suggesting that ANN has high potential in computer-aided diagnosis of lung diseases [37]. In 1998, the first automated neural technique was built to identify TB bacillus in sputum smears stained with auramine. The model's sensitivity was 93.5%, aiming to diagnose TB rapidly and accurately and reduce health risks for staff processing smear slides [38].

Similarly, in 1999, the first neural network was developed to diagnose active pulmonary tuberculosis using GRNN (general regression neural network). The model used 21 different parameters to form the input patterns and achieved sensitivity and specificity of 100% and 72%, respectively, in diagnosing active TB [39]. These machine-learning systems possess the capability to solve problems, learn from the given data, and deal with new problems. In addition to the systems mentioned above, several machine learning programs were also developed, including support vector machine (SVM) [40], decision tree (DT) [41], and random forest (RF) [42] that were applied for TB diagnosis.

The major challenge faced by all these models was diagnostic features to comply with making an accurate prediction. Furthermore, more efficient work was carried out to uphold AI advancement, leading to deep learning (DL). The DL turned up to be a useful concept in early 2010, when the integration of neural networks with algorithms (genetic algorithm [43] and fuzzy logic [44]) and single hidden layer feed-forward neural networks came into use for TB diagnosis. The capability of some deep learning approaches to predict and evaluate complex and diverse data has provided a new ray of hope for solving TB-related problems, such as drug resistance. In 2017, a deep learning model was developed to predict multidrug-resistant tuberculosis from drug-sensitive TB images obtained from computed tomography (CT). The model achieved good accuracy of 91.11% as the CT images have high resolution, are cost-effective, and help in the speedy diagnosis of TB [45]. In addition, deep learning in TB diagnosis also found its footsteps in predicting the severity of TB from CT pulmonary images, fast screening, and evaluation of chest radiography, and it builds DL tools (e.g., CAD4TB, Lunit INSIGHT, qXR, InferRead DR Chest, etc.) for easy and fast predictions.

5. Overview of AI Techniques Used in TB Diagnosis

AI or machine learning algorithms encircle a diverse variety of techniques. To assist readers with a better understanding of AI-assisted TB diagnosis, we will provide a short overview of the various AI learning techniques. Most machine learning techniques used for TB diagnosis are supervised learning, unsupervised learning, and semi-supervised learning. The choice of ML technique depends on the nature of the requirement, and each of the learning methods has its advantage and disadvantage (Table 2). Supervised learning is a process where the learning involves a set of input data (X) and output data (Y), and the training mode aims to search for a pattern in the provided data that would correlate with the coveted output data [46]. A fully automated CAD system effective for TB diagnosis was proposed to combine deep features with hand-crafted features. The authors used supervised learning and pre-trained CNN frameworks to detect TB in chest X-ray images that have minimized the pre-processing time and diagnosis performance, leading to an early screening of the disease [47].

Unsupervised learning is when only the input (X), but no comparable output data, is present [48]. The data are unlabeled in an unsupervised system. The process aims to train the model by extracting features from the data that could be used to cluster the input data into different units. In such a case, the algorithm learns from an elementary structure in the data to identify and give an interesting pattern [49]. The main difference between supervised and unsupervised learning is that unsupervised learning does not use a feedback signal to examine the standard solutions, making it less accurate and computationally complex [50]. In recent years, supervised and unsupervised learning was used in Bogota, DC, Colombia, to build two models using an artificial neural network to diagnose the disease and cluster data. The dataset was extracted based on sex, age, AIDS status, and other medical conditions of the subjects. The models probed supervised learning for disease diagnosis and unsupervised learning for data clustering from available information. The models showed a specificity of 71% and a sensitivity of 97% for TB diagnosis, giving an advantage of fast and low execution cost over traditional methods [51]. Similarly, in Rio de Janeiro, Brazil, two ANN models were developed and evaluated for diagnosing PTB in hospitalized patients. The first model used supervised learning for classification purposes, and the second used unsupervised learning to create risk groups. These predictive models were proposed to be promising tools for the early diagnosis of patients having radiological and clinical doubt of PTB [52].

An intercede of supervised and unsupervised learning [53] is known as semi-supervised learning. This AI technique utilizes a vast number of data in which only a few labeled data are available. This makes it widely applicable to real-world problems where it can increase the application of unlabeled data either by modification or reprioritization of hypotheses attained from limited tagged data [54]. For example, one of the studies used semi-supervised learning to arbitrate whether an unlabeled database could be used to train and enhance the accuracy of the machine learning model used to diagnose TB on chest X-ray images. The trained ML model showed good accuracy and could identify relevant features for TB diagnosis that the radiologists falsified. This learning technique could also significantly decrease the need for large, organized data even when the database labels were absent or noisy [55]. A specialized form of semi-supervised learning is active learning (AL), in which the model can contend with the problem of inadequate tagged training data in various ways [56]. For example, the model can request the user or any other information source to find the tags for the untagged data, for which the input data is least sure. A CAD system was developed using active learning for the detection of TB. This described learning method improved the algorithm to build a highly accurate system and helped narrow down the intrinsic uncertainty of the model while reducing the efforts for labeling [57].

Transfer learning has been one of the most popular machine learning techniques in recent years. This learning process provides relaxation from the common concept that the test and the training data should have, i.e., the same pattern and features [58]. In this way, the model learns valuable information from the old data source and transfers it to the new one by fine-tuning some parameters specific to the required output. This leads to an increase in the predictive efficiency of the target source. This learning technique was used to diagnose TB from chest X-ray images reliably. A dataset of 3500 TB infected and 3500 non-TB normal chest X-ray images were created. This database was used to transfer learning of already existing neural network models trained, authenticated, and tested to categorize TB and normal chest X-ray images. The best-performing model achieved high accuracy with 96.62% sensitivity and 96.51% specificity in diagnosing TB using chest X-ray images [59]. A CAD system was developed to detect TB with a hybrid approach, i.e., an ensemble of a deep model with a classifier. The approach increased the system's performance, but retraining the deep model was time-consuming. This limitation was overcome by using a transfer learning approach where the existing models were fine-tuned with a few epochs of data, and the training time was reduced by a large extent [60].

Table 2. Merits and limitations of the various machine learning techniques used in TB diagnosis.

S.No.	Learning Technique	Merits	Limitations	Refs.
1.	Supervised Learning	• High accuracy. • Helps solve problems based on previous data training.	• Labeled training data are required. • High quality and enough data needed.	[46]
2.	Unsupervised Learning	• It is ideal for unknown or raw data.	• Less accurate. • Unlike the supervised approach, cannot specify the output data.	[48]
3.	Semi-supervised Learning	• It can use both labeled and unlabeled data.	• Cannot manage unseen data.	[54]
4.	Transfer Learning	• Reduces the time required to build a model.	• The model works only when the input and target models' problems are the same.	[58]

6. Construction of AI Model in TB Diagnosis

The application of a specific AI algorithm in TB diagnosis is a process that needs a proper understanding of the problems involved. The necessary steps in model construction include defining the problem, collecting adequate and related data, designing the AI algorithm's architecture, training and evaluating the model, and correctly interpreting the output [61] (Figure 2). The first step involves problem identification, selecting the appropriate machine learning process, and an algorithm depending on the investigation problem [62]. The problem data can be divided into generative and discriminative inputs. The next step is to prepare a suitable model structure with appropriate algorithms such as

SVM, RF, DT, ANN, etc., and fix model parameters with a clear idea about the problem. The parameters of the algorithms vary from one to another [63]. For example, in a neural network, the number of hidden layers and neurons can be the criterion, and the number of kernels can be a criterion in SVM. After the model structure is resolved, the dataset must be prepared. The quality and the quantity of the input data play a crucial role in determining the quality of the model under development. Once the model's structure and input dataset are ready, the model's training and evaluation are done. This training step aims to reduce the prediction error and increase the model's efficiency. The final developed model should express the relation between the parameters and the developer's purpose of model building. If the essential goal is not met, the model can be fine-tuned using pertinent data to accomplish the objective [63,64].

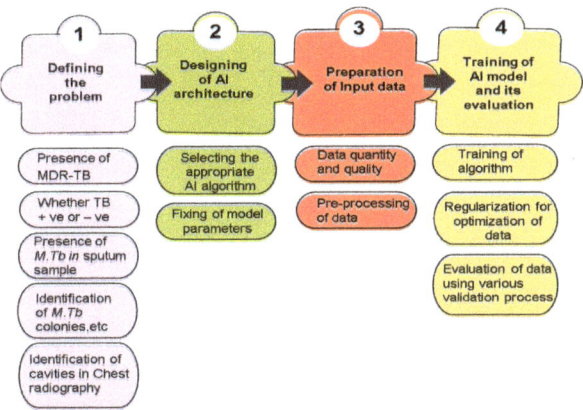

Figure 2. Steps involved in the construction of AI model for TB diagnosis.

6.1. Preparation of Input Data

The input data/dataset used for the model's training plays an important part, as it determines the model's overall performance. Nevertheless, preparing the correct data is laborious and time-demanding work [65]. Before data preparation, one should understand the needs of the training set, i.e., representation of the complexity and type of data required, the quantity of the domain-specific input data, and its distribution in the internal space [66,67]. The quality of the training set also depends on the occupying space with possible input data required for making the prediction. The model can be pre-processed if inadequate data are available [65,68]. Here, in this article, some guidance for these problems has been provided.

6.2. Input Databases Used in TB Diagnosis

The most used input datasets for TB diagnosis are the Shenzhen Dataset and Montgomery County chest X-ray dataset. Nonetheless, there are limitations constitutive of these datasets. Compared to the training model size, these datasets are small, leading to more computational memory and time. For example, Lakhani et al. [69] used AlexNet (60 million parameters) and GoogleNet (7 million parameters) as input training models for TB diagnosis. These are the most frequently used deep learning models, pre-trained on many images (besides TB radiography). Table 3 summarizes the various datasets used for developing AI models in TB diagnosis. As such, many parameters for sparse data result in more memory usage.

Similarly, evaluation using many parameters is also error-prone (overfitting). Various improved dataset models have been introduced to overcome such problems, such as the shufflenetV2 [70] model for TB diagnosis. This dataset model is more specific, accurate, has fast prediction, and uses a lightweight neural network. The other limitations include early diagnosis of multidrug-resistant TB and differentiating it from different types of

TB. This calls for an AI model requirement trained to diagnose multidrug-resistant TB in its early stage. A ResNeXt 50 CNN classifier was developed using transfer learning to identify whether the person has MDR-TB or DS-TB. ResNeXt 50 is a CNN model with 50 hidden deep layers that are easy to use and have a highly modular structure for image classification [71].

Table 3. Various datasets used in TB diagnosis.

S. No.	Name of the Database	Developed by	Features of the Database	Ref.
		Chest X-ray Dataset		
1.	Shenzhen dataset	Partnership with Shenzhen No.3 People's Hospital, Guangdong Medical College, Shenzhen, China	• Consists of a total of 662 anterior chest X-ray images. • In total, 336 images are TB cases (including pediatric chest x-rays) and 326 images are normal cases.	[72]
2.	Montgomery County chest X-ray dataset (MC)	Partnership with the Department of Health and Human Services, Montgomery County, Maryland, USA	• Consists of a total of 138 anterior chest X-rays from the Montgomery County TB screening program. • In total, 58 images are TB cases and 80 are normal cases.	[72]
3.	PadChest	Radiologist at San Juan Hospital, Spain	• Consists of a total of 160,000 images and their associated reports. • It contains a total of 152 images of TB cases.	[73]
4.	ChestX-ray8 dataset	Radiologist at NIH Clinic center, Bethesda, Maryland, USA, as a part of routine care	• Consist of a total of 112,120 anterior chest X-ray images. • In total, there are 51,760 abnormal images (18,898 TB related) and 60,360 normal chest X-rays.	[9]
5.	Belarus TB Portal dataset	TB specialist at Minsk city, capital of Belarus, Europe	• Consists of a total of 304 images of confirmed TB cases.	[74]
6.	TBX11K dataset	Media Computing Lab, Nankai University, China	• Consists of a total of 11,200 images. • In total, 924 images are of TB cases.Comprises of four classes: active TB, latent TB, healthy and unhealthy but non-TB.	[75]
7.	8-Bit dataset-A	Radiologist at National Institute of Tuberculosis and Respiratory Diseases, New Delhi, India	• Consists of a total of 156 images, where 78 images are TB cases, and the other 78 images are non-TB cases.	[76]
8.	14-Bit dataset-B	Radiologist at National Institute of Tuberculosis and Respiratory Diseases, New Delhi, India	• Consists of a total of 150 images, where 75 images are TB cases, and the other 75 images are non-TB cases.	[76]
		Sputum Smear Microscopy Image Dataset		
9.	ZNSM iDB	Jaypee University of Information Technology, Solan, India	• Consists of image data compiled from seven different datasets by using three different light field microscopes. • TB diagnosis is made on three main domains: autofocusing, auto stitching, and auto-grading of TB bacillus.	[77]

6.3. Quantity and Quality of Input Data

Input data are one of the essential parts of model construction that need close attention. For example, suppose the dataset's size is insufficient for the learning process; the training task leads to overfitting and errors and increases the chances of model incapability to generalize the new data efficiently. In such a case, the training model's performance should be checked as to whether it is acceptable. In an unacceptable case, the model normalization [78] can be carried out, and even still the model is not benefited, so some reconstruction or tuning of the model is required. Generally, learning the training data should be a possible task even with a less optimized structure, so it is better to focus on the model's architecture rather than collecting more data. However, even if the reconstruction of the model or use of another algorithm does not improve, it is time to check the quality of training data for errors, logical correspondence between input and output data, and balanced training data distribution [79].

Moreover, it is better to retrain the model on unlabeled as it gives an inefficient performance, which will conclude that the model is forming a meaningful link with training data. However, even if the model performance is still unacceptable, it is recommended to collect more data. The primary consideration here includes the high cost of collecting data, which can be overcome by optimizing the model [80]. This can be done by selecting suitable parameters, advanced architectures, regular normalization of the structure, and a preference for high-quality data at an affordable cost [78,80].

7. Advancing with Deep Learning

Deep learning is a machine learning technique in which machines learn to perform classification/prediction tasks directly from the input data [81]. Building deep learning models with high accuracy requires a combination of signals with different weights (where the dataset can be adjusted according to weights to give an expected response for a given input), which passes the results successively deeper in the multi-layer neural network framework until an output layer [79]. Multiple learnable stages make this approach more useful in tackling complex problems. "Deep" here refers to the number of hidden layers in the network, i.e., it can have numerous hidden layers compared to traditional neural networks. Deep learning has been widely used for bioinformatics and computational biology [82]. With increased training data and powerful computational capacity, conventional machine learning methods have transformed into advanced machine learning models (Figure 3).

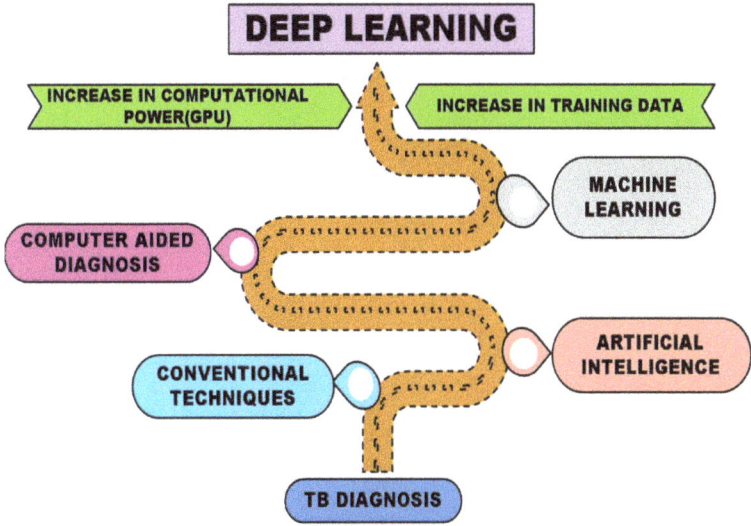

Figure 3. Evolution of artificial intelligence in TB diagnosis.

7.1. Convolutional Neural Networks (CNN)

CNN is a deep learning class that uses feed-forward artificial neural networks to analyze images [83]. It is considered state of the art for image classification due to the connectivity pattern between its neurons, which are arranged so that they respond to overlapping regions building the visual field. It consists of many hidden layers, out of which the important ones are the pooling layer and fully connected (FC) layers. The pooling layer reduces the image's spatial size without changing the depth, and the FC layers are generally placed before the final output layer, where the image classification process starts [84]. CNN is motivated by biological processes and variations of multi-layer neural networks designed to use minimal amounts of pre-processing [85]. Moreover, due to its non-requirement of domain knowledge, it can extract and learn meaningful features by segregating the target classes during the training phase [83] (Figure 4).

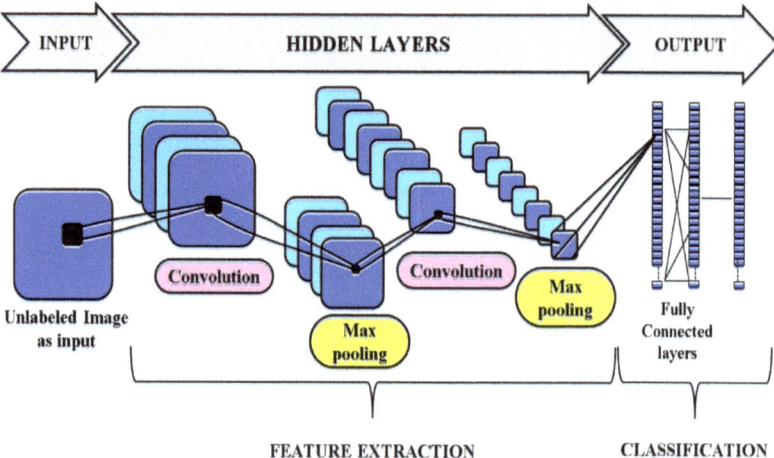

Figure 4. Working on a basic CNN model.

7.2. Does CNN Make Our Job Easier in TB Diagnosis?

CNN is a remarkable combination of math and biology with a bit of a mist of computer science. It has been a significant invention in image processing and machine vision. The conception of CNN depicts the probability of the data (images) into certain classes on the same basis as the human brain works [84]. For example, when a human looks at an image, they classify it into different types based on its characteristic features. Similarly, the computer algorithm can organize the image by identifying the low-level features such as curves and edges at initial levels and gradually generating more intense concepts with high-level features through a series of hidden layers (convolutional layer, pooling layer, fully connected layer) [83]. Similarly, a CNN model learns distinguishing features from the TB dataset and tries to classify a new input image as a TB or non-TB case (Figure 5). Details of steps required to build a CNN model for TB diagnosis using chest X-ray images are as follows.

Input for a convolutional layer: The input for a CNN model is in the form of images. These images are resized into an optimal size and transferred to the hidden layers. Each hidden layer consists of kernels or filters or neurons put over some portion of the input image subjected to the neurons' size [86]. The CNN model compares images fraction by fraction, and each fraction is known as a feature. Each feature is like a mini-image, and each neuron is a feature identifier [68]. For example, one of the filters identifies the curves in the chest X-ray image as a feature. When the input image passes through this filter, it will locate the curves present in the image. Similarly, there will be other filters for identifying features such as a straight line, curves bending to the right, curves bending to the left, or straight edges in the input image. Furthermore, the greater the number of filters, the greater the identification depth, leading to more information about the input image [87].

Activation of the convolutional layer: Each filter can identify a specific feature in the input image. When the image passes through the filter, it searches for that feature in the image. Once the filter spots the feature, it can identify the features that lead to activation of the filter [87]. The filter further moves to spot the specific feature in the input image. This leads to forming an activation map of that filter for the feature in the image. The value generated by the activation map of the filter gives an idea about the percentage of that feature present in the input image [88]. For example, we will consider a filter of dimensions (8 × 8) as a curve identifier (Figure 6). When a chest X-ray image passes through this filter, it will try to spot the image's curves.

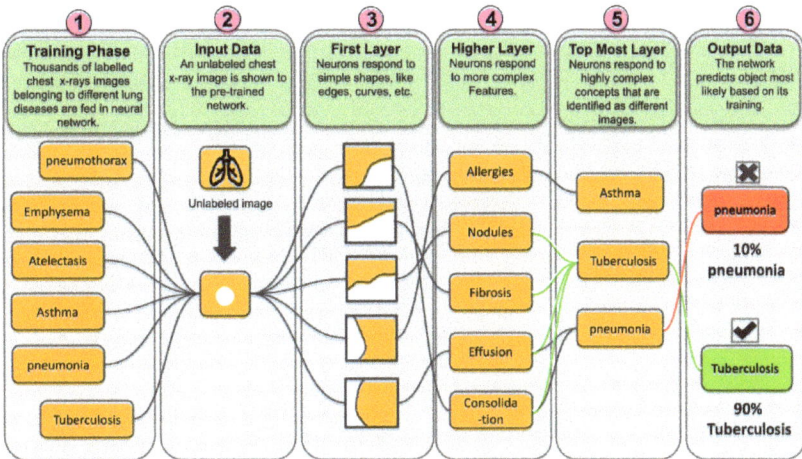

Figure 5. Representation of working of a CNN model for TB diagnosis.

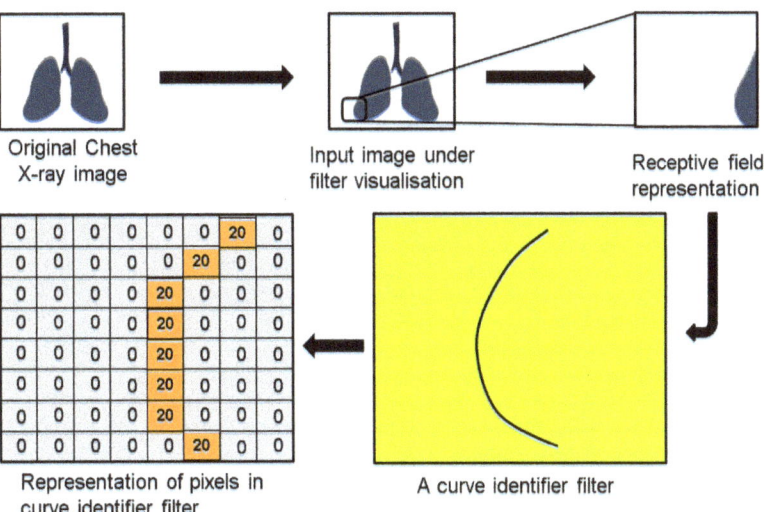

Figure 6. Curve identifier filter and its activation for a chest X-ray image.

When the filter identifies a feature, it will try to match the pixels of the input image and the pixels of the filter. Furthermore, suppose an image section responds to the matching process, leading to the generation of a value (the sum of the multiplication of filter pixels with the input image) and an activation map [89]. The higher the value generated by the activation map, the greater the presence of that feature in the image, i.e., it shows some type of curve in the input image that caused the activation of the filter and vice versa. This is only for one filter; similarly, many filters are present for each feature. Furthermore, the activation map of one filter acts as the input for the next filter, identifying another feature and forming a new activation map. This series of feature identification carries on, creating a more complex activation map [88].

Pooling layers: The pooling layer is another essential layer (the max-pooling layer (Figure 7)) in the CNN model that shrinks down a large image while preserving the essential data. It means that it keeps the maximum value of the pixel window, i.e., the best fit of the feature within the pixel window, and makes the output have few pixels but with the same number of features [88]. For example, in a chest radiograph, the max-pooling layer will be done for each feature, such as the shape of the cavity, opacity area, density of the cavity, etc. This layer helps in reducing the computation load and solves the problem of the system being hyper-literal [90].

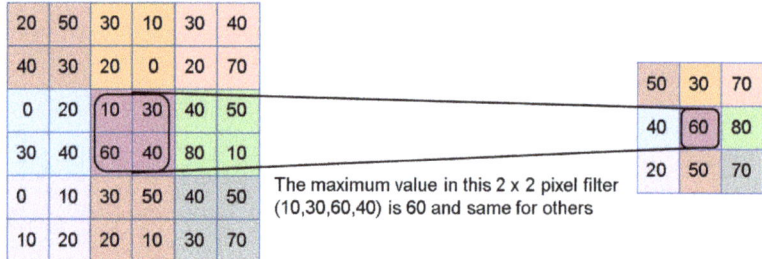

The maximum value in this 2 x 2 pixel filter (10,30,60,40) is 60 and same for others

Rectified Feature Map Representation

Figure 7. Working of max pooling layer from rectified feature map.

Extracting the output from fully connected layers (FCL): The fully connected layers in the CNN model convert the highly filtered images into votes. FCL is the primary building unit of the traditional neural network, which treats the input images as a single unit instead of two-dimensional blocks [90,91]. An FCL looks for high-value features that strongly complement a particular category and have respective weights. When the model is analyzed, it gives the correct probabilities for various categories [92]. For example, suppose the algorithm must decide that the input images are TB manifested. In that case, it will show high values in the activation maps that represent high-level features, like the opacity of the cavity, size of the cavity, lesions in lung space, etc. This will be followed by studying and interpreting the probability values for confirmation of TB in the chest X-ray image [93].

Data interpretation and explainable AI (XAI) for decision making of the CNN model: The output values obtained from the CNN model now need to be interpreted for the prediction of TB in the chest X-ray image [94]. This can be done by using explainable AI (XAI), where explainability is the ability of the AI model to explain decision making in an accessible form for medical experts in a broader range, thus making it easy to understand how a decision has been reached. There are two types of explainable AI techniques, i.e., post-hoc and intrinsic [95]. In the post-hoc method, we can approximately understand the behavior of the black box based on the decision set and perturbation-based methods, in which the relationship between prediction and feature values is extracted. This method includes class activation mapping (CAM), gradient-weighted class activation mapping (Grad-CAM), score class activation mapping (Score-CAM), Shapley Additive explanation, and principal component analysis (PCA) [96]. On the other hand, in intrinsic methods, we can understand the decision-making procedure as it accounts for which part of the input data is responsible for classification in any type of classifier. This method includes rule-based learner, logistic regression, decision tree, and Bayesian model [97].

Many research groups have reported the use of the DL models for the detection of TB by including transfer learning in the CNN model for diagnosis of TB using pre-trained models and also by varying the deep-layer CNN model parameters. A CNN model was developed using a chest X-ray dataset to diagnose TB by replacing the complexity of the pre-processing seen in DT analysis with a generalized model. It used transfer learning to train the model and the hidden layers for detection to help achieve high accuracy, i.e., with or without augmentation. The work concluded that applying CNN models could help bypass the need to build segmented algorithms, which can be time-consuming and require expertise [87]. A CNN-based LIRA (Lesion Image Recognition and Analysis) model was built to evaluate lesions obtained from pulmonary TB tissues. The study was to overcome shortcomings such as reproducibility and efficiency of histopathology studies. The LIRA model used seven pathology features, including three different lesion types from pulmonary tissue. The proposed model gave good results [98]. The FC-SVNN (fractional crow search-based deep convolutional neural network) model was proposed, which was used to classify and detect TB in a patient. The analysis for severity was conducted by extraction of features, which is detected using an adaptive fractional crow deep convolutional neural network (AFC-CNN), the modified version of the FC algorithm. The detection of TB severity using the model helped determine the level of infection [99]. Using the CNN model, a two-stage classification method (TSCM) was built to classify tuberculosis culture. The researchers used transfer learning for the small and imbalanced dataset, balanced using SMOTE (synthetic minority over-sampling technique). The model could boost 98% recall and 99% precision on non-negative class, which indicated successful detection of anomalies in the culture [100].

A deep CNN model was presented that used transfer learning to detect tuberculosis from the X-ray images. It used many pre-train CNN models i.e., MobileNet, ResNet, Xception, EfficientNet, and Inception for extracting features from the input image. It was concluded that datasets having extracted ROI gave high accuracy and better results in the detection of TB. The researchers also reported the use of two visualization techniques, i.e., grad-CAM, which helps in consolidating the medical expert diagnosis, and T-SNE, which helps in explaining the training efficiency of the trained model [101]. A simple, faster, and high-accuracy CNN model was proposed to overcome the overfitting problem and can be easily installed in mobiles. The model showed an accuracy of 86% and used a grad-CAM visualization technique for the detection of tuberculosis [102]. Similarly, a deep learning model was proposed to reliably detect TB from CXR images based on image preposing, image data augmentation, and segmentation followed by DL classification methods. It used transfer learning to classify TB and non-TB cases from the pre-trained deep CNN models. Further, it also used the Score-CAM visualization method to show that the model learns from the regions of segmented lung areas and produces the results for the diagnosis of TB with high precision, accuracy, and sensitivity, i.e., 97.34%, 97.07%, and 97.07%, respectively [59].

8. Integration of Deep Learning with Advanced Algorithms in TB Diagnosis

The power of neural networks can be amplified by integrating it with other algorithms such as fuzzy logic, genetic algorithm, and artificial immune system. These integrated systems have been applied for TB diagnosis and have proven to be useful (Figure 8).

8.1. Adaptive Neuro-Fuzzy Inference System

Fuzzy logic (FL) is a technique that handles numeric data and linguistic knowledge simultaneously; it is the rule-based mapping of a set of input values to a single output value. It maps the numeric value to numeric values [103]. Fuzzy logic presents an inference morphology that incorporates human reasoning capabilities in knowledge-based systems. Neural networks can recognize patterns, classify data, and predict events effectively, but the models cannot explain how patterns are classified or recognized. On the other hand, fuzzy systems are good at computing and explaining decisions, but they fail to adapt to new environmental conditions [104,105]. An adaptive neuro-fuzzy inference system (ANFIS) was used to diagnose tuberculosis. The model used input parameters such as sputum, chest X-ray, weight loss, etc., as TB symptoms for a rule-based fuzzy system to make output decisions. The work is under consideration for rural areas where the availability of doctors is difficult [106]. The work was extended by building an ANFIS model having 159 distinct rules and a backpropagation algorithm that would help in minimizing errors in the output. It also used a triangular fuzzifier for the fuzzification and MATLAB software results [107]. A neuro-fuzzy methodology was developed to diagnose TB in which eleven TB symptoms were used as input in MATLAB 7.0 software for the ANFIS experiment. The evaluation of the system was done by using the Trapezoidal membership function and backpropagation algorithm. The model was efficient in learning in a shorter time and gave good results [108].

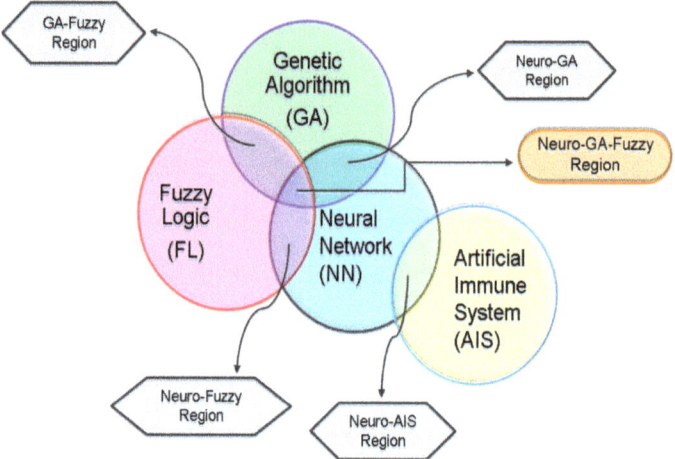

Figure 8. Integration of deep learning with fuzzy logic, genetic algorithm, and artificial immune system.

8.2. Genetic Algorithm with Deep Learning

Genetic algorithms (GAs) are commonly used to build high-quality solutions to search for problems by relying on bio-inspired operators such as mutation, crossover, and selection [109]. GAs were mainly used to simulate the environments and behaviors of entities in a population. A genetic algorithm creates a sample from the population at its very core by a random selection process. Then, it scores each member of the population based on some goal called a fitness function. Next, the mutation process selects the sample closest to the fitness function, breeds the best population members to produce more like them, and kills off the rest (survival of the fittest and all). This process is repeated multiple times, and each iteration through these steps is called a generation [110]. Genetic algorithms were trendy before Neural Networks (NNs) [111]. Since NNs require big data while GAs do not, genetic algorithms are used in artificial intelligence, like other search algorithms, to search a subset of potential solutions [109].

The genetic-neuro approach was used to study its application in diagnosing tuberculosis. A backpropagation algorithm classifier with the Levenberg—Marquardt algorithm was used to train the model, where nine features were selected for developing the dataset. GA was used for the extraction of individual features having importance. The GA-NN model could classify 96.3% correctly from the test data [112]. Similarly, a hybrid algorithm was built to diagnose chest diseases, including tuberculosis. An ANN having backpropagation algorithms was used to evaluate the output error and calculate the error gradient. It conducted a comparative study of chest diseases using the genetic-neuro method and concluded it to be a valuable tool for early TB diagnosis [113].

Genetic-Neuro-Fuzzy Inference System (GENFIS)

An inference system integrates a genetic algorithm, neural network, and fuzzy logic to develop an adaptive model that can carry out self-training for imprecise and uncertain data. A genetic-neuro-fuzzy inferential method was used to diagnose TB. The model was studied with a case study of 10 patients with the help of the MATLAB 7.9 version. The evaluation of the model was done using the medical records of 100 patients. GNFIS was optimized using a decision support engine, giving sensitivity and accuracy of 60% and 70%, respectively [114].

Similarly, a GENFIS model was applied for the early diagnosis of tuberculosis. Again, they used a decision support system to evaluate 100 patients' medical records. In this, 70% of data were used as training data, 15% for validation, and the rest for measuring the model's performance. The proposed model gave sensitivity and accuracy of 72% and 82%, respectively [115].

8.3. Artificial Immune System (AIS) with Deep Learning

AIS is a new AI technique that is starting to grow through many interdisciplinary researchers' collaborative efforts. AIS is developed using the core ideas, theories, and components of the immune system. It aims at solving problems such as pattern recognition, classification, elimination, and optimization, which are complex and require high computational power [116]. The natural immune system principles are found in the human body, forming the basis of the AIS tools. The powerful information processing capabilities of the biological immune system (BIS) are an area of significant research for multiple reasons, mainly the distributed nature of its memory and decentralized control mechanisms from an informational perspective. Such computational models are believed to solve many science and engineering problems [117]. Diagnosis for chest diseases such as tuberculosis via proper interpretation of the disease data is a significant classification problem.

Furthermore, AIS has the potential to provide an efficient way of solving chest disease diagnosis problems. Using AIS in Turkey, a study was conducted to diagnose tuberculosis. The dataset was prepared from a chest disease hospital using patients' epicrisis reports. The classification accuracy obtained was 90% with AIS and MLNN with LM (Levenberg—Marquardt) algorithm [118]. An AIRS (artificial immune recognition system) incorporated with a fuzzy logic controller was used to create an unsupervised hybrid machine learning model. This hybrid system showed bioinspired ways to help doctors in their diagnostic conclusions [119].

A new hybrid system, SAIRS2, was built to diagnose TB by incorporating AIRS with the SVM classifier. The study's primary purpose was to reduce the loss of diversity and overcome the existing selection pressure. It used the dataset to build the SAIRS2 model, which was analyzed using WEKA (Waikato Environment for Knowledge Analysis), a machine learning program [120]. The author also integrated AIRS with real-world tournament selection (RWTS), forming a new hybrid system, RAIRS2, to diagnose TB. RWTS is one of the favored and applicable tournament selection mechanisms in genetic algorithms that help control the population size and overcome the selection pressure [121]. Using a computational model UISS (universal immune system simulator), an agent-based modeling method with AIS was used to diagnose TB. The model helped understand the underlying TB pathogenesis and its interaction with the patient's immune system [122].

9. Tools Built Using Deep Learning Techniques

For many years, TB management has been approached according to a paradigm of symptomatic active infection and asymptomatic latent disease. However, in 2015, the end TB strategy specifically outlined some policies for increasing the TB diagnosis capacity across the high tuberculosis burden countries [123]. These policies prioritize rapid diagnosis using various advanced tools, mainly drug resistance. In the past few years, many computer-aided diagnostic tools using deep learning have been built for fast screening and triaging a quick and efficient screen of a large population, helping identify people needing further treatment. These CNN-based tools provide a labor-saving and structured interpretation of TB-related images [124,125] In addition, an online resource has recently been launched [https://www.ai4hlth.org/ (accessed on 3 July 2022)] by Foundation for Innovative New Diagnostics (FIND) and the Stop TB Partnership. This resource center will provide relevant data for several computer-assisted products in areas with limited access to radiologists and low-resource countries with a high TB burden (Table 4).

Table 4. Available and upcoming TB diagnostic tools built using the deep learning techniques.

Sl.No	Name of the Tool	Design Stage	Advised Age Group	Process Time	Product Development Method	Refs.
Tools with CE-marked Certification *						
1.	**CAD4TB** (Delft Imaging, the Netherlands)	Available for sale	4+ years	Less than 20 s	• Supervised learning • CNN • RNN	[126]
2.	**Infer Read DR Chest** (InferVISION, Beijing, China)	Available for sale	16+ years (approved), 12–18 years recommended	Less than 5 s	• Supervised learning • CNN • RNN	[127]
3.	**JLD02K** (JVIEWER-X) (JLK, Seoul, South Korea)	Available for sale	10+ years	15–20 s	• Supervised learning • CNN • DBN	[128]
4.	**Lunit INSIGHT CXR** (Lunit, Seoul, South Korea)	Available for sale	14+ years	≈20 s per on X-ray	• Supervised learning • CNN	[129]
5.	**qXR** (Qure.ai, Mumbai, India)	Available for sale	6+ years (approved), 2+ years recommended	Less than a minute	• Uses DL for analyzing chest X-ray	[130]
Tools with pending Certification						
1.	**AXIR** (Radisen, Seoul, South Korea)	Validation	16+ years	Less than 20 s	• Supervised learning • CNN	[131]
2.	**T-Xnet** (Artelus, Bangalore, India)	Validation	18+ years	Max. 10 s	• Supervised learning • CNN • RNN	[132]
3.	**DxTB** (DeepTek, Delaware, USA)	Available for sale	14+ years	≈2 s	• Supervised and unsupervised learning • CNN • RNN	[133]
4.	**Dr. CADx** (Dr CADx, Bulawayo, Zimbabwe)	Validation	16+ years	Less than a minute	• Supervised learning • CNN • RNN	[134]
5.	**XrayAME** (Epcon, Antwerp, Belgium)	Available for sale	18+ years	20 s	• Supervised learning • CNN • RNN	[135]
6.	**JF CXR-1** (JF Healthcare, Nanchang, China)	Available for sale	15+ years	≈1–5 s	• Supervised learning • CNN • RNN	[136]

* CE-marked certification ensures that the product complies with the specific standards of safety, efficacy, quality, and performance set by the European Union Directives.

Amongst all the tools mentioned, a few tools such as CAD4TB, Lunit INSIGHT CXR, and qXR have been validated with real-time parameters. In August 2018 in Korea, for the first time Lunit Insight CXR nodule, version 1, Lunit Inc., was approved by the government for analyzing the CXR of adults. Again in October 2019, Lunit Insight CXR MCA, version 2, based on ResNet34, was approved in Korea, and in March 2020 it was applied for all patient chest radiograph detection. From then until February 2021, around 56,192 CXR of adults have been analyzed considering the posteroanterior and anteroposterior views. This software can diagnose three forms of lesion, i.e., pneumothorax, nodule, and consolidation, and also lesions with an abnormality score of more than 15%. The image analysis and upload of results by AI happened in less than one minute, thus reducing the scan time and giving a board interaction. Lunit Insight CXR, version 3, was approved in October 2020 and installed in March 2021 in the hospital in Korea. It could detect eight types of lesions, i.e., fibrosis, pleural effusion, pneumoperitoneum, nodule, atelectasis, consolidation, cardiomegaly, and pneumothorax, and had an additional visualization method, i.e., grayscale contour maps. It could analyze around 106,230 CXR until February 2022. These AI CAD could not only diagnose the disease but also optimize the workflow by reducing the mean time to report critical and urgent cases [137].

In Dhaka, Bangladesh, a study was conducted to evaluate five commercially available AI CAD, i.e., Lunit INSIGHT CXR (version 4.9.0), CAD4TB (version 7), qXR (version 3), InferRead DR (version 2), and JF CXR-1 (version 2) between May 15, 2014 to October 4, 2016. People aged 15 years or above were referred to three TB diagnostic centers in Dhaka. All the participants were screened for symptoms and received an Xpert MTB/RIF test and digital anterior-posterior chest X-ray. These were evaluated by the five commercially available AI CAD and three registered radiologists. The performances of all the AI algorithms were compared with each other and with that of the radiologist, and also with the WHO Target Product Profile (TPP) of triage tests. Around 23954 people were analyzed for tuberculosis, and all AI algorithms outperformed all radiologists. All the AI algorithms maintained 90% sensitivity and helped in reducing of the number of Xpert tests required in TB diagnosis. The major disadvantage of all the AI algorithms was that they gave worse performance for the older age group, i.e., >60 years, and also for people having history of tuberculosis [138].

In Kharachi, Pakistan, a study was conducted at the Indus Hospital where two AI algorithms CAD4TB version 6.0 (CAD4TBv6) and qXR version 2.0 (qXRv2) were compared with a mycobacterial culture of two sputa as reference. The study included 2198 participants, out of which 2198 were HIV-negative and 272 were pulmonary tuberculosis confirmed by culture examination. Both software showed minimum value (CAD4TBv6 sensitivity 0.93, non-inferiority $p < 0.0001$; qXR sensitivity 0.93, non-inferiority $p = 0.0002$; CAD4TBv6 specificity 0.69, $p = 0.0003$; qXR specificity 0.75, $p < 0.0001$) for the test for non-inferiority as recommended by WHO, having a non-inferiority limit of 0.05. It was also seen that for both the software, the sensitivity was low in the case of smear-negative pulmonary TB and for women in CAD4TBv6. Furthermore, the specificity was low in men, those having a previous history of tuberculosis, older age groups, and those with low body mass index [139].

10. Conclusions and Future Aspect

Advances in AI techniques, particularly in deep learning (DL), have been supported by improved hardware storage such as LSPC (large-scale parallel computing), GPU (graphics processing unit), and TPU (tensor processing unit) [140], as well as big data. Accomplishment in the fields such as image and voice recognition has brought AI more public acceptance and new hopes for diagnosing disease. Machine learning has exceeded human expertise in several areas when seen in terms of performance. Therefore, it is no surprise but more promising when applied to TB diagnosis. AI approaches in TB diagnosis are mainly integrated for early disease diagnosis, focusing on TB symptoms and drug resistance. Successful DL model examples for TB diagnosis are at the fore. For instance, ImageCLEF is a forum established in 2003 that evaluates images and cross-languages retrieval by organizing conferences [141]. It is a platform that sees participation from both industrial and academic researchers in machine vision and pattern recognition, computer—human interaction, and medical informatics as a few classes in the ImageCLEF campaign [141]. In 2018, a classifier was developed to identify whether the patient has MDR tuberculosis or drug-sensitive tuberculosis based on the patient's CT scan. It secured the best accuracy and second position in AUC evaluation at ImageCLEF 2018 tuberculosis conference [71]. In Peru, a deep learning model was developed on similar grounds to identify TB based on its types. The developed model was promising and later planned to be implemented into mobile devices for TB diagnosis [142].

Regardless of significant success in the past, AI implementation in TB diagnosis is still challenging due to the acquirement of quality; thus, adequate and problem-solving data remain a challenge. Data compilation is easy when we see it in the computer vision field, as the chosen data are highly reliable and form a large dataset. However, a horse will always be a horse and cannot be an elephant. Unfortunately, it is not the same in disease diagnosis as many reasons will hinder producing good quality and sufficient data to form a dataset. On the one hand, the data collected from different experimental sources highly depends on the variant experimental conditions applied, which might give different or opposite results. This is due to our complicated biological system, which shows various symptoms and drug resistance for the same disease and a drug. On the other hand, a vast range of data is available, depending on the nature of the requirement and the necessity to build a high-quality dataset.

One solution to the kettle of fish is developing an algorithm that can deal with different or insufficient datasets. In 2019, a constructed DL model was trained using only the chest radiograph to detect TB. This model was trained using NIH and Shenzhen datasets [72] and the Belarus Tuberculosis Portal dataset [143]. However, this dataset was not of high quality since it still needed further chest image upgrading, and its distinctive quality focused solely on TB diagnosis [102]. Another critical challenge is to utilize and stick to the principle of removing unwanted data to achieve more refinement and a task-oriented standards set. In 2017, a DL model was pre-trained on millions of images using AlexNet and GoogLeNet datasets, containing many images, including chest radiographs. This model required significant computer storage space to work efficiently, even for a small job of TB detection using chest X-ray images [69]. At the same time, a dataset was proposed that required lesser storage memory and a cheaper processor as it required storage only in mega-FLOPs in contrast to AlexNet and GoogLeNet datasets that required storage in Giga–FLOPs [102].

The deep learning methods integrated with other neuro-fuzzy, genetic algorithms and artificial immune systems are the most promising subdomain for TB diagnosis. These systems increase the system's sensitivity, specificity, and accuracy since they take biological information. Therefore, we can expect to see these integrated algorithms for a much improved and increased success rate in TB diagnosis in the coming years. However, overfitting (a modeling error in which a function fits too closely to a set of limited data points) and understanding the internal mechanism of the CNN model to make specific decisions are the limitations. This overfitting is mainly because of a limited dataset for accurate TB diagnosis and nevertheless, much research related to DL and the integrated system has been taking place, which might help overcome this limitation. Furthermore, the advancement in technology has led to the development of visualization methods. These techniques help in the better interpretation of CNN model decision making by visual representation. These techniques also provide transparency to the model by visualizing the reason behind interference, thus making it more interpretable and understandable for humans. Therefore, this increases the confidence in the output data of the CNN model [59].

In brief, AI has shown its potential in various diagnostic fields. However, its application will increase research as the adoption of AI-specific domains is still in its initial stage. AI can be proven to be an elixir for many deadly diseases and its early diagnosis. Nonetheless, acceptance of new technology is a slow process as it involves duplicating work and overcoming many setbacks involved with the process. However, AI will bring specific changes in TB diagnosis, and hence there will be an advancement in the research field.

Author Contributions: M.S., G.V.P., S.A.K., M.B., H.S.A. and L.A. conceptualized and designed the study. M.S. performed the literature analysis and wrote the original manuscript draft. G.V.P., L.A., M.B., H.S.A., S.A.K. and N.M.B. revised the manuscript. B.A., A.R.A., A.R.A., A.H.G. and N.M.B. edited, and extended the final draft. All authors have read and agreed to the published version of the manuscript.

Funding: Funding was received from Indian Council of Medical Research (RFC No. ECD/Adhoc/27/2019-20 dt 27.08.2019).

Institutional Review Board Statement: Not applicable.

Informed Consent Statement: Not applicable.

Data Availability Statement: Not applicable.

Acknowledgments: The authors are thankful to Indian Council of Medical Research (ICMR), New Delhi for funding and the Principal, JSS College of Pharmacy, JSS Academy of Higher Education and Research, Mysore, India, for providing necessary facilities.

Conflicts of Interest: The authors declare no conflict of interest.

References

1. WHO. World Health Organization Global Tuberculosis Report 2020. 2020. Available online: http://apps.who.int/iris (accessed on 3 July 2022).
2. Cole, S.T.; Riccardi, G. New tuberculosis drugs on the horizon. *Curr. Opin. Microbiol.* **2011**, *14*, 570–576. [CrossRef] [PubMed]
3. Reid, M.J.A.; Arinaminpathy, N.; Bloom, A.; Bloom, B.R.; Boehme, C.; Chaisson, R.; Chin, D.P.; Churchyard, G.; Cox, H.; Ditiu, L.; et al. Building a tuberculosis-free world: The Lancet Commission on tuberculosis. *Lancet* **2019**, *393*, 1331–1384. [CrossRef]
4. Melendez, J.; Sánchez, C.I.; Philipsen, R.H.H.M.; Maduskar, P.; Dawson, R.; Theron, G.; Dheda, K.; Van Ginneken, B. An automated tuberculosis screening strategy combining X-ray-based computer-aided detection and clinical information. *Sci. Rep.* **2016**, *6*, 25265. [CrossRef]
5. Dye, C.; Williams, B.G. Criteria for the control of drug-resistant tuberculosis. *Proc. Natl. Acad. Sci. USA* **2000**, *97*, 8180–8185. [CrossRef] [PubMed]
6. Xu, T.; Cheng, I.; Long, R.; Mandal, M. Novel coarse-to-fine dual scale technique for tuberculosis cavity detection in chest radiographs. *Eurasip J. Image Video Process.* **2013**, *2013*, 3. [CrossRef]
7. Song, Y.L.; Yang, Y. Localization algorithm and implementation for focal of pulmonary tuberculosis chest image. In Proceedings of the 2010 International Conference on Machine Vision and Human-machine Interface, Kaifeng, China, 24–25 April 2010; pp. 361–364. [CrossRef]
8. Jaeger, S.; Karargyris, A.; Antani, S.; Thoma, G. Detecting tuberculosis in radiographs using combined lung masks. In Proceedings of the Annual International Conference of the IEEE Engineering in Medicine and Biology Society, San Diego, CA, USA, 28 August–1 September 2012; pp. 4978–4981. [CrossRef]
9. Sathitratanacheewin, S.; Sunanta, P.; Pongpirul, K. Deep learning for automated classification of tuberculosis-related chest X-Ray: Dataset distribution shift limits diagnostic performance generalizability. *Heliyon* **2020**, *6*, e04614. [CrossRef]
10. Vajda, S.; Karargyris, A.; Jaeger, S.; Santosh, K.C.; Candemir, S.; Xue, Z.; Antani, S.K.; Thoma, G.R. Feature Selection for Automatic Tuberculosis Screening in Frontal Chest Radiographs. *J. Med. Syst.* **2018**, *42*, 146. [CrossRef]
11. Cao, Y.; Liu, C.; Liu, B.; Brunette, M.J.; Zhang, N.; Sun, T.; Zhang, P.; Peinado, J.; Garavito, E.S.; Garcia, L.L.; et al. Improving Tuberculosis Diagnostics Using Deep Learning and Mobile Health Technologies among Resource-Poor and Marginalized Communities. In Proceedings of the 2016 IEEE First International Conference on Connected Health: Applications, Systems and Engineering Technologies (CHASE), Washington, DC, USA, 27–29 June 2016; pp. 274–281. [CrossRef]
12. Hwang, S.; Kim, H.-E.; Jeong, J.; Kim, H.-J. A novel approach for tuberculosis screening based on deep convolutional neural networks. In Proceedings of the Medical Imaging 2016: Computer-Aided Diagnosis, San Diego, CA, USA, 27 February–3 March 2016; Volume 9785, p. 97852W. [CrossRef]
13. Berthel, S.J.; Cooper, C.B.; Fotouhi, N. Chapter One—Tuberculosis. In *Medicinal Chemistry Approaches to Tuberculosis and Trypanosomiasis*; Annual Reports in Medicinal Chemistry Series; Elsevier: Amsterdam, The Netherlands, 2019; Volume 52, pp. 1–25.
14. Richeldi, L. An Update on the Diagnosis of Tuberculosis Infection. *Am. J. Respir. Crit. Care Med.* **2006**, *174*, 736–742. [CrossRef]
15. Subbaraman, R.; Nathavitharana, R.R.; Mayer, K.H.; Satyanarayana, S.; Chadha, V.K.; Arinaminpathy, N.; Pai, M. Constructing care cascades for active tuberculosis: A strategy for program monitoring and identifying gaps in quality of care. *PLoS Med.* **2019**, *16*, e1002754. [CrossRef]
16. Jasmer, R.M.; Nahid, P.; Hopewell, P.C. Latent Tuberculosis Infection. *J. Gastroenterol. Hepatol.* **2015**, *30*, 13–26. [CrossRef]
17. Noubissi, E.C.; Katte, J.-C.; Sobngwi, E. Diabetes and HIV. *Curr. Diabetes Rep.* **2018**, *18*, 125. [CrossRef] [PubMed]
18. Sharma, S.K.; Mohan, A. Miliary Tuberculosis. *ASM J. Microbiol. Spectr.* **2017**, *5*, 491–513. [CrossRef]
19. Mbuagbaw, L.; Guglielmetti, L.; Hewison, C.; Bakare, N.; Bastard, M.; Caumes, E.; Jachym, M.F.; Robert, J.; Veziris, N.; Khachatryan, N.; et al. Outcomes of bedaquiline treatment in patients with multidrug-resistant tuberculosis. *Emerg. Infect. Dis.* **2019**, *25*, 936–943. [CrossRef]
20. Bhirud, P.; Joshi, A.; Hirani, N.; Chowdhary, A. Rapid Laboratory Diagnosis of Pulmonary Tuberculosis. *Int. J. Mycobacteriol.* **2017**, *6*, 296–301. [CrossRef] [PubMed]
21. Miotto, P.; Zhang, Y.; Cirillo, D.M.; Yam, W.C. Drug resistance mechanisms and drug susceptibility testing for tuberculosis. *Respirology* **2018**, *23*, 1098–1113. [CrossRef] [PubMed]
22. World Health Organisation. Chest Radiography in Tuberculosis. 2016. Available online: http://www.who.int (accessed on 3 July 2022).
23. Steingart, K.R.; Steingart, M.; Ng, V.; Hopewell, P.C.; Ramsay, A.; Cunningham, J.; Urbanczik, R.; Perkins, M.; Aziz, M.A.; Pai, M. Fluorescence versus conventional sputum smear microscopy for tuberculosis: A systematic review. *Lancet Infect. Dis.* **2006**, *6*, 570–581. [CrossRef]
24. Ojha, A.; Banik, S.; Melanthota, S.K.; Mazumder, N. Light emitting diode (LED) based fluorescence microscopy for tuberculosis detection: A review. *Lasers Med. Sci.* **2020**, *35*, 1431–1437. [CrossRef]

25. Cruciani, M.; Scarparo, C.; Malena, M.; Bosco, O.; Serpelloni, G.; Mengoli, C. Meta-Analysis of BACTEC MGIT 960 and BACTEC 460 TB, with or without Solid Media, for Detection of Mycobacteria. *J. Clin. Microbiol.* **2004**, *42*, 2321–2325. [CrossRef]
26. Uplekar, M.; Weil, D.; Lonnroth, K.; Jaramillo, E.; Lienhardt, C.; Dias, H.M.; Falzon, D.; Floyd, K.; Gargioni, G.; Getahun, H.; et al. WHO's new End TB Strategy. *Lancet* **2015**, *385*, 1799–1801. [CrossRef]
27. Steingart, K.R.; Sohn, H.; Schiller, I.; Kloda, L.A.; Boehme, C.C.; Pai, M.; Dendukuri, N. Xpert® MTB/RIF assay for pulmonary tuberculosis and rifampicin resistance in adults. *Cochrane Database Syst. Rev.* **2013**, *1*, CD009593. [CrossRef]
28. Ling, D.I.; Zwerling, A.A.; Pai, M. GenoType MTBDR assays for the diagnosis of multidrug-resistant tuberculosis: A meta-analysis. *Eur. Respir. J.* **2008**, *32*, 1165–1174. [CrossRef] [PubMed]
29. World Health Organisation. The Use of Molecular Line Probe Assays for the Detection of Resistance to Second-Line Anti-Tuberculosis Drugs: Policy Guidance. 2019. Available online: https://apps.who.int/iris/handle/10665/246131 (accessed on 3 July 2022).
30. World Health Organisation. The Use of Loop-Mediated Isothermal Amplification (TB-LAMP) for the Diagnosis of Pulmonary Tuberculosis: Policy Guidance. 2016. Available online: https://apps.who.int/iris/handle/10665/249154 (accessed on 3 July 2022).
31. Virenfeldt, J.; Rudolf, F.; Camara, C.; Furtado, A.; Gomes, V.; Aaby, P.; Petersen, E.; Wejse, C. Treatment delay affects clinical severity of tuberculosis: A longitudinal cohort study. *BMJ Open* **2014**, *4*, e004818. [CrossRef] [PubMed]
32. Zhou, L.; He, X.; He, D.; Wang, K.; Qin, D. Biosensing Technologies for *Mycobacterium tuberculosis* Detection: Status and New Developments. *Clin. Dev. Immunol.* **2011**, *2011*, 1–9. [CrossRef] [PubMed]
33. Gupta, S.; Kakkar, V. Recent technological advancements in tuberculosis diagnostics—A review. *Biosens. Bioelectron.* **2018**, *115*, 14–29. [CrossRef] [PubMed]
34. Rosenblatt, F. The perceptron: A probabilistic model for information storage and organization in the brain. *Psychol. Rev.* **1958**, *65*, 386–408. [CrossRef]
35. Abe, H.; Kumazawa, S.; Taji, T.; Sasaki, S.I. Applications of computerized pattern recognition: A survey of correlations between pharmacological activities and mass spectra. *Biol. Mass Spectrom.* **1976**, *3*, 151–154. [CrossRef]
36. Maliwan, N.; Reid, R.W.; Pliska, S.R.; Bird, T.J.; Zvetina, J.R. Direct diagnosis of tuberculosis by computer assisted pattern recognition gas chromatographic analysis of sputum. *Biomed. Chromatogr.* **1991**, *5*, 165–170. [CrossRef]
37. Asada, N.; Doi, K.; MacMahon, H.; Montner, S.M.; Giger, M.L.; Abé, C.; Wu, Y. Potential usefulness of an artificial neural network for differential diagnosis of interstitial lung diseases: Pilot study. *Radiology* **1990**, *177*, 857–860. [CrossRef]
38. Veropoulos, K.; Campbell, C.; Learmonth, G.; Knight, B.; Simpson, J. The Automated Identification of Tubercle Bacilli using Image Processing and Neural Computing Techniques. In *ICANN 1998. Perspectives in Neural Computing*; Niklasson, L., Bodén, M., Ziemke, T., Eds.; Springer: London, UK, 1998; pp. 797–802. [CrossRef]
39. El-Solh, A.A.; Hsiao, C.-B.; Goodnough, S.; Serghani, J.; Grant, B.J. Predicting Active Pulmonary Tuberculosis Using an Artificial Neural Network. *Chest* **1999**, *116*, 968–973. [CrossRef]
40. Hearst, M.A.; Dumais, S.T.; Osuna, E.; Platt, J.; Scholkopf, B. Support Vector Machines. *IEEE Intell. Syst. Their Appl.* **1998**, *13*, 18–28. [CrossRef]
41. El-Solh, A.; Mylotte, J.; Sherif, S.; Serghani, J.; Grant, B.J. Validity of a decision tree for predicting active pulmonary tuberculosis. *Am. J. Respir. Crit. Care Med.* **1997**, *155*, 1711–1716. [CrossRef] [PubMed]
42. Ho, T.K. Random Decision Forests. In Proceedings of the 3rd International Conference on Document Analysis and Recognition, Montreal, QC, Canada, 14–16 August 1995; pp. 278–282. [CrossRef]
43. Osman, M.K.; Ahmad, F.; Saad, Z.; Mashor, M.Y.; Jaafar, H. A genetic algorithm-neural network approach for *Mycobacterium tuberculosis* detection in Ziehl-Neelsen stained tissue slide images. In Proceedings of the 2010 10th International Conference on Intelligent Systems Design and Applications, Cairo, Egypt, 29 November–1 December 2010; pp. 1229–1234. [CrossRef]
44. Semogan, A.R.C.; Gerardo, B.D.; Tanguilig, B.T.; De Castro, J.T.; Cervantes, L.F. A rule-based fuzzy diagnostics decision support system for tuberculosis. In Proceedings of the 2011 Ninth International Conference on Software Engineering Research, Management and Applications, Baltimore, MD, USA, 10–12 August 2011; pp. 60–63. [CrossRef]
45. Gao, X.W.; Qian, Y. Prediction of Multidrug-Resistant TB from CT Pulmonary Images Based on Deep Learning Techniques. *Mol. Pharm.* **2018**, *15*, 4326–4335. [CrossRef] [PubMed]
46. Raymond, J.L.; Medina, J.F. Computational Principles of Supervised Learning in the Cerebellum. *Annu. Rev. Neurosci.* **2018**, *41*, 233–253. [CrossRef] [PubMed]
47. Ayaz, M.; Shaukat, F.; Raja, G. Ensemble learning based automatic detection of tuberculosis in chest X-ray images using hybrid feature descriptors. *Phys. Eng. Sci. Med.* **2021**, *44*, 183–194. [CrossRef]
48. Weber, M.; Welling, M.; Perona, P. Unsupervised learning of models for recognition. In *Computer Vision—ECCV 2000. ECCV 2000. Lecture Notes in Computer Science*; Springer: Berlin, Heidelberg, 2000; Volume 1842, pp. 18–32. [CrossRef]
49. Meier, N.R.; Sutter, T.M.; Jacobsen, M.; Ottenhoff, T.H.M.; Vogt, J.E.; Ritz, N. Machine Learning Algorithms Evaluate Immune Response to Novel *Mycobacterium tuberculosis* Antigens for Diagnosis of Tuberculosis. *Front. Cell. Infect. Microbiol.* **2021**, *10*, 594030. [CrossRef]
50. Karmani, P.; Chandio, A.A.; Karmani, V.; Soomro, J.A.; Korejo, I.A.; Chandio, M.S. Taxonomy on Healthcare System Based on Machine Learning Approaches: Tuberculosis Disease Diagnosis. *Int. J. Comput. Digit. Syst.* **2020**, *9*, 1199–1212. [CrossRef]
51. Orjuela-Cañón, A.D.; Mendoza, J.E.C.; García, C.E.A.; Vela, E.P.V. Tuberculosis diagnosis support analysis for precarious health information systems. *Comput. Methods Programs Biomed.* **2018**, *157*, 11–17. [CrossRef]

52. Aguiar, F.S.; Torres, R.C.; Pinto, J.V.F.; Kritski, A.L.; Seixas, J.M.; Mello, F.C.Q. Development of two artificial neural network models to support the diagnosis of pulmonary tuberculosis in hospitalized patients in Rio de Janeiro, Brazil. *Med. Biol. Eng. Comput.* **2016**, *54*, 1751–1759. [CrossRef]

53. Kumar, A.; Padhy, S.K.; Takkar, B.; Chawla, R. Artificial intelligence in diabetic retinopathy: A natural step to the future. *Indian J. Ophthalmol.* **2019**, *67*, 1004–1009. [CrossRef]

54. Van Engelen, J.E.; Hoos, H.H. A survey on semi-supervised learning. *Mach. Learn.* **2019**, *109*, 373–440. [CrossRef]

55. Kim, T.K.; Yi, P.H.; Hager, G.D.; Lin, C.T. Refining dataset curation methods for deep learning-based automated tuberculosis screening. *J. Thorac. Dis.* **2020**, *12*, 5078–5085. [CrossRef] [PubMed]

56. Reker, D.; Schneider, P.; Schneider, G.; Brown, J.B. Active learning for computational chemogenomics. *Future Med. Chem.* **2017**, *9*, 381–402. [CrossRef] [PubMed]

57. Melendez, J.; van Ginneken, B.; Maduskar, P.; Philipsen, R.H.H.M.; Ayles, H.; Sanchez, C.I. On Combining Multiple-Instance Learning and Active Learning for Computer-Aided Detection of Tuberculosis. *IEEE Trans. Med. Imaging* **2015**, *35*, 1013–1024. [CrossRef] [PubMed]

58. Buchanan, B.G. Expert systems: Working systems and the research literature. *Expert Syst.* **1986**, *3*, 32–50. [CrossRef]

59. Rahman, T.; Khandakar, A.; Kadir, M.A.; Islam, K.R.; Islam, K.F.; Mazhar, R.; Hamid, T.; Islam, M.T.; Kashem, S.; Bin Mahbub, Z.; et al. Reliable Tuberculosis Detection Using Chest X-ray with Deep Learning, Segmentation and Visualization. *IEEE Access* **2020**, *8*, 191586–191601. [CrossRef]

60. Rashid, R.; Khawaja, S.G.; Akram, M.U.; Khan, A.M. Hybrid RID Network for Efficient Diagnosis of Tuberculosis from Chest X-rays. In Proceedings of the 2018 9th Cairo International Biomedical Engineering Conference (CIBEC), Cairo, Egypt, 20–22 December 2018; pp. 167–170. [CrossRef]

61. Kuddus, A.; Meehan, M.T.; White, L.J.; McBryde, E.S.; Adekunle, A.I. Modeling drug-resistant tuberculosis amplification rates and intervention strategies in Bangladesh. *PLoS ONE* **2020**, *15*, e0236112. [CrossRef]

62. Xu, J.; Xue, K.; Zhang, K. Current status and future trends of clinical diagnoses via image-based deep learning. *Theranostics* **2019**, *9*, 7556–7565. [CrossRef]

63. Ko, C.-H.; Cheng, M.-Y. Hybrid use of AI techniques in developing construction management tools. *Autom. Constr.* **2003**, *12*, 271–281. [CrossRef]

64. Riad, N.; Arditi, D.; Mohammadi, J. A conceptual model for claim management in construction: An ai approach. *Comput. Struct.* **1991**, *40*, 67–74. [CrossRef]

65. Miller, D.D. The medical AI insurgency: What physicians must know about data to practice with intelligent machines. *NPJ Digit. Med.* **2019**, *2*, 62. [CrossRef]

66. Mittelstadt, B.; Russell, C.; Wachter, S. Explaining explanations in AI. In Proceedings of the Conference on Fairness, Accountability, and Transparency (FAT* '19), Atlanta, GA, USA, 29–31 January 2019; pp. 279–288. [CrossRef]

67. Hase, P.; Bansal, M. Evaluating Explainable AI: Which Algorithmic Explanations Help Users Predict Model Behavior? In Proceedings of the 58th Annual Meeting of the Association for Computational Linguistics, Online, 4 May 2020; pp. 5540–5552. [CrossRef]

68. Liu, S.; Deng, W. Very deep convolutional neural network based image classification using small training sample size. In Proceedings of the 2015 3rd IAPR Asian Conference on Pattern Recognition (ACPR), Kuala Lumpur, Malaysia, 3–6 November 2015; pp. 730–734. [CrossRef]

69. Lakhani, P.; Sundaram, B. Deep Learning at Chest Radiography: Automated Classification of Pulmonary Tuberculosis by Using Convolutional Neural Networks. *Radiology* **2017**, *284*, 574–582. [CrossRef] [PubMed]

70. Che, J.; Ding, H.; Zhou, X. Chejiao at ImageCLEFmed Tuberculosis 2020: CT Report Generation Based on Transfer learning. In Proceedings of the CLEF2020 Working Notes. CEUR Workshop Proceedings, Thessaloniki, Greece, 22–25 September 2020; pp. 22–25.

71. Gentili, A. ImageCLEF2018: Transfer learning for deep learning with CNN for tuberculosis classification. *CEUR Workshop Proc.* **2018**, *2125*, 6–12.

72. Jaeger, S.; Candemir, S.; Antani, S.; Wáng, Y.-X.J.; Lu, P.-X.; Thoma, G. Two public chest X-ray datasets for computer-aided screening of pulmonary diseases. *Quant. Imaging Med. Surg.* **2014**, *4*, 475–477. [CrossRef] [PubMed]

73. Filho, M.E.C.; Galliez, R.M.; Bernardi, F.A.; de Oliveira, L.L.; Kritski, A.; Santos, M.K.; Alves, D. Preliminary Results on Pulmonary Tuberculosis Detection in Chest X-Ray Using Convolutional Neural Networks. In *Computational Science—ICCS 2020. ICCS 2020*; Lecture Notes in Computer Science Series; Springer: Cham, Switzerland, 2020; Volume 12140, pp. 563–576. [CrossRef]

74. Belarus Tuberculosis Database and TB Portal. Available online: http://tuberculosis.by/ (accessed on 3 July 2022).

75. Liu, Y.; Wu, Y.-H.; Ban, Y.; Wang, H.; Cheng, M.-M. Rethinking computer-aided tuberculosis diagnosis. In Proceedings of the IEEE Computer Society Conference on Computer Vision and Pattern Recognition, Seattle, WA, USA, 13–19 June 2020; pp. 2643–2652. [CrossRef]

76. Chauhan, A.; Chauhan, D.; Rout, C. Role of Gist and PHOG Features in Computer-Aided Diagnosis of Tuberculosis without Segmentation. *PLoS ONE* **2014**, *9*, e112980. [CrossRef] [PubMed]

77. Shah, M.I.; Mishra, S.; Yadav, V.K.; Chauhan, A.; Sarkar, M.; Sharma, S.K.; Rout, C. Ziehl–Neelsen sputum smear microscopy image database: A resource to facilitate automated bacilli detection for tuberculosis diagnosis. *J. Med. Imaging* **2017**, *4*, 027503. [CrossRef]

78. Srivastava, N.; Hinton, G.; Krizhevsky, A.; Sutskever, I.; Salakhutdinov, R. Dropout: A simple way to prevent neural networks from overfitting. *J. Mach. Learn. Res.* **2014**, *15*, 1929–1958.

79. Denil, M.; Shakibi, B.; Dinh, L.; Ranzato, M.; de Freitas, N. Predicting parameters in deep learning. *Adv. Neural Inf. Process. Syst.* **2013**, *26*, 1–9.

80. Gregory, R.W.; Henfridsson, O.; Kaganer, E.; Kyriakou, S.H. The Role of Artificial Intelligence and Data Network Effects for Creating User Value. *Acad. Manag. Rev.* **2021**, *46*, 534–551. [CrossRef]

81. LeCun, Y.; Bengio, Y.; Hinton, G. Deep learning. *Nature* **2015**, *521*, 436–444. [CrossRef]

82. Schmidhuber, J. Deep Learning in Neural Networks: An Overview. *Neural Netw.* **2015**, *61*, 85–117. [CrossRef]

83. Zhang, Q.; Zhang, M.; Chen, T.; Sun, Z.; Ma, Y.; Yu, B. Recent advances in convolutional neural network acceleration. *Neurocomputing* **2018**, *323*, 37–51. [CrossRef]

84. Shin, H.-C.; Roth, H.R.; Gao, M.; Lu, L.; Xu, Z.; Nogues, I.; Yao, J.; Mollura, D.; Summers, R.M. Deep Convolutional Neural Networks for Computer-Aided Detection: CNN Architectures, Dataset Characteristics and Transfer Learning. *IEEE Trans. Med. Imaging* **2016**, *35*, 1285–1298. [CrossRef] [PubMed]

85. Chauhan, R.; Ghanshala, K.K.; Joshi, R.C. Convolutional Neural Network (CNN) for Image Detection and Recognition. In Proceedings of the 2018 First International Conference on Secure Cyber Computing and Communication (ICSCCC), Jalandhar, India, 15–17 December 2018; IEEE: Piscataway, NJ, USA; pp. 278–282. [CrossRef]

86. Abbas, A.; Abdelsamea, M.M. Learning Transformation for Automated classification of manifestation of Tuberculosis using Convolutional Neural Network. In Proceedings of the 2018 13th International Conference on Computer Engineering and Systems (ICCES), Cairo, Egypt, 18–19 December 2018; pp. 122–126. [CrossRef]

87. Ahsan, M.; Gomes, R.; Denton, A. Application of a convolutional neural network using transfer learning for tuberculosis detection. In Proceedings of the 2019 IEEE International Conference on Electro Information Technology (EIT), Brookings, SD, USA, 20–22 May 2019; pp. 427–433. [CrossRef]

88. Andika, L.A.; Pratiwi, H.; Handajani, S.S. Convolutional neural network modeling for classification of pulmonary tuberculosis disease. *J. Physics: Conf. Ser.* **2020**, *1490*, 012020. [CrossRef]

89. Lopez-Garnier, S.; Sheen, P.; Zimic, M. Automatic diagnostics of tuberculosis using convolutional neural networks analysis of MODS digital images. *PLoS ONE* **2019**, *14*, e0212094. [CrossRef]

90. Msonda, P.; Uymaz, S.A.; Karaağaç, S.S. Spatial Pyramid Pooling in Deep Convolutional Networks for Automatic Tuberculosis Diagnosis. *Trait. Du Signal* **2020**, *37*, 1075–1084. [CrossRef]

91. Zhang, Y.-D.; Nayak, D.R.; Zhang, X.; Wang, S.-H. Diagnosis of secondary pulmonary tuberculosis by an eight-layer improved convolutional neural network with stochastic pooling and hyperparameter optimization. *J. Ambient Intell. Humaniz. Comput.* **2020**, 1–18. [CrossRef]

92. Liu, C.; Cao, Y.; Alcantara, M.; Liu, B.; Brunette, M.; Peinado, J.; Curioso, W. TX-CNN: Detecting tuberculosis in chest X-ray images using convolutional neural network. In Proceedings of the 2017 IEEE International Conference on Image Processing (ICIP), Beijing, China, 17–20 September 2017; pp. 2314–2318. [CrossRef]

93. Rohilla, A.; Hooda, R.; Mittal, A. TB Detection in Chest Radiograph Using Deep Learning Architecture. *Int. J. Adv. Res. Sci. Eng.* **2017**, *6*, 1073–1084.

94. Vilone, G.; Luca, L. Notions of explainability and evaluation approaches for explainable artificial intelligence. *Inf. Fusion* **2021**, *76*, 89–106. [CrossRef]

95. Adadi, A.; Berrada, M. Explainable AI for Healthcare: From Black Box to Interpretable Models. In *Advances in Intelligent Systems and Computing*; Springer: Singapore, 2020; Volume 1076, pp. 327–337. [CrossRef]

96. Barredo Arrieta, A.; Díaz-Rodríguez, N.; Del Ser, J.; Bennetot, A.; Tabik, S.; Barbado, A.; Garcia, S.; Gil-Lopez, S.; Molina, D.; Benjamins, R.; et al. Explainable Explainable Artificial Intelligence (XAI): Concepts, taxonomies, opportunities and chal-lenges toward responsible AI. *Inf. Fusion* **2020**, *58*, 82–115. [CrossRef]

97. Doshi-Velez, F.; Been, K. Towards a rigorous science of interpretable machine learning. *arXiv* **2017**, arXiv:1702.08608.

98. Asay, B.C.; Edwards, B.B.; Andrews, J.; Ramey, M.E.; Richard, J.D.; Podell, B.K.; Gutiérrez, J.F.M.; Frank, C.B.; Magunda, F.; Robertson, G.T.; et al. Digital Image Analysis of Heterogeneous Tuberculosis Pulmonary Pathology in Non-Clinical Animal Models using Deep Convolutional Neural Networks. *Sci. Rep.* **2020**, *10*, 6047. [CrossRef] [PubMed]

99. Chithra, R.S.; Jagatheeswari, P. Severity detection and infection level identification of tuberculosis using deep learning. *Int. J. Imaging Syst. Technol.* **2020**, *30*, 994–1011. [CrossRef]

100. Chang, R.I.; Chiu, Y.H.; Lin, J.W. Two-stage classification of tuberculosis culture diagnosis using convolutional neural network with transfer learning. *J. Supercomput.* **2020**, *76*, 8641–8656. [CrossRef]

101. Nafisah, S.I.; Ghula, M. Tuberculosis detection in chest radiograph using convolutional neural network architecture and explainable artificial intelligence. *Neural Comput. Appl.* **2022**, 1–21. [CrossRef]

102. Pasa, F.; Golkov, V.; Pfeiffer, F.; Cremers, D.; Pfeiffer, D. Efficient deep network architectures for fast chest X-ray tuberculosis screening and visualization. *Sci. Rep.* **2019**, *9*, 6268. [CrossRef]

103. Ahmadi, H.; Gholamzadeh, M.; Shahmoradi, L.; Nilashi, M.; Rashvand, P. Diseases diagnosis using fuzzy logic methods: A systematic and meta-analysis review. *Comput. Methods Programs Biomed.* **2018**, *161*, 145–172. [CrossRef]

104. Sharma, T.; Singh, V.; Sudhakaran, S.; Verma, N. Fuzzy based Pooling in Convolutional Neural Network for Image Classification. In Proceedings of the IEEE International Conference on Fuzzy Systems, New Orleans, LA, USA, 23–26 June 2019; pp. 1–6. [CrossRef]

105. Kang, C.; Yu, X.; Wang, S.H.; Guttery, D.S.; Pandey, H.M.; Tian, Y.; Zhang, Y. A Heuristic Neural Network Structure Relying on Fuzzy Logic for Images Scoring. *IEEE Trans. Fuzzy Syst.* **2021**, *29*, 34–45. [CrossRef]

106. Shrivastava, A.K.; Rajak, A. Modeling Pulmonary Tuberculosis using Adaptive Neuro Fuzzy Inference System. *Int. J. Innov. Res. Comput. Sci. Technol.* **2016**, *4*, 24–27. [CrossRef]

107. Shrivastava, A.K.; Rajak, A.; Bhardwaj, S. Detection of tuberculosis based on multiple parameters using ANFIS. In Proceedings of the 3rd International Conference on Innovative Applications of Computational Intelligence on Power, Energy and Controls with their Impact on Humanity, CIPECH 2018, Ghaziabad, India, 1–2 November 2018; pp. 120–124. [CrossRef]

108. Goni, I.; Ngene, C.U.; Manga, I.; Nata'ala, A. Intelligent System for Diagnosing Tuberculosis Using Adaptive Neuro-Fuzzy. *Asian J. Res. Comput. Sci.* **2018**, *2*, 1–9. [CrossRef]

109. Oreski, S.; Oreski, G. Genetic algorithm-based heuristic for feature selection in credit risk assessment. *Expert Syst. Appl.* **2014**, *41*, 2052–2064. [CrossRef]

110. Brabazon, A.; O'Neill, M.; McGarraghy, S. Genetic algorithm. *Nat. Comput. Algorithms* **2015**, *28*, 21–42. [CrossRef]

111. Maulik, U.; Bandyopadhyay, S. Genetic algorithm-based clustering technique. *Pattern Recognit.* **2000**, *33*, 1455–1465. [CrossRef]

112. Geetha, P.V.; Lukshmi, R.A.; Venkatesan, P. Tuberculosis Disease Classification using Genetic-neuro Expert System. *Indian J. Sci. Technol.* **2014**, *7*, 421–425. [CrossRef]

113. Vally, D.; Sarma, C.H.V. Diagnosis Chest Diseases Using Neural Network and Genetic Hybrid Algorithm. *Int. J. Eng. Res. Appl.* **2015**, *5*, 20–26.

114. Omisore, M.O.; Samuel, O.W.; Atajeromavwo, E.J. A Genetic-Neuro-Fuzzy inferential model for diagnosis of tuberculosis. *Appl. Comput. Informatics.* **2017**, *13*, 27–37. [CrossRef]

115. Vathana, R.B.; Balasubramanian, R. Genetic-Neuro-Fuzzy Inferential Model for Tuberculosis Detection. *Int. J. Appl. Eng. Res.* **2018**, *13*, 13308–13312.

116. Greensmith, J.; Whitbrook, A. Aickelin Artificial Immune Systems. *Int. J. Recent Res. Appl. Stud.* **2010**, *3*, 21–448. [CrossRef]

117. Dasgupta, D.; Yu, S.; Nino, F. Recent advances in artificial immune systems: Models and applications. *Appl. Soft Comput. J.* **2011**, *11*, 1574–1587. [CrossRef]

118. Er, O.; Yumusak, N.; Temurtas, F. Diagnosis of chest diseases using artificial immune system. *Expert Syst. Appl.* **2012**, *39*, 1862–1868. [CrossRef]

119. Shamshirband, S.; Hessam, S.; Javidnia, H.; Amiribesheli, M.; Vahdat, S.; Petković, D.; Gani, A.; Kiah, L. Tuberculosis disease diagnosis using artificial immune recognition system. *Int. J. Med. Sci.* **2014**, *11*, 508–514. [CrossRef]

120. Saybani, M.R.; Shamshirband, S.; Hormozi, S.G.; Wah, T.Y.; Aghabozorgi, S.; Pourhoseingholi, M.A.; Olariu, T. Diagnosing tuberculosis with a novel support vector machine-based artificial immune recognition system, Iran. *Red Crescent Med. J.* **2015**, *17*, e24557. [CrossRef]

121. Saybani, M.R.; Shamshirband, S.; Golzari, S.; Wah, T.Y.; Saeed, A.; Kiah, L.M.; Balas, V.E. RAIRS2 a new expert system for diagnosing tuberculosis with real-world tournament selection mechanism inside artificial immune recognition system. *Med. Biol. Eng. Comput.* **2016**, *54*, 385–399. [CrossRef] [PubMed]

122. Pappalardo, F.; Russo, G.; Pennisi, M.; Sgroi, G.; Palumbo, G.A.P.; Motta, S.; Fichera, E. An agent based modeling approach for the analysis of tuberculosis-Immune system dynamics. In Proceedings of the 2018 IEEE International Conference on Bioinformatics and Biomedicine, BIBM, Madrid, Spain, 3–6 December 2019; pp. 1386–1392. [CrossRef]

123. World Health Organization (WHO). The End TB Strategy. 2013. Available online: http://www.who.int (accessed on 3 July 2022).

124. World Health Organization (WHO). Operational Handbook on Tuberculosis. 2020. Available online: http://www.who.int (accessed on 3 July 2022).

125. Qin, Z.Z.; Naheyan, T.; Ruhwald, M.; Denkinger, C.M.; Gelaw, S.; Nash, M.; Creswell, J.; Kik, S.V. A new resource on artificial intelligence powered computer automated detection software products for tuberculosis programmes and implementers. *Tuberculosis* **2021**, *127*, 102049. [CrossRef]

126. AI4HLTH Resource Database. Product Profile: Delft Imaging. 2020. Available online: http://www.delft.care (accessed on 3 July 2022).

127. AI4HLTH Resource Database. Product Profile: Infervision. 2020. Available online: http://www.infervision.com (accessed on 3 July 2022).

128. AI4HLTH Resource Database. Product Profile: JLK. 2020. Available online: http://www.jlkgroup.com (accessed on 3 July 2022).

129. AI4HLTH Resource Database. Product Profile: Lunit. 2020. Available online: http://www.lunit.io (accessed on 3 July 2022).

130. AI4HLTH Resource Database. Product Profile: Qure. ai. 2020. Available online: http://www.qure.ai (accessed on 3 July 2022).

131. AI4HLTH Resource Database. Product Profile: Radisen. 2020. Available online: http://www.radisentech.com (accessed on 3 July 2022).

132. AI4HLTH Resource Database. Product Profile: Artelus. 2020. Available online: https://www.artelus.com/ (accessed on 3 July 2022).

133. AI4HLTH Resource Database. Product Profile: DeepTek Inc. 2020. Available online: https://www.deeptek.ai (accessed on 3 July 2022).

134. AI4HLTH Resource Database. Product Profile: Dr CADx. 2020. Available online: https://www.drcadx.com (accessed on 3 July 2022).
135. AI4HLTH Resource Database. Product Profile: EPCON. 2021. Available online: https://www.epcon.ai (accessed on 3 July 2022).
136. AI4HLTH Resource Database. Product Profile: JF Healthcare. 2021. Available online: http://www.jfhealthcare.com/ (accessed on 3 July 2022).
137. Lee, S.; Hyun, J.S.; Sungwon, K.; Eun-Kyung, K. Successful Implementation of an Artificial Intelligence-Based Computer-Aided Detection System for Chest Radiography in Daily Clinical Practice. *Korean J. Radiol.* **2022**, *23*, e52. [CrossRef] [PubMed]
138. Qin, Z.Z.; Shahriar, A.; Mohammad, S.S.; Kishor, P.; Ahammad SS, A.; Tasneem, N.; Rachael, B.; Sayera, B.; Jacob, C. Tuberculosis detection from chest x-rays for triaging in a high tuberculosis-burden setting: An evaluation of five artificial intelligence algorithms. *Lancet Digit. Health* **2021**, *3*, e543–e554. [CrossRef]
139. Khan, F.A.; Arman, M.; Gamuchirai, T.; Ahsana, N.; Syed, K.A.; Andrea, B.; Dick, M.; James, C.J.; Aamir, J.K.; Saima, S. Chest x-ray analysis with deep learning-based software as a triage test for pulmonary tuberculosis: A prospective study of diagnostic accuracy for culture-confirmed disease. *Lancet Digit. Health* **2020**, *2*, e573–e581. [CrossRef]
140. Gawehn, E.; Hiss, J.A.; Brown, J.B.; Schneider, G. Advancing drug discovery via GPU-based deep learning. Expert Opinion on Drug Discovery. *Expert Opin. Drug Discov.* **2018**, *13*, 579–582. [CrossRef]
141. ImageCLEF-The CLEF Cross Language Image Retrieval Track | ImageCLEF/LifeCLEF-Multimedia Retrieval in CLEF. 2003. Available online: https://www.imageclef.org/ (accessed on 3 July 2022).
142. Alcantara, M.F.; Cao, Y.; Liu, C.; Liu, B.; Brunette, M.; Zhang, N.; Sun, T.; Zhang, P.; Chen, Q.; Li, Y.; et al. Improving Tuberculosis Diagnostics using Deep Learning and Mobile Health Technologies among Resource-poor Communities in Perú. *Smart Health* **2017**, *1*, 66–76. [CrossRef]
143. Hartigan, M.A.; Wong, J.A. Algorithm AS 136: A k-Means Clustering Algorithm. *J. R. Stat. Soc. C Appl.* **2017**, *28*, 100–108. [CrossRef]

Article

EWOA-OPF: Effective Whale Optimization Algorithm to Solve Optimal Power Flow Problem

Mohammad H. Nadimi-Shahraki [1,2,*], Shokooh Taghian [1,2], Seyedali Mirjalili [3,4,*], Laith Abualigah [5,6], Mohamed Abd Elaziz [7,8,9,10] and Diego Oliva [11]

1   Faculty of Computer Engineering, Najafabad Branch, Islamic Azad University, Najafabad 8514143131, Iran; sh.taghian@sco.iaun.ac.ir
2   Big Data Research Center, Najafabad Branch, Islamic Azad University, Najafabad 8514143131, Iran
3   Centre for Artificial Intelligence Research and Optimisation, Torrens University Australia, Brisbane, QLD 4006, Australia
4   Yonsei Frontier Lab, Yonsei University, Seoul 03722, Korea
5   Faculty of Computer Sciences and Informatics, Amman Arab University, Amman 11953, Jordan; aligah.2020@gmail.com
6   School of Computer Sciences, University Sains Malaysia, Gelugor 11800, Malaysia
7   Department of Mathematics, Faculty of Science, Zagazig University, Zagazig 44519, Egypt; abd_el_aziz_m@yahoo.com
8   Artificial Intelligence Research Center (AIRC), Ajman University, Ajman 346, United Arab Emirates
9   Department of Artificial Intelligence Science & Engineering, Galala University, Suez 435611, Egypt
10 School of Computer Science and Robotics, Tomsk Polytechnic University, 634050 Tomsk, Russia
11 Departamento de Innovación Basada en la Información y el Conocimiento, Universidad de Guadalajara, CUCEI, Guadalajara 44430, Mexico; diego.oliva@cucei.udg.mx
*   Correspondence: nadimi@iaun.ac.ir (M.H.N.-S.); ali.mirjalili@torrens.edu.au (S.M.)

Citation: Nadimi-Shahraki, M.H.; Taghian, S.; Mirjalili, S.; Abualigah, L.; Abd Elaziz, M.; Oliva, D. EWOA-OPF: Effective Whale Optimization Algorithm to Solve Optimal Power Flow Problem. *Electronics* **2021**, *10*, 2975. https://doi.org/10.3390/electronics10232975

Academic Editor: Maciej Ławryńczuk

Received: 25 October 2021
Accepted: 26 November 2021
Published: 29 November 2021

Publisher's Note: MDPI stays neutral with regard to jurisdictional claims in published maps and institutional affiliations.

Abstract: The optimal power flow (OPF) is a vital tool for optimizing the control parameters of a power system by considering the desired objective functions subject to system constraints. Meta-heuristic algorithms have been proven to be well-suited for solving complex optimization problems. The whale optimization algorithm (WOA) is one of the well-regarded metaheuristics that is widely used to solve different optimization problems. Despite the use of WOA in different fields of application as OPF, its effectiveness is decreased as the dimension size of the test system is increased. Therefore, in this paper, an effective whale optimization algorithm for solving optimal power flow problems (EWOA-OPF) is proposed. The main goal of this enhancement is to improve the exploration ability and maintain a proper balance between the exploration and exploitation of the canonical WOA. In the proposed algorithm, the movement strategy of whales is enhanced by introducing two new movement strategies: (1) encircling the prey using Levy motion and (2) searching for prey using Brownian motion that cooperate with canonical bubble-net attacking. To validate the proposed EWOA-OPF algorithm, a comparison among six well-known optimization algorithms is established to solve the OPF problem. All algorithms are used to optimize single- and multi-objective functions of the OPF under the system constraints. Standard IEEE 6-bus, IEEE 14-bus, IEEE 30-bus, and IEEE 118-bus test systems are used to evaluate the proposed EWOA-OPF and comparative algorithms for solving the OPF problem in diverse power system scale sizes. The comparison of results proves that the EWOA-OPF is able to solve single- and multi-objective OPF problems with better solutions than other comparative algorithms.

Keywords: optimization; metaheuristic algorithms; optimal power flow; whale optimization algorithm

1. Introduction

Over the past decades, metaheuristic algorithms (MAs) have become more prevalent in solving optimization problems in various fields of industry and science [1]. The widespread usage of MAs for solving different optimization problems verified their ability for solving complex problems with difficulties such as non-linear constraints, multi-modality of the problem, and a non-convex search landscape [1,2]. Metaheuristics are a class of general-purpose stochastic algorithms that can be applied to any optimization problem [3]. Despite exact algorithms, metaheuristics allow tackling complex problems by providing satisfactory solutions in a reasonable time [4]. MAs estimate the approximate optimal solution of the problem by sampling the solution space to find or generate better solutions. Many combinatorial optimization problems were solved using metaheuristic algorithms in diverse engineering fields such as civil, mechanical, electrical, industrial, and system engineering. Several new optimization algorithms have been proposed recently due to the emergence of the no free lunch (NFL) theorem [5], which states that no particular optimization algorithm can solve all problems of all kinds of complexities. It is also discovered that using the same algorithm on the same problem yields varied results depending on the various parameter settings.

The inspiration and imitation of creatures' behaviors led to many effective metaheuristics to find the optimum solution for different problems. The MAs based on their source of inspiration can be broadly classified into two main categories: evolutionary and swarm intelligence algorithms. The algorithms that imitate an evolutionary phenomenon in nature are classified as evolutionary algorithms. These algorithms improve a randomly generated population of solutions for a particular optimization problem by employing evolutionary principles. Genetic algorithm (GA) [6], genetic programming (GP) [7], evolution strategy (ES) [8], evolutionary programming (EP) [9], and differential evolution (DE) [10] are the most well-known algorithms in this category. Swarm intelligence algorithms mimic simple behaviors of social creatures in which the individuals cooperate and interact collectively to find promising regions. Some of the best known and recently proposed swarm intelligence algorithms are particle swarm optimization (PSO) [11], the bat algorithm (BA) [12], krill herd (KH) [13], the grey wolf optimizer (GWO) [14], the whale optimization algorithm (WOA) [15], the salp swarm algorithm (SSA) [16], the squirrel search algorithm (SSA) [17], the African vultures optimization algorithm (AVOA), and the Aquila optimizer (AO) [18] algorithm.

On the other hand, the optimal power flow (OPF) is a non-linear and non-convex problem that is considered one of the power system's complex optimization problems [19]. OPF adjusts both continuous and discrete control variables to optimize specified objective functions by satisfying the operating constraints [20]. From the perspective of industries and power companies, minimizing the operational cost and maximizing the reliability of power systems are two primary objectives. Since a slight modification in power flow can considerably raise the running expense of power systems, the OPF focuses on the economic aspect of operating power systems [21]. Non-linear programming [22], Newton algorithm [23], and quadratic programming [24] are some of the classical optimization algorithms that have been employed to tackle the OPF problem. Although these algorithms can sometimes find the global optimum solution, they have some drawbacks such as getting trapped in local optima, a high sensitivity to initial potions, and the inability to deal with non-differentiable objective functions [25–27]. Thus, it is essential to develop effective optimization algorithms to overcome these shortcomings and deal with such challenges efficiently.

Regarding MA, the whale optimization algorithm (WOA) is a swarm-based algorithm inspired by the hunting behavior of humpback whales in nature. The humpback whales use the bubble-net hunting technique to encircle and catch their prey that are in collections of fishes close to water level. The whales go down the surface and dive into the prey, then swarm in a spiral-shaped path while they start creating bubbles. The whales' spiral movement radius narrows when prey get closer to the surface, enabling them to attack. WOA consists of three phases: encircling the prey, bubble-net attacking, and searching for the prey. WOA has been used to solve a wide range of optimization problems in different applications including feature selection [28], software defect prediction [29], clustering [30,31], classification [32,33], disease diagnosis [34], image segmentation [35,36], scheduling [37], forecasting [38,39], parameter estimation [40], global optimization [41], and photovoltaic energy generation systems [42,43]. Even though WOA is employed to tackle a wide variety of optimization problems, it still has flaws such as premature convergence, the imbalance between exploration and exploitation, and local optima stagnation [44,45].

This paper proposes an effective whale optimization algorithm for solving the optimal power flow problem (EWOA-OPF). The EWOA-OPF improves the movement strategy of whales by introducing two new movement strategies: (1) encircling the prey using Levy motion and (2) searching for prey using Brownian motion that cooperate with canonical bubble-net attacking. The reason for these changes is to maintain an appropriate balance between exploration and exploitation and enhance the exploration ability of the WOA, resulting in more precise solutions when solving problems. To validate the proposed EWOA-OPF algorithm, a comparison among well-known optimization algorithms is established under single- and multi-objective functions of the OPF. Standard IEEE 6-bus, IEEE 14-bus, IEEE 30-bus, and IEEE 118-bus test systems are used to evaluate the proposed EWOA-OPF and comparative algorithms for solving OPF problems in diverse power system scale sizes. The results were compared with four state-of-the-art algorithms consisting of particle swarm optimization (PSO) [11], krill herd (KH) [13], the grey wolf optimizer (GWO) [14], and the whale optimization algorithm (WOA) [15] and two recently proposed algorithms, the salp swarm algorithm (SSA) [16] and the Aquila optimizer (AO) [18] algorithm. The comparison of results proves that the EWOA-OPF can solve single- and multi-objective OPF problems with better solutions than other comparative algorithms.

The rest of the paper is organized as follows: the related works are reviewed in Section 2. Section 3 presents the OPF problem formulation and objective functions. Section 4 contains the mathematical model of WOA. Section 5 presents the proposed EWOA-OPF. The experimental evaluation of EWOA-OPF and comparative algorithms on OPF is presented in Section 6. Finally, the conclusion and future work are given in Section 7.

2. Related Work

The purpose of optimization is to find the global optimum solution among numerous candidate solutions. Traditional optimization methods have several drawbacks when solving complex and complicated problems that require considerable time and cost optimization. Metaheuristic algorithms have been proven capable of handling a variety of continuous and discrete optimization problems [46] in a wide range of applications including engineering [47–49], industry [50,51], image processing and segmentation [52–54], scheduling [55,56], photovoltaic modeling [57,58], optimal power flow [59,60], power and energy management [61,62], planning and routing problems [63–65], intrusion detection [66,67], feature selection [68–72], spam detection [73,74], medical diagnosis [75–77], quality monitoring [78], community detection [79], and global optimization [80–82]. In the following, some representative metaheuristic algorithms from the swarm intelligence category used in our experiments are described. Then, some metaheuristic algorithms were used to solve OPF are highlighted.

Swarm intelligence algorithms mimic the collective behavior of creatures in nature such as birds, fishes, wolves, and ants. The main principle of these algorithms is to deal with a population of particles that can interact with each other. Eberhart and Kennedy proposed the particle swarm optimization (PSO) [11] method, which simulates bird flocks' foraging and navigation behavior. It is derived from basic laws of interaction amongst birds, which prefer to retain their flight direction considering their current direction, the local best position gained so far, and the global best position that the swarm has discovered thus far. The PSO algorithm concurrently directs the particles to the best optimum solutions by each individual and the swarm. The krill herd (KH) [13] algorithm is a population-based metaheuristic algorithm based on the krill individual herding behavior modeling. The KH algorithm repeats the three motions and searches in the same direction until it finds the optimum answer. Other krill-induced movements, foraging activity, and random diffusion all have an impact on the position.

Another well-known swarm intelligence algorithm is the grey wolf optimizer (GWO) [14], which is inspired by grey wolves in nature that look for the best approach to pursue prey. In nature, the GWO algorithm uses the same method, following the pack hierarchy to organize the wolves' pack's various responsibilities. GWO divides pack members into four divisions depending on each wolf's involvement in the hunting process. The four groups are alpha, beta, delta, and omega, with alpha being the finest hunting solution yet discovered. The salp swarm algorithm (SSA) [16] is another recent optimizer that is based on natural salp swarm behavior. As a result, it creates and develops a set of random individuals within the problem's search space. Following that, the chain's leader and followers must update their location vectors. The leader salp will assault in the direction of a food supply, while the rest of the salps can advance towards it. The Aquila optimizer (AO) [18] is one of the latest proposed algorithms in the swarm intelligence category that simulates the prey-catching behavior of Aquila in nature. In AO, four methods were used to emulate this behavior consisting of selecting the search space by a high soar with a vertical stoop, exploring within a diverge search space by contour flight with short glide attack, exploiting within a converge search space by low flight with slow descent attack, and swooping by walk and grab prey.

Regardless of the nature of the algorithm, the majority of the metaheuristics, especially the population-based algorithms, have two standard contrary criteria in the search process: the exploration of the search space and the exploitation of the gained best solutions. In exploitation, the promising regions are explored more thoroughly for generating similar solutions to improve the previously obtained solution. In exploration, non-explored regions must be visited to be sure that all regions of the search space are evenly explored and that the search is not only limited to a reduced number of regions. Excessive exploitation decreases diversity and leads to premature convergence, whereas excessive exploration leads to gradual convergence [83]. Thus, metaheuristic algorithms try to balance between the exploration and exploitation that has a crucial impact on the performance of the algorithm and the gained solution [84]. Furthermore, real-world problems require achieving several objectives that are in conflict with one another such as minimizing risks, maximizing reliability, and minimizing cost. There is only one objective function to be optimized and only one global solution to be found in a single-objective problem. However, in multi-objective problems, as there is no single best solution, the aim is to find a set of solutions representing the trade-offs among the different objectives [85].

Although metaheuristic algorithms have several merits over classical optimization algorithms, such as the simple structure, independence to the problem, the gradient-free nature, and finding near-global solutions [14], they may encounter premature convergence, local optima entrapment, and the loss of diversity. In this regard, improved variants of these algorithms have been proposed, each of which adapted to tackle such weaknesses [86–88]. Additionally, the significant growth of metaheuristic algorithms has resulted in a trend of solving OPF problems by using population-based metaheuristic algorithms. In the literature, the OPF was solved by using black hole (BO) [89], teaching–learning based optimization (TLBO) [90] algorithms, the krill herd (KH) algorithm [91], the equilibrium optimizer (EO) algorithm [92], and the slime mould algorithm (SMA) [93]. Additionally, some studies used the modified and enhanced version of the canonical swarm intelligence algorithms for solving OPF with different test systems such as the modified shuffle frog leaping algorithm (MSLFA) for multi-objective optimal power flow [94] that added a mutation strategy to overcome the problem of being trapped in local optima.

Another work proposed an improved grey wolf optimizer (I-GWO) [95] to improve the GWO search strategy with a dimension learning-based hunting search strategy to deal with exploration and exploitation imbalances and premature convergence weaknesses. In [96], quasi-oppositional teaching–learning based optimization (QOTLBO) proposed to improve the convergence speed and quality of obtained solutions by using quasi-oppositional based learning (QOBL). In [97], particle swarm optimization with an aging leader and challengers (ALC-PSO) algorithm was applied to solve the OPF problem by using the concept of the leader's age and lifespan. The aging mechanism can avoid the premature convergence of PSO and result in better convergence. An improved artificial bee colony optimization algorithm was based on orthogonal learning (IABC) [98] to adjust exploration and exploitation. In [99], the modified sine–cosine algorithm (MSCA) was aimed to reduce the computational time with sufficient improvement in finding the optimal solution and feasibility. The MSCA benefits from using Levy flights cooperated by the strategy of the canonical sine–cosine algorithm to avoid local optima. In the high-performance social spider optimization algorithm (NISSO) [100], the canonical SSO algorithm was modified by using two new movement strategies that resulted in faster convergence to the optimal solution and finding better solutions in comparison to comparative algorithms.

3. OPF Problem Formulation and Objective Functions

The optimal power flow (OPF) is regarded as a fundamental tool for the effective design and operation of the power networks. The main aim of OPF is to find the optimum values of control variables for different objective functions while satisfying the system equality and inequality constraints within the permitted boundaries. The mathematical formulation and description of OPF single- and multi-objective functions are presented in detail as follows.

3.1. OPF Problem Formulation

The OPF is a non-linear and non-convex optimization problem that aims to find the best set of the power system's control variables and satisfy the desired objective function. The OPF problem is mathematically formulated [101] as shown in Equation (1):

$$
\begin{aligned}
&Min\ F(x,u) \\
&Subject\ to:\ g(x,u) = 0, \\
&\qquad\qquad\ h(x,u) \le 0,
\end{aligned}
\tag{1}
$$

where F is the objective function to be minimized, x is the vector of dependent (state) variables, u is the vector of independent (control) variables, and g and h represent equality and inequality constraints, respectively. Accordingly, vector x, which consists of slack bus power P_{G1}, load bus voltage V_L, generator reactive power output Q_G, and transmission line loading S_l, is presented by Equation (2),

$$
x = [P_{G1}, V_{L1}, \ldots, V_{LNL}, Q_{G1}, \ldots, Q_{GNG}, S_{l1}, \ldots, S_{INTL}]
\tag{2}
$$

where NL, NG, and NTL are the number of load buses, number of generators, and number of transmission lines, respectively. u is the vector of control variables, consisting of generator active power outputs P_G (except at the slack bus P_{G1}), generator voltages V_G, transformer tap settings T, and shunt VAR compensations Q_C, which is presented as Equation (3),

$$
u = [P_{G2}, \ldots, P_{GNG}, V_{G1}, \ldots, V_{GNG}, T_1, \ldots, T_{NT}, Q_{C1}, \ldots, Q_{CNC}]
\tag{3}
$$

where NT and NC are the number of the regulating transformer and VAR compensator units, respectively.

3.2. OPF Objective Functions

In this paper, two objectives are considered to deal with the OPF problem: an economical issue, the total fuel cost minimization of power generation, and a technical issue, which is a voltage profile improvement.

Case 1: Total fuel cost minimization.

The total fuel cost minimization is considered as the single-objective function for the OPF problem, which is a quadratic function of real power generations of generators in a system. The minimization of the overall fuel cost of a power generator is considered and calculated by Equation (4),

$$f_1 = \sum_{i=1}^{NG} f_i(P_{Gi}) = \sum_{i=1}^{NG} (a_i + b_i\, P_{Gi} + c_i\, P_{Gi}^2) \tag{4}$$

where a_i, b_i, and c_i are the cost coefficients of the i-th generator. For P_{Gi} (in MW), a_i, b_i, and c_i are considered in \$/hr, \$/MWh, and S/MW2h. The voltages of all load buses are limited in the range of 0.95 to 1.05 p.u.

Case 2: Voltage profile improvement.

The purpose of this multi-objective function is to minimize the fuel cost and improve the voltage profile by minimizing the load bus voltage deviations from 1.0 p.u. The objective function is calculated as shown in Equation (5),

$$f_2 = \sum_{i=1}^{NG} (a_i + b_i\, P_{Gi} + c_i\, P_{Gi}^2) + W_v \sum_{i=1}^{NL} |V_i - 1.0| \tag{5}$$

where the weighting factor W_v = 200. Notice that Equation (5) merges two objectives with a weight in a single equation to properly handle the multi-objective problem.

4. The Whale Optimization Algorithm (WOA)

The whale optimization algorithm (WOA) [15] is inspired by the hunting behavior used by humpback whales in nature. The humpback whales use the bubble-net hunting technique to encircle and catch their prey that are in groups of small fishes. In WOA, the best whale position is considered as prey position X^* and the other whales update their position according to the X^*. In WOA, three behaviors of whales are encircling prey, bubble-net attacking (exploitation), and searching for prey (exploration), modeled as in the following definitions.

Encircling prey: The first step in the whales' hunting process is surrounding the prey. Whales can detect the position of the prey and begin to surround them. Therefore, in WOA, the current best whale X^* is considered as prey or being close to the prey. All other whales update their position according to the X^* by Equations (6) and (7):

$$D = |C \times X^*(t) - X(t)| \tag{6}$$

$$X(t+1) = X^*(t) - A \times D \tag{7}$$

where t is the iteration counter and D is the calculated distance between the prey $X^*(t)$ and the whale $X(t)$. A and C are coefficient vectors that are calculated by Equations (8) and (9):

$$A = 2 \times a \times r - a(t) \tag{8}$$

$$C = 2 \times r \tag{9}$$

where the value of a is linearly decreased from 2 to 0 over the course of the iterations, and r is a random number in [0, 1].

Bubble-net attacking: Whales spin around the prey within a shrinking encircling technique or spiral updating position. This behavior is modeled by Equation (10),

$$X(t+1) = \begin{cases} X^*(t) - A \times D & if\ p < 0.5 \\ D' \times e^{bl} \times \cos(2 \times \pi \times l) + X^*(t) & if\ p \geq 0.5 \end{cases} \tag{10}$$

where p is a random number in [0,1] and shows the probability of updating whales' positions based on a shrinking encircling technique (if $p < 0.5$) or a spiral updating position (if $p > 0.5$). A is a random value in $[-a, a]$ where a is linearly decreased from 2 to 0 over the course of the iterations. In the spiral updating position, D' represents the distance between the current whale X and the prey X^*, b represents a constant used to define the spiral movement shape, and l is a random number in $[-1, 1]$.

Searching for prey: In order to find new prey, whales conduct a global search through the search space. This is completed when the absolute value of vector A value is greater or equal to 1, and it will be an exploration, else it will be exploitation. In the exploration phase, the whales update their position concerning a random whale X_{rand} instead of the best whale X^*, which is calculated using Equations (11) and (12):

$$D = |C \times X_{rand} - X(t)| \tag{11}$$

$$X(t+1) = X_{rand} - A \times D \tag{12}$$

where X_{rand} is a randomly selected whale from the current population.

5. Effective Whale Optimization Algorithm to Solve Optimal Power Flow (EWOA-OPF)

While WOA is easy to implement and applicable for solving a wide range of optimization problems, it has insufficient performance to solve complex problems. The algorithm suffers from premature convergence to local optima and an insufficient balance between exploration and exploitation. Such problems lead to inadequate performance of the WOA when used to solve complex problems. Motivated by these considerations, an enhanced version of the WOA algorithm named the effective whale optimization algorithm (EWOA-OPF) is proposed for solving the optimal power flow problem. Since maintaining an appropriate balance between exploration and exploitation can prevent premature convergence and control the global search ability of the algorithm, the canonical WOA's strategies, encircling the prey and searching for prey, are replaced by two new movement strategies. This modification aims to enhance the exploitative and explorative capabilities of WOA which leads to obtaining accurate solutions when solving problems. In the following, the proposed EWOA-OPF is explained in detail.

Initializing step: N whales are randomly generated and distributed in the search space within the predefined range [LB, UB] using Equation (13).

$$X_{i,j}(t) = LB_j + (UB_j - LB_j) \times rand(0, 1) \tag{13}$$

where X_{ij} is the position of the i-th whale in the j-th dimension, LB_j and UB_j are the lower and upper bound of the j-th dimension, and the $rand$ is a uniformly distributed random variable between 0 and 1, respectively. The fitness value of whale X_i in the t-th iteration is calculated by the fitness function $f\,(X_i\,(t))$, and the whale with better fitness is considered as X^*, which is the best solution obtained.

Encircling prey using Levy motion: Whales update their position by considering the position of X^* and the Levy-based pace scale PS^L by Equation (14),

$$X_{i,j}(t+1) = X_j^*(t) + 0.5 \times C \times PS_{i,j}^L \tag{14}$$

where $X_j^*(t)$ is the j-th dimension of the best whale, C is a linearly decreased coefficient from 1 to 0 over the course of iterations, and $PS_{i,j}^L$ is the j-th dimension of the i-th row of pace scale calculated by Equation (15).

$$PS_{i,j}^L = M_{i,j}^L \times (X_j^*(t) \times M_{i,j}^L - X_{i,j}(t)) \tag{15}$$

$M_{i,j}^L$ is a randomly generated number based on Levy movement, which is calculated by Equation (16),

$$M = \frac{u}{|v|^{1/\beta}} \times 0.05 \tag{16}$$

where u and v follow the Gaussian distribution which is calculated by Equations (17) and (18),

$$u \sim (0, \sigma_u^2), \ v \sim (0, \sigma_v^2) \tag{17}$$

$$\sigma_u = \left[\frac{\Gamma(1+\beta) \times \sin(\pi\beta/2)}{\Gamma((1+\beta)/2) \times \beta \times 2^{\beta-1/2}} \right]^{1/\beta}, \ \sigma_v = 1 \tag{18}$$

where Γ is a Gamma function and $\beta = 1.5$.

Bubble-net attacking: Whales spin around the prey within a shrinking encircling technique and spiral updating position. This behavior is as same as canonical WOA and calculated by Equations (19) and (20),

$$D' = |X^*(t) - X(t)| \tag{19}$$

$$X_{i,j}(t+1) = D' \times e^{bl} \times \cos(2 \times \pi \times l) + X_j^*(t) \tag{20}$$

where D' is the distance between the current whale X and the prey X^*, b represents a constant used to define the spiral movement shape by the whales, and l is a random number in $[-1, 1]$.

Searching for prey using Brownian motion: Whales update their position by considering the position of X^* and the Brownian-based pace scale PS^B by Equation (21),

$$X_{i,j}(t+1) = X_{i,j}(t) + A \times rand \times PS_{i,j}^B \tag{21}$$

where A is a decreasing coefficient calculated by Equation (8), $rand$ is a random number, and PS^B is Brownian-based pace scale which is calculated by Equation (22),

$$PS_{i,j}^B = M_{i,j}^B \times (X_j^*(t) - M_{i,j}^B \times X_{i,j}(t)) \tag{22}$$

where $M_{i,j}^B$ is a random number based on normal distribution representing the Brownian motion.

After determining the new position of the whales, their fitness is calculated and the prey position X^* is updated. The search process is iterated until the predefined number of iterations (*MaxIter*) is reached. The pseudo-code of the proposed EWOA-OPF is shown in Algorithm 1.

Algorithm 1 The EWOA-OPF algorithm

    Input: $N, D, MaxIter$
    Output: The global optimum (X^*)
1: **Begin**
2: $iter = 1$.
3: Randomly distribute N whales in the search space.
4: Evaluating the fitness and set X^*.
5: **While** $iter \leq MaxIter$
6:    **For** $i = 1: N$
7:      Caculating coefficients $a, A, C,$ and l.
8:      **For** $j = 1: D$
9:        **If** $(p < 0.5)$
10:        **If** $(|A| < 1)$
11:          $stepsize_{i,j} = M_{i,j}^L \times (M_{i,j}^L \times X_j^*(t) - X_{i,j}(t))$
12:          $X_{i,j}(t+1) = X_j^*(t) + 0.5 \times C \times stepsize_{i,j}$
13:        **Elseif** $(|A| \geq 1)$ and $(iter < MaxIter/3)$
14:          $stepsize_{i,j} = M_{i,j}^B \times (X_j^*(t) - M_{i,j}^B \times X_{i,j}(t))$
15:          $X_{i,j}(t+1) = X_{i,j}(t) + A \times rand \times stepsize_{i,j}$
16:        **End if**
17:        **Elseif** $(p > 0.5)$
18:        $D' = |X^*(t) - X(t)|$
19:        $X_{i,j}(t+1) = D' \times e^{bl} \times \cos(2 \times \pi \times l) + X_j^*(t)$
20:        **End if**
21:      **End for**
22:    **End for**
23:    Evaluating fitness and update X^*.
24:    $iter = iter + 1$.
25: **End while**
26: **Return** the global optimum (X^*).
27: **End**

---

6. Experimental Evaluation

In this section, the performance evaluation of the proposed EWOA-OPF was assessed over two cases based on three IEEE bus systems. The obtained results are compared with four state-of-the-art algorithms consisting of particle swarm optimization (PSO) [11], krill herd (KH) [13], the grey wolf optimizer (GWO) [14], the whale optimization algorithm (WOA) [15], and two recently proposed algorithms, the salp swarm algorithm (SSA) [16] and the Aquila optimizer (AO) [18] algorithm.

6.1. Experimental Environment

The performance of the proposed EWOA-OPF was evaluated using the IEEE 6-bus, IEEE 14-bus, IEEE 30-bus, and IEEE 118-bus test systems and the gained results were compared with six state-of-the-art and recently proposed swarm intelligence algorithms. The proposed algorithm and all the comparative algorithms implemented in MATLA R2018a and all the experiments were run on a CPU, Intel Core(TM) i7-6500U 2.50 GHz and 16.00 GB RAM. The parameters of the comparative algorithms in all experiments were the same as the recommended settings in their original works, as shown in Table 1.

Table 1. Parameter settings.

Algorithms	Parameters Value
PSO	$c_1 = c_2 = 2$
KH	$V_f = 0.02$, $D^{max} = 0.005$, $N^{max} = 0.01$
GWO	a was linearly decreased from 2 to 0
WOA	a = [20], b = 1
SSA	$c_1, c_2, c_3 = $ rand [0, 1]
AO	$\alpha = 0.1$

The algorithms were run 20 times in all experiments, and the population size (*N*) and the maximum number of iterations (*MaxIter*) were set to 50 and 200, respectively. The experimental results are reported based on the optimal values of decision variables (DVs) and objective variables for each bus system in Tables 2–9. Moreover, the last three rows of each table indicate the total cost ($/h), power losses (MW), and voltage deviation (p.u.) of each algorithm for Case 1 and Case 2.

6.2. IEEE 6-Bus Test System

This test system contains seven control variables: two generator voltages, two transformers tap changing, two VAR shunt injection capacitances, and one active generator power of the PV bus, as shown in Figure 1.

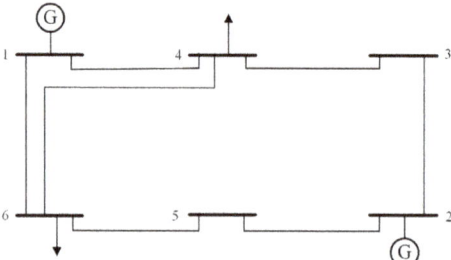

Figure 1. IEEE 6-bus test system single-line diagram.

The obtained optimal value of design variables and the optimized value of the total fuel cost of the system under Case 1 and Case 2 are shown in Tables 2 and 3. Additionally, the convergence curves of the obtained fitness for all algorithms are illustrated in Figure 2. It is seen that the total fuel cost decreased to 403.536 ($/h) by WOA and EWOA-OPF. It can be seen that the OPF results in Case 2 obtained by both WOA and EWOA-OPF are better than other algorithms in terms of the total cost.

Table 2. Results of OPF for IEEE 6-bus test system on Case 1.

DVs	PSO	KH	GWO	WOA	SSA	AO	EWOA-OPF
P_{G2} (MW)	100.000	100.000	100.000	100.000	100.000	100.000	100.000
V_{G1} (p.u.)	1.100	1.100	1.100	1.100	1.100	1.100	1.100
V_{G2} (p.u.)	1.150	1.150	1.150	1.150	1.150	1.150	1.150
$T_{(6-5)}$ (p.u.)	0.936	0.936	0.932	0.935	0.923	0.930	0.935
$T_{(4-3)}$ (p.u.)	1.023	1.023	1.025	1.024	0.975	1.026	1.024
Q_{C4} (MVAR)	5.000	5.000	5.000	5.000	5.000	5.000	5.000
Q_{C6} (MVAR)	5.500	5.500	5.500	5.500	5.499	5.500	5.500
Cost ($/h)	403.537	**403.536**	403.548	**403.536**	404.011	403.555	**403.536**
Ploss (MW)	19.581	19.581	19.583	19.581	19.579	19.584	19.581
VD (p.u.)	0.160	0.160	0.160	0.160	0.139	0.161	0.160

Table 3. Results of OPF for IEEE 6-bus test system on Case 2.

DVs	PSO	KH	GWO	WOA	SSA	AO	EWOA-OPF
P_{G2} (MW)	100.000	100.000	100.000	100.000	99.973	100.000	100.000
V_{G1} (p.u.)	1.100	1.100	1.100	1.100	1.100	1.100	1.100
V_{G2} (p.u.)	1.150	1.150	1.150	1.150	1.150	1.150	1.150
$T_{(6-5)}$ (p.u.)	0.900	0.910	0.909	0.905	0.931	0.901	0.905
$T_{(4-3)}$ (p.u.)	0.927	0.928	0.928	0.927	0.931	0.928	0.927
Q_{C4} (MVAR)	5.000	5.000	5.000	5.000	4.768	5.000	5.000
Q_{C6} (MVAR)	5.500	5.500	5.500	5.500	5.468	5.500	5.500
Cost ($/h)	405.372	**405.221**	405.241	405.294	405.230	405.291	405.291
Ploss (MW)	19.749	19.737	19.739	19.743	19.744	19.739	19.742
VD (p.u.)	0.119	0.120	0.120	0.120	0.123	0.120	0.120

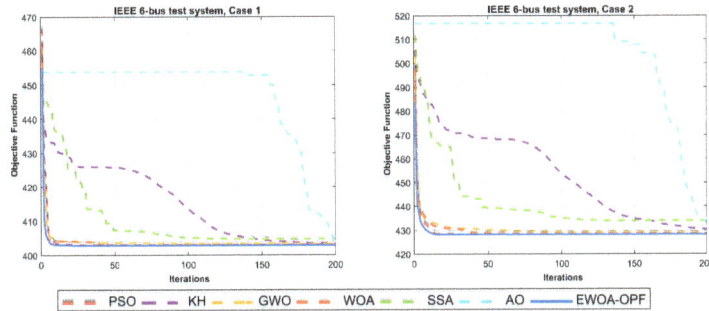

Figure 2. Curves for all test systems on Cases 1 and 2.

6.3. IEEE 14-Bus Test System

The IEEE 14-bus test system is shown in Figure 3, and contains five generation (PV) buses, while nine of those are defined as load (PQ) buses. The detailed results of the objective functions, active and reactive power outputs of generator units, transmission losses, and convergence times of the system are given in Tables 4 and 5 on Case 1 and Case 2 to make an effective comparison. Furthermore, the convergence of the obtained fitness of OPF for EWOA-OPF and comparative algorithms on the IEEE 14 bus standard test system over the curse of iterations is shown in Figure 4. The objective function values for EWOA-OPF are reported as 8079.957 and 8083.308 ($/h). It is evident that the EWOA-OPF provides smaller values in terms of the total generation cost of generator units than those found by other comparative algorithms.

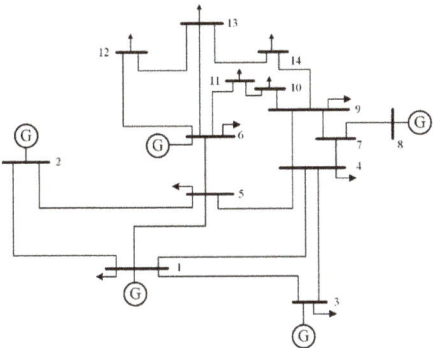

Figure 3. IEEE 14-bus test system single-line diagram.

Table 4. Results of OPF for IEEE 14-bus test system on Case 1.

DVs	PSO	KH	GWO	WOA	SSA	AO	EWOA-OPF
P_{G1} (MW)	200.444	190.585	189.364	192.574	165.346	176.495	194.278
P_{G2} (MW)	38.368	34.751	36.963	35.516	40.454	28.778	36.792
P_{G3} (MW)	30.257	27.412	39.238	24.781	28.221	0.000	27.728
P_{G6} (MW)	0.000	0.000	1.578	9.155	13.213	30.517	0.000
P_{G8} (MW)	0.000	15.510	0.707	6.267	19.744	33.309	9.458
V_{G1} (p.u.)	1.060	1.043	1.060	1.060	1.010	1.004	1.060
V_{G2} (p.u.)	1.040	1.022	1.040	1.039	0.989	0.982	1.039
V_{G3} (p.u.)	1.025	1.008	1.017	1.004	0.962	0.940	1.015
V_{G6} (p.u.)	1.060	1.013	1.023	0.989	1.031	1.002	1.032
V_{G8} (p.u.)	1.051	1.006	1.010	1.026	1.018	0.964	1.058
$T11_{(4-7)}$ (p.u.)	1.100	1.035	1.054	1.059	0.964	0.906	1.002
$T12_{(4-9)}$ (p.u.)	0.900	1.006	0.944	0.959	0.912	0.900	0.992
$T15_{(5-6)}$ (p.u.)	0.900	0.984	0.981	1.059	0.945	0.900	0.999
Q_{C14} (MVAR)	0.000	0.000	0.000	0.000	0.000	0.000	0.000
Cost ($/h)	8092.50	8098.36	8087.42	8088.39	8162.26	8226.31	**8079.95**
Ploss (MW)	10.069	9.258	8.850	9.294	7.978	10.098	9.257
VD (p.u.)	0.230	0.098	0.074	0.180	0.147	0.217	0.176

Table 5. Results of OPF for IEEE 14-bus test system on Case 2.

DVs	PSO	KH	GWO	WOA	SSA	AO	EWOA-OPF
P_{G1} (MW)	195.560	196.470	193.469	189.118	151.588	164.584	193.418
P_{G2} (MW)	37.863	32.263	33.460	34.115	45.758	23.093	36.460
P_{G3} (MW)	34.532	20.336	22.762	12.144	50.542	10.586	27.568
P_{G6} (MW)	0.000	1.635	12.138	3.029	0.200	21.020	0.000
P_{G8} (MW)	0.721	18.172	6.535	29.705	17.394	47.251	10.805
V_{G1} (p.u.)	1.060	1.041	1.060	1.060	1.050	1.040	1.060
V_{G2} (p.u.)	1.043	1.019	1.038	1.040	1.032	1.016	1.040
V_{G3} (p.u.)	1.023	1.000	1.010	1.013	1.008	1.000	1.011
V_{G6} (p.u.)	1.046	0.973	1.020	1.016	1.013	0.973	1.016
V_{G8} (p.u.)	1.017	0.986	1.020	0.991	1.014	1.035	0.995
$T11_{(4-7)}$ (p.u.)	1.061	1.006	1.037	1.024	0.957	0.993	1.012
$T12_{(4-9)}$ (p.u.)	0.900	0.996	0.968	0.937	1.040	1.041	0.942
$T15_{(5-6)}$ (p.u.)	0.900	1.003	0.968	1.000	0.950	1.002	1.003
Q_{C14} (MVAR)	0.000	0.000	0.000	0.000	0.000	0.000	0.000
Cost ($/h)	8094.47	8109.03	8093.55	8100.08	8213.16	8234.582	**8083.30**
Ploss (MW)	9.675	9.876	9.364	9.111	6.482	7.534	9.250
VD (p.u.)	0.136	0.276	0.063	0.069	0.055	0.216	0.059

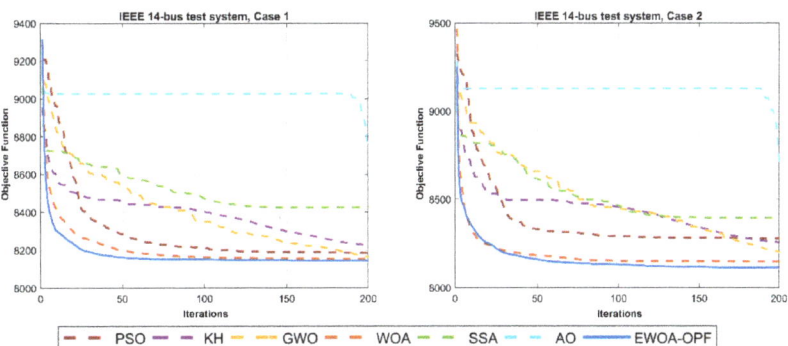

Figure 4. Curves for all test systems on Cases 1 and 2.

6.4. IEEE 30-Bus Test System

The single line diagram of the IEEE 30-bus test system is shown in Figure 5. The system consists of six generators at buses 1, 2, 5, 8, 11, and 13, four transformers in lines 6–9, 6–10, 4–12, and 27–28, and nine shunt VAR compensation buses. The lower and upper bounds of the transformer tap are set to 0.9 and 1.1 p.u. The minimum and maximum values of the shunt VAR compensations are 0.0 and 0.05 p.u. The lower and upper limit values of the voltages for all generator buses are set to be 0.95 and 1.1 p.u. The optimal settings of control variables, total fuel cost, power loss, and voltage deviations for Cases 1 and 2 are shown in Tables 6 and 7. The variation of the gained fitness are illustrated in Figure 6 for all algorithms under both cases. In Case 1, it is observed that the system total fuel cost is greatly reduced as an initial state to 799.210 ($/h) using EWOA-OPF. In Case 2, a comparison demonstrates the superiority of EWOA-OPF to achieve a better solution with a total fuel cost of 805.545 ($/h).

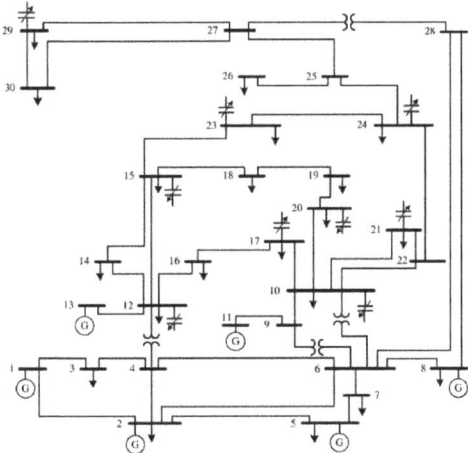

Figure 5. IEEE 30-bus test system single-line diagram.

Table 6. Results of OPF for IEEE 30-bus test system on Case 1.

DVs	PSO	KH	GWO	WOA	SSA	AO	EWOA-OPF
P_{G1} (MW)	186.001	178.261	177.251	178.805	165.059	166.312	176.804
P_{G2} (MW)	48.821	47.974	46.115	43.572	44.385	52.911	48.745
P_{G5} (MW)	15.000	21.483	19.094	23.058	24.002	21.586	21.437
P_{G8} (MW)	20.839	20.924	17.184	20.004	24.540	26.316	20.911
P_{G11} (MW)	10.000	12.219	16.178	14.994	15.025	13.957	12.128
P_{G13} (MW)	13.459	12.000	16.839	12.000	18.323	12.000	12.019
V_{G1} (p.u.)	1.072	1.076	1.079	1.079	1.092	1.100	1.100
V_{G2} (p.u.)	1.043	1.056	1.058	1.059	1.075	1.057	1.088
V_{G5} (p.u.)	1.007	1.025	1.027	1.035	1.046	0.992	1.061
V_{G8} (p.u.)	1.032	1.021	1.033	1.035	1.049	0.999	1.070
V_{G11} (p.u.)	0.957	1.065	1.074	1.063	1.083	1.078	1.100
V_{G13} (p.u.)	1.100	1.029	1.059	1.038	1.059	1.039	1.100
$T11_{(6-9)}$ (p.u.)	1.100	1.010	0.968	1.019	1.029	1.036	0.994
$T12_{(6-10)}$ (p.u.)	0.900	1.020	0.990	0.994	0.977	0.996	0.989
$T15_{(4-12)}$ (p.u.)	1.037	0.966	1.007	1.021	1.066	1.100	1.015
$T36_{(28-27)}$ (p.u.)	0.944	1.013	0.970	1.015	1.012	0.971	0.973
Q_{C10} (MVAR)	5.000	2.098	0.114	2.201	1.809	5.000	0.355
Q_{C12} (MVAR)	5.000	2.686	1.602	3.965	1.774	0.306	1.092
Q_{C15} (MVAR)	0.000	1.990	0.753	3.562	2.577	5.000	0.178
Q_{C17} (MVAR)	0.000	2.639	1.501	4.597	2.819	0.000	5.000
Q_{C20} (MVAR)	0.286	2.062	1.204	5.000	2.551	0.000	4.978
Q_{C21} (MVAR)	4.994	1.934	0.049	1.875	1.371	0.000	5.000
Q_{C23} (MVAR)	1.436	2.966	3.517	5.000	2.673	0.000	5.000
Q_{C24} (MVAR)	0.000	2.348	1.191	5.000	3.279	5.000	4.999
Q_{C29} (MVAR)	5.000	2.732	0.583	4.735	4.040	0.242	0.788
Cost ($/h)	806.703	801.885	803.112	801.817	803.305	806.287	**799.210**
Ploss (MW)	10.720	9.460	9.261	9.033	7.935	9.682	8.643
VD (p.u.)	0.463	0.353	0.517	0.468	0.600	0.456	1.526

Table 7. Results of OPF for IEEE 30-bus test system on Case 2.

DVs	PSO	KH	GWO	WOA	SSA	AO	EWOA-OPF
P_{G1} (MW)	193.906	159.718	145.215	176.996	159.796	183.686	176.804
P_{G2} (MW)	42.785	53.259	58.991	39.732	40.416	36.729	48.745
P_{G5} (MW)	15.889	20.452	26.123	23.435	29.202	20.718	21.437
P_{G8} (MW)	10.000	24.105	30.949	17.597	26.431	13.352	20.911
P_{G11} (MW)	10.830	21.550	14.851	18.724	16.173	11.677	12.128
P_{G13} (MW)	21.888	13.099	15.191	16.712	19.497	27.878	12.019
V_{G1} (p.u.)	1.022	1.036	1.049	1.027	1.048	1.064	1.100
V_{G2} (p.u.)	1.000	1.022	1.033	1.014	1.033	1.039	1.088
V_{G5} (p.u.)	0.988	1.011	1.020	1.004	0.998	1.012	1.061
V_{G8} (p.u.)	0.996	1.006	1.000	1.012	1.009	0.977	1.070

Table 7. *Cont.*

DVs	PSO	KH	GWO	WOA	SSA	AO	EWOA-OPF
V_{G11} (p.u.)	1.090	1.019	1.010	1.053	1.039	1.100	1.100
V_{G13} (p.u.)	1.074	1.024	1.003	1.010	0.995	0.996	1.100
$T11_{(6-9)}$ (p.u.)	1.033	0.972	0.997	0.981	1.015	0.944	0.994
$T12_{(6-10)}$ (p.u.)	0.900	0.964	0.913	0.944	0.928	0.983	0.989
$T15_{(4-12)}$ (p.u.)	1.089	0.987	0.948	0.986	0.933	0.968	1.015
$T36_{(28-27)}$ (p.u.)	0.923	0.949	0.958	0.957	0.959	0.974	0.973
Q_{C10} (MVAR)	5.000	2.217	1.967	0.357	3.498	0.742	0.355
Q_{C12} (MVAR)	0.000	2.640	1.557	0.584	2.436	1.777	1.092
Q_{C15} (MVAR)	5.000	2.362	4.142	3.343	2.599	0.495	0.178
Q_{C17} (MVAR)	5.000	3.897	2.464	4.523	1.632	0.000	5.000
Q_{C20} (MVAR)	0.071	2.093	2.620	3.869	2.186	0.038	4.978
Q_{C21} (MVAR)	0.000	2.875	4.097	0.603	1.961	1.792	5.000
Q_{C23} (MVAR)	0.000	3.119	1.089	2.762	2.245	4.221	5.000
Q_{C24} (MVAR)	0.000	5.000	4.178	2.537	2.451	0.080	4.999
Q_{C29} (MVAR)	0.000	2.500	4.387	2.130	2.307	5.000	0.788
Cost ($/h)	813.781	807.572	812.395	808.216	811.942	815.714	**805.545**
Ploss (MW)	11.897	8.784	7.920	9.796	8.116	10.641	9.963
VD (p.u.)	0.211	0.157	0.146	0.159	0.163	0.289	0.126

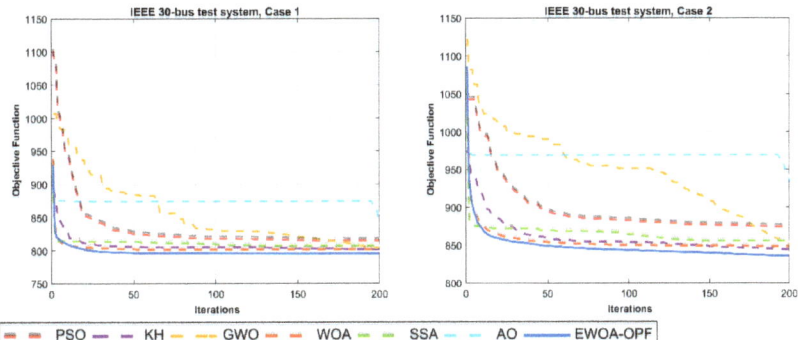

Figure 6. Curves for all test systems on Cases 1 and 2.

6.5. IEEE 118-Bus Test System

The IEEE 118-bus test system is used to evaluate the efficiency of the proposed EWOA-OPF in solving a larger power system. As shown in Figure 7, this bus test system has 54 generators, 186 branches, 9 transformers, 2 reactors, and 12 capacitors. It has 129 control variables considered for 54 generator active powers and bus voltages, 9 transformer tap settings, and 12 shunt capacitor reactive power injections. All buses have voltage limitations between 0.94 and 1.06 p.u. Within the range of 0.90–1.10 p.u., the transformer tap settings are evaluated. Shunt capacitors have available reactive powers ranging from 0 to 30 MVAR. Because of having too many design variables for Cases 1 and 2 in this experiment, the detailed results are shown in Tables A1 and A2 in the Appendix A and the final results are compared in Tables 8 and 9. The convergence curves of the obtained fitness for all algorithms is also illustrated in Figure 8.

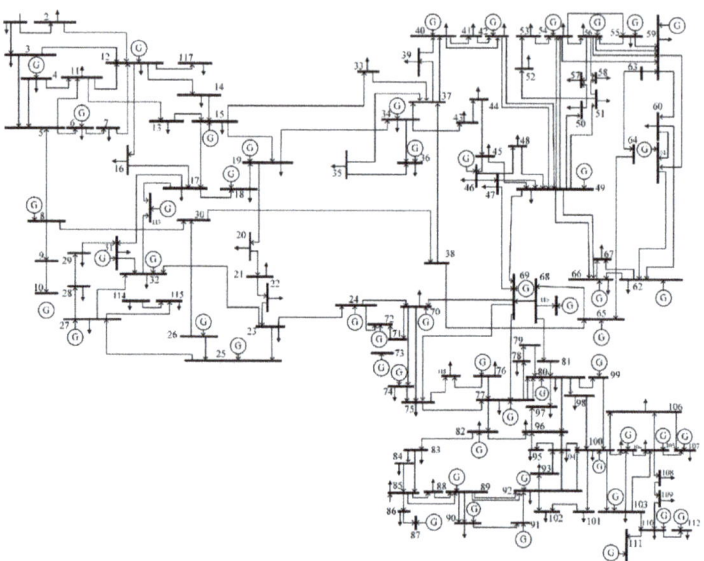

Figure 7. IEEE 118-bus test system single-line diagram.

Table 8. Final results of OPF for IEEE 118-bus test system on Case 1.

Final Results	PSO	KH	GWO	WOA	SSA	AO	EWOA-OPF
Cost ($/h)	151,751.61	155,696.34	145,902.97	144,856.49	150,655.22	159,974.6	**142,756.67**
Ploss (MW)	114.431	188.555	135.040	76.802	77.663	71.23298	78.865
VD (p.u.)	2.953	1.579	2.217	0.405	0.804	4.251571	2.816

Table 9. Final results of OPF for IEEE 118-bus test system on Case 2.

Final Results	PSO	KH	GWO	WOA	SSA	AO	EWOA-OPF
Cost ($/h)	163,613.92	155,696.40	153,293.89	145,078.86	152,484.28	164,684.39	**140,175.80**
Ploss (MW)	242.265	188.555	88.693	77.031	77.139	60.940	79.990
VD (p.u.)	3.059	1.579	1.082	0.668	0.902	3.997	1.625

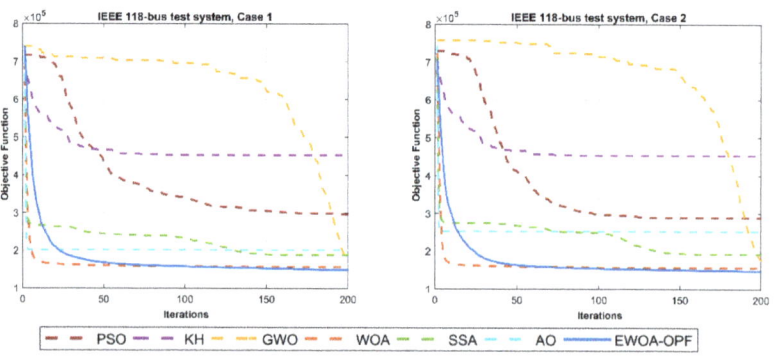

Figure 8. Curves for all test systems on Cases 1 and 2.

In Case 1 of this experiment, the comparison of results tabulated in Table 8 reveals that the proposed EWOA-OPF has the ability to converge to a better-quality solution. The total fuel cost obtained by EWOA-OPF is reduced to 142,756.67 $/h, which is less than the canonical WOA and other comparative algorithms. Table 9 compares solutions found by EWOA-OPF and other algorithms for Case 2. In this case, numerical results confirm the superiority of EWOA-OPF where it reaches the minimum fuel cost 140,175.80 $/h. The final results demonstrate that the proposed EWOA-OPF algorithm can be effectively used to solve both single- and multi-objective large-scale OPF problems.

7. Conclusions and Future Work

This paper proposes an effective whale optimization algorithm for solving optimal power flow problems (EWOA-OPF). The OPF is a non-linear and non-convex problem that is considered a vital tool for the effective design and operation of power systems. Despite the applicability of the whale optimization algorithm (WOA) in solving complex problems, its performance is degraded when the dimension size of the OPF's test system is increased. In this regard, the movement strategy of whales is modified by introducing two new movement strategies: (1) encircling the prey using Levy motion and (2) searching for prey using Brownian motion that cooperate with canonical bubble-net attacking. The main purpose of EWOA-OPF is to improve explorative capability and maintain a proper balance between the exploration and exploitation of the canonical WOA. The effectiveness and scalability of the proposed EWOA-OPF algorithm were experimentally evaluated using standard IEEE 6-bus, IEEE 14-bus, IEEE 30-bus, and IEEE 118-bus test systems to optimize single- and multi-objective functions of the OPF under the system constraints. To validate the gained results, a comparison among six well-known optimization algorithms is established. The comparison of results proves that the EWOA-OPF can solve single- and multi-objective OPF problems with better solutions than other comparative algorithms as well as large-dimensional OPF problems. In future work, the EWOA-OPF can be used to solve many-objective (more than three objective functions) OPF problems.

Author Contributions: Conceptualization, M.H.N.-S.; Methodology, M.H.N.-S. and S.T.; Software, M.H.N.-S. and S.T.; Validation, M.H.N.-S., S.T., S.M., L.A., M.A.E. and D.O.; Formal analysis, M.H.N.-S. and S.T.; Investigation, M.H.N.-S. and S.T.; Resources, M.H.N.-S., S.T. and S.M.; Data curation, M.H.N.-S. and S.T.; Writing, M.H.N.-S. and S.T.; Original draft preparation, M.H.N.-S. and S.T.; Writing—review and editing, M.H.N.-S., S.T., S.M., L.A., M.A.E. and D.O.; Visualization, M.H.N.-S. and S.T.; Supervision, M.H.N.-S. and S.M.; Project administration, M.H.N.-S. and S.M. All authors have read and agreed to the published version of the manuscript.

Funding: This research received no external funding.

Institutional Review Board Statement: Not applicable.

Informed Consent Statement: Not applicable.

Data Availability Statement: Not applicable.

Conflicts of Interest: The authors declare no conflict of interest.

Appendix A

The detailed results for Cases 1 and 2 on the IEEE-118 bus test system including the decision variables (DVs) value and the final results of the total fuel cost (cost), power losses (ploss), and voltage deviation (VD) are shown in Tables A1 and A2.

Table A1. Results of OPF for IEEE 118-bus test system on Case 1.

Panel 1

DVs	PSO	KH	GWO	WOA	SSA	AO	EWOA-OPF
PG01	100.00	63.99	44.15	31.56	47.96	67.99	199.90	40.18
PG04	100.00	43.12	67.03	10.67	34.94	71.84	115.30	28.36
PG06	0.00	83.32	51.47	79.00	37.76	63.04	79.44	94.42
PG08	0.00	21.41	66.11	19.28	46.89	38.21	91.47	19.71
PG10	369.27	50.82	316.49	67.17	294.08	67.83	70.59	52.53
PG12	185.00	54.87	155.30	49.67	105.77	33.71	69.52	71.53
PG15	0.00	16.18	37.85	46.06	59.55	39.87	35.99	19.63
PG18	100.00	73.77	36.07	86.08	68.21	80.48	88.93	37.97
PG19	100.00	24.16	36.81	64.94	55.74	62.41	41.98	44.80
PG24	0.00	83.05	53.87	23.63	28.87	37.36	66.60	39.63
PG25	0.00	256.00	134.84	41.57	142.71	92.14	0.95	0.95
PG27	0.00	54.21	49.17	251.51	209.89	111.55	0.94	0.99
PG31	100.00	39.43	2.38	39.33	46.55	79.86	0.94	0.98
PG32	0.00	70.26	15.93	73.25	55.69	43.14	0.94	0.95
PG34	0.00	87.62	10.12	35.57	44.37	36.56	0.94	0.94
PG36	0.00	36.18	51.18	37.84	51.05	65.81	0.96	0.97
PG40	100.00	40.81	73.59	51.00	43.65	70.72	0.96	0.95
PG42	0.00	26.53	69.97	17.67	60.45	70.85	0.96	0.95
PG46	0.00	37.26	49.94	45.09	48.92	78.99	0.95	0.95
PG49	304.00	88.16	2.40	160.59	46.40	45.19	0.96	1.01
PG54	0.00	29.13	61.37	42.77	108.15	103.44	0.94	0.99
PG55	100.00	51.87	31.88	8.77	56.19	147.28	0.94	0.95
PG56	100.00	28.13	66.73	32.81	51.85	42.57	0.94	0.95
PG59	255.00	42.79	83.42	41.06	46.46	26.61	0.94	0.95
PG61	260.00	139.72	139.72	126.51	116.74	68.76	0.94	0.97
PG62	0.00	17.78	52.81	66.77	108.25	115.70	0.94	0.96
PG65	0.00	298.82	285.63	6.87	38.28	132.42	0.94	0.99
PG66	492.00	103.20	402.91	122.75	242.16	28.13	0.94	0.97
PG70	0.00	11.69	304.33	74.14	277.39	340.94	0.94	0.98
PG72	100.00	4.39	6.93	53.41	55.37	410.93	0.94	0.97
PG73	0.00	70.09	21.53	3.99	53.45	231.09	0.94	0.98
PG74	100.00	20.40	15.49	84.20	56.93	26.92	0.95	0.95
PG76	0.00	77.91	55.91	46.97	44.54	32.26	0.97	0.95
PG77	0.00	77.57	49.11	31.72	52.73	33.43	0.94	0.95
PG80	577.00	250.31	180.57	461.22	57.51	90.63	0.94	0.95
PG85	100.00	30.62	84.22	6.11	230.48	65.91	0.94	0.96
PG87	0.00	46.05	37.86	8.57	36.79	83.77	0.95	0.95
PG90	125.44	526.05	604.19	128.16	51.17	184.63	0.94	1.01
PG91	100.00	18.63	16.63	37.80	321.43	82.25	0.94	0.99
PG92	0.00	52.18	7.72	31.91	50.99	32.09	0.94	0.97
PG99	0.00	56.27	13.38	67.32	49.22	40.86	0.94	0.95
		37.37	34.86	34.86	47.40	67.43	0.94	

Panel 2

DVs	PSO	KH	GWO	WOA	SSA	AO	EWOA-OPF
PG100	352.00	277.31	78.86	227.12	137.06	199.90	92.15
PG103	0.00	92.19	79.06	28.51	60.60	115.30	4.28
PG104	0.00	85.66	32.21	4.08	61.88	79.44	0.00
PG105	0.00	28.18	2.94	74.60	43.01	91.47	53.00
PG107	0.00	80.56	6.14	24.64	49.67	70.59	195.95
PG110	0.00	61.60	73.20	46.70	41.37	69.52	1.05
PG111	0.00	108.41	58.43	114.10	62.76	35.99	0.00
PG112	0.00	17.40	45.77	36.74	34.78	88.93	0.32
PG113	0.00	53.22	40.63	25.44	63.92	41.98	0.01
PG116	0.00	80.78	40.63	45.99	39.41	66.60	38.59
VG01	0.94	1.04	1.03	1.01	1.02	0.95	208.99
VG04	0.94	1.02	1.00	1.01	1.00	0.94	208.87
VG06	0.94	1.02	1.01	1.01	1.01	0.94	74.12
VG08	1.06	1.04	1.03	1.00	1.02	0.94	17.58
VG10	1.06	1.06	1.03	1.01	1.00	0.94	0.00
VG12	0.94	1.04	1.02	1.01	1.00	0.96	95.43
VG15	0.94	1.03	1.01	1.01	1.00	0.96	90.78
VG18	0.94	1.03	1.01	1.01	1.00	0.96	9.21
VG19	1.06	1.03	1.03	1.01	1.00	0.95	70.85
VG24	0.94	0.96	0.96	1.00	0.99	0.96	53.65
VG25	0.94	1.03	0.97	1.01	1.00	0.94	147.28
VG26	1.06	1.02	0.98	1.00	1.00	0.94	42.57
VG27	0.94	1.00	0.94	1.00	1.00	0.94	26.61
VG31	0.94	1.02	1.02	1.01	0.99	0.94	68.76
VG32	0.94	1.00	0.98	1.01	1.00	0.94	115.70
VG34	0.94	0.97	1.03	1.00	1.00	0.94	132.42
VG36	0.94	0.99	1.04	1.00	1.00	0.94	28.13
VG40	0.94	0.96	1.01	1.00	1.00	0.94	340.94
VG42	0.94	0.99	0.95	1.00	1.02	0.94	410.93
VG46	1.06	1.02	1.01	1.00	0.99	0.94	26.92
VG49	1.01	0.99	0.96	1.01	0.97	0.94	19.54
VG54	1.06	0.99	0.95	1.01	1.02	0.94	69.15
VG55	1.06	0.99	0.94	1.00	1.01	0.94	29.40
VG56	1.06	1.01	0.96	1.00	1.01	0.94	41.71
VG59	0.94	0.99	0.97	1.00	0.97	0.94	59.82
VG61	0.94	0.98	0.96	1.01	0.99	0.94	20.12
VG62	0.94	1.00	0.99	1.00	0.99	0.94	37.77
VG65	1.06	1.02	0.96	1.00	1.01	0.94	248.12
VG66	0.94	0.97	0.99	1.00	1.00	0.95	90.16
VG69	1.06	1.01	0.98	0.99	1.00	0.94	94.13
VG70	1.06	1.02	1.00	1.00	0.99	0.94	14.81
VG72	1.06	1.00	1.05	1.01	1.00	0.94	45.92
VG73	1.06	1.01	0.98	1.01	1.00	0.94	

Panel 3

DVs	PSO	KH	GWO	WOA	SSA	AO	EWOA-OPF
VG74	1.06	0.99	0.96	1.00	0.99	0.94	0.95
VG76	1.06	1.03	0.98	0.99	0.99	0.94	0.94
VG77	1.06	0.97	0.97	1.01	0.99	0.94	0.97
VG80	1.06	0.95	0.96	1.01	1.00	0.94	0.98
VG85	0.97	0.97	0.99	1.00	1.02	0.94	0.96
VG87	0.94	0.98	0.99	1.00	0.99	0.94	0.95
VG89	0.94	1.04	1.04	1.01	1.00	0.94	0.96
VG90	0.94	1.05	1.05	1.01	0.99	0.94	0.96
VG91	0.94	1.03	0.96	1.00	1.00	0.94	0.96
VG92	0.94	0.99	0.95	1.01	0.99	0.94	0.95
VG99	0.94	0.99	1.03	1.00	0.99	0.94	0.97
VG100	0.96	1.01	0.99	1.01	0.99	0.94	0.97
VG103	0.94	1.00	0.98	1.00	1.01	0.95	0.97
VG104	0.94	1.00	0.96	1.01	0.99	0.94	0.95
VG105	0.94	0.98	0.97	1.01	0.99	0.94	0.95
VG107	0.94	0.97	1.00	1.01	1.00	0.94	0.96
VG110	1.01	1.02	0.97	1.00	1.01	0.94	0.97
VG111	1.06	0.99	0.95	1.00	1.01	0.95	0.96
VG112	1.06	1.01	1.03	1.01	0.98	0.94	0.96
VG113	0.94	0.97	1.04	0.98	0.99	0.95	0.95
VG116	1.06	1.05	0.94	1.00	1.05	0.94	0.97
T(5-8)	1.10	1.06	0.94	0.98	1.02	0.90	0.92
T(25-26)	0.90	0.97	1.01	1.03	1.00	0.94	1.07
T(17-30)	1.10	0.94	1.07	0.98	0.99	0.90	0.92
T(37-38)	1.10	0.99	0.95	0.98	0.97	0.97	0.99
T(59-63)	1.10	1.05	0.96	1.02	1.02	0.93	1.02
T(61-64)	1.10	1.05	0.94	0.98	1.01	0.90	0.98
T(65-66)	1.10	1.06	0.97	0.98	1.03	0.96	0.90
T(68-69)	0.90	1.03	0.90	0.96	14.27	0.93	1.07
T(80-81)	0.00	27.21	0.96	22.64	10.13	0.94	0.93
QC34	30.00	11.33	22.22	19.53	20.03	30.00	20.34
QC44	30.00	4.04	22.69	10.02	11.32	30.00	9.24
QC45	30.00	18.74	14.10	24.87	12.60	30.00	0.08
QC46	0.00	19.53	21.38	5.42	15.73	30.00	23.20
QC48	0.00	6.51	6.06	16.65	18.43	30.00	2.83
QC74	0.00	18.57	4.42	20.33	18.69	30.00	26.13
QC79	0.00	23.00	12.10	2.08	17.00	30.00	25.64
QC82	0.00	6.42	25.36	20.19	13.00	30.00	15.31
QC105	30.00	21.19	5.23	1.89	12.61	30.00	14.32
QC107	30.00	6.31	15.34	25.65	13.13	30.00	15.23
QC110	0.00	6.80	7.71	13.65		30.00	3.04
			11.72				4.11

Final results

	PSO	KH	GWO	WOA	SSA	AO	EWOA-OPF
Cost ($/h)	151,751.61	155,696.34	145,902.97	144,856.49	150,655.22	159,974.6	142,756.67
Ploss (MW)	114.431	188.555	135.040	76.802	77.663	71.23298	78.865
VD (p.u.)	2.953		1.579	2.217	0.804	4.251571	2.816

Table A2. Results of OPF for IEEE 118-bus test system on Case 2.

DVs	PSO	KH	GWO	WOA	SSA	AO	EWOA-OPF
PG01	0.00	63.99	35.51	9.88	37.59	52.89	55.64
PG04	0.00	43.12	62.67	39.89	35.56	38.70	16.69
PG06	100.00	83.32	39.58	75.85	45.13	87.48	56.37
PG08	77.21	21.41	58.37	18.35	45.92	74.54	42.12
PG10	550.00	50.82	141.56	414.95	190.59	80.91	234.56
PG12	185.00	54.87	40.45	131.16	87.61	46.88	61.80
PG15	0.00	16.18	28.94	26.00	52.48	88.21	50.36
PG18	0.00	73.77	91.46	4.57	62.85	64.18	16.98
PG19	0.00	24.16	44.95	39.39	49.48	37.33	9.66
PG24	100.00	83.05	56.92	54.42	56.45	35.92	148.39
PG25	320.00	256.00	247.63	192.25	161.58	114.48	297.70
PG26	0.00	296.56	24.02	161.28	156.13	220.42	89.27
PG27	100.00	54.21	25.06	59.16	40.55	39.06	0.00
PG31	0.00	39.43	48.92	28.42	54.56	82.34	65.80
PG32	0.00	70.26	33.75	14.57	44.78	82.53	56.13
PG34	25.65	87.62	80.68	56.63	56.36	82.68	36.67
PG36	100.00	36.18	50.67	21.07	36.80	74.45	74.38
PG40	0.00	40.81	29.47	11.29	43.24	69.92	37.25
PG42	0.00	26.53	18.09	23.77	47.32	89.05	10.44
PG46	0.00	37.26	48.03	5.08	63.20	47.55	132.52
PG49	0.00	88.16	91.60	104.43	88.63	143.85	44.71
PG54	0.00	29.13	54.37	106.65	58.97	61.84	43.14
PG55	100.00	51.87	48.71	56.25	21.13	50.13	70.63
PG56	0.00	28.13	35.79	71.08	56.94	82.74	197.72
PG59	0.00	42.79	129.98	154.32	171.76	182.00	179.66
PG61	260.00	40.76	136.61	71.06	152.50	52.63	18.07
PG62	0.00	17.78	67.82	40.42	30.99	91.16	358.46
PG65	491.00	298.82	37.63	29.90	210.83	75.17	114.13
PG66	0.00	103.20	463.61	101.59	266.97	154.31	20.99
PG70	0.00	11.69	53.88	4.07	45.88	84.50	27.82
PG72	0.00	4.39	52.27	32.30	53.40	46.47	2.59
PG73	0.00	70.09	69.59	43.50	54.76	73.51	13.52
PG74	0.00	20.40	52.41	65.04	61.36	46.69	10.71
PG76	100.00	77.91	35.79	41.47	44.37	89.82	249.08
PG77	0.00	77.57	81.11	17.31	68.57	93.52	55.56
PG80	0.00	250.31	273.42	413.55	255.27	103.79	35.85
PG85	0.00	30.62	53.24	8.08	47.74	89.77	278.23
PG87	0.00	46.05	46.45	16.21	52.44	55.18	54.74
PG89	707.00	526.05	233.21	256.32	265.88	121.60	38.64
PG90	0.00	18.63	25.35	6.07	49.23	68.70	25.09
PG91	26.40	52.18	29.69	67.63	59.32	56.27	35.13
PG92	100.00	56.27	59.29	15.33	48.97	46.08	35.13
PG99	100.00	37.37	81.55	15.33	48.97	46.08	35.13
PG100	0.00	277.31	222.78	192.35	201.06	204.56	205.63
PG103	140.00	92.19	93.59	55.81	48.49	115.77	46.11
PG104	100.00	85.66	66.16	56.69	63.87	42.03	61.62
PG105	0.00	28.18	48.48	43.03	54.41	61.53	19.22
PG107	100.00	80.56	29.71	51.50	43.21	74.92	80.87
PG110	0.00	61.60	34.74	59.02	57.69	46.88	1.07
PG111	136.00	108.41	65.47	35.79	74.49	50.43	55.12
PG112	0.00	17.40	37.38	65.49	60.58	36.48	81.34
PG113	0.00	53.22	76.86	75.50	61.27	39.01	18.12
PG116	0.00	80.78	46.90	9.97	55.72	37.30	48.26
VG01	0.94	1.04	0.99	1.01	0.99	0.94	0.98
VG04	0.94	1.02	1.00	1.02	1.02	0.95	0.98
VG06	1.06	1.02	1.00	1.01	1.00	0.95	1.00
VG08	1.06	1.03	0.96	1.01	1.00	0.95	0.97
VG10	0.94	1.04	1.02	1.02	1.01	0.94	0.99
VG12	0.94	1.06	1.06	1.02	1.00	0.96	1.00
VG15	0.94	1.04	0.97	1.01	1.00	0.94	0.97
VG18	0.94	1.03	1.03	1.02	1.01	0.94	0.97
VG19	0.94	0.96	0.96	1.02	0.99	0.94	0.97
VG24	1.06	1.01	0.98	1.02	0.99	0.94	0.96
VG25	0.94	0.97	1.02	1.02	0.99	0.94	0.99
VG26	0.94	1.03	1.02	1.01	1.02	0.94	0.99
VG27	1.06	1.02	0.96	1.01	0.99	0.94	0.95
VG31	1.06	1.00	1.00	1.01	1.00	0.94	0.97
VG32	1.06	1.03	0.98	1.02	0.99	0.94	0.95
VG34	0.94	0.99	0.97	1.01	0.99	0.94	0.98
VG36	0.94	0.96	1.06	1.02	0.98	0.94	0.97
VG40	0.94	0.99	0.99	1.02	0.98	0.94	0.97
VG42	0.95	1.01	0.94	1.02	1.03	0.94	1.00
VG46	1.06	1.03	1.02	1.02	0.99	0.96	1.04
VG49	0.98	0.97	0.99	1.01	1.02	0.94	1.01
VG54	0.94	0.99	1.02	1.02	1.01	0.94	1.00
VG55	0.94	1.01	1.05	1.02	1.01	0.94	1.00
VG56	0.94	0.98	1.03	1.02	1.00	0.94	0.99
VG59	1.06	0.99	1.04	1.01	1.00	0.97	1.00
VG61	1.06	1.00	1.03	1.02	0.99	0.94	1.00
VG62	1.06	1.02	1.02	1.02	0.99	0.94	0.95
VG65	1.03	0.97	1.01	1.01	1.02	0.94	0.95
VG66	1.06	1.02	1.01	1.01	0.99	0.94	0.99
VG69	1.06	0.98	1.04	1.02	1.01	0.96	0.99
VG70	1.06	1.00	1.03	1.02	0.98	0.94	1.01
VG72	0.94	1.01	0.96	1.01	1.02	0.94	0.99
VG73	1.06	1.00	1.05	1.02	1.02	0.94	0.97
VG74	1.06	0.99	0.99	1.02	0.98	0.94	0.96
VG76	1.06	1.03	0.96	1.01	0.98	0.94	0.95
VG77	1.04	0.97	1.00	1.01	0.99	0.94	0.98
VG80	1.06	0.95	0.99	1.02	1.01	0.95	0.99
VG85	1.06	0.97	1.04	1.02	0.98	0.94	1.02
VG87	1.06	0.98	1.04	1.02	1.01	0.94	0.96
VG89	0.94	1.05	1.02	1.01	0.97	0.94	1.06
VG90	0.94	1.03	0.94	1.01	1.02	0.94	0.96
VG91	0.94	0.99	1.00	1.01	1.00	0.94	1.03
VG92	0.94	0.99	1.01	1.02	0.99	0.94	1.00
VG99	0.94	1.01	1.03	1.02	1.00	0.96	0.95
VG100	0.94	1.00	1.00	1.02	0.98	0.94	0.99
VG103	0.94	1.00	1.02	1.02	1.00	0.95	1.00
VG104	0.94	1.00	1.00	1.01	0.98	0.94	0.97
VG105	0.94	0.98	1.00	1.00	0.98	0.94	0.99
VG107	0.96	0.97	0.97	0.98	1.00	0.94	1.00
VG110	0.98	1.02	1.02	1.01	1.01	0.94	0.97
VG111	0.94	0.97	1.03	1.01	1.00	0.94	0.97
VG112	1.06	0.99	1.02	1.01	0.99	0.94	0.97
VG113	0.94	1.01	0.99	1.01	0.97	0.94	0.96
T(5-8)	1.06	1.05	0.99	1.02	1.00	0.96	0.95
T(25-26)	0.94	0.97	0.99	1.02	0.99	0.94	0.95
T(17-30)	1.06	1.06	0.90	1.01	1.00	0.94	0.95
T(37-38)	1.10	1.00	1.00	1.01	1.02	0.98	0.97
T(59-63)	1.10	0.97	0.98	0.99	0.99	0.93	0.95
T(61-64)	1.10	0.94	0.98	1.00	1.01	0.95	0.95
T(65-66)	0.90	0.99	0.91	0.98	1.00	0.91	0.98
T(68-69)	1.10	1.05	1.00	0.98	0.98	0.90	0.98
T(80-81)	0.90	1.06	1.06	0.99	1.03	0.92	0.97
QC34	0.00	27.21	20.72	19.93	14.72	30.00	19.44
QC44	30.00	11.33	16.63	0.88	14.38	30.00	5.06
QC45	30.00	4.04	7.37	20.27	15.82	30.00	0.01
QC46	30.00	18.74	19.40	9.81	12.00	30.00	22.44
QC48	30.00	19.53	20.39	13.37	15.18	30.00	3.57
QC74	30.00	6.51	8.60	21.70	15.57	30.00	11.21
QC79	30.00	18.57	22.36	16.34	15.98	30.00	27.79
QC82	0.00	23.00	12.81	9.95	15.62	30.00	5.87
QC83	0.00	6.42	15.45	19.63	11.56	30.00	14.99
QC105	30.00	21.19	12.06	14.78	16.36	30.00	9.40
QC107	0.00	6.31	9.60	12.06	18.63	30.00	14.83
QC110	0.00	6.80	26.90	9.35		30.00	24.88

Final results

	PSO	KH	GWO	WOA	SSA	AO	EWOA-OPF
Cost ($/h)	163,613.92	155,696.40	153,293.89	145,078.86	152,484.28	164,684.39	140,175.80
Ploss (MW)	242.265	188.555	88.693	77.031	77.139	60.940	79.990
VD (p.u.)	3.059	1.579	1.082	0.668	0.902	3.997	1.625

References

1. Talbi, E.-G. *Metaheuristics: From Design to Implementation*; John Wiley & Sons: Hoboken, NJ, USA, 2009; Volume 74.
2. Coello, C.A.C. Use of a self-adaptive penalty approach for engineering optimization problems. *Comput. Ind.* **2000**, *41*, 113–127. [CrossRef]
3. Glover, F.W.; Kochenberger, G.A. *Handbook of Metaheuristics*; Springer Publishing Company: New York, NY, USA, 2006; Volume 57.
4. Mesejo, P.; Ibáñez, O.; Cordón, O.; Cagnoni, S. A survey on image segmentation using metaheuristic-based deformable models: State of the art and critical analysis. *Appl. Soft Comput.* **2016**, *44*, 1–29. [CrossRef]
5. Wolpert, D.H.; Macready, W.G. No free lunch theorems for optimization. *IEEE Trans. Evol. Comput.* **1997**, *1*, 67–82. [CrossRef]
6. Goldberg, D.E.; Holland, J.H. Genetic Algorithms and Machine Learning. 1988, pp. 95–99. Available online: https://link.springer.com/content/pdf/10.1023/A:1022602019183.pdf (accessed on 25 October 2021).
7. Koza, J.R.; Koza, J.R. *Genetic Programming: On the Programming of Computers by Means of Natural Selection*; MIT Press: Cambridge, MA, USA, 1992; Volume 1.
8. Rechenberg, I. Evolution Strategy: Optimization of Technical systems by means of biological evolution. *Holzboog Stuttg.* **1973**, *104*, 15–16.
9. Yao, X.; Liu, Y.; Lin, G. Evolutionary programming made faster. *IEEE Trans. Evol. Comput.* **1999**, *3*, 82–102. [CrossRef]
10. Storn, R.; Price, K. Differential evolution–a simple and efficient heuristic for global optimization over continuous spaces. *J. Glob. Optim.* **1997**, *11*, 341–359. [CrossRef]
11. Eberhart, R.; Kennedy, J. A new optimizer using particle swarm theory. In *Proceedings of the Sixth International Symposium on Micro Machine and Human Science, MHS'95*; Nagoya, Japan, 4–6 October 1995, pp. 39–43.
12. Yang, X.-S. A new metaheuristic bat-inspired algorithm. In *Nature Inspired Cooperative Strategies for Optimization (NICSO 2010)*; Springer: Berlin/Heidelberg, Germany, 2010; pp. 65–74.
13. Gandomi, A.H.; Alavi, A.H. Krill herd: A new bio-inspired optimization algorithm. *Commun. Nonlinear Sci. Numer. Simul.* **2012**, *17*, 4831–4845. [CrossRef]
14. Mirjalili, S.; Mirjalili, S.M.; Lewis, A. Grey wolf optimizer. *Adv. Eng. Softw.* **2014**, *69*, 46–61. [CrossRef]
15. Mirjalili, S.; Lewis, A. The whale optimization algorithm. *Adv. Eng. Softw.* **2016**, *95*, 51–67. [CrossRef]
16. Mirjalili, S.; Gandomi, A.H.; Mirjalili, S.Z.; Saremi, S.; Faris, H.; Mirjalili, S.M. Salp Swarm Algorithm: A bio-inspired optimizer for engineering design problems. *Adv. Eng. Softw.* **2017**, *114*, 163–191. [CrossRef]
17. Jain, M.; Singh, V.; Rani, A. A novel nature-inspired algorithm for optimization: Squirrel search algorithm. *Swarm Evol. Comput.* **2019**, *44*, 148–175. [CrossRef]
18. Abualigah, L.; Yousri, D.; Abd Elaziz, M.; Ewees, A.A.; Al-qaness, M.A.; Gandomi, A.H. Aquila Optimizer: A novel meta-heuristic optimization Algorithm. *Comput. Ind. Eng.* **2021**, *157*, 107250. [CrossRef]
19. Dommel, H.W.; Tinney, W.F. Optimal power flow solutions. *IEEE Trans. Power Appar. Syst.* **1968**, 1866–1876. [CrossRef]
20. Radosavljević, J.; Klimenta, D.; Jevtić, M.; Arsić, N. Optimal power flow using a hybrid optimization algorithm of particle swarm optimization and gravitational search algorithm. *Electr. Power Compon. Syst.* **2015**, *43*, 1958–1970. [CrossRef]
21. Biswas, P.P.; Suganthan, P.; Amaratunga, G.A. Optimal power flow solutions incorporating stochastic wind and solar power. *Energy Convers. Manag.* **2017**, *148*, 1194–1207. [CrossRef]
22. Habibollahzadeh, H.; Luo, G.-X.; Semlyen, A. Hydrothermal optimal power flow based on a combined linear and nonlinear programming methodology. *IEEE Trans. Power Syst.* **1989**, *4*, 530–537. [CrossRef]
23. Santos, A.J.; Da Costa, G. Optimal-power-flow solution by Newton's method applied to an augmented Lagrangian function. *IEE Proc. Gener. Transm. Distrib.* **1995**, *142*, 33–36. [CrossRef]
24. Burchett, R.; Happ, H.; Vierath, D. Quadratically convergent optimal power flow. *IEEE Trans. Power Appar. Syst.* **1984**, 3267–3275. [CrossRef]
25. Roy, P.; Ghoshal, S.; Thakur, S. Biogeography based optimization for multi-constraint optimal power flow with emission and non-smooth cost function. *Expert Syst. Appl.* **2010**, *37*, 8221–8228. [CrossRef]
26. Ghasemi, M.; Ghavidel, S.; Rahmani, S.; Roosta, A.; Falah, H. A novel hybrid algorithm of imperialist competitive algorithm and teaching learning algorithm for optimal power flow problem with non-smooth cost functions. *Eng. Appl. Artif. Intell.* **2014**, *29*, 54–69. [CrossRef]
27. Islam, M.Z.; Wahab, N.I.A.; Veerasamy, V.; Hizam, H.; Mailah, N.F.; Guerrero, J.M.; Mohd Nasir, M.N. A Harris Hawks optimization based single-and multi-objective optimal power flow considering environmental emission. *Sustainability* **2020**, *12*, 5248. [CrossRef]
28. Mohammadzadeh, H.; Gharehchopogh, F.S. A novel hybrid whale optimization algorithm with flower pollination algorithm for feature selection: Case study Email spam detection. *Comput. Intell.* **2021**, *37*, 176–209. [CrossRef]
29. Zhu, K.; Ying, S.; Zhang, N.; Zhu, D. Software defect prediction based on enhanced metaheuristic feature selection optimization and a hybrid deep neural network. *J. Syst. Softw.* **2021**, *180*, 111026. [CrossRef]
30. Rahnema, N.; Gharehchopogh, F.S. An improved artificial bee colony algorithm based on whale optimization algorithm for data clustering. *Multimed. Tools Appl.* **2020**, *79*, 32169–32194. [CrossRef]

31. Kotary, D.K.; Nanda, S.J. Distributed clustering in peer to peer networks using multi-objective whale optimization. *Appl. Soft Comput.* **2020**, *96*, 106625. [CrossRef]
32. Tharwat, A.; Moemen, Y.S.; Hassanien, A.E. Classification of toxicity effects of biotransformed hepatic drugs using whale optimized support vector machines. *J. Biomed. Inform.* **2017**, *68*, 132–149. [CrossRef] [PubMed]
33. Abidi, M.H.; Umer, U.; Mohammed, M.K.; Aboudaif, M.K.; Alkhalefah, H. Automated Maintenance Data Classification Using Recurrent Neural Network: Enhancement by Spotted Hyena-Based Whale Optimization. *Mathematics* **2020**, *8*, 2008. [CrossRef]
34. Wang, M.; Chen, H. Chaotic multi-swarm whale optimizer boosted support vector machine for medical diagnosis. *Appl. Soft Comput.* **2020**, *88*, 105946. [CrossRef]
35. Lang, C.; Jia, H. Kapur's entropy for color image segmentation based on a hybrid whale optimization algorithm. *Entropy* **2019**, *21*, 318. [CrossRef]
36. Chakraborty, S.; Saha, A.K.; Nama, S.; Debnath, S. COVID-19 X-ray image segmentation by modified whale optimization algorithm with population reduction. *Comput. Biol. Med.* **2021**, *139*, 104984. [CrossRef]
37. Jiang, T.; Zhang, C.; Zhu, H.; Gu, J.; Deng, G. Energy-efficient scheduling for a job shop using an improved whale optimization algorithm. *Mathematics* **2018**, *6*, 220. [CrossRef]
38. Wang, J.; Du, P.; Niu, T.; Yang, W. A novel hybrid system based on a new proposed algorithm—Multi-Objective Whale Optimization Algorithm for wind speed forecasting. *Appl. Energy* **2017**, *208*, 344–360. [CrossRef]
39. Zhao, H.; Guo, S.; Zhao, H. Energy-related CO2 emissions forecasting using an improved LSSVM model optimized by whale optimization algorithm. *Energies* **2017**, *10*, 874. [CrossRef]
40. Yousri, D.; Allam, D.; Eteiba, M.B. Chaotic whale optimizer variants for parameters estimation of the chaotic behavior in Permanent Magnet Synchronous Motor. *Appl. Soft Comput.* **2019**, *74*, 479–503. [CrossRef]
41. Chakraborty, S.; Sharma, S.; Saha, A.K.; Chakraborty, S. SHADE–WOA: A metaheuristic algorithm for global optimization. *Appl. Soft Comput.* **2021**, *113*, 107866. [CrossRef]
42. Oliva, D.; Abd El Aziz, M.; Hassanien, A.E. Parameter estimation of photovoltaic cells using an improved chaotic whale optimization algorithm. *Appl. Energy* **2017**, *200*, 141–154. [CrossRef]
43. Liu, Y.; Feng, H.; Li, H.; Li, L. An Improved Whale Algorithm for Support Vector Machine Prediction of Photovoltaic Power Generation. *Symmetry* **2021**, *13*, 212. [CrossRef]
44. Sun, Y.; Wang, X.; Chen, Y.; Liu, Z. A modified whale optimization algorithm for large-scale global optimization problems. *Expert Syst. Appl.* **2018**, *114*, 563–577. [CrossRef]
45. Chakraborty, S.; Saha, A.K.; Chakraborty, R.; Saha, M. An enhanced whale optimization algorithm for large scale optimization problems. *Knowl. Based Syst.* **2021**, *233*, 107543. [CrossRef]
46. Taghian, S.; Nadimi-Shahraki, M.H.; Zamani, H. Comparative analysis of transfer function-based binary Metaheuristic algorithms for feature selection. In Proceedings of the 2018 International Conference on Artificial Intelligence and Data Processing (IDAP), Malatya, Turkey, 28–30 September 2018; pp. 1–6.
47. Zamani, H.; Nadimi-Shahraki, M.H.; Taghian, S.; Banaie-Dezfouli, M. Enhancement of Bernstain-Search Differential Evolution Algorithm to Solve Constrained Engineering Problems. *Int. J. Comput. Sci. Eng.* **2020**, *9*, 386–396.
48. Ghasemi, M.R.; Varaee, H. Enhanced IGMM optimization algorithm based on vibration for numerical and engineering problems. *Eng. Comput.* **2018**, *34*, 91–116. [CrossRef]
49. Gharehchopogh, F.S.; Farnad, B.; Alizadeh, A. A farmland fertility algorithm for solving constrained engineering problems. *Concurr. Comput. Pract. Exp.* **2021**, *33*, e6310. [CrossRef]
50. Ullah, I.; Hussain, I.; Singh, M. Exploiting grasshopper and cuckoo search bio-inspired optimization algorithms for industrial energy management system: Smart industries. *Electronics* **2020**, *9*, 105. [CrossRef]
51. Haber, R.; Strzelczak, S.; Miljković, Z.; Castaño, F.; Fumagalli, L.; Petrović, M. Digital twin-based Optimization on the basis of Grey Wolf Method. A Case Study on Motion Control Systems. In Proceedings of the 2020 IEEE Conference on Industrial Cyberphysical Systems (ICPS), Tampere, Finland, 10–12 June 2020; pp. 469–474.
52. Abdel-Basset, M.; Chang, V.; Mohamed, R. HSMA_WOA: A hybrid novel Slime mould algorithm with whale optimization algorithm for tackling the image segmentation problem of chest X-ray images. *Appl. Soft Comput.* **2020**, *95*, 106642. [CrossRef]
53. Naji Alwerfali, H.S.; AA Al-qaness, M.; Abd Elaziz, M.; Ewees, A.A.; Oliva, D.; Lu, S. Multi-level image thresholding based on modified spherical search optimizer and fuzzy entropy. *Entropy* **2020**, *22*, 328. [CrossRef] [PubMed]
54. Oliva, D.; Hinojosa, S.; Cuevas, E.; Pajares, G.; Avalos, O.; Gálvez, J. Cross entropy based thresholding for magnetic resonance brain images using Crow Search Algorithm. *Expert Syst. Appl.* **2017**, *79*, 164–180. [CrossRef]
55. Abualigah, L.; Diabat, A. A novel hybrid antlion optimization algorithm for multi-objective task scheduling problems in cloud computing environments. *Clust. Comput.* **2021**, *24*, 205–223. [CrossRef]
56. Zheng, J.; Wang, Y. A Hybrid Multi-Objective Bat Algorithm for Solving Cloud Computing Resource Scheduling Problems. *Sustainability* **2021**, *13*, 7933. [CrossRef]
57. Sharma, A.; Dasgotra, A.; Tiwari, S.K.; Sharma, A.; Jately, V.; Azzopardi, B. Parameter Extraction of Photovoltaic Module Using Tunicate Swarm Algorithm. *Electronics* **2021**, *10*, 878. [CrossRef]
58. Kang, T.; Yao, J.; Jin, M.; Yang, S.; Duong, T. A novel improved cuckoo search algorithm for parameter estimation of photovoltaic (PV) models. *Energies* **2018**, *11*, 1060. [CrossRef]

59. Hassan, M.H.; Kamel, S.; Selim, A.; Khurshaid, T.; Domínguez-García, J.L. A modified Rao-2 algorithm for optimal power flow incorporating renewable energy sources. *Mathematics* **2021**, *9*, 1532. [CrossRef]
60. Warid, W.; Hizam, H.; Mariun, N.; Abdul-Wahab, N.I. Optimal power flow using the Jaya algorithm. *Energies* **2016**, *9*, 678. [CrossRef]
61. Jumani, T.A.; Mustafa, M.W.; Md Rasid, M.; Hussain Mirjat, N.; Hussain Baloch, M.; Salisu, S. Optimal power flow controller for grid-connected microgrids using grasshopper optimization algorithm. *Electronics* **2019**, *8*, 111. [CrossRef]
62. Verma, P.; Alam, A.; Sarwar, A.; Tariq, M.; Vahedi, H.; Gupta, D.; Ahmad, S.; Mohamed, A.S.N. Meta-Heuristic Optimization Techniques Used for Maximum Power Point Tracking in Solar PV System. *Electronics* **2021**, *10*, 2419. [CrossRef]
63. Sayarshad, H.R. Using bees algorithm for material handling equipment planning in manufacturing systems. *Int. J. Adv. Manuf. Technol.* **2010**, *48*, 1009–1018. [CrossRef]
64. Banaie-Dezfouli, M.; Nadimi-Shahraki, M.H.; Zamani, H. A Novel Tour Planning Model using Big Data. In Proceedings of the 2018 International Conference on Artificial Intelligence and Data Processing (IDAP), Malatya, Turkey, 28–30 September 2018; pp. 1–6.
65. Yeh, W.-C.; Tan, S.-Y. Simplified Swarm Optimization for the Heterogeneous Fleet Vehicle Routing Problem with Time-Varying Continuous Speed Function. *Electronics* **2021**, *10*, 1775. [CrossRef]
66. Koryshev, N.; Hodashinsky, I.; Shelupanov, A. Building a Fuzzy Classifier Based on Whale Optimization Algorithm to Detect Network Intrusions. *Symmetry* **2021**, *13*, 1211. [CrossRef]
67. Khare, N.; Devan, P.; Chowdhary, C.L.; Bhattacharya, S.; Singh, G.; Singh, S.; Yoon, B. Smo-dnn: Spider monkey optimization and deep neural network hybrid classifier model for intrusion detection. *Electronics* **2020**, *9*, 692. [CrossRef]
68. Too, J.; Abdullah, A.R.; Mohd Saad, N. A new quadratic binary harris hawk optimization for feature selection. *Electronics* **2019**, *8*, 1130. [CrossRef]
69. Taghian, S.; Nadimi-Shahraki, M.H. A Binary Metaheuristic Algorithm for Wrapper Feature Selection. *Int. J. Comput. Sci. Eng. (IJCSE)* **2019**, *8*, 168–172.
70. Jiang, Y.; Luo, Q.; Wei, Y.; Abualigah, L.; Zhou, Y. An efficient binary Gradient-based optimizer for feature selection. *Math. Biosci. Eng. MBE* **2021**, *18*, 3813–3854. [CrossRef]
71. Mohmmadzadeh, H.; Gharehchopogh, F.S. An efficient binary chaotic symbiotic organisms search algorithm approaches for feature selection problems. *J. Supercomput.* **2021**, *77*, 1–43. [CrossRef]
72. Ewees, A.A.; Al-qaness, M.A.; Abualigah, L.; Oliva, D.; Algamal, Z.Y.; Anter, A.M.; Ali Ibrahim, R.; Ghoniem, R.M.; Abd Elaziz, M. Boosting Arithmetic Optimization Algorithm with Genetic Algorithm Operators for Feature Selection: Case Study on Cox Proportional Hazards Model. *Mathematics* **2021**, *9*, 2321. [CrossRef]
73. Mohammadzadeh, H.; Gharehchopogh, F.S. Feature Selection with Binary Symbiotic Organisms Search Algorithm for Email Spam Detection. *Int. J. Inf. Technol. Decis. Mak.* **2021**, *20*, 469–515. [CrossRef]
74. Dedeturk, B.K.; Akay, B. Spam filtering using a logistic regression model trained by an artificial bee colony algorithm. *Appl. Soft Comput.* **2020**, *91*, 106229. [CrossRef]
75. Mienye, I.D.; Sun, Y. Improved Heart Disease Prediction Using Particle Swarm Optimization Based Stacked Sparse Autoencoder. *Electronics* **2021**, *10*, 2347. [CrossRef]
76. Chattopadhyay, S.; Dey, A.; Singh, P.K.; Geem, Z.W.; Sarkar, R. COVID-19 detection by optimizing deep residual features with improved clustering-based golden ratio optimizer. *Diagnostics* **2021**, *11*, 315. [CrossRef] [PubMed]
77. Nadimi-Shahraki, M.H.; Banaie-Dezfouli, M.; Zamani, H.; Taghian, S.; Mirjalili, S. B-MFO: A Binary Moth-Flame Optimization for Feature Selection from Medical Datasets. *Computers* **2021**, *10*, 136. [CrossRef]
78. Castaño, F.; Haber, R.E.; Mohammed, W.M.; Nejman, M.; Villalonga, A.; Lastra, J.L.M. Quality monitoring of complex manufacturing systems on the basis of model driven approach. *Smart Struct. Syst.* **2020**, *26*. [CrossRef]
79. Nadimi-Shahraki, M.H.; Moeini, E.; Taghian, S.; Mirjalili, S. DMFO-CD: A Discrete Moth-Flame Optimization Algorithm for Community Detection. *Algorithms* **2021**, *14*, 314. [CrossRef]
80. Ghasemi, M.R.; Varaee, H. A fast multi-objective optimization using an efficient ideal gas molecular movement algorithm. *Eng. Comput.* **2017**, *33*, 477–496. [CrossRef]
81. Weiguo, Z.; Wang, L.; Mirjalili, S. Artificial hummingbird algorithm: A new bio-inspired optimizer with its engineering applications. *Computer Methods in Applied Mechanics and Engineering* **2022**, *388*, 114194.
82. Nama, S.; Saha, A.K.; Ghosh, S. A hybrid symbiosis organisms search algorithm and its application to real world problems. *Memetic Comput.* **2017**, *9*, 261–280. [CrossRef]
83. Chen, J.; Xin, B.; Peng, Z.; Dou, L.; Zhang, J. Optimal contraction theorem for exploration–exploitation tradeoff in search and optimization. *IEEE Trans. Syst. Man Cybern. Part A Syst. Hum.* **2009**, *39*, 680–691. [CrossRef]
84. Zamani, H.; Nadimi-Shahraki, M.H.; Gandomi, A.H. CCSA: Conscious Neighborhood-based Crow Search Algorithm for Solving Global Optimization Problems. *Appl. Soft Comput.* **2019**, *85*, 105583. [CrossRef]
85. Konak, A.; Coit, D.W.; Smith, A.E. Multi-objective optimization using genetic algorithms: A tutorial. *Reliab. Eng. Syst. Saf.* **2006**, *91*, 992–1007. [CrossRef]
86. Nadimi-Shahraki, M.H.; Taghian, S.; Mirjalili, S.; Faris, H. MTDE: An effective multi-trial vector-based differential evolution algorithm and its applications for engineering design problems. *Appl. Soft Comput.* **2020**, *97*, 106761. [CrossRef]

87. Jin, Q.; Xu, Z.; Cai, W. An Improved Whale Optimization Algorithm with Random Evolution and Special Reinforcement Dual-Operation Strategy Collaboration. *Symmetry* **2021**, *13*, 238. [CrossRef]
88. Zamani, H.; Nadimi-Shahraki, M.H.; Gandomi, A.H. QANA: Quantum-based avian navigation optimizer algorithm. *Eng. Appl. Artif. Intell.* **2021**, *104*, 104314. [CrossRef]
89. Bouchekara, H. Optimal power flow using black-hole-based optimization approach. *Appl. Soft Comput.* **2014**, *24*, 879–888. [CrossRef]
90. Bouchekara, H.; Abido, M.; Boucherma, M. Optimal power flow using teaching-learning-based optimization technique. *Electr. Power Syst. Res.* **2014**, *114*, 49–59. [CrossRef]
91. Abdollahi, A.; Ghadimi, A.A.; Miveh, M.R.; Mohammadi, F.; Jurado, F. Optimal power flow incorporating FACTS devices and stochastic wind power generation using krill herd algorithm. *Electronics* **2020**, *9*, 1043. [CrossRef]
92. Nusair, K.; Alhmoud, L. Application of equilibrium optimizer algorithm for optimal power flow with high penetration of renewable energy. *Energies* **2020**, *13*, 6066. [CrossRef]
93. Khunkitti, S.; Siritaratiwat, A.; Premrudeepreechacharn, S. Multi-Objective Optimal Power Flow Problems Based on Slime Mould Algorithm. *Sustainability* **2021**, *13*, 7448. [CrossRef]
94. Niknam, T.; rasoul Narimani, M.; Jabbari, M.; Malekpour, A.R. A modified shuffle frog leaping algorithm for multi-objective optimal power flow. *Energy* **2011**, *36*, 6420–6432. [CrossRef]
95. Nadimi-Shahraki, M.H.; Taghian, S.; Mirjalili, S. An improved grey wolf optimizer for solving engineering problems. *Expert Syst. Appl.* **2021**, *166*, 113917. [CrossRef]
96. Mandal, B.; Roy, P.K. Multi-objective optimal power flow using quasi-oppositional teaching learning based optimization. *Appl. Soft Comput.* **2014**, *21*, 590–606. [CrossRef]
97. Singh, R.P.; Mukherjee, V.; Ghoshal, S. Particle swarm optimization with an aging leader and challengers algorithm for the solution of optimal power flow problem. *Appl. Soft Comput.* **2016**, *40*, 161–177. [CrossRef]
98. Bai, W.; Eke, I.; Lee, K.Y. An improved artificial bee colony optimization algorithm based on orthogonal learning for optimal power flow problem. *Control Eng. Pract.* **2017**, *61*, 163–172. [CrossRef]
99. Attia, A.-F.; El Sehiemy, R.A.; Hasanien, H.M. Optimal power flow solution in power systems using a novel Sine-Cosine algorithm. *Int. J. Electr. Power Energy Syst.* **2018**, *99*, 331–343. [CrossRef]
100. Nguyen, T.T. A high performance social spider optimization algorithm for optimal power flow solution with single objective optimization. *Energy* **2019**, *171*, 218–240. [CrossRef]
101. Abou El Ela, A.; Abido, M.; Spea, S. Optimal power flow using differential evolution algorithm. *Electr. Power Syst. Res.* **2010**, *80*, 878–885. [CrossRef]

Article

A Hybrid Imputation Method for Multi-Pattern Missing Data: A Case Study on Type II Diabetes Diagnosis

Mohammad H. Nadimi-Shahraki [1,2,*], Saeed Mohammadi [1,2], Hoda Zamani [1,2], Mostafa Gandomi [3] and Amir H. Gandomi [4,*]

[1] Faculty of Computer Engineering, Najafabad Branch, Islamic Azad University, Najafabad 8514143131, Iran; saeed-mohamadi@sco.iaun.ac.ir (S.M.); hoda_zamani@sco.iaun.ac.ir (H.Z.)
[2] Big Data Research Center, Najafabad Branch, Islamic Azad University, Najafabad 8514143131, Iran
[3] School of Civil Engineering, College of Engineering, University of Tehran, Tehran 1417614411, Iran; mostafa.gandomi@ut.ac.ir
[4] Faculty of Engineering & Information Technology, University of Technology Sydney, Ultimo 2007, Australia
* Correspondence: nadimi@iaun.ac.ir (M.H.N.-S.); gandomi@uts.edu.au (A.H.G.)

Citation: Nadimi-Shahraki, M.H.; Mohammadi, S.; Zamani, H.; Gandomi, M.; Gandomi, A.H. A Hybrid Imputation Method for Multi-Pattern Missing Data: A Case Study on Type II Diabetes Diagnosis. *Electronics* **2021**, *10*, 3167. https:// doi.org/10.3390/electronics10243167

Academic Editor: Gongping Yang

Received: 12 November 2021
Accepted: 16 December 2021
Published: 19 December 2021

Publisher's Note: MDPI stays neutral with regard to jurisdictional claims in published maps and institutional affiliations.

Abstract: Real medical datasets usually consist of missing data with different patterns which decrease the performance of classifiers used in intelligent healthcare and disease diagnosis systems. Many methods have been proposed to impute missing data, however, they do not fulfill the need for data quality especially in real datasets with different missing data patterns. In this paper, a four-layer model is introduced, and then a hybrid imputation (HIMP) method using this model is proposed to impute multi-pattern missing data including non-random, random, and completely random patterns. In HIMP, first, non-random missing data patterns are imputed, and then the obtained dataset is decomposed into two datasets containing random and completely random missing data patterns. Then, concerning the missing data patterns in each dataset, different single or multiple imputation methods are used. Finally, the best-imputed datasets gained from random and completely random patterns are merged to form the final dataset. The experimental evaluation was conducted by a real dataset named IRDia including all three missing data patterns. The proposed method and comparative methods were compared using different classifiers in terms of accuracy, precision, recall, and F_1-score. The classifiers' performances show that the HIMP can impute multi-pattern missing values more effectively than other comparative methods.

Keywords: medical data mining; missing data pattern; single imputation; multiple imputations; hybrid imputation; diabetes diagnosis

1. Introduction

Along with the reduced physical activity and the spread of sedentary life as well as consumption of unhealthy foods, not only the diabetes affliction age has been reduced, but also its incidence rate has been increased [1–3]. According to the international diabetes federation reports, the number of diabetic patients in 2015 amounted to 415 million people, 46.5% of which, equivalent to 192.8 million people, were not aware of their disease [4]. It has been estimated that by 2040, the number of patients with diabetes all around the world will reach nearly 642 million individuals, which is more than twice the population with diabetes in 2008. Moreover, diabetes is a leading cause of mortality and an expensive medical problem [5,6]. Early and accurate diabetes diagnosis is very critical to timely treatment which can suspend the disease progression, decrease the mortality rate and control the economic burden [7–10]. Diabetes can cause serious complications on the body's organs and tissues such as cardiovascular, nephropathy, neuropathy, retinopathy, heart attacks, amputation, cancer and lead to death [11–14]. The related studies have been performed on diabetes complications as a potential negative predictor factor on other oncological diseases [15] and functional conditions such as erectile dysfunction [16]. The most common type of diabetes is are type II in which body cells can't properly use the produced insulin [17,18].

Unfortunately, the high prevalence of diabetic patients and the lack of effective and intelligent methods, which cause delay and inaccuracy in diagnosis [19–21]. Medical data mining is recognized as a powerful method that can extract hidden patterns from a huge amount of data [22–25] and provide early and accurate medical decisions [26,27]. Accordingly, many intelligent and data mining methods are developed to improve the early and accurate diagnosis from diabetes datasets [28–31]. However, the direct analysis of diabetes datasets without preprocessing results in inaccurate learning models, and erroneous medical decisions [32–34]. The diabetes data quality affects the performance of intelligent medical methods especially by their irrelevant features [35,36] and missing data which is a common problem faced with real-world diabetes datasets [37]. Efficient metaheuristic-based algorithms are introduced to select relevant and effective features and they are getting better and better with the advent of recent metaheuristic algorithms [38–41]. Missing data handling is an essential step of the medical data mining process [42–45] which is the main concern of this study.

The personal mistakes in the data collection process, nature of the features, and biological effects of features of the blood test on each other lead to the occurrence of different missing data patterns in a dataset. Recognizing the pattern of missing values is an important process in missing data imputation [46]. Little et al. [47] defined three categories of missing data, missing completely at random (MCAR), missing at random (MAR), and missing not at random (MNAR). The problem of missing value can be solved by using simple methods as well as value imputation methods [48–50]. Complete case analysis (CCA) or listwise deletion, pairwise deletion, manual filling of missing values, and use of constant global label value are among the simple methods. Imputation is a powerful method for dealing with missing data problems [51–54] which are including single imputation (SI) and multiple imputations (MI). The SI and MI methods provide desirable results on MCAR and MAR patterns, respectively; besides, the constant global label is suitable for the MNAR missing data pattern [37,55–58]. Accordingly, imputation of missing values via these methods might be introduced extra noises, biases, and poor data quality that provide less accuracy for the data model [59–64]. The presence of multi-pattern missing values can critically influence the performance of classifiers. Identifying the type of missing pattern and selecting/proposing the proper imputation method are two related issues concerning the imputation problem. Recently, a new generation of imputation methods are proposed that utilized the advantages of SI and MI methods using the hybridization schema.

In this paper, a four-layer model is introduced to hybridize imputation methods for different missing data patterns. The introduced model consists of analyzing, decomposing, imputing, and merging layers. Based on the introduced model, a hybrid imputation method named HIMP is proposed. Accordingly, first, the proposed method analyses the features and categorizes them accurately according to a variety of missing data patterns by finding the correlation between features with missing values and also specified definitions. The proposed HIMP imputes missing data with MNAR patterns and stores the results, and then it decomposes the results into two datasets D_{MCAR} and D_{MAR} including missing data with MCAR and MAR patterns, respectively. Next, D_{MCAR} is imputed using single imputation methods K-nearest neighbor (KNN) [65] and hot-deck [66] while D_{MAR} is imputed using three multiple imputation methods Markov chain Monte Carlo (MCMC) [67–69], multivariate imputation by chained equations (MICE) [70,71] and expectation maximization (Em) [72]. In this step, the imputed values estimated by each method are assessed using different classifiers to determine winner imputed methods and their D_{MCAR} and D_{MAR} datasets. Finally, HIMP merges the winner datasets to form the imputed dataset. The proposed HIMP was evaluated and compared with some other imputation methods using different classifiers in terms of accuracy, precision, recall, and F_1-score. The HIMP and comparative methods competed to impute missing values of a real-world dataset named IRDia including different patterns MAR, MNAR, and MCAR. The classifiers' performances show that the HIMP is more effective than other comparative methods. The main contributions of this study can be summarized as follows:

- Introducing a four-layer model to develop hybrid imputation methods for multi-pattern missing data;
- Proposing a hybrid imputation method (HIMP) using the introduced model;
- Collecting a real dataset named Iran diabetes (IRDia) from private medical clinics, and identifying and categorizing its missing data patterns including MCAR, MAR, and MNAR patterns;
- Evaluating the proposed HIMP by comparing its results with other imputation methods for imputing all missing data patterns of the IRDia dataset.

The rest of this paper is organized as follows: In Section 2, the background and related works are presented. In Section 3 the proposed HIMP is introduced. The experimental evaluations are provided in Section 4. Finally, Section 5 discusses and concludes the obtained finding of this study.

2. Background and Related Works

In this section, first, the missing patterns concepts are described, and then related works are briefly reviewed.

The missing pattern analysis provides descriptive measures of the relationship and connection between missing values and present values [56,73,74]. Knowing the missing patterns is useful as an exploratory step before imputation for selecting the proper data imputation methods [75–82]. The missing patterns can be classified into three categories missing completely at random (MCAR), missing at random (MAR), and missing not at random (MNAR). The real-world datasets may consist of all patterns MCAR, MAR, and MAR which are categorized in multi-pattern missing values.

Missing completely at random (MCAR) pattern: The MCAR pattern occurs completely randomly throughout the dataset. In this type of missingness, a random subset of the missing observations has distributions similar to the observed values [37,56]. If feature Y has missing values, the MCAR pattern will occur when the missing values on feature Y are independent of all the observed features and values of Y. The missing and observed distributions of Y are the same, which can be expressed as Equation (1) [83]. The MCAR pattern can be corrected using methods such as complete case analysis (CCA), pairwise deletion, initialization with a central tendency global constant, and single imputation [37,55,57,83].

$$P (Y \mid y \text{ missing}) = P (Y \mid y \text{ observed}) \tag{1}$$

Missing at random (MAR) pattern: The MAR pattern occurs randomly throughout the dataset. In MAR, the probability that a record with missing values belongs to a feature does not depend on the value of the missing value but can be dependent on the observed data [37]. In this case, the observed and missing distributions on feature Y are equal depending on some of the X observed values. In fact, according to Equation (2), the probability of missingness of observations on feature Y depends on other observations of feature X, but not on values of Y. Furthermore, the observed values are not necessarily a random sample of the assumed complete dataset [83].

$$P (Y \mid y \text{ missing}, y \text{ observed}, X) = P (Y \mid y \text{ observed}, X) \tag{2}$$

The correction method of this type of missing data pattern is multiple imputations [33,37,55,56,83]. In the MAR pattern, all the simple techniques for managing the missing values, including CCA, pairwise deletion, and use of mean representative for missing values, can lead to reduced statistical power, increased standard error, and bias of the results [37,55,84]. If the missing data pattern is of MAR type, pairwise deletion can seriously cause bias in the obtained results [83]; however, if the data do not have MAR pattern, implementing the multiple imputations can lead to errors as well biased results [56,85]. Since in the single imputation methods the overall correlation between the features is less taken into account, applying these methods in the MAR pattern might lead to inaccurate estimations [37].

Missing not at random (MNAR) pattern: This missing data pattern occurs non-randomly and due to entirely intentional reasons throughout the dataset. In one of the cases of the MNAR pattern, the feature with missingness can be logically initialized, but there is no other feature in the dataset that is conceptually associated with it. Moreover, there is another case, in which the feature cannot be initialized logically and conceptually. Furthermore, the cause of missingness can be specified using one or multiple features found in the dataset [37,49,56]. Under such conditions, the constant global label value is used to fill the blanks of the missing values [37,55,86]. According to Equation (3), in the MNAR pattern, the missing and observed values of feature Y are not equal under any condition [83]. The missing values can be corrected by using simple and imputation methods.

$$P\,(Y\mid y\ missing) \neq P\,(Y\mid y\ observed) \tag{3}$$

Real-world problems are mostly faced with different types of missing patterns which are affected in the performance of the classifier and predictor models by achieving erroneous results. Selecting the proper missing data handling is essential in preprocessing step. Many imputation methods have been developed over the years for different datasets such as real datasets of the national health and nutrition examination survey (NHANES) [87–89]. The complete-case analysis (CCA) and imputation methods are common approaches to handle missing data and achieve completeness. The CCA [48] is a simple method to handle missing data values. The CCA method is often performed when the class label is missed. In this method, all the samples containing missing values are deleted from the investigated dataset [48,50]. In pairwise deletion, those records are removed from the dataset, in which the variable or feature with missingness is used in calculations [50]. The use of a constant global label such as "unknown" value instead of the missing value in each feature can be considered as another simple missingness correction method. Another sophisticated approach to handling missing data is the imputation method that is substituting the estimated values for the missing values. The estimated values are obtained through internal and central relations of features of the dataset [55]. Missing data imputation methods are commonly divided into two groups single imputation (SI) and multiple imputations (MI).

Single imputation (SI) method: In the SI method, a value is considered instead of any missing value and, in the final analysis [37]. Among the single imputation methods, a central tendency unit such as the average or mean of records of a class is known as the concept most common (Cmc) method can be mentioned [4,48,50]. Regression imputation, mean substitution, hot-deck imputation [66], K-nearest neighbor (KNN) imputation [65], and maximum likelihood method are well-known single imputation methods [50,90,91].

Multiple imputations (MI) method: To consider the uncertainty of the value obtained for imputation relative to the unmeasured real data this method collects multiple values for each missingness in the imputation value production process [92]. To perform the multiple imputations, the missing data pattern should be of MAR type [33,37,56,83,85,86]. Some of the multiple imputation methods include Markov chain Monte Carlo (MCMC), multivariate imputation by chained equations (MICE) [70,71], and expectation-maximization (Em) [72]. The MCMC method specifies a multivariate distribution for the missing values and flows the imputation from conditional distributions by Markov chain Monte Carlo techniques. The MICE method has emerged as a systematic method for handling the missing values in the statistical literature [71,85]. The Em method performs an effective repetitive procedure to calculate the maximum likelihood estimation in the presence of the missing value [84]. The above-mentioned missing values imputation methods have no sensitivity to discreteness or continuousness of the data [92].

Many imputation methods have been developed to complete the missing data and overcome the shortcomings that occurred during the data preprocessing step. In the following, the related works proposed for imputing missing values are reviewed and discussed in three groups SI, MI, and hybrid imputation.

The CCA omits the missing values from the analysis which may lose a significant amount of useful information from the analysis [93,94]. To cover the CCA weaknesses, SI methods are developed which require less computational cost to generate a proposer value for a missing value in a dataset. Giardina et al. [95], applied the single imputation methods of K-nearest neighbors imputation, mean, and the multiple imputation method of Em in Ulster Diabetes datasets. This data has 49% maximum missingness. Randomly simulated missingness from 5% to 35% was created in the features of the Ulster dataset, but the type of the missing data pattern was not mentioned. In addition, they reported KNN and Mean as the best methods. Purwar [61] implemented single imputation and CCA methods on three datasets of Pima, WDBC, and Hepatitis with 699, 768, and 155 records, respectively, and WDBC dataset with artificially induced missing values for the correction of the missing values. The missingness rate of 25–75% was reported in the features, but the missing data pattern was not mentioned. In this study, 11 data missingness correction methods, including CCA, Cmc, and KNN, were used. Then, through clustering by the K-means algorithm and evaluating the clusters, the Cmc method was selected as the best method. Afterward, evaluation of the efficiency of the final model was obtained by the MLP classifier with the highest accuracy rate of 99.82%, 99.08%, and 99.39% for datasets of Hepatitis, Pima, and WDBC, respectively. Aljuaid [96] applied the Em, KNN, mean, and hot-deck imputation methods on five different datasets from the UCI repository with varying rates of missingness (maximum of 25%), which were used artificially and randomly. These imputation methods were applied separately on different datasets, and the result obtained by the c5.0 decision tree classifier was compared with the datasets without missing values. In this study, no exact recognition of the missing data patterns created in the dataset was expressed. According to the obtained results, the Em method yielded better results on numerical datasets; furthermore, the hot-deck method had better results in larger datasets. Moreover, the KNN method had a longer execution time in more massive datasets.

The MI methods are developed to alleviate the shortcomings of the single imputation method in handling missing values [56]. Lin [83] investigated the efficiency of the Em multiple imputation algorithm and MCMC method. In this study, these two imputation methods had no significant difference in terms of the final accuracy. The NHIS dataset with 13,017 records, 26 features, and a maximum missingness rate of 25% was used for the quality-of-life criteria, including physical, mental, and social health. The records with the missingness above 20% were deleted from the dataset. The missingness in this dataset was created artificially, and the missing data pattern was not mentioned. Mirkes [97] analyzed the TARN physical injury dataset in terms of missing values. A system of Markov non-stationary models was developed; next, these models were evaluated on 15,437 records with more than 200 features. In this study, it was noted that five repetitions could be appropriate for multiple imputations. In this study, the missingness percentage was not mentioned, and the Markov model-based multiple imputations demonstrated excellent results. Eisemann [33] used MICE multiple imputation method and regression on the breast cancer dataset of SH Research Center in Germany with 21,500 records and 13 features. Nearly 20% of the records had missingness, which was deleted from the dataset. Then, artificial missingness was created on the rest of the data. The assumed missing data pattern in this study was MAR, and the MICE method yielded desirable results. Sovilj et al. [98] developed a new method based on the gaussian mixture model and Extreme Learning Machine. The missing values are handled using the Gaussian Mixture Model and then extreme learning machine is applied for final estimation. Faisal et al. [99] proposed multiple imputations methods using the weighted nearest neighbor approach to impute missing data in which the distances are computed using the correlation among the target and candidate predictors. Blazek et al. [100] introduced a practical guide to effective multiple imputations of missing data in the context of nephrology research nephrology. Moreover, the efficient multiple imputation methods, GAMIN [101], MIRDDs [102], and MI-MOTE [103] are recently proposed.

Hybrid imputation methods for estimation of the missing values used the advantages of both single imputation and multiple imputations methods. Many algorithms are developed to combine these methods effectively. Aydilek et al. [59] presented a fuzzy c-means clustering hybrid imputation approach that utilizes the support vector regression and a genetic algorithm for estimation the missing values. Tian et al. [63] proposed a hybrid missing data completion method called multiple imputation using gray-system-theory and entropy-based on clustering (MIGEC). The MIGEC divided the non-missing data patterns into several clusters and applied the information entropy for incomplete instances in terms of the similarity metric based on gray system theory (GST) to estimate the imputed values. Gautam et al. [104] proposed hybrid imputation methods including PSO–ECM and (PSO–ECM) + MAAELM that involve particle swarm optimization (PSO), evolving clustering method (ECM), and auto-associative extreme learning machine (AAELM) for data imputation. Vazifehdan et al. [64] proposed a hybrid imputation method using a bayesian network and tensor factorization for imputing the discrete and numerical missing values, respectively, to boost the performance of the breast cancer recurrence predictor. Aleryani et al. [105] proposed the multiple imputation ensembles (MIE) for dealing with the data incompleteness. Rani et al. [62] proposed a hybrid imputation method to combine multivariate imputation by chained equations (MICE), K-nearest neighbor (KNN), mean and mode imputation methods for predicting missing values in medical datasets. Li et al. [60] proposed hybrid missing value imputation algorithms JFCM-VQNNI and JFCM-FVQNNI that are utilized the combination of the fuzzy c-means and the vaguely quantified nearest neighbor.

Xu et al. [106] proposed the MIAEC algorithm which is a missing value imputation algorithm based on the evidence chain. The MIAEC algorithm mines all relevant evidence of missing data in the dataset and then combines this evidence to produce the evidence chain for estimating the missing values. Tsai et al. [107] designed a class center-based missing value imputation (CCMVI) approach for producing effective imputation. The CCMVI is based on two modules. In the first module, the imputation threshold is determined based on the distances between the class centers and their corresponding data samples. In the second module, the threshold for missing value imputation is identified. González-Vidal et al. [108] proposed a missing data imputation framework with Bayesian maximum entropy (BME) to estimate the missing data from the internet of things applications. Mostafa et al. [109] introduced two algorithms the cumulative bayesian ridge with less NaN (CBRL) and cumulative bayesian ridge with high correlation (CBRC) for improving the accuracy of missing value imputation.

Li et al. [110] proposed a novel hybrid method coupling empirical mode decomposition and a long short-term memory deep learning network to predict missing measured signal data of structural health monitoring (SHM) systems. The generative adversarial network is the next frontier of machine learning [111] which is applied in the machine learning data imputation approach and has the potential to handle missing data accurately and efficiently. Zhang et al. [112] proposed a model of end-to-end generative adversarial network with real-data forcing to impute the missing values in a multivariate time series. The proposed model consists of an encoder network, a generator network, and a discriminator network. Faisal et.al [113] proposed a weighted imputation method for high-dimensional mixed-type datasets by nearest neighbors which use the information on similarities among samples and association among covariates. Wan et al. [114] proposed a novel collaborative clustering-based imputation method (COLI), which uses imputation quality as a key metric for the exchange of information between different clustering results.

Shahjaman et al. [115] introduced the rMisbeta algorithm as a robust iterative approach that uses robust estimators based on the minimum beta divergence method to simultaneously impute missing values and outliers. Hu et al. [116] proposed an information granule-based classifier for incomplete data and a way of representing missing entities and information granules in a unified framework. The information granule-based classifier abstracts and refines the prototypes in multi-class subspaces to capture the key structural relationship of the classes. The relocated prototypes and classification information are exploited to represent the missing values as interval information granules. Then, the incomplete data are classified and imputed as hybrid numeric and granular data. Nugroho et al. [117] proposed a class center-based firefly algorithm for retrieving missing data by considering the attribute correlation in the imputation process.

3. Proposed Hybrid Imputation (HIMP) Method for the Multi-Pattern Missing Data

In this paper, a four-layer model is introduced to develop efficient methods for imputing different missing data patterns by hybridizing some suitable imputation techniques. AS shown in Figure 1, the introduced model consists of analyzing, decomposing, imputing, and merging layers. The first layer is to analyze the original dataset and determine its different missing data patterns, and it decomposes the original dataset into different datasets in the second layer. Then, in the third layer, each decomposed dataset can be imputed using a combination of different relevant techniques to find the best possible estimation for their missing values. Finally, in the fourth layer, the best estimations gained from the third layer are merged to form the imputed dataset.

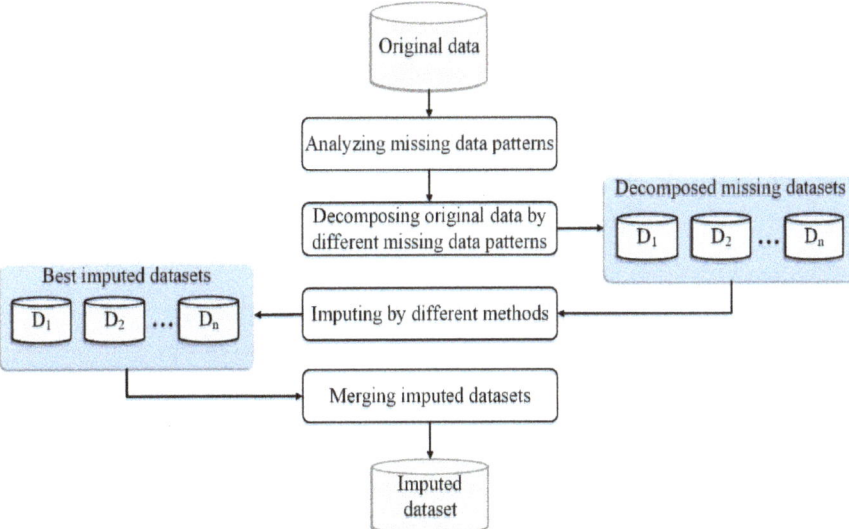

Figure 1. The introduced model for imputing multi-pattern missing data.

Based on the introduced model, a hybrid imputation method named HIMP is proposed. The pseudocode of the HIMP method is presented in Algorithm 1.

Algorithm 1. The proposed hybrid imputation (HIMP) method

Input: The original dataset (IRDia) includes different missing data patterns.
Output: Imputed dataset.
1. **Begin**
2. **Analyzing** missing data patterns.
3. **Imputing** missing data with MNAR pattern using the appropriate constant global label.
4. D ← Original dataset with imputed MNAR pattern.
5. **Decomposing** D to two databases D_{MCAR} and D_{MAR} including MCAR and MAR patterns.
6. **Single imputing** D_{MCAR} using candidate single imputation methods.
7. **Assessing** the results gained by candidate single imputation methods and selecting the winner.
8. WinnerD_{MCAR} ← The imputed D_{MCAR} gained from the winner single imputation method.
9. **Multiple imputing** D_{MAR} using candidate multiple imputation methods
10. **Assessing** the results gained by candidate multiple methods and selecting the winner.
11. WinnerD_{MAR} ← The imputed D_{MAR} gained from the winner multiple imputation method.
12. Imputed dataset ←**Merging** WinnerD_{MCAR} and WinnerD_{MAR}.
13. **End**

As shown in Figure 2, the proposed HIMP method consists of the following six steps.

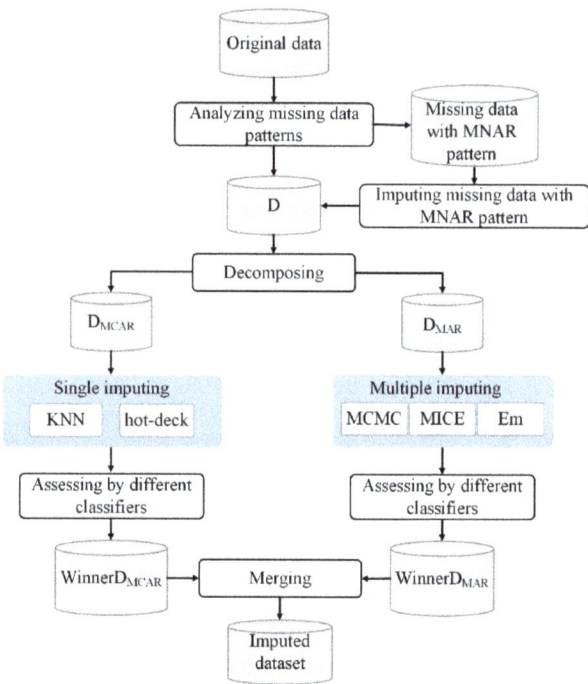

Figure 2. The proposed HIMP method.

Step 1. Analyzing missing data patterns: In this step, the original dataset with high missing data is analyzed and the missing patterns are detected.

Step 2. Imputing missing data with MNAR pattern: The features with the MNAR pattern were identified, then their missing values were imputed with appropriate constant global label values.

Step 3. Decomposing: The imputed dataset obtained from Step 2 is decomposed into two datasets D_{MCAR} and D_{MAR} with MCAR and MAR patterns by identifying the internal relationships of the variables, cause of missingness, and concerning definitions of the missing pattern and consulting with an endocrinologist.

Step 4. Single imputing: Single imputation methods including K-nearest neighbor (KNN) and hot-desk impute the MCAR patterns in the D_{MCAR} dataset. Then, the results obtained by each imputation method are assessed using different classifiers and the best results are selected as the WinnerD$_{MCAR}$.

Step 5. Multiple imputing: The multiple imputation methods including Markov chain Monte Carlo (MCMC), multivariate imputation by chained equations (MICE), and expectation-maximization (Em) were applied to the D_{MAR} datasets with the MAR pattern. Each multiple imputation method in this study generated five separate datasets. The datasets imputed by each multiple imputation method were assessed by comparing the performance of different classifiers. Then, the best results are determined as the WinnerD$_{MAR}$.

Step 6. Hybrid imputation: In the final step, the WinnerD$_{MCAR}$ and WinnerD$_{MAR}$ datasets selected from steps 4 and 5 are merged, the repetitive features are deleted, and the final dataset is formed.

4. Experimental Evaluation

In this section, first, the experimental environment and setting are described. Then, the process of clinical data collecting, features of Iran's diabetes (IRDia) dataset collected in our case study, and identifying the missing data patterns of the IRDia dataset are described. Finally, the proposed imputation method and other comparative methods are applied for imputing IRDia dataset, and then their results are assessed in terms of accuracy, precision, recall, and F_1-Score gained by different classifiers.

4.1. Experimental Environment and Setting

The proposed method was implemented using MATLAB version R 2016b and R-studio version 3.4.1 programming languages. All experiments were run using the same configuration on a personal computer, including an Intel ($^\circledR$) Core (^{TM}) i7 CPU with 3.4 GHz and 8 GB memory on Windows 10 operating system. The performance of the proposed method was evaluated using three classifiers multi-layer perceptron (MLP), classification and regression trees (CART), and K-nearest neighbors (KNN). In addition, k-fold cross-validation with k = 5 was considered to alleviate the bias caused by the random selection of the dataset.

4.2. Clinical Data Collecting and Description of IRDia Dataset

In our case study, the Iran diabetes (IRDia) dataset was collected in a 10-month process in private medical clinics. The IRDia dataset is partially considered including 2074 cases with 56 features in which 42.8% of the participants were male, and 57.2% were female. Furthermore, 26.6% of people were labeled as patients with diabetes, and 73.4% of them were labeled as patients without diabetes by the endocrinologist. The description of IRDia's features and their missing data patterns are reported in Table 1, where MP, LI, CARR, LCTV, CRM, and CMC are, respectively, standing for missing by purpose, logically imputable, logically can take a value, cause, and reason relationship, completely random missing and cause of missingness is manifest. The last column shows the type of missing data pattern for each feature by investigating relationships between the biological characteristics of the features and their conditions.

Table 1. Description of the IRDia's features and their missing data patterns (MDPs).

No.	Feature Name	MP	LI	CARR	LCTV	CRM	CMC	MDPs
F_1	Body fat	✓	-	-	✓	✓	✓	MNAR
F_2	Pregnancy	✓	-	✓	-	-	✓	MNAR
F_3	The total number of pregnancies	✓	-	✓	-	-	✓	MNAR
F_4	Pregnancy diabetes	✓	-	✓	-	-	✓	MNAR
F_5	Background of miscarriage	✓	-	✓	-	-	✓	MNAR
F_6	Background of birthing dead baby	✓	-	✓	-	-	✓	MNAR
F_7	Background of a premature baby	✓	-	✓	-	-	✓	MNAR
F_8	Macrosomia (babies weighing > 4kg)	✓	-	✓	-	-	✓	MNAR
F_9	Forearm measurement	✓	-	-	✓	✓	✓	MNAR
F_{10}	Muscle	✓	-	-	✓	✓	✓	MNAR
F_{11}	Visceral fat level	✓	-	-	✓	✓	✓	MNAR
F_{12}	Mid upper arm circumference (MUAC)	✓	-	-	✓	✓	✓	MNAR
F_{13}	Polycystic ovary syndrome (PCOS)	✓	-	✓	-	-	✓	MNAR
F_{14}	Leg width measurement	✓	-	-	✓	✓	✓	MNAR
F_{15}	Basal metabolic rate (BMR)	✓	-	-	✓	✓	✓	MNAR
F_{16}	Blood types	✓	-	-	✓	✓	✓	MNAR
F_{17}	Prostate-specific antigen (PSA)	✓	-	✓	-	-	✓	MNAR-MCAR
F_{18}	Calcium (Ca)	-	✓	-	✓	✓	-	MCAR
F_{19}	Vitamin d 25-hydroxy test	-	✓	-	✓	✓	-	MCAR
F_{20}	Iron	-	✓	-	✓	✓	-	MCAR
F_{21}	Phosphorus (PO4)	-	✓	-	✓	✓	-	MCAR
F_{22}	Sodium (NA)	-	✓	-	✓	✓	-	MCAR
F_{23}	Folic acid	-	✓	-	✓	✓	-	MCAR
F_{24}	Total iron-binding capacity (TIBC)	-	✓	-	✓	✓	-	MCAR
F_{25}	Fasting blood sugar (FBS)	✓	✓	✓	✓	-	✓	MAR
F_{26}	2-h post-prandial blood glucose (2hPG) test	✓	✓	✓	✓	-	✓	MAR
F_{27}	Glucose 5pm (G 5pm)	✓	✓	✓	✓	-	✓	MAR
F_{28}	Blood urea nitrogen (BUN)	✓	✓	✓	✓	-	✓	MAR
F_{29}	Creatinine blood test (Cr)	✓	✓	✓	✓	-	✓	MAR
F_{30}	Uric acid blood test	✓	✓	✓	✓	-	✓	MAR
F_{31}	Triglycerides blood test	✓	✓	✓	✓	-	✓	MAR
F_{32}	Cholesterol	✓	✓	✓	✓	-	✓	MAR
F_{33}	High-density lipoprotein (HDL) cholesterol	✓	✓	✓	✓	-	✓	MAR
F_{34}	Low-density lipoprotein (LDL) cholesterol	✓	✓	✓	✓	-	✓	MAR
F_{35}	Serum glutamic oxaloacetic transaminase (SGOT)	✓	✓	✓	✓	-	✓	MAR
F_{36}	Serum glutamic pyruvic transaminase (SGPT)	✓	✓	✓	✓	-	✓	MAR
F_{37}	Hemoglobin A1c (HbA1c)	✓	✓	✓	✓	-	✓	MAR
F_{38}	Potassium blood test	-	✓	-	✓	✓	-	MCAR
F_{39}	Thyroid stimulating hormone (TSH)	✓	✓	✓	✓	-	✓	MAR
F_{40}	Triiodothyronine (T3)	✓	✓	✓	✓	-	✓	MAR
F_{41}	T3 uptake (T3RU)	✓	✓	✓	✓	-	✓	MAR
F_{42}	Total thyroxine (T4) test	✓	✓	✓	✓	-	✓	MAR
F_{43}	Erythrocyte sedimentation rate (ESR 1hr)	-	✓	-	✓	✓	-	MCAR
F_{44}	C-reactive protein (CRP)	-	✓	-	✓	✓	-	MCAR
F_{45}	Alkaline phosphatase (ALP)	-	✓	-	✓	✓	-	MCAR
F_{46}	Ferritin	-	✓	-	✓	✓	-	MCAR
F_{47}	Urine culture	✓	✓	✓	✓	-	✓	MAR
F_{48}	Urine color	✓	✓	✓	✓	-	✓	MAR
F_{49}	Urine appearance	✓	✓	✓	✓	-	✓	MAR
F_{50}	Urine specific gravity	✓	✓	✓	✓	-	✓	MAR
F_{51}	Urine pH test	✓	✓	✓	✓	-	✓	MAR
F_{52}	Urine nitrate test (NT)	✓	✓	✓	✓	-	✓	MAR
F_{53}	Urine glucose test	✓	✓	✓	✓	-	✓	MAR
F_{54}	Urine ketones test	✓	✓	✓	✓	-	✓	MAR
F_{55}	Urine protein test	✓	✓	✓	✓	-	✓	MAR
F_{56}	Hemoglobin in the urine (hemoglobinuria)	✓	✓	✓	✓	-	✓	MAR

4.3. Missing Data Pattern Analysis

The IRDia dataset consists of three different missing data patterns MNAR, MCAR, and MAR which their descriptive analyses are as follows.

-MNAR pattern analysis: In the IRDia dataset, 17 features follow the MNAR pattern, among which the four features of body fat, basal metabolic rate (BMR), visceral fat, and muscle had, respectively, 1.9%, 4.5%, 2%, and 1.9% incorrect numerical values that were deleted. In this case, not only the cause of missingness was completely clear, but the missing values can also be logically initiated, and the missingness cannot be documented from other features in the dataset because these values were obtained by the signal sent and received within the individual's body. The blood group feature had 41.9% missingness. This feature can be logically measured, but missingness in this feature cannot be documented from other features. The cause of this missingness was completely clear, which was due to the participant's unawareness or non-registration of the values in the blood test. This feature was never influenced by clinical and biological factors; thus, it did not seem reasonable to impute it. These missing values were placed with a "non-determined" constant global label value.

Eight other features are related to the pregnancy features, all of which had missingness of 42.8% for male participants. Logically, there was no possible appropriate value for imputation in these values numerically. This missingness was not random, and the cause of missingness was completely clear. Furthermore, the prostate-specific antigen (PSA) feature, which was related to the prostatic enzyme measurement in men, had 57.2% missingness for females. The missingness in these nine features was initiated with the "non-determined" global constant. The MNAR pattern analysis of the IRDia is shown in Figure 3.

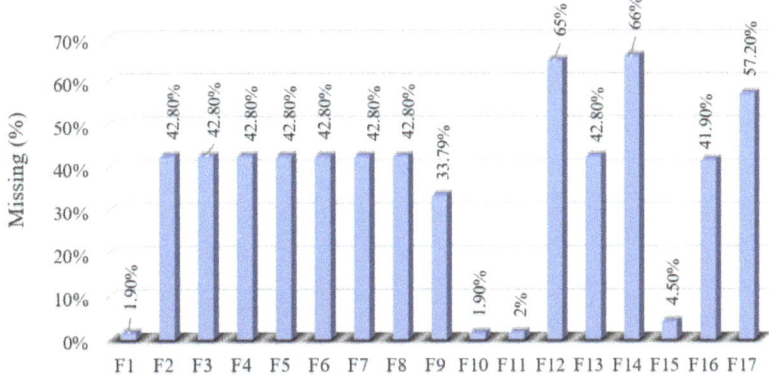

Figure 3. The MNAR pattern analysis of the IRDia dataset.

-MCAR pattern analysis: There are 13 laboratory features with missing values and there is no intermediate relationship associated with any of them on the condition of another, according to the physician. Therefore, the reasons for missingness occurrence in these features are not related to other data observations. The missingness in these features can result from completely random reasons such as operator's mistake in importing the data, lack of the patient's request for the test factor, unnecessary measurement of that factor for the participant in physician's viewpoint, or measurement of that value in near past. Therefore, the missing values in these features are categorized in the MCAR pattern. These features contributed to the diagnosis of diabetes and, thus, the imputation of the missingness in these values was necessary. The other missing values of the PSA feature were considered in this missing data pattern after initializing by the MNAR hypothesis. Figure 4 presents the percentage of the MCAR pattern of the related features in the IRDia dataset.

-MAR pattern analysis: Figure 5 shows the percentage of the MAR pattern for 27 features categorized by the endocrinologist consultation. These features can interchangeably affect each other in terms of value and lack of value. These features are interrelated and can be initiated biologically for all participants. The missingness in these features can be estimated through other features and is related to the observed values. Once missingness occurs in these features, the cause of missingness is not completely random because the missingness can be affected by the numerical range or the absence of value in another feature. The occurrence of missingness in features depends on their cause-effect relationships with each other. According to the definition of random missingness, these features include this type of missing data pattern.

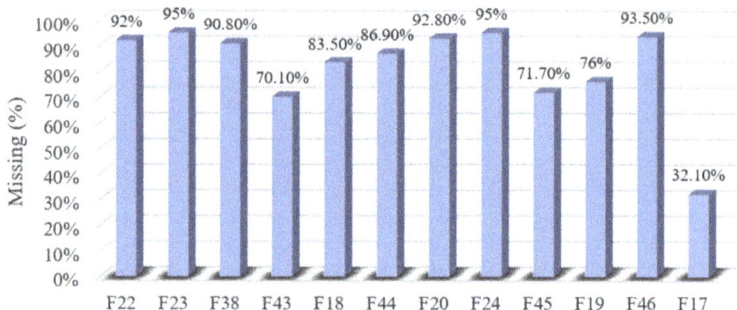

Figure 4. The MCAR pattern analysis of the IRDia dataset.

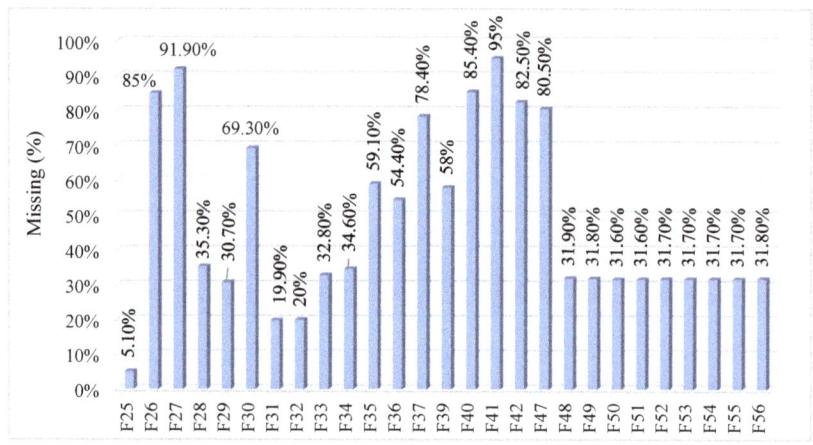

Figure 5. The MAR pattern analysis of the IRDia dataset.

4.4. Experiments and Results

In this section, the performance of the proposed HIMP method in the IRDia dataset is evaluated by the following three experiment sets. In all experiment sets, the results of the HIMP and other comparative methods are assessed using different classifiers in terms of the accuracy, precision, recall, and F_1-score using Equations (4)–(7), respectively. The true classifications are denoted by the number of true positives (TP) and the number of true negatives (TN), while misclassifications are denoted by the number of false positives (FP) and the number of false negatives (FN). In the following three experiment sets, first, the single imputation methods are performed to create the WinnerD$_{MCAR}$ dataset. Then, the multiple imputations methods are conducted to determine the WinnerD$_{MAR}$ dataset. Finally, the winner datasets selected from the single and multiple imputation methods are merged to evaluate the HIMP.

$$Accuracy\ (\%) = \frac{TN + TP}{TN + TP + FN + FP} \tag{4}$$

$$Precision\ (\%) = \frac{TP}{TP + FP} \tag{5}$$

$$Recall\ (\%) = \frac{TP}{TP + FN} \tag{6}$$

$$F_1 - score \; (\%) = \frac{TP}{TP + \frac{1}{2}(FP + FN)} \qquad (7)$$

- Single imputation experiment

  In this experiment set, the single imputation methods KNN and hot-deck compete for imputing missing values with MCAR patterns to determine the WinnerD$_\text{MCAR}$ dataset. The results reported in Table 2 show that the KNN imputation method has better performance. One of the causes of low accuracy of classification in multiple imputations could be the lack of important biological factors in the diagnosis of diabetes, such as fasting blood sugar as well as the high percentage of missingness in the imputed dataset.

Table 2. Single imputation comparison on the MCAR dataset.

Assessing Metrics (%)	Classifiers	Hot-Deck Imputation Method	KNN Imputation Method
Accuracy	MLP	75.01%	78.56%
	KNN	70.40%	74.05%
	CART	71.26%	79.05%
Precision	MLP	76.21%	77.01%
	KNN	69.34%	70.91%
	CART	68.71%	71.55%
Recall	MLP	75.28%	77.21%
	KNN	67.63%	69.18%
	CART	70.92%	72.45%
F$_1$-score	MLP	75.74%	77.11%
	KNN	68.47%	70.03%
	CART	69.80%	71.80%

- Multiple imputation experiment

  In this experiment, the Em, MICE, and MCMC multiple imputation methods are considered to impute missing values with MAR patterns in the IRDia dataset and determine the WinnerD$_\text{MAR}$ dataset by comparing the performance of different classifiers. The multiple imputation method compensates for the imputed uncertainty relative to the unmeasured data, which results in the occurrence of missingness, by generating several datasets. The classification accuracy rate of all the imputed datasets is measured by the CART decision tree classifier. Then, the dataset with the maximum accuracy rate is selected. The selected dataset is the best-imputed dataset and contains imputed data with minimum uncertainty relative to the unmeasured data. The obtained results from this experimental evaluation are reported in Table 3. The MICE method exhibited better performance than the two other methods in the IRDia dataset.

Table 3. Multiple imputation comparison on the MAR dataset.

Assessing Metrics (%)	Classifiers	Em Imputation	MCMC Imputation	MICE Imputation
Accuracy	MLP	86.34%	85.01%	91.04%
	KNN	82.66%	79.61%	83.23%
	CART	83.77%	82.95%	84.67%
Precision	MLP	82.47%	87.16%	90.50%
	KNN	81.42%	78.80%	82.23%
	CART	80.66%	79.57%	83.26%
Recall	MLP	81.09%	80.65%	86.97%
	KNN	79.65%	71.27%	85.53%
	CART	80.79%	79.15%	81.23%
F$_1$-score	MLP	81.77%	83.78%	88.70%
	KNN	80.53%	74.85%	83.85%
	CART	80.73%	79.36%	82.23%

- Evaluation of the HIMP imputation method

  Once the best single and multiple imputation methods were obtained, imputed datasets WinnerD$_{MCAR}$ and WinnerD$_{MAR}$ with the best results were used to merge the final dataset. Then, the KNN and MICE methods, which yielded the best results, were implemented separately on the entire dataset with missing values. In this experimental evaluation, the hybrid imputation method is compared with MICE [71], KNN [65], fuzzy c-means SvrGa imputation (SvrFcmGa) [59], and without the applying of imputation (along with the missing values) on the IRDia dataset. The obtained results are reported in Table 4. The experimental results demonstrated that the proposed HIMP method yields more sufficient than other imputation methods.

Table 4. Comparing the HIMP method with other imputation methods.

Assessing Metrics	Classifiers	Without-Imputation	MICE Imputation	KNN Imputation	SvrFcmGa Imputation	HIMP Method
Accuracy	MLP	75.43%	91.56%	78.56%	90.21%	94.23%
	KNN	72.31%	83.20%	74.95%	83.91%	85.91%
	CART	74.82%	84.67%	79.52%	82.49%	86.38%
Precision	MLP	73.45%	90.50%	77.01%	89.54%	91.68%
	KNN	71.59%	82.23%	70.91%	80.25%	86.47%
	CART	72.87%	83.26%	71.55%	81.12%	85.27%
Recall	MLP	71.95%	86.97%	77.21%	88.94%	96.36%
	KNN	69.53%	85.53%	69.18%	79.48%	83.94%
	CART	68.28%	81.23%	72.45%	80.67%	84.57%
F$_1$-score	MLP	72.69%	88.70%	77.11%	89.24%	93.97%
	KNN	70.55%	83.85%	70.03%	79.86%	85.19%
	CART	70.50%	82.23%	71.80%	80.89%	84.92%

Moreover, the receiver operating characteristic (ROC) curve of the best performance of the proposed HIMP method gained by using the MLP classifier is shown in Figure 6.

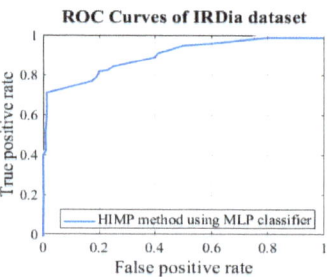

Figure 6. ROC curve of the best performance of the HIMP method.

5. Conclusions

In real-world medical datasets, the missing data usually occur with different patterns. Failure in identifying the type of missing data pattern and applying imputation methods regardless of the missingness type can reduce the performance of classifiers. Many imputation methods are developed to impute the missing data, however, most of them still do not fulfill different missing data patterns. Therefore, in this paper, first, a four-layer model consisting of analyzing, decomposing, imputing, and merging layers is presented. Then, based on the introduced model a hybrid imputation method (HIMP) is developed to cope with different missing data patterns in the real IRDia dataset collected in our case study. The HIMP consists of six steps: analyzing missing data patterns, imputing missing data with MNAR patterns, decomposing, single imputing, multiple imputing, and hybrid imputation. Since HIMP decomposes dataset imputed by its second steps into two datasets

D_{MCAR} and D_{MAR}, it can provide the best estimations by different single and multiple imputations for random and completely random missing data patterns. In fact, the HIMP personalizes the imputation of each type of missing data pattern to find the best estimations and in the end merge them to form the final imputed dataset.

In the experimental evaluation, HIMP and comparative methods were compared using different classifiers in terms of accuracy, precision, recall, and F_1-score. The single and multiple imputation experiments were tabulated in Tables 2 and 3. The obtained results of comparing the HIMP method with imputation methods reported in Table 4 demonstrated that the proposed method yields more sufficient than other imputation methods. The experimental results showed that the HIMP method can make use of the similarity between the same missing data patterns when the original dataset consisted of different missing data patterns such as the real IRDia. The classifiers' performance over IRDia dataset imputed by the HIMP method proved that the introduced model can be effectively applied to develop hybrid imputation methods for multi-pattern missing data.

In further studies, the introduced model can be applied to develop more effective hybrid imputation methods using a variety of techniques. The HIMP method can also be adapted for other complex datasets with multi-pattern missing data such as microarray gene expression data. Moreover, the HIMP can be improved using other single and multiple imputation methods.

Author Contributions: Conceptualization, M.H.N.-S. and S.M.; methodology, M.H.N.-S., S.M. and H.Z.; software, M.H.N.-S., S.M. and H.Z.; validation, M.H.N.-S., S.M. and H.Z.; formal analysis, M.H.N.-S., S.M. and H.Z.; investigation, M.H.N.-S., S.M. and H.Z.; resources, M.H.N.-S., S.M., M.G. and A.H.G.; data curation, M.H.N.-S., S.M. and H.Z.; writing, M.H.N.-S., S.M. and H.Z.; original draft preparation, M.H.N.-S., S.M. and H.Z.; writing—review and editing, M.H.N.-S., S.M., H.Z., M.G. and A.H.G.; visualization, M.H.N.-S., S.M. and A.H.G.; supervision, M.H.N.-S. and A.H.G.; project administration, M.H.N.-S. and A.H.G. All authors have read and agreed to the published version of the manuscript.

Funding: This research received no external funding.

Institutional Review Board Statement: Not applicable.

Informed Consent Statement: Not applicable.

Data Availability Statement: The data and code used in the research can be obtained from the corresponding author upon request.

Conflicts of Interest: The authors declare no conflict of interest.

References

1. Fana, S.E.; Esmaeili, F.; Esmaeili, S.; Bandaryan, F.; Esfahani, E.N.; Amoli, M.M.; Razi, F. Knowledge discovery in genetics of diabetes in Iran, a roadmap for future researches. *J. Diabetes Metab. Disord.* **2021**, *20*, 1785–1791. [CrossRef] [PubMed]
2. Nejat, N.; Hezave, A.K.M.; Pour, S.M.A.; Rezaei, K.; Moslemi, A.; Mehrabi, F. Self-care and related factors in patients with type II diabetes in Iran. *J. Diabetes Metab. Disord.* **2021**, *20*, 635–639. [CrossRef] [PubMed]
3. Tigga, N.P.; Garg, S. Prediction of type 2 diabetes using machine learning classification methods. *Procedia Comput. Sci.* **2020**, *167*, 706–716. [CrossRef]
4. Ogurtsova, K.; da Rocha Fernandes, J.; Huang, Y.; Linnenkamp, U.; Guariguata, L.; Cho, N.; Cavan, D.; Shaw, J.; Makaroff, L. IDF Diabetes Atlas: Global estimates for the prevalence of diabetes for 2015 and 2040. *Diabetes Res. Clin. Pract.* **2017**, *128*, 40–50. [CrossRef] [PubMed]
5. Farshchi, A.; Esteghamati, A.; Sari, A.A.; Kebriaeezadeh, A.; Abdollahi, M.; Dorkoosh, F.A.; Khamseh, M.E.; Aghili, R.; Keshtkar, A.; Ebadi, M. The cost of diabetes chronic complications among Iranian people with type 2 diabetes mellitus. *J. Diabetes Metab. Disord.* **2014**, *13*, 4. [CrossRef]
6. Noshad, S.; Afarideh, M.; Heidari, B.; Mechanick, J.I.; Esteghamati, A. Diabetes care in Iran: Where we stand and where we are headed. *Ann. Glob. Health* **2015**, *81*, 839–850. [CrossRef] [PubMed]
7. Swapna, G.; Vinayakumar, R.; Soman, K. Diabetes detection using deep learning algorithms. *ICT express* **2018**, *4*, 243–246.
8. Alirezaei, M.; Niaki, S.T.A.; Niaki, S.A.A. A bi-objective hybrid optimization algorithm to reduce noise and data dimension in diabetes diagnosis using support vector machines. *Expert Syst. Appl.* **2019**, *127*, 47–57. [CrossRef]
9. Kamel, S.R.; Yaghoubzadeh, R. Feature selection using grasshopper optimization algorithm in diagnosis of diabetes disease. *Inform. Med. Unlocked* **2021**, *26*, 100707. [CrossRef]

10. Qiao, L.; Zhu, Y.; Zhou, H. Diabetic retinopathy detection using prognosis of microaneurysm and early diagnosis system for non-proliferative diabetic retinopathy based on deep learning algorithms. *IEEE Access* **2020**, *8*, 104292–104302. [CrossRef]
11. Harding, J.L.; Pavkov, M.E.; Magliano, D.J.; Shaw, J.E.; Gregg, E.W. Global trends in diabetes complications: A review of current evidence. *Diabetologia* **2019**, *62*, 3–16. [CrossRef]
12. Taheri, H.; Rafaiee, R.; Rafaiee, R. Prevalence of Complications of Diabetes and Risk Factors Among Patients with Diabetes in the Diabetes Clinic in Southeast of Iran. *Iran. J. Diabetes Obes.* **2021**, *13*, 10–18. [CrossRef]
13. Schlienger, J.-L. Type 2 diabetes complications. *Presse Med.* **2013**, *42*, 839–848. [CrossRef] [PubMed]
14. Vigneri, P.; Frasca, F.; Sciacca, L.; Pandini, G.; Vigneri, R. Diabetes and cancer. *Endocr.-Relat. Cancer* **2009**, *16*, 1103–1123. [CrossRef]
15. Ferro, M.; Katalin, M.O.; Buonerba, C.; Marian, R.; Cantiello, F.; Musi, G.; Di Stasi, S.; Hurle, R.; Guazzoni, G.; Busetto, G.M. Type 2 diabetes mellitus predicts worse outcomes in patients with high-grade T1 bladder cancer receiving bacillus Calmette-Guérin after transurethral resection of the bladder tumor. *Urol. Oncol. Semin. Orig. Investig.* **2020**, *38*, 459–464. [CrossRef] [PubMed]
16. Giovannone, R.; Busetto, G.M.; Antonini, G.; De Cobelli, O.; Ferro, M.; Tricarico, S.; Del Giudice, F.; Ragonesi, G.; Conti, S.L.; Lucarelli, G. Hyperhomocysteinemia as an early predictor of erectile dysfunction: International Index of Erectile Function (IIEF) and penile Doppler ultrasound correlation with plasma levels of homocysteine. *Medicine* **2015**, *94*, e1556. [CrossRef]
17. Mellitus, D. Diagnosis and classification of diabetes mellitus. *Diabetes care* **2006**, *29*, S43.
18. Deshpande, A.D.; Harris-Hayes, M.; Schootman, M. Epidemiology of diabetes and diabetes-related complications. *Phys. Ther.* **2008**, *88*, 1254–1264. [CrossRef] [PubMed]
19. Rahaman, S. Diabetes diagnosis decision support system based on symptoms, signs and risk factor using special computational algorithm by rule base. In Proceedings of the 2012 15th International Conference on Computer and Information Technology (ICCIT), Chittagong, Bangladesh, 22–24 December 2012; pp. 65–71.
20. Omisore, O.M.; Ojokoh, B.A.; Babalola, A.E.; Igbe, T.; Folajimi, Y.; Nie, Z.; Wang, L. An affective learning-based system for diagnosis and personalized management of diabetes mellitus. *Future Gener. Comput. Syst.* **2021**, *117*, 273–290. [CrossRef]
21. Qurat-Ul-Ain, F.A.; Ejaz, M.Y. A comparative analysis on diagnosis of diabetes mellitus using different approaches–A survey. *Inform. Med. Unlocked* **2020**, *21*, 100482.
22. Golestan Hashemi, F.S.; Razi Ismail, M.; Rafii Yusop, M.; Golestan Hashemi, M.S.; Nadimi Shahraki, M.H.; Rastegari, H.; Miah, G.; Aslani, F. Intelligent mining of large-scale bio-data: Bioinformatics applications. *Biotechnol. Biotechnol. Equip.* **2018**, *32*, 10–29. [CrossRef]
23. Esfandiari, N.; Babavalian, M.R.; Moghadam, A.-M.E.; Tabar, V.K. Knowledge discovery in medicine: Current issue and future trend. *Expert Syst. Appl.* **2014**, *41*, 4434–4463. [CrossRef]
24. Fasihi, M.; Nadimi-Shahraki, M.H. Multi-class cardiovascular diseases diagnosis from electrocardiogram signals using 1-D convolution neural network. In Proceedings of the 2020 IEEE 21st International Conference on Information Reuse and Integration for Data Science (IRI), Las Vegas, NV, USA, 11–13 August 2020; pp. 372–378.
25. Bai, B.M.; Nalini, B.; Majumdar, J. Analysis and detection of diabetes using data mining techniques—a big data application in health care. In *Emerging Research in Computing, Information, Communication and Applications*; Springer: Berlin/Heidelberg, Germany, 2019; pp. 443–455.
26. Zamani, H.; Nadimi-Shahraki, M.-H. Swarm intelligence approach for breast cancer diagnosis. *Int. J. Comput. Appl.* **2016**, *151*, 40–44. [CrossRef]
27. Fasihi, M.; Nadimi-Shahraki, M.H.; Jannesari, A. A Shallow 1-D Convolution Neural Network for Fetal State Assessment Based on Cardiotocogram. *SN Comput. Sci.* **2021**, *2*, 287. [CrossRef]
28. Dagliati, A.; Marini, S.; Sacchi, L.; Cogni, G.; Teliti, M.; Tibollo, V.; De Cata, P.; Chiovato, L.; Bellazzi, R. Machine learning methods to predict diabetes complications. *J. Diabetes Sci. Technol.* **2018**, *12*, 295–302. [CrossRef]
29. Hasan, M.K.; Alam, M.A.; Das, D.; Hossain, E.; Hasan, M. Diabetes prediction using ensembling of different machine learning classifiers. *IEEE Access* **2020**, *8*, 76516–76531. [CrossRef]
30. Kavakiotis, I.; Tsave, O.; Salifoglou, A.; Maglaveras, N.; Vlahavas, I.; Chouvarda, I. Machine learning and data mining methods in diabetes research. *Comput. Struct. Biotechnol. J.* **2017**, *15*, 104–116. [CrossRef]
31. Zheng, T.; Xie, W.; Xu, L.; He, X.; Zhang, Y.; You, M.; Yang, G.; Chen, Y. A machine learning-based framework to identify type 2 diabetes through electronic health records. *Int. J. Med. Inform.* **2017**, *97*, 120–127. [CrossRef]
32. Nadimi-Shaharaki, M.H.; Ghahramani, M. Efficient data preparation techniques for diabetes detection. In Proceedings of the IEEE EUROCON 2015-International Conference on Computer as a Tool (EUROCON), Salamanca, Spain, 8–11 September 2015; pp. 1–6.
33. Eisemann, N.; Waldmann, A.; Katalinic, A. Imputation of missing values of tumour stage in population-based cancer registration. *BMC Med. Res. Methodol.* **2011**, *11*, 129. [CrossRef] [PubMed]
34. Yoo, I.; Alafaireet, P.; Marinov, M.; Pena-Hernandez, K.; Gopidi, R.; Chang, J.-F.; Hua, L. Data mining in healthcare and biomedicine: A survey of the literature. *J. Med. Syst.* **2012**, *36*, 2431–2448. [CrossRef]
35. Nadimi-Shahraki, M.H.; Banaie-Dezfouli, M.; Zamani, H.; Taghian, S.; Mirjalili, S. B-MFO: A Binary Moth-Flame Optimization for Feature Selection from Medical Datasets. *Computers* **2021**, *10*, 136. [CrossRef]
36. Zamani, H.; Nadimi-Shahraki, M.H. Feature selection based on whale optimization algorithm for diseases diagnosis. *Int. J. Comput. Sci. Inf. Secur.* **2016**, *14*, 1243.

37. Ramli, M.N.; Yahaya, A.; Ramli, N.; Yusof, N.; Abdullah, M. Roles of imputation methods for filling the missing values: A review. *Adv. Environ. Biol.* **2013**, *7*, 3861–3870.
38. Nadimi-Shahraki, M.H.; Taghian, S.; Mirjalili, S. An improved grey wolf optimizer for solving engineering problems. *Expert Syst. Appl.* **2021**, *166*, 113917. [CrossRef]
39. Zamani, H.; Nadimi-Shahraki, M.H.; Gandomi, A.H. QANA: Quantum-based avian navigation optimizer algorithm. *Eng. Appl. Artif. Intell.* **2021**, *104*, 104314. [CrossRef]
40. Nadimi-Shahraki, M.H.; Fatahi, A.; Zamani, H.; Mirjalili, S.; Abualigah, L. An Improved Moth-Flame Optimization Algorithm with Adaptation Mechanism to Solve Numerical and Mechanical Engineering Problems. *Entropy* **2021**, *23*, 1637. [CrossRef]
41. Zamani, H.; Nadimi-Shahraki, M.H.; Gandomi, A.H. CCSA: Conscious neighborhood-based crow search algorithm for solving global optimization problems. *Appl. Soft Comput.* **2019**, *85*, 105583. [CrossRef]
42. Enders, C.K. *Applied Missing Data Analysis*; Guilford Press: New York, NY, USA, 2010.
43. Fazakis, N.; Kostopoulos, G.; Kotsiantis, S.; Mporas, I. Iterative robust semi-supervised missing data imputation. *IEEE Access* **2020**, *8*, 90555–90569. [CrossRef]
44. McKnight, P.E.; McKnight, K.M.; Sidani, S.; Figueredo, A.J. *Missing Data: A Gentle Introduction*; Guilford Press: New York, NY, USA, 2007.
45. Lin, W.-C.; Tsai, C.-F. Missing value imputation: A review and analysis of the literature (2006–2017). *Artif. Intell. Rev.* **2020**, *53*, 1487–1509. [CrossRef]
46. Cismondi, F.; Fialho, A.S.; Vieira, S.M.; Reti, S.R.; Sousa, J.M.; Finkelstein, S.N. Missing data in medical databases: Impute, delete or classify? *Artif. Intell. Med.* **2013**, *58*, 63–72. [CrossRef]
47. Little, R.J.; Rubin, D.B. *Statistical Analysis with Missing Data*; John Wiley & Sons: Hoboken, NJ, USA, 2019; Volume 793.
48. Han, J.; Kamber, M.; Pei, J. Data preprocessing. In *Data Mining Concepts and Techniques*; Morgan Kaufmann: San Francisco, CA, USA, 2006; pp. 47–97.
49. Graham, J.W. Missing data analysis: Making it work in the real world. *Ann. Rev. Psychol.* **2009**, *60*, 549–576. [CrossRef]
50. Marwala, T. *Computational Intelligence for Missing Data Imputation, Estimation, and Management: Knowledge Optimization Techniques*; IGI Global: Hershey, PA, USA, 2009.
51. Thomas, R.M.; Bruin, W.; Zhutovsky, P.; van Wingen, G. Dealing with missing data, small sample sizes, and heterogeneity in machine learning studies of brain disorders. In *Machine Learning*; Elsevier: Amsterdam, The Netherlands, 2020; pp. 249–266.
52. Carpenter, J.; Kenward, M. *Multiple Imputation and Its Application*; John Wiley & Sons: Hoboken, NJ, USA, 2012.
53. Van der Heijden, G.J.; Donders, A.R.T.; Stijnen, T.; Moons, K.G. Imputation of missing values is superior to complete case analysis and the missing-indicator method in multivariable diagnostic research: A clinical example. *J. Clin. Epidemiol.* **2006**, *59*, 1102–1109. [CrossRef] [PubMed]
54. Raghunathan, K.; Soundarapandian, R.K.; Gandomi, A.H.; Ramachandran, M.; Patan, R.; Madda, R.B. Duo-stage decision: A framework for filling missing values, consistency check, and repair of decision matrices in multicriteria group decision making. *IEEE Trans. Eng. Manag.* **2019**, *68*, 1773–1785. [CrossRef]
55. Masconi, K.L.; Matsha, T.E.; Echouffo-Tcheugui, J.B.; Erasmus, R.T.; Kengne, A.P. Reporting and handling of missing data in predictive research for prevalent undiagnosed type 2 diabetes mellitus: A systematic review. *EPMA J.* **2015**, *6*, 7. [CrossRef]
56. Rezvan, P.H.; Lee, K.J.; Simpson, J.A. The rise of multiple imputation: A review of the reporting and implementation of the method in medical research. *BMC Med. Res. Methodol.* **2015**, *15*, 30.
57. Gómez-Carracedo, M.; Andrade, J.; López-Mahía, P.; Muniategui, S.; Prada, D. A practical comparison of single and multiple imputation methods to handle complex missing data in air quality datasets. *Chemom. Intell. Lab. Syst.* **2014**, *134*, 23–33. [CrossRef]
58. Rubin, D.B.; Schenker, N. Multiple imputation in health-are databases: An overview and some applications. *Stat. Med.* **1991**, *10*, 585–598. [CrossRef]
59. Aydilek, I.B.; Arslan, A. A hybrid method for imputation of missing values using optimized fuzzy c-means with support vector regression and a genetic algorithm. *Inf. Sci.* **2013**, *233*, 25–35. [CrossRef]
60. Li, D.; Zhang, H.; Li, T.; Bouras, A.; Yu, X.; Wang, T. Hybrid Missing Value Imputation Algorithms Using Fuzzy C-Means and Vaguely Quantified Rough Set. *IEEE Trans. Fuzzy Syst.* **2021**. accepted. [CrossRef]
61. Purwar, A.; Singh, S.K. Hybrid prediction model with missing value imputation for medical data. *Expert Syst. Appl.* **2015**, *42*, 5621–5631. [CrossRef]
62. Rani, P.; Kumar, R.; Jain, A. HIOC: A hybrid imputation method to predict missing values in medical datasets. *Int. J. Intell. Comput. Cybern.* **2021**, *14*, 598–661. [CrossRef]
63. Tian, J.; Yu, B.; Yu, D.; Ma, S. Missing data analyses: A hybrid multiple imputation algorithm using gray system theory and entropy based on clustering. *Appl. Intell.* **2014**, *40*, 376–388. [CrossRef]
64. Vazifehdan, M.; Moattar, M.H.; Jalali, M. A hybrid Bayesian network and tensor factorization approach for missing value imputation to improve breast cancer recurrence prediction. *J. King Saud Univ. Comput. Inf. Sci.* **2019**, *31*, 175–184. [CrossRef]
65. Malarvizhi, R.; Thanamani, A.S. K-nearest neighbor in missing data imputation. *Int. J. Eng. Res. Dev.* **2012**, *5*, 5–7.
66. Ford, B.L. An overview of hot-deck procedures. In *Incomplete Data in Sample Surveys*; Academic Press: New York, NY, USA, 1983; Volume 2, pp. 185–207.
67. Neal, R.M. *Probabilistic Inference Using Markov Chain Monte Carlo Methods*; Department of Computer Science, University of Toronto: Toronto, ON, Canada, 1993.

68. Roth, P.L.; Switzer, F.S., III. A Monte Carlo analysis of missing data techniques in a HRM setting. *J. Manag.* **1995**, *21*, 1003–1023. [CrossRef]
69. Roth, P.L.; Switzer, F.S., III; Switzer, D.M. Missing data in multiple item scales: A Monte Carlo analysis of missing data techniques. *Organ. Res. Methods* **1999**, *2*, 211–232. [CrossRef]
70. Raghunathan, T.E.; Lepkowski, J.M.; Van Hoewyk, J.; Solenberger, P. A multivariate technique for multiply imputing missing values using a sequence of regression models. *Surv. Methodol.* **2001**, *27*, 85–96.
71. Van Buuren, S.; Groothuis-Oudshoorn, K. mice: Multivariate imputation by chained equations in R. *J. Stat. Softw.* **2011**, *45*, 1–67. [CrossRef]
72. Dempster, A.P.; Laird, N.M.; Rubin, D.B. Maximum likelihood from incomplete data via the EM algorithm. *J. R. Stat. Soc. Ser. B Methodol.* **1977**, *39*, 1–22.
73. Dixon, J.K. Pattern recognition with partly missing data. *IEEE Trans. Syst. Man Cybern.* **1979**, *9*, 617–621. [CrossRef]
74. García-Laencina, P.J.; Sancho-Gómez, J.-L.; Figueiras-Vidal, A.R. Pattern classification with missing data: A review. *Neural Comput. Appl.* **2010**, *19*, 263–282. [CrossRef]
75. Norazian, M.N.; Shukri, A.; Yahaya, P.; Azam, N.; Ramli, P.; Fitri, N.F.; Yusof, M.; Mohd Mustafa Al Bakri, A. Roles of imputation methods for filling the missing values: A review. *Adv. Environ. Biol.* **2013**, *7*, 3861–3869.
76. Chowdhury, M.H.; Islam, M.K.; Khan, S.I. Imputation of missing healthcare data. In Proceedings of the 2017 20th International Conference of Computer and Information Technology (ICCIT), Dhaka, Bangladesh, 22–24 December 2017; pp. 1–6.
77. Feng, R.; Grana, D.; Balling, N. Imputation of missing well log data by random forest and its uncertainty analysis. *Comput. Geosci.* **2021**, *152*, 104763. [CrossRef]
78. Hegde, H.; Shimpi, N.; Panny, A.; Glurich, I.; Christie, P.; Acharya, A. MICE vs. PPCA: Missing data imputation in healthcare. *Inform. Med. Unlocked* **2019**, *17*, 100275. [CrossRef]
79. Jerez, J.M.; Molina, I.; García-Laencina, P.J.; Alba, E.; Ribelles, N.; Martín, M.; Franco, L. Missing data imputation using statistical and machine learning methods in a real breast cancer problem. *Artif. Intell. Med.* **2010**, *50*, 105–115. [CrossRef]
80. Liu, Z.-g.; Pan, Q.; Dezert, J.; Martin, A. Adaptive imputation of missing values for incomplete pattern classification. *Pattern Recognit.* **2016**, *52*, 85–95. [CrossRef]
81. Zhong, C.; Pedrycz, W.; Wang, D.; Li, L.; Li, Z. Granular data imputation: A framework of granular computing. *Appl. Soft Comput.* **2016**, *46*, 307–316. [CrossRef]
82. Jeong, D.; Park, C.; Ko, Y.M. Missing data imputation using mixture factor analysis for building electric load data. *Appl. Energy* **2021**, *304*, 117655. [CrossRef]
83. Lin, T.H. A comparison of multiple imputation with EM algorithm and MCMC method for quality of life missing data. *Qual. Quant.* **2010**, *44*, 277–287. [CrossRef]
84. Poolsawad, N.; Moore, L.; Kambhampati, C.; Cleland, J.G. Handling missing values in data mining—A case study of heart failure dataset. In Proceedings of the 2012 9th International Conference on Fuzzy Systems and Knowledge Discovery (FSKD), Chongqing, China, 29–31 May 2012; pp. 2934–2938.
85. Azur, M.J.; Stuart, E.A.; Frangakis, C.; Leaf, P.J. Multiple imputation by chained equations: What is it and how does it work? *Int. J. Methods Psychiatr. Res.* **2011**, *20*, 40–49. [CrossRef]
86. Rahman, S.A.; Huang, Y.; Claassen, J.; Heintzman, N.; Kleinberg, S. Combining Fourier and lagged k-nearest neighbor imputation for biomedical time series data. *J. Biomed. Inform.* **2015**, *58*, 198–207. [CrossRef] [PubMed]
87. Del Giudice, F.; Glover, F.; Belladelli, F.; De Berardinis, E.; Sciarra, A.; Salciccia, S.; Kasman, A.M.; Chen, T.; Eisenberg, M.L. Association of daily step count and serum testosterone among men in the United States. *Endocrine* **2021**, *72*, 874–881. [CrossRef] [PubMed]
88. Liu, B.; Yu, M.; Graubard, B.I.; Troiano, R.P.; Schenker, N. Multiple imputation of completely missing repeated measures data within person from a complex sample: Application to accelerometer data in the National Health and Nutrition Examination Survey. *Stat. Med.* **2016**, *35*, 5170–5188. [CrossRef] [PubMed]
89. Saint-Maurice, P.F.; Troiano, R.P.; Bassett, D.R.; Graubard, B.I.; Carlson, S.A.; Shiroma, E.J.; Fulton, J.E.; Matthews, C.E. Association of daily step count and step intensity with mortality among US adults. *Jama* **2020**, *323*, 1151–1160. [CrossRef] [PubMed]
90. Zhang, S. Nearest neighbor selection for iteratively kNN imputation. *J. Syst. Softw.* **2012**, *85*, 2541–2552. [CrossRef]
91. Lakshminarayan, K.; Harp, S.A.; Samad, T. Imputation of missing data in industrial databases. *Appl. Intell.* **1999**, *11*, 259–275. [CrossRef]
92. Rubin, D.B. *Multiple Imputation for Nonresponse in Surveys*; John Wiley & Sons: Hoboken, NJ, USA, 2004; Volume 81.
93. Zhang, Z. Missing data imputation: Focusing on single imputation. *Ann. Transl. Med.* **2016**, *4*, 9.
94. Khan, S.I.; Hoque, A.S.M.L. SICE: An improved missing data imputation technique. *J. Big Data* **2020**, *7*, 1–21. [CrossRef]
95. Giardina, M.; Huo, Y.; Azuaje, F.; McCullagh, P.; Harper, R. A missing data estimation analysis in type II diabetes databases. In Proceedings of the 2005 18th IEEE Symposium on Computer-Based Medical Systems, Dublin, Ireland, 23–24 June 2005; pp. 347–352.
96. Aljuaid, T.; Sasi, S. Proper imputation techniques for missing values in data sets. In Proceedings of the 2016 International Conference on Data Science and Engineering (ICDSE), Cochin, India, 23–25 August 2016; pp. 1–5.
97. Mirkes, E.M.; Coats, T.J.; Levesley, J.; Gorban, A.N. Handling missing data in large healthcare dataset: A case study of unknown trauma outcomes. *Comput. Biol. Med.* **2016**, *75*, 203–216. [CrossRef]

98. Sovilj, D.; Eirola, E.; Miche, Y.; Björk, K.-M.; Nian, R.; Akusok, A.; Lendasse, A. Extreme learning machine for missing data using multiple imputations. *Neurocomputing* **2016**, *174*, 220–231. [CrossRef]
99. Faisal, S.; Tutz, G. Multiple imputation using nearest neighbor methods. *Inf. Sci.* **2021**, *570*, 500–516. [CrossRef]
100. Blazek, K.; van Zwieten, A.; Saglimbene, V.; Teixeira-Pinto, A. A practical guide to multiple imputation of missing data in nephrology. *Kidney Int.* **2021**, *99*, 68–74. [CrossRef] [PubMed]
101. Yoon, S.; Sull, S. GAMIN: Generative adversarial multiple imputation network for highly missing data. In Proceedings of the IEEE/CVF Conference on Computer Vision and Pattern Recognition, Seattle, WA, USA, 13–19 June 2020; pp. 8456–8464.
102. Takahashi, M. Multiple imputation regression discontinuity designs: Alternative to regression discontinuity designs to estimate the local average treatment effect at the cutoff. *Commun. Stat. Simul. Comput.* **2021**, *50*, 1–20. [CrossRef]
103. Shin, K.; Han, J.; Kang, S. MI-MOTE: Multiple imputation-based minority oversampling technique for imbalanced and incomplete data classification. *Inf. Sci.* **2021**, *575*, 80–89. [CrossRef]
104. Gautam, C.; Ravi, V. Data imputation via evolutionary computation, clustering and a neural network. *Neurocomputing* **2015**, *156*, 134–142. [CrossRef]
105. Aleryani, A.; Wang, W.; De La Iglesia, B. Multiple Imputation Ensembles (MIE) for dealing with missing data. *SN Comput. Sci.* **2020**, *1*, 134. [CrossRef]
106. Xu, X.; Chong, W.; Li, S.; Arabo, A.; Xiao, J. MIAEC: Missing data imputation based on the evidence chain. *IEEE Access* **2018**, *6*, 12983–12992. [CrossRef]
107. Tsai, C.-F.; Li, M.-L.; Lin, W.-C. A class center based approach for missing value imputation. *Knowl.-Based Syst.* **2018**, *151*, 124–135. [CrossRef]
108. González-Vidal, A.; Rathore, P.; Rao, A.S.; Mendoza-Bernal, J.; Palaniswami, M.; Skarmeta-Gómez, A.F. Missing data imputation with bayesian maximum entropy for internet of things applications. *IEEE Internet Things J.* **2020**, *8*, 16108–16120. [CrossRef]
109. Mostafa, S.M.; Eladimy, A.S.; Hamad, S.; Amano, H. CBRL and CBRC: Novel Algorithms for Improving Missing Value Imputation Accuracy Based on Bayesian Ridge Regression. *Symmetry* **2020**, *12*, 1594. [CrossRef]
110. Li, L.; Zhou, H.; Liu, H.; Zhang, C.; Liu, J. A hybrid method coupling empirical mode decomposition and a long short-term memory network to predict missing measured signal data of SHM systems. *Struct. Health Monit.* **2020**, *20*, 1778–1793. [CrossRef]
111. Park, S.-W.; Ko, J.-S.; Huh, J.-H.; Kim, J.-C. Review on Generative Adversarial Networks: Focusing on Computer Vision and Its Applications. *Electronics* **2021**, *10*, 1216. [CrossRef]
112. Zhang, Y.; Zhou, B.; Cai, X.; Guo, W.; Ding, X.; Yuan, X. Missing value imputation in multivariate time series with end-to-end generative adversarial networks. *Inf. Sci.* **2021**, *551*, 67–82. [CrossRef]
113. Faisal, S.; Tutz, G. Imputation Methods for High-Dimensional Mixed-Type Datasets by Nearest Neighbors. *Comput. Biol. Med.* **2021**, *135*, 104577. [CrossRef]
114. Wan, D.; Razavi-Far, R.; Saif, M.; Mozafari, N. COLI: Collaborative Clustering Missing Data Imputation. *Pattern Recognit. Lett.* **2021**, *152*, 420–427. [CrossRef]
115. Shahjaman, M.; Rahman, M.R.; Islam, T.; Auwul, M.R.; Moni, M.A.; Mollah, M.N.H. rMisbeta: A robust missing value imputation approach in transcriptomics and metabolomics data. *Comput. Biol. Med.* **2021**, *138*, 104911. [CrossRef] [PubMed]
116. Hu, X.; Pedrycz, W.; Wu, K.; Shen, Y. Information granule-based classifier: A development of granular imputation of missing data. *Knowl.-Based Syst.* **2021**, *214*, 106737. [CrossRef]
117. Nugroho, H.; Utama, N.P.; Surendro, K. Class center-based firefly algorithm for handling missing data. *J. Big Data* **2021**, *8*, 37. [CrossRef]

Article

A Hybrid Data Analytics Framework with Sentiment Convergence and Multi-Feature Fusion for Stock Trend Prediction

Mohammad Kamel Daradkeh [1,2]

[1] Department of Information Technology, University of Dubai, Dubai 14143, United Arab Emirates; mdaradkeh@yu.edu.jo
[2] Department of Information Technology, Yarmouk University, Irbid 21163, Jordan

Abstract: Stock market analysis plays an indispensable role in gaining knowledge about the stock market, developing trading strategies, and determining the intrinsic value of stocks. Nevertheless, predicting stock trends remains extremely difficult due to a variety of influencing factors, volatile market news, and sentiments. In this study, we present a hybrid data analytics framework that integrates convolutional neural networks and bidirectional long short-term memory (CNN-BiLSTM) to evaluate the impact of convergence of news events and sentiment trends with quantitative financial data on predicting stock trends. We evaluated the proposed framework using two case studies from the real estate and communications sectors based on data collected from the Dubai Financial Market (DFM) between 1 January 2020 and 1 December 2021. The results show that combining news events and sentiment trends with quantitative financial data improves the accuracy of predicting stock trends. Compared to benchmarked machine learning models, CNN-BiLSTM offers an improvement of 11.6% in real estate and 25.6% in communications when news events and sentiment trends are combined. This study provides several theoretical and practical implications for further research on contextual factors that influence the prediction and analysis of stock trends.

Keywords: stock market prediction; data analytics; sentiment analysis; multi-feature fusion; bidirectional long short-term memory; convolution neural network

Citation: Daradkeh, M.K. A Hybrid Data Analytics Framework with Sentiment Convergence and Multi-Feature Fusion for Stock Trend Prediction. *Electronics* **2022**, *11*, 250. https://doi.org/10.3390/electronics11020250

Academic Editors: Amir H. Gandomi, Fang Chen, Laith Abualigah and Amir Mosavi

Received: 16 November 2021
Accepted: 21 December 2021
Published: 13 January 2022

Publisher's Note: MDPI stays neutral with regard to jurisdictional claims in published maps and institutional affiliations.

1. Introduction

Financial stock markets have an immense impact on the world economy as well as on financial and social organizations. The stock market, also called the securities market, comprises an aggregated methodology for the purchase and sale of various shares at the public or private level [1]. While financial markets are associated with colossal gains, big gains also carry risks that can lead to misfortune. This makes stock market prediction an interesting but difficult endeavor, as it is extremely difficult to predict stock markets with high accuracy due to high instability, random fluctuations, anomalies, and turbulence. Typically, stock market intelligence involves analyzing stock-related data to predict stock value fluctuations based on time series data, i.e., a chronological compilation of relevant observations, such as daily sales figures and prices of stocks. Verifiable time series data from financial stock exchanges provide detailed information about a particular stock during given stock market cycle [2]. This temporal data includes opening and closing prices, highs and lows, and the volume of stocks traded during a particular time period. Fundamental and technical analysis techniques typically rely on quantitative stock data such as stock costs, volumes, and portfolios, as well as subjective data about the companies involved, their profiles, and their trading strategies [3].

The extant research on stock trend prediction has largely focused on the application of various econometric-based methods to predict stock trends based on structured and linear historical data, mainly using linear regression and parameter estimation techniques [4–7].

However, stock price fluctuations are influenced not only by historical stock trading data, but also by nonlinear factors such as political factors, investment psychology, and unexpected events. In practice, the unstructured nature of news events and their lack of linearity and consistency have rendered traditional quantitative investment analysis methods ineffective. As technology has advanced, media news has become an important signal that captures the nonlinear factors that influence stock price performance, thereby improving the accuracy of stock price forecasting. Recent studies have suggested that media news and related sentiments can influence corporate and investor behavior as well as stock market performance [8]. Similarly, stock market trends are influenced by various events such as political influences, information security events [9,10], specific news or announcements [2], and national politics [11]. With the proliferation of stock market events, financial news, and investor decisions, it is imperative to understand how these events and sentiments influence stock market trends.

Although stock price movements are stochastic and generally involve non-random events, they can still be predicted by analyzing investor behavior and trading patterns [12–14]. While econometrics-based statistical methods can rely on tentative premises, machine learning methods pose challenges due to limited interpretability, the need for manual feature selection, and the problem of overfitting. To address these issues, deep learning methods based on conventional neural networks (CNNs) and Recurrent Neural Networks (RNNs) have been used for predicting stock market trends [15–17]. By extracting the underlying features of highly unstructured data, such deep learning prediction techniques can be used to explore the complex inherent patterns of stock price movements based on time series data. CNNs and RNNs generally integrate the concept of time into the network structure and are inherently suited for processing time series data. However, neural network methods encounter the problem that the gradient disappears when the sequence of input time series data becomes too long. To solve this problem, the long short-term memory (LSTM) model has been proposed as an improved version of RNN. Recent studies have shown that the LSTM outperforms the RNN and conventional machine learning algorithms such as random forest (RF), support vector machine (SVM), and decision tree (DT) in addressing stock prediction problems based on time series data [4,18–22].

Recently, researchers have applied deep learning techniques to stock prediction using LSTMs or modified LSTMs such as PSOLSTM, Stacked LSTM, and Time-Weighted LSTM [2,6,23,24]. Stock prediction models based on LSTMs analyze the sentiment polarity of textual information as well as the sentiment polarity of media news with historical trading data as input. Nevertheless, there are a number of research problems that need to be addressed to improve stock trend prediction and performance using both quantitative and qualitative stock-related data:

- First, while quantitative stock data can provide insight into the performance of the respective stocks, many other factors also play a crucial role in this context. Various country-specific factors such as political events, corporate politics, splits and mergers of different companies as well as global events can have a strong impact on the stock market. However, identifying such events and their linkages to investors investing in the stock market is a challenging task. Such events do have a major impact on the stock market; thus, incorporating them into stock analysis and identifying their correlation with stock performance can greatly contribute to improving stock forecasts;
- Second, in addition to fluctuations resulting from a variety of events, nonlinear stock markets are also affected by the sentiment associated with these events, which can directly or indirectly affect price movements [25]. For example, using historical stock market data to predict performance at a given point in time can provide clues to the impact of public sentiment. However, it is unclear how unstructured news data can be merged with organized stock market information. Typically, sentiment data from news texts are combined with verifiable stock market information and company financial data to contribute to stock metrics [26–28]. However, this method easily loses the sentiment data in the high-dimensional financial data. Stock prediction methods

with additional sentiment aspects have been shown to be even less accurate than those without. It is expected that merging these data sources (factors) into a single intelligence would improve the prediction accuracy in the stock market. However, it is challenging to integrate the information from different data sources into one dataset for market analysis because they have different formats (numeric or text);

- Third, while there are multiple approaches to both machine learning and deep learning, recent studies show that hybrid methods can be used to overcome inherent limitations of isolated approaches, e.g., the vanishing gradient problem in RNN can be largely avoided by deep feed-forward networks. Therefore, the effectiveness of predictive models can be improved by integrating complementary techniques. According to Alotaibi [29], financial markets are inherently non-stationary, non-linear and chaotic. In a volatile stock market, determining inherent patterns requires appropriate data representation. Therefore, due to the adaptability of DNNs and LSTMs for nonlinear financial markets, we propose the integration of DNNs and BiLSTMs with stock market data and evaluate their suitability to provide deeper insights and improve the performance of stock market forecasts.

To address the above three research challenges, this study presents a hybrid data analytics framework that integrates convolutional neural networks and bidirectional long short-term memory (CNN-BiLSTM) to evaluate the impact of the convergence of news events and sentiment trends with quantitative financial data on predicting stock trends. CNN is a powerful tool for extracting event features from news text, while BiLSTM uses two LSTM networks to obtain forward and backward contextual information, which is more suitable for discriminating sentiment polarity given context and can improve sentiment analysis compared to a single LSTM [11,15,24]. In this study, we used CNN and BiLSTM because these two techniques allow us to create detailed input features based on the fact that CNN can detect relevant internal structures in time series data through convolution and pooling operations [3]. Moreover, CNN and BiLSTM algorithms have been shown to be more accurate and more resistant to perturbation than state-of-the-art methods in classifying time series data [24,30,31]. CNN and BiLSTM algorithms are therefore able to learn relationships within time series without requiring large amounts of historical time series data. Similarly, BiLSTM and CNN have already been shown to provide highly accurate results for text mining tasks that require sequential modeling information [7]. Moreover, their implementation requires less time and effort [25]. The proposed model uses objective financial events extracted from news reports, such as surcharge events, stock prices and suspension events, on the one hand; on the other hand, BiLSTM is used to analyze the sentiment polarity of news reports and calculate the sentiment values of news texts. The features of stock news, including the types of news events and sentiment values, together with the numerical financial features of the stock are used as input to the LSTM network, and the historical stock information is used to predict the future rise and fall of the stock.

The main contributions of this study are as follows:

1. A hybrid data analytics predictive framework built on CNN and BiLSTM deep learning algorithms that combines heterogeneous stock price indicators (various categories of news events, user sentiments, historical macroeconomic variables, and historical stock price data) to predict future stock price movements. Therefore, this study demonstrates that traditional quantitative analysis techniques combined with investor and expert opinions (fundamental analysis) provide more accurate predictions of stock performance;

2. We experimentally investigated the effectiveness of the proposed framework with real stock data from the Dubai Financial Market (DFM) using two case studies from the real estate and communications sectors. We provide a comparative analysis of our approach with three basic techniques to investigate the importance of features and sentiment fusion in improving the prediction performance of stock trends. The results

show that the prediction performance of machine learning models can be significantly improved by combining different stock-related information;

3. Since the stock market data were collected during the COVID-19 pandemic, the results of this study provide valid arguments to show how news events, and thus the stock market, can be affected by pandemic data. Analysis of news events during the COVID-19 pandemic, as well as the emotional state of the public through analysis of news events, can reveal the economic impact of COVID-19 on stock markets. These insights can then lead to accurate stock market forecasts. Given the recent advances in AI algorithms and the enormous amount of information about the pandemic, this study synthesizes the market data and trains a classifier to predict the direction of the next stock market movement.

The remainder of this paper is organized as follows. Section 2 reviews the current and relevant literature on stock market analysis and forecasting. Section 3 describes the techniques and methods used in this study to integrate stock-related data and analyze their impact on stock market prediction. Section 4 presents the experimental design and case study description used to evaluate the applicability of the proposed model. Section 5 reports the empirical results of this study and discusses its implications for research and practice. Finally, Section 6 presents the conclusions of this work and suggests possible avenues for future research.

2. Literature Review

Stock market prediction is an important research topic that has attracted considerable interest from both researchers and investors. Previous research on stock market prediction can be broadly divided into two main categories: econometrics-based statistical methods, which involve the analysis of time series financial data; and computational intelligence-based techniques, which incorporate both quantitative stock data and textual information [2,3,25].

Econometrics-based statistical analysis relies mainly on historical trading data, corporate financial data, and macro data to identify and describe patterns of change in stock data over time and predict future stock trends [30,32,33]. Several machine learning algorithms were used to detect patterns in the large amount of financial information, including support vector machines (SVM), artificial neural networks (ANN), Parsimonious Bayes, and Random Forest [24,34]. Jiang, Liu [35] showed that machine learning can be used to predict the future performance of individual stocks using historical stock data. Kim, Ku [36] used SVM to predict the rise and fall of individual stocks and verified the effectiveness of SVM in classifying the rise and fall of individual stocks through empirical analysis. Lahmiri [37] compared the performance of ANN and SVM in predicting stock movements and found that ANN outperformed SVM in terms of prediction accuracy, and feedforward ANN has been widely used due to its ability to predict both upward and downward movements of stocks as well as stock prices [38].

However, since stock prices are inherently unpredictable in the short term, using historical trading data to analyze stock prices has its limitations and cannot further improve the prediction results. Behavioral economics theory states that investors are susceptible to personal and social emotions in complex and uncertain decision problems [18]. The main cause of stock price changes is the reaction to new information, and news in the media can be useful as exogenous sources of information for short-term stock price prediction [13,19]. With advances in text analytics and the increasing prevalence of social media, blogs, and user-shared news, incorporating text content into stock market research has become an interesting topic. The combination of news events and social media messages to improve the predictive accuracy of forecasting models has led to the importance of developing appropriate techniques to analyze their impact on the market. In recent years, there has been an increase in the number of studies investigating the combined effect of a user's social media sentiment and web news on stock price performance. For example, Zhang, Li [39] reported a high correlation between stock price performance and public sentiment, with predictive accuracy ranging from 55% to 63%. They also proposed an extended coupled hidden Markov method to predict stock prices based on Internet news and historical stock data. Ref. [40] proposed a multi-source multi-instance learning system based on three different data sources and found that the accuracy increased when using multiple data sources compared to single sources.

With the advancement of deep learning techniques and applications, more attention has been paid to neural network-based learning models for stock price prediction that incorporate both quantitative stock data and news data. Hiransha, Gopalakrishnan [41] presented four types of deep learning architectures, i.e., multilayer perceptron (MLP), recurrent neural networks (RNN), long short-term memory (LSTM), and convolutional neural networks (CNN) for predicting a company's stock price based on available historical prices. Similarly, Nabipour, Nayyeri [20] employed RNN and LSTM to investigate whether news about stock prices and the associated sentiment polarity affect stock prices. In their study, they found that LSTM showed more accurate results with the highest model fit. They also reported that the prediction accuracy can be improved when both stock-related news texts and tweets are counted and used as input for stock price prediction. Nasir, Shaukat [42] analyzed Dow Jones index prices based on user sentiment recorded on Twitter and showed that sentiment signals embedded in news are a reliable predictor of stock prices. Polamuri, Srinivas [43] used an RNN model with gated recurrent units to predict stock movements and fused numerical features of stock prices to examine the sentiment polarity of financial news on Twitter. Similarly, Priya, Revadi [26] used CNN and RNN to study the stock trend model that includes both news headlines and technical indicators, and showed that news headlines improve prediction accuracy more than news content. Shobana and Umamaheswari [44] examined the effects of stock market signals embedded in news websites, stock bars, blogs, and other media information and found that investors responded faster and more strongly to positive sentiment.

Recently, hybrid deep learning methods have been proposed to improve the prediction performance of stock market trends. Srivastava, Zhang [45] developed a hybrid model called RCNN, which combines RNN and CNN by exploiting the advantages of both models. Their experiments showed that the combined hybrid system had a positive impact on the performance of the model when text data and technical indicators were used as input data, and the proposed model performed better than the CNN model. Another hybrid model called RNN-boost was applied to predict stock volatility [35]. It extracts LDA and sentiment features from social media data and combines them with stock technical indicators. The proposed model combines RNN and Adaboost to achieve an overall average accuracy of 66.54% [41]. The RNN model uses gated recursive units (GRUs) to predict stock prices. A combination of three forecasting models, namely SVM, adaptive neuro-fuzzy inference system and artificial neural network (ANN), has been proposed for predicting stock prices using public opinion [46]. The proposed models were evaluated using the historical stock index of the Istanbul BIST 100 index and yielded good results. Nti, Adekoya [3] investigated the predictability of stock price movements in four countries based on sentiment in tweets and found a high correlation between stock prices and tweets.

Despite the increasing development and application of hybrid data analysis techniques based on neural network learning approaches for stock market analysis, current models incorporating quantitative stock data and news data largely consider the extraction of information sentiment polarities as a support rather than an integral part of stock trend prediction. Most previous studies have used Twitter and Twitter texts as a source of information data to better convey sentiment [2,5,10,14,20,21,47]. However, considering that news reflects perceived reality and sentiment polarity is usually fuzzy, improving predictive accuracy by highlighting opinions cannot be taken for granted. Arosemena, Pérez [30] proposed to use a latent dirichlet allocation (LDA) topic model to extract keywords from tweet texts, and then analyze the sentiment features of tweet texts based on keywords as input for stock prediction. Unlike previous studies, and considering that news events are more representative of the effects of media information on stock movements than news sentiment, this study uses a multi-feature fusion method that incorporates news events and sentiment convergence to extend the numerical features of stocks and further improve the accuracy of stock prediction.

3. Methodology

The main objective of this study is to improve the accuracy of stock market trend prediction by combining news events and sentiment patterns with quantitative financial data in a hybrid CNN-BiLSTM model. The proposed research methodology is shown in Figure 1. It includes five main steps: (1) the stock-related financial data and news are separately sifted and preprocessed to create the stock database and the news database; (2) the stock news are divided into stock events, and each news event is labeled with an event type; (3) a CNN classifier is developed and trained to classify the event type; (4) the news events are labeled with a sentiment, and a news sentiment classifier is developed using BiLSTM; and (5) the stock news features and stock price features trained in steps (3) and (4) are fed into the LSTM network to evaluate their fusion fitness for predicting the rise and fall of stock trends.

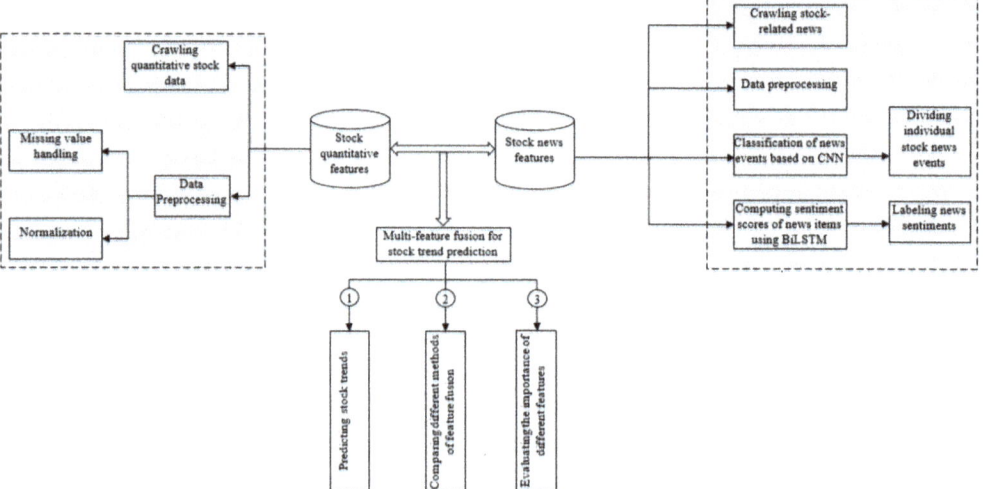

Figure 1. A hybrid CNN-BiLSTM model with multi-feature and sentiment fusion for stock trend prediction.

3.1. Extraction of Quantitative Stock Data Features

Previous research on stock market prediction has shown that various indicators such as a company's price-earnings ratio, price–net ratio, and net cash flow can help predict the performance of individual stocks [6,10,16,17,19]. To obtain the numerical financial features of a stock, we select financial data (e.g., price-earnings ratio and price-net ratio), cash flow data (e.g., inflows and sales ratios), and stock information (e.g., opening and closing prices). In addition, due to their influence on share movements, the general market index and sector index of individual shares are also used as indicators of the financial value of the stocks.

The quantitative financial features for the stocks sampled were then pre-processed to eliminate missing values. For example, if an indicator's data is missing for a particular day (e.g., during a trading pause), that day's data is removed. Moreover, given the different type and scale of the various quantitative financial indicators, using the raw values of the indicators directly may cause indicators with higher values to dominate the training and weaken the impact of indicators with smaller values. Therefore, the quantitative financial data were normalized using the z-score to ensure comparability across indicator data.

With $X_j = [x_{1j}, x_{2j}, \ldots, x_{ij}, \ldots, x_{nj}]$ as the vector consisting of the values of the j_{th} financial indicator in T_n days, and x_{ij} as the value of the j_{th} financial indicator on day i, each value in X_j is normalized by the $z - $ score, as shown in Equation (1).

$$\bar{x}_{ij} = \frac{x_{ij} - \mu_j}{\sigma_j} \tag{1}$$

where μ_j and σ_j denote the mean and standard deviation of all values of the financial indicator X_j. Table 1 illustrates the quantitative financial stock features composed of p stock indicators over T_n days, where $X_1 \sim X_p$ denote the p financial features.

Table 1. Quantitative financial stock features.

	X_1	X_2	...	X_j	...	X_p
T_1	$\bar{x}_{ij}$	$\bar{x}_{ij}$	...	$\bar{x}_{ij}$	...	$\bar{x}_{ij}$
...	...	...	...	...	...	...
T_i	$\bar{x}_{ij}$	$\bar{x}_{ij}$	...	$\bar{x}_{ij}$	...	$\bar{x}_{ij}$
...	...	...	...	...	...	...
T_n	$\bar{x}_{ij}$	$\bar{x}_{ij}$	...	$\bar{x}_{ij}$	...	$\bar{x}_{ij}$

3.2. Extraction of News Events Features

Feature extraction of news events was performed to identify and extract objective financial events from news headlines. First, the headline data was preprocessed and the Natural Language Toolkit (NLTK) word tokenizer was used to tokenize words and remove stop words. At the same time, custom stop words and a financial lexicon were added to improve the accuracy of word tokenization. The custom financial lexicon includes common financial words, codes, and abbreviations of listed companies, as well as the names of executives of listed companies. The financial news items were categorized by objective events based on the keyword field of the news items in the Dubai Financial Market (DFM) news classification, resulting in a total of 82 news events. Table 2 shows a list of selected categories of news events and their descriptive terms.

Table 2. Subcategories of news event types.

Event Category	Event Description Terms
Transactions	Suspension, resumption, inflow of funds, outflow of funds, block trade, share price, inversion, record, high
Equity	Listing, holding, acquisitions, mergers, asset reorganization, asset freeze, stock transfer
Investment & Financing	Investment, construction, issuance of offerings, issuance of bonds, convertible bonds, capital raising, pledge, dividend
Corporate Affairs	Change of registered capital, rapid development, strategic cooperation, business expansion, management reduction.
External Events	Dubai Financial Market (DFM) listing, stock market penalty, favorable rating, rating downgrade, positive policies.

3.3. Classification of News Events Based on CNN Model

To classify stock market news based on the 82 classified news events, we developed a CNN-based news classifier that includes an input layer, a convolution layer, a pooling layer, and a fully connected layer. The output of each layer is the input to the next layer [2,48]. First, the news headlines were trained using Word2Vec, and the resulting word vector matrix was used as the input to the convolutional layer. The convolution layer uses filters to convolve the word vector matrix of the headlines and generate the feature maps. The pooling layer takes samples from the feature maps and extracts the most important features in each feature map to pass to the fully connected layer. Finally, the fully connected layer obtains the final classification result of the headlines using the SoftMax function [12] and outputs the event type of the headlines. The daily news about a particular stock is counted by the CNN news classifier. For each news item input to the news classifier, a single event type is generated; therefore, the frequency of each event per day is counted to obtain the news feature matrix, as shown in Table 3. Here, $N_1 \sim N_p$ denote p news events, where $p = 82$ and n_{ij} denotes the frequency of event feature N_j on day T_i.

Table 3. News event features.

	N_1	N_2	...	N_j	...	N_p
T_1	n_{ij}	n_{ij}	...	n_{ij}	...	n_{ij}
...	...	...	...	...	...	...
T_i	n_{ij}	n_{ij}	...	n_{ij}	...	n_{ij}
...	...	...	...	...	...	...
T_n	n_{ij}	n_{ij}	...	n_{ij}	...	n_{ij}

3.4. Detection of News Text Sentiments

The news event describes an objective event, while the sentiment of a news text describes the contextual opinions about the news event, i.e., negative or positive. Therefore, to determine the sentiment of a news text, it is necessary to consider the given contextual information. To this end, BiLSTM is trained with two LSTM networks, a training sequence that starts at the beginning of the text and a training sequence that starts at the end of the text, which are connected to the same output layer. BiLSTM is able to integrate both the front and back sequence information of each point, which is more effective than a single LSTM for determining the sentiment polarity of the text [13,48]. Figure 2 shows the process of calculating the sentiment polarity of news headlines using BiLSTM.

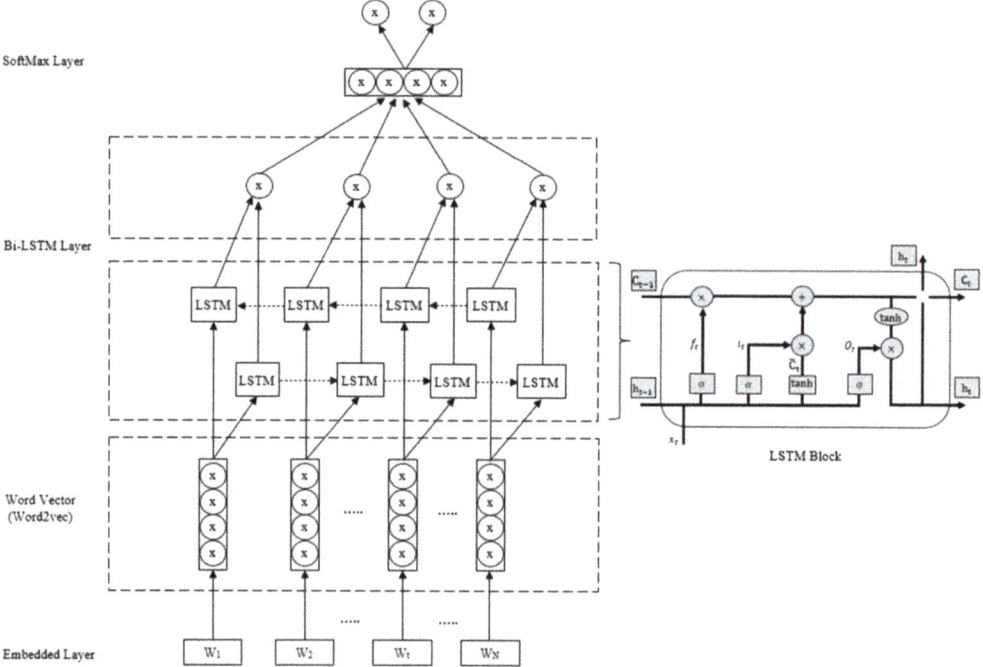

Figure 2. BiLSTM-based news sentiment analysis model.

After data preprocessing for BiLSTM-based sentiment analysis, each news headline x is truncated by a maximum of N words, and the processing step of LSTM is set to N. For headlines less than N in length, they are terminated by left zeroing. For each sampling time ($t \leq N$), the word vector x_t obtained by Word2Vec training is fed to an LSTM layer with L neurons. This neural network layer outputs an implicit state vector h_t of dimension L. Each neuron sets three threshold structures, namely forget gate f, input gate i and output gate o. Based on the past implicit state vector $h_t - 1$ and the current input x_t, it decides what information needs to be forgotten, what new information needs to be input, and what new memory information needs to be encoded to obtain h_t as output. The LSTM layer at time t is calculated as shown in Equations (2)–(7).

$$f_t = \sigma(W_f \cdot [h_{t-1}, x_t] + b_f) \tag{2}$$

$$i_t = \sigma(W_i \cdot [h_{t-1}, x_t] + b_i) \tag{3}$$

$$O_t = \sigma(W_0 \cdot [h_{t-1}, x_t] + b_0) \tag{4}$$

$$\overline{C}_t = \tanh(W_c \cdot [h_{t-1}, x_t] + b_i) \tag{5}$$

$$C_t = f_t * C_{t-1} + i_t * \overline{C}_t \tag{6}$$

$$h_t = \tanh(C_t) * O_t \tag{7}$$

First, the forget gate uses the sigmoid activation function σ to determine how meaningful the past memory is to the current memory state, and generates the coefficient f_t according to Equation (2). Next, the input gate determines how significant the current word input vector x_t is according to Equation (3) and generates the coefficient i_t. Then, the neuron updates the state C_t of the current time according to Equation (4). Finally, the output gate determines in what sense the new memory can be output based on C_t, and the implicit state h_t of the output is represented by Equation (7). In Equations (2)–(7), W_0 and b_0 denote the weight matrix and bias vector, respectively.

After the above calculation, the implicit state code h_N of the headline n at time $t = N$ is obtained. Based on h_N, the vector of the probability distribution of j in the different sentiment categories [13,14], i.e., positive and negative, is obtained by the SoftMax function as shown in Equation (8). Based on y_j, the sentiment orientation (SO) of heading n is then calculated as shown in Equation (9). Here, $SO_n \in [-1, 1]$. If $SO_n > 0$, the sentiment orientation is positive, otherwise it is negative. Assuming there are m_i news items at time T_i and the sentiment polarity of each news item is denoted by SO_j, $j = 1, 2, \ldots, m_i$, $SO_j \in [-1, 1]$, then the overall sentiment value of the news at time T_i is obtained from Equation (10). To obtain the stock news matrix, the news sentiment vector $S = [S_1, S_2, \ldots, S_j, \ldots, S_n]$ is added as a column feature to the news event matrix, as shown in Table 3.

$$y_j = \text{Softmax}(W_0 \cdot h_N + b_0) \tag{8}$$

$$SO_j = (1, -1) \cdot Y_{dj} \tag{9}$$

$$S_i = \frac{1}{m_i} \sum_{j=1}^{m_i} SO_j \tag{10}$$

3.5. Stock Trend Prediction

The final step in the proposed hybrid CNN-BiLTM model is to predict the stock trend by combining the financial feature matrix and the stock news feature matrix by date as input to the stock trend prediction model. As with forward time series modeling, the effects of backward series need not be considered when predicting the stock trend, so an LSTM rather than a BiLSTM is used to predict upward and downward stock trends. However, when the financial matrix and the news matrix are directly merged as input to the LSTM model, the problem of gradient disappearance may occur [35,48]. Therefore, two LSTM neurons were used in this study, and the financial matrix and the news matrix were input to the two LSTMs separately. Then, the results were vectorized together and fed into the fully connected neural network. Finally, the results for stock rise and fall are output. For example, if the sampling interval is one day, the rise and fall of the stock on day t is predicted based on the data of the past $t - a \sim t - 1$ days as illustrated in Figure 3.

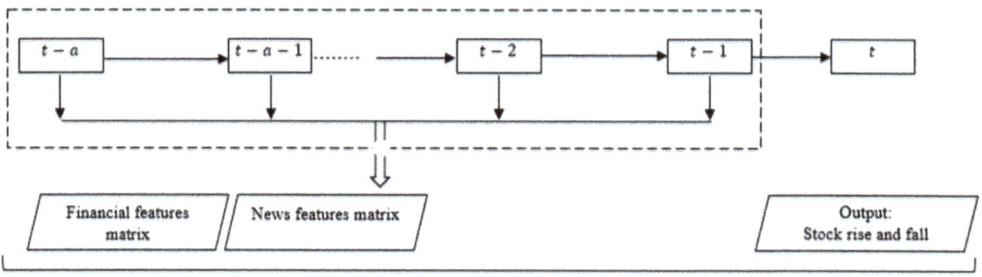

Prediction cycle per sample

Figure 3. Sample period of the stock prediction model.

4. Experiment Setup

4.1. Experiment Dataset

To evaluate the applicability of the proposed model to different sectors, we selected two stocks, Aldar Properties (ALDAR) and Emirates Telecom (ETISALAT), from the real estate development sector and the communications sector as test objects. The real estate sector is cyclical and more affected by national or international economic fluctuations. In contrast, the communications sector is defensive and less affected by cyclical fluctuations and has a relatively stable share price performance. These companies were selected because they had few missing values in their dataset. In addition, they were generally reported on extensively in the media and in web-based media platforms, allowing a considerable amount of subjective data to be collected about them.

In this experiment, a total of 12 financial stock indicators were selected to form the matrix of financial characteristics, including: opening price, minimum price, high price, closing price, net capital inflow, turnover rate, rise/fall rate, price/earnings ratio, price/net ratio, DFM general market index, and sector index. Quantitative stock data for the two companies were mainly downloaded from the Dubai Financial Market (DFM) (https://www.dfm.ae/market-data, accessed on 1 December 2021). DFM is a publicly owned company based in the United Arab Emirates. It operates in the field of financial markets and offers highly reliable and comprehensive online data on financial markets. It uses scientific verification tools and advanced management methods to keep the reliability and accuracy of the data as high as possible. The DFM database was crawled to collect a total of 18,766 news data and 29,352 financial data for ALDAR and 18,796 news data and 29,364 financial data for ETISALAT during the two-year period from 1 January 2020 to 1 December 2021. The source of the tagged data for news event classification is the DFM historical data. A total of 27,800 news events were labeled with the 82 news categories and used to train the event classification model.

4.2. Experiment Hyperparameter Settings

There are several factors that influence the performance of the CNN-based model for news event classification and the BiLSTM model for sentiment analysis, such as the dimensionality of the word vector, the size of the convolutional window, the number of iterations, and the number of filters. In the experiments, the performance of the model was evaluated by 10-fold cross-validation to select the most appropriate parameter combinations. The best parameter combinations for the dataset used in this study are listed in Table 4, where Null means that this parameter setting is not required.

Table 4. Settings of the parameters for the prediction model.

Parameter	CNN	BiLSTM
Word vector dimensionality	300	300
Number of convolution kernels	96	Null
Convolution kernel size	3, 4, 5	Null
Dropout	0.5	0.5
Batch size	128	128
Number of iterations	10	20
Header interception length	Null	15
Number of single-layer LSTM neurons	Null	[256, 256]

4.3. Evaluation Indicators

The most commonly applied measures of precision, recall, and F1 were used to evaluate the classification results in this study. As illustrated in Equations (11)–(13), the precision, recall, and F1 measures for classifying the i_{th} category of news events were expressed by Pre_i, R_i, and $F1_i$, respectively. Where TP_i is the number of samples that were correctly classified into category i; FP_i is the number of samples that were incorrectly classified into category i; and FN_i is the number of samples that originally belonged to category i but were incorrectly classified into other categories.

$$Pre_i = \frac{TP_i}{TP_i + FP_i} \tag{11}$$

$$R_i = \frac{TPi}{TP_i + FN_i} \tag{12}$$

$$F1_i = \frac{2 \times Pre_i \times R_i}{Pre_i + R_i} \tag{13}$$

5. Empirical Results and Discussion

5.1. News Event Classification

The empirical results of news event classification are shown in Table 5. To verify the performance of the CNN-based news event classifier, it was compared with the SVM and maximum entropy methods [9–12] for news event classification. SVM is widely investigated and applied for modeling, classification, and data-driven error detection as it has been shown to be powerful and generalizable, while maximum entropy is a linear logit model with proven classification capabilities. In the experiment, 90% of the dataset with a total of 25,020 news items was used as the training set and 10% of the dataset with a total of 2780 news items was used as the test set. For time series data, the temporal dimension of the observations means that we cannot randomly divide them into cohorts. Instead, we need to split the data and take into account the temporal sequence in which the samples were observed. For this reason, we used the train-test split method, which takes into account the temporal sequence of observations [49,50]. The training and testing data sets for the stock market forecasting model were divided as follows: data from 1 January 2020 to 31 July 2021 were used to train the model, and data from 1 August 2021 to 1 December 2021 were used to test and validate the applicability of the model. For the dataset analyzed in this study, the CNN-based news classifier achieved an accuracy of 93.0% in the training dataset and 87.7% in the testing dataset, outperforming the SVM-based and Maxent-based news classifiers (see Table 5).

Table 5. Comparison of accuracy rate of news event classification.

Model	Dataset	
	Training Set	Test Set
SVM	90.8%	85.2%
Maxent	72.0%	69.4%
CNN	93.0%	87.7%

Table 6 shows the classification results of the CNN-based news classifier for different news events, as well as the precision, recall, and F1 measures for the different news events. Due to space limitations, only selected event types are listed. High recall and F1 values indicate better predictive power and accuracy of the message events. As shown in Table 6, most event types with high recall and high F1 values belong to the corporate news category. In general, the content of news events of different companies does not greatly differ, and the news events have certain templates with good classification performance. News events with poor classification performance are mostly predictions of stock price trends; both good and bad trends vary greatly in the news content of different sectors and companies, making the classification accuracy relatively poor.

Table 6. Evaluation of classification performance for each news event class (partial categories).

Categories of News Events with Relatively High Classification Performance				Categories of News Events with Weak Classification Performance			
Sample of News Event Categories				Sample of News Event Categories			
News Events Category	Precision	Recall	F1	News Events Category	Precision	Recall	F1
Listed on DFM	1.00	1.00	1.00	Declining performance	0.64	0.58	0.61
Suspension	0.98	1.00	0.99	Favorable policies	0.81	0.65	0.72
Business Change	1.00	1.00	1.00	Change of capital	1.00	0.22	0.36
Winning Bids	1.00	1.00	1.00	Hiring of Executives	0.50	0.40	0.44
Convertible bonds	0.97	0.97	0.97	Performance growth	0.68	0.73	0.71
Pledges	1.00	1.00	1.00	Expected decline	0.67	0.61	0.64
Stock Exchange Inquiries	0.94	1.00	0.97	Spread news	0.42	0.47	0.44
Delisting	1.00	1.00	1.00	Favorable News	0.46	0.65	0.54

Table 7 shows the results of news sentiment classification. BiLSTM-based news sentiment classification achieved 94.1% accuracy in the training set and 91.1% in the test set. SVM-based news sentiment classification achieved the second-best performance with 85.5% and 80.2% accuracy in the training set and the test set, respectively; Maxent-based news sentiment classification was the worst. These trained news sentiment classification models were used to classify the news datasets from ALDAR and ETISALAT, calculate the news sentiment scores, and generate the news sentiment vector matrix.

Table 7. Comparison of news sentiment classification accuracy.

Model	Dataset	
	Training Set	Test Set
SVM	85.5%	80.2%
Maxent	81.7%	75.1%
BiLSTM	94.1%	91.1%

5.2. Stock Trend Prediction

To test the effectiveness of the proposed hybrid CNN-BiLSTM model in improving the prediction of stock trends, we conducted an experiment comparing the effects of the convergence of news events and sentiment trends with quantitative financial data in predicting stock trends based on the following layers of feature fusion:

(1) LSTM with financial features only: stock trend prediction with financial features only;

(2) LSTM with news infusion: stock trend prediction using financial features and news features, as shown in Table 3;

(3) LSTM with news events and sentiment fusion: stock trend prediction using financial features, news event features, and sentiment features;

(4) GBDT with news event and sentiment fusion: stock prediction based on gradient boosting decision tree model (GBDT) [22] with the same inputs as proposed in model no. (3). GBDT is a highly generalized decision tree algorithm that can effectively avoid overfitting and resist noise by training multiple weak regression tree classifiers over multiple iterations [11]. The performance of LSTM and GBDT in predicting stocks is compared under the same input constraints.

The threshold for stock rise and fall was set to 1%, i.e., if the rise is above the threshold of 1%, it is classified as stock rise, which is represented by 1; conversely, a fall above the threshold of 1% is classified as stock fall, which is represented by 0. The sampling interval of the model was set to $a = 14$, the data from day $t - 13$ to day $t - 1$ were entered, and the result of predicting the rise and fall of stocks on day t was outputted. The accuracy of the stock trend prediction for different layers of feature fusion is shown in Table 8.

Table 8. Accuracy of prediction of stock trend for different layers of feature fusion.

Layers of Feature Fusion	ALDAR Stock	ETISALAT Stock
LSTM with only financial stock features	0.699	0.646
LSTM with financial features and news events	0.754	0.785
LSTM with financial features, news events and sentiment fusion	0.781	0.812
GBDT with financial features, news events and sentiment fusion	0.625	0.654

As shown in Table 8, both the LSTM model with news events and the LSTM model with news events and sentiment fusion improved the stock prediction accuracy compared to the LSTM model using only quantitative financial features. The prediction accuracy of ALDAR individual stocks improved from 0.699 to 0.754 and 0.781, an increase of 7.8% and 11.6%, respectively. The predictive accuracy of ETISALAT individual stocks improved from 0.646 to 0.785 and 0.812, representing increases of 21.4% and 25.6%, respectively. Consequently, the qualitative information contained in stock market news has a positive impact on the prediction of stock trends. In particular, the convergence of news events and sentiment trends with quantitative financial data seems to have a significant impact on improving the prediction of stock trends. Compared with the GBDT model, the LSTM model is more advantageous in predicting stock trends because it improves the prediction performance to a certain extent.

Examining the applicability of the model to both sectors, the results show that the LSTM model performed better in the real estate sector than in the communications sector when only the financial characteristics were used. However, when combining news and financial features, the LSTM model performed better in the communications sector than in the real estate sector. Thus, the applicability of the model in this study is higher for the communications sector, which is also consistent with the expectation that defensive sectors have more stable stock prices compared to more cyclical sectors. To visually demonstrate the effectiveness of the proposed model in predicting stock price movements, Figures 4 and 5 show the prediction results of the proposed model for the two stocks ETISALAT and ALDAR from 1 August to 1 December, 2021, respectively, using the test dataset.

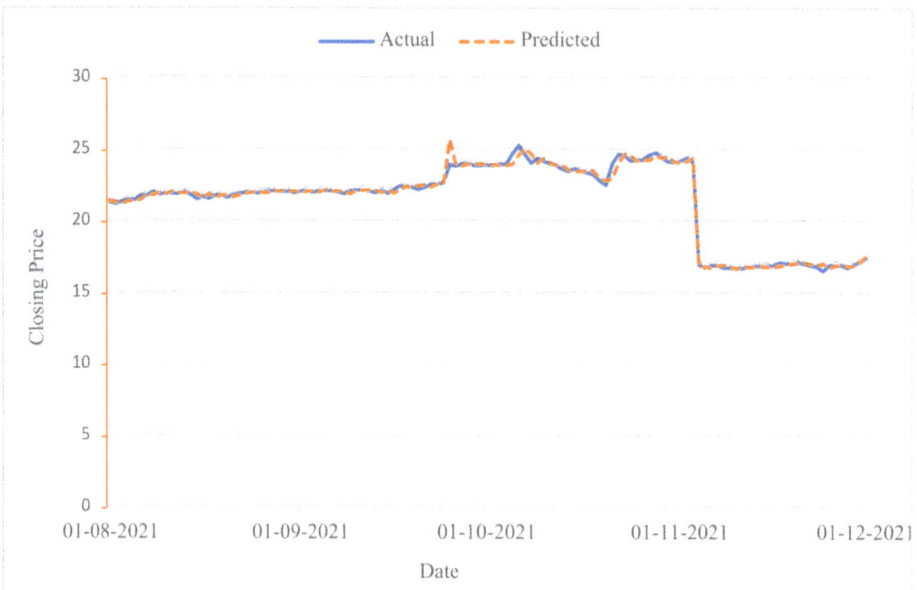

Figure 4. Stock trend prediction for ETISALAT from 1 August to 1 December 2021.

Figure 5. Stock trend prediction for ALDAR from 1 August to 1 December 2021.

Since stock trend prediction is a dichotomous classification problem, the resulting output is either a rising trend or a falling trend. To illustrate the impact of trend prediction, we consider a sample interval of 13 days. If the prediction result on day 14 is rising, the predicted closing price is set as the sum of the actual closing price on day 13 and the difference between the actual closing prices on day 13 and on day 14. Conversely, it is set to the difference between the actual closing price on day 13 and the actual closing prices on days 13 and 14. In Figures 4 and 5, the results of the stock movement prediction and the actual situation are essentially the same, suggesting a good performance of the model in predicting individual stock fluctuations.

5.3. Comparison of Features Significance

To evaluate and compare the importance and contribution of different features in predicting stock trends, we used the ranking function that ranks the features according to their importance in the final GDBT model [13]. The results of the GBDT model to evaluate the importance of different features for two stocks, ALDAR and ETISALAT, are shown in Figures 6 and 7. Considering the large number of dimensions of input features, we classified the quantitative and qualitative features used in this study into 5 categories, namely: (1) the importance of stock price-related features (calculated by summing the importance of opening price, closing price, high price, low price, rise and fall, and the spread between rise and fall); (2) the importance of cash flow features (calculated by summing the importance of net cash inflow and turnover rate); (3) the importance of the company's financial features (calculated by summing the importance of the price-earnings ratio and the price-earnings ratio); (4) the importance of the general market index and the sector index (calculated by summing the importance of the DFM index and the sector index); and finally (5) the importance of the news and sentiment features (calculated by summing the importance of the news events and the sentiment features).

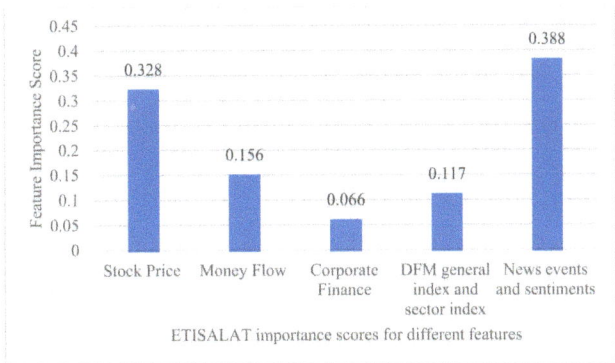

Figure 6. Ranking of features according to their importance for the final GDBT model (ETISALAT stock).

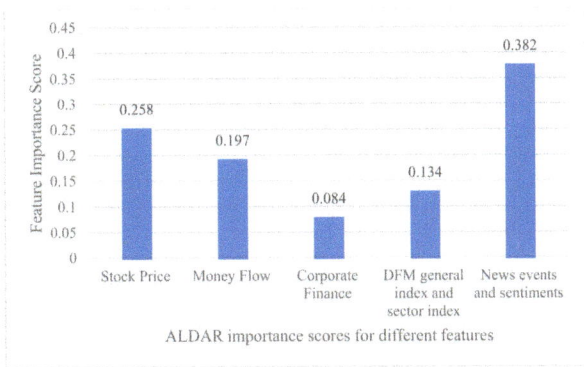

Figure 7. Ranking of features according to their importance for the final GDBT model (ALDAR stocks).

5.4. Analysis of the Rise and Fall Threshold

The value of the thresholds for rising and falling prices affects the labeling of stocks that rise or fall, and thus the performance of the prediction models. In the experiments, we set the thresholds from 1% to 8%, with 1% as the step size, to test the prediction effect of the different models for the two stocks of ALDAR and ETISALAT. The experimental results are shown in Figures 8 and 9.

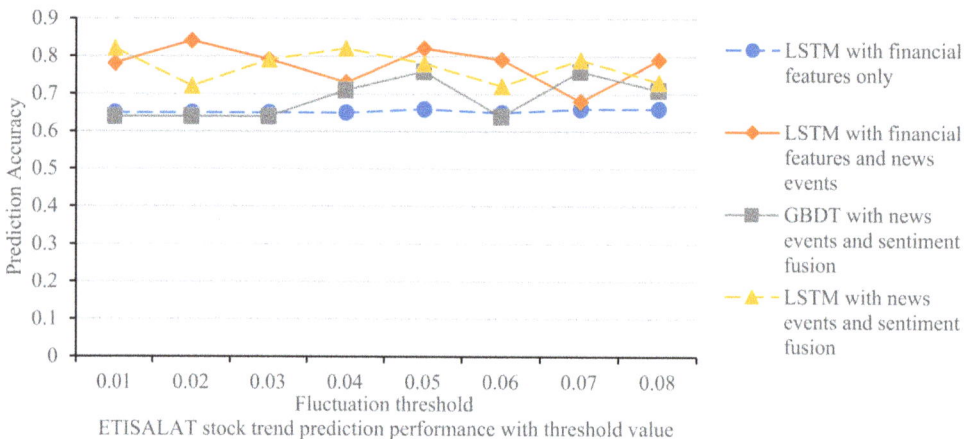

ETISALAT stock trend prediction performance with threshold value

Figure 8. The effect of threshold value on stock trend prediction model (ETISALAT).

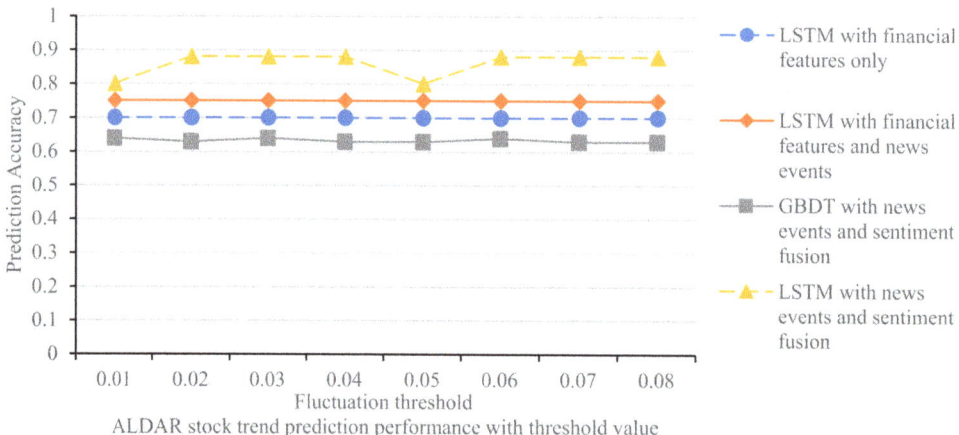

ALDAR stock trend prediction performance with threshold value

Figure 9. The effect of threshold value on stock trend prediction model (ALDAR).

Several findings can be derived from the experimental results. First, the predictive accuracy of the model does not increase or decrease linearly when the threshold is increased from 0.01 to 0.08, but fluctuates randomly. The threshold affects the labeling of stock price increases and decreases in the interval [0.01, 0.08], which in turn affects the accuracy of the prediction model. The threshold value is set to eliminate the effect of fluctuations in this part of the data on the model, and the specific value can be determined by combining experience and experimental tests. Second, the LSTM model with news event integration and the LSTM model with news event and sentiment integration outperforms the LSTM model with financial features for all thresholds, confirming that integrating media news features into the stock trend prediction model can improve the stock prediction accuracy.

Finally, the comparison of Figures 8 and 9 shows that the performance of the different models in predicting ALDAR's stock movements is essentially consistent with the changes in the rise and fall thresholds. Examining the financial stock source data, we find that only 1.5% of the ALDAR stock rise and fall data are between 0.01 and 0.08, which is a relatively small percentage; therefore, changing the label of this portion of the data has limited impact on the model's predictive performance. In contrast, 5% of the data for ETISALAT shares is between 0.01 and 0.08; therefore, changing the threshold has a greater impact on the model's predictive performance.

6. Limitations and Future Research

This study has a number of limitations that should be considered when interpreting the results. First, the effects of different estimation cycles on the prediction of stock trends were not considered in the proposed CNN-BiLSTM model. Second, the current study relies on a single stock-related information source, which may limit the predictive power of the proposed model. Indeed, stock markets are typically influenced by a variety of text-based information sources, such as monetary news, online media, websites, or corporate statements [8,14,31,38,51,52]. These information sources differ in the way they influence monetary economic entities. Public opinion on online media, news information, and the opinion of monetary news writers, as well as the officiality of improvised statements, can influence the performance of stock prices in different ways. Therefore, it is equally important to study the combination of information from different sources to understand the impact of news information on predicting stock trends. These strategies can be used and extended to include news content from web-based media and monetary news to create a more comprehensive feature map. Sector and market-related information can additionally be used to tap into and explore the realm of organization-related texts (e.g., stock-related texts and administration-related texts) for stock market research.

Possible research and development directions to improve the accuracy of stock forecasts can be considered from two perspectives. First, given that the magnitude of the increase in stock investment has a large impact on investment profitability, the predictive accuracy of the model could be examined by classifying stock investment into four categories (small increase, large increase, small decrease, and large decrease). Second, other stock-related control variables, such as return and crash risk, can be included in the forecasting model and the effects of these control variables on stock forecasting performance can be compared. Since the BiLSTM-based commentary sentiment analysis method takes a long time to train the model, the method could be further developed in the future. In future work, the method could be investigated to effectively speed up the training process of the model. Further experiments with representations from different but related corpus, new deep learning techniques such as generative adversarial network (GAN) models and graph-based deep learning models can be investigated. The applications of graph-based deep learning not only allow us to tap into the rich values underlying existing graph data, but also help us to naturally model relational data as graphs. Hybrid models that integrate different machine learning and deep learning models can also be explored.

7. Conclusions

This paper presents a hybrid CNN-BiLSTM model with multi-feature fusion for predicting stock trends. The objective is to improve the prediction accuracy by incorporating news events and sentiment trends in the media as market signals that influence stock trends into the stock prediction model. We selected two stocks from the real estate sector and the communications sector as objects to test the effectiveness of the proposed model. The stock trend prediction model presented in this paper shows that integrating quantitative stock data with non-numerical stock signals from media events and sentiment trends leads to better stock performance. Specifically, the results show that the prediction accuracy of the proposed model is 11.6% and 25.6% higher than that of the benchmarked methods for two stocks in the real estate and communication sectors, respectively. The relatively high applicability of the model for the communications sector is consistent with the expectation that defensive sectors (e.g., the communications sector) have more stable stock prices than more cyclical sectors (e.g., the real estate sector). This paper also examines the importance of the characteristics that influence stock trend prediction models. The analysis shows that stock price characteristics are the most important, followed by news characteristics, while company financial characteristics are the least important.

Funding: This research received no external funding.

Data Availability Statement: Please refer to https://www.dfm.ae/market-data (accessed on 20 December 2021).

Conflicts of Interest: The author declares no conflict of interest.

References

1. Nguyen, T.H.; Shirai, K.; Velcin, J. Sentiment analysis on social media for stock movement prediction. *Expert Syst. Appl.* **2015**, *42*, 9603–9611. [CrossRef]
2. Thakkar, A.; Chaudhari, K. Fusion in stock market prediction: A decade survey on the necessity, recent developments, and potential future directions. *Inf. Fusion* **2020**, *65*, 95–107. [CrossRef] [PubMed]
3. Nti, I.K.; Adekoya, A.F.; Weyori, B.A. A novel multi-source information-fusion predictive framework based on deep neural networks for accuracy enhancement in stock market prediction. *J. Big Data* **2021**, *8*, 17. [CrossRef]
4. Padhi, D.K.; Padhy, N.; Bhoi, A.K.; Shafi, J.; Ijaz, M.F. A Fusion Framework for Forecasting Financial Market Direction Using Enhanced Ensemble Models and Technical Indicators. *Mathematics* **2021**, *9*, 2646. [CrossRef]
5. Panwar, B.; Dhuriya, G.; Johri, P.; Yadav, S.S.; Gaur, N. Stock Market Prediction Using Linear Regression and SVM. In Proceedings of the 2021 International Conference on Advance Computing and Innovative Technologies in Engineering (ICACITE), Greater Noida, India, 4–5 March 2021; pp. 629–631.
6. Patil, P.; Parasar, D.; Charhate, S. A Literature Review on Machine Learning Techniques and Strategies Applied to Stock Market Price Prediction. In Proceedings of the DDCIOT 2021, Udaipur, India, 20–21 March 2021.
7. Peng, Y.; Albuquerque, P.H.M.; Kimura, H.; Saavedra, C.A.P.B. Feature selection and deep neural networks for stock price direction forecasting using technical analysis indicators. *Mach. Learn. Appl.* **2021**, *5*, 100060. [CrossRef]
8. Shields, R.; El Zein, S.A.; Brunet, N.V. An Analysis on the NASDAQ's Potential for Sustainable Investment Practices during the Financial Shock from COVID-19. *Sustainability* **2021**, *13*, 3748. [CrossRef]
9. Song, D.; Baek, A.M.C.; Kim, N. Forecasting Stock Market Indices Using Padding-Based Fourier Transform Denoising and Time Series Deep Learning Models. *IEEE Access* **2021**, *9*, 83786–83796. [CrossRef]
10. Walkshäusl, C. Predicting Stock Returns from the Pricing and Mispricing of Accounting Fundamentals. *Q. Rev. Econ. Financ.* **2021**, *81*, 253–260. [CrossRef]
11. Wu, D.; Wang, X.; Su, J.; Tang, B.; Wu, S. A Labeling Method for Financial Time Series Prediction Based on Trends. *Entropy* **2020**, *22*, 1162. [CrossRef]
12. Yadav, K.; Yadav, M.; Saini, S. Stock values predictions using deep learning based hybrid models. *CAAI Trans. Intell. Technol.* **2021**, *25*, 1600214. [CrossRef]
13. Yun, K.K.; Yoon, S.W.; Won, D. Prediction of stock price direction using a hybrid GA-XGBoost algorithm with a three-stage feature engineering process. *Expert Syst. Appl.* **2021**, *186*, 115716. [CrossRef]
14. Zahara, S.; Sugianto. Multivariate Time Series Forecasting Based Cloud Computing for Consumer Price Index Using Deep Learning Algorithms. In Proceedings of the 2020 3rd International Seminar on Research of Information Technology and Intelligent Systems (ISRITI), Yogyakarta, Indonesia, 10–11 December 2020; pp. 338–343. [CrossRef]
15. Lin, Y.; Liu, S.; Yang, H.; Wu, H.; Jiang, B. Improving stock trading decisions based on pattern recognition using machine learning technology. *PLoS ONE* **2021**, *16*, e0255558. [CrossRef]
16. Lu, R.; Lu, M. Stock Trend Prediction Algorithm Based on Deep Recurrent Neural Network. *Wirel. Commun. Mob. Comput.* **2021**, *2021*, 5694975. [CrossRef]
17. Lyócsa, Š.; Stašek, D. Improving stock market volatility forecasts with complete subset linear and quantile HAR models. *Expert Syst. Appl.* **2021**, *183*, 115416. [CrossRef]
18. Mo, D.; Chen, Y. Projecting Financial Technical Indicators into Networks as a Tool to Build a Portfolio. *IEEE Access* **2021**, *9*, 39973–39984. [CrossRef]
19. Nabipour, M.; Nayyeri, P.; Jabani, H.; Mosavi, A.; Salwana, E.; Shahab, S. Deep Learning for Stock Market Prediction. *Entropy* **2020**, *22*, 840. [CrossRef]
20. Nabipour, M.; Nayyeri, P.; Jabani, H.; Shahab, S.; Mosavi, A. Predicting Stock Market Trends Using Machine Learning and Deep Learning Algorithms Via Continuous and Binary Data; a Comparative Analysis. *IEEE Access* **2020**, *8*, 150199–150212. [CrossRef]
21. Nayak, S.C.; Misra, B.B. Estimating stock closing indices using a GA-weighted condensed polynomial neural network. *Financial Innov.* **2018**, *4*, 21. [CrossRef]

22. Nti, I.K.; Adekoya, A.F.; Weyori, B.A. A comprehensive evaluation of ensemble learning for stock-market prediction. *J. Big Data* **2020**, *7*, 20. [CrossRef]
23. Zhao, H. Futures price prediction of agricultural products based on machine learning. *Neural Comput. Appl.* **2020**, *33*, 837–850. [CrossRef]
24. Chopra, R.; Sharma, G.D. Application of Artificial Intelligence in Stock Market Forecasting: A Critique, Review, and Research Agenda. *J. Risk Financial Manag.* **2021**, *14*, 526. [CrossRef]
25. Shah, D.; Isah, H.; Zulkernine, F. Stock Market Analysis: A Review and Taxonomy of Prediction Techniques. *Int. J. Financ. Stud.* **2019**, *7*, 26. [CrossRef]
26. Priya, S.; Revadi, R.; Terence, S.; Immaculate, J. A Novel Framework to Detect Effective Prediction Using Machine Learning. In *Security Issues and Privacy Concerns in Industry 4.0 Applications*; Wiley Online Library: Bridgewater, NJ, USA, 2021; pp. 179–194. [CrossRef]
27. Saleh, A.; Baiwei, L. Dengue Prediction Using Deep Learning with Long Short-Term Memory. In Proceedings of the 2021 1st International Conference on Emerging Smart Technologies and Applications (eSmarTA), Sana'a, Yemen, 10–12 August 2021; pp. 1–5.
28. Shaila, S.; Monish, L.; Rajlaxmi, P. Real-Time Problems to Be Solved by the Combination of IoT, Big Data, and Cloud Technologies. In *Challenges and Opportunities for the Convergence of IoT, Big Data, and Cloud Computing*; Sathiyamoorthi, V., Ed.; IGI Global: Hershey, PA, USA, 2021; pp. 265–276. [CrossRef]
29. Alotaibi, S.S. Ensemble Technique with Optimal Feature Selection for Saudi Stock Market Prediction: A Novel Hybrid Red Deer-Grey Algorithm. *IEEE Access* **2021**, *9*, 64929–64944. [CrossRef]
30. Arosemena, J.; Pérez, N.; Benítez, D.; Riofrío, D.; Flores-Moyano, R. Stock Price Analysis with Deep-Learning Models. In Proceedings of the 2021 IEEE Colombian Conference on Applications of Computational Intelligence (ColCACI), Cali, Colombia, 26–28 May 2021; pp. 1–6.
31. Jaggi, M.; Mandal, P.; Narang, S.; Naseem, U.; Khushi, M. Text Mining of Stocktwits Data for Predicting Stock Prices. *Appl. Syst. Innov.* **2021**, *4*, 13. [CrossRef]
32. Arjun, R.; Suprabha, K. Forecasting banking sectors in Indian stock markets using machine intelligence. *Int. J. Hybrid Intell. Syst.* **2019**, *15*, 129–142. [CrossRef]
33. Assous, H.F.; Al-Rousan, N.; Al-Najjar, D.; Al-Najjar, H. Can International Market Indices Estimate TASI's Movements? The ARIMA Model. *J. Open Innov. Technol. Mark. Complex.* **2020**, *6*, 27. [CrossRef]
34. Chen, Y.-S.; Sangaiah, A.K.; Chen, S.-F.; Huang, H.-C. Applied Identification of Industry Data Science Using an Advanced Multi-Componential Discretization Model. *Symmetry* **2020**, *12*, 1620. [CrossRef]
35. Jiang, M.; Liu, J.; Zhang, L.; Liu, C. An improved Stacking framework for stock index prediction by leveraging tree-based ensemble models and deep learning algorithms. *Phys. A Stat. Mech. Its Appl.* **2019**, *541*, 122272. [CrossRef]
36. Kim, S.; Ku, S.; Chang, W.; Song, J.W. Predicting the Direction of US Stock Prices Using Effective Transfer Entropy and Machine Learning Techniques. *IEEE Access* **2020**, *8*, 111660–111682. [CrossRef]
37. Lahmiri, S. A predictive system integrating intrinsic mode functions, artificial neural networks, and genetic algorithms for forecasting S&P500 intra-day data. *Intell. Syst.* **2020**, *27*, 55–65. [CrossRef]
38. Nazari, E.; Biviji, R.; Farzin, A.H.; Asgari, P.; Tabesh, H. Advantages and Challenges of Information Fusion Technique for Big Data Analysis: Proposed Framework. *Biostat. Epidemiol.* **2021**, *7*, 189–216. [CrossRef]
39. Zhang, X.; Li, Y.; Wang, S.; Fang, B.; Yu, P.S. Enhancing stock market prediction with extended coupled hidden Markov model over multi-sourced data. *Knowl. Inf. Syst.* **2018**, *61*, 1071–1090. [CrossRef]
40. Zhang, X.; Qu, S.; Huang, J.; Fang, B.; Yu, P. Stock Market Prediction via Multi-Source Multiple Instance Learning. *IEEE Access* **2018**, *6*, 50720–50728. [CrossRef]
41. Hiransha, M.; Gopalakrishnan, E.A.; Vijay, K.M.; Soman, K.P. NSE Stock Market Prediction Using Deep-Learning Models. *Procedia Comput. Sci.* **2018**, *132*, 1351–1362. [CrossRef]
42. Nasir, A.; Shaukat, K.; Khan, K.I.; Hameed, I.A.; Alam, T.M.; Luo, S. Trends and Directions of Financial Technology (Fintech) in Society and Environment: A Bibliometric Study. *Appl. Sci.* **2021**, *11*, 10353. [CrossRef]
43. Polamuri, S.R.; Srinivas, K.; Mohan, A.K. Multi model-Based Hybrid Prediction Algorithm (MM-HPA) for Stock Market Prices Prediction Framework (SMPPF). *Arab. J. Sci. Eng.* **2020**, *45*, 10493–10509. [CrossRef]
44. Shobana, G.; Umamaheswari, K. Forecasting by Machine Learning Techniques and Econometrics: A Review. In Proceedings of the 2021 6th International Conference on Inventive Computation Technologies (ICICT), Coimbatore, India, 20–22 January 2021.
45. Srivastava, P.; Zhang, Z.; Eachempati, P. Deep Neural Network and Time Series Approach for Finance Systems: Predicting the Movement of the Indian Stock Market. *J. Organ. End User Comput.* **2021**, *33*, 204–226. [CrossRef]
46. Gao, Y.; Wang, R.; Zhou, E. Stock Prediction Based on Optimized LSTM and GRU Models. *Sci. Program.* **2021**, *2021*, 4055281. [CrossRef]
47. Xie, M.; Li, H.; Zhao, Y. Blockchain financial investment based on deep learning network algorithm. *J. Comput. Appl. Math.* **2020**, *372*, 112723. [CrossRef]
48. Xu, G.; Meng, Y.; Qiu, X.; Yu, Z.; Wu, X. Sentiment Analysis of Comment Texts Based on BiLSTM. *IEEE Access* **2019**, *7*, 51522–51532. [CrossRef]

49. Peach, R.L.; Greenbury, S.F.; Johnston, I.G.; Yaliraki, S.N.; Lefevre, D.J.; Barahona, M. Understanding learner behaviour in online courses with Bayesian modelling and time series characterisation. *Sci. Rep.* **2021**, *11*, 2823. [CrossRef] [PubMed]
50. Bergmeir, C.; Benítez, J.M. On the use of cross-validation for time series predictor evaluation. *Inf. Sci.* **2012**, *191*, 192–213. [CrossRef]
51. Eachempati, P.; Srivastava, P.R.; Kumar, A.; Tan, K.H.; Gupta, S. Validating the impact of accounting disclosures on stock market: A deep neural network approach. *Technol. Forecast. Soc. Chang.* **2021**, *170*, 120903. [CrossRef]
52. Ghosh, I.; Sanyal, M.K. Introspecting predictability of market fear in Indian context during COVID-19 pandemic: An integrated approach of applied predictive modelling and explainable AI. *Int. J. Inf. Manag. Data Insights* **2021**, *1*, 100039. [CrossRef]

Article

Enhanced Credit Card Fraud Detection Model Using Machine Learning

Noor Saleh Alfaiz * and Suliman Mohamed Fati

College of Computer and Information Sciences, Prince Sultan University, Riyadh 11586, Saudi Arabia; smfati@yahoo.com or sgaber@psu.edu.sa
* Correspondence: mrnoor220@gmail.com

Abstract: The COVID-19 pandemic has limited people's mobility to a certain extent, making it difficult to purchase goods and services offline, which has led the creation of a culture of increased dependence on online services. One of the crucial issues with using credit cards is fraud, which is a serious challenge in the realm of online transactions. Consequently, there is a huge need to develop the best approach possible to using machine learning in order to prevent almost all fraudulent credit card transactions. This paper studies a total of 66 machine learning models based on two stages of evaluation. A real-world credit card fraud detection dataset of European cardholders is used in each model along with stratified K-fold cross-validation. In the first stage, nine machine learning algorithms are tested to detect fraudulent transactions. The best three algorithms are nominated to be used again in the second stage, with 19 resampling techniques used with each one of the best three algorithms. Out of 330 evaluation metric values that took nearly one month to obtain, the All K-Nearest Neighbors (AllKNN) undersampling technique along with CatBoost (AllKNN-CatBoost) is considered to be the best proposed model. Accordingly, the AllKNN-CatBoost model is compared with related works. The results indicate that the proposed model outperforms previous models with an AUC value of 97.94%, a Recall value of 95.91%, and an F1-Score value of 87.40%.

Keywords: credit card fraud; fraud detection; machine learning; CatBoost; XGBoost; random forest; class imbalance

Citation: Alfaiz, N.S.; Fati, S.M. Enhanced Credit Card Fraud Detection Model Using Machine Learning. *Electronics* **2022**, *11*, 662. https://doi.org/10.3390/electronics11040662

Academic Editors: Amir H. Gandomi, Fang Chen and Laith Abualigah

Received: 19 December 2021
Accepted: 14 February 2022
Published: 21 February 2022

1. Introduction

As the world is heading to a cashless society, there will be more and more dependency on making online transactions. Modern fraud does not require fraudsters to be physically in the crime locations. They can perform their diabolical activities at the comfort of their homes with many ways of hiding their identities. Such identity hiding techniques include using a VPN, routing the victim's traffic through the Tor network, etc., and it is not easy to trace them back.

The impact of online financial losses cannot be underestimated. Once fraudsters steal card details, they can use the cards themselves or sell the card details to other people, as is the case in India, where the card details of around 70 million people are being sold on the dark web [1]. One of the most serious credit card fraud incidents in recent memory that took place in the UK resulted in GBP 17 million total in financial losses. The incident occurred after a group of international fraudsters conspired to steal the detail information of more than 32,000 credit cards in the mid-2000s [2]. This incident is considered to be the biggest card fraud in history. Thus, the lack of effective security systems results in billion-dollar losses due to credit card fraud [3]. Both cardholders, while using their cards, and card issuers, while processing the transactions, are being reassured that all transactions are benign. Conversely to this belief, fraudsters intend to deceive financial institutions and cardholders into believing that the fraudulent transactions are legitimate.

In addition, there are some fraudulent transactions that happen continuously to obtain financial gain without the knowledge of both card issuers and cardholders. Both authorized institutions and cardholders sometimes do not know that they have fraudulent transactions, and this is the darkest side of credit card transactions. With that in mind, it is a very challenging process to detect fraudulent activity amongst thousands of genuine transactions, especially when fraudulent transactions are significantly less than the genuine ones [4].

There are many fraud detection techniques that help to prevent fraud in the financial industry, such as predictive analytics and data mining, especially modeling algorithms that incorporate clustering techniques and anomaly detection [5]. However, all these techniques cannot be performed without machine learning algorithms, whether they are supervised or unsupervised, which can be effective in credit card fraud classification [6]. However, those machine learning algorithms encounter countless numbers of challenges when trying to detect all fraudulent activity [7].

In the ideal machine learning model, the commonly used evaluation metrics must be at the highest values. In the hopes of moving closer to this ideal model, there are many improvements needed in this arena. The challenges facing credit card fraud detection depend on many factors, such as machine learning algorithms, cross-validation techniques, and resampling techniques. Considering these factors can enhance the performance of the model that can be validated by the evaluation metrics.

In a real-world problem, it is extremely rare to have a balanced dataset to work with, which means that the classification algorithm undermines the importance of the minority class in the dataset in most cases. As a matter of fact, the minority class is the most significant aspect of the classification process, especially in credit card fraud detection. Due to the unbalanced distribution of the classes in the dataset, the proposed approach highlights the imbalance class issue using various resampling techniques after choosing the best machine learning algorithms. Not only are the resampling techniques considered in this paper, but so too are the improved cross-validation (CV) techniques as well.

This paper proposes an advanced approach in terms of choosing the best machine learning algorithm in combination with the best resampling technique. This approach is based on an analysis at two stages using performance evaluation metrics. The first stage aims to analyze nine machine learning algorithms with their default parameters. The nine algorithms are Logistic Regression (LR) [8], K-Nearest Neighbors (KNN) [9], Decision Tree (DT) [10], Naïve Bayes (NB) [11], Random Forest (RF) [9], Gradient Boosting Machines (GBM) [12], Light Gradient Boosting Machine (LightGBM) [13], Extreme Gradient Boosting (XGBoost) [14], and Category Boosting (CatBoost) [15]. Out of these nine algorithms, only the best three algorithms are nominated to be use in the second stage. The second stage aims to analyze 19 resampling techniques with each one of the selected three algorithms from the first stage. These 19 resampling techniques are categorized as follows: 11 undersampling, 6 oversampling, and 2 with combinations of both undersampling and oversampling techniques at once. Furthermore, this stage aims to select the best combination of both algorithm and resampling technique to obtain the best proposed model based on the best overall performance.

This innovative approach stands out by exploring different ways to address the class imbalance issue in the dataset. This is shown in terms of comparing the best machine learning algorithms and using stratified K-fold CV and resampling techniques. Using this number of various algorithms and techniques gives a promising result, especially given that it took nearly one month just to obtain all the evaluation metric values.

The rest of the paper is structured as follows. In the second section, related work is reviewed. The third section describes the proposed approach. In the fourth section, the experimental results are discussed. Finally, the conclusion and future work are summarized in the fifth section.

2. Related Work

Given the importance of credit card fraud, there are renowned techniques to impede this diabolical activity. Not only do financial institutions and banks provide the convenience of financial services, but they also do not hesitate to be the front line protectors of cardholders. In addition, they invest and develop various techniques, including the state-of-the-art machine learning techniques that many systems heavily depend on.

One of these techniques used is DT. It is easy to implement, but it needs to check each transaction one by one [16]. Khatri et al. [17] analyzed various models with an imbalanced European credit card fraud detection (ECCFD) dataset. They did not consider using any resampling techniques. The results indicated that DT was generally the best, with good Recall (79.21%), Precision (85.11%), and time (5 s), while KNN was better in regard to Recall (81.19%), Precision (91.11%), but not with time (463 s).

Another technique involves using LightGBM. Taha and Malebary [18] conducted their experiment on two datasets using LightGBM. The first one is the ECCFD dataset, and the second one is the UCSD-FICO Data Mining Contest 2009 dataset. Using a 5-fold version of the K-Fold CV, they calculated the average values. They compared it to their Optimized Light Gradient Boosting Machine (OLightGBM), which included hyper-parameter tuning with other state-of-the-art algorithms. They found that OLightGBM achieved the highest scores in both datasets. In the first dataset, OLightGBM achieved 90.94% in Area under the Receiver Operating Characteristic Curve (AUC) measures, 98.40% in Accuracy, 40.59% in Recall, 97.34% in Precision, and 56.95% in $F1$-Score. Similarly, in the second dataset, OLightGBM achieved 92.88% in AUC, 98.35% in Accuracy, 28.33% in Recall, 91.72% in Precision, and 43.27% in $F1$-Score.

Another research direction focused on LR and KNN, whereby Vengatesan et al. [19] examined the performance of LR and KNN on the imbalanced ECCFD dataset. The findings were that KNN achieved the best Precision of 95%, Recall of 72%, and $F1$-Score of 82%. In addition, Puh and Brkić [20] studied the performance of different algorithms, namely, RF, the Support Vector Machine (SVM), and LR, on the dataset of European cardholders. They tackled the imbalance class issue in the dataset using the Synthetic Minority Oversampling Technique (SMOTE). SMOTE and LR were used to create their models with some changes in the parameters of the algorithm. The LR parameter C was set to 100 and L2-Regulation was used. They created two models using LR in terms of the learning process. The first one involves static learning and the other one involves incremental learning. The results showed that the AUC score was 91.14% with static learning and the AUC score was 91.07% with incremental learning. The Average Precision score was 73.37% with static learning, and the Average Precision score was 84.13% with incremental learning.

Other researchers focused on RF. Hema [21] evaluated the ECCFD dataset without addressing the imbalanced class issue using three algorithms, which were RF, LR, and Category Boosting (CatBoost). Hema found that RF gave better overall results in terms of Accuracy (99.95%), Precision (91.95%), Recall (79.2%), F1-Score (85.1%), MCC (85.31%), and AUC (89%). Kumar et al. [22] conducted a basic study using RF on the ECCFD dataset. They found that the accuracy of RF was 90%.

Some other researchers considered using an Artificial Neural Network (ANN), which simulates how a human brain works [23]. Asha and KR [24] used SVM, KNN, and ANN models on the ECCFD dataset. The results showed that the ANN was the best among the other models, with an Accuracy of 99.92%, a Precision of 81.15%, and a Recall of 76.19%. Dubey et al. [1] conducted an experiment on the Credit Card Customer dataset with the use of ANN. That processed the data in the first layer, which was the input layer, and then the hidden layer, which had 15 neurons and the use of the RELU activation function, and then the output layer, which used the Sigmoid activation function. Eventually, their approach resulted in 99.92% Accuracy, 99.96% Recall, 99.96% Precision, and 99.96% $F1$-Score values. Varmedja et al. [25] conducted their research by splitting the ECCFD in a 80:20 ratio. The algorithms they used were LR, RF, NB, Multilayer Perceptron, and ANN. The imbalanced issue of the dataset was addressed using SMOTE. Each model was updated through multiple epochs depending on the tolerance for the optimization. Their findings indicated that RF achieved the best results in terms of Accuracy (99.96%), Recall (81.63%), and Precision (96.38%).

Local Outlier Factor (LOF) and Isolation Forest (iForest) have been used in some studies. LOF detects outliers based on the local density [26], while iForest also detects outliers based on a tree structure [27]. One of these studies was performed by John and Naaz [28], as they used both LOF and iForest on the ECCFD dataset. They did not address the imbalanced class issue in the dataset, and the results indicated that LOF showed the highest accuracy rate of 97%.

Looking at related work, there are some aspects need to be considered to detect fraudulent activity in credit card transactions. Each approach has its own methodology to enhance the overall performance of their proposed models. However, a machine learning algorithm can have a certain result in one approach, and different results in the other ones. To obtain a better idea on which algorithm performs the best, increasing the number of algorithms used in the experiment should be considered. The imbalance class issue is very common in datasets. Thus, not addressing this issue can lead to poor performance. This issue can be tackled by using stratified CV and resampling techniques, with a significant number of resampling techniques that can be used in experiments. Moreover, the number of evaluation metrics is important for evaluating the model's performance from different angles. Some previous works lack one or more of these aspects. Consequently, an unprecedented approach is proposed.

3. Proposed Approach

The approach is divided into two stages, where the results of the first stage are used as inputs for the second one. The two stages are illustrated in Figure 1.

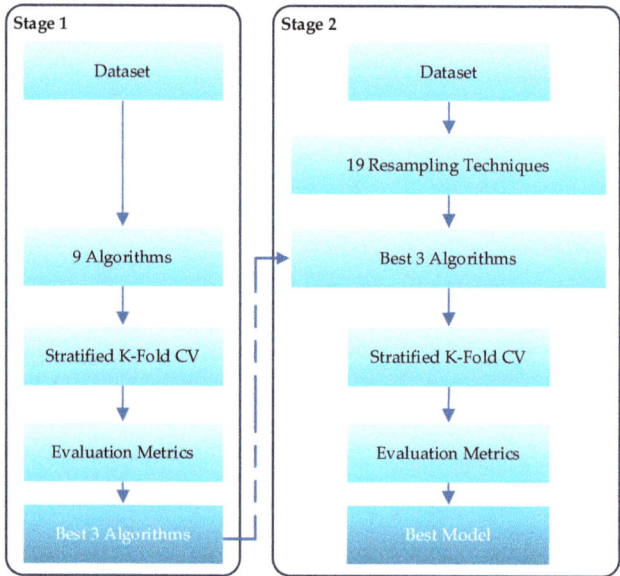

Figure 1. Overall proposed approach.

3.1. Simulation Environment

The simulation environment can be categorized as follows:

3.1.1. Software

The experiment is performed using a 64-bit Windows 10 virtual machine on a server that is equipped with Anaconda Navigator 1.10.0, Jupyter Notebook 6.1.4, and Python 3.8. The libraries used in the Anaconda Navigator environment are Scikit-Learn, Pandas, Numpy, Seaborn, Matplotlib, and Imbalanced-Learn, along with machine learning classifiers.

3.1.2. Hardware

The following points reflect the hardware environment:

- Processor: Intel(R) Xeon(R) CPU D-1527 @ 2.20 GHz 2.19 GHz.
- RAM: 7.00 GB.

The server itself has four CPU cores, and the virtual machine only uses three CPU cores with six threats.

3.2. Dataset

The dataset that is used with this proposed approach is a real-world dataset obtained from Kaggle [29]. It contains transactions made by credit cards in September 2013 by European cardholders that occurred over two days published by Universite Libre de Bruxelles. There are 492 instances of fraud out of 284,807 transactions with 31 features, namely 'Time', 'V1' to 'V28', 'Amount', and 'Class'. This dataset is widely used by many researchers and practitioners found in the related work section; hence, this dataset is chosen to compare the evaluation metric values of our proposed model with theirs.

Preprocessing is not always needed when the dataset meets certain criteria. One of these criteria is to check if there are any missing values that may affect the prediction. When exploring the data, we see that each feature in the dataset has 284,807 values, which means that none of these features is missing any values. Thus, preprocessing is not needed. Figure 2 shows the correlation matrix along with the heat map. The correlation matrix is an advantageous technique that helps us to decide if there is any need to remove a certain feature. Since the correlation matrix shows that all features are related to the 'Class' feature regardless of whether the correlation is strong or weak, this leads us to the conclusion that there is no need to pull out any feature; hence, there is no need to preprocess the dataset. Another reason is that the features from 'V1' to 'V28' are the result of a PCA dimensionality reduction transformation. This was performed because the original data of these features contain sensitive information. Due to the fact that the dataset is already processed, the preprocessing stage is deliberately avoided to obtain a more realistic approach.

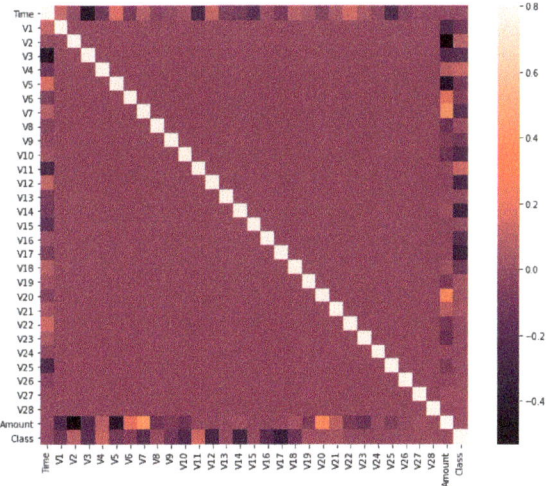

Figure 2. Correlation matrix.

3.3. Algorithms

There are nine machine learning algorithms that are being used in the first stage of the proposed approach. They are LR, KNN, DT, NB, RF, GBM, LightGBM, XGBoost, and finally CatBoost. Each one of these machine learning algorithms' parameters is set to default, except KNN, where the value of "n_neighbors" is set to 3. Only the best 3 algorithms that achieve the highest performance from the first stage are used again in the second stage, as is shown in Figure 1. Each algorithm is explained as follows.

3.3.1. Logistic Regression

This is one of the traditional machine learning algorithms that is still used today due to its quick analysis and simple method of processing the features of a class. The ability of LR to associate various factors, especially with strong ones, and its ability to adjust to different factors depend on predictor variables and the outcome. LR uses values that are greater than 1 and less than 0 to treat the anomalies in the dataset, and it is not limited to classifying and predicting binominal outcomes, but also multinomial outcomes as well, and it uses the sigmoid function to estimate the values of parameters' coefficients [7]. When LR examines the values of the attributes during an ongoing transaction, it tells us whether the transaction should continue or not, as it is used for clustering [30].

3.3.2. K-Nearest Neighbors

This is a classifier that is used for classification and regression problems. One of its advantages is that it increases the credit card detection rate and decreases false alarm rates. It works based on similarity measures. Thus, it stores all instances that are accessible and arranges new ones [9]. It uses statistical learning techniques, and it works well in supervised machine learning systems, as there is a learning stage that is used to obtain the necessary knowledge, which enables it to classify major differences. However, in unsupervised learning techniques, the training stage is not required. There are three factors in KNN: the distance metrics, the distance rule, and the K value. Distance metrics help to locate the nearest neighbor of any incoming data point, the distance rule classifies the new data point into a class when it is processing its features in relation to the data points in its neighborhood, and the K value is the number of neighbors with which to compare it [7].

3.3.3. Decision Tree

This is a computational method that aims to classify and predict. It has a tree-like process, including a root node, leaf node, and branch. Each internal node indicates a test based on its attributes, the outcome of the test indicates each branch, and the class label holds each leaf node [10]. The process happens recursively when a similarity tree is defined, where the nodes are labelled with attribute names and edges. Those labelled values are attributes that satisfy some conditions and leaves that contain an intensity factor, which is defined as the ratio of the number of transactions that satisfy these conditions over the total number of legitimate transaction in the behavior [31].

3.3.4. CatBoost

There are some classifiers that belong to the DT family, such as CatBoost, which is a cutting-edge, open-source form of gradient boosting for the DT library developed by Yandex researchers and engineers [15]. CatBoost is highly versatile and can be used with a wide range of applications and problems.

3.3.5. XGBoost

Another classifier is XGBoost, which belongs to the DT family, and it is a decision tree-based ensemble machine learning classifier. XGBoost uses a gradient boosting framework that consists of a set of classification and regression trees (CART) [14].

3.3.6. GBM

GBM is another classifier that belongs to the DT family that uses an ensemble technique. It aims to improve Accuracy using an ensemble of trees instead of a single tree, and this algorithm is used for regression and classification, as outlined by Friedman [12,32].

3.3.7. LightGBM

Another algorithm is LightGBM, which is commonly used as a fast, distributed, high-performance, and open-source gradient boosting framework. LightGBM is developed by Microsoft and is based on DT algorithms [13].

3.3.8. Naïve Bayes

This is a supervised machine learning classifier that can be trained to predict future instances of the target class. NB is known to be a powerful probabilistic method that takes advantage of feature and class information from the dataset, which enables it to predict instances in the future [33,34]. "Naïve" is a description of how this technique works because it treats each attribute independently based on the class variable, whether it is present or absent, and "Bayes" is a description of how it calculates the probability of the class correctness [11]. Although NB has a simple mechanism, this algorithm produces good results in many complicated real-world problems.

3.3.9. Random Forest

When encountering a classification or regression problem, the ensemble method, also known as the RF method, can deal with both by growing many decision trees in a way that each tree acts as a weak learner, and those trees are added together, and they become a robust learner [9]. One of the advantages of an RF is that it is effective and fast when handling imbalanced datasets, even when the imbalanced datasets have thousands of features [35]. The way that an RF works is that each tree provides a classification vote for a class. The new object is created, and it is given maximum votes into the class.

3.4. Resampling Techniques

Resampling techniques are commonly used to tackle the imbalance class issue in a dataset [36]. When looking at the dataset used here, the total number of valid cases is 284,315 and the total number of fraud cases is 492. That means that the valid cases are 99.827% of the total number of cases; meanwhile, the fraud cases are only 0.173% of the total number of cases. Certainly, the dataset is highly unbalanced. Thus, resampling techniques come in handy, as the imbalance class issue is related to the performance of the algorithms [37]. There are 3 main categories of resampling techniques: undersampling, oversampling, and the combination of both undersampling and oversampling.

3.4.1. Undersampling

Undersampling techniques are known to provide a compact balanced training set, and one of the advantages of this kind of technique is that it reduces the cost of the learning phase [38]. One of the issues of undersampling techniques is the removal of a large chunk of the training set, especially when the majority class instances are tremendously huge, which leads to the loss of significant cases that would, in turn, lead to difficulties in classification and prediction.

3.4.2. Oversampling

Unlike undersampling, the development of oversampling methods aims to preserve the majority class instances and replicate the minority class instances in order to tackle the issue of imbalanced training set. The issue with this kind of technique is that it may lead to poor performance of the model in some cases because it may be hard to generate the minority data in the training set [39,40].

3.4.3. Combination of Both Undersampling and Oversampling

This combination aims to use both undersampling and oversampling techniques at the same time. By merging these techniques, the imbalance class issue is addressed differently.

3.4.4. The 19 Resampling Techniques

Table 1 states the 19 resampling techniques that are used in the proposed approach, and they are as follows:

- Eleven undersampling techniques.
- Six oversampling techniques.
- Two combinations of both undersampling and oversampling techniques at once.

Table 1. Nineteen Resampling Techniques.

Type	Technique	Abbreviation
Undersampling	Random Undersampling	RUS
	Condensed Nearest Neighbor	CNN
	Tomek	Tomek
	One-Sided Selection	OSS
	Edited Nearest Neighbors	ENN
	Repeated Edited Nearest Neighbors	RENN
	All K-Nearest Neighbors	AllKNN
	Neighborhood Cleaning Rule	NCR
	Near Miss 1	NM1
	Near Miss 2	NM2
	Instance Hardness Threshold	IHT
Oversampling	Random Oversampling	ROS
	Synthetic Minority Oversampling Technique	SMOTE
	Adaptive Synthetic	ADASYN
	Borderline SMOTE 1	Border1
	Borderline SMOTE 2	Border2
	SVM SMOTE	SVMSM
Both Undersampling and Oversampling	SMOTEENN	SMENN
	SMOTETomek	SMTomek

There are two versions of Near Miss, and that is the reason why both NM1 and NM2 are used. Similarly, there are two versions of Borderline SMOTE; the first one is Borderline1, and the second one is Borderline2.

3.5. Stratified K-Fold Cross-Validation

Due to the high sensitivity of the credit card fraud issue, evaluating machine learning models must involve rigorous procedures. A single iteration of evaluating a model may not provide an accurate validation of the model. Thus, the multiple iteration method is the right method to ensure that the model goes through a rigid examination to obtain robust performance.

Provided that multiple iterations are necessary to examine the proposed models, one cannot simply use K-fold cross-validation (CV) when there is an improved version of it. The improved version is stratified K-fold CV. This technique comes in handy, especially when considering that a highly unbalanced dataset may cause a major issue for machine learning algorithms. Despite the fact that K-fold CV is widely used, stratified K-fold CV is used to validate the models of the proposed approach, as it is recommended by Scikit-Learn Developers [41]. Stratified K-fold CV aims to consider the proportion of the minority class in each fold; thus, the minority class is similarly distributed.

Figure 3 shows how stratified K-fold CV is used throughout the proposed approach in both stages. The data are randomly divided in each iteration, with 80% forming part of the training set and 20% forming part of the test set in a very organized manner, which does not lead to data leakage when training the model. The average value of the total of the 5 iterations is considered to be the final value when evaluating the model using evaluation metrics.

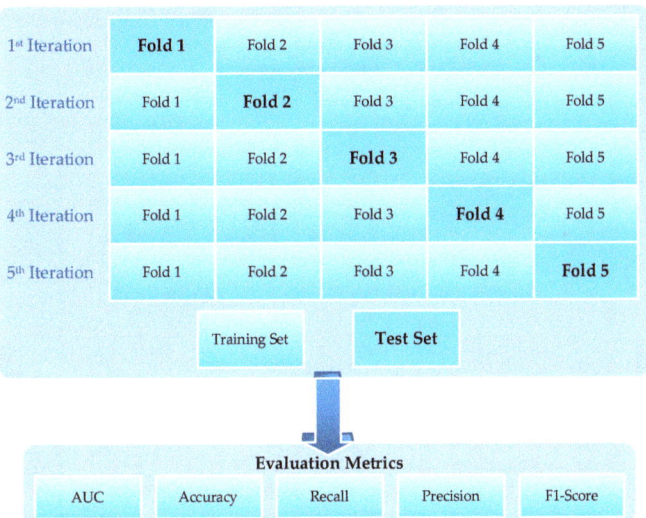

Figure 3. Stratified K-fold cross-validation with evaluation metrics.

3.6. Evaluation Metrics

Each one of the 66 models in both stages is evaluated based on the Area under the Receiver Operating Characteristic Curve (AUC), *Accuracy, Recall, Precision*, and F1-Score. All evaluation metrics used in the proposed approach depend on a confusion matrix in one way or another [42]. A confusion matrix, sometimes referred to as an error matrix [43], is one of the traditional ways to evaluate machine learning model performance that provides four outcomes. They are True Positive (*TP*), False Negative (*FN*), True Negative (*TN*), and False Positive (*FP*) [44–46].

The Receiver Operating Characteristics (ROC) curve provides a graphical representation of the classification model performance. The False Positive Rate (FPR) is plotted on the *x*-axis and the True Positive Rate (TPR) is on the *y*-axis in the ROC space. The AUC calculates the whole two-dimensional area underneath the whole ROC curve. This can be achieved by calculating the collective performance of all potential classification thresholds [47].

Accuracy, which is also known as the error rate, is one method to find out how often the classifier classifies a data point properly [48]. Equation (1) [49] shows the Accuracy calculated as the ratio of the correct classified cases (fraud (*TP*) and non-fraud (*TN*)) to the whole pool of cases.

$$Accuracy = \frac{TP + TN}{TP + FN + TN + FP} \tag{1}$$

Precision and *Recall* are evaluation metrics that work in different ways to achieve different results. There is often a trade-off between *Precision* and *Recall*. If *Precision* is higher, *Recall* becomes lower, and if *Precision* is lower, *Recall* becomes higher [50]. *Precision*, also called the Positive Predictive Value, evaluates the correct prediction of the positive cases out of the total positive cases, as is shown in Equation (2):

$$Precison = Positive\ Predicted\ Value = \frac{TP}{TP + FP} \tag{2}$$

Recall, also known as True Positive Rate (*TPR*) and *Sensitivity* [51], is one of the most important evaluation metrics used in detecting fraudulent credit card transactions. Its importance relies on its ability to catch positive cases. The higher the *Recall* value is, the more the detection of fraudulent activity is increased. As a result, it is important to obtain the higher *Recall* value as much as possible to avoid missing any cases of fraud, even though the proposed model may obtain a reasonable amount of *FP*, but not at the expense of *FN* as far as possible. *Recall* is expressed in Equation (3):

$$Recall = Sensitivity = TPR = \frac{True\ Positive}{Total\ Positives} = \frac{TP}{TP + FN} \qquad (3)$$

Precision is important, but it is not as important as *Recall*. *Precision* is concerned about the actual *TP* cases of all predicted positive cases. Nonetheless, having a reasonable amount of *FP* cases made by the proposed model is acceptable as long as the proposed model does not compromise on *FN* cases as much as possible. For this reason, *Recall* is more important than *Precision* in credit card fraud detection. On the other hand, F1-Score evaluates the performance of the model by combining the *Precision* and *Recall* values. When comparing between two or more models, the F1-Score is considered among other evaluation metrics [52]; hence, the classifier with the highest F1-Score must be chosen, as is stated in [6]. Equation (4) is the expression of F1-Score:

$$F1 = 2 \times \frac{Precision \times Recall}{Precision + Recall} \qquad (4)$$

The AUC, *Accuracy*, *Recall*, *Precision*, and F1-Score evaluation metrics give 330 values for each one of the 66 models that are used in the proposed approach across both stages.

4. Results

4.1. The First Stage: Algorithm Comparison

Referring to Figure 1, the first stage provides an initial assessment of how well each machine learning algorithm performs. These algorithms are LR, KNN, DT, NB, RF, GBM, LightGBM, XGBoost, and CatBoost.

Table 2 shows that CatBoost, XGBoost, and RF achieve the highest AUC values. With regard to Accuracy, all algorithms achieve similar values above 99%. However, this evaluation metric does not reflect the overall performance of these nine algorithms. Recall, which is a significant evaluation metric due to its intolerance to any fraudulent activity, gives similar results to the AUC. Regarding Precision, CatBoost, XGBoost, RF, and DT achieve the highest values. With regard to F1-Score, CatBoost, XGBoost, and RF achieve the highest values. NB achieves the lowest values in terms of AUC and Recall, whereas KNN achieves the lowest values in terms of Precision and F1-Score.

Table 2. Algorithms without Resampling Techniques.

Classifier	AUC	Accuracy	Recall	Precision	F1-Score
LR	0.8483	0.9989	0.6971	0.6462	0.6688
KNN	0.9180	0.9984	0.8375	0.0956	0.1711
DT	0.8722	0.9991	0.7449	0.7724	0.7581
NB	0.5736	0.9929	0.1478	0.6485	0.2405
RF	0.9742	0.9996	0.9487	0.7846	0.8588
GBM	0.8841	0.9990	0.7688	0.6034	0.6615
LightGBM	0.6246	0.9959	0.2499	0.5612	0.3410
XGBoost	0.9760	0.9996	0.9523	**0.8008**	0.8698
Catboost	**0.9804**	**0.9996**	**0.9612**	0.7967	**0.8711**

The takeaway from the first stage of assessment is that CatBoost achieved high scores virtually on each evaluation metric. Nonetheless, XGBoost is competing aggressively against CatBoost, and achieves a slightly higher Precision metric than CatBoost. RF is closely behind CatBoost and XGBoost, as it achieves an equal Accuracy metric value to CatBoost and XGBoost. Therefore, the chosen three machine learning algorithms from the first stage are CatBoost, XGBoost, and RF.

4.2. The Second Stage: Resampling Techniques

Tables 3–5 show the results of the second stage when integrating the chosen three algorithms from the first stage with the three resampling technique types. These types are undersampling, oversampling, and the combination of both undersampling and oversampling techniques at the same time. The first row of Tables 3–5 shows the evaluation metric results of the algorithm without any resampling techniques. The next 11 rows show the resulting values of the undersampling techniques, which are RUS, CNN, Tomek, OSS, ENN, RENN, AllKNN, NCR, NM1, NM2, and IHT. The next six rows show the resulting values of the oversampling techniques including ROS, SMOTE, ADASYN, Border1, Border2, and SVMSM. The last two rows of Tables 3–5 show the resulting values of the combined undersampling and oversampling techniques. The two techniques are SMENN and SMTomek.

Table 3. CatBoost with Resampling Techniques.

Technique	AUC	Accuracy	Recall	Precision	F1-Score
Without	0.9804	**0.9996**	0.9612	0.7967	0.8711
RUS	0.5331	0.9776	0.0663	0.9065	0.1234
CNN	0.7496	0.9982	0.4994	0.8597	0.6306
Tomek	0.9768	**0.9996**	0.9539	0.7947	0.8670
OSS	**0.9806**	**0.9996**	**0.9616**	0.7948	0.8699
ENN	0.9791	**0.9996**	0.9586	0.7947	0.8689
RENN	0.9782	**0.9996**	0.9568	0.8029	0.8730
AllKNN	0.9794	**0.9996**	0.9591	0.8028	**0.8740**
NCR	0.9792	**0.9996**	0.9587	0.7967	0.8702
NM1	0.5037	0.7698	0.0075	0.9350	0.0149
NM2	0.5005	0.0160	0.0017	**0.9939**	0.0035
IHT	0.5007	0.0300	0.0018	**0.9939**	0.0035
ROS	0.9045	0.9994	0.8093	0.8435	0.8256
SMOTE	0.8627	0.9992	0.7256	0.8476	0.7811
ADASYN	0.8327	0.9990	0.6657	0.8435	0.7431
Border1	0.9139	0.9994	0.8281	0.8231	0.8253
Border2	0.8869	0.9993	0.7741	0.8313	0.8014
SVMSM	0.9291	0.9995	0.8585	0.8231	0.8403
SMENN	0.8486	0.9991	0.6975	0.8414	0.7617
SMTomek	0.8295	0.9990	0.6593	0.8435	0.7400

To find out the best model, going through each one of these evaluation metrics can help us obtain a better idea.

4.2.1. AUC

When looking at Tables 3–5 in regard to AUC, OSS improves all three algorithms, especially CatBoost and XGBoost. Unlike RENN, which improves RF, it does not improve both CatBoost and XGBoost the same way. Therefore, the best model for AUC is CatBoost with OSS.

4.2.2. Accuracy

Tables 3–5 show that the maximum Accuracy value is 99.96%, which is nearly 100%. There are many models that achieve an extremely high score for Accuracy. As such, the best model cannot be determined based on Accuracy. In spite of the inconclusive high scores achieved, IHT and NM2 are extremely poor in this arena. Therefore, this is an alarming indication that these two resampling techniques should not be considered.

4.2.3. Recall

It is shown in Tables 3–5 that CatBoost achieves the highest value, while XGBoost and RF are closely behind CatBoost, in regard to Recall. The highest Recall score is 96.16%, which is achieved by CatBoost with OSS. Significantly, OSS always seems to improve all three chosen algorithms, which is a good indication of this undersampling technique.

Table 4. XGBoost with Resampling Techniques.

Technique	AUC	Accuracy	Recall	Precision	F1-Score
Without	0.9760	**0.9996**	0.9523	0.8008	0.8698
RUS	0.5210	0.9638	0.0422	0.9146	0.0806
CNN	0.7058	0.9976	0.4119	0.8638	0.5558
Tomek	0.9748	**0.9996**	0.9499	0.8008	0.8689
OSS	**0.9769**	**0.9996**	**0.9541**	0.7947	0.8669
ENN	0.9727	**0.9996**	0.9457	0.8049	0.8695
RENN	0.9737	**0.9996**	0.9477	0.8029	0.8692
AllKNN	0.9725	**0.9996**	0.9453	0.8008	0.8670
NCR	0.9714	**0.9996**	0.9431	0.8009	0.8659
NM1	0.5026	0.6754	0.0054	0.9472	0.0107
NM2	0.5004	0.0105	0.0017	**0.9959**	0.0035
IHT	0.5008	0.0413	0.0018	0.9939	0.0036
ROS	0.9598	**0.9996**	0.9200	0.8252	0.8697
SMOTE	0.9306	0.9995	0.8614	0.8394	0.8501
ADASYN	0.9203	0.9995	0.8408	0.8435	0.8420
Border1	0.9647	**0.9996**	0.9298	0.8231	**0.8730**
Border2	0.9458	0.9995	0.8920	0.8231	0.8561
SVMSM	0.9650	**0.9996**	0.9304	0.8089	0.8652
SMENN	0.9319	0.9995	0.8640	0.8333	0.8483
SMTomek	0.9227	0.9995	0.8457	0.8415	0.8434

Table 5. RF with Resampling Techniques.

Technique	AUC	Accuracy	Recall	Precision	F1-Score
Without	0.9742	**0.9996**	0.9487	0.7846	0.8588
RUS	0.5303	0.9753	0.0608	0.9065	0.1140
CNN	0.7911	0.9987	0.5824	0.8577	0.6924
Tomek	0.9776	**0.9996**	0.9556	0.7825	0.8604
OSS	0.9756	**0.9996**	0.9516	0.7927	0.8648
ENN	0.9740	0.9995	0.9484	0.7765	0.8537
RENN	**0.9789**	**0.9996**	**0.9582**	0.7886	0.8651
AllKNN	0.9759	**0.9996**	0.9521	0.7907	0.8636
NCR	0.9733	**0.9996**	0.9470	0.7927	0.8629
NM1	0.5040	0.7802	0.0081	0.9350	0.0160
NM2	0.5011	0.2504	0.0023	0.9918	0.0046
IHT	0.5008	0.0332	0.0018	**0.9959**	0.0035
ROS	0.9766	**0.9996**	0.9536	0.7886	0.8632
SMOTE	0.9495	0.9995	0.8994	0.8313	0.8639
ADASYN	0.9453	0.9995	0.8908	0.8272	0.8578
Border1	0.9712	**0.9996**	0.9427	0.7988	0.8647
Border2	0.9640	**0.9996**	0.9282	0.8110	0.8656
SVMSM	0.9767	**0.9996**	0.9537	0.7927	**0.8657**
SMENN	0.9453	0.9995	0.8909	0.8273	0.8578
SMTomek	0.9466	0.9995	0.8935	0.8313	0.8612

4.2.4. Precision

Precision is also important in order to obtain a high F1-Score, as is the case with Recall. When a model gives an extremely low score in Recall and it gives an extremely high score in Precision, this indicates that this model is not able to classify the real positive cases out of all classified positive cases accurately because the model has a high assumption of classified positive cases. That is, there are significantly more stipulated positive cases than the real number of positive cases. This is the reason why the model gives a low Recall value. However, high values demonstrate the improvement in the classification of the real positive cases as positives. That is the reason why the model gives a high value in Precision. After all, the models' results in both Recall and Precision achieved by IHT and NM2 followed by NM1 must not be considered to be reflective of good performance. That is because they achieve extremely low Recall values, even though they achieve extremely high Precision values, as is shown in Tables 3–5.

4.2.5. F1-Score

This evaluation metric is tremendously valuable. It can give a significant indication of the best model so far. CatBoost still achieves the highest results virtually on all the evaluation metrics, including the *F1*-Score. The highest *F1*-Score value is 87.40% and is achieved by the AllKNN undersampling technique along with CatBoost, among other *F1*-Score values in Tables 3–5.

It is noticeable that some resampling techniques perform well, such as RENN and AllKNN, while other ones perform badly, such as RUS, NM1, NM2, and IHT. This is related to how each technique resamples the dataset. This study not only shows the best combination of a machine learning algorithm and resampling technique, but it also shows the ones that should not be considered in future.

4.3. Comparison with Previous Works

After the careful analysis of 66 models and 330 evaluation metric values that took nearly a month to be obtained, the best proposed model is AllKNN along with CatBoost (AllKNN-CatBoost). To put this into perspective, the proposed model is compared with previous works with the same dataset and similar approaches in Table 6.

Table 6. RF with Resampling Techniques.

Paper	Yr.	Model	AUC	Acc.	Recall	Prc.	F1
[21]	2021	RF	0.8900	0.9995	0.7920	0.9195	0.8510
[18]	2020	LGBM+Hyper-Parameter	0.9094	0.9840	0.4059	**0.9734**	0.5695
[19]	2020	KNN			0.7200	0.9500	0.8200
[17]	2020	KNN			0.8119	0.9111	
[24]	2021	ANN		0.9992	0.7619	0.8115	
[25]	2019	RF+SMOTE		**0.9996**	0.8163	0.9638	
[20]	2019	LR+SMOTE+ StaticLearning	0.9114				
[28]	2019	LOF		0.9700			
[22]	2019	RF		0.9000			
Ours	2021	AllKNN-CatBoost	**0.9794**	**0.9996**	**0.9591**	0.8028	**0.8740**

As one of main objectives of this paper is to address the imbalance class issue, and this can be looked at in terms of CV and resampling techniques. None of the previous works mentioned in Table 6 used stratified CV. The proposed model uses stratified CV, which can help to address the imbalance class issue, whereas [18] considered using K-fold CV, which overlooks the proportion of minority class in each fold. The other aspect of addressing the imbalance class issue is the use of resampling techniques. When using resampling techniques such as SMOTE in [20,25], the overall performance is very reasonable. However, when the resampling techniques are not used, the overall performance may be adversely impacted, as is the case in [21,28].

When looking at Table 6, the proposed model indeed outperforms other models in terms of AUC, Recall, and F1-Score. In regard to Accuracy, AllKNN-CatBoost still achieves a very good value, even though it is tied with the model found in [25]. However, AllKNN-CatBoost does not outperform the other models in terms of Precision despite the outstanding performance. However, it is reasonably acceptable to generate some FP cases, but not at the expense of FN cases as far as possible. In other words, it is bearable to be extra cautious and classify a reasonable number of valid cases as fraudulent, but not to classify fraudulent cases as valid. Thus, obtaining a very high Recall value shows that AllKNN-CatBoost does improve credit card fraud detection without compromising on the detection of fraudulent cases as much as possible. Unlike some previous works that were concerned with one or more evaluation metrics, the proposed model is evaluated based on several evaluation metrics.

The importance of this work lies in comparing different algorithms while addressing the imbalance class issue using stratified CV and resampling techniques. In addition, it considers using multiple evaluation metrics to obtain a better idea on how well the proposed model performs. Considering these aspects enhances the detection of fraudulent activity in credit card transactions. However, this work is limited in considering only one dataset, unlike some other works that have considered more than one dataset, as is the case in [18].

5. Conclusions and Future Work

With increased dependency on online transactions and credit cards, fraudsters and criminals are developing their means to seize other people's money. Nevertheless, a proactive approach must be considered by harnessing artificial intelligence and machine learning tools to aggressively tackle this issue, regardless of how sophisticated the countermeasures are.

The proposed approach is constructed based on two stages. The first stage aims to nominate the best three machine learning algorithms out of nine algorithms. The second stage aims to integrate the best three algorithms with nineteen resampling techniques. Each model in both stages is evaluated based on the Area under the Receiver Operating Characteristic Curve (AUC), Accuracy, Recall, Precision, and F1-Score. In the first stage, the nine algorithms are Logistic Regression (LR), K-Nearest Neighbors (KNN), Decision Tree (DT), Naïve Bayes (NB), Random Forest (RF), Gradient Boosting Machines (GBM), Light Gradient Boosting Machine (LightGBM), Extreme Gradient Boosting (XGBoost), and Category Boosting (CatBoost). In the second stage, the 19 resampling techniques are divided as follows: 11 undersampling, 6 oversampling, and 2 combinations of both undersampling and oversampling techniques. The total number of models in both stages are 66, with their 330 evaluation metric values that took nearly one month to obtain. The best model out of all these is AllKNN along with CatBoost (AllKNN-CatBoost). Finally, AllKNN-CatBoost is compared with previous works with the same dataset and similar approaches. Indeed, AllKNN-CatBoost outperforms previous models in terms of AUC (97.94%), Recall (95.91%), and F1-Score (87.40%).

Future work may include using another dataset and other optimization algorithms. Some of these algorithms are Monarch Butterfly Optimization (MBO) [53], Earthworm Optimization Algorithm (EWA) [54], Elephant Herding Optimization (EHO) [55], Moth Search (MS) algorithm [56], Slime Mold Algorithm (SMA), and Harris Hawks Optimization (HHO) [57].

Author Contributions: Conceptualization, methodology, validation, formal analysis, investigation, and visualization, N.S.A. and S.M.F.; software and writing—original draft preparation, N.S.A.; writing—review and editing, S.M.F. All authors have read and agreed to the published version of the manuscript.

Funding: The authors would like to acknowledge the support of Prince Sultan University for paying the Article Processing Charges (APC) for this publication.

Conflicts of Interest: The authors declare no conflict of interest.

References

1. Dubey, S.C.; Mundhe, K.S.; Kadam, A.A. Credit Card Fraud Detection using Artificial Neural Network and BackPropagation. In Proceedings of the 2020 4th International Conference on Intelligent Computing and Control Systems (ICICCS), Rasayani, India, 13–15 May 2020; pp. 268–273. [CrossRef]
2. Martin, T. Credit Card Fraud: The Biggest Card Frauds in History. Available online: https://www.uswitch.com/credit-cards/guides/credit-card-fraud-the-biggest-card-frauds-in-history/ (accessed on 22 January 2022).
3. Zhang, X.; Han, Y.; Xu, W.; Wang, Q. HOBA: A novel feature engineering methodology for credit card fraud detection with a deep learning architecture. *Inf. Sci.* **2019**, *557*, 302–316. [CrossRef]
4. Makki, S.; Assaghir, Z.; Taher, Y.; Haque, R.; Hacid, M.-S.; Zeineddine, H. An experimental study with imbalanced classification approaches for credit card fraud detection. *IEEE Access* **2019**, *7*, 93010–93022. [CrossRef]

5.   McCue, C. *Advanced Topics. Data Mining and Predictive Analysis*; Butterworth-Heinemann: Oxford, UK, 2015; pp. 349–365.
6.   Berad, P.; Parihar, S.; Lakhani, Z.; Kshirsagar, A.; Chaudhari, A. A Comparative Study: Credit Card Fraud Detection Using Machine Learning. *J. Crit. Rev.* **2020**, *7*, 1005.
7.   Jain, Y.; Namrata, T.; Shripriya, D.; Jain, S. A comparative analysis of various credit card fraud detection techniques. *Int. J. Recent Technol. Eng.* **2019**, *7*, 402–403.
8.   Tolles, J.; Meurer, W.J. Logistic regression: Relating patient characteristics to outcomes. *JAMA* **2016**, *316*, 533–534. [CrossRef] [PubMed]
9.   Shirodkar, N.; Mandrekar, P.; Mandrekar, R.S.; Sakhalkar, R.; Kumar, K.C.; Aswale, S. Credit card fraud detection techniques–A survey. In Proceedings of the 2020 International Conference on Emerging Trends in Information Technology and Engineering (ic-ETITE), Shiroda, India, 13–15 May 2020; pp. 1–7. [CrossRef]
10.   Gaikwad, J.R.; Deshmane, A.B.; Somavanshi, H.V.; Patil, S.V.; Badgujar, R.A. Credit Card Fraud Detection using Decision Tree Induction Algorithm. *Int. J. Innov. Technol. Explor. Eng. IJITEE* **2014**, *4*, 66–67.
11.   Zareapoor, M.; Seeja, K.; Alam, M.A. Analysis on credit card fraud detection techniques: Based on certain design criteria. *Int. J. Comput. Appl.* **2012**, *52*, 35–42. [CrossRef]
12.   Friedman, J.H. Greedy function approximation: A gradient boosting machine. *Ann. Stat.* **2001**, *29*, 1189–1232. [CrossRef]
13.   Microsoft. LightGBM. Available online: https://github.com/microsoft/LightGBM (accessed on 22 January 2021).
14.   XGBoost Developers. Introduction to Boosted Trees. Available online: https://xgboost.readthedocs.io/en/latest/tutorials/model.html (accessed on 22 January 2022).
15.   Yandex Technologies. CatBoost. Available online: https://yandex.com/dev/catboost/ (accessed on 22 January 2022).
16.   Delamaire, L.; Abdou, H.; Pointon, J. Credit card fraud and detection techniques: A review. *Banks Bank Syst.* **2009**, *4*, 61.
17.   Khatri, S.; Arora, A.; Agrawal, A.P. Supervised machine learning algorithms for credit card fraud detection: A comparison. In Proceedings of the 2020 10th International Conference on Cloud Computing, Data Science & Engineering (Confluence), Noida, India, 29–31 January 2020; pp. 680–683. [CrossRef]
18.   Taha, A.A.; Malebary, S.J. An intelligent approach to credit card fraud detection using an optimized light gradient boosting machine. *IEEE Access* **2020**, *8*, 25579–25587. [CrossRef]
19.   Vengatesan, K.; Kumar, A.; Yuvraj, S.; Kumar, V.; Sabnis, S. Credit card fraud detection using data analytic techniques. *Adv. Math. Sci. J.* **2020**, *9*, 1185–1196. [CrossRef]
20.   Puh, M.; Brkić, L. Detecting credit card fraud using selected machine learning algorithms. In Proceedings of the 2019 42nd International Convention on Information and Communication Technology, Electronics and Microelectronics (MIPRO), Zagreb, Croatia, 20–24 May 2019; pp. 1250–1255. [CrossRef]
21.   Hema, A. Machine Learning methods for Discovering Credit Card Fraud. *Int. Res. J. Comput. Sci.* **2020**, *8*, 1–6.
22.   Kumar, M.S.; Soundarya, V.; Kavitha, S.; Keerthika, E.; Aswini, E. Credit card fraud detection using random forest algorithm. In Proceedings of the 2019 3rd International Conference on Computing and Communications Technologies (ICCCT), Chennai, India, 21–22 February 2019; pp. 149–153. [CrossRef]
23.   Patidar, R.; Sharma, L. Credit card fraud detection using neural network. *Int. J. Soft Comput. Eng. IJSCE* **2011**, *1*, 32–38.
24.   Asha, R.; KR, S.K. Credit card fraud detection using artificial neural network. *Glob. Trans. Proc.* **2021**, *2*, 35–41. [CrossRef]
25.   Varmedja, D.; Karanovic, M.; Sladojevic, S.; Arsenovic, M.; Anderla, A. Credit card fraud detection-machine learning methods. In Proceedings of the 2019 18th International Symposium Infoteh-Jahorina (Infoteh), Novi Sad, Serbia, 20–22 March 2019; pp. 1–5. [CrossRef]
26.   Breunig, M.M.; Kriegel, H.P.; Ng, R.T.; Sander, J. LOF: Identifying density-based local outliers. In Proceedings of the 2000 ACM SIGMOD International Conference on Management of Data, Dallas, TX, USA, 15–18 May 2000; pp. 93–104. [CrossRef]
27.   Liu, F.T.; Ting, K.M.; Zhou, Z.H. Isolation forest. In Proceedings of the 2008 Eighth IEEE International Conference on Data Mining, Ballarat, VIC, Australia, 15–19 December 2008; pp. 413–422. [CrossRef]
28.   John, H.; Naaz, S. Credit card fraud detection using local outlier factor and isolation forest. *Int. J. Comput. Sci. Eng* **2019**, *7*, 1060–1064. [CrossRef]
29.   Dal Pozzolo, A.; Caelen, O.; Johnson, R.A.; Bontempi, G. Calibrating probability with undersampling for unbalanced classification. In Proceedings of the 2015 IEEE Symposium Series on Computational Intelligence, Cape Town, South Africa, 7–10 December 2015; pp. 159–166. [CrossRef]
30.   Sahin, Y.; Duman, E. Detecting credit card fraud by ANN and logistic regression. In Proceedings of the 2011 International Symposium on Innovations in Intelligent Systems and Applications, Istanbul, Turkey, 15–18 June 2011; pp. 315–319.
31.   Kokkinaki, A.I. On atypical database transactions: Identification of probable frauds using machine learning for user profiling. In Proceedings of the 1997 IEEE Knowledge and Data Engineering Exchange Workshop, Nicosia, Cyprus, 4 November 1997; p. 109.
32.   Piryonesi, S.M.; El-Diraby, T.E. Data analytics in asset management: Cost-effective prediction of the pavement condition index. *J. Infrastruct. Syst.* **2020**, *26*, 04019036. [CrossRef]
33.   Maes, S.; Tuyls, K.; Vanschoenwinkel, B.; Manderick, B. Credit card fraud detection using Bayesian and neural networks. In Proceedings of the 1st International Naiso Congress on Neuro Fuzzy Technologies, Brussel, Belgium, 16–19 January 2002; pp. 261–270.

34. Syeda, M.; Zhang, Y.Q.; Pan, Y. Parallel granular neural networks for fast credit card fraud detection. In Proceedings of the 2002 IEEE World Congress on Computational Intelligence. 2002 IEEE International Conference on Fuzzy Systems. FUZZ-IEEE'02. Proceedings (Cat. No. 02CH37291), Atlanta, GA, USA, 12–17 May 2002; pp. 572–577. [CrossRef]
35. Seeja, K.; Zareapoor, M. Fraudminer: A novel credit card fraud detection model based on frequent itemset mining. *Sci. World J.* **2014**, *2014*, 1–10. [CrossRef]
36. Scikit-Learn-Contrib. Imbalanced-Learn. Available online: https://github.com/scikit-learn-contrib/imbalanced-learn (accessed on 22 January 2022).
37. He, H.; Garcia, E.A. Learning from imbalanced data. *IEEE Trans. Knowl. Data Eng.* **2009**, *21*, 1263–1284. [CrossRef]
38. Dal Pozzolo, A.; Caelen, O.; Bontempi, G. When is undersampling effective in unbalanced classification tasks? In Proceedings of the Joint European Conference on Machine Learning and Knowledge Discovery in Databases, Porto, Portugal, 7–11 September 2015; pp. 200–215.
39. García, V.; Mollineda, R.A.; Sánchez, J.S. On the k-NN performance in a challenging scenario of imbalance and overlapping. *Pattern Anal. Appl.* **2008**, *11*, 269–280. [CrossRef]
40. Cieslak, D.A.; Chawla, N.V. Start globally, optimize locally, predict globally: Improving performance on imbalanced data. In Proceedings of the 2008 Eighth IEEE International Conference on Data Mining, Notre Dame, IN, USA, 15–19 December 2008; pp. 143–152.
41. Scikit-Learn Developers. 3.1. Cross-validation: Evaluating Estimator Performance. Available online: https://scikit-learn.org/stable/modules/cross_validation.html (accessed on 22 January 2022).
42. Hanley, J.A.; McNeil, B.J. The meaning and use of the area under a receiver operating characteristic (ROC) curve. *Radiology* **1982**, *143*, 29. [CrossRef]
43. Stehman, S.V. Selecting and interpreting measures of thematic classification accuracy. *Remote Sens. Environ.* **1997**, *62*, 77. [CrossRef]
44. Fawcett, T. An introduction to ROC analysis. *Pattern Recognit. Lett.* **2006**, *27*, 862. [CrossRef]
45. Powers, D.M. Evaluation: From precision, recall and F-measure to ROC, informedness, markedness and correlation. *arXiv* **2020**, arXiv:2010.16061.
46. Chicco, D.; Tötsch, N.; Jurman, G. The Matthews correlation coefficient (MCC) is more reliable than balanced accuracy, bookmaker informedness, and markedness in two-class confusion matrix evaluation. *BioData Min.* **2021**, *14*, 1–22. [CrossRef] [PubMed]
47. Google Developers. Classification: ROC Curve and AUC. Available online: https://developers.google.com/machine-learning/crash-course/classification/roc-and-auc (accessed on 22 January 2022).
48. DeepAI. Accuracy (Error Rate). Available online: https://deepai.org/machine-learning-glossary-and-terms/accuracy-error-rate (accessed on 22 January 2022).
49. Guido, S.; Müller, A.C. *Introduction to Machine Learning with Python A Guide for Data Scientists*; O'Reilly: Sebastopol, CA, USA, 2021; p. 282.
50. C3, AI. Precision. Available online: https://c3.ai/glossary/machine-learning/precision/ (accessed on 22 January 2022).
51. Masís, S. *Interpretable Machine Learning with Python: Learn to Build Interpretable High-Performance Models with Hands-On Real-World Examples*; Packt Publishing Ltd.: Birmingham, UK, 2021; p. 81.
52. Prusti, D.; Rath, S.K. Fraudulent transaction detection in credit card by applying ensemble machine learning techniques. In Proceedings of the 2019 10th International Conference on Computing, Communication and Networking Technologies (ICCCNT), Rourkela, India, 6–8 July 2019; pp. 1–6. [CrossRef]
53. Wang, G.-G.; Deb, S.; Cui, Z. Monarch butterfly optimization. *Neural Comput. Appl.* **2019**, *31*, 1995–2014. [CrossRef]
54. Ghosh, I.; Roy, P.K. Application of earthworm optimization algorithm for solution of optimal power flow. In Proceedings of the 2019 International Conference on Opto-Electronics and Applied Optics (Optronix), Kolkata, India, 18–20 March 2019; pp. 1–6. [CrossRef]
55. Wang, G.-G.; Deb, S.; Coelho, L.d.S. Elephant herding optimization. In Proceedings of the 2015 3rd International Symposium on Computational and Business Intelligence (ISCBI), Xuzhou, China, 7–9 December 2015; pp. 1–5. [CrossRef]
56. Wang, G.-G. Moth search algorithm: A bio-inspired metaheuristic algorithm for global optimization problems. *Memetic Comput.* **2018**, *10*, 151–164. [CrossRef]
57. Heidari, A.A.; Mirjalili, S.; Faris, H.; Aljarah, I.; Mafarja, M.; Chen, H. Harris hawks optimization: Algorithm and applications. *Future Gener. Comput. Syst.* **2019**, *97*, 849–872. [CrossRef]

Article

Classification of Glaucoma Based on Elephant-Herding Optimization Algorithm and Deep Belief Network

Mona A. S. Ali [1,2,*], Kishore Balasubramanian [3], Gayathri Devi Krishnamoorthy [4], Suresh Muthusamy [5], Santhiya Pandiyan [6], Hitesh Panchal [7], Suman Mann [8], Kokilavani Thangaraj [9], Noha E. El-Attar [10], Laith Abualigah [11,*] and Diaa Salama Abd Elminaam [12,13,*]

[1] Computer Science Department, College of Computer Science and Information Technology, King Faisal University, Al Ahsa 400, Saudi Arabia
[2] Computer Science Department, Faculty of Computers and Artificial Intelligence, Benha University, Benha 12311, Egypt
[3] Department of Electrical and Electronics Engineering, Mahalingam College of Engineering and Technology (Autonomous), Coimbatore 642001, India; bkishore1979@gmail.com
[4] Department of Electronics and Communication Engineering, NGP Institute of Technology, Coimbatore 641001, India; gayathridevi@drngpit.ac.in
[5] Department of Electronics and Communication Engineering, Kongu Engineering College (Autonomous), Coimbatore 638001, India; infostosuresh@gmail.com
[6] Department of Computer Science and Engineering, Kongu Engineering College (Autonomous), Coimbatore 638001, India; santhiyaashok172@gmail.com
[7] Department of Mechanical Engineering, Government Engineering College, Patan 384265, India; engineerhitesh2000@gmail.com
[8] Department of Information Technology, Maharaja Surajmal Institute of Technology, New Delhi 110005, India; sumanmann@msit.in
[9] Department of Electrical and Electronics Engineering, College of Engineering and Technology (Autonomous), Coimbatore 641001, India; kokime.t@gmail.com
[10] Department of Information System, Faculty of Computers and Artificial Intelligence, Benha University, Benha 12311, Egypt; noha.ezzat@fci.bu.edu.eg
[11] Faculty of Computer Sciences and Informatics, Amman Arab University, Amman 11953, Jordan
[12] Information Systems Department, Faculty of Computers and Artificial Intelligence, Benha University, Benha 12311, Egypt
[13] Computer Science Department, Faculty of Computer Science, Misr International University, Cairo 12585, Egypt
* Correspondence: m.ali@kfu.edu.sa (M.A.S.A.); aligah.2020@gmail.com (L.A.); diaa.salama@miuegypt.edu.eg (D.S.A.E.)

Citation: Ali, M.A.S.; Balasubramanian, K.; Krishnamoorthy, G.D.; Muthusamy, S.; Pandiyan, S.; Panchal, H.; Mann, S.; Thangaraj, K.; El-Attar, N.E.; Abualigah, L.; et al. Classification of Glaucoma Based on Elephant-Herding Optimization Algorithm and Deep Belief Network. *Electronics* 2022, *11*, 1763. https://doi.org/10.3390/electronics11111763

Academic Editor: Maciej Ławryńczuk

Received: 11 April 2022
Accepted: 23 May 2022
Published: 2 June 2022

Publisher's Note: MDPI stays neutral with regard to jurisdictional claims in published maps and institutional affiliations.

Abstract: This study proposes a novel glaucoma identification system from fundus images through the deep belief network (DBN) optimized by the elephant-herding optimization (EHO) algorithm. Initially, the input image undergoes the preprocessing steps of noise removal and enhancement processes, followed by optical disc (OD) and optical cup (OC) segmentation and extraction of structural, intensity, and textural features. Most discriminative features are then selected using the ReliefF algorithm and passed to the DBN for classification into glaucomatous or normal. To enhance the classification rate of the DBN, the DBN parameters are fine-tuned by the EHO algorithm. The model has experimented on public and private datasets with 7280 images, which attained a maximum classification rate of 99.4%, 100% specificity, and 99.89% sensitivity. The 10-fold cross validation reduced the misclassification and attained 98.5% accuracy. Investigations proved the efficacy of the proposed method in avoiding bias, dataset variability, and reducing false positives compared to similar works of glaucoma classification. The proposed system can be tested on diverse datasets, aiding in the improved glaucoma diagnosis.

Keywords: optic disc; optic cup; elephant-herding optimization; deep belief network; circle Hough transform; modified Wiener filter; reliefF algorithm; glaucoma

1. Introduction

Glaucoma is a type of ocular neuropathy which threatens vision if left untreated [1]. It is a gradual condition that develops as the ocular pressure rises [2]. Nearly 80 million people are affected by glaucoma globally [3]. Optic nerves are impaired gradually due to high ocular pressure [4,5]. Approximately 75–80% of the glaucoma cases are identified only at the developed stage, which cannot be cured. One cannot visualize any known symptoms of glaucoma except for narrowing of vision at a later stage [6]. The progression is slow and painful at certain levels [6]. It requires lifelong treatment, and it is impossible to reinstate vision loss. Hence, early detection of glaucoma and treatment stands as the best means of prevention. Concerning the fundamental issue, there is a critical need to build a system that can function well without the need for excessive equipment, qualified medical practitioners, or time. Computer-assisted techniques could help detect the disease at its early stages using advanced machine-learning and deep-learning methods. Trained deep-learning models could take advantage of minor changes, such as retinal layer thinning, that human specialists cannot notice.

Nevertheless, the optic nerve damage precipitated slowly develops, and as symptoms stem from it, the disease advances significantly [7]. Nevertheless, the most up-to-date technology can probably hinder glaucoma development in patients [8,9]. Figure 1 shows sample images of normal and glaucomatous eyes.

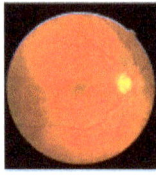   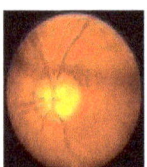

(**a**) Normal eye   (**b**) Glaucomatous eye

Figure 1. Eye shape (normal and glaucomatous eye).

To scrutinize various glaucoma traits, ophthalmologists utilize confocal scanning laser ophthalmoscopy (CSLO) [10], Heidelberg retina tomography (HRT), optical coherence tomography (OCT), along with fundus images [11]. For instance, numerous retinal features, optic nerves head (ONH), peripapillary atrophy, and retinal nerve fiber layer, are perceived for glaucoma diagnosis [12]. Assessment of increased IOP, abnormal visual field (V.F.), damaged ONH, etc. are usually investigated for glaucoma [13–15]. The OD is split into three disparate areas: the cup (central region), the neuroretinal rim, and parapapillary atrophy [16,17]. The white cup-like structure located in the disc center is the OC. The ratio of OC size to OD size is normally an important measure analyzed in glaucoma diagnosis, denoted as the cup-disc ratio (CDR). The main contributions of this paper can be summarized as follow:

1. Developing an optimized model employing a deep belief network classifier (DBN);
2. Employing modified Wiener filter (MWF), circular Hough transform (CHT), and Otsu's thresholding for OD and OC segmentation, respectively;
3. Generating a distinct hybrid feature set to aid in diagnosis;
4. Selecting relevant features through the ReliefF algorithm based on predictive importance weights;
5. Fine-tuning DBN by elephant-herding optimization algorithm (EHO);
6. Investigating the model's robustness to noise such as Gaussian and salt-pepper;
7. Analyzing the isolated and combined feature set contribution in glaucoma identification.

The paper is structured as follows: Section 2 outlines various works related to the proposed method. Section 3 presents the adopted architecture of the method proposed. Experimental outcomes along with dataset preparation are explored in Section 4. The conclusion is elucidated in Section 5.

2. Related Works

A brief literature review based on feature extraction and neural network classifier for glaucoma detection is elucidated in this section. Raja et al. [18] described a statistical feature extraction method based on the hyper analytic wavelet transformation (HWT) in which statistical characteristics were extracted and passed to a support vector machine (SVM). The particle swarm algorithm is used to adjust the HWT and SVM-RB simultaneously to get the optimum fit. Issac, A. et al. [19] and Koh J.E. et al. [20] presented a similar feature extraction strategy for glaucoma classification. Haralick's features-centered categorization of glaucoma using back propagation neural networks (BPNN) was suggested by Samanta et al. [21]. The results of the experiment revealed good accuracy, sensitivity, and specificity.

Acharya, U. et al. [22] proposed an effective technique that included preprocessing, picture convolving with filter banks, and the chosen features fed into the KNN classifier. Jun et al. [23] demonstrated a super-pixel-based OD and OC segmentation model for diagnosing glaucoma. The unreliable results exhibited scope for improvement. Gift and Nirmal [24] suggested gray wolf optimized NN produce enhanced accuracy for glaucoma detection through a sequence of steps. Preprocessing, image normalization and feature extraction were done, and the features were given to the GWO-NN classifier. Anushikha et al. [25] presented an automated diagnostic system utilizing wavelet features from the segmented OD, which was extorted for analysis in addition to classification. Experimental outcomes signified an accuracy of 0.947. Ajesh et al. [26] reported a new multi-feature extraction approach for glaucoma identification and classification by integrating discrete wavelet transform (DWT) and ML algorithms that produced an accuracy of 95% in glaucoma identification.

For fine-imaging analysis, DWT was computationally intensive. Diaz-Pinto et al. [27] provided an automatic technique using retinal structural features and Luv color space for OD and OC segmentation, obtaining 81% specificity and 87% sensitivity. Studies have reported numerous methodologies for recognizing glaucoma through CAD. They use either conventional machine learning, deep learning, or both. Several works related to the diagnosis of glaucoma using CNN have been demonstrated in the literature [28–32]. The CNN employed was constructed from scratch, and different datasets were used to investigate the models. Data augmentation via rotation, random flip, image translation, etc. was performed to increase the dataset size artificially. OCT images were also used to segment the retinal vasculature apart from the fundus images. The deep networks were employed to extract and learn the layer properties of the retina using a pretrained backbone network and reinforcement learning. A multiscale feature generated could then be used on modules, such as the encoder–decoder, to retrieve retinal information and capture finer retinal boundaries. Many optimization algorithms are also used to solve the various optimization problems. A blended approach is adopted in our method, where the features extracted are selected and passed to an optimized deep network for classification.

3. Proposed Method

This paper reports using the DBN classifier, a robust, novel, and efficient glaucoma detection method on retinal fundus images (RFI). Input is acquired from fundus databases and preprocessed for noise removal using MWF. Utilizing CHT, the OD is then segmented from the noise-removed image. The OC is cropped from the OD image using Otsu's thresholding algorithm. Structural and functional features are extorted and fed to the DBN classifier. The EHO algorithm optimizes DBN's parameters to obtain a minimum cost function and the best solution for healthy and glaucomatous classification. Figure 2 illustrates the schematic diagram of the system.

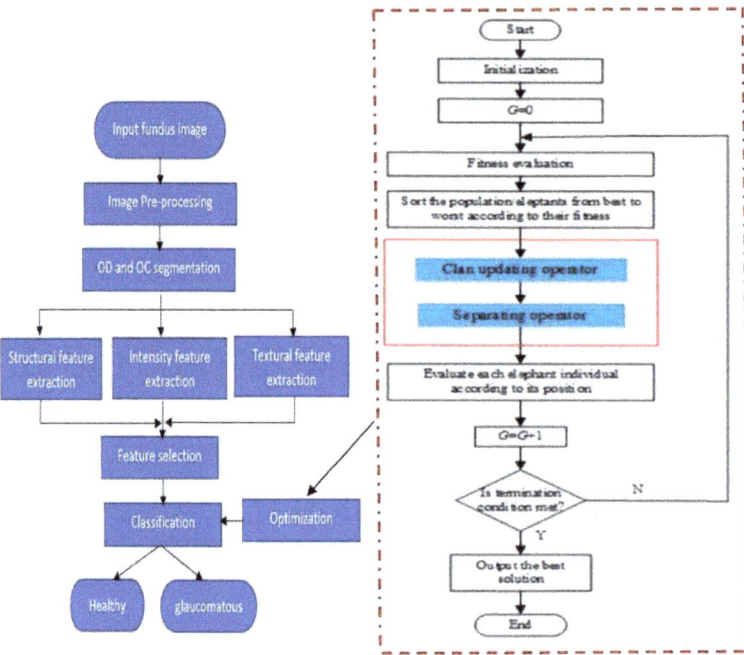

Figure 2. Flow diagram of the proposed approach.

3.1. Preprocessing

The fundus image collected must be preprocessed to highlight the vessel and other morphological features. Given the benefits of grayscale images, RBG is converted to grayscale first [33], then filtered to remove background noise [34]. A modified Wiener filter is employed to prevent impulse noise while preserving the edges [35]. The noise reduction aims to protect crucial structural content for disease detection, besides determining noisy pixels [36].

3.2. OD and OC Segmentation

OD segmentation is done on the image after noise removal. First, the OD location is identified. Subsequently, edges are calculated through the Canny edge filter. As the OD in the retina is a circular object, the circle detection Hough transform (CHT) is applied to identify the area. The boundary positions along with the region of the OD are obtained. The ROI termed OD is cropped from the original image for further OC segmentation. The OC is segmented from pre-segmented OD using Otsu's thresholding [37].

3.3. Feature Extraction

Structural, textural, and intensity-based features contributing to the disease diagnosis are extorted in this phase [38]. Table 1 lists the set of features generated through this process.

Table 1. List of features extracted.

Structural Features	Cup to Disc Ratio (CDR), Neuro Retinal Rim (NRR), Cup Shape
Textural features	Wavelet-based features, gray level co-occurrence matrix (GLCM) features—energy, correlation, homogeneity, contrast, and entropy gray-level run length—low gray level run emphasis, gray level non-uniformity, segmentation-based fractal texture analysis (SFTA)
Intensity features	Brightness, color moments, super pixels, enhanced local binary pattern (ELBP), speeded-up robust feature (SURF), pyramid histogram of oriented gradients (PHOG), local energy-based shape histogram (LESH)

Using the procedure described above, the 111 features extracted are then selected using the relief F algorithm before being fed to DBN for classification.

3.4. Feature Selection

This stage is critical because rarely discernible characteristics are deleted, putting the modeling process under more computational strain. In this work, the ReliefF algorithm is preferred for dimensionality reduction due to its promising results, as explained in [38]. ReliefF ranks features according to their weight participation, with the most active features being placed first. As illustrated in Figure 3, other features contribute far less to the last features. As a result, we can choose the 15 most potent features based on their weight and exclude characteristics that add to the model's computational cost.

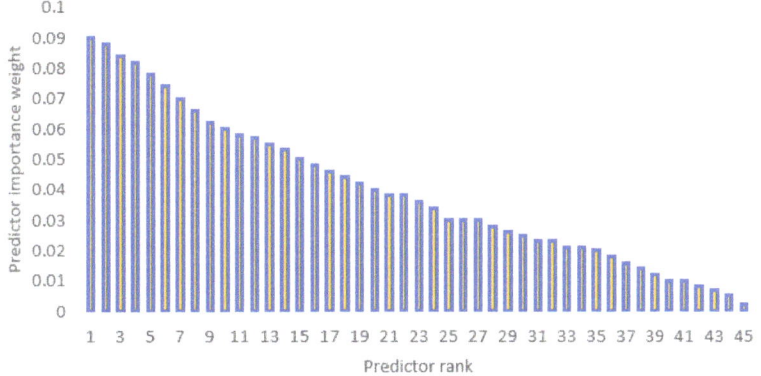

Figure 3. Weight ranking of features.

ReliefF chooses T, some instances at random, but subsequently, k searches for the closest same-class neighbors, which are referred to as the nearest hit values of H. The k-nearest neighbors are the one–one scores among the multiple classes, also known as the M(T) nearest misses. The number of nearest neighbors is set at three in our study. The 111 features are reduced to 15 optimal features based on their participation at the top of the weighted list for the highest accuracy using the procedure described above. The remaining ones are ignored because there is not much difference in output, which increases the computing weight of a model. Figure 4 depicts cumulative accuracy vs. a number of features, and 15 contribute more than the total variations.

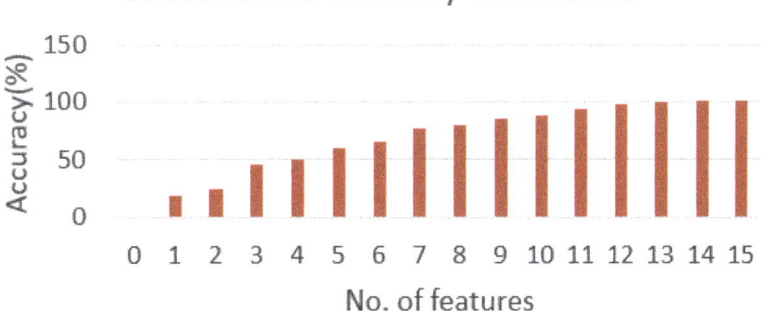

Figure 4. Cumulative accuracy vs. no. of features.

3.5. Classification

3.5.1. Deep Belief Networks (DBN)

The DBN class of neural network (NN) can be considered a generative model that uses a set of Boltzmann machines as basic building elements [39]. Each layer of the DBNs has a restricted Boltzmann machine (RBM). DBN extracts H.L. features from the data slated for training to improve the between-classes separation power. The training is performed on all the layers through supervised mode, and the backward propagation mode modifies the weight in the network to reduce over-fitting. This work develops a DBN model trained using greedy layer-wise learning [40] by stacking up RBMs, as shown in Figure 5.

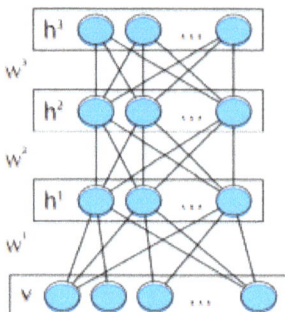

Figure 5. Stacked up RBMs model DBN.

RBM concentrates on a particular layer during its learning procedure and ignores others. We assume we have a DBN with L levels, with Wi being the RBM's weight matrix at layer i. In addition, the hidden units at the ith layer form the layer (i + 1) input unit. In the model proposed, the set of weight matrices is assigned as W = {W1, W2, W3} and the set of hidden layers as h = {h1, h2, h3}. The weight matrix between layers ith and (i + 1), which is denoted by Wi, while the jth hidden layer is denoted by hj. The following energy function was used to compute the combined distribution of the hidden and visible layers:

$$p(v,h) = \frac{e^{-E(v,h)}}{\sum_{v,h} e^{-E(v,h)}} \tag{1}$$

where $E(v,h)$ denotes RBM's energy function,

$$E(v,h) = -\sum_{i=1} a_i v_i - \sum_{j=1} b_j h_j - \sum_{i,j} v_i h_j W_{ij} \tag{2}$$

W_{ij} denotes the weight between the visible and the hidden layer, a_i and b_j describe the visible and hidden layer coefficients. This study uses the stochastic gradient descent (SGD) method following log-likelihood (L.L.) to accomplish optimal training. This is accomplished by optimizing the RBM's parameters a, b, and wij. The derivatives of the $\log p(v,h)$ w.r.t W_{ij}, a_i and b_j must be computed to update the weights and biases. The resulting equations are

$$W^{t+1} = W^t + \eta \left(p(h \mid v)v^T - p(h \mid v)v^T \right) - \lambda W^t + \alpha \Delta W^{t-1} \tag{3}$$

$$a^{t+1} = a^t + \eta(v - \tilde{v}) + \alpha \Delta a^{t-1} \tag{4}$$

$$b^{t+1} = b^t + \eta \left(p(h \mid v) - p\left(\tilde{h} \mid \tilde{v}\right) \right) + \alpha \Delta b^{t-1} \tag{5}$$

where $p(h_j = 1 \mid v) = \sigma(\sum_{i=1}^{m} w_{ij} v_i + b_j)$, $p(v_i = 1 \mid h) = \sigma(\sum_{j=1}^{n} w_{ij} h_j + a_i)$, and $\sigma(\cdot)$ represents the logistic sigmoid function. $\tilde{v}$ and $\tilde{h}$ denote the reconstructed v and h, respectively.

N is the number of hidden nodes, η, the learning ratio, α, the momentum weight, and λ, the weight decay. The weight matrix and accompanying bias vectors of the visible and hidden nodes are learned using contrastive divergence (CD) and persistent contrastive divergence (PCD). This optimization process uses the BP with the conventional gradient ascent algorithm to tune the weight matrices to optimal values. The optimization algorithm considers the outcome of an extra layer built over the DBN after its previous greedy training to minimize some error metrics. Softmax, or logistic units, are frequently used in this layer.

3.5.2. Elephant Herd Optimization (EHO) Algorithm

The EHO algorithm was introduced by Wang et al. in 2015 [41]. Elephants behave socially and encompass a complex structure of calves and females. An elephant group comprises numerous clans with a matriarch as the leader and her calves or other related females. A female forms a clan. EHO concerns the succeeding assumptions.

- The elephant group is classified into clans, and each such clan comprises specific elephants.
- A specific number of male elephants (ME) depart their clan to live independently.
- Each clan has a leader termed the matriarch.

The matriarch group keeps the best solution in the elephant herd. The entire elephant population is divided into j clans. Matriarch ci influences the new position of each elephant ci. The elephant j in clan ci can be calculated using

$$x_{new,\ c_{i,j}} = x_{c_{ij}} + a \times \left(x_{best,\ c_i} - x_{c_{i,j}} \right) \times r \tag{6}$$

where $x_{new,\ c_{i,j}}$ indicated the new position and $x_{c_{ij}}$ denotes the old position for elephant j in the clan ci. $x_{best,\ c_i}$ represents matriarch c_i, which denotes the best elephant. $a \in [0,1]$ shows a scaling factor, $r \in [0,1]$. The best elephant is computed for each clan using

$$x_{new,ci,j} = \beta \times x_{center,\ ,i} \tag{7}$$

Here, $\beta \in [0,1]$ indicates the second parameter that guides the impact of the $x_{center,ci,d}$ delineated in

$$x_{center,ci,d} = \frac{1}{n_{ci}} \times \sum_{j=1}^{n_{ci}} x_{ci,j,d} \tag{8}$$

where $1 \leq d \leq D$, and nci represent the number of elephants in clan $x_{ci,j,d}$ is the d_{th} dimension of individual elephant $x_{ci,j,d}$ the center of clan ci ($x_{center,ci,d}$) can be updated (Equation (8)). The separating process could be modelled as a separation operator when tackling optimization issues. In each clan, the worst valued elephants are moved to the next position indicated by

$$x_{worst,\ d} = x_{min} + (x_{max} - x_{min} + 1) \times rand \tag{9}$$

Here the lower and upper bands of the search space are indicated by x_{min} and x_{max}, respectively. $rand \in [0,1]$ signifies the random value picked from the uniform distribution.

The EHO algorithm was examined for various benchmark set functions and in medical diagnosis [42–46], showing better results. This study employs the EHO algorithm for DBN parameter optimization. The output of the DBN model is grounded in weights and the biases of preceding layers in the network. EHO does not employ the previous individuals in the later updating process as other optimization algorithms. EHO is a swarm-inspired algorithm that deals with global optimization missions characterized by clan updating and searching operations. EHO does not resort to relaxation and is less vulnerable to noise. They perform better in constrained, optimized environments. High convergence rate and low localization errors with less execution time are the important characteristics of EHO. The algorithm can tackle non-convex ML problems directly.

3.5.3. Fine Tuning of DBM

The learning rate, hidden units, momentum weight, and weight decay are the four basic parameters set up in most RBMs. The use of traditional methods for computing the error function is an NP-hard problem due to its complexity and differentiation. Meta-heuristics have been employed to solve this issue. The EHO algorithm is used to optimize the DBN training by fine tuning the parameters in this work. Here, the parameters set are

$$n \in [5, 100], \ \eta \in [0.1, 0.9], \ \lambda \in [0.1, 0.9] \ and \ \alpha \in [0.00001, 0.01]$$

A fitness function must be designed to steer the searching process to attain the best answers to meet the objectives. Mean squared error (*MSE*) is adopted as the fitness function. It measures the error between the output and the desired value and is given by

$$MSE = \frac{1}{T} \sum_{j=1}^{N} \sum_{i=1}^{T} (D_j(i) - Y_j(i))^2 \tag{10}$$

where *T*—data number, *N*—number of the output layers.

The EHO looks for a collection of DBN parameters that minimizes *MSE*. $D_j(i)$ denotes the value from the *j*th unit in the DBN's output layer at the time 't', $Y_j(i)$ represents the *j*th factor of the desired value. The process is repeated until the halting criteria is met.

The optimization steps of EHO are as follows:

1. Set the EHO parameters and initialize the population.
2. Evaluate the individual fitness value (RMSE) of the DBN, as per the learning rate and the number of batch learning. Identify the optimal individual.
3. Check if the termination condition is reached; if so, end the iteration and output the result; or else, go to the next step.
4. Update each individual position. Reinitialize the individuals beyond the lower and upper limits.
5. Start a new iteration by updating the optimal individual.

4. Results and Discussion

Evaluation of the proposed model's performance is presented in this section. The experiment is executed in MATLAB with the following specifications: the Intel Core i7 Processor, Windows 10, 3.20 GHz CPU speed, and 4GB RAM.

4.1. Dataset Preparation

This work uses DRISHTI–GS1, ACRIMA, ORIGA-Light, and LAG datasets for evaluation. The images were captured utilizing a Canon CR-1 fundus camera at 2336 × 3504 resolution with a 45° FOV and a disparate acquisition setting. The dataset used in the methodology is from public and private datasets annotated by an ophthalmologist who has over 15 years of experience in the field. The list of databases is depicted in Table 2. A total of 7280 images obtained from various public and private databases are used for investigating the proposed system's performance after eliminating a few irrelevant images. Images are trained and tested in the ratio of 70:30, respectively.

Table 2. Dataset labeling.

Database/Images	Normal	Glaucoma	Total	Type
DRISHIT-GSI [44]	12	89	101	Public
ACRIMA [29,45]	309	396	705	Public
OTIHS-lihjy [46]	482	368	650	Public
LAG [47]	3432	2392	5824	Private
Total	**4235**	**3045**	**7280**	

Images that are preprocessed are subjected to OD and OC segmentation. Sample images and results of the segmentation are given below in Figure 6.

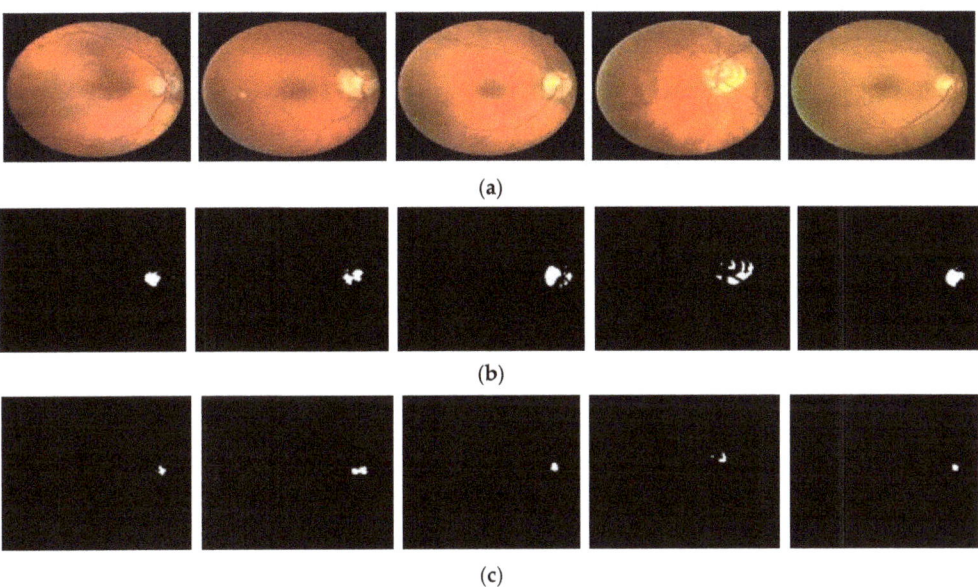

Figure 6. Results: (**a**) original image; (**b**) OD segmented image; (**c**) OC segmented image.

4.2. Performance Analysis

Experiments are done to show the efficacy of the DBN–EHO on different fundus datasets. Initially, the investigations are performed to show the efficacy of EHO in optimizing the DBN. EHO is compared with meta-heuristic algorithms, such as artificial bee colony (ABC), firefly algorithm (FA), harmony search (HS), cuckoo search (CS), particle swarm optimization algorithms (PSO), and differential evolution algorithms (DE). A hold-out technique with 20 training and test sets generated at random, subjected to 10 iterations for each RBM learning procedure, and a mini-batch of 20 are performed for consistent comparisons with other works. Five agents of over 50 iterations are employed to achieve convergence using all strategies in tests. Control parameters for all the algorithms are outlined in Table 3.

Table 3. Control parameters of all algorithms.

Algorithm	Parameters
ABC	N = 30, MCN = 100, limit = 20
HS	HMCR = 0.7, PAR = 0.7, $\eta = 1$
FA	$\gamma = 1$, $\beta_0 = 1$, $\alpha = 0.2$, $MCN = 100$
CS	$\alpha = 0.1$, pa = 0.25
PSO	Wmax = 0.9, Wmin = 0.2, C1 = 2, C2 = 2
DE	F = 0.8, C = 0.5
EHO	nClan = 5, $\alpha = 0.25$, $\beta = 0.05$

In Table 4, the *MSE* values of each algorithm on the original LAG dataset considering DBN. A Wilcoxon signed-rank test with a 0.05 significance level is utilized to analyze the method statistically. It is observed from Table 4 that EHO outperformed all the other algorithms in terms of the lowest MSE employing fewer layers. ABC and FA algorithms have also performed well next to EHO.

Table 4. Average MSE over the LAG dataset.

Algorithm	Layer-1		Layer-2		Layer-3	
	CD	PCD	CD	PCD	CD	PCD
ABC	0.0891	0.8940	0.0881	0.0884	0.0880	0.0878
HS	0.1259	0.1345	0.1256	0.1169	0.1158	0.1156
FA	0.0864	0.0864	0.864	0.0860	0.0864	0.0862
CS	0.1146	0.1146	0.1176	0.1175	0.1164	0.1162
PSO	0.1086	0.1086	0.0988	0.0992	0.1045	0.1046
DE	0.1250	0.1254	0.1254	0.1254	0.1158	0.1156
EHO	0.0756	0.0756	0.0778	0.0778	0.0776	0.774

Taking the performance of EHO, the performance of the proposed work is assessed by finding 'true positive' (*TP*), 'true negative' (*TN*), 'false positive' (*FP*), and 'false negative' (*FN*) values. TP denotes the instances wherein glaucoma is detected correctly. *TN* shows the condition wherein a person with no glaucoma is classified correctly. *FP* indicates the number of negative instances recognized as positive. Positive instances recognized as negative are indicated by *FN*. Precision, accuracy, F-score, specificity, recall, sensitivity, and MCC (Mathew's correlation coefficient) are used in this work, as in Table 5.

Table 5. Performance Metrics.

Parameters	Expression
Sensitivity (%)	$\frac{TP}{TP+FN} \times 100$
Specificity (%)	$\frac{TN}{TN+FP} \times 100$
Accuracy (%)	$\frac{TP+TN}{TP+FN+TN+FP} \times 100$
Precision (%)	$\frac{TP}{TP+FP} \times 100$
Recall (%)	$\frac{TP}{TP+FN} \times 100$
F-score (%)	$2 \times \frac{(Precision)(Recall)}{Precision+Recall} \times 100$
Mathew's correlation coefficient (MCC) (%)	$\frac{(TP \times TN)-(FP \times FN)}{\sqrt{(TP+FP)(TP+FN)(TN+FP)(TN+FN)}} \times 100$

The performance of the proposed work on individual datasets is provided in Table 6. It is inferred that a maximum accuracy of 99.34% on the ACRIMA dataset is attained, followed by 99.31% on the LAG dataset. The classification rate is between 96.95% and 99.34%, ensuring that the DBN–EHO performed better in all the datasets. This indicates that the images in the set are captured under different illuminations. Specificity of 100% on the LAG dataset shows that the model can reduce false positive rates.

Table 6. Performance of the proposed method employing DBN and EHO.

Dataset	Acc (%)	Sens (%)	Spec (%)	Prec (%)	Recall (%)	F-Score (%)	MCC
Drishti-GS1	96.95	98.56	97.44	97.69	96.86	97.68	0.749
ACRIMA	99.34	97.1	98.2	88.92	95.3	93.5	0.772
ORIGA	98.51	94.73	98.7	98.55	97.92	95.32	0.784
LAG	99.31	99.89	100	96.73	94.56	95.64	0.789

The impact of isolated and combined feature sets on the diagnosis of glaucoma in the LAG dataset is depicted in Table 7. The extraction of isolated features yielded an enhanced result, increasing the algorithm's efficiency. When the features are combined, an accuracy of 99.3% is obtained. When the features are combined, better accuracy of 99.34% is obtained. The feature contribution indicates that the DBN optimization also contributes to appreciable performance as the accuracy ranges from 95% to 99% on different kinds of features.

Table 7. Impact of features in detecting glaucoma from LAG dataset.

Features	Accuracy (%)	Sensitivity (%)	Specificity (%)
Structural (SF)	94.87	95.32	93.52
Intensity (IF)	95.98	89.23	92.41
Textural (TF)	96.21	97.28	99.33
SF + IF	95.86	90.74	95.21
SF + TF	96.78	94.23	97.56
IF + TF	90.88	95.79	94.35
Selected features	99.31	99.89	100

The feature contribution indicates that the DBN optimization also contributes to appreciable performance as the accuracy ranges from 95% to 99% on different kinds of features. A 10-fold cross validation done to reduce bias during testing enhances the algorithm's robustness and reduces the classifier's misclassification rate. From Table 8, it is seen that the cross-validation accuracy across the datasets is appreciably high, ensuring that the model is free from bias. The model applies to a wide range of datasets, compensating for any imbalance. Figure 7 highlights the proposed work against various performance metrics.

Table 8. 10-fold cross validation results.

Dataset	Accuracy (%)
Drishti-GS1	97.1
ACRIMA	98.5
ORIGA	96.2
LAG	97.8

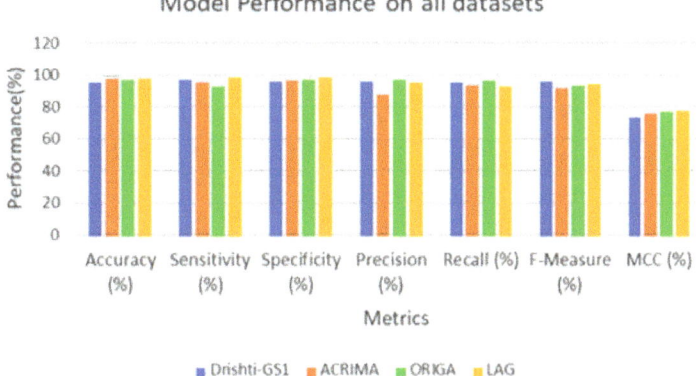

Figure 7. Results of the proposed work on all the datasets.

A 10-fold CV is carried out to reduce bias during testing, and the results are shown in Table 8.

From Table 8, it is seen that the cross-validation accuracy across the datasets is appreciably high, ensuring that the model is free from bias. The model applies to a wide range of datasets, compensating for any imbalance.

Table 9 reports the outcomes of the classifier when compared with similar conventional ML classifiers, such as K-nearest neighbor (KNN), random forest (RF), support vector machine (SVM), and DBN without optimization. The DBN attains a more appreciable performance than the conventional ML classifiers. The DBN, when optimized for weight by EHO, still achieves better performance across all the datasets.

Table 9. Performance analysis with dissimilar classifiers.

Dataset	Classifier	Accuracy (%)	Sensitivity (%)	Specificity (%)
Drishti-GS	KNN	95.34	90.47	93.08
	RF	94.50	91.34	92.33
	SVM	95.86	96.87	96.87
	DBN	96.23	97.56	96.62
	DBN–EHO	**96.95**	**98.56**	**97.44**
ACRIMA	KNN	95.66	90.86	93.78
	RF	94.32	91.24	90.84
	SVM	97.06	96.64	96.12
	DBN	97.26	98.16	97.06
	DBN–EHO	**99.34**	**97.1**	**98.2**
ORIGA-Light	KNN	94.22	96.86	97.08
	RF	91.34	88.56	89.75
	SVM	94.88	95.56	96.69
	DBN	96.06	97.65	97.81
	DBN–EHO	**98.51**	**94.73**	**98.7**
LAG	KNN	94.24	95.56	95.85
	RF	92.78	90.89	91.48
	SVM	95.60	95.68	96.45
	DBN	97.54	95.67	97.43
	DBN–EHO	**99.31**	**100**	**99.89**

From Table 9, it is seen that the DBN classifier attains a more appreciable performance than the conventional ML classifiers. The DBN, when optimized for weight by EHO, still achieves better performance across all the datasets. Furthermore, to assess the robustness of the model, salt-pepper and Gaussian noise are added to the LAG dataset (original image set). Gaussian noise is predominant if the images were captured under low illumination. Salt-pepper noise is an impulse noise occurring owing to intense and sparse disturbances. Figure 8 depicts the original and noise-added image (sample). Experimentation is performed with Gaussian noise and salt-pepper noise, with the variance (σ) and noise density (d) varying from 0.1 to 0.5, respectively, and the result is reported in Figure 9.

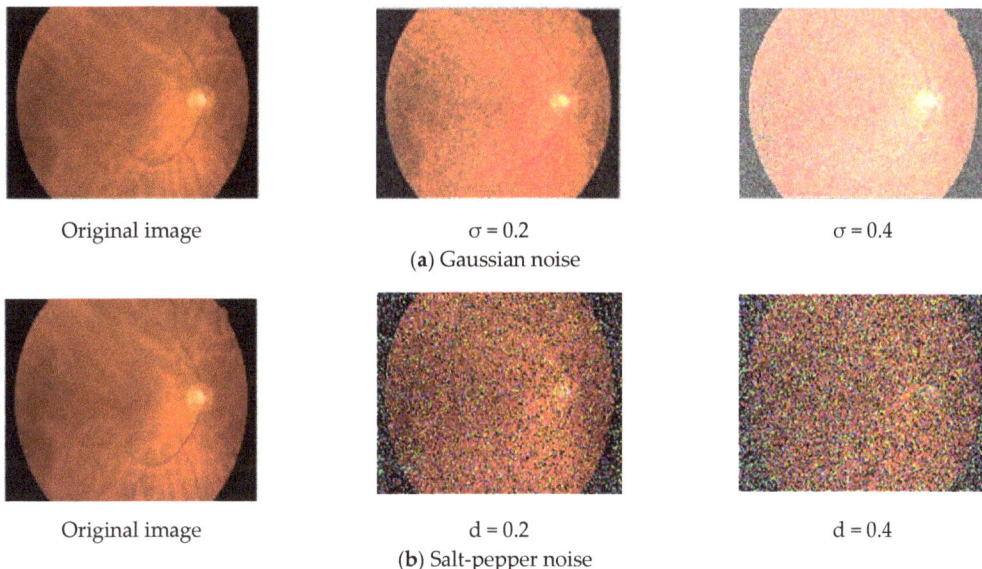

Figure 8. Sample fundus images with noise added.

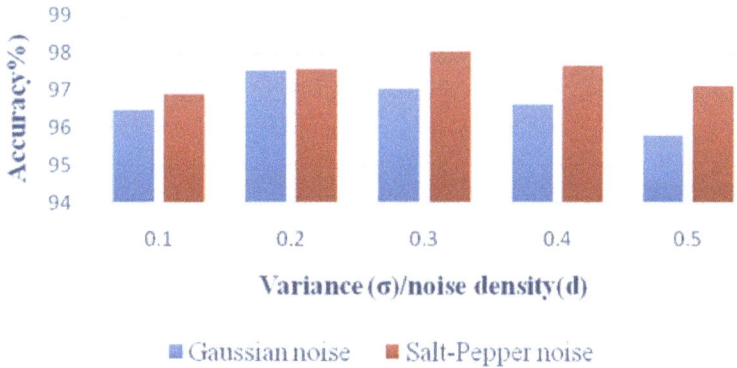

Figure 9. Recognition rate on degraded images of the LAG dataset.

It is seen from Figure 9 that the accuracy remains fairly the same. This demonstrates that the suggested model is extremely robust in both original and degraded datasets.

Table 10 compares the proposed model with well-known CNN models employing transfer learning. Transfer learning is applied to the DRISHTI-GS1 dataset, as the number of images is small. It is inferred that our model can work well compared to well-known, pre-trained models using transfer learning. Table 11 illustrates a comparison of similar other techniques and our technique in diagnosing glaucoma. Many optimization algorithms are also used to solve the other various optimization problems [48–64].

Table 10. Comparison of DBN-EHO with CNN models employing transfer learning.

Dataset	Classifier	Accuracy (%)	Sensitivity (%)	Specificity (%)
Drishti-GS	AlexNet	93.84	91.57	92.88
	GoogLeNet	95.46	90.34	93.36
	VGG16	94.12	95.77	96.42
	DBN-EHO	**96.95**	**98.56**	**97.44**

Table 11. Comparison of proposed work.

References	Features/Methods	Classifier Used	Images	Performance (%)
Karthikeyan and Rengarajan [65]	GLCM	BPN	Local dataset	Accuracy—95
Issac, A. et al. [19]	CDR, NRR, blood vessel features	SVM and ANN	67	Accuracy—94.11 Sensitivity—100
Mookiah et al. [66]	Discrete wavelet and HOS	SVM	60	Accuracy—95 Sensitivity—93.3 Specificity—96.67
Gifta [24]	GLCM, HOG, SURF	Gray Wolf Optimized NN	N.A.	Accuracy—93.1 Sensitivity—91.6 Specificity—94.1
Acharya, U.R. et al. [22]	6 features from LM filter bank	KNN	NA	Accuracy—95.8
Koh, J.E. et al. [20]	PHOG, SURF features	KNN	910	Accuracy—96.21 Sensitivity—97.42
Samanta et al. [21]	Haralick features	BPN	60	Accuracy—96.26 Sensitivity—90.43 Specificity—99.5
Acharya et al. [67]	Texture and HOF	RF	60	Accuracy—91
Acharya et al. [68]	Gabor transformation and principal component analysis	SVM	510	Accuracy—93.10; sensitivity—89.75; specificity—96.20
Yadav et al. [69]	Homogeneity, Contrast, energy, correlation, entropy	N.N.	20	Accuracy—72
Maheshwari et al. [70]	Entropy and fractal	SVM	488	Accuracy—95.19
Bajwa M. N et al. [71]	ROI, Scaling	2-Stage CNN	ORIGA	AUC—0.87
Raghavendra et al. [72]	-	20 layer CNN	1426	Accuracy—98.13
Chen et al. [73]	-	16 layer CNN	SECS, ORIGA	AUC—0.881
Proposed Work	**Structural, intensity, and texture features**	**DBN and EHO**	**7280**	**Accuracy—99.34 Sensitivity—100 Specificity—99.89**

5. Conclusions

Glaucoma is a class of ocular neuropathy wherein the optic nerve gets vandalized, resulting in permanent vision loss. Glaucoma detection in RFI using the DBN classifier is proposed in this work. Input images from different public databases are enhanced through the preprocessing phase. The OD and OC are then segmented using CHT and Otsu's thresholding. The various structural, intensity, and textural features are extorted from the segmented OC and OD images and fed to the DBN classifier optimized by the EHO algorithm. To investigate the performance, the technique is compared with classifier techniques, such as R.F., KNN, SVM, pre-trained CNNs, etc. Experimental outcomes exhibit the performance of the DBN classifier in recognizing the absence or presence of glaucoma accurately compared to other approaches. The proposed work concentrates on some of the important features contributing to glaucoma disease. The ReliefF algorithm selects the features before feeding them to the classifier for classifying them into either healthy or glaucomatous. The classifier performance is improved through an optimization technique where EHO does the weight update process. Dataset imbalance is also minimized as the model showed better training accuracy when images were selected randomly from each set using 10-fold cross validation. One potential drawback of this method is that it is unclear whether the attained specificities and sensitivities will be generalizable to real-world patient populations with common comorbidities, such as cataracts and surface ocular disease, which can degrade the input image quality. The performance of the computational hardware needs to be improved, along with network structure refinement and data dimension reduction, to attain competitively better computational speed. In the future, a universal domain adaptation method for various datasets (both public and private) is needed to be developed using hybrid weighted deep adversarial learning [74] and adaptive on-line validation [75]. In the future, the detection of glaucoma systems will be enhanced using the feature selection and ranking phase with different hybrid optimization algorithms. Besides, granular computing will be embedded in deep neural networks (granulated CNN) to enhance the computation speed significantly.

Author Contributions: Conceptualization, M.A.S.A., D.S.A.E., N.E.E.-A. and L.A.; methodology, M.A.S.A., D.S.A.E., N.E.E.-A. and L.A.; software, M.A.S.A., D.S.A.E., N.E.E.-A. and L.A.; validation K.B., G.D.K., S.M. (Suresh Muthusamy), S.P., H.P., S.M. (Suman Mann) and K.T.; formal analysis, K.B., G.D.K., S.M. (Suresh Muthusamy), S.P., H.P., S.M. (Suman Mann) and K.T.; investigation, M.A.S.A., D.S.A.E., N.E.E.-A. and L.A.; resources, M.A.S.A., D.S.A.E., N.E.E.-A. and L.A.; data curation, M.A.S.A., D.S.A.E., N.E.E.-A. and L.A.; writing—original draft preparation, K.B., G.D.K., S.M. (Suresh Muthusamy), S.P., H.P., S.M. (Suman Mann) and K.T.; writing—review and editing, M.A.S.A., D.S.A.E., N.E.E.-A. and L.A.; visualization, M.A.S.A., D.S.A.E., N.E.E.-A. and L.A.; project administration, D.S.A.E.; funding acquisition, M.A.S.A. All authors have read and agreed to the published version of the manuscript.

Funding: This Research is funded by Deanship of Scientific Research, King Faisal University, Saudi Arabia [Project No. GRANT716].

Acknowledgments: This work was supported by the Deanship of Scientific Research, Vice Presidency for Graduate Studies and Scientific Research, King Faisal University, Saudi Arabia [Project No. GRANT716].

Conflicts of Interest: The authors declare no potential conflicts of interest and funding.

References

1. Quigley, H.A.; Broman, A.T. The number of people with glaucoma worldwide in 2010 and 2020. *Br. J. Ophthalmol.* **2006**, *90*, 262–267. [CrossRef] [PubMed]
2. Dervisevic, E.; Pavlja, S.; Dervisevic, A.; Kasumovic, S.S. Challenges in early glaucoma detection. *Med. Arch.* **2017**, *70*, 203–207. [CrossRef] [PubMed]
3. Kassebaum, N.J.; Bertozzi-Villa, A.; Coggeshall, M.S.; A Shackelford, K.; Steiner, C.; Heuton, K.R.; Gonzalez-Medina, D.; Barber, R.; Huynh, C.; Dicker, D.; et al. Global, regional, and national levels and causes of maternal mortality during 1990–2013: A systematic analysis for the Global Burden of Disease Study 2013. *Lancet* **2014**, *384*, 980–1004. [CrossRef]
4. What Is Glaucoma? Available online: https://www.glaucoma.org/glaucoma/optic-nerve-cupping.php (accessed on 1 May 2021).
5. McMonnies, C.W. Intraocular pressure and glaucoma: Is physical exercise beneficial or a risk? *J. Optom.* **2016**, *9*, 139–147. [CrossRef]
6. Types of Glaucoma. Available online: http://www.glaucoma-association.com/about-glaucoma/types-of-glaucoma/chronic-glaucoma (accessed on 1 May 2021).
7. Blindness. Available online: https://www.who.int/health-topics/blindness-and-vision-loss (accessed on 2 May 2021).
8. Chandrika, S.; Nirmala, K. Analysis of CDR detection for glaucoma diagnosis. *Int. J. Eng. Res. Appl.* **2014**, *2*, 23–27.

9. Al-Bander, B.; Al-Nuaimy, W.; Al-Taee, M.; Zheng, Y. Automated glaucoma diagnosis using deep learning approach. In Proceedings of the 14th International Multi-Conference on Systems, Signals & Devices (SSD), Marrakech, Morocco, 28–31 March 2017; pp. 207–210.
10. Mardin, C.Y.; Horn, F.K.; Jonas, J.B.; Budde, W.M. Preperimetric glaucoma diagnosis by confocal scanning laser tomography of the optic disc. *Br. J. Ophthalmol.* **1999**, *83*, 299–304. [CrossRef]
11. Adhi, M.; Duker, J.S. Optical coherence tomography—Current and future applications. *Curr. Opin. Ophthalmol.* **2013**, *24*, 213–221. [CrossRef]
12. Septiarini, A.; Khairina, D.M.; Kridalaksana, A.H.; Hamdani, H. Automatic Glaucoma Detection Method Applying a Statistical Approach to Fundus Images. *Healthc. Inform. Res.* **2018**, *24*, 53–60. [CrossRef]
13. Thorat, S.; Jadhav, S. Optic disc and cup segmentation for glaucoma screening based on super pixel classification. *Int. J. Innov. Adv. Comput. Sci.* **2015**, *4*, 167–172.
14. Kavitha, K.; Malathi, M. Optic disc and optic cup segmentation for glaucoma classification. *Int. J. Adv. Res. Comput. Sci. Technol.* **2014**, *2*, 87–90. [CrossRef]
15. Manju, K.; Sabeenian, R.S. Robust CDR calculation for glaucoma identification. *Biomed. Res.* **2018**. [CrossRef]
16. Mahalakshmi, V.; Karthikeyan, S. Clustering based optic disc and optic cup segmentation for glaucoma detection. *Int. J. Innov. Res. Comput. Commun. Eng.* **2014**, *2*, 3756–3761.
17. Almazroa, A.; Burman, R.; Raahemifar, K.; Lakshminarayanan, V. Optic Disc and Optic Cup Segmentation Methodologies for Glaucoma Image Detection: A Survey. *J. Ophthalmol.* **2015**, *2015*, 180972. [CrossRef] [PubMed]
18. Raja, C.; Gangatharan, N. A Hybrid Swarm Algorithm for optimizing glaucoma diagnosis. *Comput. Biol. Med.* **2015**, *63*, 196–207. [CrossRef] [PubMed]
19. Issac, A.; Sarathi, M.P.; Dutta, M.K. An adaptive threshold based image processing technique for improved glaucoma detection and classification. *Comput. Methods Programs Biomed.* **2015**, *122*, 229–244. [CrossRef]
20. Koh, J.E.W.; Ng, E.Y.K.; Bhandary, S.V.; Laude, A.; Acharya, U.R. Automated detection of retinal health using PHOG and SURF features extracted from fundus images. *Appl. Intell.* **2017**, *48*, 1379–1393. [CrossRef]
21. Samanta, S.; Ahmed, S.K.; Salem, M.A.; Nath, S.S.; Dey, N.; Chowdhury, S.S. Haralick features based automated glaucoma classification using back propagation neural network. In Proceedings of the 3rd International Conference on Frontiers of Intelligent Computing: Theory and Applications (FICTA), Bhubaneswar, India, 14–15 November 2014; Springer: Cham, Switzerland, 2015; pp. 351–358.
22. Cheng, J.; Liu, J.; Xu, Y.; Yin, F.; Wong, D.W.; Tan, N.M.; Tao, D.; Cheng, C.Y.; Aung, T.; Wong, T.Y. Superpixel classification based optic disc and optic cup segmentation for glaucoma screening. *IEEE Trans. Med. Imaging* **2013**, *32*, 1019–1032. [CrossRef]
23. Singh, A.; Dutta, M.K.; ParthaSarathi, M.; Uher, V.; Burget, R. Image processing based automatic diagnosis of glaucoma using wavelet features of segmented optic disc from fundus image. *Comput. Methods Programs Biomed.* **2016**, *124*, 108–120. [CrossRef]
24. Ajesh, F.; Ravi, R.; Rajakumar, G. Early diagnosis of glaucoma using multi-feature analysis and DBN based classification. *J. Ambient. Intell. Humaniz. Comput.* **2021**, *12*, 4027–4036. [CrossRef]
25. Diaz, A.; Morales, S.; Naranjo, V.; Alcocer, P.; Lanzagorta, A. Glaucoma diagnosis by means of optic cup feature analysis in color fundus images. In Proceedings of the 24th European Signal Processing Conference (EUSIPCO), Budapest, Hungary, 29 August–2 September 2016; pp. 2055–2059.
26. Gómez-Valverde, J.J.; Antón, A.; Fatti, G.; Liefers, B.; Herranz, A.; Santos, A.; Sánchez, C.I.; Ledesma-Carbayo, M.J. Automatic glaucoma classification using color fundus images based on convolutional neural networks and transfer learning. *Biomed. Opt. Express* **2019**, *10*, 892–913. [CrossRef]
27. Diaz-Pinto, A.; Morales, S.; Naranjo, V.; Köhler, T.; Mossi, J.M.; Navea, A. CNNs for automatic glaucoma assessment using fundus images: An extensive validation. *Biomed. Eng. Online* **2019**, *18*, 29. [CrossRef] [PubMed]
28. Raghavendra, U.; Fujita, H.; Bhandary, S.V.; Gudigar, A.; Tan, J.H.; Acharya, U.R. Deep convolution neural network for accurate diagnosis of glaucoma using digital fundus images. *Inf. Sci.* **2018**, *441*, 41–49. [CrossRef]
29. Orlando, J.I.; Prokofyeva, E.; del Fresno, M.; Blaschko, M.B. Convolutional neural network transfer for automated glaucoma identification. In Proceedings of the 12th International Symposium on Medical Information Processing and Analysis, Tandil, Argentina, 5–7 December 2016.
30. Chen, X.; Xu, Y.; Wong, D.W.; Wong, T.Y.; Liu, J. Glaucoma detection based on deep convolutional neural network. In Proceedings of the 2015 37th annual international conference of the IEEE engineering in medicine and biology society (EMBC), Milan, Italy, 25–29 August 2015; pp. 715–718.
31. Staal, J.; Abràmoff, M.D.; Niemeijer, M.; Viergever, M.A.; Van Ginneken, B. Ridge-based vessel segmentation in color images of the retina. *IEEE Trans. Med. Imaging* **2004**, *23*, 501–509. [CrossRef]
32. Hani, A.F.; Soomro, T.A.; Fayee, I.; Kamel, N.; Yahya, N. Identification of noise in the fundus images. In Proceedings of the 2013 IEEE International Conference on Control System, Computing and Engineering, Penang, Malaysia, 29 November–1 December 2013; pp. 191–196.
33. Nagu, M.; Shanker, N. Image De-Noising by Using Median Filter and Weiner Filter. *Int. J. Innov. Res. Comput. Commun. Eng.* **2014**, *2*, 5641–5649.
34. Aliskan, A.; Çevik, U. An Efficient Noisy Pixels Detection Model for C.T. Images using Extreme Learning Machines. *Teh. Vjesn. —Tech. Gaz.* **2018**, *25*, 679–686. [CrossRef]

35. Raj, P.A.; George, A. FCM and Otsu's Thresholding based Glaucoma Detection and its Analysis using Fundus Images. In Proceedings of the 2nd International Conference on Intelligent Computing, Instrumentation and Control Technologies (ICICICT), Kannur, India, 5–6 July 2019; pp. 753–757.

36. Urbanowicz, R.J.; Meeker, M.; La Cava, W.; Olson, R.S.; Moore, J.H. Relief-based feature selection: Introduction and review. *J. Biomed. Inform.* **2018**, *85*, 189–203. [CrossRef]

37. Rosa, G.; Papa, J.; Costa, K.; Passos, L.; Pereira, C.; Yang, X. Learning Parameters in Deep Belief Networks Through Firefly Algorithm. In Proceedings of the IAPR Workshop on Artificial Neural Networks in Pattern Recognition. In Artificial Neural Networks in Pattern Recognition. ANNPR 2016, Ulm, Germany, 28–30 September 2016; Lecture Notes in Computer Science. Springer: Cham, Switzerland, 2016; pp. 138–149.

38. Hinton, G.E.; Osindero, S.; Teh, Y.-W. A Fast Learning Algorithm for Deep Belief Nets. *Neural Comput.* **2006**, *18*, 1527–1554. [CrossRef]

39. Wang, G.-G.; Deb, S.; Coelho, L.d.S. Elephant Herding Optimization. In Proceedings of the 3rd International Symposium on Computational and Business Intelligence (ISCBI 2015), Bali, Indonesia, 7–8 December 2015; pp. 1–5.

40. Li, J.; Lei, H.; Alavi, A.H.; Wang, G.-G. Elephant Herding Optimization: Variants, Hybrids, and Applications. *Mathematics* **2020**, *8*, 1415. [CrossRef]

41. Nayak, M.; Das, S.; Bhanja, U.; Senapati, M.R. Elephant herding optimization technique based neural network for cancer prediction. *Inform. Med. Unlocked* **2020**, *21*, 100445. [CrossRef]

42. Sivaswamy, J.; Krishnadas, S.R.; Joshi, G.D.; Jain, M.; Tabish, A.U.S. Drishti-GS: Retinal image dataset for optic nerve head (ONH) segmentation. In Proceedings of the IEEE 11th International Symposium on Biomedical Imaging (ISBI), Beijing, China, 29 April–2 May 2014; pp. 53–56.

43. Khan, S.M.; Liu, X.; Nath, S.; Korot, E.; Faes, L.; Wagner, S.K.; Keane, P.A.; Sebire, N.J.; Burton, M.J.; Denniston, A.K. A global review of publicly available datasets for ophthalmological imaging: Barriers to access, usability, and generalisability. *Lancet. Digit. Health* **2021**, *3*, e51–e66. [CrossRef]

44. Zhang, Z.; Yin, F.S.; Liu, J.; Wong, W.K.; Tan, N.M.; Lee, B.H.; Cheng, J.; Wong, T.Y. ORIGA[(light)]: An on-line retinal fundus image database for glaucoma analysis and research. In Proceedings of the 2010 Annual International Conference of the IEEE Engineering in Medicine and Biology, Buenos Aires, Argentina, 31 August–4 September 2020; pp. 3065–3068.

45. Li, L.; Xu, M.; Wang, X.; Jiang, L.; Liu, H. Attention Based Glaucoma Detection: A Large-Scale Database and CNN Model. In Proceedings of the IEEE/CVF Conference on Computer Vision and Pattern Recognition (CVPR), Long Beach, CA, USA, 15–20 June 2019; pp. 10563–10572.

46. Karthikeyan, S.; Rengarajan, N. Performance Analysis of Gray Level Co-Occurrence Matrix Texture Features for Glaucoma Diagnosis. *Am. J. Appl. Sci.* **2014**, *11*, 248–257. [CrossRef]

47. Mookiah, M.R.; Acharya, U.R.; Lim, C.M.; Petznick, A.; Suri, J.S. Data mining technique for automated diagnosis of glaucoma using higher order spectra and wavelet energy features. *Knowl.-Based Syst.* **2012**, *33*, 73–82. [CrossRef]

48. Danandeh Mehr, A.; Rikhtehgar Ghiasi, A.; Yaseen, Z.M.; Sorman, A.U.; Abualigah, L. A novel intelligent deep learning predictive model for meteorological drought forecasting. *J. Ambient. Intell. Humaniz. Comput.* **2022**, *24*, 1–5. [CrossRef]

49. Gharaibeh, M.; Almahmoud, M.; Ali, M.Z.; Al-Badarneh, A.; El-Heis, M.; Abualigah, L.; Altalhi, M.; Alaiad, A.; Gandomi, A.H. Early Diagnosis of Alzheimer's Disease Using Cerebral Catheter Angiogram Neuroimaging: A Novel Model Based on Deep Learning Approaches. *Big Data Cogn. Comput.* **2021**, *6*, 2. [CrossRef]

50. Gandomi, A.H.; Chen, F.; Abualigah, L. Machine Learning Technologies for Big Data Analytics. *Electronics* **2022**, *11*, 421. [CrossRef]

51. Houssein, E.H.; Hassaballah, M.; Ibrahim, I.E.; AbdElminaam, D.S.; Wazery, Y.M. An automatic arrhythmia classification model based on improved Marine Predators Algorithm and Convolutions Neural Networks. *Expert Syst. Appl.* **2022**, *187*, 115936. [CrossRef]

52. Houssein, E.H.; Abdelminaam, D.S.; Hassan, H.N.; Al-Sayed, M.M.; Nabil, E. A Hybrid Barnacles Mating Optimizer Algorithm with Support Vector Machines for Gene Selection of Microarray Cancer Classification. *IEEE Access* **2021**, *9*, 64895–64905. [CrossRef]

53. Houssein, E.H.; Abdelminaam, D.S.; Ibrahim, I.E.; Hassaballah, M.; Wazery, Y.M. A Hybrid Heartbeats Classification Approach Based on Marine Predators Algorithm and Convolution Neural Networks. *IEEE Access* **2021**, *9*, 86194–86206. [CrossRef]

54. Elminaam, D.A.; Ibrahim, S.A. Building a robust heart diseases diagnose intelligent model based on RST using lem2 and modlem2. In Proceedings of the 32nd IBIMA Conference, Seville, Spain, 15–16 November 2018; pp. 5733–5744.

55. Abd Elminaam, D.S.; Elashmawi, W.H.; Ibraheem, S.A. HMFC: Hybrid MODLEM-Fuzzy Classifier for Liver Diseases Diagnose. *Int. Arab. J. E Technol.* **2019**, *5*, 100–109.

56. Nadimi-Shahraki, M.H.; Taghian, S.; Mirjalili, S.; Ewees, A.A.; Abualigah, L.; Elaziz, M.A. MTV-MFO: Multi-Trial Vector-Based Moth-Flame Optimization Algorithm. *Symmetry* **2021**, *13*, 2388. [CrossRef]

57. Nadimi-Shahraki, M.H.; Taghian, S.; Mirjalili, S.; Abualigah, L.; Elaziz, M.A.; Oliva, D. EWOA-OPF: Effective Whale Optimization Algorithm to Solve Optimal Power Flow Problem. *Electronics* **2021**, *10*, 2975. [CrossRef]

58. Nadimi-Shahraki, M.H.; Fatahi, A.; Zamani, H.; Mirjalili, S.; Abualigah, L. An Improved Moth-Flame Optimization Algorithm with Adaptation Mechanism to Solve Numerical and Mechanical Engineering Problems. *Entropy* **2021**, *23*, 1637. [CrossRef] [PubMed]

59. Elminaam, D.S.A.; Neggaz, N.; Ahmed, I.A.; Abouelyazed, A.E.S. Swarming Behavior of Harris Hawks Optimizer for Arabic Opinion Mining. *Comput. Mater. Contin.* **2021**, *69*, 4129–4149. [CrossRef]

60. AbdElminaam, D.S.; Neggaz, N.; Gomaa, I.A.E.; Ismail, F.H.; Elsawy, A. AOM-MPA: Arabic Opinion Mining using Marine Predators Algorithm based Feature Selection. In Proceedings of the 2021 International Mobile, Intelligent, and Ubiquitous Computing Conference (MIUCC), Cairo, Egypt, 26–27 May 2021; pp. 395–402. [CrossRef]

61. Shaban, H.; Houssein, E.H.; Pérez-Cisneros, M.; Oliva, D.; Hassan, A.Y.; Ismaeel, A.A.K.; AbdElminaam, D.S.; Deb, S.; Said, M. Identification of Parameters in Photovoltaic Models through a Runge Kutta Optimizer. *Mathematics* **2021**, *9*, 2313. [CrossRef]

62. Deb, S.; Houssein, E.H.; Said, M.; Abdelminaam, D.S. Performance of Turbulent Flow of Water Optimization on Economic Load Dispatch Problem. *IEEE Access* **2021**, *9*, 77882–77893. [CrossRef]

63. Abdul-Minaam, D.S.; Al-Mutairi, W.M.E.S.; Awad, M.A.; El-Ashmawi, W.H. An Adaptive Fitness-Dependent Optimizer for the One-Dimensional Bin Packing Problem. *IEEE Access* **2020**, *8*, 97959–97974. [CrossRef]

64. El-Ashmawi, W.H.; Elminaam, D.S.A.; Nabil, A.M.; Eldesouky, E. A chaotic owl search algorithm based bilateral negotiation model. *Ain Shams Eng. J.* **2020**, *11*, 1163–1178. [CrossRef]

65. Acharya, U.R.; Dua, S.; Du, X.; Chua, C.K. Automated diagnosis of glaucoma using texture and higher order spectra features. *IEEE Trans. Inf. Technol. Biomed.* **2011**, *15*, 449–455. [CrossRef]

66. Acharya, U.R.; Ng, E.Y.; Eugene, L.W.; Noronha, K.P.; Min, L.C.; Nayak, K.P.; Bhandary, S.V. Decision support system for the glaucoma using Gabor transformation. *Biomed. Signal Process. Control* **2015**, *15*, 18–26. [CrossRef]

67. Yadav, D.; Sarathi, M.P.; Dutta, M.K. Classification of glaucoma based on texture features using neural networks. In Proceedings of the 2014 Seventh International Conference on Contemporary Computing (IC3), Noida, India, 7–9 August 2014; pp. 109–112.

68. Maheshwari, S.; Pachori, R.B.; Kanhangad, V.; Bhandary, S.V.; Acharya, U.R. Iterative variational mode decomposition based automated detection of glaucoma using fundus images. *Comput. Biol. Med.* **2017**, *88*, 142–149. [CrossRef]

69. Bajwa, M.N.; Malik, M.I.; Siddiqui, S.A.; Dengel, A.; Shafait, F.; Neumeier, W.; Ahmed, S. Two-stage framework for optic disc localization and glaucoma classification in retinal fundus images using deep learning. *BMC Med. Inform. Decis. Mak.* **2019**, *19*, 1–6.

70. Shehab, M.; Abualigah, L.; Shambour, Q.; Abu-Hashem, M.A.; Shambour, M.K.Y.; Alsalibi, A.I.; Gandomi, A.H. Machine learning in medical applications: A review of state-of-the-art methods. *Comput. Biol. Med.* **2022**, *145*, 105458. [CrossRef] [PubMed]

71. Ezugwu, A.E.; Ikotun, A.M.; Oyelade, O.O.; Abualigah, L.; Agushaka, J.O.; Eke, C.I.; Akinyelu, A.A. A comprehensive survey of clustering algorithms: State-of-the-art machine learning applications, taxonomy, challenges, and future research prospects. *Eng. Appl. Artif. Intell.* **2022**, *110*, 104743. [CrossRef]

72. Liu, Q.; Li, N.; Jia, H.; Qi, Q.; Abualigah, L. Modified Remora Optimization Algorithm for Global Optimization and Multilevel Thresholding Image Segmentation. *Mathematics* **2022**, *10*, 1014. [CrossRef]

73. Gharaibeh, M.; Alzu'Bi, D.; Abdullah, M.; Hmeidi, I.; Al Nasar, M.R.; Abualigah, L.; Gandomi, A.H. Radiology Imaging Scans for Early Diagnosis of Kidney Tumors: A Review of Data Analytics-Based Machine Learning and Deep Learning Approaches. *Big Data Cogn. Comput.* **2022**, *6*, 29. [CrossRef]

74. Zhang, W.; Li, X.; Ma, H.; Luo, Z.; Li, X. Universal Domain Adaptation in Fault Diagnostics with Hybrid Weighted Deep Adversarial Learning. *IEEE Trans. Ind. Inform.* **2021**, *17*, 7957–7967. [CrossRef]

75. Zhang, W.; Li, X.; Li, X. Deep learning-based prognostic approach for lithium-ion batteries with adaptive time-series prediction and online validation. *Measurement* **2020**, *164*, 108052. [CrossRef]

 *electronics*

 MDPI

Article

A Novel Method for the Classification of Butterfly Species Using Pre-Trained CNN Models

Fathimathul Rajeena P. P. [1,*], Rasha Orban [2], Kogilavani Shanmuga Vadivel [3], Malliga Subramanian [3], Suresh Muthusamy [4], Diaa Salam Abd Elminaam [5,6,*], Ayman Nabil [6], Laith Abulaigh [7,8], Mohsen Ahmadi [9] and Mona A. S. Ali [1,2,*]

1   Computer Science Department, College of Computer Science and Information Technology, King Faisal University, Al Ahsa 400, Saudi Arabia
2   Computer Science Department, Faculty of Computers and Artificial Intelligence, Benha University, Benha 12311, Egypt; rasha.abdelkreem@fci.bu.edu.eg
3   Department of Computer Science and Engineering, Kongu Engineering College (Autonomous), Erode 638001, Tamil Nadu, India; kogilavani.sv@gmail.com (K.S.V.); mallinishanth72@gmail.com (M.S.)
4   Department of Electronics and Communication Engineering, Kongu Engineering College (Autonomous), Erode 638001, Tamil Nadu, India; infostosuresh@gmail.com
5   Information Systems Department, Faculty of Computers and Artificial Intelligence, Benha University, Benha 12311, Egypt
6   Computer Science Department, Faculty of Computer Science, Misr International University, Cairo 12585, Egypt; ayman.nabil@miuegypt.edu.eg
7   Faculty of Information Technology, Middle East University, Amman 11953, Jordan; aligah.2020@gmail.com
8   Faculty of Computer Sciences and Informatics, Amman Arab University, Amman 11953, Jordan
9   Department of Industrial Engineering, Urmia University of Technology (UUT), Urmia P.O. Box 57166-419, Iran; mohsen.ahmadi@ine.uut.ac.ir
*   Correspondence: fatimah.rajeena@kfu.edu.sa (F.R.P.P.); diaa.salama@fci.bu.edu.eg (D.S.A.E.); m.ali@kfu.edu.sa (M.A.S.A.)

Citation: Rajeena P. P., F.; Orban, R.; Vadivel, K.S.; Subramanian, M.; Muthusamy, S.; Elminaam, D.S.A.; Nabil, A.; Abulaigh, L.; Ahmadi, M.; Ali, M.A.S. A Novel Method for the Classification of Butterfly Species Using Pre-Trained CNN Models. *Electronics* **2022**, *11*, 2016. https://doi.org/10.3390/electronics11132016

Academic Editor: George A. Papakostas

Received: 15 May 2022
Accepted: 20 June 2022
Published: 27 June 2022

Publisher's Note: MDPI stays neutral with regard to jurisdictional claims in published maps and institutional affiliations.

Abstract: In comparison to the competitors, engineers must provide quick, low-cost, and dependable solutions. The advancement of intelligence generated by machines and its application in almost every field has created a need to reduce the human role in image processing while also making time and labor profit. Lepidopterology is the discipline of entomology dedicated to the scientific analysis of caterpillars and the three butterfly superfamilies. Students studying lepidopterology must generally capture butterflies with nets and dissect them to discover the insect's family types and shape. This research work aims to assist science students in correctly recognizing butterflies without harming the insects during their analysis. This paper discusses transfer-learning-based neural network models to identify butterfly species. The datasets are collected from the Kaggle website, which contains 10,035 images of 75 different species of butterflies. From the available dataset, 15 unusual species were selected, including various butterfly orientations, photography angles, butterfly lengths, occlusion, and backdrop complexity. When we analyzed the dataset, we found an imbalanced class distribution among the 15 identified classes, leading to overfitting. The proposed system performs data augmentation to prevent data scarcity and reduce overfitting. The augmented dataset is also used to improve the accuracy of the data models. This research work utilizes transfer learning based on various convolutional neural network architectures such as VGG16, VGG19, MobileNet, Xception, ResNet50, and InceptionV3 to classify the butterfly species into various categories. All the proposed models are evaluated using precision, recall, F-Measure, and accuracy. The investigation findings reveal that the InceptionV3 architecture provides an accuracy of 94.66%, superior to all other architectures.

Keywords: butterfly species; transfer-learning techniques; data augmentation; classification; convolutional neural network

1. Introduction

The study of butterflies is among the most fundamental in ecology, and it is carried out all around the world. The variety of butterfly species in the ecosystem ranges from 15,000 to 21,000 [1]. Butterfly identification and classification is difficult due to the great similarities of different species and the inability to distinguish between them. Furthermore, the number of biologists and technical staff has decreased dramatically. Moths and butterflies are members of the Animalia order [2]. The Animalia order has existed since the Jurassic period and exists today. The scales are one of the fascinating aspects of the Lepidoptera [3,4]. The entire body is covered, including the bodies, wings, and beaks. The Lepidoptera family contains many species with various wing shapes and colors, making identification of such a big number of species difficult. An automatic butterfly species identification system must be developed to decrease the burden of manual butterfly species classification [5].

In the traditional butterfly identification approach, the desired butterfly species must be personally trapped using a trap [6,7]. This method wastes effort and time and damages the insect because it must be kept in tight spaces for a long time to distinguish between the belly and the wings [8]. At the same time, the butterfly's traits must be recognized using an encyclopedia, which is enormous and cumbersome to transport on a field trip. Nur Nabila Kamaron Arzar et al. [9] have concentrated upon GoogLeNet, a pre-trained CNN architectural model. The Black Veined Tiger, Chocolate Grass Yellow, Grey Pansy, and Plain Lacewing are several varieties of insects that are often encountered throughout Asia. They employed a variety of transfer-learning techniques to identify different butterfly species. One hundred and twenty photos of four different varieties of butterflies were only tested and achieved 90.5% overall identification accuracy. However, in this approach, they utilized a small dataset for training the model. Ayadalmryad et al. in [10] proposed an automated butterfly genus reorganization model using deep-learning-based neural architecture. They gathered 44,569 pictures of 104 distinct butterfly genus in various butterfly poses. Butterfly species were identified using a convolutional neural network. Experiments on ten common butterfly species revealed that the procedure successfully identified different types of butterflies.

Juanying al [11] have presented the latest partitioning and augmentation strategy for the biological morpho database, which is severely unbalanced. They discovered the Retina Net is the better deep-learning-based neural network model for identifying morpho varieties depending upon genus photos taken in vivid settings. The best result they could obtain was 79.7% in terms of MAP. Zhao et al. [12] utilized a recurrent convolutional neural network to create automated morpho-classification and discrimination in various ecological situations, with an average classification accuracy of 70.4%. Mehre et al. [13] analyzed the structural information of several insect photos. It is possible to ensure the capacity to classify species of butterflies. Using two surface characteristics called bidirectional patterning (LBP) and a grey-level co-occurrence matrix, they examined 19 different species of the pyridine butterfly family, totaling 190 butterfly photographs (GCLM). The accuracy of LBP and GLCM was 90.45 % and 91.25%, respectively.

Sedaemeltekkara et al. [14] focused on a convolutional neural network applied to 7148 photos of six butterfly species used in the study, with 80% of the dataset being assigned for training purposes and 20% for testing purposes, and the model run with the appropriate parameters. They were able to achieve an accuracy of 89.73%. Miao et al. [15] classified butterfly photos acquired from camera traps, and researchers are using transfer-learning approaches. They train the picture datasets using CNN with VGC16 and ResNet-50 algorithms. In their model, they used a total of 111,467 images from 20 different species. On average, the model's accuracy is 87.5%. Alimboyong C et al. [16] mentioned how the butterfly species are classified using deep-neural-learning architecture. They used 4234 photos from 12 different species. Five convolutional neural layers and two fully linked layers make up the model. The training, validation, and testing percentages are roughly 70%, 20%, and 10%, respectively. The estimation's overall accuracy is 90.15%. They also talk about how to use various architectures such as VGG16, GoogleLeNet, ResNet, or transfer learning to build the same, different, or a larger number of datasets in the future. The proposed work considers these models for classifying the butterfly species.

Lim et al. [17] developed a model for automatic butterfly identification. On 30 species, they utilized the Inception V3 model. They have an 84% accuracy rate on average in their work. Following that, the author discussed the applicability and classification of butterfly species. Liong et al. [18] employed the YOLO method for automatic butterfly labeling in this study. According to the author, their developed architecture is a good mix for the mess of small sampling along with high accuracy in automatic butterfly species detection and recognition. With 5695 pictures, they looked at 14 species from 11 genera. Both specimens and ecological photography are depicted in this image. Finally, they were able to reach an accuracy of 89.35%. Mayo et al. [19] demonstrated that data-mining steps could be used to recognize species. They used WEKA, a data-mining software that includes, among other classifiers, naive Bayes, instantiation learning, random forests, decision trees, and support vector machines. Using SVM, WEKA was able to accurately categorize live moths by species with an accuracy of 85%.

From the above findings, it is understood that the detection and characterization of butterflies are not obvious due to the variety of taxonomy, higher parallels, and attributes, and the classification of butterflies has low accuracy and slow recognition. In addition, the number of taxonomists and skilled technologists has collapsed [20]. Butterfly diagnosis, notably at the advanced level, is required for critical themes such as species conservation research, reducing insect damage to agricultural plants, and biodiversity protection. An efficient and performing model which can define species even in small datasets may reduce the need for experts on the subject or reduce the time spent for identification [21]. Distinguishing among species of butterflies requires experience and time, which are both not always attainable. Still, the need for specialists will be reduced after developing software that detects butterfly species by extracting data from photos. There seem to be two major issues with the current computer perception of butterflies based on image processing research [22,23]. Firstly, gathering the butterfly dataset is tough, recognizing caterpillars is time-consuming labor for biologists, and the insect dataset's quantity of caterpillars is not thorough. Second, the butterfly images utilized in learning are pattern images with evident morphological characters rather than ecological images of butterflies in the wild [24]. Additionally, the evident disparities between two images make it difficult to combine research and manufacturing, and the accuracy rate is low [25]. Many optimization algorithms are also used to solve the various optimization problems [26–38].

The above literature survey motivates us to develop a system to detect butterfly species type automatically without any human intervention. At the same time, it has to reduce the burden of science students who are analyzing the butterfly insects for their study purpose. In order to do this, the proposed research work applies transfer-learning algorithms to classify butterfly species automatically. Initially, machine-learning algorithms are utilized for classification, which require human effort to construct features from the dataset. Automatic feature extraction is performed with domain knowledge when we utilize transfer-learning algorithms. The transfer-learning algorithms contain multiple layers to extract low-level and high-level features from the dataset. A convolutional neural network is a famous transfer-learning network that detects the most significant features from the dataset without any human intervention.

The proposed system utilizes 15 rare species collected from Kaggle, consisting of 1761 butterfly species images split into training, testing, and validation dataset images. If the data provided to the transfer-learning model is large, then the model predicts the results more accurately. For this small dataset with a large number of classes, data augmentation is helpful to improve the performance by creating new images to train the model. Data augmentation is a regularization technique used to manage the overfitting of data. Data augmentation activities such as padding, random rotating, re-scaling, vertical and horizontal flipping, translation, cropping, and zooming are applied to the image dataset. Initially, several CNN-based transfer-learning algorithms such as VGG16, VGG19, MobileNet, Xception, ResNet50, and InceptionV3 are applied with this dataset, and accuracy is evaluated. To improve the accuracy of these models, data augmentation is applied to the same dataset, and once again, all the models are evaluated with the augmented dataset.

The main contribution of this research work is:

- Apply the data augmentation technique in order to obtain various combinations of original butterfly species.
- Apply the transfer learning technique to detect the type of the butterfly species without harming them physically. These augmented, i.e., transformed, data that are applied to various pre-trained CNN models help to improve the accuracy.

The rest of the paper is organized as follows: The literature overview of recent studies on butterfly species identification is discussed in Section 2. The data sets utilized, data augmentation techniques, and different state-of-the-art CNN-based transfer-learning models for butterfly species classification are discussed in Section 3. The performance evaluation of various classifiers is discussed in Section 4. The conclusion, as well as the future scope, is presented in Section 5.

2. Related Works

Zhu et al. [39] classified lepidopteran insect images, an integrative region matched, and the dual-complex discrete wavelet approach was presented. They tested their method on a collection of 100+ lepidopterous insects from 18 genera, and the recognition accuracy was found to be 84.47%. Silva et al. [40] wanted to see which feature selection strategies and classifiers were best for identifying honeybee subspecies among the seven feature pickers and classification methods available. In their experiments, they discovered that the best combination was the naive Bayes classifier and the mutual information extraction of features.

Wen et al. [41] incorporated local and global information for insect classification; researchers developed a model that incorporates K nearest neighbor classification (KNNC), regular densities predicated sequential classification model (NDLC), minimal level fewest linear classification algorithm (MLSLC), the nearest mean classifier (NMC), and decision tree (DT). Their experimental results showed an 86.6% classification rate when assessed on images taken during actual field trapping for training.

Kaya et al. [42] proposed two different local binary patterns (LPB) descriptors for detecting special textures in images. The first is based on the distance between the sequential neighbors of a center pixel. In contrast, the second is based on the central pixel parameter determining the neighbors in the same orientation. They used laboratory-based photos of 140 morphos obtained in Van, Turkey to evaluate their descriptors for identifying butterfly species. The artificial neural network has the greatest accuracy of 90.71% in classifying butterflies.

Faithpraise et al. [43] extracted structural information and used ANN to construct an automatic detection algorithm for copepod species. They assessed an overall accuracy of 93.13 % using seven copepod traits from 240 reference photos. Xie et al. [44] used advanced multiple-task sparse representation and multiple-kernel learning approaches; additional efforts were towards a classification method to categorize butterfly imagery. They applied the conceptual approach to the trial on 24 prevalent farming systems species and contrasted it to some newer approaches.

Feng et al. [45], relying on flap features of butterfly photos, improved an insect species recognition and retrieving method. Their recovery method is built upon the CBIR framework, which also does not require a formal confirmation but provides users with a range of matches. Abeysinghe et al. [46] used multilayer Siamese networks to build a completely computerized system for identifying snake species. Even though the original snake dataset is limited, they could attain consistent results. Alsing et al. [47] created genuine CNN infrastructure based on domain adaptation to detect post-it locations and then converted these algorithms to be used on smartphones and tablets. The fastest RCNN ResNet50 structure had the highest MAP (mean average precision) of 99.33%, but it took 20,018 milliseconds to infer.

Hernandez et al. [48] used a computational approach to categorize 740 species and 11,198 samples in a dataset. They were 91.65% accurate with fish, 92.87% with flora, and 91.25 % for butterflies. Iamsaata et al. [49] used the extreme learning machines (ELM) to categorize the butterflies and compare these results to the SVM algorithm. The ELM approach has a 90.37% accuracy, which is somewhat higher than the support vector machine (SVM).

Kang et al. [50] produced a unique neural network to classify butterflies based on the shape of their wings, with an accuracy of 80.3%. Bouzalmat et al. [51] used PCA and SVM to analyze two feature collections, the ATT and IFD datasets, which achieved 90.24 % and 66.8% accuracy. The literature survey identified that all models applied to butterfly species classification obtained 91.25%.

The above literature survey helps to understand that various machine-learning and deep-learning models are used to identify the butterfly species type. At present, pre-trained CNN models are very much used in classification and produce better accuracy also. The goal of this research work is to apply these pre-trained CNN models for the classification of butterfly species to improve the accuracy of machine-learning and deep-learning models. In addition to that, the proposed work adopts the data augmentation technique to produce a large dataset which will be helpful to predict the butterfly species correctly. A detailed description of data augmentation is discussed in Section 3.

3. Proposed System Methodology

Transfer-learning models, particularly convolutional neural networks, have performed well on image classification tasks. However, these models rely on a large dataset to produce accurate results and to avoid overfitting. The proposed work classifies butterfly species images into various classes using pre-trained transfer-learning models.

3.1. Dataset Description

To carry out this research work, the data set consists of 15 species of butterfly images, 1761 training images, 75 testing images of each fifteen classes, and 75 validation images of each fifteen classes chosen from Kaggle. All images were reduced to 350×350 pixels because they were of various resolutions. The input images include various features, such as occlusion and backdrop complexity, because they were captured with wide field-of-view cameras. Table 1 lists the name and number of shots in the dataset for each butterfly genus.

Table 1. Dataset Description.

Genus	Training Dataset	Testing Dataset	Validation Dataset
Africangaint Swallowtail	107	75	75
American Snoot	119	75	75
Atala	143	75	75
Banded Peacock	116	75	75
Becker's White	105	75	75
Bkue Morphs	138	75	75
Crescent	108	75	75
Eastern Coma	133	75	75
Large Marble	112	75	75
Metamark	116	75	75
Painted Lady	116	75	75
Purple Hairstreak	107	75	75
Silver Spot Skipper	113	75	75
Tropical Leawing	119	75	75
Yellow Swallow Tail	118	75	75
Total	**1761**	**1125**	**1125**

3.2. Data Augmentation

Data augmentation enhances the size and quality of training datasets. In the proposed model, all the original images are transformed by applying various transformation functions in each epoch using the Image Data Generator from the Keras framework. The newly generated images have different variations of the same image and are applied to transfer-learning models. Figure 1 represents the data augmentation process applied to the butterfly species dataset. The butterfly species image dataset containing the original batch of images is fed into the Image Data Generator image augmentation object, which produces a randomly transformed batch of images.

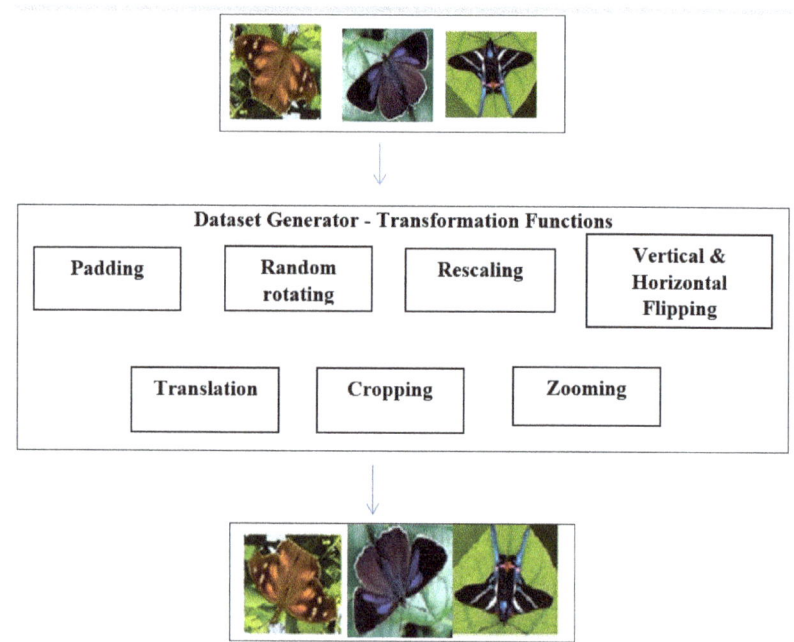

Figure 1. Data Augmentation Process.

3.2.1. Cropping

Cropping is the process of positioning and squaring the entire image at a random location. A parameter determines the diagonal relative position just on image pixels. The square will be the same size as the picture if the value is 0, with no cropping. If the crop square is 50%, it will crop half of the source images in horizontal and vertical directions.

3.2.2. Rescaling

A layer that rescales input data to a new range as part of the pre-processing process. This layer rescales every input value (typically an image) by multiplying by the scale and adding an offset. The size of it varies based on the range. The squares will be the same dimension as the input if the scale is reduced to 0. The square will be in a randomized region around half the dimension and height and width of the object if the percentage is set to 50%.

3.2.3. Horizontal Flips

The horizontal flip argument specifies a Boolean value that flips the images horizontally. True causes them to be horizontally flipped. The vertical flip argument specifies a Boolean value that flips the images vertically.

3.2.4. Fill Mode

When you rotate an image, some pixels will move outside of the image, leaving an empty region that needs to be filled in. The default value for the fill mode option is "nearest," which simply replaces the empty region with the closest pixel values.

3.2.5. Shear Range

Shear range = 0.2 says that the image will be sheared by 20%. Zoom range denotes a 20 % zoom-in and zoom-out range. Horizontal flip = True is set for mirror reflection. Fill mode is the most significant argument of Image Data Generator. There is some room left behind after the image shifts by 20%.

3.2.6. Width Shift

The width shift range is a floating-point value between 0.0 and 1.0 that determines the absolute limit of the fraction of the overall breadth. The image will be relocated to the left or right at irregular intervals.

3.2.7. Height Shift

It works the same as width_shift_range but shifts vertically (up or down).

3.2.8. Rotation Range

By passing an integer number in the rotation range argument to the Image Data Generator class, you can rotate images arbitrarily between 0 and 360 degrees. Some pixels will migrate outside the image as it is rotated, leaving an empty region that must be filled in.

3.3. Transfer-Learning Models

Transfer learning has risen to prominence as a crucial study area for artificial intelligence applications in recent years. Every day, the usage rate rises due to significant accomplishments in corresponding fields of speech recognition, computational linguistics, and human–computer interaction. Transfer-learning algorithms are based upon convolutional neural networks, influenced by the simplicity of synapses in a human mind. They have come to the forefront due to their effectiveness in learning. Transfer-learning methods can address the issue of feature extraction techniques by dynamically eliminating distinctive traits from the provided input data. Transfer learning requires a lot more labeled data than traditional neural networks. Transfer learning has become increasingly significant in problem solving because of the tremendous rise in available data. Many scientists in data analytics have noticed these remarks; CNNs are an upwards inter-feed-forward neural net regarding animal vision. A convolutional neural network is a deep-learning neural architecture used to classify images, discover similarities, and recognize objects. CNN, primarily employed for image classification, is now being used in practically every field where categorization is required. The basic convolutional neural architecture contains many numbers of numerous convolutions layers and maxpooling layers in succession, one to many fully linked parts, and finally, a classification output layer. Pre-trained transfer-learning neural prediction approaches such as VGG16, VGG19, MobileNet, Xception, ResNet50, and InceptionV3 are employed to classify the image. The proposed system workflow is represented in Figure 2.

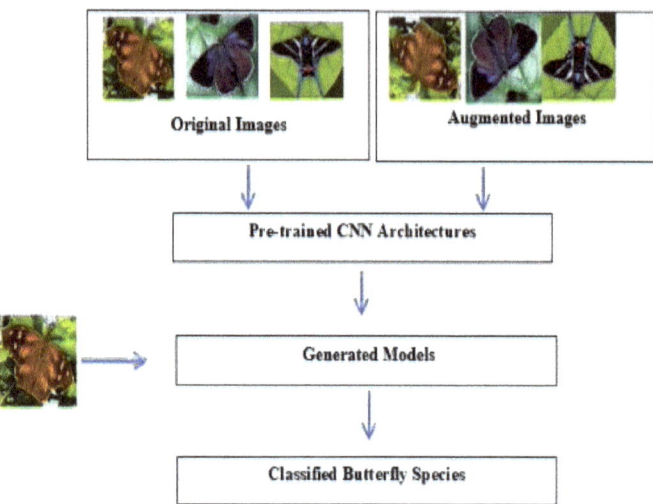

Figure 2. The proposed system's workflow.

3.3.1. VGG16

VGG16 is a CNN model developed by VGG at Oxford University. Alex Net, the channel's replacement, emerged in 2012. VGG16 has eight levels, three fully associated layers, seven max-pooling layers upon layer, and one SoftMax layer. As part of the ImageNet contest, the architecture has been designed. The convolution blocks' width is set to a tiny number. The width parameter is extended by two after each max-pooling operation until it reaches 512. The VGG16 has an image size of 224 × 224 pixels. Spatial cushioning was used to maintain the picture's pixel density. The VGG16 network, which has been declared accessible, can be used to do similar functionality. The modeling can be leveraged for transfer learning in certain systems, such as Keras. These supply pre-trained weights can generate custom models with modest adjustments and produce higher accuracy.

VGG16 without Data Augmentation

The input shape of the image is 350 × 350 pixels. The trainable layer in the base model is set as false, the model is sequential, and the activation function is sigmoid. The optimizer used in SGD has a learning rate of 0.0001 and the loss is categorical cross entropy. It has been validated for ten epochs. For input layer_2, the output shape is (None, 350, 350, 3) and the parameter is 0. For inblock1_conv1 layer, the output shape is (None, 350, 350, 64). The parameter 1792 is connected to the block2_conv2 where the output shape is (None, 350, 350, 64) and the parameter 36,928 is connected to the max-pooling layer where the output shape is (None, 350, 250, 64) and the parameter is 0. The same follows until block5 layer and the global_max_pooling layer where the output shape is (None, 10, 10, 512) and the parameter is 0. The flatten layer has output shape of (None, 51,200) and the parameter is 0. For the dense layer, the output shape is (None, 1024) and the parameter is 52,429,824 which is connected to the dropout layer where the output shape is (None, 1024) and the parameter is 0, which is connected to the dense layer which has the output shape of (None, 15) and the parameter of 15,375. The total number of parameters is 67,159,887 and the trainable parameters is 67,159,887 and the total non-trainable parameters is 0. The model has been trained for 10 epochs. In epoch 1, the loss value is 2.8380 and the value accuracy is 0.1411; in epoch2, the loss value is 2.1099 and the value accuracy is 0.3195, followed by an increase in the value accuracy and decrease in the value loss. In the 10th epoch, the loss is 0.0334 and the value accuracy is 0.9903. Thus, the model VGG16 without data augmentation has achieved the accuracy of 85.33%.

VGG16 with Data Augmentation

ImageDataGenerator is used for image pre-processing. The values for the parameters are rescale = 1.0/255.0, horizontal flip = True, fill mode = 'nearest', zoom range = 0.2, shear range = 0.2, width_shift_range = 0.2, height_shift_range = 0.2, and the rotation angle is 0.2. The batch size is 5, and the class mode is categorical. The input shape of the image is 350 × 350 pixels, and the pooling layer is the max-pooling layer. The model is the sequential model, and the activation function is sigmoid, the optimizer used in SGD with the learning rate of 0.0001, and the loss is categorical cross entropy. It has been validated for ten epochs. In epoch one the loss value is 2.6083, and the value accuracy is 0.1367. In epoch2, the loss value is 2.1047, and the value accuracy is 0.3749 followed by increase in the value accuracy and decrease in the value loss. In the 10th epoch, the loss is 0.3815, and the value accuracy is 0.8764. Thus, the model VGG16 with data augmentation has achieved an accuracy of 86.99%, and the loss value is 0.5347.

3.3.2. VGG19

VGG19 is a neural network trained on over a billion images in ImageNet. A laptop, keyboard, pencils, and a range of creatures are among the 1000 object classes the 19-layer network can classify photos into. As a result, the system has amassed a library of rich feature descriptions for a wide series of frames. VGGNet is architecture that stacks convolutional layers with tiny 33 receptive fields in blocks before adding a max-pooling layer. They use 11 convolutions in one network configuration to boost the nonlinearity of the decision function without modifying the convolutional layers' receptive fields. We use the VGG19 design, which includes 19 weight layers, in this study.

VGG19 without Data Augmentation

The input shape of the image is 350 × 350 pixels. The num_class is 15, and the dropout layer is 0.25; it uses sigmoid as an activation function. The optimizer used is Adam, with a learning rate of 0.0001. The loss is categorical cross entropy, where the trainable layer is set as false the input layer_2, where the output shape is (None, 350, 350, 3) and the parameter is 0. In block1_ conv1 layer, the output shape is (None, 350, 350, 64). The parameter 1792 is connected to the block2_conv2 where the output shape is (None, 350, 350, 64) and the parameter is 36,928, connected to the max-pooling layer where the output shape is (None, 350, 250, 64) and the parameter is 0. The same follows until block5 layer and the global_max_pooling layer where the output shape is (None,10, 10, 512) and the parameter is 0. The flatten layer has output shape of (None, 51, 200) and the parameter is 0. In the dense layer, the output shape is (None, 1024) and the parameter is 52,429,824 which is connected to the dropout layer the output shape is (None, 1024) and the parameter is 0 which is connected to the dense layer which has the output shape of (None, 15) and the parameter of 15,375. The total number of parameters is 72,469,583. It has been validated for 10 epochs. In epoch 1, the loss value is 2.5518 and the value accuracy is 0.2323; in epoch2, the loss value is 1.0219 and the value accuracy is 0.6720 followed by increase in the value accuracy and decrease in the value loss. In the 10th epoch, the loss is 0.0088 and the value accuracy is 0.9994. Thus, the model VGG19 without data augmentation has achieved the accuracy of 90.66%.

VGG19 with Data Augmentation

ImageDataGenerator is used for image pre-processing. The values for the parameters are rescale = 1.0/255.0, horizontal_flip = True, fill_mode = 'nearest', zoom_range = 0.2, shear_range = 0.2, width_shift_range = 0.2, height_shift_range = 0.2, and the rotation angle is 0.2. The batch size is 5 and the class mode is categorical. The input shape of the image is 350 × 350 pixels, it used relu as activation function, and the dropout is 0.2. The final sigmoid layer with 4 nodes for classification output uses sigmoid as activation function. The optimizer used is RMSprop with the learning rate of 0.0001 and the loss is categorical cross entropy. It has been validated for 10 epochs. In epoch 1, the loss value is 2.6922 and the value accuracy is 0.1276; in epoch2 the loss value is 2.1818 and the value accuracy is 0.3206, followed by increase in the value accuracy and decrease in the value loss. In the 10th epoch, the loss is 0.4017 and the value accuracy is 0.8736. Thus, the model VGG19 with data augmentation has achieved the accuracy of 92.00% and the loss value is 0.3694.

3.3.3. MOBILENET

MobileNet employs depth-wise differentiated convolution layer. The set of parameters is significantly reduced when compared to a system using normal convolution layers of same depth in the networks. Light weighted deep-learning neural networks are constructed as a result. MobileNets are built using depth-wise separable convolution layers. Every insight-detachable convolutional layer is composed of a depth-wise convolution as well as a pointwise fully connected layer. A standard MobileNet's number of parameters can be reduced to 4.2 million by adjusting the width multiplier hyperparameter. The size of the input image is 350×350 pixels.

MobileNet without Data Augmentation

The input shape of the image is 350×350 pixels. The trainable layer in base model is set as false, the model is sequential and the activation function is sigmoid. SGD is employed as the optimizer, with a detection rate of 0.0001 and a loss of categorical crossing entropy. In input layer_2, the output shape is (None, 350, 350, 3) and the parameter is 0. In conv1 layer, the output shape is (None, 175, 175, 32) and the parameter is 864, which connected to the batch normalization layer where the output shape is (None, 175, 175, 32) and the parameter is 128, which is connected to the relu layer where the output shape is (None, 175, 175, 32) and the parameter is 0. In depth-wise layer, the output shape is (None, 175, 175, 32) and the parameter is 288, which is connected to the batch normalization layer. It is followed as same for 13 relu functions. The flatten layer has output shape of (None, 165888) and the parameter is 0 which is connected to the mixed_10; in the dense, the output shape is (None, 1024) and the parameter shape is 1,049,600, which is connected to the flatten layer; in the dropout layer, the output shape is (None, 1024) and the parameter is 0 which is connected to the dense layer, which has the output shape (None, 15) and the parameter is 15,375, which is connected to the dropout layer. The total number of parameters is 4,293,839 and the trainable parameters are 4271.951 and the total non-trainable parameters are 21,888. It has been validated for 10 epochs. In epoch 1, the loss value is 5.1287 and the value accuracy is 0.0860; in epoch2, the loss value is 3.5716 and the value accuracy is 0.1350, followed by increase in the value accuracy and decrease in the value loss. In the 10th epoch, the loss is 1.3671 and the value accuracy is 0.5774. Thus, the model MobileNet with data augmentation has achieved the accuracy of 75.99% and the loss value of 0.7950.

MobileNet with Data Augmentation

Image Data Generator is used for image pre-processing. The values for the parameters are rescale = 1.0/255.0, horizontal_flip = True, fill_mode = 'nearest', zoom_range = 0.2, shear_range = 0.2, width_shift_range = 0.2, height_shift_range = 0.2, and the rotation angle is 0.2. The batch size is 5 and the class mode is categorical. The input shape of the image is 350×350 pixels. The trainable layer in base model is set as false, the model is sequential and the activation function is sigmoid. The optimizer used is SGD with the learning rate of 0.0001 and the loss is categorical cross entropy. It has been validated for 10 epochs. In epoch 1, the loss value is 5.1428 and the value accuracy is 0.0742; in epoch2, the loss value is 3.5890 and the value accuracy is 0.1492, followed by increase in the value accuracy and decrease in the value loss. In the 10th epoch, the loss is 1.0231 and the value accuracy is 0.6925. Thus, the model MobileNet with data augmentation has achieved an accuracy of 81.33% and the loss value is 0.8082.

3.3.4. XCEPTION

The Inception network has been phased out in favor of the Xception network. Xception is a term used to describe extreme inception. The Xception architecture employs larger values with separate convolutional parts rather than traditional fully connected layers. Xception accesses various spatial and bridge correlations, which in CNN-extracted features can be entirely disconnected. Inception's basic architecture has been preserved a little longer than Xception, about 36, whereas convolution in the Xception architecture could be broken into 14 possible paths. After the initial and last levels are removed, every level has a persistent remnant link surrounding it. The incoming image is converted to identify the likelihood in each output of acquiring cross-channel similarities. The depth-wise 11 convolution approach is then applied. Rather than 3D mappings, the interconnections can be represented as a 2D + 1D mapping. Inception commences with a 2D area connection, which 1D space correlations would precede.

Xception without Data Augmentation

The input shape of the image is 350×350 pixels. The trainable layer in base model is set as false, the model is sequential and the activation function is sigmoid. The optimizer used is SGD with the learning rate of 0.0001 and the loss is categorical cross entropy. It has been validated for 10 epochs. In the input layer_1, the output shape is (None, 350, 350, 3) and the parameter is 0. In the conv1 layer, the output shape is (None, 175, 175, 32), and the parameter is 864 is connected to the input_layer1 where the output shape is (None, 175, 175, 32) and the parameter is 128, which is connected to the activation layer where the output shape is (None, 175, 175, 32) and the parameter is 0. In the depth-wise layer, the output shape is (None, 175, 175, 32), and the parameter is 0, which is connected to the batch normalization layer. The same follows until block14 layer and the global_max_pooling layer where the output shape is (None, 2048) and the parameter is 0, which is connected to the block14. The flatten layer has an output shape of (None, 2048), and the parameter is 0, which is connected to the global max-pooling layer; in the dense layer, the output shape is (None, 1024) and the parameter shape is 2,098,176 which is connected to the flatten layer; in the dropout layer, the output shape is (None, 1024) and the parameter is 0 which is connected to the dense layer; finally, in the dense layer, the output shape is (None, 15) and the parameter is 15,375 which is connected to the dropout layer. The total number of parameters is 22,975,031, the trainable parameters is 22,920,503, and the total non-trainable parameters is 54,528. In epoch 1, the loss value is 1.1388 and the value accuracy is 0.6657; in epoch2, the loss value is 1.0308 and the value accuracy is 0.6953 followed by increase in the value accuracy and decrease in the value loss. In the 10th epoch, the loss is 0.6127, and the value accuracy is 0.8286. Thus, the model Xception without data augmentation has achieved an accuracy of 87.99%.

Xception with Data Augmentation

ImageDataGenerator is used for image pre-processing. The values for the parameters are rescale = 1.0/255.0, horizontal_flip = True, fill_mode = 'nearest', zoom_range = 0.2, shear_range = 0.2, width_shift_range = 0.2, height_shift_range = 0.2, and the rotation angle is 0.2. The batch size is 5 and the class mode is categorical. The input shape of the image is 350×350 pixels; the pooling layer is max-pooling layer. The model is sequential models and the activation function is sigmoid; the optimizer used is SGD with the learning rate of 0.0001 and the loss is categorical cross entropy. It has been validated for 10 epochs. In epoch 1, the loss value is 1.1388 and the value accuracy is 0.9957; in epoch2, the loss value is 1.0308 and the value accuracy is 0.6953 followed by increase in the value accuracy and decrease in the value loss. In the 10th epoch, the loss is 0.6127 and the value accuracy is 0. 8286. Thus, the model Xception with data augmentation has achieved an accuracy of 87.99%.

3.3.5. RESNET50

ResNet differs from other standard subsequent communication networks, including VGGNet and Alex Net, because it has segments and sub-module structures different from other architectures. It may be preferable to shift to the lower layer and ignore the level transitions. ResNet's architecture addresses this situation, and the network's success rate improves by reducing the challenge of recalling the system. ResNet is a 177-layer neural network. There is information on how multi-interconnections will be established in conjunction with the large-scale project. This model has been trained on photos with a size of $224 \times 224 \times 3$.

Resnet50 without Data Augmentation

The input shape of the image is 350×350 pixels. It uses a sigmoid as an activation function. The optimizer used is SGD with the learning rate of 0.0001 and the loss is categorical cross entropy, where the trainable layer is set as false. In input layer_2, the output shape is (None, 350, 350, 3) and the parameter is 0. In conv1_pad layer, the output shape is (None, 350, 350, 3) and the parameter is 0 which is connected to the input1 layer, where the output shape is (None, 350, 350, 64) and the parameter is 9427, which is connected to the batch normalization layer where the output shape is (None, 175, 175, 64) and the parameter 256, which is connected to the conv1 layer. The same follows until block5 layer and the global_max_pooling where layer the output shape is (None, 2048) and the parameter is 0. The flatten layer has output shape of (None, 2048) and the parameter is 0. In the dense layer, the output shape is (None, 1024) and the parameter is 209,8176, which is connected to the dropout layer where the output shape is (None, 1024) and the parameter is 0, which is connected to the flatten layer which has the output shape of (None, 1024) and the parameter is 15,375. The total number of parameters is 25,701,263, the non-trainable parameter is 2,113,551 and the non-trainable parameters is 23,587,712. It has been validated for 10 epochs. In epoch 1, the loss value is 3.7351 and the value accuracy is 0.0746; in epoch2, the loss value is 3.2707 and the value accuracy is 0.0866 followed by increase in the value accuracy and decrease in the value loss. In the 10th epoch, the loss is 2.2222 and the value accuracy is 0.2882. Thus, the model ResNet50 with data augmentation has achieved an accuracy of 38.66%.

Resnet50 with Data Augmentation

ImageDataGenerator is used for image pre-processing. The values for the parameters are rescale = 1.0/255.0, horizontal_flip = True, fill_mode = 'nearest', zoom_range = 0.2, shear_range = 0.2, width_shift_range = 0.2, height_shift_range = 0.2, and the rotation angle is 0.2. The batch size is 5 and the class mode is categorical. The input shape of the image is 350×350 pixels. The trainable layer in base model is set as false, the model is sequential and the activation function is sigmoid. The optimizer used is SGD with the learning rate of 0.0001 and the loss is categorical cross entropy. It has been validated for 10 epochs. In epoch 1, the loss value is 3.4661 and the value accuracy is 0.1071; in epoch2, the loss value is 2.6349 and the value accuracy is 0.1726, followed by increase in the value accuracy and decrease in the value loss. In the 10th epoch, the loss is 2.1626 and the value accuracy is 0.3013. Thus, the model Xception with data augmentation has achieved an accuracy of 43.99%.

3.3.6. INCEPTIONV3

Inception is an add-on to the Xception architecture that uses a complexity-separated convolution layer instead of the standard convolution layers. The Inception model is a neural network that helps classify objects in images. Another term for Inception is Google Net. During the training phase, the ImageNet dataset is utilized. The photographs for Inception must have a resolution of $299 \times 299 \times 3$. By lowering dimensions with a layered 11 convolution layer, Inception convolutional neural networks can deliver more effective computing and deep connections. The components were developed to address issues such as computation complexity and generalization, among many others.

InceptionV3 without Data Augmentation

The input shape of the image is 350×350 pixels; it used relu as an activation function and the dropout is 0.2. The final sigmoid layer with 4 nodes for classification output uses sigmoid as an activation function. The optimizer used is RMSprop with the learning rate of 0.0001 and the loss is categorical cross entropy. In input layer1, output shape is (None, 350, 350, 3) and the parameter is 0. In conv2d layer, the output shape is (None, 174, 174, 32, 864) and the parameter is 0, which is connected to the input1. In the batch normalization layer, the output shape is (None, 174, 174, 32, 96) and the parameter is 96 which is connected to the output layer of conv2d. In activation layer, the output shape is (None, 174, 174, 32, 0) and the parameter is 0, which is connected to the batch normalization layer, and in conv2d_1 layer the output shape is (None, 172,172, 32, 9216) and the parameter is 96; this is connected to the output layer of batch normalization layer 1. This is followed by the activation function of 93 where the output shape is (None, 9, 9, 192) and the parameter is 0 which is connected to the (activation_85, mixed9_1, concatenate_1 and activation_93); the flatten layer has output shape of (None, 165888). The parameter is 0 which is connected to the mixed_10; in the dense layer, the output shape is (None, 1024) and the parameter shape is 169,870,336 which is connected to the flatten layer; in the dropout layer, the output shape is (None, 1024) and the parameter is 0, which is connected to the dense layer which has the output shape of (None, 15). The parameter 15,375 is connected to the dropout layer. The total number of parameters is 191,688,495, trainable parameters is 169,885,711 and the total non-trainable parameters is 21,802,784. It has been validated for 10 epochs. In epoch 1, the loss value is 117.8563 and the value accuracy is 0.2437; in epoch2, the loss value is 4.8096 and the value accuracy is 0.2688 followed by increase in the value accuracy and decrease in the value loss. In the 10th epoch, the loss is 2.2486 and the value accuracy is 0.4243. Thus, the model inception without data augmentation has achieved the accuracy of 42.66%.

InceptionV3 with Data Augmentation

ImageDataGenerator is used for image pre-processing. The values for the parameters are rescale = 1.0/255.0, horizontal_flip = True, fill_mode = 'nearest', zoom_range = 0.2, shear_range = 0.2, width_shift_range = 0.2, height_shift_range = 0.2, and the rotation angle is 0.2. The batch size is 5 and the class mode is categorical. The input shape of the image is 350×350 pixels, it used relu as an activation function and the dropout is 0.2. The final sigmoid layer with 4 nodes for classification output uses sigmoid as an activation function. The optimizer used is RMSprop with the learning rate of 0.0001 and the loss is categorical cross entropy. It has been validated for 10 epochs. In epoch 1, the loss value is 3.0758 and the value accuracy is 0.5011; in epoch2, the loss value is 1.1765 and the value accuracy is 0.7187 followed by increase in the value accuracy and decrease in the value loss. In the 10th epoch, the loss is 0.4305 and the value accuracy is 0.9060. Thus, the model Inception with data augmentation has achieved an accuracy of 94.66%, and the loss is 0.8228.

4. Performance Evaluation

Each and every model has a model parameter that is internal to the specific model and its value is estimated from the given data. To improve the performance of the models, we can tune the parameters such as epochs, learning rate, etc., of each pre-trained model, and the detailed explanation about parameter tuning is mentioned in Sections 3.3.1–3.3.6. Certain activation functions are employed to lessen the nonlinearity in a neuron's output. The output's gradient-activating function determines the kind of forecasts the system can generate. For all of the models in the present scheme, the Softmax layer is used as the activation function. The network output, SoftMax, is utilized in the deep network to forecast a multinomial probability distribution. The "loss" is the network's prediction error, while the "loss function" is the process for computing it. The loss function also calculates the gradients. The weights of the neural network are updated using gradients. Categorical cross entropy were used to multi-task the classification tasks. It can be any possible category, and the model should decide the best among the ones. Image augmentation increases the amount of data used to train the network. The datasets are broken into three sections: training, validation, and testing datasets. Training is the collection of dataset samples used to learn how to adjust the input data to obtain the desired output. Validation is a set of dataset samples used to fine-tune the input dataset's sample of a classifier. After training and validating the data for ten epochs, the class species of the images is calculated. The outcomes were determined by assessing performance indicators, loss, and value accuracy. The parameters such as batch size, image dimension, optimizer, activation function, and loss function used for the state-of-the-art CNN-based pre-trained transfer-learning models are represented in Table 2.

Table 2. Parameters of CNN based pre-trained transfer-learning Models.

Performance Measures	VGG16	VGG19	MobileNet	Xception	ResNet50	Inception V3
Batch Size	5	5	5	5	5	5
Image Dimension	350×350	350×350	350×350	350×350	350×350	350×350
Optimizer	SGD	Adam	SGD	SGD	SGD	RMSprop
Activation Function	Sigmoid	Sigmoid	Sigmoid	Sigmoid	Sigmoid	Sigmoid
Loss Function	Categorical Cross entropy	Categorical Cross entropy	Categorical Cross entropy	Categorical Cross entropy	Categorical Cross entropy	Categorical Cross entropy

4.1. Accuracy and Loss Values of Pre-Trained Transfer Learning Models

Pre-trained CNN models such as VGG16, VGG19, MobileNet, Xception, and ResNet50 have far more hyperparameters in reality than InceptionV3. The Inception V3 model concentrates on the convolution operation of 3×3 filters in phase one and padding together with max-pooling layers of 2×2 filters in stride two, rather than having a bunch of hyperparameters. As a result, Inception V3's classification performance is better at detecting the butterfly's genus representations. All of the models' accuracy and loss values are plotted against epochs from Figure 3a,f.

The accuracy value represents the performance of the model. In general, the loss value represents the sum of errors in the model. A good model should exhibit lower loss and higher accuracy. From Figure 3a,f, it is understood that the lowest loss and highest error are achieved in the Inception V3 model. This best accuracy is obtained due to label smoothing, 7×7 convolutions, and auxiliary classifier features of the Inception V3 model.

4.2. Accuracy of Pre-Trained Transfer Learning Models

Table 3 compares the performance of models that use data augmentation vs. models that do not use data augmentation. The results suggest that pre-trained transfer-learning CNN models perform better when identifying species of butterflies in imagery.

Table 3. Accuracy of pre-trained CNN based transfer-learning Models.

Models	Without Data Augmentation	With Data Augmentation
InceptionV3	**42.66**	**94.66**
VGG19	90.66	92.00
Xception	81.33	87.99
VGG16	85.33	86.66
MobileNet	75.99	81.33
ResNet50	38.66	43.99

The InceptionV3 method uses a normal dense architecture to mimic a sparse CNN. Because only a few hidden neurons are required, the spacing of convolutional filters in a particular kernel size is reduced to a minimum. Convolution layers of varying sizes are also used to collect features from different scales. As a result, the InceptionV3 model is the best for attaining greater accuracy.

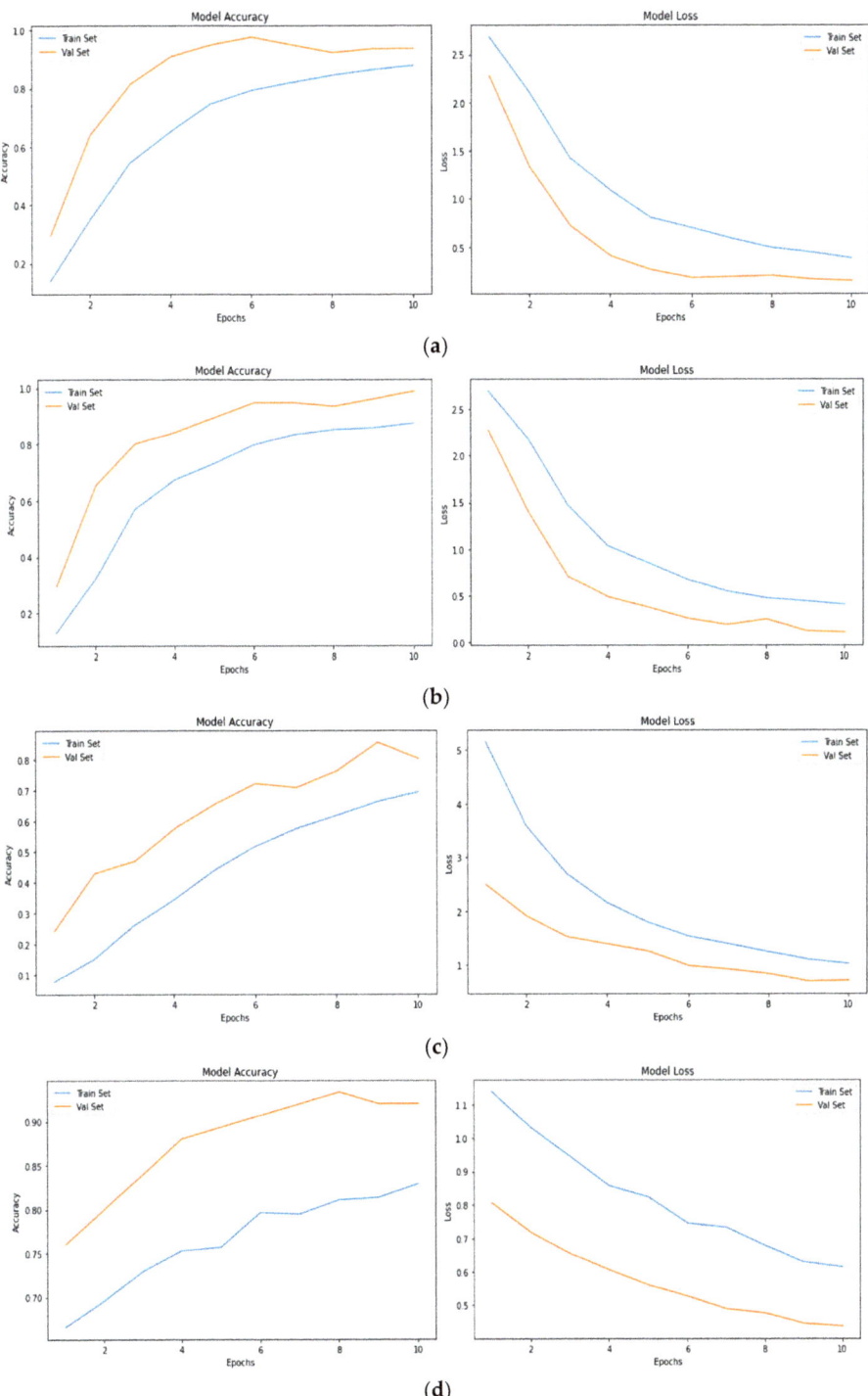

Figure 3. *Cont.*

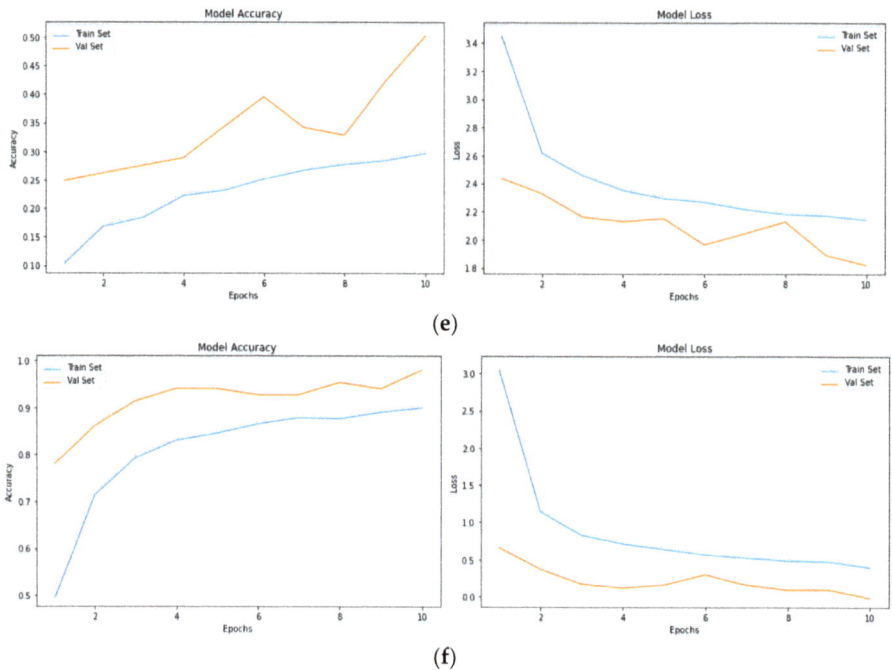

(e)

(f)

Figure 3. (**a**) Accuracy and Loss values of VGG16 Model. (**b**) Accuracy and Loss values of VGG19 Model. (**c**) Accuracy and Loss values of MobileNet Model. (**d**) Accuracy and Loss values of Xception Model. (**e**) Accuracy and Loss values of ResNet50 Model. (**f**) Accuracy and Loss values of Inception V3 Model.

4.3. Precision, Recall, F1-Score of Inception V3 Model

The precision, recall, and F1-score of the Inception V3 model are shown in Table 4. The result shows that the highest precision of 1 is obtained for 11 classes out of 15 classes, indicating that these 11 classes of butterfly species are predicted accurately. Similarly, 11 classes obtained the recall value of 1, meaning that most of the relevant images were retrieved. F1-score is the weighted average of precision and recall.

Table 4. Precision, Recall, F1-Score of Inception V3 model with data augmentation.

Species Classes	Precision	Recall	F1-Score	Support
African Giant Swallowtail	1.00	1.00	1.00	5
American Snoot	0.83	1.00	0.91	5
Atala	1.00	1.00	1.00	5
Banded Peacock	0.83	1.00	0.91	5
Becker's White	1.00	1.00	1.00	5
Blue Morpho	0.83	1.00	0.91	5
Crescent	1.00	0.80	0.89	5
Eastern Coma	1.00	1.00	1.00	5
Large Marble	1.00	1.00	1.00	5
Metalmark	1.00	1.00	1.00	5
Painted Lady	0.83	1.00	0.91	5
Purple Hairstreak	1.00	0.60	0.75	5
Silver Spot Skipper	1.00	1.00	1.00	5
Tropical Leafwing	1.00	0.80	0.89	5
Yellow Swallow Tail	1.00	1.00	1.00	5

4.4. Confusion Matrix

The confusion matrix obtained by the Inception V3 model with data augmentation is shown in Figure 4. The result shows that out of 15 classes, 12 classes were correctly classified, whereas images in 3 classes such as a crescent, purple hairstreak, and tropical leafwing were wrongly classified by the Inception V3 model.

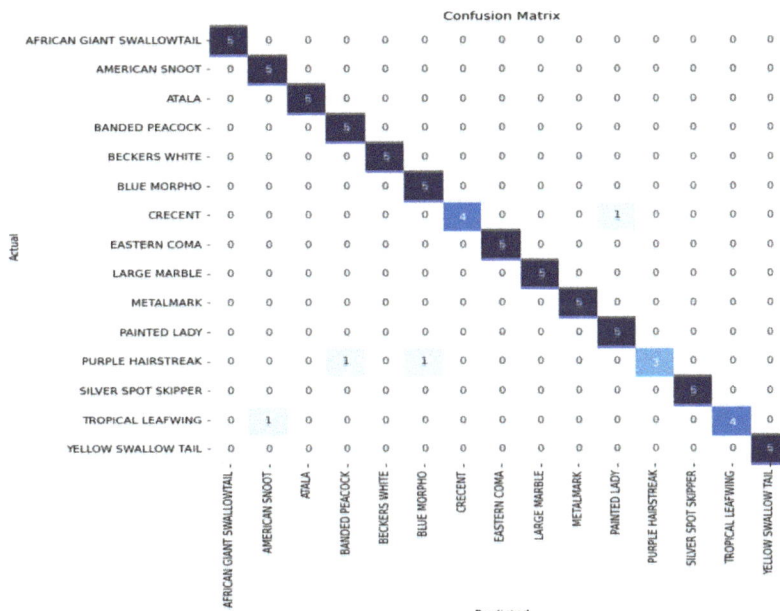

Figure 4. Confusion Matrix for InceptionV3.

5. Conclusions and Future Scope

The proposed research work aimed to help science students to analyze butterfly species type without harming them by applying pre-trained CNN models. In order to achieve better accuracy, these pre-trained models require a large dataset which is prepared by applying data transformation techniques. The proposed system compares ubiquitous and effective pre-trained transfer-learning models for identifying the specific species of butterflies by analyzing butterfly species visuals. Data augmentation is used to gain more pictures because the species images collected by Kaggle are restricted. Transfer-learning algorithms are recommended to provide efficient results by identifying butterfly species. Pre-trained transfer-learning neural network models such as VGG16, VGG19, MobileNet, Xception, ResNet50, and Inception V3 are employed in this proposed work. The models categorize fifteen different species of butterflies, and their performance is validated using a test dataset, yielding anticipated efficiency for all of them. Performance indicators, including accuracy, precision, recall, and F1-score, assess the model's performance. Out of all models, InceptionV3 with data augmentation has the highest accuracy of 94.64% among all the transfer learning models. The confusion matrix presented in Section 4.4 depicts that this model was able to predict 12 classes correctly out of 15 classes. This research work mainly concentrates on obtaining the best model to classify butterflies among all the pre-trained CNN models. However, the limitation lies in the fact that the data used for classification are purely images. This work can be further extended to obtain multiple input images from real-time videos taken which contain multimodal data, i.e., both images and sounds of species and then apply this multimodal data into pre-trained models. In future work, we are planning to increase the test sets to improve the accuracy of the evaluation results.

Author Contributions: Data curation, D.S.A.E., R.O., A.N., M.A.S.A. and K.S.V.; Formal analysis, F.R.P.P., D.S.A.E., R.O., A.N., M.A.S.A., K.S.V., M.S., S.M., L.A., M.A. and M.A.; Funding acquisition, F.R.P.P. and K.S.V.; Investigation, D.S.A.E. and S.M.; Methodology, F.R.P.P., D.S.A.E., K.S.V., M.S., S.M., L.A., M.A., R.O., A.N., M.A.S.A. and M.A.; Project administration, D.S.A.E.; Resources, F.R.P.P. and M.A.; Supervision, D.S.A.E. and M.S.; Validation, D.S.A.E., R.O., A.N., M.A.S.A., K.S.V., S.M., M.A. and M.A.; Visualization, D.S.A.E. and L.A.; Writing—original draft, F.R.P.P., D.S.A.E., K.S.V., M.S., S.M., L.A., M.A. and M.A.; Writing—review and editing, F.R.P.P., D.S.A.E., K.S.V., R.O., A.N., M.A.S.A. and M.A. All authors have read and agreed to the published version of the manuscript.

Funding: This research was funded by Deanship of Scientific Research, King Faisal University, grant number GRANT725 and The APC was funded by Deanship of Scientific Research, King Faisal University.

Conflicts of Interest: The authors declare no potential conflict of interest.

References

1. Fauzi, F.; Permanasari, A.E.; Setiawan, N.A. Butterfly Image Classification Using Convolutional Neural Net-work (CNN). In Proceedings of the 2021 3rd International Conference on Electronics Representation and Algorithm (ICERA), Yogyakarta, Indonesia, 29–30 July 2021; pp. 66–70.
2. Fan, L.; Zhou, W. An Improved Contour Feature Extraction Method for the Image Butterfly Specimen. In *3D Imaging Technologies— Multidimensional Signal Processing and Deep Learning*; Springer: Singapore, 2021; pp. 17–26.
3. Ali, M.A.S.; Balasubramanian, K.; Krishnamoorthy, G.D.; Muthusamy, S.; Pandiyan, S.; Panchal, H.; Mann, S.; Thangaraj, K.; El-Attar, N.E.; Abualigah, L.; et al. Classification of Glaucoma Based on Elephant-Herding Optimization Algorithm and Deep Belief Network. *Electronics* **2022**, *11*, 1763. [CrossRef]
4. Chen, X.; Wang, B.; Gao, Y. Gaussian Convolution Angles: Invariant Vein and Texture Descriptors for Butterfly Species Identifica-tion. In Proceedings of the 2020 25th International Conference on Pattern Recognition (ICPR), Milan, Italy, 10–15 January 2021; pp. 5798–5803.
5. Min, F.; Xiong, W. Butterfly Image Generation and Recognition Based on Improved Generative Adversarial Networks. In Proceedings of the 2021 4th International Conference on Robotics, Control and Automation Engineering (RCAE), Wuhan, China, 4–6 November 2021; pp. 40–44. [CrossRef]
6. Xi, T.; Wang, J.; Han, Y.; Lin, C.; Ji, L. Multiple butterfly recognition based on deep residual learning and image analysis. *Èntomol. Res.* **2022**, *52*, 44–53. [CrossRef]
7. Houssein, E.H.; Abdelminaam, D.S.; Hassan, H.N.; Al-Sayed, M.M.; Nabil, E. A hybrid barnacles mating optimizer algorithm with support vector machines for gene selection of microarray cancer classification. *IEEE Access* **2021**, *9*, 64895–64905. [CrossRef]
8. Marta, S.; Luccioni, A.; Rolnick, D. Spatiotemporal Features Improve Fine-Grained Butterfly Image Classification. In Proceedings of the Conference on Neural Information Processing Systems. 2020. Available online: https://s3.us-east-1.amazonaws.com/climate-change-ai/papers/neurips2020/63/paper.pdf (accessed on 14 May 2022).
9. Houssein, E.H.; Hassaballah, M.; Ibrahim, I.E.; AbdElminaam, D.S.; Wazery, Y.M. An automatic arrhythmia classification model based on improved marine predators algorithm and convolutions neural networks. *Expert Syst. Appl.* **2022**, *187*, 115936. [CrossRef]
10. Almryad, A.; Kutucu, H. Automatic Detection of Butterflies by convolutional neural networks. *Eng. Sci. Technol. Int. J.* **2020**, *23*, 189–195.
11. Houssein, E.H.; Abdelminaam, D.S.; Ibrahim, I.E.; Hassaballah, M.; Wazery, Y.M. A hybrid heartbeats classification approach based on marine predators algorithm and convolution neural networks. *IEEE Access* **2021**, *9*, 86194–86206. [CrossRef]
12. Zhao, R.; Li, C.; Ye, S.; Fang, X. Deep-red fluorescence from isolated dimers: A highly bright excimer and imaging in vivo. *Chem. Sci.* **2001**, *291*, 213–225.
13. Nijhout, H.F. Elements of butterfly wing patterns. *J. Exp. Zool.* **2001**, *291*, 213–225. [CrossRef]
14. Pinzari, M.; Santonico, M.; Pennazza, G.; Martinelli, E.; Capuano, R.; Paolesse, R.; Di Rao, M.; D'Amico, A.; Cesaroni, D.; Sbordoni, V.; et al. Chemically mediated species recognition in two sympatric Grayling butterflies. *PLoS ONE* **2018**, *13*, e0199997. [CrossRef]
15. Austin, G.T.; Riley, T.J. Portable bait traps for the study of butterflies. *Trop. Lepid. Res.* **1995**, *6*, 5–9.
16. Ries, L.; Debinski, D.M.; Wieland, M.L. Conservation value of roadside prairie restoration to butterfly community. *Conserv. Biol.* **2001**, *15*, 401–411. [CrossRef]
17. Fina, F.; Birch, P.; Young, R.; Obu, J.; Faithpraise, B.; Chatwin, C. Automatic plant pest detection and recognition using k-means clustering algorithm and correspondence filters. *Int. J. Adv. Biotechnol. Res.* **2013**, *4*, 189–199.
18. Leow, L.K.; Chew Li Chong, V.C.; Dhillon, S.K. Automated identification of copepods using digital image processing and artificial neural network. *BMC Bioinf.* **2015**, *16*, S4. [CrossRef] [PubMed]
19. Mayo, M.; Watson, A.T. Automatic species identification of live moths. *Knowl. Based Syst.* **2007**, *20*, 195–202. [CrossRef]

20. Tan, A.; Zhou, G.; He, M. Rapid Fine-Grained Classification of Butterflies Based on FCM-KM and Mask R-CNN Fusion. *IEEE Access* **2020**, *8*, 124722–124733. [CrossRef]

21. Salama AbdELminaam, D.; Almansori, A.M.; Taha, M.; Badr, E. A deep facial recognition system using computational intelligent algorithms. *PLoS ONE* **2020**, *15*, e0242269. [CrossRef]

22. Kartika, D.S.Y.; Herumurti, D.; Rahmat, B.; Yuniarti, A.; Maulana, H.; Anggraeny, F.T. Combining of Extraction Butterfly Image using Color, Texture and Form Features. In Proceedings of the 6th Information Technology International Seminar (ITIS), Surabaya, Indonesia, 14–16 October 2020; pp. 98–102.

23. Rodrigues, R.; Manjesh, R.; Sindhura, P.; Hegde, S.N.; Sheethal, A. Butterfly species identification using convolutional neural network. *Int. J. Res. Eng. Sci. Manag.* **2020**, *3*, 245–246.

24. Theivaprakasham, H. Identification of Indian butterflies using Deep Convolutional Neural Network. *J. Asia-Pacific Èntomol.* **2021**, *24*, 329–340. [CrossRef]

25. Lin, Z.; Jia, J.; Gao, W.; Huang, F. Fine-grained visual categorization of butterfly specimens at sub-species level via a convolutional neural network with skip-connections. *Neurocomputing* **2020**, *384*, 295–313. [CrossRef]

26. Zhu, L.-Q.; Zhang, Z. Insect recognition based on integrated region matching and dual tree complex wavelet transform. *J. Zhejiang Univ. Sci. C* **2011**, *12*, 44–53. [CrossRef]

27. da Silva, F.L.; Sella, M.L.G.; Francoy, T.M.; Costa, A.H.R. Evaluating classification and feature selection techniques for honeybee subspecies identification using wing images. *Comput. Electron. Agric.* **2015**, *114*, 68–77. [CrossRef]

28. Wen, C.; Guyer, D. Image-based orchard insect automated identification and classification method. *Comput. Electron. Agric.* **2012**, *89*, 110–115. [CrossRef]

29. Kaya, Y.; Kaycı, L. Application of artificial neural network for automatic detection of butterfly species using color and texture features. *Visual Comput.* **2014**, *30*, 71–79. [CrossRef]

30. Xie, C.; Zhang, J.; Li, R.; Li, J.; Hong, P.; Xia, J.; Chen, P. Automatic classification for field crop insects via multiple-task sparse representation and multiple-kernel learning. *Comput. Electron. Agric.* **2015**, *119*, 123–132. [CrossRef]

31. Feng, L.; Bhanu, B.; Heraty, J. A software system for automated identification and retrieval of moth images based on wing attributes. *Pattern Recognit.* **2016**, *51*, 225–241. [CrossRef]

32. Abeysinghe, C.; Welivita, A.; Perera, I. Snake image classification using Siamese networks. In Proceedings of the 2019 3rd In-ternational Conference on Graphics and Signal Processing, Hong Kong, China, 1–3 June 2019; pp. 8–12. [CrossRef]

33. Alsing, O. Mobile Object Detection Using Tensorflow Lite and Transfer Learning. Master's Thesis, KTH School of Electrical Engineering and Computer Science (EECS), Stockholm, Sweden, 2018.

34. Hernandez-Serna, A.; Jim'enez-Segura, L.F. Automatic identification of species with neural networks. *PeerJ* **2014**, *2*, e563. [CrossRef]

35. Iamsaata, S.; Horataa, P.; Sunata, K.; Thipayanga, N. Improving butterfly family classification using past separating features extraction in extreme learning machine. In *Proceedings of the 2nd International Conference on Intelligent Systems and Image Processing*; The Institute of Industrial Applications Engineers: Kitakyushu, Fukuoka, Japan, 2014.

36. Kang, S.-H.; Cho, J.-H.; Lee, S.-H. Identification of butterfly based on their shapes when viewed from different angles using an artificial neural network. *J. Asia-Pacific Entomol.* **2014**, *17*, 143–149. [CrossRef]

37. Bouzalmat, A.; Kharroubi, J.; Zarghili, A. Comparative Study of PCA, ICA, LDA using SVM Classifier. *J. Emerg. Technol. Web Intell.* **2014**, *6*, 64–68. [CrossRef]

38. Xin, D.; Chen, Y.-W.; Li, J. Fine-Grained Butterfly Classification in Ecological Images Using Squeeze-And-Excitation and Spatial Attention Modules. *Appl. Sci.* **2020**, *10*, 1681. [CrossRef]

39. Zhu, L.; Spachos, P. Towards Image Classification with Machine Learning Methodologies for Smartphones. *Mach. Learn. Knowl. Extr.* **2019**, *1*, 1039–1057. [CrossRef]

40. Rashid, M.; Khan, M.A.; Alhaisoni, M.; Wang, S.-H.; Naqvi, S.R.; Rehman, A.; Saba, T. A Sustainable Deep Learning Framework for Object Recognition Using Multi-Layers Deep Features Fusion and Selection. *Sustainability* **2020**, *12*, 5037. [CrossRef]

41. Alzubaidi, L.; Fadhel, M.; Al-Shamma, O.; Zhang, J.; Santamaría, J.; Duan, Y.; Oleiwi, S. Towards a Better Understanding of Transfer Learning for Medical Imaging: A Case Study. *Appl. Sci.* **2020**, *10*, 4523. [CrossRef]

42. Barbedo, J.G.A. Detecting and Classifying Pests in Crops Using Proximal Images and Machine Learning: A Review. *AI* **2020**, *1*, 312–328. [CrossRef]

43. Fang, X.; Jie, W.; Feng, T. An Industrial Micro-Defect Diagnosis System via Intelligent Segmentation Region. *Sensors* **2019**, *19*, 2636. [CrossRef]

44. Elminaam, D.S.A.; Neggaz, N.; Ahmed, I.A.; Abouelyazed, A.E.S. Swarming Behavior of Harris Hawks Optimizer for Arabic Opinion Mining. *Comput. Mater. Contin.* **2021**, *69*, 4129–4149. [CrossRef]

45. AbdElminaam, D.S.; Neggaz, N.; Gomaa, I.A.E.; Ismail, F.H.; Elsawy, A. AOM-MPA: Arabic Opinion Mining using Marine Predators Algorithm-based Feature Selection. In Proceedings of the 2021 International Mobile, Intelligent, and Ubiquitous Computing Conference (MIUCC), Cairo, Egypt, 26–27 May 2021; IEEE: Piscataway, NJ, USA, 2021; pp. 395–402.

46. Shaban, H.; Houssein, E.H.; Pérez-Cisneros, M.; Oliva, D.; Hassan, A.Y.; Ismaeel, A.A.; Said, M. Identification of Parameters in Photovoltaic Models through a Runge Kutta Optimizer. *Mathematics* **2021**, *9*, 2313. [CrossRef]

47. Deb, S.; Houssein, E.H.; Said, M.; Abdelminaam, D.S. Performance of Turbulent Flow of Water Optimization on Economic Load Dispatch Problem. *IEEE Access* **2021**, *9*, 77882–77893. [CrossRef]

48. Abdul-Minaam, D.S.; Al-Mutairi, W.M.E.S.; Awad, M.A.; El-Ashmawi, W.H. An adaptive fit-ness-dependent optimizer for the one-dimensional bin packing problem. *IEEE Access* **2020**, *8*, 97959–97974. [CrossRef]
49. El-Ashmawi, W.H.; Elminaam, D.S.A.; Nabil, A.M.; Eldesouky, E. A chaotic owl search algorithm based bilateral negotiation model. *Ain Shams Eng. J.* **2020**, *11*, 1163–1178. [CrossRef]
50. Espejo-Garcia, B.; Malounas, I.; Vali, E.; Fountas, S. Testing the Suitability of Automated Machine Learning for Weeds Identification. *AI* **2021**, *2*, 34–47. [CrossRef]
51. Valade, S.; Ley, A.; Massimetti, F.; D'Hondt, O.; Laiolo, M.; Coppola, D.; Walter, T.R. Towards global volcano monitoring using multisensor sentinel missions and artificial intelligence: The MOUNTS monitoring system. *Remote Sens.* **2019**, *11*, 1528. [CrossRef]

Article

Scientometric Analysis and Classification of Research Using Convolutional Neural Networks: A Case Study in Data Science and Analytics

Mohammad Daradkeh [1,2,*], Laith Abualigah [3,4], Shadi Atalla [1] and Wathiq Mansoor [1]

[1] College of Engineering and Information Technology, University of Dubai, Dubai 14143, United Arab Emirates; satalla@ud.ac.ae (S.A.); wmansoor@ud.ac.ae (W.M.)
[2] Faculty of Information Technology and Computer Science, Yarmouk University, Irbid 21163, Jordan
[3] Faculty of Computer Sciences and Informatics, Amman Arab University, Amman 11953, Jordan; aligah.2020@gmail.com
[4] Faculty of Information Technology, Middle East University, Amman 11831, Jordan
* Correspondence: mdaradkehc@ud.ac.ae

Abstract: With the increasing development of published literature, classification methods based on bibliometric information and traditional machine learning approaches encounter performance challenges related to overly coarse classifications and low accuracy. This study presents a deep learning approach for scientometric analysis and classification of scientific literature based on convolutional neural networks (CNN). Three dimensions, namely publication features, author features, and content features, were divided into explicit and implicit features to form a set of scientometric terms through explicit feature extraction and implicit feature mapping. The weighted scientometric term vectors are fitted into a CNN model to achieve dual-label classification of literature based on research content and methods. The effectiveness of the proposed model is demonstrated using an application example from the data science and analytics literature. The empirical results show that the scientometric classification model proposed in this study performs better than comparable machine learning classification methods in terms of precision, recognition, and F1-score. It also exhibits higher accuracy than deep learning classification based solely on explicit and dominant features. This study provides a methodological guide for fine-grained classification of scientific literature and a thorough investigation of its practice.

Keywords: scientific literature; thematic classification; scientometric; deep learning; convolutional neural network (CNN)

Citation: Daradkeh, M.; Abualigah, L.; Atalla, S.; Mansoor, W. Scientometric Analysis and Classification of Research Using Convolutional Neural Networks: A Case Study in Data Science and Analytics. *Electronics* **2022**, *11*, 2066. https://doi.org/10.3390/electronics11132066

Academic Editor: José D. Martín-Guerrero

Received: 26 May 2022
Accepted: 28 June 2022
Published: 30 June 2022

Publisher's Note: MDPI stays neutral with regard to jurisdictional claims in published maps and institutional affiliations.

1. Introduction

In recent years, the number of new research disciplines and practices has grown manyfold, leading to an internal diversification of research and greater interdisciplinary interactions. This evolution of interdisciplinary research paradigms has led to the development of new research foci, organization of interdisciplinary conferences, establishment of international scientific societies, and creation of new journals, among others [1]. As the landscape of scientific disciplines continues to differentiate, classification systems are being developed to better reflect this dynamic reality and facilitate the study of knowledge production and dissemination, and as such can serve important classification functions [2–5]. Scientometric analysis and the classification of scientific literature provides an indispensable basis for the evaluation and synthesis of published literature and improves the efficiency of researchers' information search. At the same time, it helps academic institutions and scientific literature management platforms analyze the development direction of disciplines [6], facilitates the exploration of knowledge production and dissemination, and accelerates the rapid development of scientific research [7,8]. Acknowledging the advantages of scientometric analysis, it has been widely used to evaluate leading scientific researchers or publications [9], examine the structure of a scientific field's network [10,11], reveal emerging issues [12], and help researchers study the development of research fields and disciplines by categorizing documents along multiple dimensions [4].

Typically, scientometric studies focus on broad classification of published articles based on primary or secondary subjects or disciplines. Currently, scientometric studies classify publications using generic classification systems, such as the Web of Science (WoS) subject categories and the Field of Science and Technology Classification (FOS) [9]. In their current form, these systems are too broad to adequately reflect the more complex, fine-grained cognitive reality; therefore, their scope is limited and they only indicate broad scientific domains or general disciplines. Empirical studies [5] as well as theoretical arguments by researchers [13] emphasize the need for fine-grained classification approaches. A recent study by Wahid et al. [11] found that focused research communities can be distinguished based on publication associations, and publication practices and patterns may vary within these communities. However, fine-grained classification is challenging for researchers because it is not clear to what extent authors in particular fields collaborate to disseminate new findings and knowledge [9,14,15]. Such finer classification usually involves two aspects. First, it narrows the disciplinary focus of a particular research area into categories; for example, the literature on data science and analytics can be further divided into big data analytics, business analytics, business intelligence, machine learning, predictive modeling, and deep learning. Second, the classification dimension includes research content and research method; for example, a research paper can be classified as business analytics based on its content and as empirical research based on its research methodology.

Recently, there has been a resurgence of interest in applying machine learning methods to scientometric classification and analysis of scientific literature, as these algorithms have achieved acceptable results in text analysis and classification. Commonly used machine learning algorithms include support vector machines (SVM), Naive Bayes classifiers, and the K-nearest neighbor model (KNN) [16]. However, with the abundance and diversity of scientific research and the exponential increase in scientific output, classification methods based on general scientometric information and traditional machine learning methods have shown significant shortcomings in terms of coarse classification and insufficient accuracy [1,9,17]. Moreover, the data elements used by existing scientific literature classification systems are primarily derived from explicit scientometric information such as titles, abstracts, and keywords. Nevertheless, data elements may also have implicit relationships such as journal names, authors, research institution names, and research content and method [6,10,18,19]. The same journal, author, or research institution are more likely to focus on certain research content and methods, even if there is no direct relationship between them. Therefore, to improve the accuracy and performance of scientific literature classification, it is imperative to study and integrate these implicit relationships along with the explicit features of scientific publications.

To this end, this study develops a deep learning approach for scientometric analysis and classification of scientific literature based on convolutional neural network (CNN), aiming at dual-label classification of literature based on research content and method. We demonstrate the efficacy of the proposed model using an application example from the data science and analytics literature. The empirical results show that the scientometric classification model proposed in this study performs better than comparable machine learning classification methods in terms of precision, recognition, and F1-score. It also exhibits higher accuracy than deep learning classification based only on explicit and dominant features. It is worth noting, though, that this study only considered publications from a single domain, namely data science and analytics. Nevertheless, we investigate the use of textual content to classify publications in three major databases and platforms (Scopus, ProQuest, and EBSCOhost). As will be discussed in more detail below, we aim to classify these data science and analytics abstracts into granular subcategories, since an article can be assigned to multiple categories simultaneously. The novelty of this study is that we applied a unique approach to validate the data collected for our machine learning experiments and were able to assign multiple sub-disciplinary categories to a single article. The results of this study may therefore open up new opportunities to understand knowledge production and dissemination in the emerging sub-disciplines of data science and analytics at a more detailed level.

2. Literature Review

Scientometrics is a field of study concerned with the quantitative analysis of textual features and characteristics of scientific literature [7,8,14]. It can be considered as the science of science. The goal of scientometrics is to evaluate the development of a scientific field, influence of scientific publications, patterns of authorship, and production processes of scientific knowledge. Typically, scientometrics is concerned with monitoring research, evaluating the scientific contribution of authors, journals, and specific works, and assessing the dissemination of scientific knowledge [20]. As part of these approaches, researchers develop methodological principles for deriving information from communication activities and use specific methods to achieve these goals, including citation analysis, social network analysis, syndicated terminology analysis, and text mining [16]. Scientometric studies usually focus on authorship or measurement of journal or professional association contributions. However, they may also examine terms that appear in titles, abstracts, full texts of book chapters and journal articles, or keywords assigned by editors to published articles or publishing houses [9,21–23]. González-Alcaide et al. [24] used scientometric analysis to identify the main research interests and directions on Chagas cardiomyopathy in the MEDLINE database. Specifically, they identify research patterns and trends on Chagas cardiomyopathy. Similarly, Mosallaie et al. [12] used scientometric analysis approaches to identify trends in artificial intelligence in cancer research, while Wahid et al. [11] applied scientometric analysis and group-level comparative analysis of Pakistani authors to determine their scientific productivity. The body of scientific knowledge in a particular area of interest provides a comprehensive description and representation of previous and current knowledge on that particular topic. Therefore, a comprehensive and quantitative analysis of such literature sources provides valuable insight into the evolving research interest in the field and can provide a comprehensive picture of the topics and their current status and relevance.

Scientometric analysis is based on the breakdown and disclosure of relationships between different research contributions (articles), from which statistical indices are calculated to reveal research paradigms and emerging trends [13]. In scientometric studies, scientific literature is often classified using abstracts, keywords, and titles. For example, Hernandez-Alvarez et al. [23] used high-frequency keywords in abstracts, manually identified important terms to generate knowledge domains, and divided the literature into multiple knowledge domains by calculating the similarity between them to classify the literature. Similarly, Kim et al. [25] used keywords and abstracts as raw data to create a document terminology matrix representing the frequency of terms in the accounting literature. Makabate et al. [3] used a grounded theory approach to code the terms collected in the abstracts and classify research methods. Nosratabadi et al. [26] extracted feature terms from titles and abstracts based on lexicality, filtered them, calculated feature term frequencies to characterize the documents as feature vectors, and classified them using association rules. Ozcan et al. [10] constructed a literature topic matrix and a topic-feature term matrix based on the titles and abstracts of patent documents to identify topics for technological innovations. In addition, several researchers have attempted to construct features from external resources to improve classification accuracy. For example, Purnomo et al. [27] used external feature information such as Wikipedia and news sites to improve the accuracy of literature classification. Bhatt et al. [28] used Medical Subject Headings (MeSH) as the basis for selecting key terms related to stem cells as feature vectors to characterize the literature. Ho and Shekofteh [29] selected patent classification codes to create a technical lexicon. They characterized the literature as vectors based on the Derwent Manual Code (DMC) to create a patent manual code matrix and build a technical knowledge map of the patent literature.

In recent years, machine learning methods have been widely used to improve the accuracy of scientometric classification and analysis of scientific literature, as these algorithms have achieved acceptable results in text classification. For example, Eykens et al. [9] used supervised machine learning methods (gradient boosting and Naive polynomial Bayes) to classify social science articles based on textual data. Similarly, Huang et al. [2] improved the NB algorithm by using local weighting to improve classification performance. Makabate et al. [3] compared the performance of KNN and SVM algorithms in classifying scientific literature in data analytics. As deep learning algorithms have evolved, convolutional neural networks (CNNs) have been shown to automatically learn features from text and reduce manual input of feature information, resulting in better text classification capabilities than traditional machine learning algorithms. In their study, Salazar-Reyna et al. [30] applied different machine learning algorithms to classify documents and found that deep learning algorithms are superior to traditional machine learning algorithms. Sood et al. [4] performed a multi-level classification of 1.7 million documents information in an international scientific journal index based on CNN models and obtained satisfactory scientometric classification results.

Machine learning methods using neural networks and BERT (Transformers Bidirectional Encoder Representations) models have also been used separately to vectorize and reveal relationships between scholarly articles. Kandimalla et al. [31] presented a comprehensive characterization study using neural networks and word embedding models to organize articles by WoS topic categories and focused on the use of these moderately novel NLP strategies to vectorize logical distributions. The researchers show that such frameworks perform excellently in grouping samples, achieving a normal F-score of 0.76, with values ranging from 0.5 to 0.95 for each topic category. As a result, subcategories with too many record pairs are either grouped or removed from the current study because they negatively affect classification performance. In addition, documents with more than one classification continue to be excluded. The authors conclude that their analysis shows that the managed learning approach scales better than strategies based on reference clusters. Dunham et al. [32] train SciBERT classifiers on arXiv metadata, which are then used to develop a model for distinguishing the important artificial intelligence distributions in WoS, digital science dimensions, and Microsoft academic. The authors report that F1 values range from 0.58 to 0.85 for the four classifications in the artificial intelligence domain.

Machine learning and deep learning algorithms have been used in scientometric research mainly based on explicit scientometric information and features such as abstracts, keywords, and titles. However, in addition to these explicit features embedded in the literature, scientometric information also includes journal name, author name, and institution name. These relevant contents, however, are still scarcely investigated. Wang et al. [18] found that the classification accuracy of data elements such as journal title, author, and institution added directly to the feature vector does not improve regardless of whether traditional machine learning or deep learning algorithms are used, but decreases significantly. According to their findings, this is mainly due to the fact that the technical terms referring to research content and method can be obtained from abstracts, keywords, and titles. At the same time, there are almost no technical terms in the journal, author, and institution names that can directly characterize literature information. Each journal defines its research focus and emphasizes specific research methods, each author has their research expertise and focuses on research methods, and each research institution or team also develops specific research areas and common research methods. Throughout this study, we conjecture that these data have implicit features that relate to research content and research method. Therefore, our primary goal is to use the implicit textual features of scientific publications to classify them into pre-established discipline-specific categories. As we elaborate below, we intend to classify these scientific literature documents into granular subcategories, implying that a scientific publication can be simultaneously assigned to one or more categories.

3. Model Development

To classify scientific literature, scientometric information is used as a basis, an initial feature matrix is created by feature extraction, and terms vectorization is performed. In this study, scientometric data are divided into explicit and implicit features, where abstract, keywords, and title are explicit features, while journal title, authors, and institutions are implicit features. Explicit and implicit features differ significantly in their identification methods; explicit features can be easily identified by their direct association with the classification label [33]. In contrast, there are no obvious linguistic and syntactic clues for identifying implicit features; instead, they must be determined based on their deep semantic features and are usually those features that are not directly associated with the classification label [34]. Therefore, identifying implicit features is still one of the most difficult tasks in scientometric analysis and classification of literature. A very effective and useful method to extract implicit features is to use association rules to identify the implicit feature by finding the association of a certain feature with the classification labels; in this study, the classification labels are presented as research content and research method. For the explicit features, the feature terms are extracted directly from the literature documents. For the implicit features, feature mapping is performed to make them explicit. In this way, a vector of feature terms is created and applied to Word2Vec to build a term vector model that feeds the CNN deep learning model. The CNN deep learning algorithm is then used for feature extraction and fine-grained classification, i.e., dual-label classification for research content and method. The output layer of the CNN model implements dual-label classification of research content and research method simultaneously.

The research methodology used in this study is detailed in Figure 1. This process is divided into three main phases: (1) creation of scientometric features and stopword lexicons. This involves creating the scientometric feature lexicon and stopword list by selecting titles, abstracts, and keywords of all documents in the training set to improve the accuracy of the features; (2) creation of the feature matrix and vectorization. This involves dividing the scientometric information into explicit features (abstract, title, and keywords) and implicit features (author, journal name, and institution). For the explicit features, term tokenization and stop word removal are performed; for the implicit features, feature mapping is performed to make the implicit features explicit. A feature word vector based on scientometric information is created and used as input data for the CNN classification model; and (3) literature analysis and classification using CNNs, where the form research content (C) × research method (M) is developed in the output layer of the CNN model to achieve dual-label classification of the literature.

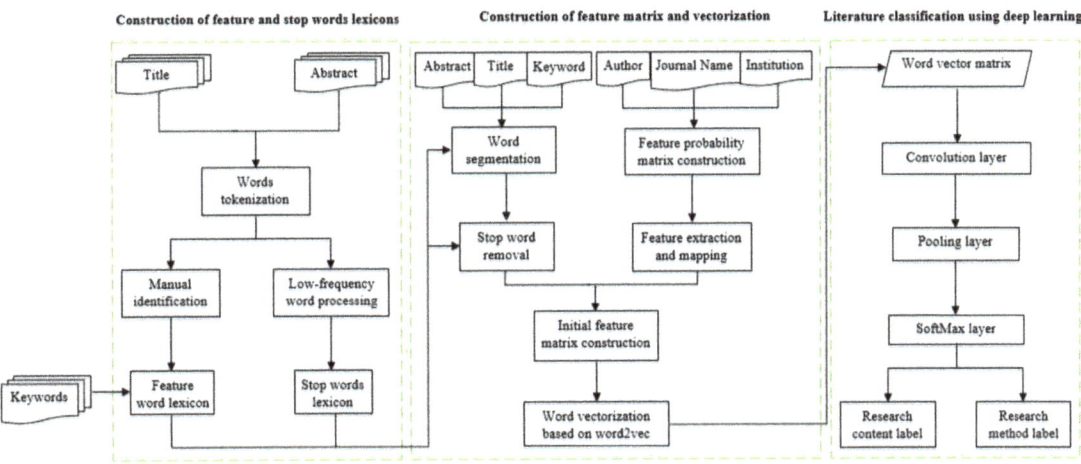

Figure 1. Scientometric analysis and classification of scientific literature using CNN.

In machine learning applications, dual-label classification involves assigning two target labels to each document instance. Dual-label classification is a variant of the classification problem that requires assigning two target labels to each document. Deep learning neural networks are an example of an algorithm that inherently supports dual-label classification problems. As such, they have been widely used in recent years, particularly in text analysis and opining mining, e.g., citation annotation [35], text categorization [21], movie genre categorization [36], and web mining [37]. These applications typically involve a significant number of labels, and the number of labels continues to increase with new applications. Therefore, describing samples with only a single label is challenging [38]. In this study, we address the problem of dual-label classification in the context of scientometric classification of literature, where labels for research content and method must be assigned to each document with high descriptive accuracy. The task of dual-label classification is to train a function to predict the unknown sample and return two target labels for each of the documents. In contrast to traditional classification, dual-label classification represents a sample by an eigenvector and two target labels, instead of just one exclusive label. The traditional classification approach consists of training different classification prediction labels separately. This approach is characterized by low training and testing efficiency and reasonable memory consumption when the set of target labels is quite large [36,39,40].

3.1. Building Stop and Feature Terms Lexicons

Building feature and stop terms lexicons is an integral part of data preprocessing. The lexicon of feature terms is used as a custom dictionary to improve the accuracy of automatic term tokenization. The lexicon of stop terms helps filter out the noise in the term tokenization results, improving the deep learning model's performance and avoiding the phenomenon of overfitting. This study builds a feature lexicon and a stop term lexicon for the literature domain based on all the data elements of title, abstract, and key terms in the training set. The feature term lexicon consists of three main parts. First, given the importance of key words in scientometric information, all key words were included in the feature term lexicon. Second, the feature term lexicon included high-frequency terms (greater than or equal to 5) included in titles and abstracts. Finally, typical terms describing the literature topics were included in the feature term lexicon in coordination with the knowledge of subject matter experts. Validation of terms for inclusion in the final lexicon was performed using two methods: validation by three subject matter experts and comparison with existing terms from the data science and analytics literature [4,30,41,42]. The final validated lexicon of feature terms will be used in downstream literature classification tasks by helping to select appropriate data science terms from publication platforms/databases (e.g., ProQuest, EBSCOhost, and Scopus) and pre-annotating these terms to support the development of a deep-learning application for classifying mentions of data science and analytics in the literature. Further explanation of the derived terms in the final lexicon can be found in Section 4.1.

In this study, only the English Snowball list [43] was initially used for the stop word lexicon, but the results were not satisfactory. After analysis, we found two main reasons for this situation. First, there are more formal descriptive terms in the scientific literature, such as "together with", "pointed out", "in agreement with", and other sentence-initial terms, which can easily mislead the machine learning procedure. Second, terms with low frequency (less than 5) and insignificant categorical features are prone to overfitting in machine learning. Therefore, in addition to Porter's English snowball list, the stopword lexicon in this study includes sentence-initial terms and terms with low frequency and unclear categorical features. Compared to Porter's English snowball list [43], our stopword lexicon consists of frequently mentioned terms related to open source tools (e.g., KNIME, RapidMiner, Weka, and MS Power BI), programming languages, and libraries (e.g., Python, R Script, STATA, SQL, and NLP).

3.2. Feature Matrix Construction and Vectorization

In text mining applications, deep learning models can automatically find features from distributed term vectors, which are highly portable and efficient to learn compared to conventional machine learning algorithms such as support vector machines (SVM) and conditional random fields (CRF) [44,45]. However, the quality of initial features still affects the efficiency of deep learning, and low-quality features tend to be overfitted or underfitted [46]. In this study, the data elements in scientometric information are divided into explicit and implicit features and processed separately.

3.2.1. Extraction of Explicit Features

First, key terms are directly added to the key term set K. A lexicon of feature terms and stop terms is then added, and the title and abstract are segmented with a tokenization tool to form the title feature set T and abstract feature set S, respectively. This process is shown in Equations (1)–(3) as follows:

$$K = (k_1, k_2, \ldots, k_r) \tag{1}$$

$$T = (t_1, t_2, \cdots, t_P) \tag{2}$$

$$S = (s_1, s_2, \cdots, s_q) \tag{3}$$

where k_r is the r_{th} term in the key terms, t_P is the p_{th} term in the title, and s_q is the q_{th} term in the abstract. Note that r, p, and q are variables for each document. To determine the length of the subsequent term vectors, three hyperparameters, $R\ (\geq r)$, $P\ (\geq p)$, and $Q\ (\geq q)$, are needed to determine the length of K, T, and S, respectively. The incomplete part is filled with 0, as shown in Equations (4)–(6).

$$K = (k_1, k_2, \ldots, k_r, \overbrace{0, \ldots, 0}^{R-r}) \tag{4}$$

$$T = (t_1, t_2, \cdots, t_P, \overbrace{0, \ldots, 0}^{P-p}) \tag{5}$$

$$S = (s_1, s_2, \cdots, s_q, \overbrace{0, \ldots, 0}^{Q-q}) \tag{6}$$

3.2.2. Implicit Feature Mapping

The institution name, journal name, and authors in the scientometric information are implicitly related to the research content or research methods of the literature. In the field of data science and analytics, academic articles published by computer science schools, for example, may focus on "applications of data analytics," while articles published by business schools may focus on "business analytics and decision making". Scholarly articles published in data analytics journals typically focus on data analytics applications and techniques, while scholarly articles published in healthcare journals typically focus on the application of data analytics in healthcare. In addition, collaboration with other researchers may change the research content or methodology. Similarly, an author usually uses a relatively specific type of research method and focuses on a particular research area, but when the author collaborates with other authors, the research content or method may change. Therefore, in this study, the scientometric information implicit in the names of the institution, journal, and authors is made explicit using feature mapping and then added to the original feature matrix. The mapping procedure for author, journal, and institution features is presented below:

(1) Author feature processing. The authors are associated with the domain literature, and the implicit feature of authorship is made explicit according to the co-occurrence frequency of the authors with the research content and research method involved in the

published literature [47]. Figure 2 shows the process of generating research method labels for different types of authors.

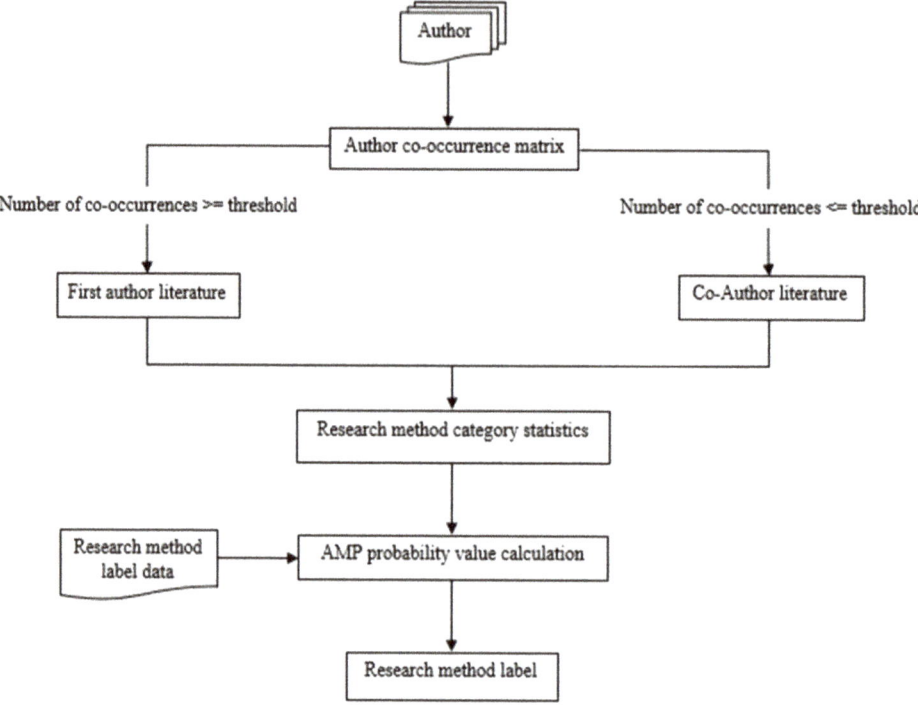

Figure 2. Author features mapping process.

The author co-occurrence matrix is constructed based on the author co-authorship relationship of domain literature. If the number of co-occurrences (i.e., co-authorship frequency) exceeds a specified threshold, the two authors are considered to have a stable collaborative relationship in a particular area of academic research and are considered co-authors for feature mapping; otherwise, only the first author is considered for feature mapping. Specifically, the frequency distribution table of "author–research method" is generated by first counting the frequency of co-authors (or first authors) according to the research method category. The probability value of the research method used by different authors is then calculated as AMP, shown in Equation (7). AMP indicates the percentage of papers authored by a particular author using a particular research method. For example, if author-1 publishes 10 papers, of which 5 papers use a mixed methods approach, then the AMP is 0.50 (50%). The larger the AMP value, the stronger the preference of an author for a certain research method. Finally, the "author–research method" probability distribution table is generated.

$$AMP_i(a) = \frac{m_{ia}}{\sum_{i=1}^{M} m_{ia}} \tag{7}$$

In Equation (7), M denotes the category of research method in the paper and m_{ia} denotes the frequency of the i_{th} research method used by author a. Based on the probability distribution table, authors are assigned to the explicit features of the research method. First, the threshold value for the AMP transformation probability is set, then the label for the research content with the largest AMP value that satisfies the threshold value is selected, and the authors are assigned to this label. The threshold value is a hyperparameter, and after experimentation, it is assumed that the threshold value is set to 0.7.That is, if an author's AMP value is greater than 0.7, the author is assigned to that research method label; otherwise, the placeholder 0 is used. Table 1 shows an example of the assignment of authors to research method labels. Author-1 is mapped to research method-2, co-author-2 is mapped to research method-1, author-5 is mapped to research method-3, while author-3 and co-author-4 are replaced by placeholder 0.

Table 1. Example of author–research method probability distribution.

	Research Method-1	Research Method-2	Research Method-3	Research Method-4
Author-1	0	1	0	0
Co-Author-2	0.8	0.2	0	0
Author-3	0	0	0.5	0.5
Co-Author-4	0.6	0	0.4	0
Author-5	0	0	1	0

(2) Journal feature processing. Similar to the author feature processing, the journal name is associated with the domain literature and mapped to the research content and research method explicit features. Taking the research content as an example, the processing flow is shown in Figure 3.

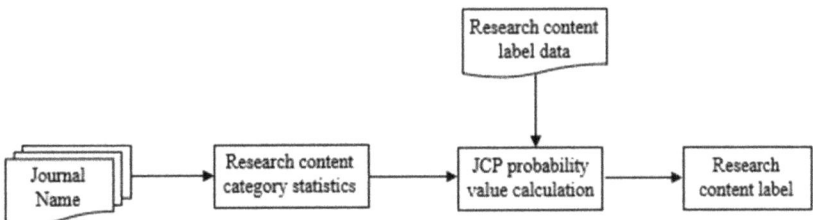

Figure 3. Journal features mapping process.

First, the frequency of different research contents of each journal was calculated using the journal title as the object to generate a frequency distribution table of journal–research content. The probability value of research content label for each journal was calculated as JCP, as shown in Equation (8). Again, the higher the value of JCP, the stronger the preference of a journal for a specific research content. A "journal–research content" probability distribution table is then generated based on JCP.

$$JCP_i(j) = \frac{C_{ij}}{\sum_{i=1}^{C} C_{ij}} \tag{8}$$

In Equation (8), C represents the category of the research content in the literature and C_{ij} represents the frequency of journal j for the i_{th} label of the research content. Based on the probability distribution table, the journal name is mapped to the explicit features of the research content. First, the JCP transformation probability threshold is set, and then the journal name is transformed to research content labels greater than or equal to the threshold. If there are no labels that meet the threshold or the number of labels is insufficient, a placeholder 0 is used instead. Assuming that the threshold is set to 0.33, labels for research content are added to the set of journal title mappings if the JCP value of research content is greater than 0.33. Table 2 shows examples of journal titles mapped to research content labels. The mapping set for journal-1 is (research content-1, research content-4, 0), the mapping set for journal-3 is (research content-3, research content-4, research content-5), and the mapping set for journal-5 is (0, 0, 0).

Table 2. Example of a journal–research content probability distribution.

	Research Content-1	Research Content-2	Research Content-3	Research Content-4	Research Content-5
Journal-1	0.60	0	0	0.40	0
Journal-2	0.15	0.10	0.75	0	0
Journal-3	0	0	0.34	0.33	0.33
Journal-4	0	1	0	0	0
Journal-5	0.25	0	0.20	0.25	0.30

(3) Research institution features mapping. The research institution is linked to the published article and mapped to the research content and research method explicit features. For instance, the processing flow of mapping the institution to the research content is shown in Figure 4.

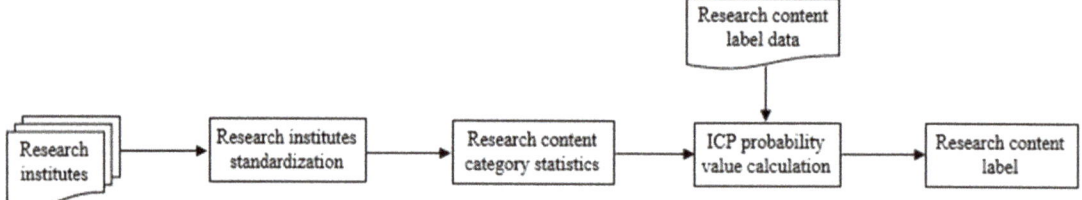

Figure 4. Features mapping process for research institutions.

The research institutions were first treated as follows: (i) if more than one research institution exists in the literature, only the first research institution is selected; (ii) regular expressions perform the classification of primary and secondary research institutions. Considering that the first-level research institution such as "XXXX University" basically cannot indicate the research content of the domain literature, only second-level research institutions, such as the Faculty of Economics and Management and the Faculty of Engineering, were retained for feature mapping. After that, the probability values of "research content" and "research method" labels were calculated for each research institution, and feature mapping was performed in the same way as journal mapping.

First, the frequency of the different research content for each institution name was calculated to create a frequency distribution table of institution–research content. The probability value of the research content label for each institution was calculated as ICP, as shown in equation (9). The higher the value of ICP, the stronger an institution's preference for a particular research content. Then, based on ICP, a probability distribution table of "institution–research content" is constructed.

$$ICP_i(j) = \frac{C_{ij}}{\sum_{i=1}^{C} C_{ij}} \tag{9}$$

In Equation (9), C represents the category of the research content in the literature and C_{ij} represents the frequency of institution j for the i_{th} label of the research content. Based on the probability distribution table, the institution name is mapped to the explicit features of research content. First, the ICP transformation probability threshold is set, and then the institution name is transformed to research content labels greater than or equal to the threshold. If there are no labels that meet the threshold or the number of labels is insufficient, a placeholder 0 is used instead. Assuming that the threshold is set to 0.33, labels for research content are added to the set of institution name mappings if the ICP value of research content is greater than 0.33. Table 2 shows examples of institution names mapped to research content labels. The mapping set for institution-1 is (research content-1, research content-4, 0), the mapping set for institution-3 is (research content-3, research content-4, research content-5), and the mapping set for institution-5 is (0, 0, 0).

3.2.3. Term Vectorization/Embeddings

The processed explicit and implicit features are added to the feature term embedding array D as shown in Equation (10).

$$D = [K, T, S, A, J, I] \tag{10}$$

Here, K, T, S, A, J, and I represent the processed data on the keywords, title, abstract, authors names, journal name, and institution name, respectively.

Then, D is converted into a term vectorization using Word2Vec, forming the initialized feature matrix for the subsequent CNN model. Word2Vec is a flat neural network model that maps terms into a multidimensional numerical space, where the position in the numerical space indicates the semantic information of the term [48]. To compute the term embeddings, we used Skip-gram, a Word2Vec term vector model method, to predict the occurrence probability of contextual environment terms based on the central term. The use of pre-trained term vectors greatly improves the classification performance of CNN models [49]. Consistent with Timoshenko and Hauser [50], in this study, we set the sliding window size c to 5 and the term vector dimension d to 20 to define the parameters of the Skip-gram Word2Vec model. The array D^* is the input for the term vector model, and the output is a term vector matrix $D^* \in i^{d \times n}$, which is used as the input for the CNN model.

3.3. Deep Learning for Literature Classification

Compared to traditional machine learning algorithms, deep learning models have performed better in classifying large-scale texts [42,51,52]. Deep learning models can learn high-level features at a deep level, starting from primary features at a superficial level by connecting neurons [26]. The specified input data are first fed to a feature extraction network, and the extracted features are then fed to a classification network. For the term vector matrix D^* built in this study, the deep-learning model CNN can learn both the aggregated features and the detailed features contained in the various scientometric information. An important advantage of CNNs is that they have the ability to automatically extract features [2]. A typical convolutional layer usually uses a pooling function in its last phase to change the output of the layer. In this study, we used max-pooling [30], one of the widely used pooling functions that returns the maximum output within a rectangular neighborhood. Max-pooling is a pooling operation that computes the maximum value for patches of a feature map and uses it to create a down-sampled (pooled) feature map. The result is down-sampled or pooled feature maps that highlight the most present feature in the field, rather than the average presence of the feature as in the case of average pooling. In practice, this method has been shown to perform better than average pooling in automated feature extraction, such as feature extraction in text mining applications [37,38].

As shown in Figure 5, the CNN model consists of an input layer, a convolution layer, a pooling layer, and a SoftMax layer, and uses a gradient descent method to inversely adjust the weighting parameters [30]. The input layer of the CNN is the term vector matrix D^*, and the convolution layer performs the convolution operation on the original feature matrix with multiple convolution kernels to form the feature map. The feature map is then pooled to reduce the dimensionality and set the threshold. The pooling layer filters out the unusable features and keeps the essential features. Finally, the SoftMax layer converts the sampled output vectors from the pooling layer into probability values for the literature content and method, using a fully connected SoftMax function to predict article categories.

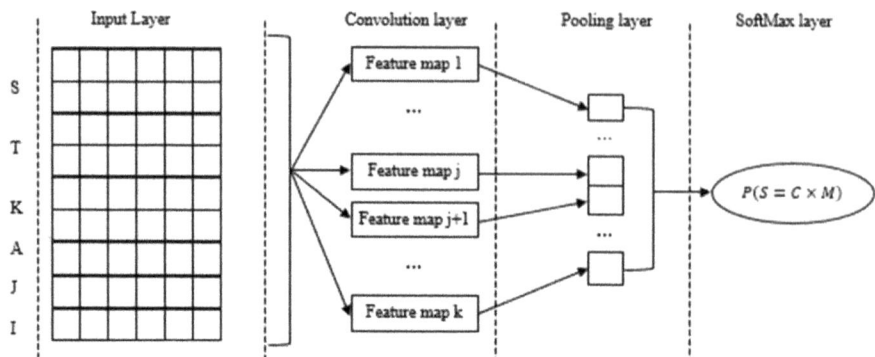

Figure 5. Structure of the CNN model.

For a collection of research content set S, both research content and research method are used as the output of the CNN model, and the resulting combination is modeled as in Equation (11).

$$S = C \times M \tag{11}$$

where C denotes the research content labels set, M denotes the research method labels set, and S denotes the combination of research content and research method labels, thereby achieving dual-label classification. The specific process is shown in Figure 6. For example, assuming that there are 4 research methods and 8 types of research content in a certain field, then 32 topic labels need to be defined, namely topic label 1, topic label 2, and up to topic label 32. If a paper is labeled with "Topic Label 32", it means that its research content and research method are "Research Content 8" and "Research Method 4" respectively.

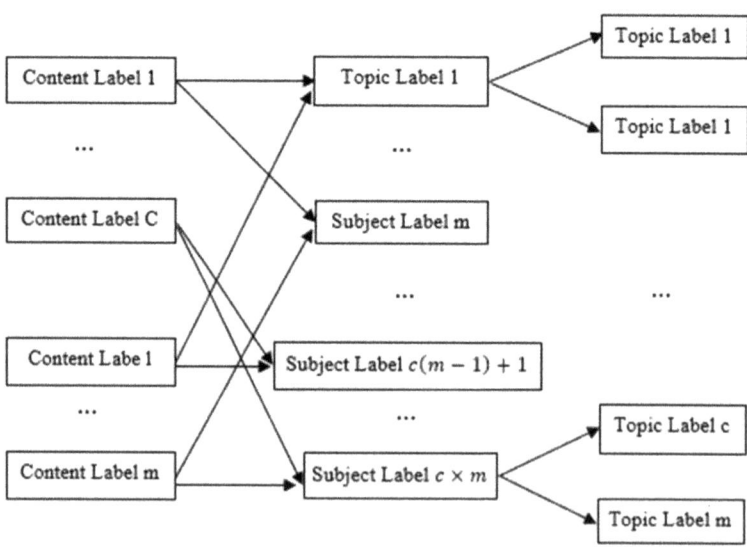

Figure 6. Process of implementing dual-label classification of literature.

4. Experimental Validation

To validate the utility and effectiveness of the above classification model, this study analyzes research content and method from the data science and analytics literature. Data science and analytics span multiple domains and disciplines; therefore, there is no general agreement in the literature on their scope, dimensions, and the characteristics of their components and interactions [53–57]. Salazar-Reyna et al. [30] described data mining, machine learning, and software tools as three overlapping subsystems of data science along two dimensions (i.e., experimental versus theoretical; descriptive versus prescriptive). Purnomo et al. [27] developed a schematic representation of the major domains that comprise data science and analytics (i.e., domain knowledge, statistics/mathematics, and computer science) and their overlap (i.e., machine learning, biostatistics, and data science). The literature is replete with publications on the use of data science, data analytics, and machine learning algorithms in various application areas such as healthcare, business, decision making, and marketing. However, it is unclear to what extent researchers in this field collaborate to share new insights and important results [30]. Therefore, a systematic approach to fine-grained classification of the currently published literature in the field of data science and analytics would be helpful to categorize these scholarly publications in the field of data science and analytics into granular subcategories and to establish future directions for the development and refinement of this area of research.

4.1. Data Source and Collection

The preliminary protocol for the search design included the use of five individual search terms (data science, data analytics, big data analytics, machine learning, and business analytics), three platforms (Scopus, ProQuest, and EBSCOhost), the use of Boolean operational rules (AND/OR), searching across all domains, and the primary exclusion criterion—publication in English-language journals. This search approach was repeatedly tested and modified to obtain a final set of appropriate guidelines for the study setting. To increase the exploratory nature of the search, we added synonyms (e.g., data mining, big datasets, and business intelligence) and techniques (e.g., data processing, text mining, machine learning, neural networks, and deep learning) to the original search terms, as well as the term data science (given the lack of uniformity between data analytics and data science in publications and academic texts) with the Boolean operator OR to the original search terms. To increase sensitivity, the Boolean operator was implemented in the abstracts rather than in all data elements or in the entire text content, which helps to control the scope.

The search covered the period from 2000 to 2022, and a total of 8874 records containing titles, study institutes, journals, keywords, abstracts, and other information were retrieved. After removing duplicates, processing errors, and missing values, 7647 records were finally sampled for annotation. The 7647 articles contain 13,977 key terms, and the most frequently occurring term is data analytics, with a total of 136 occurrences. A total of 785 journals are included, with the highest frequency for a single journal being 291 (*International Journal of Data Science and Analytics*—Springer) and 560 journals occurring more than twice. A total of 6785 research institutions are included, with the highest publication frequency for a single research institution being 82 (Boston University School of Information Management) and 1899 occurring more than twice. A total of 10,568 authors are recorded, with the highest frequency for a single author being 33 and 2262 authors occurring more than twice. The distribution of high-frequency terms, journals, and research institutions is shown in Table 3.

Table 3. Example of a journal—research content probability distribution.

	Research Content-1	Research Content-2	Research Content-3	Research Content-4	Research Content-5
Institution-1	0.60	0	0	0.40	0
Institution-2	0.15	0.10	0.75	0	0
Institution-3	0	0	0.34	0.33	0.33
Institution-4	0	1	0	0	0
Institution-5	0.25	0	0.20	0.25	0.30

4.2. Manual Annotation

We identified 22 classification features and divided them into two categories: research content and research method. This was achieved through a preliminary literature review based on the classification method described by Luo et al. [58]. As shown in Table 4, these 22 labels describe the main research areas of data science and analysis. In terms of research content labels, "self-service analytics" refers to niche areas of data science and analytics research, such as augmented data analytics and self-service business analytics [59,60]. This study classifies research that uses mainly qualitative research methods to analyze concepts or interpretive strategies as theoretical research in terms of research methodology. Research that mainly uses econometric or quantitative methods to examine cross-sectional or time-series data at the macro and micro levels is classified as empirical research. Research that focuses on organizational behavior by constructing models and using specific data to analyze specific cases is classified as case studies. Systematic literature review (SLR) refers to applying data science and analytical techniques in various application areas, such as healthcare, marketing, and decision-making [30].

Table 4. Frequency distribution of high-frequency terms, journals, and research institutions.

Subject Terms	Frequency	Journal	Frequency	Research Institution	Frequency
Data analytics	136	*International Journal of Data Science and Analytics*	291	Boston University	82
Big data analytics	131	*Data Science Journal*	290	California Institute of Technology	77
Machine learning	109	*International Journal of Data Science and Analytics*	233	Case Western Reserve University	75
Deep learning	77	*Intelligent Data Analysis*	179	Cornell University	68
Business analytics	73	*International Journal of Behavioral Analytics*	166	Davidson College	66
Business intelligence	72	*MIS Quarterly*	133	University of Chicago	65
Deep learning and neural networks	68	*Data Science and Management*	115	University of Georgia	57
Data mining	68	*Intelligent Data Analysis*	115	University of Michigan	52
Artificial intelligence	67	*The Journal of Finance and Data Science*	106	University of Notre Dame	46
Internet of Things	63	*Statistical Analysis and Data Mining*	85	University of Pennsylvania	44

Considering the highly specialized nature of scientific literature and the uniformity of citation standards [32,61], we used experts for manual citation annotation rather than the popular crowdsourcing model. Citation and annotation of data under the crowdsourcing model is often performed by many non-experts, which improves citation efficiency but is not suitable for citing highly specialized scientific literature. As for the specific operations, we mainly use subject matter experts to identify a set of feature terms for each research content label (see Table 5) and combine the position and frequency of occurrence of the feature terms for research content labels. When more than two types of research content occur in an article, the research content labels are sorted by the frequency of the feature terms, and the research content labels with a high feature terms' frequency are selected.

Table 5. Topic labels of the literature.

Categories	Topic Labels	No.
Research Content	Machine learning; business analytics; business intelligence; decision support systems; Internet of Things; big data analytics; deep learning and neural networks; data visualization, financial analytics; marketing analytics; data mining, text analytics, sentiment analytics, artificial intelligence, predictive analytics, operation research; prescriptive analytics; self-service analytics.	18
Research Method	Theoretical studies; empirical studies; case studies; systematic literature review (SLR)	4
Total		22

To ensure the accuracy of the annotation results, annotations were made independently by two master's students in data science and analytics research according to the annotation rules above. If the annotation results of two or more coders matched, the label category of the article was determined. The intercoder reliability and agreement between the two coders was tested using Krippendorff's alpha threshold as a measure of evaluator quality [62]. In general, a Krippendorff's alpha (α) of 0.80 is considered an acceptable level of intercoder reliability and agreement [63]. However, when the annotation results of the two coders did not match, the article and intercoder agreement were reviewed by the subject matter experts. The final intercoder reliability in this process, as measured by Krippendorff's alpha coefficient, was 83%, suggesting an acceptable level of intercoder agreement.

4.3. Experimental Analysis

4.3.1. Evaluation Criteria

The classification of the research areas in the literature was evaluated using precision, recall, and $F1$ measure. The method used in this study is to consider the class labels to be evaluated as individual positive classes and the other classes as negative classes and to construct a confusion matrix for each class label. The number of samples correctly assigned to a class label is TP, the number of samples incorrectly assigned to that label is FP, the number of samples correctly assigned to other class labels is TN, and the number of samples incorrectly assigned to other class labels is FN. The values P, R, and $F1$ are obtained from Equations (12)–(14).

$$P = \frac{TP}{TP + FP} \tag{12}$$

$$R = \frac{TP}{TP + FN} \tag{13}$$

$$F1 = \frac{2 \times P \times R}{P + R} \tag{14}$$

4.3.2. Comparative Analysis

The data science and analytic literature classification results are shown in Tables 6–8. Table 6 shows the classification accuracy of our model for the topic categories of data science and analytic literature. Table 7 shows the classification accuracy of our proposed model based on different initial feature constructs. Table 8 shows the classification accuracy of our model compared to other machine learning benchmark models.

Table 6. Annotation features of disciplinary categories in data science and analytics.

Research Content Label	Main Feature Terms
Machine learning	Database, computer vision, supervised learning, unsupervised learning, Reinforcement learning, neural network, classification, clustering, association rule mining.
Business analytics	Business, decision support systems, statistical model, descriptive analytics, diagnostic analytics, predictive analytics, prescriptive analytics, quantitative methods.
Business intelligence	Database, data warehouse, visualization, descriptive analytics, business performance management, key performance indicators, dashboard, scorecards, decision support.
Decision support systems	Online reviews, pricing research, consumer preferences.
Big data analytics	Recommendation algorithms, cloud computing.
Deep learning and neural networks	Deep learning, neural networks, long short-term memory.
Data visualization	Visualization techniques, graphics, descriptive analytics, data representation, communication, decision support.
Internet of Things	IoT data analytics, cloud computing, real-time streaming, network, smart manufacturing, interconnected devices, cloud manufacturing, fog computing, smart city.
Text analytics	Natural language processing text classification, topic modeling, social media, document frequency, corpus, lexicon, online reviews.
Sentiment analytics	Machine learning, user-generated content, opinion mining, voice, users, customers, subjective information, computational linguistics, biometrics, social network analysis.
Predictive analytics	Machine learning, predictive model, statistical analysis, supervised learning, unsupervised learning, reinforcement learning, classification, feature selection.
Artificial intelligence	Machine learning, augmented analytics, robotics, self-service analytics, deep learning, neural networks, decision making.
Operations research	Problem solving, optimization, decision making, prescriptive analytics, management science, simulation, supply chain management, planning, enterprise resource planning, risk management.
Prescriptive analytics	Management science, business performance management, optimization, decision making, sensitivity analysis.
Data mining	Statistics and modeling techniques, clickstream data.
Self-service analytics	Business user, report, dashboard, data-driven organizations, citizen data scientist, ad hoc analysis, queries, reports.
Financial analytics	Ad hoc analysis, forecast, business questions, financial data, financial risk.
Marketing analytics	Marketing campaigns, customer analytics, marketing channels, customer behavior, online reviews, brand management.

Table 7. Classification results of data science and analytics literature topic categories.

Research Topics		Performance Indicators		
Category	Label	P	R	F1-Score
Research Content	Machine learning	0.95	0.95	0.95
	Business analytics	0.93	0.92	0.92
	Business intelligence	0.91	0.94	0.92
	Decision support systems	0.84	0.84	0.84
	Big data analytics	0.85	0.81	0.83
	Deep learning and neural networks	0.88	0.82	0.85
	Data visualization	0.87	0.91	0.89
	Internet of Things	0.59	0.56	0.57
	Text analytics	0.94	0.93	0.93
	Sentiment analytics	0.93	0.89	0.91
	Predictive analytics	0.88	0.84	0.86
	Artificial intelligence	0.88	0.88	0.88
	Operations research	0.88	0.86	0.87
	Prescriptive analytics	0.88	0.88	0.88
	Data mining	0.91	0.92	0.91
	Self-service analytics	0.89	0.85	0.87
	Financial analytics	0.74	0.74	0.74
	Marketing analytics	0.74	0.77	0.75
Research Method	Theoretical research	0.72	0.76	0.74
	Empirical research	0.93	0.91	0.92
	Qualitative research	0.91	0.89	0.90
	Case study	0.61	0.66	0.63
	Systematic literature review	0.72	0.79	0.75

Table 8. Comparison of data science and analytics literature topic classification results with different data inputs and preprocessing.

Input Data and Preprocessing	Performance Indicators					
	Research Content			Research Method		
	P	R	F1	P	R	F1
Classification model of this study	0.73	0.74	0.73	0.88	0.84	0.86
By directly adding the journal name, author, and institution	0.62	0.61	0.61	0.74	0.71	0.72
Title and abstract only	0.72	0.73	0.72	0.76	0.75	0.75
Using only English Snowball stop term list [43]	0.70	0.71	0.70	0.76	0.77	0.76

As shown in Table 6, among the classification results of data science and analytics literature, machine learning has the highest *F*1 value of 95%, while the Internet of Things has the lowest *F*1 value of 57%. The *F*1 values of Financial Analytics and Marketing Analytics are relatively low, while the *F*1 values of the other research topics and categories are above 80%. The analysis shows that the research content with poor classification results has a relatively wide range of literature studies. For example, the research content in the literature labeled as the Internet of Things and related to data science and analytics has a lower coverage rate. The inconsistency of the research content leads to a wide dispersion of literature features in the categories of the Internet of Things, and the classification results are relatively poor. For research method, except for the case study category, which has a low $F1$ value, the $F1$ value is above 85% for all other categories, and the classification results are superior. We found that the proportion of literature using case studies in data science and analytics is relatively small for the case study category, accounting for only 7.36% of the total labeled literature. The small amount of literature may lead to poor feature extraction and overfitting of the model for the case study research method.

We conduct comparative experiments using different methods to investigate the usefulness of the original feature matrix created in this study. The experiments are based on the research method proposed in this study, in which only one feature term is changed at a time while the other feature terms remain unchanged. The results are shown in Table 7. The accuracy rate of the title information-based literature classification model for research content classification is 72%, the recall rate is 73%, and the macro F1 value is 74%. The accuracy rate for research method classification is 88%, the recall rate is 80%, and the macro $F1$ value is 81%. The macro F1 values for research content and research method decreased by 9% and 11%, respectively, by directly including the original data of authors, institutions, and journal titles in the feature matrix. When using the CNN algorithm to classify documents, which was applied by other researchers who used only article titles and abstract data [9], the macro $F1$ values for research content and research method were 2% and 3%, respectively. When the lexicon of domain features is not included in the data preprocessing and the original data is classified by Porter's English Snowball stop term list only, the macro $F1$ values for research content and research method differ by 4%. This is clear evidence that mapping author, institution name, and journal name features and creating an initial feature matrix help improve the model's classification performance.

To test the effectiveness of the CNN algorithm for fine-grained classification of scientific literature, we used common machine learning algorithms as benchmark experiments, including Naïve Bayes classifier, support vector machines (SVM), and k-nearest neighbor (KNN) [42,64,65]. All feature terms were used identically in the experiments, but the models were different. The empirical results in Table 9 show that the best classification results are obtained with the classification model of this study (based on the CNN algorithm). The NB algorithm performs better in document topic classification than the traditional machine learning algorithms, but the gap is more obvious than the CNN algorithm. The macro $F1$ values of the research content classification results differ by 9% and the research method differs by 13%.

Table 9. Classification results of literature topics in data science and analytics using different models.

Model	Performance Indicators					
	Research Content			Research Method		
	P	R	F_1	P	R	F_1
Fine-grained classification model based on CNN	0.72	0.73	0.74	0.88	0.80	0.81
SVM	0.57	0.60	0.58	0.69	0.41	0.51
NBM	0.64	0.67	0.65	0.70	0.67	0.68
KNN	0.50	0.50	0.50	0.69	0.45	0.54

Overall, the comparative analysis in Tables 7 and 8 shows that the method proposed in this study improves the macro $F1$ values of literature classification results. This proves the effectiveness of the method proposed in this study in addressing the problem of fine-grained classification of scientific literature.

4.3.3. Limitations and Future Research

Thematic classification of published literature based on scientometric information also presents several challenges.

First, caution is needed when generalizing the results of this work because each research method has different biases, such as database bias (resulting from the use of a limited database) and interpretation bias (resulting from the use of multiple researchers' interpretations of the content of publications). To reduce the impact of these biases in this study, the authors used multiple platforms to collect relevant publications (ProQuest, EBSCOhost, and Scopus). Each of these platforms has access to different databases. Since the data used in the experiments of this paper are relatively small, further large-scale literature classification experiments should be conducted to validate the proposed method's effectiveness further.

Second, due to the complexity of the research topics and the multidisciplinary nature of the literature, it is not easy to make a coherent classification of the scientific literature. In this study, we only classify the topics based on the most frequently occurring terms, which may lead to an inaccurate classification. For example, in the literature on data science and analytics, we named machine learning, predictive analytics, and business analytics based on the frequency of the feature terms; however, the classification result of the model is machine learning, which shows the inadequacy of the output in a single category. In further research, the output layer of the CNN model should be improved to develop a multi-category output and increase the accuracy of literature topic classification.

Third, in deep learning, the feature extraction and modeling steps are performed automatically after data training. Future research could therefore be devoted to improving the proposed method by incorporating feature selection techniques such as principal component analysis (PCA), regularization, matching pursuit, random projection, random forests, and LASSO.

Finally, another problem is that the classifications of the literature are partially based on the manual coding of subject matter experts who have determined the labels for the subcategories; this imposes certain subjective limitations. Further research should consider a combination of machine learning algorithms and expert knowledge to identify research topics in the literature and improve the model's ability to classify the literature automatically.

5. Conclusions

Advancement and development in a particular area of research are illustrated by the ever-growing body of scientific literature. This accumulation of literature describes various developments and innovations that occur over time and contains potentially valuable information that can be evaluated and classified to explain current emerging trends. In this study, we present a scientometric classification and analysis model for scientific literature based on convolutional neural networks (CNNs). Three dimensions, namely publication features, author features, and content features, were divided into explicit and implicit features to form a set of scientometric terms through explicit feature extraction and implicit feature mapping. First, we filter this scientometric information that characterizes the literature topic and build a lexicon of features and stop terms based on all scientometric titles, key terms, and abstracts in the training set. We then extract the explicit features such as keywords, titles, and abstracts from the scientometric information and map the implicit features such as authors, journal titles, and institutions to create a feature map. The feature map is then trained with weighted term vectors and used as input to the CNN model. Finally, the CNN model is used to perform a dual-label classification based on the published literature and articles' research content and methods.

The development of such an updated classification scheme is illustrated by a case study from the data science and analytics literature. The empirical results show that the macro F1 values of the proposed model for the two categories of research content and research method are 0.74 and 0.81, respectively. Compared to traditional machine learning methods, the classification results are significantly better and outperform the results obtained using only explicit features. Building a multi-faceted and fine-grained classification framework based on this approach provides the opportunity to explore interactions between disciplines (i.e., inter- and intra-disciplinary knowledge flows) in more detail, and allows for more detailed identification of inconsistencies between different classification systems. By using a minimal set of textual data, the approach presented in this study can be practically generalized to other datasets (e.g., artificial intelligence and big data analytics literature). Additional bibliographic metadata would likely improve the overall performance of the classification method. An interesting avenue would be to use full text, which provides more textual data and better accuracy of explicit features mapping and transformation. Additionally, it would be very promising to study and analyze in detail the classification ambiguities resulting from the algorithms' predictions.

Drawing on the findings and limitations of the current study, we believe that future research should focus on intensifying theoretical and applied research in this area in four directions: Assessing the costs and benefits of data science and analytics applications, conducting normative analytics studies, using data science and analytics to analyze the decision-making process, and validating the proposed research methods in a short period of time in different contexts using different databases and publishing platforms. Therefore, we believe that our work will stimulate similar future studies to explore the limits of machine learning and data science classification capabilities.

Author Contributions: Conceptualization, M.D.; methodology, M.D. and S.A.; software, S.A.; validation, M.D. and S.A.; formal analysis, M.D.; investigation, M.D.; resources, M.D. and W.M.; data curation, M.D.; writing—original draft preparation, M.D.; writing—review and editing, W.M. and L.A.; visualization, W.M.; supervision, W.M.; project administration, M.D., W.M. and L.A. All authors have read and agreed to the published version of the manuscript.

Funding: This research received no external funding.

Conflicts of Interest: The authors declare no conflict of interest.

References

1. Serenko, A. A structured literature review of scientometric research of the knowledge management discipline: A 2021 update. *J. Knowl. Manag.* **2021**, *25*, 1889–1925. [CrossRef]
2. Huang, H.; Zhu, D.; Wang, X. Evaluating scientific impact of publications: Combining citation polarity and purpose. *Scientometrics* **2021**, *126*, 1–25. [CrossRef]
3. Makabate, C.T.; Musonda, I.; Okoro, C.S.; Chileshe, N. Scientometric analysis of BIM adoption by SMEs in the architecture, construction and engineering sector. *Eng. Constr. Arch. Manag.* 2021; *ahead of print*. [CrossRef]
4. Sood, S.K.; Kumar, N.; Saini, M. Scientometric analysis of literature on distributed vehicular networks: VOSViewer visualization techniques. *Artif. Intell. Rev.* **2021**, *54*, 6309–6341. [CrossRef]
5. Zhang, Z.; Tam, W.; Cox, A. Towards automated analysis of research methods in library and information science. *Quant. Sci. Stud.* **2021**, *2*, 698–732. [CrossRef]
6. Adnani, H.; Cherraj, M.; Bouabid, H. Similarity indexes for scientometric research: A comparative analysis. *Malays. J. Libr. Inf. Sci.* **2020**, *25*, 31–48.
7. Liakata, M.; Saha, S.; Dobnik, S.; Batchelor, C.; Rebholz-Schuhmann, D. Automatic recognition of conceptualization zones in scientific articles and two life science applications. *Bioinformatics* **2012**, *28*, 991–1000. [CrossRef]
8. Wickett, K.; Sacchi, S.; Dubin, D.; Renear, A.H. Identifying content and levels of representation in scientific data. *Proc. Am. Soc. Inf. Sci. Technol.* **2012**, *49*, 1–10. [CrossRef]
9. Eykens, J.; Guns, R.; Engels, T.C.E. Fine-grained classification of social science journal articles using textual data: A comparison of supervised machine learning approaches. *Quant. Sci. Stud.* **2021**, *2*, 89–110. [CrossRef]
10. Ozcan, S.; Boye, D.; Arsenyan, J.; Trott, P. A Scientometric Exploration of Crowdsourcing: Research Clusters and Applications. *IEEE Trans. Eng. Manag.* **2020**, *64*, 1–15. [CrossRef]
11. Wahid, N.N.; Warraich, M.T. Group level scientometric analysis of Pakistani authors. COLLNET. *J. Scientometr. Inf. Manag.* **2021**, *15*, 287–304.
12. Mosallaie, S.; Rad, M.; Schiffauerova, A.; Ebadi, A. Discovering the evolution of artificial intelligence in cancer research using dynamic topic modeling. *Collnet J. Sci. Inf. Manag.* **2021**, *15*, 225–240. [CrossRef]
13. Andriamamonjy, A.; Saelens, D.; Klein, R. A combined scientometric and conventional literature review to grasp the entire BIM knowledge and its integration with energy simulation. *J. Build. Eng.* **2019**, *22*, 513–527. [CrossRef]

14. Hernández-Alvarez, M.; Gomez, J. Survey about citation context analysis: Tasks, techniques, and resources. *Nat. Lang. Eng.* **2016**, *22*, 327–349. [CrossRef]
15. Ravenscroft, J.E.; Liakata, M.; Clare, A.; Duma, D. Measuring scientific impact beyond academia: An assessment of existing impact metrics and proposed improvements. *PLoS ONE* **2017**, *12*, e0173152. [CrossRef]
16. Iqbal, S.; Hassan, S.-U.; Aljohani, N.R.; Alelyani, S.; Nawaz, R.; Bornmann, L. A decade of in-text citation analysis based on natural language processing and machine learning techniques: An overview of empirical studies. *Scientometrics* **2021**, *126*, 6551–6599. [CrossRef]
17. Wang, G.; Cheng, L.; Lin, J.; Dai, Y.; Zhang, T. Fine-grained classification based on multi-scale pyramid convolution networks. *PLoS ONE* **2021**, *16*, e0254054. [CrossRef]
18. Wang, M.; Zhang, J.; Jiao, S.; Zhang, X.; Zhu, N.; Chen, G. Important citation identification by exploiting the syntactic and contextual information of citations. *Scientometrics* **2020**, *125*, 2109–2129. [CrossRef]
19. Accuosto, P.; Saggion, H. Mining arguments in scientific abstracts with discourse-level embeddings. *Data Knowl. Eng.* **2020**, *129*, 101840. [CrossRef]
20. Mercer, R.E.; Di Marco, C. The Importance of Fine-Grained Cue Phrases in Scientific Citations. In *Advances in Artificial Intelligence. Canadian AI 2003. Lecture Notes in Computer Science (Lecture Notes in Artificial Intelligence)*; Xiang, Y., Chaib-draa, B., Eds.; Springer: Berlin/Heidelberg, Germany, 2003; Volume 2671. [CrossRef]
21. An, X.; Sun, X.; Xu, S.; Hao, L.; Li, J. Important citations identification by exploiting generative model into discriminative model. *J. Inf. Sci.* **2021**, *48*, 0165551521991034. [CrossRef]
22. Caselli, T.; Sprugnoli, R.; Moretti, G. Identifying communicative functions in discourse with content types. *Lang. Resour. Eval.* **2021**, *56*, 417–450. [CrossRef] [PubMed]
23. Hernández-Alvarez, M.; Gomez Soriano, J.M.; Martínez-Barco, P. Citation function, polarity and influence classification. *Nat. Lang. Eng.* **2017**, *23*, 561–588. [CrossRef]
24. González-Alcaide, G.; Salinas, A.; Ramos, J. Scientometrics analysis of research activity and collaboration patterns in Chagas cardiomyopathy. *PLoS Neglected Trop. Dis.* **2018**, *12*, e0006602. [CrossRef] [PubMed]
25. Kim, M.C.; Nam, S.; Wang, F.; Zhu, Y. Mapping scientific landscapes in UMLS research: A scientometric review. *J. Am. Med. Inform. Assoc.* **2020**, *27*, 1612–1624. [CrossRef]
26. Nosratabadi, S.; Mosavi, A.; Duan, P.; Ghamisi, P.; Filip, F.; Band, S.; Reuter, U.; Gama, J.; Gandomi, A. Data Science in Economics: Comprehensive Review of Advanced Machine Learning and Deep Learning Methods. *Mathematics* **2020**, *8*, 1799. [CrossRef]
27. Purnomo, A.; Rosyidah, E.; Firdaus, M.; Asitah, N.; Septiano, A. Data Science Publication: Thirty-Six Years Lesson of Scientometric Review. In Proceedings of the 2020 International Conference on Information Management and Technology (ICIMTech), Bandung, Indonesia, 13–14 August 2020.
28. Bhatt, C.; Kumar, I.; Vijayakumar, V.; Singh, K.U.; Kumar, A. The state of the art of deep learning models in medical science and their challenges. *Multimedia Syst.* **2021**, *27*, 599–613. [CrossRef]
29. Ho, Y.-S.; Shekofteh, M. Performance of highly cited multiple sclerosis publications in the Science Citation Index expanded: A scientometric analysis. *Mult. Scler. Relat. Disord.* **2021**, *54*, 103112. [CrossRef]
30. Salazar-Reyna, R.; Gonzalez-Aleu, F.; Granda-Gutierrez, E.M.; Diaz-Ramirez, J.; Garza-Reyes, J.A.; Kumar, A. A systematic literature review of data science, data analytics and machine learning applied to healthcare engineering systems. *Manag. Decis.* **2020**, *60*, 300–319. [CrossRef]
31. Kandimalla, B.; Rohatgi, S.; Wu, J.; Giles, C.L. Large Scale Subject Category Classification of Scholarly Papers With Deep Attentive Neural Networks. *Front. Res. Metrics Anal.* **2021**, *5*. [CrossRef]
32. Dunham, J.; Melot, J.; Murdick, D. Identifying the Development and Application of Artificial Intelligence in Scientific Text. *arXiv* **2020**, arXiv:abs/2002.07143.
33. Vortmann, L.-M.; Putze, F. Combining Implicit and Explicit Feature Extraction for Eye Tracking: Attention Classification Using a Heterogeneous Input. *Sensors* **2021**, *21*, 8205. [CrossRef] [PubMed]
34. Aljohani, N.; Fayoumi, A.; Hassan, S. An in-text citation classification predictive model for a scholarly search system. *Scientometrics* **2021**, *126*, 5509–5529. [CrossRef]
35. Aljuaid, H.; Iftikhar, R.; Ahmad, S.; Asif, M.; Afzal, M.T. Important citation identification using sentiment analysis of in-text citations. *Telematics Informatics* **2021**, *56*, 101492. [CrossRef]
36. Rajput, N.; Grover, B. A multi-label movie genre classification scheme based on the movie's subtitles. *Multimed. Tools Appl.* **2022**, *81*, 1–22. [CrossRef]
37. Setyanto, A.; Laksito, A.; Alarfaj, F.; Alreshoodi, M.; Kusrini; Oyong, I.; Hayaty, M.; Alomair, A.; Almusallam, N.; Kurniasari, L. Arabic Language Opinion Mining Based on Long Short-Term Memory (LSTM). *Appl. Sci.* **2022**, *12*, 4140. [CrossRef]
38. Sagnika, S.; Mishra, B.S.P.; Meher, S.K. An attention-based CNN-LSTM model for subjectivity detection in opinion-mining. *Neural Comput. Appl.* **2021**, *33*, 17425–17438. [CrossRef]
39. Wang, L.; Liu, Y.; Di, H.; Qin, C.; Sun, G.; Fu, Y. Semi-Supervised Dual Relation Learning for Multi-Label Classification. *IEEE Trans. Image Process.* **2021**, *30*, 9125–9135. [CrossRef]
40. Zhao, D.; Gao, Q.; Lu, Y.; Sun, D. Learning view-specific labels and label-feature dependence maximization for multi-view multi-label classification. *Appl. Soft Comput.* **2022**, *124*, 109071. [CrossRef]

41. Gryncewicz, W.; Sitarska-Buba, M. Data Science in Decision-Making Processes: A Scientometric Analysis. *Eur. Res. Stud. J.* **2021**, *24*, 1061–1067. [CrossRef]
42. Sarker, I. Machine Learning: Algorithms, Real-World Applications and Research Directions. *SN Comput. Sci.* **2021**, *2*, 16. [CrossRef]
43. Porter, M. Snowball: A Language for Stemming Algorithms. 2001. Available online: http://snowball.tartarus.org/texts/introduction.html (accessed on 23 April 2020).
44. Xu, G.; Meng, Y.; Qiu, X.; Yu, Z.; Wu, X. Sentiment Analysis of Comment Texts Based on BiLSTM. *IEEE Access* **2019**, *7*, 51522–51532. [CrossRef]
45. Daradkeh, M. Analyzing Sentiments and Diffusion Characteristics of COVID-19 Vaccine Misinformation Topics in Social Media: A Data Analytics Framework. *Int. J. Bus. Anal.* **2021**, *9*, 55–88. [CrossRef]
46. Daradkeh, M. Organizational Adoption of Sentiment Analytics in Social Media Networks: Insights from a Systematic Literature Review. *Int. J. Inf. Technol. Syst. Approach* **2022**, *15*, 15–45.
47. Guo, D.; Chen, H.; Long, R.; Lu, H.; Long, Q. A Co-Word Analysis of Organizational Constraints for Maintaining Sustainability. *Sustainability* **2017**, *9*, 1928. [CrossRef]
48. Kozlowski, A.; Taddy, M.; Evans, J. The Geometry of Culture: Analyzing the Meanings of Class through Word Embeddings. *Am. Sociol. Rev.* **2019**, *84*, 905–949. [CrossRef]
49. Ravikiran, M.; Nonaka, Y.; Mariyasagayam, N. A Sensitivity Analysis (and Practitioners' Guide to) of DeepSORT for Low Frame Rate Video. In Proceedings of the 2020 IEEE International Conference on Big Data (Big Data), Atlanta, GA, USA, 10–13 December 2020.
50. Timoshenko, A.; Hauser, J. Identifying Customer Needs from User-Generated Content. *Mark. Sci.* **2019**, *38*, 1–20. [CrossRef]
51. Najafabadi, M.M.; Villanustre, F.; Khoshgoftaar, T.M.; Seliya, N.; Wald, R.; Muharemagic, E. Deep learning applications and challenges in big data analytics. *J. Big Data* **2015**, *2*, 1. [CrossRef]
52. Schmidt, J.; Marques, M.R.G.; Botti, S.; Marques, M.A.L. Recent advances and applications of machine learning in solid-state materials science. *npj Comput. Mater.* **2019**, *5*, 83. [CrossRef]
53. Medeiros, M.N.; Hoppen, N.; Maçada, A. Data science for business: Benefits, challenges and opportunities. *Bottom Line* **2020**, *33*, 149–163. [CrossRef]
54. Provost, F.; Fawcett, T. Data Science and its Relationship to Big Data and Data-Driven Decision Making. *Big Data* **2013**, *1*, 51–59. [CrossRef]
55. Vicario, G.; Coleman, S. A review of data science in business and industry and a future view. *Appl. Stoch. Model. Bus. Ind.* **2020**, *36*, 6–18. [CrossRef]
56. Waller, M.A.; Fawcett, S. Data Science, Predictive Analytics, and Big Data: A Revolution That Will Transform Supply Chain Design and Management. *J. Bus. Logist.* **2013**, *34*, 77–84. [CrossRef]
57. Wimmer, H.; Aasheim, C. Examining Factors that Influence Intent to Adopt Data Science. *J. Comput. Inf. Syst.* **2019**, *59*, 43–51. [CrossRef]
58. Luo, J.; Huang, S.; Wang, R. A fine-grained sentiment analysis of online guest reviews of economy hotels in China. *J. Hosp. Mark. Manag.* **2021**, *30*, 71–95. [CrossRef]
59. Daradkeh, M. Determinants of Self-Service Analytics Adoption Intention: The Effect of Task-Technology Fit, Compatibility, and User Empowerment. *J. Organ. End User Comput. (JOEUC)* **2019**, *31*, 19–45. [CrossRef]
60. Daradkeh, M.; Al-Dwairi, R. Self-Service Business Intelligence Adoption in Business Enterprises: The Effects of Information Quality, System Quality, and Analysis Quality. In *Operations and Service Management: Concepts, Methodologies, Tools, and Applications*; A. Information Resources Management, IGI Global: Hershey, PA, USA, 2018; pp. 1096–1118.
61. Brack, A.; D'Souza, J.; Hoppe, A.; Auer, S.; Ewerth, R. Domain-Independent Extraction of Scientific Concepts from Research Articles. Advances in Information Retrieval. In Proceedings of the 42nd European Conference on IR Research, ECIR 2020, Lisbon, Portugal, 14–17 April 2020; Part I, 12035. pp. 251–266.
62. Krippendorff, K. *Content analysis: An Introduction to Its Methodology*; Sage: Thousand Oaks, CA, USA, 2012.
63. Daradkeh, M. Determinants of visual analytics adoption in organizations: Knowledge discovery through content analysis of online evaluation reviews. *Inf. Technol. People* **2019**, *32*, 668–695. [CrossRef]
64. Mukhamediev, R.; Symagulov, A.; Kuchin, Y.; Yakunin, K.; Yelis, M. From Classical Machine Learning to Deep Neural Networks: A Simplified Scientometric Review. *Appl. Sci.* **2021**, *11*, 5541. [CrossRef]
65. Wang, J.; Lu, Y. A novel CNN model for fine-grained classification with large spatial variants. *J. Phys. Conf. Ser.* **2020**, *1544*, 012138. [CrossRef]

Article

Real-Time Facemask Detection for Preventing COVID-19 Spread Using Transfer Learning Based Deep Neural Network

Mona A. S. Ai [1,2,*], **Anitha Shanmugam** [3], **Suresh Muthusamy** [4], **Chandrasekaran Viswanathan** [5], **Hitesh Panchal** [6], **Mahendran Krishnamoorthy** [7], **Diaa Salama Abd Elminaam** [8,9,*] and **Rasha Orban** [2]

1   Computer Science Department, College of Computer Science and Information Technology, King Faisal Unversity, Hofuf 31982, Saudi Arabia
2   Computer Science Department, Faculty of Computers and Artificial Intelligence, Benha University, Benha 12311, Egypt; mona.abdelbaset@fci.bu.edu.eg (M.A.S.A.); rasha.abdelkreem@fci.bu.edu.eg (R.O.)
3   Department of Information Technology, Kongu Engineering College (Autonomous), Perundurai 638060, Tamil Nadu, India; anithame@kongu.ac.in
4   Department of Electronics and Communication Engineering, Kongu Engineering College (Autonomous), Perundurai 638060, Tamil Nadu, India; infostosuresh@gmail.com
5   Department of Medical Electronics, Vellalar College of Engineering and Technology, Thindal 638012, Tamil Nadu, India; vc4sachin@gmail.com
6   Department of Mechanical Engineering, Government Engineering College, Gandhinagar 382028, Gujarat, India; engineerhitesh2000@gmail.com
7   Department of Electrical and Electronics Engineering, Jansons Institute of Technology, Karumathampatti, Coimbatore 641659, Tamil Nadu, India; mahae1987@gmail.com
8   Information Systems Department, Faculty of Computers and Artificial Intelligence, Benha University, Benha 12311, Egypt
9   Computer Science Department, Faculty of Computer Science, Misr International University, Cairo 12585, Egypt
*   Correspondence: m.ali@kfu.edu.sa (M.A.S.A.); diaa.salama@fci.bu.edu.eg (D.S.A.E.)

Citation: Ai, M.A.S.; Shanmugam, A.; Muthusamy, S.; Viswanathan, C.; Panchal, H.; Krishnamoorthy, M.; Elminaam, D.S.A.; Orban, R. Real-Time Facemask Detection for Preventing COVID-19 Spread Using Transfer Learning Based Deep Neural Network. *Electronics* **2022**, *11*, 2250. https://doi.org/10.3390/electronics11142250

Academic Editors: Amir H. Gandomi, Fang Chen, Laith Abualigah, Amir Mosavi and Daniel Morris

Received: 14 April 2022
Accepted: 12 July 2022
Published: 18 July 2022

Abstract: The COVID-19 pandemic disrupted people's livelihoods and hindered global trade and transportation. During the COVID-19 pandemic, the World Health Organization mandated that masks be worn to protect against this deadly virus. Protecting one's face with a mask has become the standard. Many public service providers will encourage clients to wear masks properly in the foreseeable future. On the other hand, monitoring the individuals while standing alone in one location is exhausting. This paper offers a solution based on deep learning for identifying masks worn over faces in public places to minimize the coronavirus community transmission. The main contribution of the proposed work is the development of a real-time system for determining whether the person on a webcam is wearing a mask or not. The ensemble method makes it easier to achieve high accuracy and makes considerable strides toward enhancing detection speed. In addition, the implementation of transfer learning on pretrained models and stringent testing on an objective dataset led to the development of a highly dependable and inexpensive solution. The findings provide validity to the application's potential for use in real-world settings, contributing to the reduction in pandemic transmission. Compared to the existing methodologies, the proposed method delivers improved accuracy, specificity, precision, recall, and F-measure performance in three-class outputs. These metrics include accuracy, specificity, precision, and recall. An appropriate balance is kept between the number of necessary parameters and the time needed to conclude the various models.

Keywords: deep learning; facemask; computer vision; CNN; COVID-19

1. Introduction

The research supporting people wearing masks in public locations to prevent COVID-19 transmission is advancing rapidly. Disease spread can be delayed by physically separating sick persons from others, taking additional precautions, and minimizing the probability of transmission per interaction. A mask minimizes transmissibility per encounter in laboratory and clinical settings by limiting the transmission of contaminated respiratory particles. When public mask-wearing is widespread, it effectively reduces virus spread [1]. Recently, researchers at the University of Edinburgh published a study to better understand the COVID-19 pandemic response measures. Wearing a face mask or other covering over the nose and mouth was proven to significantly minimize the risk of coronavirus spread by avoiding the forward distance traveled by an individual's exhaled air [2]. Face mask detection is determining whether or not someone is wearing a mask. In computer vision and pattern recognition, face detection is a crucial component. The face is recognized using various machine learning techniques [3]. The existing systems have several flaws, including high feature complexity and low detection accuracy. Face identification approaches based on deep convolutional neural networks (CNNs) have been popular in increasing detection performance [4]. Even though many academicians have worked hard to develop fast face detection and recognition algorithms, there is a significant difference between 'detection of the face under mask' and 'detection of mask over face'. In practice, it is difficult to spot mask abuse. The key challenge is the dataset limitation. Mask-wearing status datasets are often minimal and merely identify the presence of masks. There is very little study on detecting masks over the face in the literature. The proposed research intends to create a technique that can accurately detect masks over the face in public places (such as airports, train stations, crowded markets, and bus stops) to prevent coronavirus transmission, thus contributing to public health. Furthermore, detecting faces with or without a mask in public is difficult due to the little data available for detecting masks on human faces, making the model difficult to train. As a result, the concept of transfer learning is utilized to transfer learned kernels from networks trained on a large dataset for similar face detection.

In this pandemic situation, there is a need to monitor the people wearing masks to control the spread of COVID-19. It is necessary to alert the people to wear masks properly in public places by comparing the captured image with the datasets. If CCTV cameras record videos, the faces appear small, hazy, and low-resolution. Because people do not always stare straight at the camera, the facial angles change. These real-world videos differ significantly from those obtained by webcams or selfie cameras, making face mask recognition in practice much more difficult. Residual blocks were integrated into the depth-wise separable convolution layer developed by MobileNetV2. Residual networks enable deep network training by creating the network using residual models. Residual network ResNet50V2 is one of the fastest object detection techniques for face detection using CNN. Inception-ResNetV2 is a convolutional neural architecture based on the Inception family of architectures that includes residual connections (which replace the filter concatenation stage in the Inception). Efficient Net examines neural network scaling, thereby simultaneously scaling the network's width, resolution, and depth. The objective was to create a face detector using ResNet50V2 to improve the efficiency of identifying faces with better accuracy and speed. The system's goal was to reduce manual labor by identifying people through video analysis and determining whether or not they are wearing masks. A heuristic evaluation with numerous users was conducted to examine usability, concluding that the implemented system is more user-friendly, faster, and more efficient than existing solutions. A unified approach of ResNet50V2 combines many features and classifiers, where all features can be used to identify the mask through video detection. ResNet50V2 can identify multiple objects in a single frame or image, providing better accuracy since many persons can be in a single frame. ResNet50V2 correctly identifies and warns the user with better accuracy compared toResNet101V2. The object recognition algorithm performs better only when the images are captured, and it takes more time to process the image and produce the output. Comparatively, ResNet50V2 gives the result by detecting the object in the video stream. The proposed method is faster, more efficient, and more accurate.

The main contributions of the proposed work (techniques and benefits) are as follows:

1. A real-time system was built for determining whether a person on a webcam is wearing a mask or not.
2. A balanced dataset for a facemask with a nearly one-to-one imbalance ratio was generated using random oversampling (ROS).
3. An object detection approach (ensemble) combined a one-stage and two-stage detector to recognize objects from real-time video streams with a short inference time (high speed) and high accuracy.
4. Transfer learning was utilized in ResNet50V2 for fusing high-level semantic information in diverse feature maps by extracting new features from learned characteristics.
5. An improved affine (bounding box) transformation was applied in the cropped region of interest (ROI) as there are many changes in the size of the face and location.

The remainder of the paper is arranged as follows: Section 2 presents the literature review. The proposed methodology is given in Section 3. Section 4 provides the implementation results and discussion. Lastly, the conclusions and future work are specified in Section 5.

2. Literature Review

Transfer learning is an approach in which knowledge acquired by a CNN from provided and related data is used to solve the problem. Deep learning networks pretrained on previous datasets can be fine-tuned to achieve high accuracy with a smaller dataset. The methods which are used for deep learning are discussed below. Sethi et al. [5] proposed a multigranularity masked face recognition model developed using MobileNetV2 and achieved 94% accuracy. Sen et al. [6] built a system that differentiates those who use face masks and those who do not utilizing a series of photographs and videos. The suggested method employed the MobileNetV2 model and Python's PyTorch and OpenCV for mask detection, with 79.24% accuracy. Balaji et al. [7] included an entrance system to public locations that distinguish persons who wear masks from those who do not. Furthermore, if a person violates the rule of wearing a facemask, this device produces a beep as an alert. The video was captured with a Raspberry-PI camera and then converted into pictures for further processing. The usage of masks significantly slow the virus's spread, according to Cheng et al. [8]. It was determined that YOLO v3-tiny (You Only Look Once) can detect mask use in real time. It is also small, fast, and excellent for real-time detection and mobile hardware deployment. Sakshi et al. [9] created a face mask detector based on MobileNetV2 architecture utilizing Keras/TensorFlow. The model was changed to guarantee face mask recognition in real-time video or still pictures. The ultimate goal is to employ computer vision to execute the concept in high-density areas, such as hospitals, healthcare facilities, and educational institutions. Using a featured image pyramid and focus loss, a single-stage object detector can detect dense objects in images over several layers. Jiang et al. [10] proposed a two-stage detector that achieves amazing accuracy and speeds comparable to the single-stage detector. It divides a picture into GxG grids, each providing N-bound box predictions. Each bounding box can only have one class during the prediction, preventing the network from finding smaller items. Redmon et al. [11] introduced YOLO, which uses a one-phase prediction strategy with impressive inference time, but the localization accuracy was low for small images. YOLOv2 with batch normalization, a high-resolution classifier, and anchor boxes were added to the YOLO network.

YOLOv3 is an improved version of YOLOv2, featuring a new feature extraction network, a better backbone classifier, and multiscale prediction. Although Kumar et al. [12] suggested a two-stage detector with high object detection accuracy, it is limited for video surveillance due to sluggish real-time inference speed. Although Morera et al. [13] suggested YOLOv3, it achieved the same classification accuracy as a single-shot detector (SSD). Furthermore, YOLOv3's inference demands significant CPU resources, making it unsuitable for embedded systems. SSD networks outperform YOLO networks due to their compact filters of convolution type, extensive feature maps, and estimation across manifolds. The YOLO network has two fully linked layers, while the SSD network utilizes varied-sized convolutional layers. The region-based convolutional neural network (R-CNN) presented by Girshick et al. [14] was the first CNN implementation for object detection and localization on a large scale. The model generated state-of-the-art results when tested on standard datasets. R-CNN first extracts a set of item proposals using a selective search strategy and then forecasts items and related classes using an SVM (support vector machine) classifier. He et al. [15] introduced SPPNet, which is a categorization system for gathering features and feeding them into a fully connected layer. SPNN can create feature maps in a single-shot detection for the whole image, resulting in a nearly 20-fold boost in object detection time over R-CNN. Both the detector and the regressor are trained simultaneously without changing the network configurations. Girshick et al. [16] introduced fast R-CNN in which the region of interest (RoI) pooling layer is used to fine-tune the model. Nguyen et al. [17] proposed fast R-CNN, which is an extension of R-CNN and SPPNet. Although fast R-CNN efficiently integrates the properties of R-CNN and SPPNet, its detection speed is still inferior to single-stage detectors. Fu et al. [18] proposed faster R-CNN, which combines fast R-CNN and RPN. It achieves nearly cost-free region proposals by gradually integrating individual components of the object detection system (e.g., proposal detection, feature extraction, and bounding box regression) in a single step. Even though this integration breaks beyond the fast R-CNN speed bottleneck, the subsequent detection stage has computation redundancy. The region-based fully convolutional network (R-FCN) method supports backpropagation for both training and inference, according to Dvornik et al. [19]. Liang et al. [20] introduced the feature pyramid network (FPN) to recognize nonuniform objects; however, academics rarely employ this network due to its high processing costs and memory requirements. He et al. [21] proposed mask R-CNN to improve faster R-CNN by utilizing segmented mask estimates on each RoI. Most existing systems use images to identify the presence or absence of a mask. Fewer algorithms give output with more than a 90% accuracy rate in video streaming. The users are also detected through images, but this works efficiently only when they remain stationary, posing a problem for real-time implementation. Capturing the user's image and then determining the presence/absence of a mask takes more time and is a little more complicated than in video streaming. ResNet50V2 correctly identifies the presence/absence of a mask with better accuracy compared to MobileNetV2. The video analysis method can be used for face mask detection. Of all the approaches proposed in the literature, ResNet50V2 appears to be the most promising face mask detection as it uses a fast and accurate object detection algorithm. The ResNet50V2 approach allows the accuracy of determining mask wearing in a video and identification/extraction of the pixels associated with each individual.

The existing literature study has some limitations, which are summarized as follows:

a. Various models have been pretrained on standard datasets, but only a limited number of datasets handle facemask detection to overcome the COVID-19 spread.

b. Due to the limitedness of facemask datasets, varying degrees of occlusion and semantics are essential for numerous mask types.

c. However, none of them are ideal for real-time video surveillance systems.

According to Roy et al., surveillance devices are constrained by a lack of processing power and memory [22]. As a result, these devices necessitate efficient object detection models capable of performing real-time surveillance while using minimal memory and maintaining high accuracy. Although one-stage detectors are suitable for video surveillance in many applications, hey have limited accuracy [23]. Two-stage detectors offer accurate detection in case of multifaceted input at the expense of high computing time [24]. The aforementioned factors require creating a combined surveillance device, thereby saving computing time with improved accuracy. To obtain the required image complexity score, each image is represented in a pyramid, extracted features are combined, and L2 normalization is performed. The input samples chosen for analysis should always be balanced, containing the appropriate number of samples belonging to each class label. Handling an imbalanced dataset is important for better classification [25,26]. According to the papers described above, deep learning architectures are rapidly being applied to facemask detection to prevent COVID-19 spread using a transfer learning-based deep neural network [27–34]. Other deep learning [35–42] and optimization algorithms are also used to solve various optimization problems [43–51]. However, several gaps in using deep learning systems for real-time implementation and prevention strategies must be addressed, as indicated [52–57].

3. Proposed Methodology

Figure 1 shows the proposed real-time face mask detection system, which is implemented in two phases (training and deployment). The training and deployment phase algorithms are given in Algorithms 1 and 2, respectively. The training phase consists of 11 steps ranging from dataset collection to image classification (the dataset is classified into three classes: face with the correct mask, face with an incorrect mask, and face without a mask). In the first step, the data frame is extracted using OpenCV, followed by random oversampling to balance the unequal number of classes by performing imbalance computation and random oversampling (ROS) using ρ. In the third step, image augmentation and face detection are applied by passing through many convolutional layers, which extract feature maps. In the next step, transfer learning is implemented by replacing the last predicting layer of the pretrained model with its predicting layers to implement fine-tuned transfer learning. Finally, in the last step, a pretrained classification model, ResNet50V2, is applied to classify images. The training phase is applied to the MAFA dataset [56] described in the next section. The deployment phase consists of 12 steps ranging from data collection (live video) to displaying personal information (such as identity and name) and violation information (such as location, timestamp, camera type, ID, and violation category, e.g., face without a mask and face with an incorrect mask). In the first step, the data frame is extracted using OpenCV, followed by image complexity prediction to identify whether the image is soft or hard. Object classification using a semi-supervised approach is applied. In the next step, transfer learning is implemented by replacing the last predicting layer of the pretrained model with its predicting layers to implement fine-tuned transfer learning. Finally, identity prediction by applying a pretrained classification model, ResNet50V2, is the last step in classifying images.

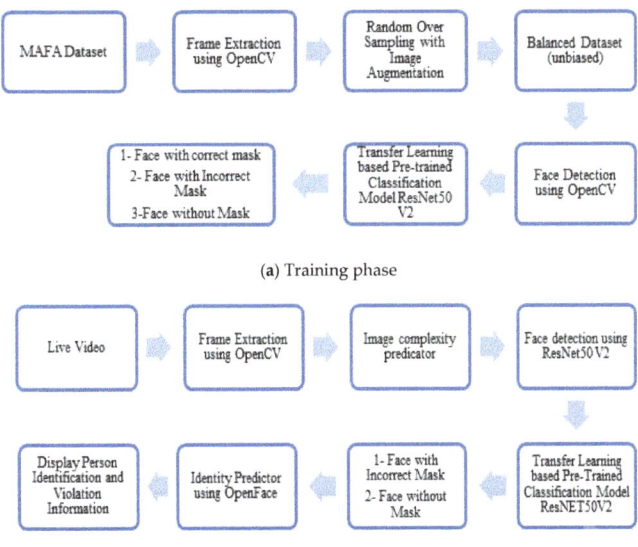

(a) Training phase

(b) Deployment phase

Figure 1. The proposed real-time model for face mask detection.

Algorithm 1. Training phase

Input:	MAFA dataset containing videos
Processes:	Frame extraction, random oversampling, image augmentation, face detection and transfer learning with pretrained classification
Frame extraction using OpenCV:	
Step 1:	Split the video captured using cv2.VideoCapture(<path_of_video>) through inbuilt camera into frames and save using cv2.imwrite()
Random over sampling:	
Step 2:	Unequal number of classes is balanced by performing imbalance computation and ROS using ρ $\rho = \frac{\text{count}(\text{majority}(Di))}{\text{count}(\text{minority}(Di))}$, where D_{mi} and D_{ma} are majority and minority classes of D,
Image augmentation and Face detection:	
Step 3:	At various locations, the image is passed through a large number of convolutional layers, which extract feature maps.
Step 4:	In each of those feature maps, a 4×4 filter is used to determine a tiny low default box and predict each box's bounding box offset.
Step 5:	Five predictions are included in each bounding box output: x, y, w, h, and confidence. The centroid of the box is represented by x and y in relation to the grid cell limits
Step 6:	Conditional class probabilities are also predicted in each grid cell, Pr(class | object)
Step 7:	The truth boxes are matched with the expected boxes using intersection over union (IOU), $Intersection over union (IOU) = \frac{\text{area of overlap}}{\text{area of union}}$.
Transfer Learning:	
Step 8:	Replace last predicting layer of the pretrained model with its own predicting layers to implement fine-tuned transfer learning.
Step 9:	Generic features are learnt by the network's initial lower layers from the pretrained Model, and its weights are frozen and not modified during the training.
Step 10:	Task-specific traits are learned at higher layers which can be pretrained and fine-tuned.
Pre-trained classification:	
Step 11:	Apply pretrained classification model, ResNET50V2 to classify images.
Output:	Images in the dataset are classified into three classes: face with correct mask, face with incorrect mask, and face without mask.

Algorithm 2. Deployment phase	
Input:	Live video
Processes:	Frame extraction, image complexity predictor, transfer learning with pretrained classification and identity prediction
Frame extraction:	
Step 1:	Split the video captured using cv2.VideoCapture(<path_of_video>) through inbuilt camera into frames and save using cv2.imwrite()
Step 2:	Face detection using MobileNetV2 and ResNET50V2 is performed by comparing with trained images
Step 3:	During testing, class-specific confidence scores are obtained using $\Pr(\text{Class} \mid \text{Object}) \times \Pr(\text{Object}) \times [0U = \Pr(\text{Class}) \times 10U.$
Step 4:	The truth boxes are matched with the expected boxes using IOU, $\text{Intersection over union} = \frac{\text{area of overlap}}{\text{area of union}}.$
Image Complexity Prediction:	
Step 5:	To identify whether the image is soft or hard, object classification using semi-supervised approach is applied.
Step 6:	For predicting the class of soft pictures, the MobileNet-SSD model is used, $L = 1/N(\text{Lclass} + \text{Lbox}),$ where N is the total number of matched boxes with the final set of matched boxes, Lbox is the L1 smooth loss indicating the error of matched boxes, and Lclass is the softmax loss for classification.
Step 7:	For predicting challenging pictures, a faster RCNN based on ResNet50V2 is used.
Transfer Learning:	
Step 8:	Replace last predicting layer of the pretrained model with its own predicting layers to implement fine-tuned transfer learning.
Step 9:	Generic features are learnt by the network's initial lower layers from the pretrained Model, and its weights are frozen and not modified during the training.
Step 10:	Task-specific traits are learned at higher layers which can be pre-trained and fine-tuned.
Pre-trained classification:	
Step 11:	By applying pretrained classification model, ResNet50V2, images are classified into face with mask, face with no mask, and face with incorrect mask.
Identity prediction:	
Step 12:	OpenFace is applied to detect the face is with or without mask. Affine transformation is applied to detect the non-mask faces.
Output:	Display the personal information such as identity and name and violation information (such as location, timestamp, camera type, ID, and violation category, e.g., face without mask and face with incorrect mask).

In the proposed model for face mask detection, a simple and user-friendly system brings comfort to users. It uses a web camera as its hardware requirement and processes the video captured. The web camera can be placed where the shop's entrance, hotels, offices, etc., are visible so that a face mask can be easily detected. In the proposed methodology, the video is processed using transfer learning and an efficient deep learning method for detecting the face mask. The proposed solution is applied to the face mask dataset, i.e., MAFA (benchmark dataset), to check the efficiency of the proposed solution. The dataset name is face mask data consisting of 15,000 images with 7500 people wearing masks and 7500 images with people not wearing masks (Samples of the pictures from the dataset can be found in Figure 2, obtained from MAFA https://www.kaggle.com/datasets/revanthrex/mafadataset (accessed on 1 November 2021)).

(**a**) Samples of people wearing masks from the MAFA dataset

(**b**) Samples of people without masks from the MAFA dataset

Figure 2. Face mask dataset, samples for each class from the MAFA dataset.

Learning more features using learning algorithms is difficult due to the face mask dataset's small size and various image complexities. Transfer learning based on deep learning is used to pass knowledge learned from a source task to a related target task. It is also used to train the network more quickly, reliably, and cost-effectively. The proposed work generally consists of preprocessing with an image complexity predictor, pretrained classifier, and identity predictor.

The image is scaled, and the dataset is unbiased in the first step. Then, the image is divided into soft and hard types according to complexity. For predicting the class of soft pictures, the MobileNet-SSD model is used. For predicting challenging images, a faster RCNN based on ResNet50V2 is used. In the second step, transfer learning is applied. The classifier model classifies into three classes: face detection with a correct mask, face detection with an incorrect mask, and face detection with no mask. Personal identification and violation information are then displayed for further action. A full description of the three phases of the planned architecture is provided below.

3.1. Dataset Characteristics

This paper conducted experiments using the medical face mask dataset, i.e., MAFA [56], published by Shiming Ge. The MAFA dataset consists of 35,803 masked faces with a minimum size of 32 × 32. The faces in this dataset have a different orientation and occlusion degree. We selected 15,000 images that contained frontal faces from MAFA. The dataset was divided into three parts for training, validation, and testing with 11,000, 2000, and 2000 images, respectively. Figure 2 shows sample images from the MAFA dataset. The data are presented in Figure 2, adapted from [58].

3.2. Image Prepocessing and Face Detection

Bias denotes a dataset with an unequal number of classes. This bias was balanced, and frames were extracted from the videos and resized to 128 × 128 pixels. Data augmentation is a widely used approach for getting the most out of a data source. In CNN, the initial layers are in charge of extracting generic visual elements such as edges and textures. The subsequent layers look for more specific qualities on the basis of the preceding attributes. This procedure is applied for numerous layers until high-value semantic traits can be detected, such as detecting eyes or noses. Finally, the categorization is carried out using a traditional neural network. Variety of the training set can be obtained from changes made to the photos such as rotations, translations, or zooming.

The transfer learning approach is preferable in the case of limited samples available in the training set. Then, the dataset can be increased to a large size by performing a different arrangement of faces on a template. However, this cannot be meticulously followed in real time. Hence, face detection is achieved by removing the image boundaries with no useful information. For this purpose, an effective approach called rapid object detection with a boosted cascade of simple features is utilized.

OpenCV considers a snapshot of a live video in a given location and converts it into frames. The facial photos are extracted and used to distinguish the person not wearing a mask on their face. Face features are extracted from photos using the ResNet50V2 model, and these features are subsequently learned using many hidden layers. An alarm sound will be played to a person without a mask whenever the model recognizes someone without a mask. The various steps in image augmentation for classification are illustrated in Figure 3. The data are presented in Figure 3, adapted from [58].

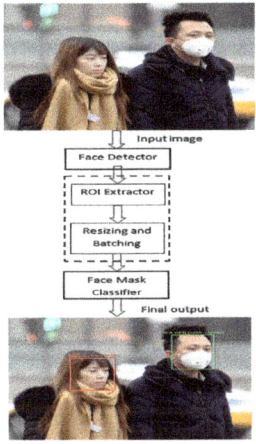

Figure 3. Steps in image augmentation for classification.

3.3. Image Complexity Prediction

The image complexity predictor uses a semi-supervised object classification strategy to split the data into soft or hard images. This strategy is preferred when limited labeled and unlabeled data are present in the dataset. Then, the soft images are processed using a single-stage detector, and hard images are processed using the two-stage detector. Compared with trained images, the predictor optimizes face detection accuracy and computational time while detecting faces using MobileNetV2 and ResNet50V2. A fully connected layer follows two convolutional layers with 512 neurons and a read-out layer with 10 neurons in the curriculum learning network. This helps in learning harder images step by step and is included in class labels, producing high accuracy even for small networks. The algorithm for the image complexity predictor is shown in Algorithm 3.

Algorithm 3. Image complexity predictor	
Input:	Images from the MAFA dataset containing videos
Processes:	Single- and two-stage detectors
Step 1:	Split soft images (very few people in an image) and hard images (group of people in different poses and locations with background).
Step 2:	Apply a single-stage detector to process soft images.
Step 3:	Apply a two-stage detector to process hard images.
Output:	Set of region proposals (R denotes image left position with height and width, and G denotes bounding box around the image)

3.4. Transfer Learning-Based Pretrained Classification Model

Transfer learning was founded on developing learning by transferring information from a previously learned task to a new task. There are two stages in transfer learning. In the initial feature extraction phase, only the classification layers are trained; however, in the second phase of fine-tuning, all layers in the system are retrained. Transfer learning using MobileNetV2, VGG19, ResNet50V2, AlexNet, and InceptionV3 is shown in Figure 4. The data are presented in Figure 4, adapted from [58].

AlexNet has five convolutional layers and three fully connected layers. It employs ReLu, which is much quicker than sigmoid, and adds a dropout layer after each FC layer to reduce overfitting. By substituting large kernel-sized filters (11 and five in the first and second convolutional layers, respectively) with multiple 3×3 kernel-sized filters one after the other, VGG19 outperforms AlexNet. The activations in Inception are sparsely connected, which means that not all 512 output channels are connected to all 512 input channels.

ResNet50V2 was fine-tuned with five additional layers: a 5×5 average pooling layer, a flattening layer, and a dense rectified linear unit (ReLU) layer with 128 neurons and 0.5 dropouts of an output layer consisting of softmax function as the activation function.

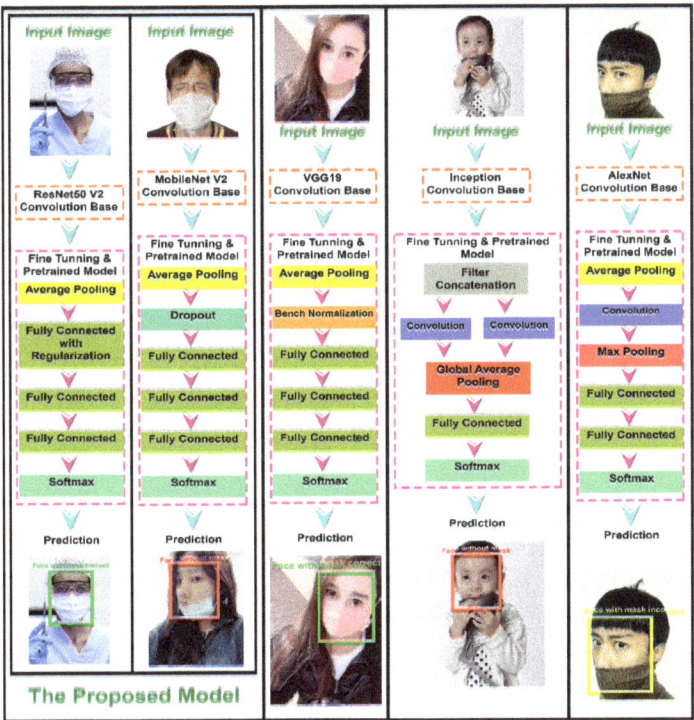

Figure 4. Transfer learning using MobileNetV2, VGG19, ResNet50V2, AlexNet, and InceptionV3.

3.5. Identity Prediction

The identity predictor is applied using OpenFace 0.20 for detecting faces with or without a mask. For processing non-masked faces, an affine transformation is applied, as shown in Figure 5. The data are presented in Figure 3, adapted from [56]. The pair (R, G) represents the region proposal where $R = (Rx, Ry, Rw, Rh)$ represents the pixel coordinates of the center of proposals along with width and height, and $G = (Gx, Gy, Gw, Gh)$ represents coordinates of each ground-truth bounding box. After applying the affine transformation, bounding box regression is applied for moving information from the region proposal (R) to bounding box (G), representing ground truth with no loss of information. Then, a scale-invariant transformation is performed on pixel coordinates of R, and then log space transformation is applied on the R's width and height. $Tx(R)$, $Ty(R)$, $Tw(R)$, and $Th(R)$ represent the corresponding four transformations, and coordinates of the ground-truth box are obtained using Equations (1)–(4).

$$G_x = T_x(R_x) + R_x, \tag{1}$$

$$G_y = T_y(R_y) + R_y, \tag{2}$$

$$G_w = T_w(R_w) + R_w, \tag{3}$$

$$G_h = T_h(R_h) + R_h, \tag{4}$$

where $f_6(R)$ represents the linear function of $Pool_6$ feature of R. The equation for $T_i(R)$ is shown in Equation (5).

$$T_i(R) = w_i f_6(R), \tag{5}$$

where w_i represents the weight learned by optimizing the regression, as given by Equation (6).

$$w_i = \sum_{n \in R} (t_i^n - \hat{w} f_6(R^n))^2 + \lambda |\hat{w}_i|^2,$$ (6)

where t_i represents the regression target which is related to coordinates, width, and height of region proposal pair (R, G) as denoted in Equations (7)–(10), respectively.

$$t_x = \frac{G_x - R_x}{R_w}.$$ (7)

$$t_y = \frac{G_y - R_y}{R_h}.$$ (8)

$$t_w = \log\left(\frac{G_x}{R_w}\right).$$ (9)

$$t_h = \log\left(\frac{G_h}{R_h}\right).$$ (10)

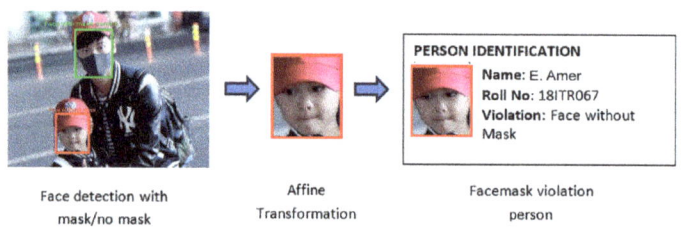

Figure 5. Localizing a face without a mask using affine transformation.

3.6. Loss Function and Optimization

In classification theory, the loss function and objective function transfer estimated distributions onto true distributions. This function's output should be minimized using an optimization method. Classification and regression losses are used in the single-shot detector. The confidence level in the predictions of each bounding box produced by the network is measured by the classification loss. Categorical cross-entropy is used to calculate this loss, as given by Equation (11).

$$Loss = \sum t(x) \log(e(x)),$$ (11)

where $t(x)$ and $e(x)$ represent true and estimated distributions over categorical variables, respectively. The regression loss is the difference between the network's predicted bounding boxes and the ground-truth bounding box.

3.7. Control of Overfitting

Even though data augmentation and an unbiased dataset are used, the model must be generalized to fit any pattern in the input and respond with appropriate results. When the time to train the model increases, the model becomes overfitted. To reduce the overfitting problem to a negligible value, the feature selection process is performed with a better optimizer.

3.8. Evaluation Parameters

The standard evaluation parameters such as accuracy, recall (sensitivity), precision, F-measure, and specificity are calculated on the basis of the number of true positives (TP), the number of true negatives (TN), the number of false negatives (FN), and the number of false positives (FP) as given in Equations (12)–(16).

$$\text{Accuracy} = \frac{(TN + TP)}{(TN + TP + FN + FP)}. \tag{12}$$

$$\text{Precision} = \frac{TP}{(TP + FP)}. \tag{13}$$

$$\text{Recall} = \frac{TP}{(TP + FN)}. \tag{14}$$

$$F - \text{measure} = \frac{(\mathbf{2} \times \text{Precision} \times \text{Recall})}{(\text{Precision} + \text{Recall})}. \tag{15}$$

$$\text{Specificity} = \frac{TN}{(TN + FP)}. \tag{16}$$

The TP, TN, FN, and FP values are calculated using the confusion matrix in Table 1, and the corresponding formulas are given below.

Table 1. Confusion matrix.

		Predicted Values		
		Face Wearing Mask Correctly	Face Wearing Mask Incorrectly	Face Wearing No Mask
Actual values	Face wearing mask correctly	a	b	c
	Face wearing mask incorrectly	d	e	f
	Face wearing no mask	g	h	i

- Face wearing mask correctly:

$$TP = a.$$

$$FN = b + c.$$

$$FP = d + g.$$

$$TN = e + f + h + i.$$

- Face wearing mask incorrectly:

$$TP = e.$$

$$FN = d + f.$$

$$FP = b + h.$$

$$FP = b + h.$$

- Face wearing no mask:

$$TP = i.$$

$$FN = g + h.$$

$$FP = c + f.$$

$$TN = a + b + d + e.$$

Inference time represents the time spent reading from the input image to the final class prediction.

The number of trainable and nontrainable parameters present in different layers affects the capability of prediction, the complexity of the model, and the amount of memory required. The confusion matrix values combining all comparison models are depicted in Table 2.

Table 2. Confusion matrix results for all comparison models.

		Predicted Value		
		face wearing mask correctly	face wearing mask incorrectly	face wearing no mask
Actual Values	face wearing mask correctly	0.94	0.058	0.002
	face wearing mask incorrectly	0.079	0.9	0.021
	face wearing no mask	0.005	0.00497	0.99

4. Results and Discussion

The proposed algorithm was implemented in Python, and the integrated development environment was PyCharm, a popular Python IDE created by JetBrains to conduct Python language programming. The experiment was set up by loading different pretrained models using the Charm package (https://github.com/JetBrains/awesome-pycharm (accessed on 11 July 2022)) run on an Intel(R) Core i7 2.80 GHz CPU with 8 GB RAM and the Windows 10 operating system. The proposed system uses MaskedFace-Net (MFN) and Flickr-Faces-HQ Dataset (FFHQ) with 67,193 pictures of faces with a correct mask, 66,899 pictures of a face with an incorrect mask, and 66,535 pictures of a face with no mask. Figure 6a–d exhibit the accuracy of face mask detection for various models.

After numerous experiments, it was discovered that translation and zoom operations did not affect the results. Finally, the training dataset was rotated and flipped horizontally randomly in the range of $[-5°, +5°]$.

The proposed technique with a multilayer convolutional network for recognizing objects from color images achieves larger mAP, more frames to increase speed, and acceptable accuracy. The training accuracy increases sharply and becomes stable at epoch 2 due to a balanced dataset in ResNet50V2, as depicted in Figure 6a. The training and validation accuracy differs at the maximum by 25% at epoch 2.5 in VGG19, as shown in Figure 6b. The training and validation accuracy differs at the initial epoch and becomes stable at epoch 1 in InceptionV3, as shown in Figure 6c. The training and validation accuracy is the same at every epoch of the execution in MobileNetV2, as shown in Figure 6d.

The accuracy of the ResNet50V2 model was higher when compared to other models, namely, VGG19, MobileNetV2, and InceptionV3, by 2.92, 0.44, and 3.38, and by 9.49, 1.31, and 4.9 when using the biased dataset in both training and validation phases, respectively, as depicted in Figure 7.

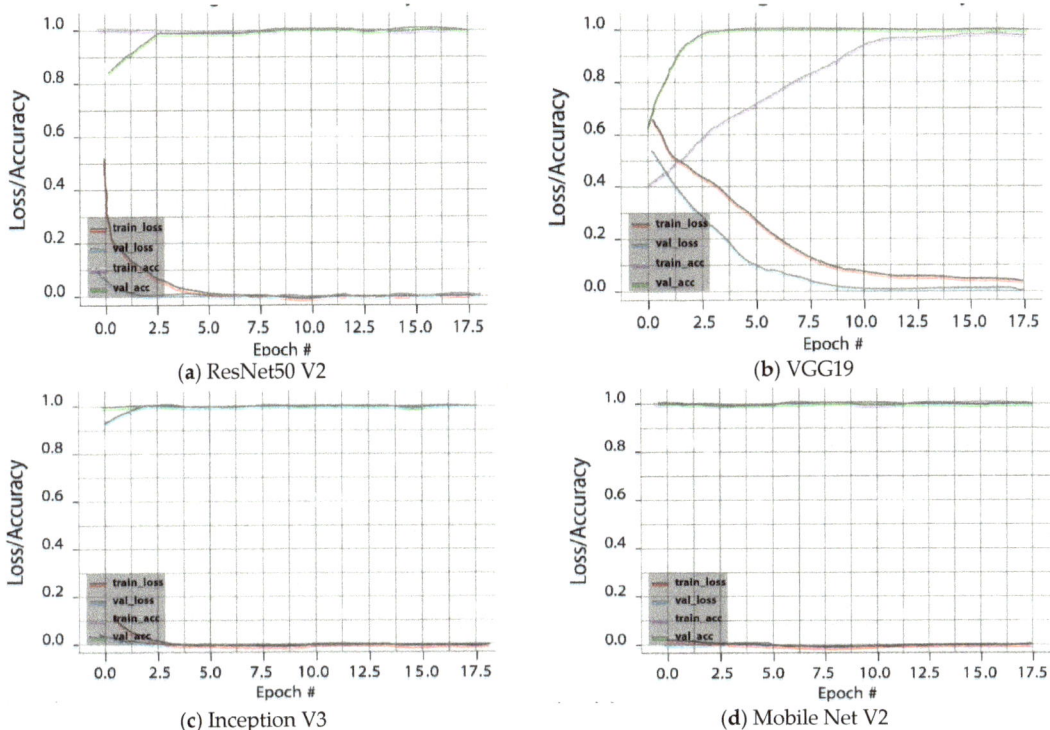

Figure 6. Accuracy and loss of face mask detection in different models.

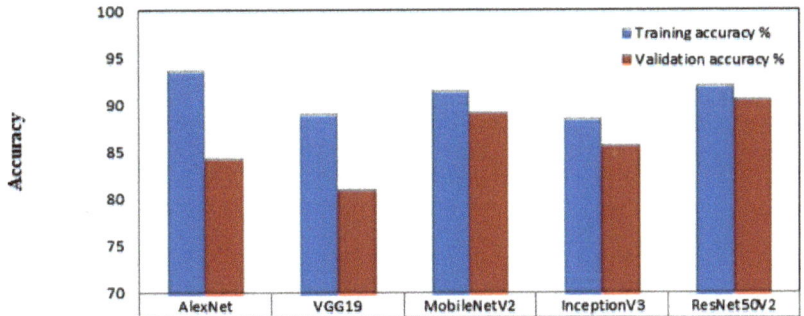

Figure 7. Training and validation accuracy in face mask detection.

The input picture size was 840 × 840 with a batch size of 2 in strong ResNet50V2 backbone, while the input image size is 640 × 640 with a batch size of 32 in light MobileNetV2backbone. Although multiple network components can improve detection performance, the ResNet50V2 backbone achieved the greatest improvement in several parameters with the balanced dataset. ResNet50V2 showed an improvement in parameters precision, recall, F-measure, accuracy, and specificity by 1.22, 3.21, 0.43, and 2.22 and by 0.17, 2.13, 0.16, and 1.08, respectively when compared to AlexNet and MobileNetV2 (see Figure 8).

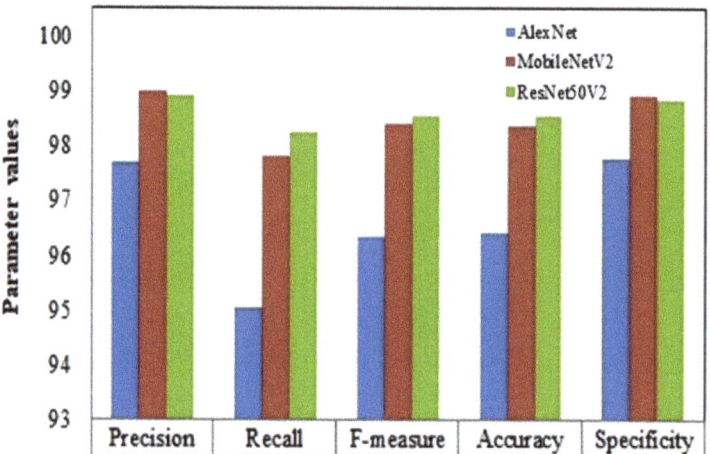

Figure 8. Performance of various parameters in the face mask detection.

The total number of trainable and nontrainable parameters in ResNet50V2 was 24 million; hence, high computation cost was incurred, whereas, in MobileNetV2, VGG19, and InceptionV3, is the numbers were 2.4 million, 20 million, and 22 million, respectively. MobileNetV2 uses Dropout in the fully connected network, such that the number of parameters in the network is greatly reduced compared to ResNet50V2. InceptionV3 uses filter concatenation in the convolution layer rather than the connected layer to reduce the number of parameters. As VGG19 uses batch normalization in the connected layer, the number of parameters is reduced. MobileNetV2 extracts features using depth-wise convolutions and adjusts channel numbers using channel-wise convolutions; hence, the computational cost of MobileNetV2 is substantially lower than networks utilizing traditional convolutions. Thus, MobileNetV2 performs well in real-time object detection using surveillance devices with less memory consumption.

ResNet50V2 achieved 97% when averaging precision, recall, and F1-score values as the bias was removed among the three classes of facemask detection. Compared to other models, MobileNetV2, InceptionV3, and VGG19, ResNet50V2 led to improvements by 0.5%, 6.5%, and 3%, as shown in Table 3. ResNet50V2's inference time was reduced by 4 ms, while InceptionV3, VGG19, and MobileNetV2's inference times were reduced by 2 ms. The integrated system used MobileNet-SSD for face detection and ResNet50V2 as the backbone for facemask classification; hence, high accuracy with decreased inference time was obtained. A deep neural network is costly since it demands substantial computing power and requires time to train huge datasets. Deep-learning-based transfer learning is utilized to pretrain the ResNet50V2 network faster and cost-effectively by deleting the batch normalization layer in the network at test time. As faster R-CNN uses RPN, it is more efficient in generating ROI and runs at 10 ms per image. The parameter values for different models are denoted in Table 3.

Figure 9a–d show various screenshots illustrating facemask detection with three-class outputs.

The four pretrained models, ResNet50V2, MobileNetV2, InceptionV3, and VGG19, were compared for performance analysis. ResNet50V2 was the optimal model in terms of inference time, error rate, detection speed, and memory usage among the compared models. Figure 9 shows screenshots of three-class face mask detection. The data are presented in Figure 9, adapted from [58].

Table 3. Different models and their parameter values.

Models	Total Number of Trainable and Nontrainable Parameters	Precision	Recall	F1-score	Inference Time (ms)	Training Accuracy	Validation Accuracy
MobileNetV2	2,422,339	0.97	0.96	0.97	15	91.49	89.18
VGG19	20,090,435	0.94	0.94	0.94	11	89.01	81
InceptionV3	22,065,443	0.91	0.9	0.91	9	88.55	85.59
ResNet50V2	**23,827,459**	**0.97**	**0.97**	**0.97**	**7**	**91.93**	**90.49**

(**a**) Face with correct and incorrect mask detection (**b**) Face with and without mask detection in two-person group

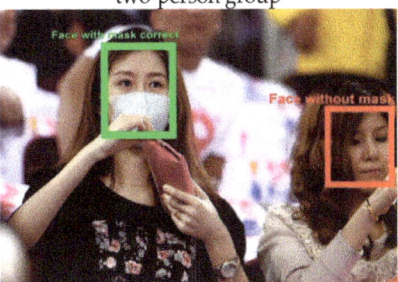

(**c**) Face with and without mask detection in three-person group (**d**) Face with and without mask detection in three-person group

Figure 9. Screenshots of three-class face mask detection.

5. Comparison with Related Works and Discussion

Developing a system that can be easily embedded in a device that can be utilized in public spaces to aid in the prevention of COVID-19 transmission requires more accurate face detection, precise localization of the individual's identity, and avoidance of overfitting. To further demonstrate the quality of the proposed model, we compared AlexNet, MobileNet, and YOLO baseline models in terms of accuracy, precision, and recall for detecting human images with and without a mask. Table 4 summarizes the outcomes of this comparison, demonstrating that the proposed system outperformed other models in terms of accuracy, precision, and recall. Experiments demonstrated that the proposed system can accurately detect faces and masks while consuming less inference time and memory than previously developed methods. To address the data imbalance issue identified in the previously published dataset, efforts were made to create an entirely new, unbiased dataset that is well suited for mask detection tasks related to COVID-19, among other applications.

Table 4. Performance comparison of different methods in terms of accuracy (AC) and average precision (ap).

Reference	Methodology	Classification	Detection	Result
(Ejaz et al., 2019) [59]	PCA	Yes	No	AC = 70%
(Ud Din et al., 2020) [60]	GAN	Yes	Yes	-
Proposed	Improved ResNetV2	Yes	Yes	AC = 91.93% AP = 97% Recall = 97% F-Score = 97%

6. Improvement in Accuracy Using MAFA Dataset in the Proposed Method

- In the original imbalanced MAFA dataset, random oversampling was applied to obtain the balanced dataset, and image augmentation was also performed to improve the accuracy.
- In a large dataset ranging from simple to complex images, transfer learning was applied to pretrain the parameters, especially for small objects, which also improved the accuracy of the model.
- In the fine-tuning phase of transfer learning, all the layers in the system were pretrained. Accordingly, the optimum value for each parameter was obtained, which was used to improve the accuracy of the model.
- Using MobileNetV2 for face detection and ResNet50V2 for mask detection improved the accuracy of the system.
- Two-stage detection for classifying images according to groups, distant views, and occlusions also improved the accuracy but at the cost of computational time.
- The batch normalization layer in ResNet50V2 for pretraining the parameters and L2 normalization to accurately predict the image complexity were used to improve the accuracy of the system.

7. Conclusions

The proposed work presented a deep-learning-based solution for identifying masks over faces in public locations to reduce coronavirus community spread. The ensemble approach aids in reaching high accuracy, but it also significantly improves detection speed. Furthermore, transfer learning on pretrained models and rigorous testing on an unbiased dataset resulted in a reliable and low-cost solution. The findings support this application's viability in real-world scenarios, thus helping to prevent pandemic spread. Compared with existing approaches, the proposed method achieved better performance in terms of accuracy, specificity, precision, recall, and F-measure in three-class outputs. A proper tradeoff was maintained between several required parameters and inference time using different models. To improve the proposed method's performance, different datasets with different sizes can be used for medical face masking detection. Furthermore, data can be pretrained using new deep learning methods, which can result in a huge number of features in the datasets. Hence, to improve accuracy, we can apply a new metaheuristic algorithm for solving the image classification problem based on feature selection. Moreover, to improve the accuracy of the new metaheuristic algorithm, we can use hybrid algorithms or a different operator to enhance the exploitation stage, such as random opposition-based learning (ROBL) and opposition-based learning (OBL) to prevent local optima and accelerate the convergence. Future work can be expanded to include other mask-wearing issues to improve accuracy. The developed model can be implemented using surveillance devices for biometric applications, especially in polluted industries with facial landmark detection and face masks.

Author Contributions: Conceptualization, M.A.S.A., A.S., S.M., C.V., H.P., M.K., R.O. and D.S.A.E.; Data curation M.A.S.A., A.S., S.M., C.V., H.P., M.K., R.O. and D.S.A.E.; Formal analysis, M.A.S.A.,

A.S., S.M., C.V., H.P., M.K., R.O. and D.S.A.E.; Funding, M.A.S.A. acquisition; Methodology, M.A.S.A., A.S., S.M., C.V., Hitesh Panchal Investigation, M.K., R.O. and D.S.A.E.; Supervision; M.A.S.A., A.S., S.M., C.V., H.P., M.K., R.O. and D.S.A.E.; Software, M.A.S.A., A.S., S.M., C.V., H.P., M.K., R.O. and D.S.A.E.; Validation, M.A.S.A., A.S., S.M., C.V., H.P., M.K., R.O. and D.S.A.E.; Writing—original draft; Writing—review & editing M.A.S.A., A.S., S.M., C.V., H.P., M.K., R.O. and D.S.A.E. All authors have read and agreed to the published version of the manuscript.

Funding: This research was funded by the Deanship of Scientific Research, King Faisal University, grant number GRANT207, and the APC was funded by the Deanship of Scientific Research, King Faisal University.

Acknowledgments: This work was supported by the Deanship of Scientific Research, Vice Presidency for Graduate Studies and Scientific Research, King Faisal University, Saudi Arabia (Project No. GRANT207).

Conflicts of Interest: The authors declare no conflict of interest.

Abbreviation

CNN	Convolutional neural network
ResNet	Residual network
ROI	Region of interest
YOLO	You only look once
R-CNN	Region-based convolutional neural network
ROS	Random oversampling
IOU	Intersection over union
MFN	MaskedFace-Net
FFHQ	Flickr-Faces-HQ Dataset
ROBL	Random opposition-based learning
OBL	Opposition-based learning

References

1. Howard, J.; Huang, A.; Li, Z.; Tufekci, Z.; Zdimal, V.; van der Westhuizen, H.-M.; von Delft, A.; Price, A.; Fridman, L.; Tang, L.-H.; et al. An evidence review of face masks against COVID-19. *Proc. Natl. Acad. Sci. USA* **2021**, *118*, e2014564118. [CrossRef] [PubMed]
2. Godoy, L.R.G.; Jones, A.E.; Anderson, T.N.; Fisher, C.L.; Seeley, K.M.; Beeson, E.A.; Zane, H.K.; Peterson, J.W.; Sullivan, P.D. Facial protection for healthcare workers during pandemics: A scoping review. *BMJ Glob. Health* **2020**, *5*, e002553. [CrossRef] [PubMed]
3. Nanni, L.; Ghidoni, S.; Brahnam, S. Handcrafted vs. non-handcrafted features for computer vision classification. *Pattern Recognit.* **2017**, *71*, 158–172. [CrossRef]
4. Erhan, D.; Szegedy, C.; Toshev, A.; Anguelov, D. Scalable Object Detection using Deep Neural Networks. In Proceedings of the IEEE Conference on Computer Vision and Pattern Recognition, Columbus, OH, USA, 23–28 June 2014; pp. 2147–2154.
5. Sethi, S.; Kathuria, M.; Kaushik, T. Face mask detection using deep learning: An approach to reduce risk of Coronavirus spread. *J. Biomed. Inform.* **2021**, *120*, 103848. [CrossRef]
6. Sen, S.; Sawant, K. Face mask detection for COVID-19 pandemic using pytorch in deep learning. *IOP Conf. Ser. Mater. Sci. Eng.* **2021**, *1070*, 012061. [CrossRef]
7. Balaji, S.; Balamurugan, B.; Kumar, T.A.; Rajmohan, R.; Kumar, P.P. A Brief Survey on AI Based Face Mask Detection System for Public Places. *Ir. Interdiscip. J. Sci. Res.* **2021**, *5*, 108–117.
8. Cheng, G.; Li, S.; Zhang, Y.; Zhou, R. A Mask Detection System Based on Yolov3-Tiny. *Front. Soc. Sci. Technol.* **2020**, *2*, 33–41.
9. Sakshi, S.; Gupta, A.K.; Yadav, S.S.; Kumar, U. Face Mask Detection System using CNN. In Proceedings of the 2021 IEEE International Conference on Advanced Computing and Innovative Technologies in Engineering (ICACITE), Greater Noida, India, 4–5 March 2021; pp. 212–216.
10. Jiang, M.; Fan, X.; Yan, H. RetinaMask: A Face Mask Detector. 2020. Available online: http://arxiv.org/abs/2005.03950 (accessed on 5 April 2021).
11. Redmon, J.; Divvala, S.; Girshick, R.; Farhadi, A. You only look once: Unified, real-time object detection. In Proceedings of the IEEE Computer Society Conference on Computer Vision and Pattern Recognition, Las Vegas, NV, USA, 27–30 June 2016; Volume 2016, pp. 779–788.
12. Kumar, Z.; Zhang, J.; Lyu, H. Object detection in real time based on improved single shot multi-box detector algorithm. *EURASIP J. Wirel. Commun. Netw.* **2020**, *1*, 1–18. [CrossRef]
13. Morera, Á.; Sánchez, Á.; Moreno, A.B.; Sappa, Á.D.; Vélez, J.F. SSD vs. YOLO for Detection of Outdoor Urban Advertising Panels under Multiple Variabilities. *Sensors* **2020**, *20*, 4587. [CrossRef]

14. Girshick, R.; Donahue, J.; Darrell, T.; Malik, J. Region-Based Convolutional Networks for Accurate Object Detection and Segmentation. *IEEE Trans. Pattern Anal. Mach. Intell.* **2015**, *38*, 142–158. [CrossRef]
15. He, K.; Zhang, X.; Ren, S.; Sun, J. Spatial Pyramid Pooling in Deep Convolutional Networks for Visual Recognition. *IEEE Trans. Pattern Anal. Mach. Intell.* **2015**, *37*, 1904–1916. [CrossRef] [PubMed]
16. Girshick, R. Fast R-CNN. In Proceedings of the IEEE International Conference on Computer Vision (ICCV), Santiago, Chile, 7–13 December 2015; pp. 1440–1448.
17. Nguyen, N.-D.; Do, T.; Ngo, T.D.; Le, D.-D. An Evaluation of Deep Learning Methods for Small Object Detection. *J. Electr. Comput. Eng.* **2020**, *2020*, 3189691. [CrossRef]
18. Fu, C.-Y.; Liu, W.; Ranga, A.; Tyagi, A.; Berg, A.C. DSSD: Deconvolutional Single Shot Detector. *arXiv* **2017**, arXiv:1701.06659.
19. Dvornik, N.; Shmelkov, K.; Mairal, J.; Schmid, C. BlitzNet: A Real-Time Deep Network for Scene Understanding. In Proceedings of the IEEE International Conference on Computer Vision, Venice, Italy, 22–29 October 2017.
20. Liang, Z.; Shao, J.; Zhang, D.; Gao, L. Small Object Detection Using Deep Feature Pyramid Networks. In *Lecture Notes in Computer Science*; Springer: Berlin, Germany, 2018; Volume 11166, pp. 554–564. [CrossRef]
21. He, K.; Gkioxari, G.; Dollar, P.; Girshick, R. Mask R-CNN. In Proceedings of the IEEE International Conference on Computer Vision, Venice, Italy, 22–29 October 2017; pp. 2980–2988.
22. Roy, B.; Nandy, S.; Ghosh, D.; Dutta, D.; Biswas, P.; Das, T. MOXA: A Deep Learning Based Unmanned Approach For Real-Time Monitoring of People Wearing Medical Masks. *Trans. Indian Natl. Acad. Eng.* **2020**, *5*, 509–518. [CrossRef]
23. Ionescu, R.T.; Alexe, B.; Leordeanu, M.; Popescu, M.; Papadopoulos, D.P.; Ferrari, V. How hard can it be? Estimating the difficulty of visual search in an image. In Proceedings of the IEEE Conference on Computer Vision and Pattern Recognition, Las Vegas, NV, USA, 27–30 June 2016; pp. 2157–2166.
24. Soviany, P.; Ionescu, R.T. Optimizing the Trade-Off between Single-Stage and Two-Stage Deep Object Detectors using Image Difficulty Prediction. In Proceedings of the 2018 20th International Symposium on Symbolic and Numeric Algorithms for Scientific Computing (SYNASC), Timisoara, Romania, 20–23 September 2018. [CrossRef]
25. Devi Priya, R.; Sivaraj, R.; Anitha, N.; Devisurya, V. Forward feature extraction from imbalanced microarray datasets using wrapper based incremental genetic algorithm. *Int. J. Bio-Inspired Comput.* **2020**, *16*, 171–180. [CrossRef]
26. Devi Priya, R.; Sivaraj, R.; Anitha, N.; Rajadevi, R.; Devisurya, V. Variable population sized PSO for highly imbalanced dataset classification. *Comput. Intell.* **2021**, *37*, 873–890.
27. Chen, K. MMDetection: Open MMLab Detection Toolbox and Benchmark. *arXiv* **2019**, arXiv:1906.07155.
28. Goyal, H.; Sidana, K.; Singh, C. A real time face mask detection system using convolutional neural network. *Multimed. Tools Appl.* **2022**, *81*, 14999–15015. [CrossRef]
29. Farman, H.; Khan, T.; Khan, Z.; Habib, S.; Islam, M.; Ammar, A. Real-Time Face Mask Detection to Ensure COVID-19 Precautionary Measures in the Developing Countries. *Appl. Sci.* **2022**, *12*, 3879. [CrossRef]
30. Mbunge, E.; Simelane, S.; Fashoto, S.G.; Akinnuwesi, B.; Metfula, A.S. Application of deep learning and machine learning models to detect COVID-19 face masks—A review. *Sustain. Oper. Comput.* **2021**, *2*, 235–245. [CrossRef]
31. Tomás, J.; Rego, A.; Viciano-Tudela, S.; Lloret, J. Incorrect Facemask-Wearing Detection Using Convolutional Neural Networks with Transfer Learning. *Healthcare* **2021**, *9*, 1050. [CrossRef] [PubMed]
32. Jiang, X.; Gao, T.; Zhu, Z.; Zhao, Y. Real-Time Face Mask Detection Method Based on YOLOv3. *Electronics* **2021**, *10*, 837. [CrossRef]
33. Hussain, S.; Yu, Y.; Ayoub, M.; Khan, A.; Rehman, R.; Wahid, J.; Hou, W. IoT and Deep Learning Based Approach for Rapid Screening and Face Mask Detection for Infection Spread Control of COVID-19. *Appl. Sci.* **2021**, *11*, 3495. [CrossRef]
34. Awan, M.J.; Bilal, M.H.; Yasin, A.; Nobanee, H.; Khan, N.S.; Zain, A.M. Detection of COVID-19 in Chest X-ray Images: A Big Data Enabled Deep Learning Approach. *Int. J. Environ. Res. Public Health* **2021**, *18*, 10147. [CrossRef]
35. Ardabili, S.; Mosavi, A.; Várkonyi-Kóczy, A.R. Systematic review of deep learning and machine learning models in biofuels research. In *Engineering for Sustainable Future*; Springer: Cham, Switzerland, 2020; pp. 19–32. [CrossRef]
36. Abdelminaam, D.S.; Ismail, F.H.; Taha, M.; Taha, A.; Houssein, E.H.; Nabil, A. Coaid-deep: An optimized intelligent framework for automated detecting COVID-19 misleading information on Twitter. *IEEE Access* **2021**, *9*, 27840–27867. [CrossRef] [PubMed]
37. Emadi, M.; Taghizadeh-Mehrjardi, R.; Cherati, A.; Danesh, M.; Mosavi, A.; Scholten, T. Predicting and Mapping of Soil Organic Carbon Using Machine Learning Algorithms in Northern Iran. *Remote Sens.* **2020**, *12*, 2234. [CrossRef]
38. Salama AbdELminaam, D.; Almansori, A.M.; Taha, M.; Badr, E. A deep facial recognition system using intelligent computational algorithms. *PLoS ONE* **2020**, *15*, e0242269. [CrossRef]
39. Mahmoudi, M.R.; Heydari, M.H.; Qasem, S.N.; Mosavi, A.; Band, S.S. Principal component analysis to study the relations between the spread rates of COVID-19 in high risks countries. *Alex. Eng. J.* **2020**, *60*, 457–464. [CrossRef]
40. Ardabili, S.; Mosavi, A.; Várkonyi-Kóczy, A.R. Advances in Machine Learning Modeling Reviewing Hybrid and Ensemble Methods. In *Engineering for Sustainable Future*; Springer: Cham, Switzerland, 2020; pp. 215–217. [CrossRef]
41. AbdElminaam, D.S.; ElMasry, N.; Talaat, Y.; Adel, M.; Hisham, A.; Atef, K.; Mohamed, A.; Akram, M. HR-Chat bot: Designing and Building Effective Interview Chat-bots for Fake CV Detection. In Proceedings of the 2021 International Mobile, Intelligent, and Ubiquitous Computing Conference (MIUCC), Cairo, Egypt, 26–27 May 2021; pp. 403–408. [CrossRef]
42. Rezakazemi, M.; Mosavi, A.; Shirazian, S. ANFIS pattern for molecular membranes separation optimization. *J. Mol. Liq.* **2018**, *274*, 470–476. [CrossRef]

43. Torabi, M.; Hashemi, S.; Saybani, M.R.; Shamshirband, S.; Mosavi, A. A Hybrid clustering and classification technique for forecasting short-term energy consumption. *Environ. Prog. Sustain. Energy* **2018**, *38*, 66–76. [CrossRef]
44. Ardabili, S.; Abdolalizadeh, L.; Mako, C.; Torok, B.; Mosavi, A. Systematic Review of Deep Learning and Machine Learning for Building Energy. *Front. Energy Res.* **2022**, *10*, 786027. [CrossRef]
45. Houssein, E.H.; Hassaballah, M.; Ibrahim, I.E.; AbdElminaam, D.S.; Wazery, Y.M. An automatic arrhythmia classification model based on improved Marine Predators Algorithm and Convolutions Neural Networks. *Expert Syst. Appl.* **2021**, *187*, 115936. [CrossRef]
46. Deb, S.; Abdelminaam, D.S.; Said, M.; Houssein, E.H. Recent Methodology-Based Gradient-Based Optimizer for Economic Load Dispatch Problem. *IEEE Access* **2021**, *9*, 44322–44338. [CrossRef]
47. Elminaam, D.S.A.; Neggaz, N.; Ahmed, I.A.; Abouelyazed, A.E.S. Swarming Behavior of Harris Hawks Optimizer for Arabic Opinion Mining. *Comput. Mater. Contin.* **2021**, *69*, 4129–4149. [CrossRef]
48. Band, S.S.; Ardabili, S.; Sookhak, M.; Chronopoulos, A.T.; Elnaffar, S.; Moslehpour, M.; Csaba, M.; Torok, B.; Pai, H.-T.; Mosavi, A. When Smart Cities Get Smarter via Machine Learning: An In-Depth Literature Review. *IEEE Access* **2022**, *10*, 60985–61015. [CrossRef]
49. Mohammadzadeh, S.D.; Kazemi, S.-F.; Mosavi, A.; Nasseralshariati, E.; Tah, J.H. Prediction of compression index of fine-grained soils using a gene expression programming model. *Infrastructures* **2019**, *4*, 26. [CrossRef]
50. Deb, S.; Houssein, E.H.; Said, M.; Abdelminaam, D.S. Performance of Turbulent Flow of Water Optimization on Economic Load Dispatch Problem. *IEEE Access* **2021**, *9*, 77882–77893. [CrossRef]
51. Abdul-Minaam, D.S.; Al-Mutairi, W.M.E.S.; Awad, M.A.; El-Ashmawi, W.H. An Adaptive Fitness-Dependent Optimizer for the One-Dimensional Bin Packing Problem. *IEEE Access* **2020**, *8*, 97959–97974. [CrossRef]
52. Mosavi, A.; Golshan, M.; Janizadeh, S.; Choubin, B.; Melesse, A.M.; Dineva, A.A. Ensemble models of GLM, FDA, MARS, and RF for flood and erosion susceptibility mapping: A priority assessment of sub-basins. *Geocarto Int.* **2020**, 2541–2560. [CrossRef]
53. Mercaldo, F.; Santone, A. Transfer learning for mobile real-time face mask detection and localization. *J. Am. Med. Inform. Assoc.* **2021**, *28*, 1548–1554. [CrossRef]
54. Teboulbi, S.; Messaoud, S.; Hajjaji, M.A.; Mtibaa, A. Real-Time Implementation of AI-Based Face Mask Detection and Social Distancing Measuring System for COVID-19 Prevention. *Sci. Program.* **2021**, *2021*, 8340779. [CrossRef]
55. Hussain, D.; Ismail, M.; Hussain, I.; Alroobaea, R.; Hussain, S.; Ullah, S.S. Face Mask Detection Using Deep Convolutional Neural Network and MobileNetV2-Based Transfer Learning. *Wirel. Commun. Mob. Comput.* **2022**, *2022*, 1536318. [CrossRef]
56. Shaban, H.; Houssein, E.H.; Pérez-Cisneros, M.; Oliva, D.; Hassan, A.Y.; Ismaeel, A.A.; AbdElminaam, D.S.; Deb, S.; Said, M. Identification of parameters in photovoltaic models through a runge kutta optimizer. *Mathematics* **2021**, *9*, 2313. [CrossRef]
57. Houssein, E.H.; Abdelminaam, D.S.; Hassan, H.N.; Al-Sayed, M.M.; Nabil, E. A hybrid barnacles mating optimizer algorithm with support vector machines for gene selection of microarray cancer classification. *IEEE Access* **2021**, *9*, 64895–64905. [CrossRef]
58. Vibhuti; Jindal, N.; Singh, H.; Rana, P.S. Face mask detection in COVID-19: A strategic review. *Multimedia Tools Appl.* **2022**, 1–30. [CrossRef] [PubMed]
59. Ejaz, M.S.; Islam, M.R.; Sifatullah, M.; Sarker, A. Implementation of principal component analysis on masked and non-masked face recognition. In Proceedings of the 2019 1st International Conference on Advances in Science, Engineering and Robotics Technology (ICASERT), Dhaka, Bangladesh, 3–5 May 2019; pp. 1–5.
60. Din, N.U.; Javed, K.; Bae, S.; Yi, J. A Novel GAN-Based Network for Unmasking of Masked Face. *IEEE Access* **2020**, *8*, 44276–44287. [CrossRef]

 *electronics*

Article

A Survey of Trajectory Planning Techniques for Autonomous Systems

Imran Mir [1,2,*], **Faiza Gul** [3], **Suleman Mir** [4], **Mansoor Ahmed Khan** [1], **Nasir Saeed** [5], **Laith Abualigah** [6,7], **Belal Abuhaija** [8,*] and **Amir H. Gandomi** [9,*]

1   School of Avionics & Electrical Engineering, College of Aeronautical Engineering, National University of Sciences and Technology (NUST), Islamabad 44000, Pakistan
2   Department of Avionics Engineering, Air University, Aerospace & Aviation Campus Kamra, Islamabad 43570, Pakistan
3   Department of Electrical Engineering, Air University, Aerospace & Aviation Campus Kamra, Islamabad 43600, Pakistan
4   Electrical Department, Fast-National University of Computer & Emerging Sciences, Peshawar 25124, Pakistan
5   Department of Electrical and Communication Engineering, United Arab Emirates University (UAEU), Al Ain 15551, United Arab Emirates
6   Hourani Center for Applied Scientific Research, Al-Ahliyya Amman University, Amman 11831, Jordan
7   Faculty of Information Technology, Middle East University, Amman 11831, Jordan
8   Department of Computer Science, Wenzhou-Kean University, Wenzhou 325015, China
9   Faculty of Engineering and Information Technology, University of Technology Sydney, Ultimo, NSW 2007, Australia
*   Correspondence: imran.mir@aack.au.edu.pk (I.M.); babuhaij@kean.edu (B.A.); gandomi@uts.edu.au (A.H.G.)

Citation: Mir, I.; Gul, F.; Mir, S.; Khan, M.A.; Saeed, N.; Abualigah, L.; Abuhaija, B.; Gandomi, A.H. A Survey of Trajectory Planning Techniques for Autonomous Systems. *Electronics* **2022**, *11*, 2801. https://doi.org/10.3390/electronics11182801

Academic Editor: Mahmut Reyhanoglu

Received: 28 June 2022
Accepted: 29 August 2022
Published: 6 September 2022

Publisher's Note: MDPI stays neutral with regard to jurisdictional claims in published maps and institutional affiliations.

Abstract: This work offers an overview of the effective communication techniques for space exploration of ground, aerial, and underwater vehicles. We not only comprehensively summarize the trajectory planning, space exploration, optimization, and other challenges encountered but also present the possible directions for future work. Because a detailed study like this is uncommon in the literature, an attempt has been made to fill the gap for readers interested in path planning. This paper also includes optimization strategies that can be used to implement terrestrial, underwater, and airborne applications. This study addresses numerical, bio-inspired, and hybrid methodologies for each dimension described. Throughout this study, we endeavored to establish a centralized platform in which a wealth of research on autonomous vehicles (on the land and their trajectory optimizations), airborne vehicles, and underwater vehicles, is published.

Keywords: aerial vehicle; ground robotics; hybridization; exploration; trajectory planning

1. Introduction

The significance of ground autonomous vehicles began with the DARPA (Defense Advanced Research Projects Agency) urban challenge in 2007 [1,2]; this concept later extended to the development of aerial vehicles. Different concepts were also applied to flight dynamics techniques to improve flight stability. Optimization algorithms for the path findings of ground robotics [3–7] and aerial vehicles [8–12] include numerous applications. Since the 1970s, path planning has received a lot of attention, and it has been used to address issues in a variety of sectors, from simple geographical route planning to selecting an acceptable action sequence to achieve a certain objective. Path planning can be employed in fully-known or partially-known surroundings, as well as in completely new situations, where data from system-mounted sensors are used to update environmental maps and instruct the robot/planned AV's movements.

To keep the robot moving from the start state to the goal location through various intermediate stages, a proper trajectory is constructed as a series of actions. Every choice made by path planning algorithms is determined by the information that is currently accessible, as well as by other factors, such as the Euclidean distance computation's calculation of the shortest distance to the target point (i.e., certain objectives are required to be fulfilled). In terms of optimization, the best path must travel the fewest distances, be free of obstacles and collisions, and take the least amount of time to arrive at the desired state.

In the last decade, multiple path planning methods have been formulated for land and aerial vehicles using the trajectory optimization problem. These trajectory optimization problems are distinguished into two groups: (i) heuristics and, (ii) non-heuristic methods. The former uses the trade-off in producing optimal solutions but gives computationally effective results and the latter uses mathematical derivations, which are computationally expensive [13].

For mobile robots or aerial vehicles, autonomous navigation is a crucial tool. It aids in reducing their reliance on human assistance. However, it does involve several jobs or difficulties to accomplish, such as path planning. This assignment entails determining the optimal course of action for obtaining a robot from its current condition to the target state. Both states may, for example, represent the objective and the starting positions, respectively. This plan of action takes the shape of a path, which is also known as a route in other works. In general, path planning algorithms aim to find the optimal path or at least a close approximation to it. The optimal route refers to the best path, in the sense that it is the outcome of minimizing one or more objective optimization functions. This path, for example, may be the one that takes the least amount of time. This is crucial in operations such as search-and-rescue [14], for example, catastrophe victims may request assistance in life-or-death circumstances. Another optimization function to consider could be the energy of the robot. In the case of planetary exploration, this is critical since rovers have limited energy resources available.

For collision avoidance of a mobile robot in a dynamic scenario, Rath et al. [15] considered a virtual disc in front of the mobile robot that was centered at the mobile robot's heading angle. According to some specified regulations, the crossing angle between the disc and the obstacles was computed and continually modified in the direction of the mobile robot. To tackle the motion-planning problem, ANNs and radial basis neural networks are utilized to forecast the movements of dynamic barriers.

An efficient path planning algorithm must meet four requirements. First, in actual static situations, the motion planning approach must always be capable of identifying the best path. Second, it must be adaptable to changing conditions. Third, it must be consistent with and strengthen the self-referencing strategy selected. Fourth, it must keep the complexity, data storage, and computing time to a minimum. A survey article on land/aerial and underwater has been given by a number of scholars. However, these surveys are insufficient to offer information on their navigation [16]. A detailed examination of individual navigational strategies has been presented in this research. The purpose of the suggested survey articles on vehicle navigation is to discover the research gaps and potential for innovation in a certain field.

The route generation and optimization problem can be tackled using deterministic (numerical) approaches, nature-inspired algorithms, or a combination of these techniques. To calculate the precise solution, there are several numerical techniques available, including the iterative method [17], Runge Kutta [18], Newton–Raphson method [19], and the bisection method [20]. These techniques can be utilized to locate any type of answer. These algorithms are used to tackle path planning, trajectory optimization, and a variety of other vehicle versions for autonomous vehicles. Nature-inspired approaches are based on the social hierarchy of animals and birds such as ants, bees, and flies [21–24]. There are a great number of different algorithms, which are inspired by the Grey Wolf Optimizer, Whale Optimization, the Deer Hunting Algorithm, the Slap Swarm Algorithm, the Grasshopper Algorithm, the Ant Lion Optimizer, the Moth Flame Optimizer, simulated annealing, the Arithmetic Algorithm, the Harmony Search Algorithm, the Aquila Optimizer, and the Owl Search Algorithm [25–33].

Path planning for autonomous vehicles is also known as a multi-objective optimization since it involves achieving many goals, such as generating optimal routes while avoiding obstacles that evade the capability [34]. Route planning for agents can be divided into different categories based on how they complete a task in a given environment, namely: (i) reactive computing, (ii) soft computing, (iii) optimal control, and (iv) C-space search, refer to Figure 1.

Figure 1. Schematic showing different path planning methods.

The first idea is defined as: if the vehicle has access to or knowledge of the surrounding region prior to the start of its voyage, it is inferred as a priori information. The latter, on the other hand, involves the vehicle lacking information about the surrounding region [35–37]. The surrounding space can also be divided as dynamic or static; when the obstacles are in motion, it is called dynamic motion and when the objects are not in motion, it is known as a static motion [35,38–41]. Therefore, it is evident the optimization of path planning and space exploration techniques have gained significant importance in the research community (due to their vast applicability and diversity). Several authors have used different industrial robots to implement the algorithms and validate their effectiveness and robustness. Table 1 depicts such few robotic parameters mentioned in the different studies.

Table 1. Various parameters for robotics.

Panel	Sensor	Software	Map Testing
ROSbot 2.0 [42]	-	Ros Operating System	Lab-based
Pioneer 3-DX [43]	Camera	Xilinx, GA-IP FPGA	Lab based
MATLAB (ROS system) [44]	–	ROS (SLAM)	Garage map
Aria P3-DX [45]	–	Saphira software	simple environment
Husarian ROSbot [46]	LiDAR	ROS	Lab

1.1. Objective and Contents

This research examines numerical approaches along with nature-inspired techniques, and their integration with each other (or individually), for navigation and obstacle avoidance utilized for land, aerial, and underwater vehicles. This research is aimed at providing academics with the most up-to-date knowledge for path optimization and environment modeling. This paper compares several algorithms and shows how they can be implemented in various contexts. The following is a list of this review's contributions:

- **Consolidation of relevant work:** Human drivers have an amazing ability to simultaneously perceive a vehicle's environment while steadily performing the essential motion movements. Globally, researchers are working on replicating the maneuverable capabilities of human drivers in designing autonomous guided vehicles that are simple in design, provide safety, and are efficient) [47–51]. Therefore, this study strives to provide valuable insight into the land, aerial, and underwater vehicles for readers in-order to understand their utilities in the industry and research.

- **Limitations and the way forward:** Another major contribution of this research involved identifying the impediments associated with path optimization and obstacle avoidance using numerical and nature-inspired methods. Characteristics that do not contribute toward finding the optimal trajectory optimization for ground and aerial vehicles are identified and categorized into two categories: (i) numerical methods and nature-inspired techniques: limitations; (ii) numerical methods and nature-inspired techniques: restrictions. A complete way forward is also suggested.

1.2. Paper Organization

The paper is organized in the following manner. Section 2 elaborates on the fundamentals regarding the trajectory planning. Section 3 presents detailed information regarding the numerical methods, bio-inspired algorithms, and hybrid algorithms involved in land, aerial, and underwater vehicles. Section 4 contains an elaborated description of the challenges involved in land, aerial, and underwater vehicles. The paper ends with our conclusion in Section 5.

2. Trajectory Planning Fundamentals

To formulate the desired trajectories, the trajectory planning problem is treated as an optimization problem. With the exception of simple problems (such as the infinite horizon linear quadratic problem [52]), these optimization problems must be solved numerically. Such techniques can be divided into three major methods—dynamic programming, direct methods, and indirect methods [53].

In the 1970s, there was interest in path planning [54]; in the following years, it has been used to solve problems in a variety of sectors, from straightforward geographical route planning to the choice of an appropriate action sequence that is necessary to achieve a specific goal. When information is obtained from system-mounted sensors and updated environmental maps, path planning can be employed in fully or partially known surroundings as well as in completely new environments to guide the desired motion of the robot [46,55]. Finding a single solution to this NP-hard problem is not the goal; rather, it is to find the best possible answer, one that travels the shortest distance, makes the fewest maneuvers, and avoids all known obstacles. The global planner often divides this module into two parts: the local planner, which recalculates the initial plan to account for potential dynamic impediments, and the global planner, which employs a priori knowledge of the environment to produce the best path, if any.

The created plan consists of a set of waypoints for both the global $P_i = (x_i, y_i)^T$ and the local $P_i = (x_i, y_i, \theta_i)^T, \epsilon\ R^2 \times S^1$, where S is the navigation plane on which the vehicle can drive. Learning-based approaches have begun to demonstrate their effectiveness in resolving motion planning issues. They either use human-designed incentive functions or learn workable solutions from previous successful planning experiences to direct the robot's movement. In general, supervised/unsupervised learning and reinforcement learning can be used to categorize learning-based approaches to robot motion planning. Four requirements are critical for effective path planning; Algorithm 1. First, in realistic static situations, the motion planning technique must always be able to identify the best path. Second, it needs to be scalable to dynamic contexts. Third, it must continue to be beneficial to (and compatible with) the selected self-referencing strategy. The complexity, data storage, and computing time must all be kept to a minimum [56]. Realizing the importance of path planning, this research introduces a wide range of path planning algorithms for all three domains of ground, aerial, and underwater applications.

Algorithm 1 Integrated CME-Adaptive Aquila Optimizer.

1: Set nRbt, iteration, agent start position
2: Define utility of unknown space = 1
3: **while** iter = iter + 1 **do**
4:     **for** all nRbt **do**
5:         Initialize coordinates of V_c
6:         Determine the cost of V_c
7:         Subtract RU_c^i & V_c
8:         Utilize X1, X2, X3, and X4
9:         Update the X(iter + 1) position
10:        Re-select the agent position
11:        Reduce RU_j^{gc} on X(t + 1)
12:    **end for**
13:    Determine G1, G2 & QF
14: **end while**
15: return the solution

Trajectory Planning: Mathematical Framework

Essentially, all numerical methods for solving the trajectory planning problem involve iterative mechanisms with a finite number of unknowns and known variables, subject to static, dynamic, and linkage constraints. This functionality is demonstrated through Figure 2. The flow chart elaborates the fundamental steps adopted in the trajectory planning algorithm beginning with user-defined input data for the stated problem to the computation of the final trajectory.

Conventionally the problem is configured as a multiple-domain optimal control problem [57]. In this, $v \in [1, ..., V]$ is the phase number, V is the total number of phases, M_y is the output dimension, M_u is the input dimension, M_q is the integral dimension, and M_s is the dimension of the static parameters. The optimal control problem then tries to determine the state, $z^{(v)}(t) \in \mathbb{R}^{M_y^{(v)}}$, control, $u^{(v)}(t) \in \mathbb{R}^{M_u^{(v)}}$, integrals $q^{(v)} \in \mathbb{R}^{M_q^{(v)}}$, start time, $t_0(p) \in R$, phase terminal time, $t_f(p) \in R$, in all phases $p \in [1, ..., P]$, along with the static parameters $s \in \mathbb{R}^{M_s}$, which minimize the objective function in Equation (1)

$$T = \left[\sum_{v=1}^{v} [\Phi^{(vp)}(x^{(v)}(t_0), t_0^{(v)}, x^{(v)}(t_f), t_f^{(v)}, q^{(v)}) + \int_{t_0^{(v)}}^{t_f^{(v)}} L^{(v)}(x^{(v)}(t), u^{(v)}(t), q^{(v)} dt)] \right] \quad (1)$$

subject to constraints in Equation (2), inequality path constraints in Estimates (3), boundary constraints in Estimates (4), and linkage constraints in Estimates (5).

$$\dot{z}^{(v)} = f^{(v)}(z^{(v)} u^{(z)} t; a^{(v)}), \quad v = 1, ...V \quad (2)$$

$$C_{min}^{(v)} \leq C(v)(z^{(v)}, u^{(v)}, t; q^{(v)}) \leq C_{max}, \quad v = 1, ...V \quad (3)$$

$$\phi_{min}^{(v)} \leq \phi(v)(x^{(V)}(t_0), t0o, z^{(v)}(t_f), t_f, ; q^{(v)}) \leq \phi_{max}, \quad v = 1, ...V \quad (4)$$

$$K_{min}^{(r)} \leq K^{(r)}(z^{(v_1^r)}(t_f), t_f^{(v_1^r)}; q^{(v_1^r)}, x^{(v_r^r)}(t_0), t_0^{(v_r^r)}; q^{(v_r^r)}) \leq L_{max^{(r)}}) \quad (5)$$

$$where \; [v_1, v_r \in [v = 1, ...V]], r = [1, ...K]$$

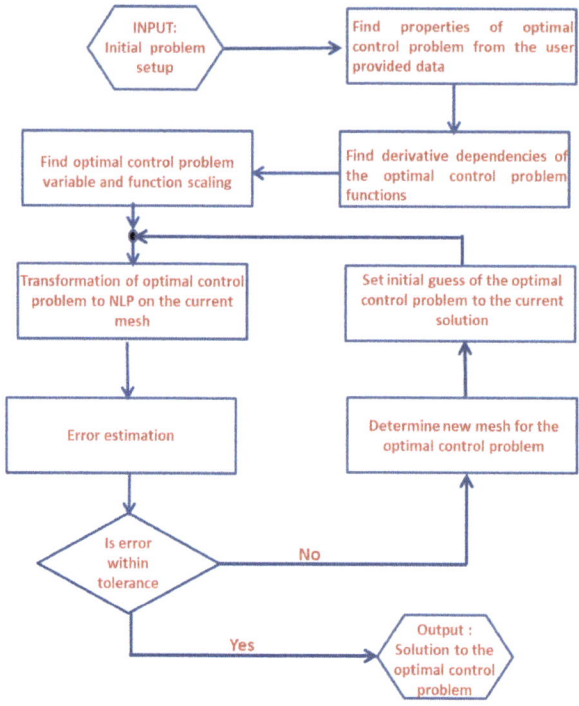

Figure 2. Conventional operational flow chart of trajectory planning algorithm.

The required state and control variables are then calculated using polynomial interpolation as elaborated in Equation (6)

$$z(\tau) \approx Z(\tau) = \sum_{i=1}^{N} Z_i \cdot K_i(\tau), \quad \tau \in [-1, 1] \tag{6}$$

where $L_i(\tau) = \prod_{j=0, j \neq i}^{N} \frac{\tau - \tau_j}{\tau_i - \tau_j}$, $i = 0, 1 \dots N$.

The control is then determined using Equation (7)

$$u(\tau) \approx U(\tau) = \sum_{i=1}^{N} Z_i \cdot K_i^*(\tau), \quad \tau \in [-1, 1] \tag{7}$$

where $L_i^*(\tau) = \prod_{j=1, j \neq i}^{N} \frac{\tau - \tau_j}{\tau_i - \tau_j}$, $i = 1 \dots N$. From Equation (6), $\dot{x}(\tau)$ is approximated by $\dot{X}(\tau)$ (see Equation (8))

$$\dot{z}(\tau) \approx \dot{Z}(\tau) \tag{8}$$

The continuous cost function of Equation (1) is approximated using a quadrature given by Equation (9)

$$J = \Phi(Z_0, t_0, Z_f, t_f) + \frac{t_f - t_o}{2} \sum_{b=1}^{N} w_k \cdot g(X_b, U_b, \tau_b; t_0, t_f) \tag{9}$$

where w_b are the weights. The boundary constraint of Estimates. (4) is expressed as in Equation (10)

$$\phi(X_0, t_0, X_f, t_f) = 0 \tag{10}$$

The cost function and algebraic constraints in Equation (9) define the transformed problem, whose solution is an approximate solution to the original trajectory planning problem from the time t_0 to t_f.

This fundamental framework has been utilized by various research studies for numerous applications and is now considered a pretty robust and widely acceptable technique for ground, aerial, space, and underwater trajectory optimization problems [58–75].

3. Relevant Studies

In this section, we will present an in-depth analysis and review of major studies performed for space exploration for autonomous systems. As elaborated earlier, path planning, space exploration, and trajectory optimization problems can be solved utilizing numerical techniques, bio-inspired algorithms, and the hybridization of these techniques with each other. In the beginning, deterministic methods or numerical methods were employed for path planning and other jobs. However, due to their inability to generate random solutions and computationally expensive nature, they were replaced by other algorithms. With growing interest, research areas have expanded and introduced bio-inspired techniques based on swarm, ant, reptile, etc., to solve trajectory planning, obstacle avoidance, and trajectory optimization. It is often seen that no single algorithm or technique can guarantee the desired results; therefore, it is common practice to integrate techniques to achieve higher accuracy and design a system more efficiently. This whole process is called the hybridization of algorithms/techniques [76].

The analysis will comprehensively cover the numerical, bio-inspired, and hybrid optimization techniques utilized for aerial, surface, and subsurface purposes.

3.1. Numerical Techniques

The implementation of algorithms for obtaining numerical solutions is a part of numerical analysis. It entails mathematical analysis on a theoretical level. The numerical methodologies, and their utilities found in land, aerial, and undersea vehicles, are presented in this section.

3.1.1. Applications to Aerial Vehicles

The most predominant feature involved in any aerial vehicle system is the sensor performance. Numerous sensors, such as radar, LiDAR, and sonar, are linked with the efficiency of aerial vehicles and their dynamics. In [77–79], the authors efficiently utilized radar to detect fast-moving targets, whereas the authors of [80,81] employed LiDAR for airborne purpose. Moreover, the authors of [82] utilized sonar for similar purposes. Important scholarly contributions in this aspect are summarized in Table 2. Various algorithms [83–85] have been developed to control the flight mechanics of UAVs. Few have presented and implemented the leader–follower strategy for accurate outcomes. The following is a list of works that are related to this one: Hasircioglu et al. [86] implemented the GA algorithm for 3D UAV flights for multiple missions. Nikolos et al. [87] used the evolutionary algorithm to increase the robustness and efficiency. Similarly, many researchers have worked on the obstacle avoidance of UAVs. One way is to add a penalty function in the objective function to catch the error [88]. Mansury et al. [89] came up with the penalty function in a planned path when a collision occurred.

One method added a penalty to its objective function as the planned path neared an obstacle, while another approach imposed a penalty only when the planned path resulted in a collision. Obstacles can also be treated as flight-restricted areas in lieu of a single point. Zhao et al. [90,91] converted an optimal control problem into parameter optimization via a collocation approach (numerically-solved with the software, Nonlinear Programming Solver (NPSOL)) [92]. NPSOL is a suite of Fortran 77 subroutines designed to solve a non-linear programming problem. NPSOL uses sequential quadratic programming (SQP) algorithm, in which the search direction is the solution of a quadratic programming subproblem. The step size at each iteration is iteratively selected to produce a sufficient decrease in an augmented Lagrangian merit function. After successful convergence, solutions of the NPSOL program represent a locally optimal solution to the non-linear programming problem. Zhang et al. [93] followed the nature-inspired technique that birds follow and developed an algorithm for a target using the Tau theory.

Table 2. Scholarly contributions.

Ref	Sensors	Contribution
Moses et al. [94]	Radar Sensor	The authors presented the overall efficiency of radar and put forward the novel design of lightweight X-band radar sensor for UAVs. The Doppler effect caused the propulsion of the UAV, which provided safe and easy identification of the target and efficient maneuverability to avoid collisions. The authors noted that the proposed design is scalable and can be used for larger vehicles.
Hugler et al. [95]	Radar Sensor	The authors presented a detailed study on the advantages of radar with UAVs for detecting obstacles, such as their velocity and angular rates. They also provided the range tendency and the multi-target detection in the angular range of $\pm 60°$ in azimuth. They conducted experimental work.
Mohamed et al. [80]	Radar Sensor	The authors highlighted the predominant features involved in radar sensors for detecting obstacles. They concluded that radar sensors have the capability to withstand weather conditions, making them suitable for outdoor applications. They can perfectly determine the sizes and shapes of obstacles while detecting them; however, the exact dimensions cannot be retrieved due to the low output resolutions of radar sensors.
Asvadi et al. [96]	Velodyne LiDAR	The authors presented the work of Velodyne LiDAR. A static 2D map was constructed, which was continuously compared with a previously constructed map using GPS/IMU.
Azim et al. [97]	Velodyne LiDAR	The researchers studied the obstacle detection and representation using OctoMap. They formulated the entire area with the Velodyne LiDAR sensor using spatial clustering and GPU for position correction.

3.1.2. Applications to Ground Vehicles

Curve interpolation planners, such as clothoid, polynomial, spline, and Bézier curves, are common in online route planning. Because the behavior of the curve is specified by a few control points or parameters, these planners are comparable to graph search techniques and have minimal computing costs. However, the resultant path's optimality cannot be guaranteed, and the dynamic restrictions of a robot are not taken into account during the planning phase (because the sizes of the curves in obstacles vary), necessitating a smoothing step. The clothoid curve introduces a novel way to reduce the route length and curvature change [98]. The suggested technique produces a closed-form solution to link two clothoid sets for the position of a waypoint in this approach, which considers two points on the plane. This method lowers the robot's rapid changes in curvature and sideslip and improves movement performance. Zhang et al. [99] measured unmanageable divergence. This statistic was used to build a system to transition between numerous predictive controllers, reducing the controller's return time while maintaining predictive accuracy. The authors of [100] created a smooth route by combining RRT* (rapidly-exploring random trees) and spline approaches. The suggested bidirectional Spline-RRT* method is based on the cubic curve and meets both start and target position direction restrictions. This approach is unlike any previous route planning algorithm, and the robot's solution is sub-optimal yet workable.

3.1.3. Application to Underwater Vehicle (AUV)

The navigation and controls of autonomous underwater vehicle systems have reached the same level of importance as ground and aerial vehicles. Ocean vehicle navigation is another name for them. It is also crucial to discuss the AUV system's connected literature. Autonomous underwater vehicles, such as ground and aerial vehicles, require path planning to navigate in the best possible way. However, in comparison to ground and airborne vehicles, the water environment has several problems because of data transmission, sensing range, and power limits.

Because of the constantly shifting bandwidth channel, communicating successfully underwater is difficult. As a result, deciding which path to follow for autonomous underwater vehicles is a difficult task. Path planning and trajectory planning are two types of motion planning. The first one is described as the numerous waypoints in which a vehicle must travel to reach the destination point, while the latter is defined as the time required to complete the journey. Underwater, the GPS system is not available and with weak communication power, it is extremely hard to set the routes for AUVs. Soylu et al. [101] presented an algorithm with an adaptive term; it works on the concept of control, although it is only concerned with maritime vehicles. An underwater vehicle uncertainty estimator (limited to 4 DOF systems defined by a diagonal inertia matrix) is proposed. The authors of [102] suggested a unique technique that consisted of two steps: (i) the creation of a velocity control algorithm in terms of the normalized generalized velocity components (NGVC) as a tool for analysis, and, (ii) its application to the vehicle dynamics inquiry. The algorithm is defined in terms of the altered equations of motion resulting from the decomposition of the inertia matrix. The author proposed approach is appropriate for fully-operated underwater vehicles and may be used to conduct numerical testing of the assumed model before conducting an actual experiment. The simulation on a 6 DOF underwater vehicle demonstrates the usefulness of the suggested technique.

A nonlinear MPC (model predictive control) is proposed in [103] for an autonomous underwater vehicle. A receding horizon optimization framework with a spline template was used to address the path planning issue. Once the current local optimal path is created, it is used as the vehicle's reference trajectory. A nonlinear model predictive control (MPC) system is used to simultaneously manage the depth of the AUV and to interact amicably with the dynamic route planning method. For tracking control, a combination of the path planning result and MPC is employed. A path planning approach using MPC is suggested to select the maneuvers mode for autonomous cars in dynamic conditions [104].

3.2. Bio-Inspired Techniques

This section provides information about trajectory planning for land, airborne, and undersea vehicles, as well as different nature-inspired techniques. The primary idea behind path optimization approaches is to define route planning as an optimization problem that takes into account the robot's intended performance and restrictions. This method can determine the best path between the start and target points.

Siddique et al. [105] investigated meta-heuristic and nature-inspired algorithms that mimic natural events in natural sciences. Many academics have tackled the challenge of ground and aerial vehicle trajectory planning and obstacle avoidance using an optimization algorithm that replicates the behavior of live organisms, such as fish, ants, bees, whales, wolves, and bats. [106–111]. They are referred to as unconventional approaches. These algorithms are known as bio-inspired approaches, and they have been used in engineering to solve challenging mathematical issues [112]. A few bio-inspired algorithms and their summaries are presented in Table 3.

Table 3. Nature-inspired algorithms.

Technique	Seminal Work
ANN [113,114]	Depends on self-organizing maps.
ABC [115–117]	The algorithm is used for optimization and imitates the bee colony pattern for the food search. Classified into three : (i) employed bees, (ii) onlooker bees, and (iii) scouts.
GA [118–126]	Extension of evolutionary algorithms; they depend on operators, e.g., mutation, crossover, and selection operators.
SA [127]	A probabilistic method employed for searching the global minima. It depends on the physical phenomena in solidifying fluids, such as metals.
GWO [21,128]	Depends on the hierarchical distribution of wolves. A mathematical model is obtained on how wolves hunt and prey.
AO [28,129]	Depends on mathematical operators, i.e addition, subtraction, multiplication, and division. Its popularity stems from its ease of use, with fewer parameters, making it straightforward to execute and adaptable to a wide range of applications.
WO [22,130,131]	Inspired by the hunting behavior of whales. They have an advantage because of their hunting strategies.

3.2.1. Application to Aerial Vehicles

Zhang et al. [128] focused on obtaining an ideal flying route while avoiding hazards in a battle area. They exhibited Grey Wolf Optimizer (GWO) performance on an unmanned combat aerial vehicle (UCAV; also known as a combat drone, colloquially shortened as drone or battlefield UAV) in a 2D environment. The safest path is determined by connecting nodes while avoiding risks. The simulation results were astounding, demonstrating that an unmanned combat aerial vehicle (UCAV) is more capable than a contemporary algorithm. Similarly, Qu et al. [132] blended the methods to accomplish successful route planning in UAVs. They merged the Grey Wolf Optimizer (GWO) with the Symbiotic Organisms Search (SOS) to present another variant optimizer—the Grey Wolf Optimizer (SGWO) and the Modified Symbiotic Organisms Search (MSOS), called HSGWO-MSOS. The stochastic parameters involved in the algorithm were intelligently adjusted to further enhance the convergence rate. For analysis, a linear difference equation was utilized, and the cubic B-spline curve approach was used to smooth the flight trajectory. The experimental findings show that the proposed algorithm HSGWO-MSOS delivers more viable outputs and is more efficient in conducting the flight trajectory.

Lewis et al. [133] presented a particle swarm optimization path-finding (PSOP) for UAV navigation purposes. The method was employed to control the flock of drones; based on this, a model known as drone flock control (DFC) was constructed. The model is combined with Reynolds flocking and the AI method for obstacle avoidance for UAVs in an unknown space. Majd Saied et al. [134] looked at a variety of unmanned aerial vehicles. The suggested concept uses the Artificial Bee Colony (ABC; inspired by the intelligent foraging behavior of honey bees) method to calculate velocity to avoid obstacles and maintain track of flight data. The simulations were run in MATLAB using various case situations.

3.2.2. Application to Ground Vehicles

In situations with dynamic impediments, Han et al. [126] employed genetic algorithms to identify the shortest pathways. Marco Cruz et al. [39] generated an ideal path by using the ABC method to perform local searches, which progressively created a path without colliding by correlating the mobile robot's start and end points, and then using evolutionary programming to optimize the practical path. GWO has an atypical condition of local optima avoidance, according to Sen Zhang et al. [128], which increases the likelihood of discovering reasonable approximations of the optimal weighted total cost of this path. Furthermore, due to the strong utilization of the GWO, the accuracy of the generated optimal values for weighted sum cost is quite high. Janglova et al. [135] demonstrated the use of a NN to navigate a wheeled mobile robot in a mostly unknown area. To build a collision-free route, they employed two NN-based techniques. The first neural mechanism used sensory input to discover clear space, while another NN avoided the nearest impediment to find a safe path (to prevent human guidance during the navigation procedure). Gasparri et al. [136] offered real-time navigation in a hallway, lobby, and built floor environments using a single mobile robot system. Abbas et al. [137] developed an upgraded BFO algorithm to improve the path planning performance of a wheeled robot.

3.2.3. Application to Underwater Vehicles

Shen et al. [103] designed a multi-AUV target search with a bio-inspired neural network that could successfully design search trajectories. A fuzzy algorithm was added to the bio-inspired neural network to smooth out the AUV obstacle avoidance trajectory. Unlike existing algorithms that require repeat training to obtain the essential parameters, the suggested technique obtains all of the required parameters without the requirement for learning or training.

Kahlil et al. [138] presented an enhanced cooperative route planning model. This research focused on the search and tracking of an underwater object. To obtain the best results, the mission was separated into search and tracing stages, with the goal of increasing the search space and decreasing the terminal error. The improvement was conducted utilizing the improved whale algorithm. The simulated results show that the suggested technique provides superior outcomes for the search and tracing phase, an improved computing performance, and well-achieved optimization for cooperative path planning of large-scale complicated issues. Daqi Zhu et al. [139] proposed a new rapid marching-based method to extract a continuous route from an environment while taking into consideration the underwater current. Yilmaz et al. [140] proposed the path planning issue as an optimization framework and mixed it with an integer linear programming-based technique. All of the approaches described above were evaluated in two-dimensional (2D) settings, which did not fulfill the actual requirements for AUV route planning. Hu et al. [141], by utilizing a control rule with an attractive force toward a target and a repulsive force against obstacles, produced a vision-based autonomous robotic fish capable of 3D mobility.

An improved self-organizing map and a velocity synthesis approach were presented for multi-AUV route planning in a 3D underwater workspace [142]. Those approaches have their own benefits, but there are certain flaws that need to be investigated further. For example, vision-based approaches perform poorly in an underwater environment; certain evolution-based methods are difficult to compute; and methods based on the premise that underwater habitats are totally known are unsuitable for the real world. Yuan and Qu [143] devised an optimum real-time collision-free AUV route in an unknown 3D underwater environment. The 3D motion planning issue was reduced to a 2D problem in their technique, resulting in a significant reduction in processing costs.

3.3. Hybrid Techniques

After elaborating on numerical and nature-inspired techniques, this section presents detailed information on hybridized algorithms and their related path optimization for land, aerial, and underwater applications.

3.3.1. Application to Aerial Vehicles

Hassan et al. [144] used the traveling salesman method for maximum UAV area coverage. The authors integrated PSO with the GA algorithm to suggest multiple paths for multiple UAVs and to further propose the parallel version of both algorithms. The authors intelligently exploited PSO and GA to avoid local minima and to pick up the quality of the output in a minimum amount of time. Statistical data obtained from the simulated results prove that the proposed method provides promising results. Arantes et al. [145] presented the integration of the genetic algorithm with the visibility graph method to decode the path in an uncertain environment under convex-shaped obstacles. The path was further decoded by linear programming methods to solve each individual path separately. Under the set, 50 different maps that proposed heuristic approaches were tested and the obtained outputs depicted promising results.

Dhargupta et al. [146] presented the integration of RL with the GWO algorithm for a smoother and more efficient flight path for UAVs. Furthermore, the authors in [132] presented a novel algorithm for UAV path planning by combining RL with the GWO optimizer. The algorithm helps in generating a refined clean trajectory for UAVs. The adjustment of stochastic parameters for GWO helps in generating a smoother path. Similarly, a number of authors have also worked on obstacle avoidance. Bouhamed et al. [147] came up with an efficient UAV that glided and, at the same time, avoided static and dynamic objects. The authors utilized the deep deterministic policy gradient (DDPG) learning algorithm, which used a reward function to help detect the target and avoid obstacles. The reward function also helped to diminish the distance between the UAV's initial step to its final step. A penalty function was added to catch the anomaly in the algorithm. Another method was presented by Challita et al. [148], which depicts numerous sub-challenges for UAVs. The authors discussed the intervention cause during path planning from the ground.

3.3.2. Application to Ground Vehicles

Pengchao Zhang et al. [149] argued that combining classical algorithms with heuristic programming algorithms based on AI yields beneficial outcomes. To modify the functions of path smoothness and path planning, the classic quickly exploring random tree approach was combined with a neural network. The simulations were run in real-time to test the viability of the modified method, which produced better outcomes when dealing with navigation challenges. Faiza et al. [150] presented a novel approach for space surfing by combining the deterministic method with an up-to-date bio-inspired method. The coordinated multi-agent exploration combined with the Arithmetic Algorithm helped to achieve a rate of exploration much higher when compared to contemporary methods. The rates of the failed simulation runs were also lesser than the compared algorithms. Bakdi et al. [151] demonstrated a robot with a camera for trajectory planning. All data obtained from the environment was processed using IM techniques, and GA was utilized to generate the best trajectory to connect the starting point with the destination point. GA was also used with a piecewise cubic Hermite interpolating polynomial to smoothen the route. Finally, an adaptive fuzzy logic controller was used to maintain track of the vehicle's left and right wheel velocities.

3.3.3. Underwater Vehicles

Wenjie Chen et al. [152] offered a technique to obtain quality photos of underwater localization since previously-reported algorithms, such as simultaneous localization and mapping (SLAM), lacked feature-based extraction qualities, resulting in fuzzy images. To address this issue, a novel technology called visual SLAM employs generative adversarial networks to improve picture quality using assessment criteria. This increases the SLAM efficiency and delivers improved localization and accuracy. The suggested approach was tested on many photos with various amounts of turbidity in the water. For fault resilience challenges in autonomous underwater vehicles, the authors of [153] developed a moth flame optimization algorithm for AUVs. AUVs have a difficult time communicating; hence, a fast network is required to send data packets back to the station. To tackle the failure problem, MFO develops a unique fitness function. The suggested methods for AUVs have been evaluated and were found to be successful.

4. Challenges, Recommendations, and Future Directions

In this section, based on the survey of the literature work, we present a summary of the challenges encountered in the space exploration process. We then propose solutions and future directions.

4.1. Challenges Involved in Path Planning

Below are the challenges involved in path planning for vehicles.

4.1.1. Inaccurate Results

No single method guarantees 100% results, despite the number of research studies conducted on land, aerial, and underwater vehicles. In robotics, the system accuracy depends on whether the robot can reach a known place without becoming stuck to the local/global minima/maxima. If the robot evades without becoming stuck, then the accuracy of that algorithm is higher. However, for space exploration, the areas being explored by the robot(s) are measured in terms of percentages, e.g., 80%, 90%, etc. [154,155]. Further, the intrinsic limitation of nature-inspired algorithms being stuck in local/global maxima/minima is the main drawback of all bio-inspired algorithms. Aspects such as oscillations, sensor, and measurement noises, and overshooting/undershooting make the design architecture more susceptible to errors. These disadvantages have substantial impacts on the workings of algorithms, which ultimately affect the performances of autonomous vehicles.

4.1.2. Sensor Dependence

The placement of onboard sensors is the most commonly used strategy for path identification [156,157]. However, the readings obtained from such sensors are greatly impacted by noise and system oscillations; therefore, such readings are neither accurate nor precise, resulting in an uncertainty in the system output and accidental inaccuracy in the algorithm output [158].

4.1.3. Dependent on Environmental Observation

Certain algorithms rely on the surrounding information for their navigational decisions. This causes unwanted halts in the vehicle's motion. Baldoni et al. [159] addressed the same difficulty with the aid of simulations. He presented that generating an optimal efficient trajectory for any kind of mobile vehicle is hard; even so, if that vehicle is able to arrive at its intended point, no algorithm can claim to generate a smooth path for its navigation.

4.1.4. Computational Cost

Algorithm proofs are easy in a simulated world; however, the onboard implementations of algorithms are computationally expensive. Furthermore, it is necessary to consider the robot's orientation and utilize the robot's real footprint for non-circular robots working in crowded environments with small pathways (such as entrances and parking places) [160]. The cost of such planning increases for a number of reasons. First, it must be completed in at least three dimensions (x, y, and orientation). Second, it is quite expensive to estimate an action's cost. Since it entails convolution (the set of all the cells visited by the robot during execution), this cost evaluation approach typically ends up taking the longest amount of time in the planning process. For instance, a basic turn-in-place movement using a 1 by 1 m square robot operating in a 2.5 cm grid covers over 500 cells.

4.1.5. Insufficient Literature on Space Exploration

The literature depicts the number of authors that have worked on path planning for ground and aerial vehicles. The literature offers a wide range of algorithm implementations for path planning but fewer for space exploration. Even the review papers are written on path planning but not for any other type of research [161–164].

4.1.6. Simulated Work

The work was conducted using simulation methods; this served as a 'drawback' pertaining to how the developed algorithm could work in real-time [165–167].

Other challenges involved in vehicle maneuverability and algorithms are depicted in Table 4 in the form of highlights.

Table 4. Path planning challenges.

Problem Area	Improvement Areas
Noise occurrence [168]	Numerous studies have been conducted to limit and accommodate noise incidences in vehicle systems; however, this remains a difficulty. These (and other issues) significantly impede the real-time implementation of any algorithm.
Vision-based [169,170]	The difficulty comes from identifying joint points in the same dimension. This leads to uncertainty in recognizing points, resulting in conflicting interpretations of images.
ANN [171,172]	This approach has various advantages; however, it requires a large data set of the surrounding region for hidden layer tuning. The well-known backpropagation technique has its own drawbacks since it rapidly converges to local minima.

4.2. Proposed Solutions

Path planning is the most investigated topic in control engineering for land, aerial, and underwater vehicles; it has been further extended to path optimization. Different algorithms [173] involving probabilistic and non-probabilistic techniques, such as A-star; (A-star is designed as a graph traversal problem to help build a robot that can find its own course); the bug algorithm (this robot moves in the direction of the goal until an obstacle is encountered. A canonical direction is followed (clockwise) until the location of the initial encounter is reached); the bug2 algorithm (the robot always attempts to move along the line of sight toward the goal. If an obstacle is encountered, a canonical direction is followed until the line of sight is encountered); artificial potential field (a robot path planning method used to reach the goal point and avoid obstacles by using the magnetic force method, which is the attractive force to reach the goal point and the repulsive force to avoid obstacles in an unknown environment); the rolling window algorithm (this takes full advantage of local, real-time environmental data that the robot has collected; path planning is carried out online in a rolling fashion through efficient scenario prediction); PRM (probabilistic roadmap; an algorithm that builds a graph to perform motion planning), etc., have been utilized to solve optimization problems in all three domains.

These methods were further improved and the authors came up with a number of variants, namely, A*, D*, and various improvements to PRM and APF. No single method can fulfill all objectives, so the integration/hybridization of methods has become a common practice. The nature-inspired algorithms mimic social behaviors for how they appear in nature; therefore, they are modeled as complete optimization algorithms. Nature-inspired algorithms, such as the Grey Wolf Optimizer, Arithmetic Optimizer, Aquila Optimizer, Snake Optimizer, Reptile Search Optimizer, etc., are widely used in this regard. Researchers are also working on controllers, known as sliding mode controllers, adaptive controllers, and linear quadratic controllers, with a combination of nature-inspired methods. Keeping in mind the trends involved in the implementation of different algorithms, the best approach is the hybridization of methods, so that instead of benefiting from a single objective, multiple objectives can be achieved [43,150,174–176]. The important aspect to remember is that hybridization may result in increased oscillation in the system performance, additional noise, or an increase in computational complexity. Nonetheless, the added advantages after integration are not comparable to other deficiencies. The trade-off is always observed under such circumstances.

Table 5 describes each path planning category's key characteristics using the suggested categorization scheme in this study. A detailed discussion of the algorithm along with its merits and demerits is presented in the Table 5.

Table 5. Benefits and weaknesses of algorithms involved in autonomous vehicle path planning.

Algorithms	Benefits	Weakness	Implementation	Time Complexity
Fuzzy Logic	(a) It is easy to tune fuzzy rules according to need [177] (b) Logic building is easy [178] (c) Can easily integrate with bio-inspired algorithms [177]	(a) Membership functions are difficult to implement.	Simulated world and real-time	$T \geq 0(n^2)$
Neural Network	(a) Real-time implementation is easy compared to fuzzy (b) Control logic imitation is easy (c) Backpropagation is beneficial [179] (d) Dataset collection is difficult in real-time [171]	(a) Neuron layer embedded in the network results in harder implementation [171] (b) Layered structure increases the complexity [171]	Real-time and simulation	$T \geq 0(n^2)$
Genetic Algorithm	(a) Faster convergence rate [180] (b) Easily integrable with other algorithms [180] (c) Easy implementation [183]	(a) Local minima problem exists in a complex environment [181] (b) System needs a lot oftuning [182]	Simulated world	$T \geq 0(n^2)$
ABC	(a) Fewer control parameters [117] (b) Less execution time is needed [183] (c) Integrable with other algorithms [183]	(a) Weak convergence rate [184]	Simulated world	$T \geq 0(n^2)$
Arithmetic Algorithm	(a) Easy implementation [185]	(a) (Tad bit) less of a convergence rate [186]	Simulated World	$T \geq 0(n^2)$
GWO	(a) Convergence rate is fast [187] (b) Tuning of the parameter is easy [187] (c) Performs better when integrated with another algorithm [189]	(a) A bit tricky in a complex environment [188]	Simulated world	$T \geq 0(n^2)$
Moth flame	(a) Performs effectively in a complex environment [190]	(a) Suffers from premature convergence [191]	Simulated world and real-time	$T \geq 0(n^2)$
WOA	(a) Fast convergence rate [192]	(a) Not easily implementable in a dynamic environment [109]	Simulated world and real-time	$T \geq 0(n^2)$
Aquila Optimizer	(a) Effective at producing good solutions in a complex environment [193] (b) Convergence rate is faster initially	(a) Requires tuning of a lot of variables [194] (b) Becomes a tad bit slow at latter iterations [195].	Simulated world and real-time	$T \geq 0(n^2)$

4.3. Potential Future Directions

For insight into trajectory generation, the utilization of the newly developed Aquila Optimizer with widespread potential utilization is a potential direction to look into. The Aquila Optimizer (AO) is a nature-inspired algorithm [32]. This nature-inspired Aquila Optimizer—with minor modifications—was merged with multi-coordinated robot exploration. Readers may be interested in using these strategies for trajectory optimization and area surfing. Instead of employing a single robot, multiple robots can be coordinated. Another alternative route (with the same notion but a different optimization strategy) may be found in [186].

We present insight into the Aquila Optimizer (as a tentative future direction). In AO, there are two hyperparameters: quality function (QF) and G2. QF is used to bring equilibrium in the search strategies and G2 is a stochastic parameter that linearly decreases during the course of iteration; it represents the flight slope of AO, which it follows for prey during the elope movement. The findings demonstrate that when G2 < 1, G2 is a convex function, which allows for a more thorough exploration of the method in the early stages rather than abruptly converging to a limited area. Another version, the Adaptive Aquila Optimizer (AAO) based on these findings, is also proposed. In this, not only the G2 and QF are adaptively modified but the **alpha**; a hyperparameter was introduced to control the decrease of G2 function. The parameters were changed into modified adaptive functions; refer to Equations (11)–(14) and Algorithm 1. A few results are elaborated in Figure 3. Another possible direction could be found in [196].

$$alpha =$$

$$alpha_{min} + (alpha_{max} - alpha_{min}) \times \frac{f_{max} - f_{min}}{f_{avg} - f_{min}} f_{max} \leq f_{avg} \tag{11}$$

$$alpha_{min} + (alpha_{max} - alpha_{min}) \times \frac{f_{max} - f_{min}}{f_{max} - f_{avg}} f_{max} \geq f_{avg} \tag{12}$$

$$alpha^{-} = 1 - alpha(t) + eps \tag{13}$$

$$G_2' = 2 \times (1 - \frac{t}{T})^{alpha} \tag{14}$$

$$QF(t)' = t^{\frac{2 \times -1}{(1-T)^2}} \tag{15}$$

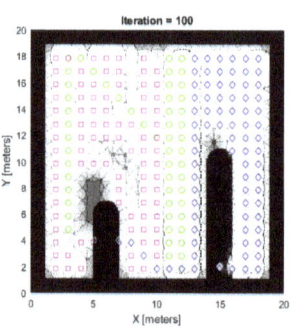
(a) **CME-AO Areas Coverage = 98.54%**

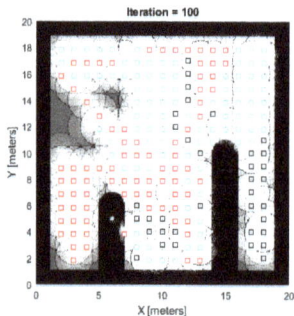
(b) **CME-AAO Area Exploration = 97.12%**

Figure 3. The simulation of CME-AO and CME-AAO exploration algorithms.

5. Conclusions

We covered a number of methods for producing the best coverage pathways in spaces and addressed different errors when executing coverage. For autonomous vehicles, trajectory planning is of fundamental importance. A lot of research has been conducted in the last decade to address the strengths and challenges of autonomous vehicles. The numerical approaches and optimization techniques used in ground, airborne, and underwater vehicles were thoroughly discussed and described in this work. From the standpoint of use on land, aerial, and underwater vehicles, a full analysis of trajectory planning and optimization was offered. Different algorithms were addressed, which were numerical strategies used for accomplishing path planning. Finally, we discussed future directions for multi-robot coverage techniques that, in addition to increasing robustness guarantees, shorten the completion times by distributing the tasks among the many robot team members.

The most pertinent conclusion points are summarized as follows:

1. **Consolidation of available information.** A detailed review of the trajectory planning and optimization is presented from the application points of view of ground (single and multi-robot), aerial, and underwater vehicles. Solutions along with future directions are presented at the end of the manuscript.
2. **Problem formulation and generation of optimal trajectories.** An explanation of how different algorithms could be integrated to build a mathematical model for planning and the formation of trajectory components were presented with a literature survey.
3. **Limitations and a way forward.** Though numerous works have reviewed robotics, aerial and underwater vehicle systems have been presented together with optimization techniques and numerical methods, and no single algorithm produced desired results or accurate output; therefore, a hybridization of different algorithms was used by researchers. Two optimization algorithms or two numerical methods together can be integrated, or a mix and match of techniques can be used to obtain the desired characteristics results.

Author Contributions: Conceptualization, I.M. and F.G.; methodology, I.M., F.G., N.S. and B.A.; software, F.G.; validation, S.M. and M.A.K.; formal analysis, F.G.; investigation, I.M. and F.G. and N.S.; resources, A.H.G. and L.A.; data curation, I.M. and F.G.; writing—original draft preparation, F.G.; writing—review and editing, F.G., I.M. and M.A.K.; visualization, F.G.; supervision, I.M. and S.M.; project administration, I.M.; funding acquisition, A.H.G. and L.A. All authors have read and agreed to the published version of the manuscript.

Funding: This research received no external funding.

Data Availability Statement: Not applicable.

Conflicts of Interest: The authors declare no conflict of interest.

Abbreviations

The following abbreviations are used in this manuscript:

UAV	Unmanned Aerial Vehicles
AUV	Autonomous Underwater Vehicles
UGVs	Unmanned Ground Vehicles
SLAM	Simultaneous Localization and Mapping
sUAV	Small Unmanned Aerial Vehicle
UAAV	Unmanned Aerial-Aquatic Vehicle
ROS	Robot Operating System
UUV	Unmanned Underwater Vehicle
GPS	Global Positioning System
IMU	Inertial Measurement Unit
MPC	Model Predictive Control
IN	Inertial Navigation
IM	Image Processing Technique
RL	Reinforcement Learning
PSO	Particle Swarm Optimization
GWO	Grey Wolf Optimization
ANN	Artificial Neural Network
GA	Genetic Algorithm
ALO	Ant Lion Optimization
WOA	Whale Optimization
MFO	Moth Flame Optimization
PRM	Probabilistic Roadmap
CNN	Convolutional Neural Network
SLI	Sylvester Law of Inertia
UWG	Underwater Glider

References

1. Berlin, T. Spirit of Berlin: An Autonomous Car for the DARPA Urban Challenge Hardware and Software Architecture. Available online: https://citeseerx.ist.psu.edu/viewdoc/download?doi=10.1.1.108.3075&rep=rep1&type=pdf (accessed on 27 June 2022).
2. Gul, F.; Mir, I.; Abualigah, L.; Sumari, P.; Forestiero, A. A Consolidated Review of Path Planning and Optimization Techniques: Technical Perspectives and Future Directions. *Electronics* **2021**, *10*, 2250. [CrossRef]
3. Aguilar, W.G.; Sandoval, S.; Limaico, A.; Villegas-Pico, M.; Asimbaya, I. Path Planning Based Navigation Using LIDAR for an Ackerman Unmanned Ground Vehicle. In Proceedings of the International Conference on Intelligent Robotics and Applications, Shenyang, China, 8–11 August 2019; pp. 399–410.
4. Le, A.V.; Nhan, N.H.K.; Mohan, R.E. Evolutionary algorithm-based complete coverage path planning for tetriamond tiling robots. *Sensors* **2020**, *20*, 445. [CrossRef] [PubMed]
5. Thoma, J.; Paudel, D.P.; Chhatkuli, A.; Probst, T.; Gool, L.V. Mapping, localization and path planning for image-based navigation using visual features and map. In Proceedings of the IEEE Conference on Computer Vision and Pattern Recognition, Long Beach, CA, USA, 15–20 June 2019; pp. 7383–7391.
6. Krell, E.; Sheta, A.; Balasubramanian, A.P.R.; King, S.A. Collision-free autonomous robot navigation in unknown environments utilizing pso for path planning. *J. Artif. Intell. Soft Comput. Res.* **2019**, *9*, 267–282. [CrossRef]
7. Vis, I.F. Survey of research in the design and control of automated guided vehicle systems. *Eur. J. Oper. Res.* **2006**, *170*, 677–709. [CrossRef]
8. Sanchez-Lopez, J.L.; Wang, M.; Olivares-Mendez, M.A.; Molina, M.; Voos, H. A real-time 3d path planning solution for collision-free navigation of multirotor aerial robots in dynamic environments. *J. Intell. Robot. Syst.* **2019**, *93*, 33–53. [CrossRef]
9. Hussain, A.; Hussain, I.; Mir, I.; Afzal, W.; Anjum, U.; Channa, B.A. Target Parameter Estimation in Reduced Dimension STAP for Airborne Phased Array Radar. In Proceedings of the 2020 IEEE 23rd International Multitopic Conference (INMIC), Bahawalpur, Pakistan, 5–7 November 2020; pp. 1–6.
10. Yi, J.H.; Lu, M.; Zhao, X.J. Quantum inspired monarch butterfly optimisation for UCAV path planning navigation problem. *Int. J. Bio-Inspired Comput.* **2020**, *15*, 75–89. [CrossRef]
11. Majeed, A.; Lee, S. A new coverage flight path planning algorithm based on footprint sweep fitting for unmanned aerial vehicle navigation in urban environments. *Appl. Sci.* **2019**, *9*, 1470. [CrossRef]
12. Hussain, A.; Anjum, U.; Channa, B.A.; Afzal, W.; Hussain, I.; Mir, I. Displaced Phase Center Antenna Processing For Airborne Phased Array Radar. In Proceedings of the 2021 International Bhurban Conference on Applied Sciences and Technologies (IBCAST), Islamabad, Pakistan, 12–16 January 2021; pp. 988–992.
13. Forestiero, A.; Mastroianni, C.; Spezzano, G. Building a peer-to-peer information system in grids via self-organizing agents. *J. Grid Comput.* **2008**, *6*, 125–140. [CrossRef]
14. Forestiero, A. Heuristic recommendation technique in Internet of Things featuring swarm intelligence approach. *Expert Syst. Appl.* **2022**, *187*, 115904. [CrossRef]
15. Rath, M.K.; Deepak, B. PSO based system architecture for path planning of mobile robot in dynamic environment. In Proceedings of the 2015 Global Conference on Communication Technologies (GCCT), Thuckalay, India, 23–24 April 2015; pp. 797–801.
16. Mir, I.; Eisa, S.A.; Maqsood, A. Review of dynamic soaring: technical aspects, nonlinear modeling perspectives and future directions. *Nonlinear Dyn.* **2018**, *94*, 3117–3144. [CrossRef]
17. Noor, M.A.; Noor, K.I.; Al-Said, E.; Waseem, M. Some new iterative methods for nonlinear equations. *Math. Probl. Eng.* **2010**, *2010*, 198943. [CrossRef]
18. Hull, T.; Enright, W.H.; Jackson, K. Runge-Kutta Research at Toronto. *Appl. Numer. Math.* **1996**, *22*, 225–236. [CrossRef]
19. Verbeke, J.; Cools, R. The Newton-Raphson method. *Int. J. Math. Educ. Sci. Technol.* **1995**, *26*, 177–193. [CrossRef]
20. Wood, G.R. The bisection method in higher dimensions. *Math. Program.* **1992**, *55*, 319–337. [CrossRef]
21. Mirjalili, S.; Mirjalili, S.M.; Lewis, A. Grey wolf optimizer. *Adv. Eng. Softw.* **2014**, *69*, 46–61. [CrossRef]
22. Mirjalili, S.; Lewis, A. The whale optimization algorithm. *Adv. Eng. Softw.* **2016**, *95*, 51–67. [CrossRef]
23. Meraihi, Y.; Ramdane-Cherif, A.; Acheli, D.; Mahseur, M. Dragonfly algorithm: A comprehensive review and applications. *Neural Comput. Appl.* **2020**, *32*, 16625–16646. [CrossRef]
24. Abualigah, L.; Shehab, M.; Alshinwan, M.; Alabool, H. Salp swarm algorithm: A comprehensive survey. *Neural Comput. Appl.* **2019**, *32*, 1–21. [CrossRef]
25. Saremi, S.; Mirjalili, S.; Lewis, A. Grasshopper optimisation algorithm: Theory and application. *Adv. Eng. Softw.* **2017**, *105*, 30–47. [CrossRef]
26. Brammya, G.; Praveena, S.; Ninu Preetha, N.; Ramya, R.; Rajakumar, B.; Binu, D. Deer hunting optimization algorithm: A new nature-inspired meta-heuristic paradigm. *Comput. J.* **2019**.: 10.1093/comjnl/bxy133. [CrossRef]
27. Mirjalili, S. The ant lion optimizer. *Adv. Eng. Softw.* **2015**, *83*, 80–98. [CrossRef]
28. Mirjalili, S. Moth-flame optimization algorithm: A novel nature-inspired heuristic paradigm. *Knowl.-Based Syst.* **2015**, *89*, 228–249. [CrossRef]
29. Ma, G.; Zhang, Y.; Nee, A. A simulated annealing-based optimization algorithm for process planning. *Int. J. Prod. Res.* **2000**, *38*, 2671–2687. [CrossRef]
30. Abualigah, L.; Diabat, A.; Mirjalili, S.; Abd Elaziz, M.; Gandomi, A.H. The arithmetic optimization algorithm. *Comput. Methods Appl. Mech. Eng.* **2021**, *376*, 113609. [CrossRef]

31. Gao, X.Z.; Govindasamy, V.; Xu, H.; Wang, X.; Zenger, K. Harmony search method: theory and applications. *Comput. Intell. Neurosci.* **2015**, *2015*, 258491. [CrossRef]
32. Abualigah, L.; Yousri, D.; Abd Elaziz, M.; Ewees, A.A.; Al-qaness, M.A.; Gandomi, A.H. Aquila Optimizer: A novel meta-heuristic optimization Algorithm. *Comput. Ind. Eng.* **2021**, *157*, 107250. [CrossRef]
33. Jain, M.; Maurya, S.; Rani, A.; Singh, V. Owl search algorithm: a novel nature-inspired heuristic paradigm for global optimization. *J. Intell. Fuzzy Syst.* **2018**, *34*, 1573–1582. [CrossRef]
34. Yiqing, L.; Xigang, Y.; Yongjian, L. An improved PSO algorithm for solving non-convex NLP/MINLP problems with equality constraints. *Comput. Chem. Eng.* **2007**, *31*, 153–162. [CrossRef]
35. Huang, W.H.; Fajen, B.R.; Fink, J.R.; Warren, W.H. Visual navigation and obstacle avoidance using a steering potential function. *Robot. Auton. Syst.* **2006**, *54*, 288–299. [CrossRef]
36. Gul, F.; Rahiman, W. An Integrated approach for Path Planning for Mobile Robot Using Bi-RRT. In Proceedings of the IOP Conference Series: Materials Science and Engineering; Terengganu, Malaysia, 27–28 August 2019; Volume 697, p. 012022.
37. Gul, F.; Rahiman, W.; Nazli Alhady, S.S. A comprehensive study for robot navigation techniques. *Cogent Eng.* **2019**, *6*, 1632046. [CrossRef]
38. Tzafestas, S.G. Mobile robot path, motion, and task planning. *Introd. Mob. Robot. Control.* **2014**, 429–478. B978-0-12-417049-0.00011-0. [CrossRef]
39. Contreras-Cruz, M.A.; Ayala-Ramirez, V.; Hernandez-Belmonte, U.H. Mobile robot path planning using artificial bee colony and evolutionary programming. *Appl. Soft Comput.* **2015**, *30*, 319–328. [CrossRef]
40. Ganeshmurthy, M.; Suresh, G. Path planning algorithm for autonomous mobile robot in dynamic environment. In Proceedings of the 2015 3rd International Conference on Signal Processing, Communication and Networking (ICSCN), Chennai, India, 26–28 March 2015; pp. 1–6.
41. Montiel, O.; Orozco-Rosas, U.; Sepúlveda, R. Path planning for mobile robots using Bacterial Potential Field for avoiding static and dynamic obstacles. *Expert Syst. Appl.* **2015**, *42*, 5177–5191. [CrossRef]
42. Tuncer, A.; Yildirim, M. Design and implementation of a genetic algorithm IP core on an FPGA for path planning of mobile robots. *Turk. J. Electr. Eng. Comput. Sci.* **2016**, *24*, 5055–5067. [CrossRef]
43. Szczepanski, R.; Bereit, A.; Tarczewski, T. Efficient Local Path Planning Algorithm Using Artificial Potential Field Supported by Augmented Reality. *Energies* **2021**, *14*, 6642. [CrossRef]
44. Chaari, I.; Koubaa, A.; Bennaceur, H.; Ammar, A.; Alajlan, M.; Youssef, H. Design and performance analysis of global path planning techniques for autonomous mobile robots in grid environments. *Int. J. Adv. Robot. Syst.* **2017**, *14*, 1729881416663663. [CrossRef]
45. Do, C.H.; Lin, H.Y. Differential evolution for optimizing motion planning of mobile robot. In Proceedings of the 2017 IEEE/SICE International Symposium on System Integration (SII), Taipei, Taiwan, 11–14 December 2017; pp. 399–404.
46. Szczepanski, R.; Tarczewski, T. Global path planning for mobile robot based on Artificial Bee Colony and Dijkstra's algorithms. In Proceedings of the 2021 IEEE 19th International Power Electronics and Motion Control Conference (PEMC), Gliwice, Poland, 25–29 April 2021; pp. 724–730.
47. Bertozzi, M.; Broggi, A.; Fascioli, A. Vision-based intelligent vehicles: State of the art and perspectives. *Robot. Auton. Syst.* **2000**, *32*, 1–16. [CrossRef]
48. Franke, U.; Gavrila, D.; Gern, A.; Görzig, S.; Janssen, R.; Paetzold, F.; Wöhler, C. From door to door—Principles and applications of computer vision for driver assistant systems. In *Intelligent Vehicle Technologies*; Elsevier: Amsterdam, The Netherlands, 2001; pp. 131–188.
49. Dickmanns, E.D.; Behringer, R.; Dickmanns, D.; Hildebrandt, T.; Maurer, M.; Thomanek, F.; Schiehlen, J. The seeing passenger car 'VaMoRs-P'. In Proceedings of the Intelligent Vehicles' 94 Symposium, Paris, France, 24–26 October 1994; pp. 68–73.
50. Nagel, H.H.; Enkelmann, W.; Struck, G. FhG-Co-Driver: From map-guided automatic driving by machine vision to a cooperative driver support. *Math. Comput. Model.* **1995**, *22*, 185–212. [CrossRef]
51. Thorpe, C.; Hebert, M.H.; Kanade, T.; Shafer, S.A. Vision and navigation for the Carnegie-Mellon Navlab. *IEEE Trans. Pattern Anal. Mach. Intell.* **1988**, *10*, 362–373. [CrossRef]
52. Kahveci, N.E.; Ioannou, P.A. Adaptive steering control for uncertain ship dynamics and stability analysis. *Automatica* **2013**, *49*, 685–697. [CrossRef]
53. Rao, A.V. A survey of numerical methods for optimal control. *Adv. Astronaut. Sci.* **2009**, *135*, 497–528.
54. Bock, H.G.; Plitt, K.J. A multiple shooting algorithm for direct solution of optimal control problems. *IFAC Proc. Vol.* **1984**, *17*, 1603–1608. [CrossRef]
55. Abualigah, L.; Elaziz, M.A.; Khodadadi, N.; Forestiero, A.; Jia, H.; Gandomi, A.H. Aquila Optimizer Based PSO Swarm Intelligence for IoT Task Scheduling Application in Cloud Computing. In *Integrating Meta-Heuristics and Machine Learning for Real-World Optimization Problems*; Springer: Berlin/Heidelberg, Germany, 2022; pp. 481–497.
56. Janet, J.A.; Luo, R.C.; Kay, M.G. The essential visibility graph: An approach to global motion planning for autonomous mobile robots. In Proceedings of the 1995 IEEE International Conference on Robotics and Automation, Nagoya, Japan, 21–27 May 1995; Volume 2; pp. 1958–1963.
57. Mir, I. Dynamics, Numeric Optimization and Control of Dynamic Soaring Maneuvers for a Morphing Capable Unmanned Aerial Vehicle. Ph.D. Thesis, National University of Sciences & Technology, Islamabad, Pakistan, 2018.

58. Schubert, K.F.; Rao, A.V. Minimum-Time Low-Earth Orbit to High-Earth Orbit Low-Thrust Trajectory Optimization. In Proceedings of the AAS/AIAA Astrodynamics Specialist Conference, Hilton Head, SC, USA, 11–15 August 2013.
59. Jodeh, N.M.; Coon, T.; Masternak, T.J.; Cobb, R.; Agte, J.S. Optimal Airborne Trajectories for Data Collected from Emplaced Ground Sensor Arrays. In Proceedings of the AIAA Guidance, Navigation, and Control Conference, National Harbor, MD, USA, 13–17 January 2014; p. 1291.
60. Kim, M.K.; Tahk, M.J.; Park, B.G.; Kim, Y.Y. Terminal Velocity Maximization of Air-to-Air Missiles in Agile Turn Phase. In *Proceedings of the MATEC Web of Conferences, Chongqing, China, 15–17 June 2016*; EDP Sciences: Les Ulis, France 2016; Volume 77, p. 07009.
61. Zhou, W.; Zhang, C.; Li, J.; Fathy, H.K. A pseudospectral strategy for optimal power management in series hybrid electric powertrains. *IEEE Trans. Veh. Technol.* **2016**, *65*, 4813–4825. [CrossRef]
62. Hong, S.M.; Seo, M.G.; Shim, S.W.; Tahk, M.J.; Lee, C.H. Sensitivity analysis on weight and trajectory optimization results for multistage guided missile. *IFAC-PapersOnLine* **2016**, *49*, 23–27. [CrossRef]
63. Dahmen, T.; Saupeand, D. Optimal pacing strategy for a race of two competing cyclists. *J. Sci. Cycl.* **2014**, *3*, 12.
64. Hu, X.; Perez, H.E.; Moura, S.J. Battery charge control with an electro-thermal-aging coupling. In Proceedings of the ASME 2015 Dynamic Systems and Control Conference. American Society of Mechanical Engineers, Columbus, OH, USA, 28–30 October 2015. [CrossRef]
65. Kodera, M.; Ogawa, H.; Tomioka, S.; Ueda, S. Multi-objective design and trajectory optimization of space transport systems with RBCC propulsion via evolutionary algorithms and pseudospectral methods. In Proceedings of the 52nd Aerospace Sciences Meeting, National Harbor, MD, USA, 13–17 January 2014; p. 0629.
66. Diwale, S.S.; Lymperopoulos, I.; Jones, C.N. Optimization of an airborne wind energy system using constrained gaussian processes. In Proceedings of the Control Applications (CCA), 2014 IEEE Conference on, Dubrovnik, Croatia, 3–5 October 2014; pp. 1394–1399.
67. Moon, Y.; Kwon, S. Lunar soft landing with minimum-mass propulsion system using H2O2/kerosene bipropellant rocket system. *Acta Astronaut.* **2014**, *99*, 153–157. [CrossRef]
68. Kaushik, H.; Mohan, R.; Prakash, K.A. Utilization of wind shear for powering unmanned aerial vehicles in surveillance application: A numerical optimization study. *Energy Procedia* **2016**, *90*, 349–359. [CrossRef]
69. Hu, X.; Li, S.; Peng, H.; Sun, F. Charging time and loss optimization for LiNMC and LiFePO4 batteries based on equivalent circuit models. *J. Power Sources* **2013**, *239*, 449–457. [CrossRef]
70. Wolf, S.; Bertschinger, R.; Saupe, D. Road cycling climbs made speedier by personalized pacing strategies. In Proceedings of the 4th International Congress on Sport Sciences Research and Technology Support, Porto, Portugal, 7–9 November 2016; pp. 109–114.
71. Coşkun, E.c. Multistage Launch Vehicle Design with Thrust Profile and Trajectory Optimization. Ph.D. Thesis, Middle East Technical University, Çankaya/Ankara, Turkey, 2014.
72. Grymin, D.J.; Farhood, M. Two-step system identification for control of small UAVs along pre-specified trajectories. In Proceedings of the American Control Conference (ACC), Portland, OR, USA, 4–6 June 2014; pp. 4404–4409.
73. Lührs, B.; Niklass, M.; Froemming, C.; Grewe, V.; Gollnick, V. Cost-benefit assessment of 2d and 3d climate and weather optimized trajectories. In Proceedings of the 16th AIAA Aviation Technology, Integration, and Operations Conference, Washington, DC, USA, 13–17 June 2016; p. 3758.
74. Peloni, A.; Rao, A.V.; Ceriotti, M. Automated Trajectory Optimizer for Solar Sailing (ATOSS). *Aerosp. Sci. Technol.* **2018**, *72*, 465–475. [CrossRef]
75. Smith, E.; Tavernini, D.; Claret, C.; Velenis, E.; Cao, D. Optimal yaw-rate target for electric vehicle torque vectoring system. In *The Dynamics of Vehicles on Roads and Tracks: Proceedings of the 24th Symposium of the International Association for Vehicle System Dynamics (IAVSD 2015), Graz, Austria, 17–21 August 2015*; CRC Press: Boca Raton, FL, USA, 2016; p. 107.
76. Gul, F.; Rahiman, W.; Alhady, S.N.; Ali, A.; Mir, I.; Jalil, A. Meta-heuristic approach for solving multi-objective path planning for autonomous guided robot using PSO–GWO optimization algorithm with evolutionary programming. *J. Ambient. Intell. Humaniz. Comput.* **2021**, *12*, 7873–7890. [CrossRef]
77. Owen, M.P.; Duffy, S.M.; Edwards, M.W. Unmanned aircraft sense and avoid radar: Surrogate flight testing performance evaluation. In Proceedings of the 2014 IEEE Radar Conference, Cincinnati, OH, USA, 19–23 May 2014; pp. 0548–0551.
78. Mir, I.; Maqsood, A.; Taha, H.E.; Eisa, S.A. Soaring Energetics for a Nature Inspired Unmanned Aerial Vehicle. In Proceedings of the AIAA Scitech 2019 Forum, San Diego, California, 7–11 January 2019; p. 1622.
79. Mir, I.; Akhtar, S.; Eisa, S.; Maqsood, A. Guidance and control of standoff air-to-surface carrier vehicle. *Aeronaut. J.* **2019**, *123*, 283–309. [CrossRef]
80. Mohamed, S.A.; Haghbayan, M.H.; Westerlund, T.; Heikkonen, J.; Tenhunen, H.; Plosila, J. A survey on odometry for autonomous navigation systems. *IEEE Access* **2019**, *7*, 97466–97486. [CrossRef]
81. Mir, I.; Maqsood, A.; Akhtar, S. Dynamic modeling & stability analysis of a generic UAV in glide phase. In Proceedings of the MATEC Web of Conferences, Beijing, China, 12–14 May 2017; EDP Sciences: Les Ulis, France, 2017; Volume 114, p. 01007.
82. Bitzinger, R.A. Chapter 2: Transition and Readjustment in Second-Tier Defence Industries: Five Case Studies. *Adelphi Ser.* **2003**, *43*, 39–62. [CrossRef]
83. Mir, I.; Taha, H.; Eisa, S.A.; Maqsood, A. A controllability perspective of dynamic soaring. *Nonlinear Dyn.* **2018**, *94*, 2347–2362. [CrossRef]

84. Mir, I.; Maqsood, A.; Akhtar, S. Optimization of Dynamic Soaring Maneuvers for a Morphing Capable UAV. In Proceedings of the AIAA Information Systems-AIAA Infotech@ Aerospace, Grapevine, TX, USA, 9–13 January 2017; p. 0678.

85. Mir, I.; Maqsood, A.; Eisa, S.A.; Taha, H.; Akhtar, S. Optimal morphing–augmented dynamic soaring maneuvers for unmanned air vehicle capable of span and sweep morphologies. *Aerosp. Sci. Technol.* **2018**, *79*, 17–36. [CrossRef]

86. Hasircioglu, I.; Topcuoglu, H.R.; Ermis, M. 3-D path planning for the navigation of unmanned aerial vehicles by using evolutionary algorithms. In Proceedings of the 10th Annual Conference on Genetic and Evolutionary Computation, Atlanta, GA, USA, 12–16 July 2008; pp. 1499–1506.

87. Caselli, S.; Reggiani, M.; Rocchi, R. Heuristic methods for randomized path planning in potential fields. In Proceedings of the 2001 IEEE International Symposium on Computational Intelligence in Robotics and Automation (Cat. No. 01EX515), Banff, AB, Canada, 29 July–1 August 2001; pp. 426–431.

88. Saska, M.; Macas, M.; Preucil, L.; Lhotska, L. Robot path planning using particle swarm optimization of Ferguson splines. In Proceedings of the 2006 IEEE Conference on Emerging Technologies and Factory Automation, Prague, Czech Republic, 20–22 September 2006; pp. 833–839.

89. Mansury, E.; Nikookar, A.; Salehi, M.E. Artificial Bee Colony optimization of ferguson splines for soccer robot path planning. In Proceedings of the 2013 First RSI/ISM International Conference on Robotics and Mechatronics (ICRoM), Tehran, Iran, 13–15 February 2013; pp. 85–89.

90. Zhao, Y.J. Optimal patterns of glider dynamic soaring. *Optim. Control. Appl. Methods* **2004**, *25*, 67–89. [CrossRef]

91. Zhao, Y.J.; Qi, Y.C. Minimum fuel powered dynamic soaring of unmanned aerial vehicles utilizing wind gradients. *Optim. Control. Appl. Methods* **2004**, *25*, 211–233. [CrossRef]

92. Gill, P.E.; Murray, W.; Saunders, M.A.; Wright, M.H. *User's Guide for NPSOL (version 4.0): A Fortran Package for Nonlinear Programming;* Technical report; Stanford Univ Ca Systems Optimization Lab: Stanford, CA, USA, 1986.

93. Zhang, Z.; Xie, P.; Ma, O. Bio-inspired trajectory generation for UAV perching. In Proceedings of the 2013 IEEE/ASME International Conference on Advanced Intelligent Mechatronics, Wollongong, Australia, 9–12 July 2013; pp. 997–1002.

94. Moses, A.; Rutherford, M.J.; Kontitsis, M.; Valavanis, K.P. UAV-borne X-band radar for collision avoidance. *Robotica* **2014**, *32*, 97. [CrossRef]

95. Hügler, P.; Roos, F.; Schartel, M.; Geiger, M.; Waldschmidt, C. Radar taking off: New capabilities for UAVs. *IEEE Microw. Mag.* **2018**, *19*, 43–53. [CrossRef]

96. Asvadi, A.; Peixoto, P.; Nunes, U. Detection and tracking of moving objects using 2.5 d motion grids. In Proceedings of the 2015 IEEE 18th International Conference on Intelligent Transportation Systems, Gran Canaria, Spain, 5–18 September 2015; pp. 788–793.

97. Azim, A.; Aycard, O. Layer-based supervised classification of moving objects in outdoor dynamic environment using 3D laser scanner. In Proceedings of the 2014 IEEE Intelligent Vehicles Symposium Proceedings, Dearborn, MI, USA, 8–11 June 2014; pp. 1408–1414.

98. Kim, Y.; Park, J.; Son, W.; Yoon, T. Modified turn algorithm for motion planning based on clothoid curve. *Electron. Lett.* **2017**, *53*, 1574–1576. [CrossRef]

99. Zhang, K.; Sprinkle, J.; Sanfelice, R.G. A hybrid model predictive controller for path planning and path following. In Proceedings of the ACM/IEEE Sixth International Conference on Cyber-Physical Systems, Seattle, WA, USA, 14–16 April 2015; pp. 139–148.

100. Sudhakara, P.; Ganapathy, V.; Sundaran, K. Optimal trajectory planning based on bidirectional spline-RRT for wheeled mobile robot. In Proceedings of the 2017 Third International Conference on Sensing, Signal Processing and Security (ICSSS), Chennai, India, 4–5 May 2017; pp. 65–68.

101. Soylu, S.; Buckham, B.J.; Podhorodeski, R.P. A chattering-free sliding-mode controller for underwater vehicles with fault-tolerant infinity-norm thrust allocation. *Ocean. Eng.* **2008**, *35*, 1647–1659. [CrossRef]

102. Herman, P. Numerical Test of Underwater Vehicle Dynamics Using Velocity Controller. In Proceedings of the 2019 12th International Workshop on Robot Motion and Control (RoMoCo), Poznań, Poland, 8–10 July 2019; pp. 26–31.

103. Shen, C.; Shi, Y.; Buckham, B. Model predictive control for an AUV with dynamic path planning. In Proceedings of the 2015 54th Annual Conference of the Society of Instrument and Control Engineers of Japan (SICE), Hangzhou, China, 28–30 July 2015; pp. 475–480.

104. Liu, C.; Lee, S.; Varnhagen, S.; Tseng, H.E. Path planning for autonomous vehicles using model predictive control. In Proceedings of the 2017 IEEE Intelligent Vehicles Symposium (IV), Los Angeles, CA, USA, 11–14 June 2017; pp. 174–179.

105. Siddique, N.; Adeli, H. Nature inspired computing: an overview and some future directions. *Cogn. Comput.* **2015**, *7*, 706–714. [CrossRef] [PubMed]

106. Zhang, Y.; Guan, G.; Pu, X. The robot path planning based on improved artificial fish swarm algorithm. *Math. Probl. Eng.* **2016**, *2016*, 3297585. [CrossRef]

107. Wang, H.J.; Fu, Y.; Zhao, Z.Q.; Yue, Y.J. An Improved Ant Colony Algorithm of Robot Path Planning for Obstacle Avoidance. *J. Robot.* **2019**, *2019*, 6097591. [CrossRef]

108. Saffari, M.; Mahjoob, M. Bee colony algorithm for real-time optimal path planning of mobile robots. In Proceedings of the 2009 Fifth International Conference on Soft Computing, Computing with Words and Perceptions in System Analysis, Decision and Control, Famagusta, North Cyprus, 2–4 September 2009; pp. 1–4.

109. Dao, T.K.; Pan, T.S.; Pan, J.S. A multi-objective optimal mobile robot path planning based on whale optimization algorithm. In Proceedings of the 2016 IEEE 13th International Conference on Signal Processing (ICSP), Chengdu, China, 6–10 November 2016; pp. 337–342.

110. Tsai, P.W.; Dao, T.K. Robot path planning optimization based on multiobjective grey wolf optimizer. In *Proceedings of the International Conference on Genetic and Evolutionary Computing, Fuzhou, China, 7–9 November 2016*; Springer: Berlin/Heidelberg, Germany, 2016; pp. 166–173.

111. Guo, J.; Gao, Y.; Cui, G. The path planning for mobile robot based on bat algorithm. *Int. J. Autom. Control.* **2015**, *9*, 50–60. [CrossRef]

112. Yang, X.S. *Nature-Inspired Metaheuristic Algorithms*; Luniver Press: Bristol, UK, 2010.

113. Surmann, H.; Kanstein, A.; Goser, K. Self-organizing and genetic algorithms for an automatic design of fuzzy control and decision systems. In Proceedings of the EUFIT'93, Aachen, Germany, 7–10 September 1993.

114. Payne, D.; Stern, J. Wavelength-switched passively coupled single-mode optical network. In Proceedings of the IOOC-ECOC, Venezia, Italy, 1–4 October 1985; Volume 85, p. 585.

115. Karaboga, D.; Akay, B. A comparative study of artificial bee colony algorithm. *Appl. Math. Comput.* **2009**, *214*, 108–132. [CrossRef]

116. Baykasoğlu, A.; Özbakır, L.; Tapkan, P. Artificial Bee Colony Algorithm and Its Application to Generalized Assignment Problem Swarm Intelligence Focus on Ant and Particle Swarm Optimization. In *Swarm Intelligence: Focus on Ant and Particle Swarm Optimization*; IntechOpen: London, UK, 2007.

117. Kamil, R.T.; Mohamed, M.J.; Oleiwi, B.K. Path Planning of Mobile Robot Using Improved Artificial Bee Colony Algorithm. *Eng. Technol. J.* **2020**, *38*, 1384–1395. [CrossRef]

118. Ismail, A.; Sheta, A.; Al-Weshah, M. A mobile robot path planning using genetic algorithm in static environment. *J. Comput. Sci.* **2008**, *4*, 341–344.

119. Mitchell, M. *An Introduction to Genetic Algorithms*; MIT Press: Cambridge, MA, USA, 1998.

120. Xin, D.; Hua-hua, C.; Wei-kang, G. Neural network and genetic algorithm based global path planning in a static environment. *J. Zhejiang Univ. Sci. A* **2005**, *6*, 549–554. [CrossRef]

121. Li, J.; Deng, G.; Luo, C.; Lin, Q.; Yan, Q.; Ming, Z. A hybrid path planning method in unmanned air/ground vehicle (UAV/UGV) cooperative systems. *IEEE Trans. Veh. Technol.* **2016**, *65*, 9585–9596. [CrossRef]

122. Lee, J.; Kang, B.Y.; Kim, D.W. Fast genetic algorithm for robot path planning. *Electron. Lett.* **2013**, *49*, 1449–1451. [CrossRef]

123. Tian, L.; Collins, C. An effective robot trajectory planning method using a genetic algorithm. *Mechatronics* **2004**, *14*, 455–470. [CrossRef]

124. Châari, I.; Koubaa, A.; Bennaceur, H.; Trigui, S.; Al-Shalfan, K. SmartPATH: A hybrid ACO-GA algorithm for robot path planning. In Proceedings of the 2012 IEEE Congress on Evolutionary Computation, Brisbane, Australia, 10–15 June 2012; pp. 1–8.

125. Geisler, T.; Manikas, T.W. Autonomous robot navigation system using a novel value encoded genetic algorithm. In Proceedings of the The 2002 45th Midwest Symposium on Circuits and Systems, 2002. MWSCAS-2002, Tulsa, OK, USA, 4–7 August 2002; Volume 3, p. III.

126. Han, W.G.; Baek, S.M.; Kuc, T.Y. Genetic algorithm based path planning and dynamic obstacle avoidance of mobile robots. In Proceedings of the 1997 IEEE International Conference on Systems, Man, and Cybernetics. Computational Cybernetics and Simulation, Orlando, FL, USA, 12–15 October 1997; Volume 3; pp. 2747–2751.

127. Liu, K.; Zhang, M. Path planning based on simulated annealing ant colony algorithm. In Proceedings of the 2016 9th International Symposium on Computational Intelligence and Design (ISCID), Hangzhou, China, 10–11 December 2016; Volume 2; pp. 461–466.

128. Zhang, S.; Zhou, Y.; Li, Z.; Pan, W. Grey wolf optimizer for unmanned combat aerial vehicle path planning. *Adv. Eng. Softw.* **2016**, *99*, 121–136. [CrossRef]

129. Hussien, A.G.; Amin, M.; Abd El Aziz, M. A comprehensive review of moth-flame optimisation: variants, hybrids, and applications. *J. Exp. Theor. Artif. Intell.* **2020**, *32*, 1–21. [CrossRef]

130. Watkins, W.A.; Schevill, W.E. Aerial observation of feeding behavior in four baleen whales: Eubalaena glacialis, Balaenoptera borealis, Megaptera novaeangliae, and Balaenoptera physalus. *J. Mammal.* **1979**, *60*, 155–163. [CrossRef]

131. Goldbogen, J.A.; Friedlaender, A.S.; Calambokidis, J.; Mckenna, M.F.; Simon, M.; Nowacek, D.P. Integrative Approaches to the Study of Baleen Whale Diving Behavior, Feeding Performance, and Foraging Ecology. *BioScience* **2013**, *63*, 90–100. [CrossRef]

132. Qu, C.; Gai, W.; Zhang, J.; Zhong, M. A novel hybrid grey wolf optimizer algorithm for unmanned aerial vehicle (UAV) path planning. *Knowl.-Based Syst.* **2020**, *194*, 105530. [CrossRef]

133. Stark, C.R.; Pyke, L.M. Dynamic pathfinding for a swarm intelligence based UAV control model using particle swarm optimisation. *Front. Appl. Math. Stat.* **2021**, *7*, 744955.

134. Saied, M.; Slim, M.; Mazeh, H.; Francis, C.; Shraim, H. Unmanned Aerial Vehicles Fleet Control via Artificial Bee Colony Algorithm. In Proceedings of the 2019 4th Conference on Control and Fault Tolerant Systems (SysTol), Casablanca, Morocco, 18–20 September 2019; pp. 80–85.

135. Janglová, D. Neural networks in mobile robot motion. *Int. J. Adv. Robot. Syst.* **2004**, *1*, 2. [CrossRef]

136. Gasparri, A.; Prosperi, M. A bacterial colony growth algorithm for mobile robot localization. *Auton. Robot.* **2008**, *24*, 349–364. [CrossRef]

137. Abbas, N.H.; Ali, F.M. Path planning of an autonomous mobile robot using enhanced bacterial foraging optimization algorithm. *Al-Khwarizmi Eng. J.* **2016**, *12*, 26–35.
Integrative approaches to the study of baleen whale diving behavior, feeding performance, and foraging ecology. *BioScience* **2013**, *63*, 90–100. [CrossRef]
138. Khalil, A.E.K.; Anwar, S.; Husnain, G.; Elahi, A.; Dong, Z. A Novel Bio-Inspired Path Planning for Autonomous Underwater Vehicle for Search and Tracing of Underwater Target. In Proceedings of the 2021 International Conference on Innovative Computing (ICIC), Online, 15–16 September 2021; pp. 1–7.
139. Zhu, D.; Li, W.; Yan, M.; Yang, S.X. The path planning of AUV based on DS information fusion map building and bio-inspired neural network in unknown dynamic environment. *Int. J. Adv. Robot. Syst.* **2014**, *11*, 34. [CrossRef]
140. Yilmaz, N.K.; Evangelinos, C.; Lermusiaux, P.F.; Patrikalakis, N.M. Path planning of autonomous underwater vehicles for adaptive sampling using mixed integer linear programming. *IEEE J. Ocean. Eng.* **2008**, *33*, 522–537. [CrossRef]
141. Hu, Y.; Zhao, W.; Wang, L. Vision-based target tracking and collision avoidance for two autonomous robotic fish. *IEEE Trans. Ind. Electron.* **2009**, *56*, 1401–1410.
142. Zhu, D.; Huang, H.; Yang, S.X. Dynamic task assignment and path planning of multi-AUV system based on an improved self-organizing map and velocity synthesis method in three-dimensional underwater workspace. *IEEE Trans. Cybern.* **2013**, *43*, 504–514. [PubMed]
143. Yuan, H.; Qu, Z. Optimal real-time collision-free motion planning for autonomous underwater vehicles in a 3D underwater space. *IET Control. Theory Appl.* **2009**, *3*, 712–721. [CrossRef]
144. Haghighi, H.; Sadati, S.H.; Dehghan, S.; Karimi, J. Hybrid form of particle swarm optimization and genetic algorithm for optimal path planning in coverage mission by cooperated unmanned aerial vehicles. *J. Aerosp. Technol. Manag.* **2020**, *12*. [CrossRef]
145. Arantes, M.d.S.; Arantes, J.d.S.; Toledo, C.F.M.; Williams, B.C. A hybrid multi-population genetic algorithm for UAV path planning. In Proceedings of the Genetic and Evolutionary Computation Conference 2016, Denver, CO, USA, 20–24 July 2016; pp. 853–860.
146. Dhargupta, S.; Ghosh, M.; Mirjalili, S.; Sarkar, R. Selective opposition based grey wolf optimization. *Expert Syst. Appl.* **2020**, *151*, 113389. [CrossRef]
147. Bouhamed, O.; Ghazzai, H.; Besbes, H.; Massoud, Y. Autonomous UAV navigation: A DDPG-based deep reinforcement learning approach. In Proceedings of the 2020 IEEE International Symposium on Circuits and Systems (ISCAS), Sevilla, Spain, 10–21 October 2020; pp. 1–5.
148. Challita, U.; Saad, W.; Bettstetter, C. Interference management for cellular-connected UAVs: A deep reinforcement learning approach. *IEEE Trans. Wirel. Commun.* **2019**, *18*, 2125–2140. [CrossRef]
149. Zhang, P.; Xiong, C.; Li, W.; Du, X.; Zhao, C. Path planning for mobile robot based on modified rapidly exploring random tree method and neural network. *Int. J. Adv. Robot. Syst.* **2018**, *15*, 1729881418784221. [CrossRef]
150. Gul, F.; Mir, S.; Mir, I. Coordinated Multi-Robot Exploration: Hybrid Stochastic Optimization Approach. In Proceedings of the AIAA SCITECH 2022 Forum, San Diego, CA & Virtual, 3–7 January 2022; p. 1414.
151. Bakdi, A.; Hentout, A.; Boutami, H.; Maoudj, A.; Hachour, O.; Bouzouia, B. Optimal path planning and execution for mobile robots using genetic algorithm and adaptive fuzzy-logic control. *Robot. Auton. Syst.* **2017**, *89*, 95–109. [CrossRef]
152. Chen, W.; Rahmati, M.; Sadhu, V.; Pompili, D. Real-time Image Enhancement for Vision-based Autonomous Underwater Vehicle Navigation in Murky Waters. In Proceedings of the International Conference on Underwater Networks & Systems, Atlanta, GA, USA, 23–25 October 2019; pp. 1–8.
153. Kumari, S.; Mishra, P.K.; Anand, V. Fault resilient routing based on moth flame optimization scheme for underwater wireless sensor networks. *Wirel. Networks* **2020**, *26*, 1417–1431. [CrossRef]
154. Buschhaus, A.; Blank, A.; Ziegler, C.; Franke, J. Highly efficient control system enabling robot accuracy improvement. *Procedia CIRP* **2014**, *23*, 200–205. [CrossRef]
155. Qiao, G.; Weiss, B.A. Accuracy degradation analysis for industrial robot systems. In Proceedings of the International Manufacturing Science and Engineering Conference, American Society of Mechanical Engineers, Los Angeles, CA, USA, 4–8 June 2017; Volume 50749, p. V003T04A006.
156. Lagisetty, R.; Philip, N.; Padhi, R.; Bhat, M. Object detection and obstacle avoidance for mobile robot using stereo camera. In Proceedings of the 2013 IEEE International Conference on Control Applications (CCA), Hyderabad, India, 28–30 August 2013; pp. 605–610.
157. Fulgenzi, C.; Spalanzani, A.; Laugier, C. Dynamic obstacle avoidance in uncertain environment combining PVOs and occupancy grid. In Proceedings of the 2007 IEEE International Conference on Robotics and Automation, Roma, Italy, 10–14 April 2007; pp. 1610–1616.
158. Michels, J.; Saxena, A.; Ng, A.Y. High speed obstacle avoidance using monocular vision and reinforcement learning. In Proceedings of the 22nd International Conference on Machine Learning, Bonn, Germany, 7–11 August 2005; pp. 593–600.
159. Baldoni, P.D.; Yang, Y.; Kim, S.Y. Development of efficient obstacle avoidance for a mobile robot using fuzzy Petri nets. In Proceedings of the 2016 IEEE 17th International Conference on Information Reuse and Integration (IRI), Pittsburgh, PA, USA, 28–30 July 2016; pp. 265–269.
160. Likhachev, M.; Ferguson, D. Planning long dynamically feasible maneuvers for autonomous vehicles. *Int. J. Robot. Res.* **2009**, *28*, 933–945. [CrossRef]

161. Sánchez-Ibáñez, J.R.; Pérez-del Pulgar, C.J.; García-Cerezo, A. Path Planning for Autonomous Mobile Robots: A Review. *Sensors* **2021**, *21*, 7898. [CrossRef]
162. Patle, B.; Pandey, A.; Parhi, D.; Jagadeesh, A.; et al. A review: On path planning strategies for navigation of mobile robot. *Def. Technol.* **2019**, *15*, 582–606. [CrossRef]
163. King, J.; Likhachev, M. Efficient cost computation in cost map planning for non-circular robots. In Proceedings of the 2009 IEEE/RSJ International Conference on Intelligent Robots and Systems, St. Louis, MO, USA, 10–15 October 2009; pp. 3924–3930.
164. Campbell, S.; O'Mahony, N.; Carvalho, A.; Krpalkova, L.; Riordan, D.; Walsh, J. Path planning techniques for mobile robots a review. In Proceedings of the 2020 6th International Conference on Mechatronics and Robotics Engineering (ICMRE), Columbus, OH, USA, 27–29 September 2020; pp. 12–16.
165. Ibrahim, M.I.; Sariff, N.; Johari, J.; Buniyamin, N. Mobile robot obstacle avoidance in various type of static environments using fuzzy logic approach. In Proceedings of the 2014 2nd International Conference on Electrical, Electronics and System Engineering (ICEESE), Kuala Lumpur, Malaysia, 9–10 December 2014; pp. 83–88.
166. Ajeil, F.H.; Ibraheem, I.K.; Azar, A.T.; Humaidi, A.J. Grid-based mobile robot path planning using aging-based ant colony optimization algorithm in static and dynamic environments. *Sensors* **2020**, *20*, 1880. [CrossRef]
167. Ali, H.; Gong, D.; Wang, M.; Dai, X. Path planning of mobile robot with improved ant colony algorithm and MDP to produce smooth trajectory in grid-based environment. *Front. Neurorobotics* **2020**, *14*, 44. [CrossRef]
168. Seraji, H.; Howard, A. Behavior-based robot navigation on challenging terrain: A fuzzy logic approach. *IEEE Trans. Robot. Autom.* **2002**, *18*, 308–321. [CrossRef]
169. Sharma, P.S.; Chitaliya, D. Obstacle avoidance using stereo vision: A survey. *Int. J. Innov. Res. Comput. Commun. Eng.* **2015**, *3*, 24–29. [CrossRef]
170. Typiak, A. Use of laser rangefinder to detecting in surroundings of mobile robot the obstacles. In Proceedings of the Symposium on Automation and Robotics in Construction, Vilnius, Lithuania, 26–29 June 2008; pp. 26–29.
171. Yang, J.; Chen, P.; Rong, H.J.; Chen, B. Least mean p-power extreme learning machine for obstacle avoidance of a mobile robot. In Proceedings of the 2016 International Joint Conference on Neural Networks (IJCNN), Vancouver, BC, Canada, 24–29 July 2016; pp. 1968–1976.
172. Haykin, S.; Network, N. A comprehensive foundation. *Neural Netw.* **2004**, *2*, 41.
173. Sun, B.; Han, D.; Wei, Q. Application of Rolling Window Algorithm to the Robot Path Planning. *Comput. Simul.* **2006**, *23*, 159–162.
174. Syed, U.A.; Kunwar, F.; Iqbal, M. Guided Autowave Pulse Coupled Neural Network (GAPCNN) based real time path planning and an obstacle avoidance scheme for mobile robots. *Robot. Auton. Syst.* **2014**, *62*, 474–486. [CrossRef]
175. Al-Mutib, K.; Abdessemed, F.; Faisal, M.; Ramdane, H.; Alsulaiman, M.; Bencherif, M. Obstacle avoidance using wall-following strategy for indoor mobile robots. In Proceedings of the 2016 2nd IEEE International Symposium on Robotics and Manufacturing Automation (ROMA), Ipoh, Malaysia, 25–27 September 2016; pp. 1–6.
176. Ahmed, A.A.; Abdalla, T.Y.; Abed, A.A. Path planning of mobile robot by using modified optimized potential field method. *Int. J. Comput. Appl.* **2015**, *113*, 6–10. [CrossRef]
177. Zhong, M.; Yang, Y.; Dessouky, Y.; Postolache, O. Multi-AGV scheduling for conflict-free path planning in automated container terminals. *Comput. Ind. Eng.* **2020**, *142*, 106371. [CrossRef]
178. Cherroun, L.; Boumehraz, M.; Kouzou, A. Mobile Robot Path Planning Based on Optimized Fuzzy Logic Controllers. In *New Developments and Advances in Robot Control*; Springer: Berlin/Heidelberg, Germany, 2019; pp. 255–283.
179. Chhotray, A.; Parhi, D.R. Navigational control analysis of two-wheeled self-balancing robot in an unknown terrain using back-propagation neural network integrated modified DAYANI approach. *Robotica* **2019**, *37*, 1346–1362. [CrossRef]
180. Naazare, M.; Ramos, D.; Wildt, J.; Schulz, D. Application of Graph-based Path Planning for UAVs to Avoid Restricted Areas. In Proceedings of the 2019 IEEE International Symposium on Safety, Security, and Rescue Robotics (SSRR), Wurzburg, Germany, 2–4 September 2019; pp. 139–144.
181. Burchardt, H.; Salomon, R. Implementation of path planning using genetic algorithms on mobile robots. In Proceedings of the 2006 IEEE International Conference on Evolutionary Computation, Vancouver, BC, Canada, 16–21 July 2006; pp. 1831–1836.
182. Su, K.; Wang, Y.; Hu, X. Robot path planning based on random coding particle swarm optimization. *Int. J. Adv. Comput. Sci. Appl.* **2015**, *6*, 58–64. [CrossRef]
183. Darwish, A.H.; Joukhadar, A.; Kashkash, M. Using the Bees Algorithm for wheeled mobile robot path planning in an indoor dynamic environment. *Cogent Eng.* **2018**, *5*, 1426539. [CrossRef]
184. Karaboga, D.; Gorkemli, B.; Ozturk, C.; Karaboga, N. A comprehensive survey: artificial bee colony (ABC) algorithm and applications. *Artif. Intell. Rev.* **2014**, *42*, 21–57. [CrossRef]
185. Agushaka, J.O.; Ezugwu, A.E. Advanced arithmetic optimization algorithm for solving mechanical engineering design problems. *PLoS ONE* **2021**, *16*, e0255703.
186. Gul, F.; Mir, I.; Abualigah, L.; Sumari, P. Multi-Robot Space Exploration: An Augmented Arithmetic Approach. *IEEE Access* **2021**, *9*, 107738–107750. [CrossRef]
187. Wu, H.S.; Zhang, F.M. Wolf pack algorithm for unconstrained global optimization. *Mathematical Problems in Engineering* **2014**, *2014*, 465082. [CrossRef]
188. Mittal, N.; Singh, U.; Sohi, B.S. Modified grey wolf optimizer for global engineering optimization. *Appl. Comput. Intell. Soft Comput.* **2016**, *2016*, 7950348. [CrossRef]

189. Liu, C.; Yan, X.; Liu, C.; Wu, H. The wolf colony algorithm and its application. *Chin. J. Electron.* **2011**, *20*, 212–216.

190. Jalali, S.M.J.; Khosravi, A.; Kebria, P.M.; Hedjam, R.; Nahavandi, S. Autonomous robot navigation system using the evolutionary multi-verse optimizer algorithm. In Proceedings of the 2019 IEEE International Conference on Systems, Man and Cybernetics (SMC), Bari, Italy, 6–9 October 2019; pp. 1221–1226.

191. Jalali, S.M.J.; Hedjam, R.; Khosravi, A.; Heidari, A.A.; Mirjalili, S.; Nahavandi, S. Autonomous robot navigation using moth-flame-based neuroevolution. In *Evolutionary Machine Learning Techniques*; Springer: Berlin/Heidelberg, Germany, 2020; pp. 67–83.

192. Chhillar, A.; Choudhary, A. Mobile Robot Path Planning Based Upon Updated Whale Optimization Algorithm. In Proceedings of the 2020 10th International Conference on Cloud Computing, Data Science & Engineering (Confluence), Noida, India, 29–31 January 2020; pp. 684–691.

193. Wang, S.; Jia, H.; Abualigah, L.; Liu, Q.; Zheng, R. An improved hybrid aquila optimizer and harris hawks algorithm for solving industrial engineering optimization problems. *Processes* **2021**, *9*, 1551. [CrossRef]

194. Mahajan, S.; Abualigah, L.; Pandit, A.K.; Altalhi, M. Hybrid Aquila optimizer with arithmetic optimization algorithm for global optimization tasks. *Soft Comput.* **2022**, *26*, 4863–4881. [CrossRef]

195. Zhao, J.; Gao, Z.M. The heterogeneous Aquila optimization algorithm. *Math. Biosci. Eng. MBE* **2022**, *19*, 5867–5904. [CrossRef] [PubMed]

196. Forestiero, A.; Papuzzo, G. Agents-based algorithm for a distributed information system in Internet of Things. *IEEE Internet Things J.* **2021**, *8*, 16548–16558. [CrossRef]

Article

A Novel Deep Learning Technique for Detecting Emotional Impact in Online Education

Shadi AlZu'bi [1,*], Raed Abu Zitar [2], Bilal Hawashin [1], Samia Abu Shanab [1], Amjed Zraiqat [1], Ala Mughaid [3], Khaled H. Almotairi [4] and Laith Abualigah [5,6,*]

1 Faculty of Science and IT, Al-Zaytoonah University of Jordan, Amman 11733, Jordan
2 Sorbonne Center of Artificial Intelligence, Sorbonne University-Abu Dhabi, Abu Dhabi 38044, United Arab Emirates
3 Department of Information Technology, Faculty of Prince Al-Hussien bin Abdullah II for IT, The Hashemite University, Zarqa 13133, Jordan
4 Computer Engineering Department, Computer and Information Systems College, Umm Al-Qura University, Makkah 21955, Saudi Arabia
5 Hourani Center for Applied Scientific Research, Al-Ahliyya Amman University, Amman 19328, Jordan
6 Faculty of Information Technology, Middle East University, Amman 11831, Jordan
* Correspondence: smalzubi@zuj.edu.jo (S.A.); aligah.2020@gmail.com (L.A.); Tel.: +962-799100034 (S.A.)

Abstract: Emotional intelligence is the automatic detection of human emotions using various intelligent methods. Several studies have been conducted on emotional intelligence, and only a few have been adopted in education. Detecting student emotions can significantly increase productivity and improve the education process. This paper proposes a new deep learning method to detect student emotions. The main aim of this paper is to map the relationship between teaching practices and student learning based on emotional impact. Facial recognition algorithms extract helpful information from online platforms as image classification techniques are applied to detect the emotions of student and/or teacher faces. As part of this work, two deep learning models are compared according to their performance. Promising results are achieved using both techniques, as presented in the Experimental Results Section. For validation of the proposed system, an online course with students is used; the findings suggest that this technique operates well. Based on emotional analysis, several deep learning techniques are applied to train and test the emotion classification process. Transfer learning for a pre-trained deep neural network is used as well to increase the accuracy of the emotion classification stage. The obtained results show that the performance of the proposed method is promising using both techniques, as presented in the Experimental Results Section.

Keywords: emotional intelligence; online education; deep learning; intelligent education; transfer learning; computer vision

Citation: AlZu'bi, S.; Abu Zitar, R.; Hawashin, B.; Abu Shanab, S.; Zraiqat, A.; Mughaid, A.; Almotairi, K.H.; Abualigah, L. A Novel Deep Learning Technique for Detecting Emotional Impact in Online Education. *Electronics* **2022**, *11*, 2964. https://doi.org/10.3390/electronics11182964

Academic Editors: George A. Papakostas and Akshya Swain

Received: 26 July 2022
Accepted: 13 September 2022
Published: 19 September 2022

Publisher's Note: MDPI stays neutral with regard to jurisdictional claims in published maps and institutional affiliations.

1. Introduction

Emotions are a vital and fundamental part of our existence. To comprehend a human's most fundamental behavior, we must examine these feelings using emotional data, such as text, voice, face, facial emotions, and facial data [1,2]. Emotion analysis is used in computer vision, image processing, and high-speed photography applications to detect movement in images [3]. Emotion analysis aims to detect emotion in an image, track a person's emotion through time, group items that move together, and determine motion direction. Human faces are thought to contain much information that humans use to make engagement decisions, and facial emotions are closely linked to perceived engagement [4].

Facial expressions reveal much about a person's feelings, intentions, and internal states [5]. Facial expression systems are a type of automatic facial expression recognition system [6]. Such systems can function reasonably, displaying spontaneous and planned behavior and contrived facial expressions [7].

Emotional analysis employs a complicated framework for understanding customer responses [8,9]. Using emoji and text analysis, this method assesses the variances in the feelings expressed by different viewers or purchasers [10]. It is a detailed examination of the feelings and intensities felt as emotions develop and change [11–13].

Unlike sentiment analysis, emotional analysis considers human emotions' nuances. It also investigates the viewer's, buyer's, or reader's intentions and impulses [14,15]. These discoveries can be quite enlightening and are simple to put into action: if boredom is the predominant emotion, spice things up with humor, creativity, or a cliffhanger moment. A confused reaction can indicate that the material is too complicated and that you must convey it differently [16].

Emotions are essential in our life, as they are inborn with the ability to influence our behaviors and judgments [17]. Faces are often the best sign of this because they convey emotions without words and may be observed by others [18]. Facial emotions are created by muscle movements beneath the skin of the face [19,20]. Emotions, according to scholars, are a significant component of nonverbal communication and a rich source of social signals, and they are crucial in understanding human behavior [21]. By examining facial expressions and mood data, researchers can gain a deeper comprehension of complicated human actions [22].

A straightforward guide to students' internal expressions is preferred to develop a successful strategy for teaching effectively and improving academic achievements [23]. This can reveal complex emotions and impulses, which are never simply black and white either for positive or negative emotions for any student [24].

Teachers could get real-time data on their pupils' engagement with educational videos. Such data could indicate whether a video causes high anxiety or low involvement. The technology could aid in determining when and why pupils become disengaged, allowing intervention before it is too late [25]. This study looks at methods for automatically detecting student involvement based on facial expressions. We investigated whether human observers can reliably judge engagement from the face. The technology could assist in understanding when and why kids get distracted and possibly intervene before it becomes a problem [26]. Automated Instructional Systems (AITS) is a type of computer-assisted instruction that reports the video viewing speed that students choose as well as the student's perception of the degree of difficulty.

In-depth emotional analysis is designed to help understand student behaviors and motivations [27]. This is the only way to properly understand how to change website or social media site content during online education. It encompasses the full range of human emotions. Emotions are strong feelings associated with each circumstance and play an important role in communication between students and teachers. Emoticons can be recognized by various features, including face, speech, and even text. Facial expressions are one of the most direct ways of communicating feelings and are necessary to appreciate a student's internal feelings [28,29]. The facial expressions of students and/or teachers can be used to understand their emotions in the learning environment.

This paper aims to map the relationship between teaching practices and student learning based on students' and teachers' emotional impact. Facial recognition algorithms extract helpful information from online platforms as image classification techniques are applied to detect the emotion of student and/or teacher faces. To validate the proposed system, an online course with students is used; the findings suggest that this technique operates well. Based on emotional analysis, several deep learning techniques are applied to train and test the emotion classification process. Transfer learning for a pre-trained deep neural network is used as well to increase the accuracy of the emotion classification stage. The obtained results show that the performance of the proposed method is promising with both techniques, as presented in the Experimental Results Section.

Application of the proposed system to a sample of online courses and in-class students resulted in an unexpected conclusion. In-class students mainly were positive and had interactive emotions such as happy, surprised, sad, and angry. Furthermore, the online students' emotions were negative faces such as contempt, disgust, fear, and natural. It is worth mentioning that the ahegao emotion appeared a few times with only online course students and never appeared with in-class students. Furthermore, according to the grades achieved, it was expected that online course students would have lower total grades based on their emotions during the class. However, the system proved the opposite: online course students achieved higher grades than in-class students.

The benefit of applying the proposed system in real life relies on grouping students into two groups based on their class emotions: those who are more engaged with face-to-face education, and the others who can get better results by attending online courses. Moreover, according to the tested sample, 67% of the students who were not interested during face-to-face education, based on their emotions, will have better results if they attend the same course virtually.

The remaining of this paper is structured as follow: Section 2 reviews the related literature. The proposed system is introduced in Section 3. Section 4 includes the experimental results and discussions. Finally, the work is concluded and future work is mentioned in Section 6.

2. Literature Review

Teachers must comprehend student efficiency in a scientific atmosphere [30]. This problem does not occur in an offline setting since the teacher can see the pupils' emotions and expressions. The concept described in this study assists teachers in adjusting their teaching approaches to match the interests, progress, and learning of their pupils [31,32].

The teacher is the most crucial element in the school, and his/her personality greatly influences student behavior, as no good educational situation can be achieved without teachers. Their values and behavior are personally affected by their characteristics and their style of dealing inside and outside the classroom [33].

A teacher who has desirable personal characteristics (based on student perception) is more able to bring about changes in their behavior and is more able to arouse their interest and direct them in the desired direction. The positive relationship between a teacher and the students allow them to learn how to lead and direct themselves [33]. Professors and teachers are the most important people affecting students, especially in the primary stages, which are considered the most important stages of study because the student acquires everything that comes to mind from information, whether negative or negative positive, at this stage.

Many types of research have been conducted since the sudden move to online education; many problems have been addressed in these research articles [34–36]. One of the important things that teachers should pay attention to is body language and facial expressions. Because the students focus on the teacher's kinetic language accurately and can even verbally describe it, they constantly monitor his movements, so attention must be paid to students' strength of observation to achieve the required communication. The effort is focused on the teacher, so he directs his physical movements, eyebrow expressions, tone of voice, the use of shoulders, and many other nonverbal movements [37].

Many previous researchers have worked on the present technique for developing emotion recognition hardware on image/pattern recognition systems [38,39]. Further, an important point that must be focused on, according to experts, is that communication with body language must be reciprocal. Students express themselves through their movements more than through speaking, and they sometimes may not dare to speak, but they express themselves through their behavior more, and the teacher must understand these movements and nonverbal signals to help with student engagement. Figure 1 illustrates a sample of teachers' emotions in the classroom.

Figure 1. A sample of teachers' emotions in the classroom.

Many earlier studies have focused on emotion analysis (EA) for various purposes. The developers of [40] have given an emotion care scheme and web-based platform to recognize people's emotional status during the continuing COVID-19 issue. They looked at eight emotions in various situations (i.e., anger, anticipation, disgust, fear, joy, sadness, surprise, and trust).

In [41], a convolutional neural network 2D (CNN-2D) input is a spectrogram built from speech sounds. Convolution layers, pooling layers, and fully connected layers are the three CNN layers that extract particular properties from spectrogram representations. When this model is used, the accuracy improves by 6.5 percent.

In [42], the authors' proposed paradigm has much promise for use in mental health care. It could identify, monitor, and diagnose a patient's mental health in a low-cost, user-friendly way. Their suggested approach employed the CK+ and FER2013 datasets to get information from AlexNet's Fully Connected Layer 6.

In [43], a group of scientists created a system that employs sensors to log and disseminate real-time mood data. The platform is intended to make it simple to prototype new computer interfaces that can detect, respond to, and adapt to human emotion. They expect it will contribute to the advancement of effective computing technology.

In [44], after being trained on a large dataset consisting of animations of the characters Tom and Jerry with a size of 8K by downloading videos from a popular YouTube channel, the proposed integrated deep neural network (DNN) correctly identifies the character, segments their face masks, and recognizes the resulting emotions. With 96 percent accuracy and an F1 score of 0.85, VGG 16 exceeded the competition. The study's primary goal was to integrate DNN and validate it on vast data to better comprehend and analyze emotions. The suggested integrated DNN includes Mask R-CNN for cartoon figure detection, and well-known learning architectures/models such as VGG16, InceptionV3, ResNet-50, and MobileNetV2.

In [45], a sophisticated Lie-Sensor is developed for detecting fraud or malicious intent and authorizing its validation. Face emotions are labeled as 'Happiness,' 'Sadness,' 'Surprise,' and 'Hate' in a suggested live emotional intelligence detector. It also uses text classification to forecast a message's label separately. Finally, it compares the two labels and determines whether the message is genuine. The authors of [46] present a method for recognizing facial expressions in photographs of people of various ages, genders, and nationalities. "Emotion sketches", simplified depictions of facial expressions, are proposed. The study explains how to get emotion sketches and confirms the method by using them to train and test neural networks. Emotion sketches were used to train three neural networks of different types in order to classify facial expressions as 'Positive', 'Negative', 'Awe' and 'Neutral'. The prediction results were encouraging, with over 70% accuracy given by each network on a query dataset.

In [47], for facial sentiment analysis, the researchers suggest a real-time streaming image-based PingPong (PP2) method, line-segment feature analysis (LFA), and convolutional recurrent neural network (CRNN) model. The accuracy of face recognition using the suggested method is compared to the loss rate for other models in a performance evaluation. This study was carried out to address security issues that may arise with driver convenience services that use video in smart automobiles. We built an encoding–decrypting procedure on videos to improve the security of real-time stream videos. Using two variable clock functions and memory, the PP2 algorithm generated random numbers. PP2LFA-CRNN models were compared to AlexNet and CRNN models. The learning rate was 96.8% in the experiment using the test dataset, which was higher than expected.

In [48], the PP2LFA-CRNN model was compared to AlexNet and CRNN models in terms of performance. The test dataset experiment's learning rate was 96.8%, which was more excellent than previous techniques (CRNN: 94.2 percent and AlexNet: 91.3 percent). The experiment revealed that a person's visual attention matches their purchasing and consumption habits. More consumer cognition research will help researchers better understand human behavior for various applications, including marketing, health care, personal qualities, wellness, and many more. In [49], the authors suggested using RIEA (relationship identification using emotion analysis) to find relationships between intelligent agents. Their study extracted emotions and mapped them onto a set of human interactions using cognitive psychology and natural language processing theories.

In [50], the authors offered a current assessment of computational analytic tools for assessing emotional facial expression in Parkinson's disease patients (PWP). An NVIDIA GeForce 920M GPU was used to develop a deep-learning-based model. Techniques for computational facial expression analysis in Parkinson's disease have many applications. Many of the proposed approaches to improving clinical assessment contain flaws. Hypomimia is a biomarker for Parkinson's disease that we believe is significant. In [51], a new software application designed as a serious game to teach children with autism how to understand and express their emotions was released. Children naturally grab objects and engage with the system with their faces. The system was assessed based on its relevance for children with autism spectrum disorder (ASD). ASD is a neurodevelopmental disease that affects a person's social skills, particularly those related to emotional awareness and recognition. These skills can be learned, especially early in life. The researchers designed a game with no distracting elements so that children's attention is focused on learning to understand emotions.

The research in [52] investigated the effects of the proportion of non-competitive people and the length of emotional and cognitive time on the evolution of cooperation. Emotion comes through people's relationships, and studies have shown that emotion greatly impacts people's decision-making. Among non-competitive individuals, the fraction of cooperators increases with the minimum, whereas in competitive individuals, the proportion of cooperators peaks at M = 5. Individual emotions being introduced into strategy evolution is congruent with real-world phenomena. Our findings will help researchers better understand how strategies and emotions co-evolve. In [53], electroencephalogram (EEG) signals were used to detect a patient's mental state. EEG-based e-healthcare systems can be deployed and used in various smart contexts. They can assist disabled people in moving or controlling various devices, computers, and artificial limbs. Participants looked at images on a 15-inch display from a distance of roughly 70 cm. The display had gaze sensors mounted, and participants wore a head cap to measure functional near-infrared spectroscopy (fNIRS) signals. The proposed approach was compared via two different types of comparison methodologies.

In [54], A team of researchers at the University of British Columbia (UBC) in Canada developed a machine-learning model that achieves state-of-the-art single-network accuracy on FER2013 without using extra training data. They adopted the VGGNet architecture, rigorously fine-tuned its hyperparameters, and experimented with various optimization methods. Without additional training data, researchers at the University of Bristol achieved the highest single-network accuracy on FER2013. They used the VGG network to build a series of experiments to test various optimization algorithms and learning rate schedulers for better prediction accuracy. This paper achieved single-network state-of-the-art classification accuracy on FER2013 using a VGGNet. They also conducted extra tuning of their model using cosine annealing and combined the training and validation datasets to improve the classification accuracy further.

In [55], the authors presented emotion analysis (EA), which determines whether or not a text has any emotion. EA has grown in popularity recently, particularly for social media applications such as tweets and Facebook posts. The authors considered several instances of public posts and focused on several emotions in a single post. In [56], the authors presented a headline emotion classification. The content words were extracted to form different word pairs with joy, disgust, fear, anger, sadness, and surprise emotions. In [57], Vasileios Hatzivassiloglou and Kathleen R. McKeown found and validated limitations from conjunctions on the positive or negative semantic orientation of conjoined adjectives from a large corpus. A log-linear regression model uses these constraints to predict if conjoined adjectives are similar.

In [58], the authors distinguished six basic emotions using supervised machine learning. The support vector machine (SVM) classifier outperformed all other classifiers. On previously unseen examples, it generalized well. In [59], the authors proposed a system that automatically recognizes facial expressions from an image and classifies emotions. The system uses a simplified 'Viola Jones Face Detection' method for face localization. The different feature vectors are combined to improve recognition and classification performance. In [60], the authors explored a couple of machine learning algorithms and feature-extraction techniques to help accurately identify human emotion. In [61], the authors reviewed the recent literature on speech emotion recognition. Thirty-two representative speech databases were reviewed from the point of view of their language, number of speakers, and emotions. The importance of choosing different classification models has been discussed.

EA has also been employed in the educational field; student and/or teacher emotions could be detected using smart systems. Many researchers have studied the effects of people's emotions on others. In [62], the authors tried to analyze online learning behaviors based on image emotion recognition. Key frames were extracted from human faces using an improved local binary pattern (LBP) and wavelet transform. The authors designed the structure for an online learning behavior analysis system. They also proposed a strategy for learning to recognize emotions through facial expressions. They extracted significant frames from facial expression photographs using an upgraded LBP and wavelet transform. The mean expression feature was then solved using many extracted key frames. Data and histograms show that the suggested technique can improve the effectiveness of image emotion recognition in experiments.

The authors of [63] established the SELCSI (Student Emotional Learning in Cultural Safety Instrument). The preliminary validity and reliability of students' emotional learning scales were discovered. This tool could help researchers better understand how nursing and midwifery students learn to practice in a culturally acceptable manner. The tool's use has significant theoretical, educational, and methodological implications. The SELCSI is a tool to assist students to understand how health students learn to engage with First Peoples and communities in a culturally appropriate manner. For nursing and midwifery education, the instrument's use has substantial theoretical, pedagogical, and methodological implications. In [64], the researchers' goal was to look at the impact of mindfulness techniques on stress perception and psychological well-being. The study included 45 graduate students split into two groups: intervention and control. Analysis of variance (ANOVA) for repeated measures was used to evaluate quantitative data, while thematic content analysis was used to analyze the interviews. The interviews revealed the presence of mixed feelings about graduate school and the development of new coping methods to deal with this work environment. In both groups, the results showed an increase in mindfulness and psychological well-being, as well as a decrease in perceived stress.

The research in [65] presents an EEG-based emotion detection method for detecting a patient's emotional state. The overall categorization accuracy was found to be 83.87 percent. Four electrodes are used to test a new technique based on the EEG database "DEAP". When compared to existing algorithms, it performs well. It uses electroencephalogram (EEG) signals to detect a patient's mental state. EEG-based e-healthcare systems can be used in a variety of smart settings. They can assist disabled people with operating or controlling various devices, computers, and prosthetic limbs. In [66], the authors presented a system to detect the engagement level of the students. The system correctly identified when students were "very engaged", "nominally engaged", and "not engaged at all". The students with the best scores also had higher concentration indexes and were more attentive to details of their work.

Concluding the literature review, artificial intelligence (AI) and recent deep learning techniques could be applied to many areas that facilitate human lives [67,68]. Furthermore, it could be applied in medical applications [69,70], recommender systems [71], job-seeking [72], smart cities and localization [73], hospitals [74,75], object tracking [76–78], software engineering [79,80], E-commerce [81], emotional analysis [82], agriculture applications [83,84], and many others [85].

3. Methodology

Face Reader is the most reliable automated method for recognizing a variety of specific qualities in facial photographs, including the nine basic or universal expressions of happiness, sadness, anger, surprise, neutrality, disdain, Ahegao, fear, and disgust. According to Paul Ekman, these emotional categories are basic or universal emotions. Face Reader can also detect a 'neutral' condition and evaluate 'contempt.' Action units, valence, arousal, gaze direction, head orientation, and personal factors such as gender and age are also calculated.

Online students exhibit varied levels of involvement while participating in these instructional activities, including boredom, annoyance, delight, neutral, bewilderment, and learning gain. Online educators must accurately and efficiently assess online learners' engagement status to give individualized pedagogical support. Automatic categorization methods extract features from various traits such as eye movement, facial expressions, gestures, and postures or physiological and neurological sensors. These methods do not interfere with learners' engagement detection in their learning environments, enabling them to be grouped into different subject areas.

The amount of arousal or alertness is commonly associated with participation in the neuroscience literature. The detected emotion of either student or the teacher are the indicators used to assess engagement and attentiveness. These methods require using computer-vision-based approaches that are not practical in real-world educational settings.

Computer-vision-based approaches can assess whether a learner is engaged in an activity. The assessment procedure is unobtrusive and simple to use, comparable to how a teacher monitors whether a pupil is motivated without disrupting his or her activity in the classroom.

3.1. Proposed System

Several datasets have been used in the proposed system; some are collected from the web, and others have been previously implemented by other researchers (more information about the dataset will be explained in detail in the next section). The proposed system employs deep learning techniques to test the emotions in the dataset after applying preprocessing stages to reduce the features and remove noise. Figure 2 illustrates the proposed system implemented to analyze teacher and student emotions.

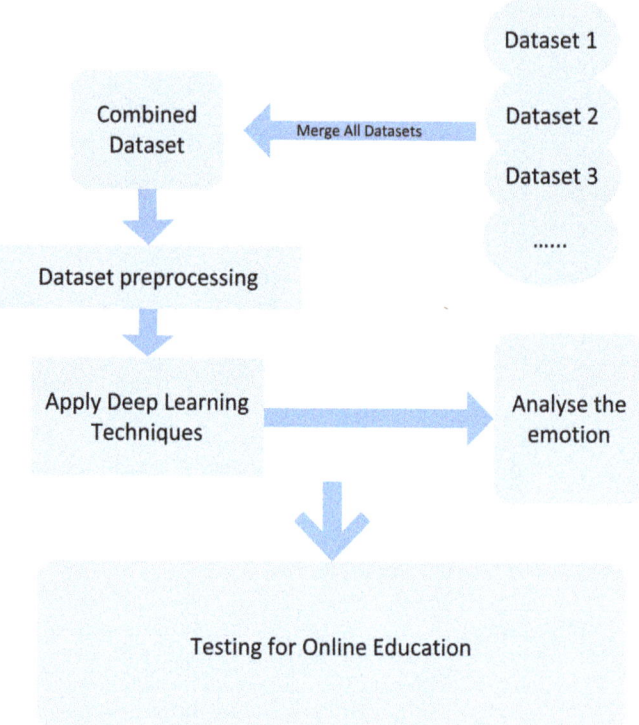

Figure 2. Proposed emotional impact detection system.

3.2. Dataset

Many available datasets can be used for EA, and some of them are employed in this research. The following describes the well-known datasets in the field.

Among the most comprehensive databases for face affect in still images, AffectNet includes category and dimensional models; 1250 emotion-related tags in English, German, Spanish, Portuguese, Arabic, and Farsi were used to collect the data.

The CK+ (Extended Cohn–Kanade Dataset) is a publicly available benchmark dataset for action unit and emotion recognition. There are 5876 images in the collection from 123 persons, with expression sequences ranging from neutral to peak. The images in the CK+ collection all share the same backdrop, are mostly grayscale, and are 640 × 490 pixels in size.

A training set of 28,000 labeled photos, a development set of 3500 annotated images, and a test set of 3500 images comprise the Fer-2013 (Facial Expression Recognition 2013) dataset. The dataset was created by combining the results of each emotion's Google image search with synonyms for the emotions. Each image in FER-2013 is tagged with one of seven emotions: happy, sad, furious, afraid, surprise, disgust, and neutral, with happiness being the most common, resulting in a 24.4 percent baseline for random guessing.

EMOTIC (Emotion Recognition in Context) is a database of photographs of people in real-life scenarios labeled with their apparent emotions. The EMOTIC dataset includes two types of emotion representation: discrete categories (a set of 26) and continuous dimensions (24) (e.g., valence, arousal, and dominance). There are 23,571 images and 34,320 people tagged in the collection. In reality, some images were hand-picked from Google's search engine.

The Google Facial Expression Comparison dataset is a popular emotion dataset with many people using it. There are labeled triplet images in the collection. The top six raters assign each triplet a label. The dataset aids in establishing which of the two faces has similar feelings in each scenario. The data are mainly used to summarize albums, determine emotions, and other similar tasks.

Ascertain is a multi-modal database for implicit personality and affects recognition that may be used to track physiological responses to assess personality traits and emotional states. The data contain 58 individuals' Big Five personality scores and emotional self-ratings, synchronously recorded EEG, ECG, galvanic skin response (GSR), and facial activity data acquired while watching affective movie clips with off-the-shelf sensors.

Dreamer is a multi-modal database that contains electroencephalogram (EEG) and electrocardiogram (ECG) information collected during affect elicitation with audio–visual stimuli. Signals from 23 people were captured in this dataset, together with the subjects' self-assessment of their affective state regarding valence, arousal, and dominance following each stimulus.

K-EmoCon is a multi-modal dataset compiled from 32 persons who participated in 16 paired social discussions. The data were gathered using three off-the-shelf wearable sensors, audio–visual video of debate participants, and continual emotional annotations.

In this paper, we collected data by downloading it from the Kaggle website, where we obtained a dataset for analyzing emotions of images with different names such as fer-2013, CK+48, jaffedbase, OAHEGA EMOTION RECOGNITION DATASET, and Natural Human Face Images for Emotion Recognition, as described in detail in Table 1. We consolidated the examples from the various datasets into a separate file for each emotion: ahegao, anger, contempt, happiness, fear, disgust, neutrality, surprise, and sad.

Then, we divided each separate file into two groups: 80% training and 20% testing. We used cross validation to optimize the training and testing percentages, as illustrated in Table 1:

Table 1. Number of dataset images used for training vs. testing.

Emotion Label	Total Images	Images/Feature	
		Training	Testing
Aheago	1205	964	241
Anger	7321	5856	1465
Contempt	208	166	42
Disgust	1015	812	203
Fear	5798	4638	1160
Happy	14,373	11,498	2875
Neutral	10,779	8623	2156
Sad	10,872	8697	2175
Surprise	6290	5032	1258
Total	57,861	46,286	11,575

In this paper, we apply several algorithms to each of our datasets separately and then to our aggregate dataset, with the aim of revealing the extent to which teachers influence students in the educational process by focusing on analyzing feelings, which is the main objective of this paper. A sample of the dataset used in this research is illustrated in Figure 3.

Figure 3. A sample of the implemented dataset.

The second step was to make the dataset stabled, so we converted all images to the same extension and size and made them gray (black and white). Our purpose is to build stabled dataset to be ready for use in many experiments in several papers for education purposes. This paper's main contribution is linking the emotional impact of both students and teachers on online education. The unbalanced data that was noticed from Table 1 will be resolved in future work as both oversampling and under-sampling techniques will be implemented and applied to the gathered dataset to make the accuracy much better according to the emotion classification process.

4. Experimental Results

4.1. Evaluation Measurements

The evaluation method is based on calculating retrieval, accuracy, and F1. For each label, we find the TP, FP, TN, and FN. Table 2 presents the Confusion Matrix.

Table 2. Confusion Matrix.

	Positive (1)	Negative (0)
Predicted Positive (1)	**True Positives (TPs)**	**False Positive (FPs)**
Predicted Negative (0)	**False Negatives (FNs)**	**True Negatives (TNs)**

The labels of the Confusion Matrix are explained below:

- Positive = the expectation was real;
- Negative = the prediction was not true;
- True = the prediction was correct;
- False = incorrect prediction.

The evaluation measurements used in the experiments are given as follows:

- Recall: the percentage of correctly assigned records in that class among all the records belonging to that class. It is given by Equation (1).

$$R = TP/(TP + FN), \tag{1}$$

- Precision: the percentage of correctly assigned records for that class among all the assigned records of that class. It is given by Equation (2).

$$P = TP/(TP + FP), \tag{2}$$

- F1: the harmonic mean between the Recall and the Precision. It is given by Equation (3).

$$F1 = (2 * R * P)/(R + P), \tag{3}$$

- Loss: the difference between the actual and the predicted result. It is given in Equation (4).

$$Loss = -(YactualLog(Ypredicted) + (1 - Yactual)Log(1 - Ypredicted)), \qquad (4)$$

4.2. Experimental Settings

For the conducted experiments, we used an Intel(R) Core(TM) i7-10870H CPU @ 2.20GHz with 32GB RAM and an Nvidia RTX 3070 GPU. For the implementation of the algorithms, we used Python 3.8.8 and MATLAB 2020b.

4.3. The Compared Deep Artificial Neural Networks

In this work for the sake of classifying images, we adopted two deep architectures: ResNet50 and a 7-layered deep CNN. ResNet50 is a CNN model that was trained on the ImageNet dataset. The model can classify an image to one of the 1000 labels available. The dataset contains millions of records, and the CNN is 50 layers deep. The pre-trained model has been widely used in various image applications. We also used another deep model that is composed of seven convolutional layers. The architecture of the model is given as follows.

```
Model: "sequential"

_____
Layer (type)                   Output Shape          Param #
=================================================================
conv2d (Conv2D)                (None, 48, 48, 64)      640

batch_normalization(BatchNo)   (None, 48, 48, 64)      256

activation (Activation)        (None, 48, 48, 64)       0

max_pooling2d (MaxPooling2D)   (None, 24, 24, 64)       0

dropout (Dropout)              (None, 24, 24, 64)       0

conv2d_1 (Conv2D)              (None, 24, 24, 128)    204928

batch_normalization_1 (Batch)  (None, 24, 24, 128)     512

activation_1 (Activation)      (None, 24, 24, 128)      0

max_pooling2d_1 (MaxPooling2    (None, 12, 12, 128)      0

dropout_1 (Dropout)            (None, 12, 12, 128)      0

conv2d_2 (Conv2D)              (None, 12, 12, 512)    590336

batch_normalization_2 (Batch)  (None, 12, 12, 512)    2048

activation_2 (Activation)      (None, 12, 12, 512)      0

max_pooling2d_2 (MaxPooling2    (None, 6, 6, 512)        0

dropout_2 (Dropout)            (None, 6, 6, 512)        0

conv2d_3 (Conv2D)              (None, 6, 6, 512)     2359808

batch_normalization_3 (Batch)  (None, 6, 6, 512)      2048

activation_3 (Activation)      (None, 6, 6, 512)        0

max_pooling2d_3 (MaxPooling2)  (None, 3, 3, 512)        0
_____
```

```
dropout_3 (Dropout)              (None, 3, 3, 512)        0
---------------------------------------------------------------
flatten (Flatten)               (None, 4608)             0
---------------------------------------------------------------
dense (Dense)                   (None, 256)              1179904
---------------------------------------------------------------
batch_normalization_4 (Batch)   (None, 256)              1024
---------------------------------------------------------------
activation_4 (Activation)       (None, 256)              0
---------------------------------------------------------------
dropout_4 (Dropout)             (None, 256)              0
---------------------------------------------------------------
dense_1 (Dense)                 (None, 512)              131584
---------------------------------------------------------------
batch_normalization_5 (Batch)   (None, 512)              2048
---------------------------------------------------------------
activation_5 (Activation)       (None, 512)              0
---------------------------------------------------------------
dropout_5 (Dropout)             (None, 512)              0
---------------------------------------------------------------
dense_2 (Dense)                 (None, 9)                4617
===============================================================
Total params: 4,479,753
Trainable params: 4,475,785
Non-trainable params: 3,968
```

4.4. Experimental Results

We conducted two sets of experiments. The first was conducted using the 7-layered deep neural network, and the second was conducted by transferring the pre-trained widely used RESNET50 architecture. The results in Table 3 illustrate the F1 measurement and loss for the 7-layered deep neural network, and after using 50 epochs and a batch size of 10, both the F1 measurement and the loss are represented in Figure 4. The F1 increased exponentially with the increase in the epochs for both the training set and the validation set until reaching a point at which the F1 increase tended to be linear. That point was reached with approximately ten epochs. It was also noted that the increase in the F1 for the training set was more than that of the validation set. This was expected due to the overfitting common in training sets. The best F1 was 0.64 for the validation and 0.68 for the training set. These readings were achieved using 50 epochs. As for the loss, it showed opposite behavior to the F1, as it started to decrease rapidly until reaching 10 epochs, at which point it started to decrease linearly. The best loss for the validation set was 0.95, whereas the best loss for the training set was 0.9.

Table 3. Accuracy of EA using 7-layered deep neural network and multiple epochs.

Epoch	Training F1	Validation F1	Training Loss	Validation Loss
10	0.6450	0.6250	0.9500	1.0000
20	0.6500	0.6290	0.9400	0.9800
30	0.6570	0.6330	0.9300	0.9700
40	0.6630	0.6370	0.9100	0.9600
50	0.6730	0.6400	0.9000	0.9500

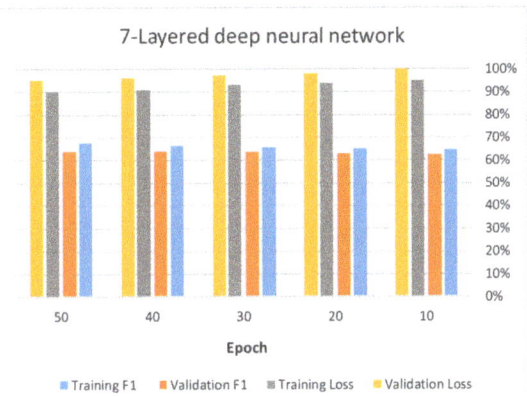

Figure 4. F1 measure and loss for training and validation stages using 7-layered deep neural network.

When the ResNet50 architecture was used instead, relatively similar performance was obtained. Using 50 epochs, it can be noticed from Table 4 that the best F1 was 0.7 for the validation set and 0.785 for the training set. As for the loss, it reached 0.8 for the validation set and 0.59 for the training set, as shown in Figure 5.

Table 4. Accuracy of EA using ResNet50 and multiple epochs.

Epoch	Training F1	Validation F1	Training Loss	Validation Loss
10	0.6800	0.6300	0.8000	0.9300
20	0.7158	0.6916	0.7660	0.8387
30	0.7503	0.6950	0.6711	0.8200
40	0.7700	0.7000	0.6200	0.8100
50	0.7850	0.7050	0.5900	0.8000

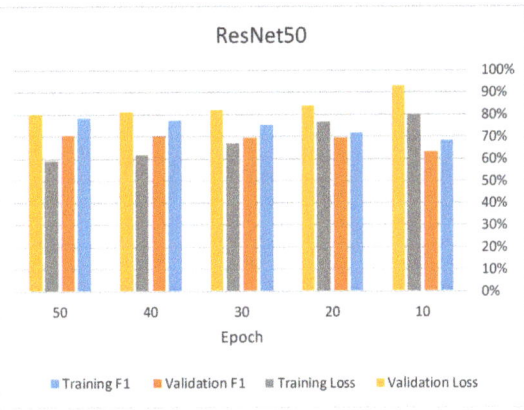

Figure 5. F1 measure and loss for training and validation stages using ResNet50.

Table 5 and Figure 6 provide the Recall per label for the 7-layered model. Table 6 and Figure 7 provide the Precision per label for the 7-layered model. Table 7 and Figure 8 provide the F1 per label for the 7-layered model based on the validation of transfer learning using the pre-trained deep neural network ResNet50. Table 8 and Figure 9 provide the Recall per label for the 7-layered model. Table 9 and Figure 10 provides the precision per label for the 7-layered model. Table 10 and Figure 11 provides the F1 per label for the 7-layered model.

Table 5. Recall per label for the 7-layered model.

Label	Recall
Ahegao	0.97
Angry	0.53
Contempt	0.98
Disgust	0.55
Fear	0.34
Happy	0.87
Neutral	0.65
Sad	0.59
Surprise	0.83
Macro Avg	0.7

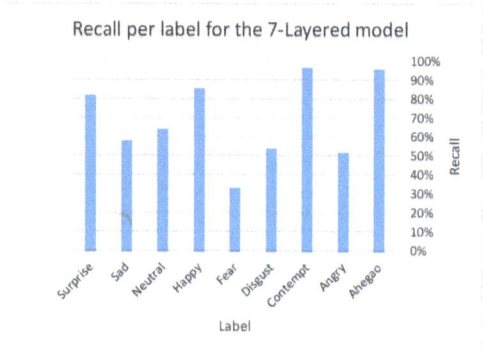

Figure 6. Recall per label for the 7-layered model.

Table 6. Precision per label for the 7-layered model.

Label	Precision
Ahegao	0.96
Angry	0.59
Contempt	0.76
Disgust	0.59
Fear	0.55
Happy	0.83
Neutral	0.57
Sad	0.52
Surprise	0.74
Macro Avg	0.68

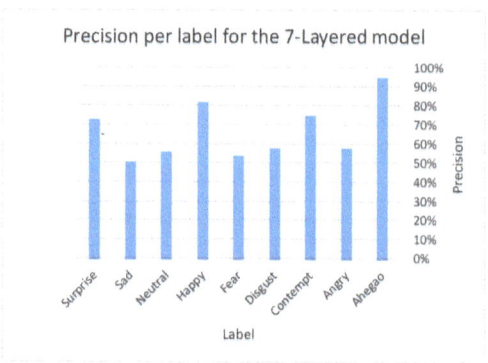

Figure 7. Precision per label for the 7-layered model.

Table 7. F1 measure per label for the 7-layered model.

Label	F1
Ahegao	0.96
Angry	0.56
Contempt	0.85
Disgust	0.57
Fear	0.42
Happy	0.85
Neutral	0.61
Sad	0.55
Surprise	0.78
Macro Avg	0.68

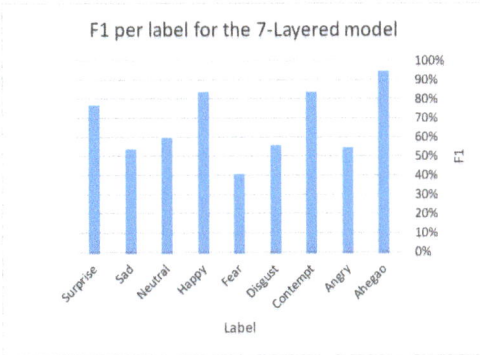

Figure 8. F1 measure per label for the 7-layered model.

Table 8. Recall per label for the pre-trained deep NN (ResNet59).

Label	Recall
Ahegao	0.94
Angry	0.59
Contempt	0.67
Disgust	0.73
Fear	0.58
Happy	0.93
Neutral	0.66
Sad	0.61
Surprise	0.78
Macro Avg	0.72

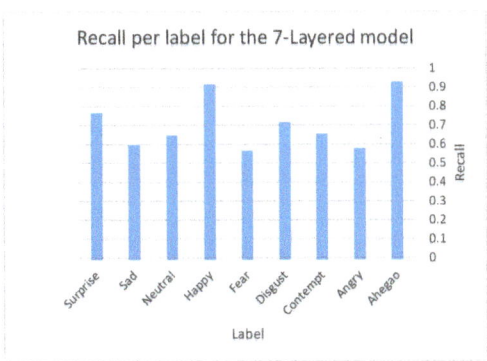

Figure 9. Recall per label for the pre-trained deep NN (ResNet59).

Table 9. Precision per label for the pre-trained deep NN (ResNet59).

Label	Precision
Ahegao	0.95
Angry	0.71
Contempt	0.11
Disgust	0.42
Fear	0.45
Happy	0.85
Neutral	0.69
Sad	0.69
Surprise	0.77
Macro Avg	0.63

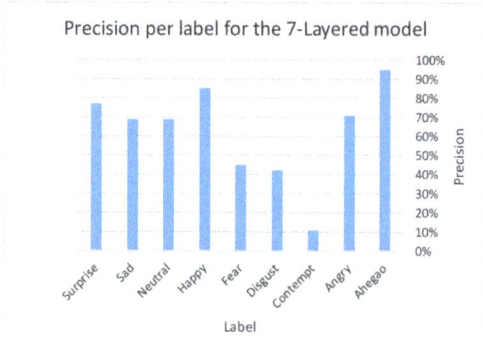

Figure 10. Precision per label for the pre-trained deep NN (ResNet59).

Table 10. F1 measure per label for the pre-trained deep NN (ResNet59).

Label	F1
Ahegao	0.95
Angry	0.64
Contempt	0.19
Disgust	0.53
Fear	0.51
Happy	0.89
Neutral	0.68
Sad	0.65
Surprise	0.77
Macro Avg	0.72

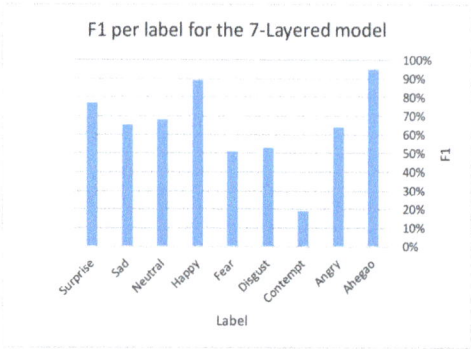

Figure 11. F1 measure per label for the pre-trained deep NN (ResNet59).

Clearly, the performance of the model varies per label. The best Precision was for the Ahegao label, and the Happy label was next. The worst Precision was for the Sad label, and the neutral label was next. As for the Recall, the best Recall was for the Contempt label, followed by Ahegao; the worst Recall was for the Fear label, followed by Angry. Regarding the F1, the labels are ranked as follows:

Ahegao → Contempt and Happy → Surprise → Neutral → Disgust and Angry → Fear

The variance of the performance per label can be attributed to the difficulty of the emotion. For example, the Happy emotion is much more evident than the Fear emotion. Therefore, it is easier for the classifier to detect the Happy emotion.

We conducted more experiments to study the effect of the number of samples per label on the performance. Based on the achieved results with the 7-layered model, Table 11 provides the F1 for each label along with the corresponding number of samples. Figures 12 and 13 illustrates the F1 for each label and the corresponding number of samples, respectively. For the results achieved using the pre-trained deep NN (ResNet50) model, Table 12 provides the F1 for each label along with the corresponding number of samples. Figures 14 and 15 illustrate the F1 for each label and the corresponding number of samples, respectively.

Table 11. F1 for each label along with the corresponding number of samples.

Label	F1	Number of Samples
Ahegao	96%	946
Angry	−56%	5856
Contempt	85%	166
Disgust	−57%	812
Fear	−42%	4638
Happy	85%	11,498
Neutral	−61%	8623
Sad	−55%	8697
Surprise	78%	5032
Macro Avg	68%	46,268

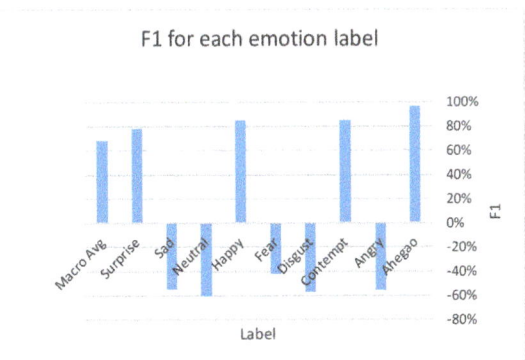

Figure 12. F1 measure for each label.

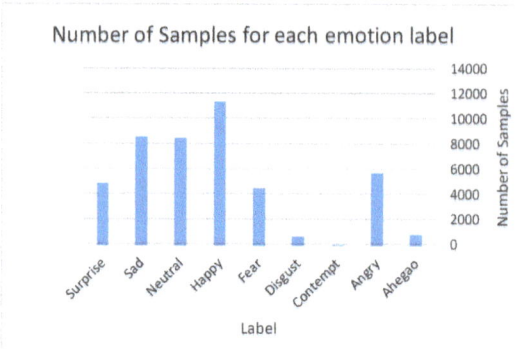

Figure 13. The corresponding number of samples for each label.

Table 12. F1 for each label along with the corresponding number of samples using ResNet50 model.

Label	F1	Number of Samples
Ahegao	95%	223
Angry	−64%	1650
Contempt	−19%	6
Disgust	−53%	124
Fear	−51%	896
Happy	89%	2701
Neutral	−68%	2297
Sad	−65%	2419
Surprise	−77%	1257
Macro Avg	72%	11,573

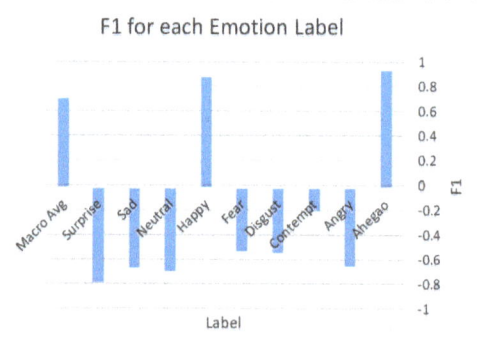

Figure 14. F1 measure for each label using ResNet50 model.

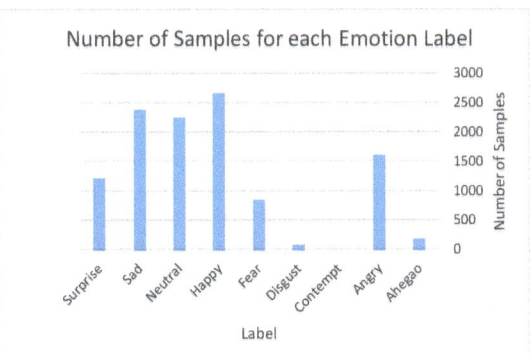

Figure 15. The corresponding number of samples for each label using ResNet50 model.

Unexpectedly, the number of samples did not have much effect on the performance. The four best F1 values were for a set of labels with various numbers of samples. To study the effect of the number of batches, we conducted a further set of experiments using batch size values increasing gradually from 32 to 128 using 10 epochs on the 7-layered model. The results are provided in Table 13 and Figure 16.

Table 13. Results based on batch size.

Batch Size	Training F1	Validation F1
32	60%	54%
64	61%	51%
96	61%	51%
128	56%	47%

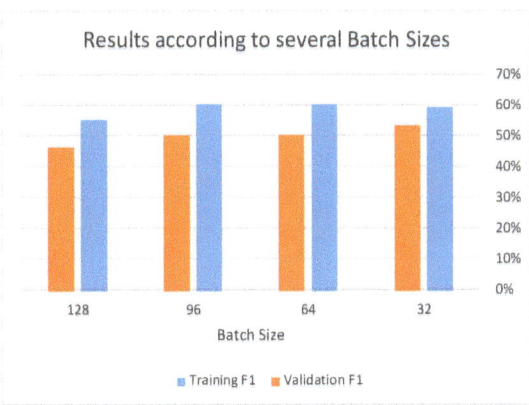

Figure 16. Results based on batch size.

From these results, it is noticeable that changing the batch size can slightly change the performance of the deep learning method. The best batch size ranged from 32–64.

5. Discussion

This study aims to analyze the acceptance of technology by students and how it affects achievements based on emotions after participating in an online course. A survey of 271 students (119 registered in face-to-face instruction, 252 registered in an online course) revealed a higher level of positive emotions than negative emotions.

Online course students had higher levels of aheago, anger, contempt, and disgust but less happy and surprise. Furthermore, the results show that students in online courses reported significantly higher grades, as technological achievements related significantly with class enjoyment.

Based on a five-point scale survey (1 = not related; 5 = very related), the following nine emotions were measured: ahegao, anger, contempt, happiness, fear, disgust, neutrality, surprise, and sad. The emotions varied in terms of valence and activation: positive activating, negative activating, positive deactivating (not measured), and negative deactivating.

For the assessment scales to show important connections with student emotions, both control and value scales and technology-related beliefs and age were included as covariates in further analyses of variance. An in-depth analysis was conducted to assess differences in students' grades for both online and face-to-face education.

Based on analyzing the conducted survey, the covariate effects can explain significant differences in students' negative emotions in both online and face-to-face education. Surprisingly, for domain-specific achievement, neither the main effect nor the covariates showed significant effects, although the t-test confirmed a significant difference between the groups.

The purpose of this research was to analyze to what extent there are differences in the experiences of specific teachers' students with respective to how their achievement is related to individual emotions; this has been evaluated by comparing students who attended the course physically with those who attended it virtually. As a result of what we conducted here, students with positive emotions have more benefits than those with negative emotions in university courses in education.

Further results regarding emotions and their appraisals showed that achievement task value was rated higher in the on-campus group, while technological control was higher in the online group. Consequently, domain-specific achievement was higher in the on-campus group. This supports the previous assumption that for some students, it seems to be difficult to learn to self-regulate.

In sum, it has been shown in this study that the learning environment might affect student achievement task value and technological control. On the other hand, the results indicate that the learning environment (i.e., online vs. face-to-face) seemed to have only weak effects on student achievement in this study.

6. Conclusions and Future Work

In this work, we propose the use of emotion detection in education. This work aims to improve educational outcomes by finding the hidden emotions of students. In order to detect emotions, we propose to use deep learning as a result of its wide use and excellent performance. In detail, we propose to use ResNet50 and a 7-layer model. After comparing the two models using various parameters, it was clear that these models performed efficiently and proved their ability to detect emotions correctly. The best-obtained F1 was 0.63 for the 7-layered model and 0.7 for ResNet50 for the validation data. As expected, the F1 measurement for the training data was slightly higher due to overfitting. Performance varied slightly when changing some deep learning parameters, such as the number of epochs and the batch size.

In future work, more architectures can be compared. Additionally, parameters of the deep neural network can be further optimized. Moreover, the use of pre-trained models can be further studied and compared with non-trained deep architectures. In addition, image enhancement techniques can help improve detection accuracy by emphasizing the essential features.

Here are some challenges and future targets: It is unclear how often the engagement detection decision should be made. What is the maximum duration of a video clip that can be assigned to a single level in the case of a short fragment? It is uncertain what criterion should be used when classifying training data.

Author Contributions: Conceptualization, S.A., A.Z. and S.A.S.; methodology, S.A. and B.H.; software, A.M. and S.A.; validation, S.A., K.H.A. and L.A.; formal analysis, S.A.S. and B.H.; investigation, L.A., A.M. and S.A.; resources, S.A.S.; data curation, S.A.S. and K.H.A.; writing—original draft preparation, S.A., K.H.A. and B.H.; writing—review and editing, S.A., R.A.Z. and B.H.; visualization, R.A.Z., A.Z., L.A., K.H.A. and A.M.; supervision, L.A. and B.H.; project administration, S.A.; funding acquisition, S.A. and R.A.Z. All authors of this research have contributed equally in this paper. All authors have read and agreed to the published version of the manuscript.

Funding: This research received no external funding.

Institutional Review Board Statement: Not applicable.

Informed Consent Statement: Not applicable.

Data Availability Statement: All data used in this research will be available upon request.

Acknowledgments: The authors would like to thank the Deanship of Scientific Research at Umm Al-Qura University for supporting this work through grant (22UQU4320277DSR11).

Conflicts of Interest: The authors declare no conflict of interest.

References

1. Walker, S.A.; Double, K.S.; Kunst, H.; Zhang, M.; MacCann, C. Emotional intelligence and attachment in adulthood: A meta-analysis. *Personal. Individ. Differ.* **2022**, *184*, 111174. [CrossRef]
2. Ghanem, B.; Rosso, P.; Rangel, F. An emotional analysis of false information in social media and news articles. *ACM Trans. Internet Technol. (TOIT)* **2020**, *20*, 1–18. [CrossRef]
3. Radlak, K.; Smolka, B. A novel approach to the eye movement analysis using a high speed camera. In Proceedings of the 2012 2nd International Conference on Advances in Computational Tools for Engineering Applications (ACTEA), Beirut, Lebanon, 12–15 December 2012; IEEE: Piscataway, NJ, USA, 2012; pp. 145–150.
4. Whitehill, J.; Serpell, Z.; Lin, Y.C.; Foster, A.; Movellan, J.R. The faces of engagement: Automatic recognition of student engagement from facial expressions. *IEEE Trans. Affect. Comput.* **2014**, *5*, 86–98. [CrossRef]
5. Olsson, A.; Ochsner, K.N. The role of social cognition in emotion. *Trends Cogn. Sci.* **2008**, *12*, 65–71. [CrossRef] [PubMed]
6. Sandbach, G.; Zafeiriou, S.; Pantic, M.; Yin, L. Static and dynamic 3D facial expression recognition: A comprehensive survey. *Image Vis. Comput.* **2012**, *30*, 683–697. [CrossRef]
7. Motley, M.T.; Camden, C.T. Facial expression of emotion: A comparison of posed expressions versus spontaneous expressions in an interpersonal communication setting. *West. J. Commun. (Includes Commun. Rep.)* **1988**, *52*, 1–22. [CrossRef]
8. Brown, S.P.; Lam, S.K. A meta-analysis of relationships linking employee satisfaction to customer responses. *J. Retail.* **2008**, *84*, 243–255. [CrossRef]
9. Park, E.; Jang, Y.; Kim, J.; Jeong, N.J.; Bae, K.; Del Pobil, A.P. Determinants of customer satisfaction with airline services: An analysis of customer feedback big data. *J. Retail. Consum. Serv.* **2019**, *51*, 186–190. [CrossRef]
10. Lou, Y.; Zhang, Y.; Li, F.; Qian, T.; Ji, D. Emoji-based sentiment analysis using attention networks. *Acm Trans. Asian -Low-Resour. Lang. Inf. Process. (TALLIP)* **2020**, *19*, 1–13. [CrossRef]
11. Rodrigo-Ruiz, D. Effect of teachers' emotions on their students: Some evidence. *J. Educ. Soc. Policy* **2016**, *3*, 73–79.
12. Wang, M.; Deng, W. Deep face recognition: A survey. *Neurocomputing* **2021**, *429*, 215–244. [CrossRef]
13. Adjabi, I.; Ouahabi, A.; Benzaoui, A.; Taleb-Ahmed, A. Past, Present, and Future of Face Recognition: A Review. *Electronics* **2020**, *9*, 1188. [CrossRef]
14. Abualigah, L.; Kareem, N.K.; Omari, M.; Elaziz, M.A.; Gandomi, A.H. Survey on Twitter Sentiment Analysis: Architecture, Classifications, and Challenges. In *Deep Learning Approaches for Spoken and Natural Language Processing*; Springer: Berlin/Heidelberg, Germany, 2021; pp. 1–18.
15. Abualigah, L.; Alfar, H.E.; Shehab, M.; Hussein, A.M.A. Sentiment analysis in healthcare: A brief review. In *Recent Advances in NLP: The Case of Arabic Language*; 2020; pp. 129–141.
16. Ransan-Cooper, H.; Lovell, H.; Watson, P.; Harwood, A.; Hann, V. Frustration, confusion and excitement: Mixed emotional responses to new household solar-battery systems in Australia. *Energy Res. Soc. Sci.* **2020**, *70*, 101656. [CrossRef]
17. Solomon, R.C. On emotions as judgments. *Am. Philos. Q.* **1988**, *25*, 183–191.
18. Torre, J.B.; Lieberman, M.D. Putting feelings into words: Affect labeling as implicit emotion regulation. *Emot. Rev.* **2018**, *10*, 116–124. [CrossRef]
19. Zhang, J.; Chen, K.; Zheng, J. Facial expression retargeting from human to avatar made easy. *IEEE Trans. Vis. Comput. Graph.* **2020**, *28*, 1274–1287. [CrossRef]
20. Yagi, S.; Nakata, Y.; Nakamura, Y.; Ishiguro, H. Can an android's posture and movement discriminate against the ambiguous emotion perceived from its facial expressions? *PLoS ONE* **2021**, *16*, e0254905. [CrossRef]
21. He, Y.; Choi, C.Y. A Study of Facial Expression of Digital Character with Muscle Simulation System. *Int. J. Adv. Smart Converg.* **2019**, *8*, 162–169.

22. Alzubi, S.; Hawashin, B.; Mughaid, A.; Jararweh, Y. Whats Trending? An Efficient Trending Research Topics Extractor and Recommender. In Proceedings of the 2020 11th International Conference on Information and Communication Systems (ICICS), Virtual, 7–9 April 2020; IEEE: Piscataway, NJ, USA, 2020; pp. 191–196.

23. Corcoran, R.P.; Cheung, A.C.; Kim, E.; Xie, C. Effective universal school-based social and emotional learning programs for improving academic achievement: A systematic review and meta-analysis of 50 years of research. *Educ. Res. Rev.* **2018**, *25*, 56–72. [CrossRef]

24. Chen, C.H.; Yang, Y.C. Revisiting the effects of project-based learning on students' academic achievement: A meta-analysis investigating moderators. *Educ. Res. Rev.* **2019**, *26*, 71–81. [CrossRef]

25. Ekman, P.; Friesen, W.V. Facial action coding system. *Environ. Psychol. Nonverbal Behav.* **1978**.

26. Littlewort, G.; Whitehill, J.; Wu, T.; Fasel, I.; Frank, M.; Movellan, J.; Bartlett, M. The computer expression recognition toolbox (CERT). In Proceedings of the 2011 IEEE International Conference on Automatic Face & Gesture Recognition (FG), Santa Barbara, CA, USA, 21–25 March 2011; IEEE: Piscataway, NJ, USA, 2011; pp. 298–305.

27. Hewson, E.R. Students' emotional engagement, motivation and behaviour over the life of an online course: Reflections on two market research case studies. *J. Interact. Media Educ.* **2018**, *1*. [CrossRef]

28. Bieniek-Tobasco, A.; McCormick, S.; Rimal, R.N.; Harrington, C.B.; Shafer, M.; Shaikh, H. Communicating climate change through documentary film: Imagery, emotion, and efficacy. *Clim. Chang.* **2019**, *154*, 1–18. [CrossRef]

29. Hong, W.; Bernacki, M.L.; Perera, H.N. A latent profile analysis of undergraduates' achievement motivations and metacognitive behaviors, and their relations to achievement in science. *J. Educ. Psychol.* **2020**, *112*, 1409. [CrossRef]

30. Anis, M.Z.A.; Susanto, H.; Mardiani, F. Analysis of the Effectiveness of MPBH: The Mains of Mandai as a Saving Food in Banjarmasin Community. In Proceedings of the 2nd International Conference on Social Sciences Education (ICSSE 2020), Virtually, 24-27 September 2020; Atlantis Press: Amsterdam, The Netherlands, 2021; pp. 89–94.

31. Danişman, Ş.; Güler, M.; Karadağ, E. The Effect of Teacher Characteristics on Student Achievement: A Meta-Analysis Study. *Croat. J. Educ.* **2019**, *21*, 1367–1398.

32. Smale-Jacobse, A.E.; Meijer, A.; Helms-Lorenz, M.; Maulana, R. Differentiated instruction in secondary education: A systematic review of research evidence. *Front. Psychol.* **2019**, *10*, 2366. [CrossRef]

33. Bitler, M.; Corcoran, S.; Domina, T.; Penner, E. Teacher Effects on Student Achievement and Height: A Cautionary Tale. NBER Working Paper No. 26480. *Natl. Bur. Econ. Res.* **2019**, *14*, 900–924.

34. Abdallah, M.; Jaber, K.M.; Salah, M.; Jawad, M.A.; AlQbailat, N.; Abdalla, A. An E-learning Portal Quality Model: From Al-Zaytoonah University Students' Perspective. In Proceedings of the 2021 International Conference on Information Technology (ICIT), Amman, Jordan, 14–15 July 2021; IEEE: Piscataway, NJ, USA, 2021; pp. 553–557.

35. Jaber, K.M.; Abduljawad, M.; Ahmad, A.; Abdallah, M.; Salah, M.; Alhindawi, N. E-learning Mobile Application Evaluation: Al-Zaytoonah University as a Case Study. *Int. J. Adv. Soft Comput. Its Appl.* **2021**, *3*, 13. [CrossRef]

36. Maqableh, M.; Alia, M. Evaluation online learning of undergraduate students under lockdown amidst COVID-19 Pandemic: The online learning experience and students' satisfaction. *Child. Youth Serv. Rev.* **2021**, *128*, 106160. [CrossRef]

37. H'mida, C.; Kalyuga, S.; Souissi, N.; Rekik, G.; Jarraya, M.; Khacharem, A. Is the human movement effect stable over time? The effects of presentation format on acquisition and retention of a motor skill. *J. Comput. Assist. Learn.* **2022**, *38*, 167–177. [CrossRef]

38. Nikam, R.D.; Lee, J.; Choi, W.; Banerjee, W.; Kwak, M.; Yadav, M.; Hwang, H. Ionic Sieving Through One-Atom-Thick 2D Material Enables Analog Nonvolatile Memory for Neuromorphic Computing. *Small* **2021**, *17*, 2103543. [CrossRef] [PubMed]

39. Marini, M.; Ansani, A.; Paglieri, F.; Caruana, F.; Viola, M. The impact of facemasks on emotion recognition, trust attribution and re-identification. *Sci. Rep.* **2021**, *11*, 1–14. [CrossRef] [PubMed]

40. Gupta, V.; Jain, N.; Katariya, P.; Kumar, A.; Mohan, S.; Ahmadian, A.; Ferrara, M. An emotion care model using multimodal textual analysis on COVID-19. *Chaos Solitons Fractals* **2021**, *144*, 110708. [CrossRef]

41. Indira, D. An Enhanced CNN-2D for Audio-Visual Emotion Recognition (AVER) Using ADAM Optimizer. *Turk. J. Comput. Math. Educ. (TURCOMAT)* **2021**, *12*, 1378–1388.

42. Fei, Z.; Yang, E.; Li, D.D.U.; Butler, S.; Ijomah, W.; Li, X.; Zhou, H. Deep convolution network based emotion analysis towards mental health care. *Neurocomputing* **2020**, *388*, 212–227. [CrossRef]

43. McDuff, D.; Rowan, K.; Choudhury, P.; Wolk, J.; Pham, T.; Czerwinski, M. A multimodal emotion sensing platform for building emotion-aware applications. *arXiv* **2019**, arXiv:1903.12133.

44. Jain, N.; Gupta, V.; Shubham, S.; Madan, A.; Chaudhary, A.; Santosh, K. Understanding cartoon emotion using integrated deep neural network on large dataset. *Neural Comput. Appl.* **2021**, 1–21. [CrossRef]

45. Patel, F.; Patel, N.; Bharti, S.K. Lie-Sensor: A Live Emotion Verifier or a Licensor for Chat Applications using Emotional Intelligence. *arXiv* **2021**, arXiv:2102.11318.

46. COSTACHE, A.; POPESCU, D. Emotion Sketches: Facial Expression Recognition in Diversity Groups. *Sci. Bull.* **2021**, *83*, 29–40.

47. Kim, C.M.; Kim, K.H.; Lee, Y.S.; Chung, K.; Park, R.C. Real-time streaming image based PP2LFA-CRNN model for facial sentiment analysis. *IEEE Access* **2020**, *8*, 199586–199602. [CrossRef]

48. Zamani, H.; Abas, A.; Amin, M. Eye tracking application on emotion analysis for marketing strategy. *J. Telecommun. Electron. Comput. Eng. (JTEC)* **2016**, *8*, 87–91.

49. Qamar, S.; Mujtaba, H.; Majeed, H.; Beg, M.O. Relationship identification between conversational agents using emotion analysis. *Cogn. Comput.* **2021**, *13*, 673–687. [CrossRef]

50. Sonawane, B.; Sharma, P. Review of automated emotion-based quantification of facial expression in Parkinson's patients. *Vis. Comput.* **2021**, *37*, 1151–1167. [CrossRef]
51. Garcia-Garcia, J.M.; Penichet, V.M.; Lozano, M.D.; Fernando, A. Using emotion recognition technologies to teach children with autism spectrum disorder how to identify and express emotions. *Univers. Access Inf. Soc.* **2021**, 1–17. [CrossRef]
52. Chen, W.; Wang, J.; Yu, F.; He, J.; Xu, W.; Wang, R. Effects of emotion on the evolution of cooperation in a spatial prisoner's dilemma game. *Appl. Math. Comput.* **2021**, *411*, 126497. [CrossRef]
53. Pizarro, R.; Bekios-Calfa, J. Emotion recognition using multimodal matchmap fusion and multi-task learning. *Iet Digit. Libr.* **2021**.
54. Khaireddin, Y.; Chen, Z. Facial emotion recognition: State of the art performance on FER2013. *arXiv* **2021**, arXiv:2105.03588.
55. Alzu'bi, S.; Badarneh, O.; Hawashin, B.; Al-Ayyoub, M.; Alhindawi, N.; Jararweh, Y. Multi-label emotion classification for Arabic tweets. In Proceedings of the 2019 Sixth International Conference on Social Networks Analysis, Management and Security (SNAMS), Granada, Spain, 22–25 October 2019; IEEE: Piscataway, NJ, USA, 2019; pp. 499–504.
56. Kozareva, Z.; Navarro, B.; Vázquez, S.; Montoyo, A. UA-ZBSA: A headline emotion classification through web information. In Proceedings of the Fourth International Workshop on Semantic Evaluations (SemEval-2007), Prague, Czech Republic, 23–24 June 2007; pp. 334–337.
57. Hatzivassiloglou, V.; McKeown, K. Predicting the semantic orientation of adjectives. In Proceedings of the 35th Annual Meeting of the Association for Computational Linguistics and 8th Conference of the European Chapter of the Association for Computational Linguistics, Madrid, Spain, 7–12 July 1997; pp. 174–181.
58. Chaffar, S.; Inkpen, D. Using a heterogeneous dataset for emotion analysis in text. In *Canadian Conference on Artificial Intelligence*; Springer: Berlin/Heidelberg, Germany, 2011; pp. 62–67.
59. Jayalekshmi, J.; Mathew, T. Facial expression recognition and emotion classification system for sentiment analysis. In Proceedings of the 2017 International Conference on Networks & Advances in Computational Technologies (NetACT), Thiruvananthapuram, India, 20–22 July 2017; IEEE: Piscataway, NJ, USA, 2017; pp. 1–8.
60. Song, Z. Facial Expression Emotion Recognition Model Integrating Philosophy and Machine Learning Theory. *Front. Psychol.* **2021**, *12*. [CrossRef]
61. Koolagudi, S.G.; Rao, K.S. Emotion recognition from speech: A review. *Int. J. Speech Technol.* **2012**, *15*, 99–117. [CrossRef]
62. Wang, S. Online Learning Behavior Analysis Based on Image Emotion Recognition. *Trait. Signal* **2021**, *38*. [CrossRef]
63. Mills, K.; Creedy, D.K.; Sunderland, N.; Allen, J. Examining the transformative potential of emotion in education: A new measure of nursing and midwifery students' emotional learning in first peoples' cultural safety. *Nurse Educ. Today* **2021**, *100*, 104854. [CrossRef] [PubMed]
64. Ali, M.; Mosa, A.H.; Al Machot, F.; Kyamakya, K. EEG-based emotion recognition approach for e-healthcare applications. In Proceedings of the 2016 Eighth International Conference on Ubiquitous and Future Networks (Icufn), Vienna, Austria, 5–8 July 2016; IEEE: Piscataway, NJ, USA, 2016; pp. 946–950.
65. Moroto, Y.; Maeda, K.; Ogawa, T.; Haseyama, M. Human Emotion Estimation Using Multi-Modal Variational AutoEncoder with Time Changes. In Proceedings of the 2021 IEEE 3rd Global Conference on Life Sciences and Technologies (LifeTech), Nara, Japan, 9–11 March 2021; IEEE: Piscataway, NJ, USA, 2021; pp. 67–68.
66. Sharma, P.; Joshi, S.; Gautam, S.; Maharjan, S.; Filipe, V.; Reis, M.J. Student engagement detection using emotion analysis, eye tracking and head movement with machine learning. *arXiv* **2019**, arXiv:1909.12913.
67. Danandeh Mehr, A.; Rikhtehgar Ghiasi, A.; Yaseen, Z.M.; Sorman, A.U.; Abualigah, L. A novel intelligent deep learning predictive model for meteorological drought forecasting. *J. Ambient. Intell. Humaniz. Comput.* **2022**, 1–15. [CrossRef]
68. Sumari, P.; Syed, S.J.; Abualigah, L. A novel deep learning pipeline architecture based on CNN to detect Covid-19 in chest X-ray images. *Turk. J. Comput. Math. Educ. (TURCOMAT)* **2021**, *12*, 2001–2011.
69. AlZu'bi, S.; Jararweh, Y.; Al-Zoubi, H.; Elbes, M.; Kanan, T.; Gupta, B. Multi-orientation geometric medical volumes segmentation using 3d multiresolution analysis. *Multimed. Tools Appl.* **2018**, 1–26. [CrossRef]
70. Al-Zu'bi, S.; Hawashin, B.; Mughaid, A.; Baker, T. Efficient 3D medical image segmentation algorithm over a secured multimedia network. *Multimed. Tools Appl.* **2021**, *80*, 16887–16905. [CrossRef]
71. Hawashin, B.; Aqel, D.; Alzubi, S.; Elbes, M. Improving recommender systems using co-appearing and semantically correlated user interests. *Recent Adv. Comput. Sci. Commun. (Formerly: Recent Patents Comput. Sci.)* **2020**, *13*, 240–247. [CrossRef]
72. AlZu'bi, S.; Aqel, D.; Mughaid, A.; Jararweh, Y. A multi-levels geo-location based crawling method for social media platforms. In Proceedings of the 2019 Sixth International Conference on Social Networks Analysis, Management and Security (SNAMS), Granada, Spain, 22–25 October 2019; IEEE: Piscataway, NJ, USA, 2019; pp. 494–498.
73. Elbes, M.; Alrawashdeh, T.; Almaita, E.; AlZu'bi, S.; Jararweh, Y. A platform for power management based on indoor localization in smart buildings using long short-term neural networks. *Trans. Emerg. Telecommun. Technol.* **2020**, e3867. [CrossRef]
74. AlZu'bi, S.; AlQatawneh, S.; ElBes, M.; Alsmirat, M. Transferable HMM probability matrices in multi-orientation geometric medical volumes segmentation. *Concurr. Comput. Pract. Exp.* **2019**, *32*, e5214. [CrossRef]
75. Alasal, S.A.; Alsmirat, M.; Baker, Q.B.; Alzu'bi, S. Lumbar disk 3D modeling from limited number of MRI axial slices. *Int. J. Electr. Comput. Eng.* **2020**, *10*, 4101.
76. Alsarayreh, M.A.; Alia, M.A.; Maria, K.A. A novel image steganographic system based on exact matching algorithm and key-dependent data technique. *J. Theor. Appl. Inf. Technol.* **2017**, *95*.

77. Alqatawneh, S.; Jaber, K.M.; Salah, M.; Yehia, D.B.; Alqatawneh, O. Employing of Object Tracking System in Public Surveillance Cameras to Enforce Quarantine and Social Distancing Using Parallel Machine Learning Techniques. *Int. J. Adv. Soft Comput. Its Appl.* **2021**, *13*. [CrossRef]

78. Rezaee, H.; Aghagolzadeh, A.; Seyedarabi, M.H.; Al Zu'bi, S. Tracking and occlusion handling in multi-sensor networks by particle filter. In Proceedings of the 2011 IEEE GCC Conference and Exhibition (GCC), Dubai, United Arab Emirates, 19–22 February 2011; IEEE: Piscataway, NJ, USA, 2011; pp. 397–400.

79. Muhairat, M.; ALZu'bi, S.; Hawashin, B.; Elbes, M.; Al-Ayyoub, M. An Intelligent Recommender System Based on Association Rule Analysis for Requirement Engineering. *J. Univers. Comput. Sci.* **2020**, *26*, 33–49. [CrossRef]

80. Lafi, M.; Hawashin, B.; AlZu'bi, S. Maintenance requests labeling using machine learning classification. In Proceedings of the 2020 Seventh International Conference on Software Defined Systems (SDS), Paris, France, 20–23 April 2020; IEEE: Piscataway, NJ, USA, 2020; pp. 245–249.

81. Alsmadi, A.; AlZu'bi, S.; Hawashin, B.; Al-Ayyoub, M.; Jararweh, Y. Employing deep learning methods for predicting helpful reviews. In Proceedings of the 2020 11th International Conference on Information and Communication Systems (ICICS), Irbid, Jordan, 7–9 April 2020; IEEE: Piscataway, NJ, USA, 2020; pp. 7–12.

82. Maria, K.A.; Zitar, R.A. Emotional agents: A modeling and an application. *Inf. Softw. Technol.* **2007**, *49*, 695–716. [CrossRef]

83. Aqel, D.; Al-Zubi, S.; Mughaid, A.; Jararweh, Y. Extreme learning machine for plant diseases classification: A sustainable approach for smart agriculture. *Clust. Comput.* **2021**, 1–14. [CrossRef]

84. AlZu'bi, S.; Hawashin, B.; Mujahed, M.; Jararweh, Y.; Gupta, B.B. An efficient employment of internet of multimedia things in smart and future agriculture. *Multimed. Tools Appl.* **2019**, *78*, 29581–29605. [CrossRef]

85. Alkhatib, K.; Khazaleh, H.; Alkhazaleh, H.A.; Alsoud, A.R.; Abualigah, L. A New Stock Price Forecasting Method Using Active Deep Learning Approach. *J. Open Innov. Technol. Mark. Complex.* **2022**, *8*, 96. [CrossRef]

 *electronics*

Article

Design Research Insights on Text Mining Analysis: Establishing the Most Used and Trends in Keywords of Design Research Journals

Muneer Nusir [1,*], Ali Louati [1], Hassen Louati [2], Usman Tariq [3], Raed Abu Zitar [4], Laith Abualigah [5,6,7,8] and Amir H. Gandomi [9,10,*]

1   College of Computer Engineering and Sciences, Prince Sattam bin Abdulaziz University, Alkharj 16278, Saudi Arabia
2   ISG, SMART Lab, University of Tunis, Avenue de la Liberté, Bouchoucha, Le Bardo, Tunis 2000, Tunisia
3   College of Business Administration, Prince Sattam bin Abdulaziz University, Alkharj 16278, Saudi Arabia
4   Sorbonne Center of Artificial Intelligence, Sorbonne University-Abu Dhabi, Abu Dhabi 38044, United Arab Emirates
5   Hourani Center for Applied Scientific Research, Al-Ahliyya Amman University, Amman 19328, Jordan
6   Faculty of Information Technology, Middle East University, Amman 11831, Jordan
7   Faculty of Information Technology, Applied Science Private University, Amman 11931, Jordan
8   School of Computer Sciences, Universiti Sains Malaysia, Pulau Pinang 11800, Malaysia
9   Faculty of Engineering & Information Technology, University of Technology Sydney, Ultimo, NSW 2007, Australia
10 University Research and Innovation Center (EKIK), Óbuda University, 1034 Budapest, Hungary
*   Correspondence: moneer.techno@gmail.com (M.N.); gandomi@uts.edu.au (A.H.G.)

Citation: Nusir, M.; Louati, A.; Louati, H.; Tariq, U.; Zitar, R.A.; Abualigah, L.; Gandomi, A.H. Design Research Insights on Text Mining Analysis: Establishing the Most Used and Trends in Keywords of Design Research Journals. *Electronics* **2022**, *11*, 3930. https://doi.org/10.3390/electronics11233930

Academic Editor: George A. Papakostas

Received: 22 October 2022
Accepted: 25 November 2022
Published: 28 November 2022

Publisher's Note: MDPI stays neutral with regard to jurisdictional claims in published maps and institutional affiliations.

Abstract: Design research topics attract exponentially more attention and consideration among researchers. This study is the first research article that endeavors to analyze selected design research publications using an advanced approach called "text mining". This approach speculates its results depending on the existence of a research term (i.e., keywords), which can be more robust than other methods/approaches that rely on contextual data or authors' perspectives. The main aim of this research paper is to expand knowledge and familiarity with design research and explore future research directions by addressing the gaps in the literature; relying on the literature review, it can be stated that the research area in the design domain still not built-up a theory, which can unify the field. In general, text mining with these features allows increased validity and generalization as compared to other approaches in the literature. We used a text mining technique to collect data and analyzed 3553 articles collected in 10 journals using 17,487 keywords. New topics were investigated in the domain of design concepts, which included attracting researchers, practitioners, and journal editorial boards. Such issues as co-innovation, ethical design, social practice design, conceptual thinking, collaborative design, creativity, and generative methods and tools were subject to additional research. On the other hand, researchers pursued topics such as collaborative design, human-centered design, interdisciplinary design, design education, participatory design, design practice, collaborative design, design development, collaboration, design theories, design administration, and service/product design areas. The key categories investigated and reported in this paper helped in determining what fields are flourishing and what fields are eroding.

Keywords: keywords analysis; design research; visualization trends; text mining; research directions; design insights

1. Introduction

The topic and/or discipline of design is becoming very important and relatively young but has matured rapidly in the last decade with the increased use of digital phenomena in different fields [1]. As a result, research related to design is growing exponentially.

Scholars/researchers are investigating and exploring a variety of disciplines of Design research and disseminating under several of the fields (i.e., engineering, CAD, management, ergonomics, business, education, and art and design); to extend the experience and knowledge in this domain for this arena [2].

The design was defined by a range of variety of design research definitions. Many definitions point to the importance of this subject in several design domains [1,3–5]. Rachel Cooper, one of the founders and editorial chairs of 'The Design Journal' was defined 'Design' in his journal publication which is called 'Design Research Comes of Age' as an initial trial issue published in 1997 (volume 0, issue 1) stated: "When we say 'design' we mean: the design disciplines covering products, places, and communication (i.e., graphic design, information design, product and industrial design, fashion and textiles, interior design and designer/maker issues), design management (design strategy, design policy, marketing and design, design and manufacturing, innovation), design theory (design methods, psychology, and design, creativity and design), Eco and environmental design, gender issues in design. We anticipate these topics will be addressed from an educational, historical, technological, or practical perspective. We believe these disciplines can provide a rich perspective, each informing and contributing to the depth and breadth of design research" [6].

Ralph and Wand [7] defined the concept of design after they reviewed of literature of existing definitions and stated: "The report views the design activity as a process, executed by an agent, to generate a specification of an object based on: the environment in which the object will exist, the goals ascribed to the object, the desired structural and behavioral properties of the object (requirements), a given set of component types (primitives), and constraints that limit the acceptable solutions.

The main and/or major directions in Design research are related to anyone who really is so interested in design to cultivate his/her understanding of how designers think and work [8,9]. Moreover, design offers designers/non-designers the opportunity to create/create effective, efficient, original, and impressive designs. In this sense, the design goes beyond a set of design tools or practical skills and is a process [8]. Nevertheless, the design concept is expanding to include more diverse disciplines and disciplines. Therefore, it is essential to add value and quality to our lives as humans [10,11].

The movement of Design research as a discipline toward facing dilemmas in the coming years. Design research as a discipline and the concept of 'Design' has seen tremendous extension/enlargement of interest in recent years; in particular, from management, health, education, design industry, ICT and its applications, and business books as Design terms considers an interdisciplinary [12,13]. Moreover, the amount of Design research is growing with the increase in the number of journals, conferences, books, and magazines dedicated to design as a discipline. Design research is an interdisciplinary topic that covers various sciences (i.e., social, practical, computer, health, education, engineering, culture, history sciences, etc.). Several studies [8,14–16], reviewed Design research as a discipline to achieve a foundational understanding of this domain. These studies focus on a variety of topics cover ranging from investigating the main research streams on the 'Design research' concept. The primary research topics identified in the literature are concerned with the ability not just to build rigorous depth of knowledge but also the breadth of the discipline. Design research has consistently identified innovation, users, materials, production, etc. However, some domains in Design research (i.e., social innovation, policy design, open design, and design for specific industries and engineering, such as design for health, culture, education, IT, and design against crime are becoming very popular [4].

The main aim of this research study is to investigate and comprehend the dominant areas or subfields of design research through an analysis of indexed keywords that were included in journal publications' abstracts (i.e., research articles). Our analysis focused on keywords related to journal articles in design research. To the best of our knowledge, this study is the first documented effort to use a cutting-edge method termed "text mining" to examine the chosen Design research articles in a research article. This method/approach hypothesizes that its results depend on a study term's existence (i.e., keywords), which can be more reliable than other methods/approaches that rely on contextual data or authors' opinions. Text mining also takes into account its frequency to reflect the dominance and applicability of a phrase or keyword in the data.

This research's motivation can easily be noticed when you think about the difference between this study and Google scholar or other search engines. Web searches, in general, may resemble text mining, but there are significant differences. Based on specific search keywords, search is the retrieval of documents or other results. The output typically consists of a hyperlink to text or information located elsewhere and a brief description of what can be found at the other end of the link. These kinds of searches are frequently carried out using search engines like Google, Yahoo, or Bing, and your company may also use an enterprise search solution.

Finding the entire existing work is the goal of using its material. The purpose of text mining is to analyze text. Instead of just looking for, linking to, and retrieving papers that contain specific data, the objective is to extract useful information. In contrast to searches, the outcomes of text mining depend on the researcher's intended use of the data. While search functionality aids users in locating the particular document(s) they need, text mining goes far beyond search to identify specific facts and claims in the literature to create new value. The work is the first attempt to use text mining to examine research directions in design research.

This paper contributes to Design research and practice by detecting/exploring main research trends in the design research discipline and spotting light on previous and new prospective research priorities. Additionally, this research study provides perceptions/observations concerning new dimensions important in the design and associated areas. Compared to other literature methodologies, text mining with these qualities typically allows for higher applicability and validity. The Findings of this study reveal the research interest and the trends of the design research discipline. This research study utilized one of the largest samples of publications (i.e., papers). A total of 17,486 words from design journals were used in this research report. A quantitative analysis was conducted to prevent author bias when analyzing research and how we look at and analyze the data collected. Future scholars might examine and cluster the information acquired in this research study (data available in Appendix A can be used manually). The following section presents Design research directions and the research methods conducted in state of the art. The third section illustrates this research paper's research method and questions. Section four describes a report of results by analyzing and discussing data results. Finally, conclusions, including contributions and limitations, are stated in the fifth section. The popular design terms and abbreviations, are listed in Appendices A and B sequentially.

2. Design Research

The following two sections will review the previous studies and related works on design research dimensions and research methods conducted or applied. It is essential to investigate such topics to examine how text mining will contribute to identifying correct dimensions not reported in the previous research.

2.1. Design Research Dimensions

The term 'design' is a strategy or portrayal formed to demonstrate the aspect and purpose or mechanisms of an entity modeling before it is prepared [17,18]. Studies within the field of design may be perceived to be evolving. However, some associated design methodologies' castigations, such as, production, organizational designs, comprehensive design vocabulary emerges, strategic planning, engineering design and interface design have an extended post [19–21]. Chai et al. [22] Explored the fundamental subjects of design study by retaining a bibliometric and system breakdown. The research examined references and co-records from design use cases. As an alternative to exhausting the typical study routine of grouping writer co-citations, this research miner conducts the study at the discrete publication level [23].

Anthropological contributors directed a methodical diagramming study to categorize and examine thirty crucial pragmatic case studies on software outlining applications, consisting of twenty-four original researches and six replications, to describe the study design of experiential research. It was observed that by exhausting shared trials and modus operandi, academics can design novel training, reproduce in effect studies, and be able to associate the outcomes. Nonetheless, the authors witnessed that multiple framework issues (such as tentative measures, usages, and partaker familiarities) limited the comparability level of the results.

It is essential to know how we define "design", "design study", and "prospect" of design examination. Chakrabarti et al. [24] identified three categories of associations that must exist: (1) design occurrences, (2) design study arrays, and (3) relations and models to indicate the design study. They offered an introduction classification for the two of these and described the likely methods of achieving each. The understanding of (a) internal growth and (b) external acknowledgment for widely suggested applications was enhanced by this consolidation. It suggested developing (a) a maiden classification of singularities allied to design, (b) a maiden categorization of design study domains, (c) a data warehouse of design study research articles, and (d) a dictionary of expressions and notions used in the research articles within respective study zone [25]. Domain-specific design goals included product launch time, market portion, benefits, industrialization capacity, budget, assemblage, innovation, discernability, aesthetics, and functional value. Utilizing this, the subject matter "Design for budget" developed further diligently and was associated with "Design for life" than, at a guess to, "Design for appropriateness".

Numerous aspects of the design environment were measured; thus, modeling progression can be utilized hands-on. The modeling method of this reasoning reflects the impact of the properties of the informal setting and the features of the producer. Nonetheless, there are rare instances of associating and relating the expert's setting and features to the design element. To accomplish this phenomenon, projected study adapted [26] predicament-resolution to conduct design discipline research in a controlled manner. This progression contained the subsequent five phases (a) problem designation, (b) exploration and analysis, (c) resolution scheme, (d) execution, and (e) assessment [26].

This broadsheet [27] discovers the density and reasoning liability allied to quantified optimal research. The difficulty is examined about design dimensions such as the sum of accessible substitutes (i.e., numerous design dimensions), the number of characteristics used to outline these options, the sum of stages for those traits, the array of feature points, and the number of particular circumstances offered to each respondent. These design scopes are methodically diversified according to a trial design in an initial design order; the following option encompassed the characteristics of respective substitutes (e.g., portable epochs and mobility rate mechanisms). To research the difficulty of the trial author detailed a 'heteroskedastic logit prototypical' with the rule limitation described as a task of the scheme dimensions. This permitted them to detach the properties of optimal intricacy from the borderline efficacy approximations. Research outcomes illustrate that five design dimensions distress the optimal discrepancy or disturb selection reliability [28–30].

A study [28] was conducted to classify the features of design studies in restraints other than design discipline. The design was diligently created and improved through tight relationships with various inculcations. Researchers developed a framework for interpreting the controversial interdisciplinary practice of design projects [29]. The taxonomy of design research, and the significance of design relations. Investigators adopted this outline to examine, illustrate and choose what categories of lessons on design have been directed in the collective disciplines and what style of design they were cast off for. The examined argument may benefit discourse logical and communication obstacles to design-positioned, design-correlated, or design-worn study diagonal use cases. The review also donates to the expansion of sagacity of the synthesizing perspective for the title "design". Though analyzing the subjective material to comprehend the feeling of design in varying attainments took a while, this understanding did ensure a few precincts.

2.2. Research Methods Conducted in the Design

Service dominance reasoning that provides a practical design. Rooted in the fundamental concept of service dominance, the critical co-concept, two essential perspectives are helpful for novelty testing of the services involved. On the one hand, the focus is on integrating resources within and between different levels of care that can demonstrate different value potentials and thus improve perspectives [30–32]. The second is service-dominant reasoning, competing with recipients individually for control and viewing co-concepts of valuation as reserve assimilation and shared service-providing actors that value concepts beyond established decision-making sites. It is worth mentioning that service-dominant logic portrays deficiencies in the applied procedures that enterprises consider as prerequisites to monitor the ways they can collect the distinct comprehensions into the value of co-conception and redesign their possessions to transform through augmentation of significance [32].

Another study used the text-mining approach in the design research [33]. Nie and Sun [34] used this approach, building on her two dimensions of bibliometrics and network analysis to identify academic sector themes. Specifically, we evaluated design research fields using bibliometrics and clarified research themes in each academic field of design research using network analysis. Various design techniques are classified step by step and presented as a collection of subsystems [35]. In this framework, the design progression includes the theoretical concept of a "new entity or system" at the highest level of illustration, with the more salient elements predominating at, the lower levels of representation. Illustrated Broadside [36] proclaims that program design is a new dimension in design. To articulate this argument, researchers propose: (a) Hypothesis: It is true that procedure consists of design, (b) Counter-thesis: Procedure implies design. (c) Fusion: Abandon Hypothesis: The program indeed contains design results. Process design is a (novel) part of design research and training. It is fair to conclude that inventors have directed additional research areas to answer existent complications and an innovative epoch of Computer-Assisted Strategy Design is evolving under the direction of program informatics with significant prospects for design. The mixture of examination, applications, and learning in procedure design presents countless chances for transnational design groups [34].

The previously mentioned work by Kavousi et al. [37] shows that meta-reasoning is a crucial part of planning knowledge initiation and improvement and is a significant portion of innovative progression in design. Furthermore, the subsequent prototypical clarifies how modules of meta-reasoning relate and offer understanding to researchers in the quest to boost design progression and its effects on users. In another study [33], researchers deciphered a Multidisciplinary Design Optimization (MDO) problem in which the progress of stabilizer-contrived yields is tailored for different consumers in dissimilar market subdivisions. Three sectors, i.e., consumer inclination modeling, additive manufacturing (AM) assembly valuation, and physical technicalities, are unified in the MDO problem. The prime choices of modules, resources, AM progressions, and dimensional limitations were examined to exploit the functionality effectiveness, contesting discrete consumers' particular routine necessities and diminishing the overall budget. The study smeared an unbiased heritable procedure with the anticipated gene scrambling configuration to resolve the MDO problem. The MDO delivered a set of possible policy resolutions from which the producer would choose the suitable ones grounded on its market approach. In addition, the study in [35] investigated the positioning of the research field through keyword identification in the design research field using an exploratory survey of the emails' corpus. A related study was conducted by Lloyd [38] on design research society to investigate many themes in design disciplines, such as objects, experiences, practices, and networks; design and translation; and design for tangible, embedded, and networked technologies based on the systematic view of design.

The aspect-based sentiment analysis (ABSA) consists of two subtasks—aspect term extraction and aspect sentiment prediction. Existing methods deal with both subtasks in a pipeline manner, in which some problems in performance and real application exist.

Ref. [36] investigates the end-to-end ABSA and proposes a novel multitask Multiview network (MTMVN) architecture. Specifically, the architecture takes the unified ABSA as the central task, with the two subtasks as auxiliary tasks. Meanwhile, the representation obtained from the branch network of the main task is regarded as the global view, whereas the representations of the two subtasks are considered two local arguments with different emphases. Through multitask learning, the main task can be facilitated by more accurate aspect boundary and sentiment polarity information. Furthermore, Most State-Of-The-Art (SOTA) Neural Machine Translation (NMT) systems today achieve outstanding results based only on large parallel corpora. The large-scale parallel corpora for high-resource languages is easily obtainable. However, the translation quality of NMT for morphologically rich languages is still unsatisfactory, mainly because of the data sparsity problem encountered in Low-Resource Languages (LRLs). In the low-resource NMT paradigm, Transfer Learning (TL) has been developed into one of the most efficient methods. It is not easy to train the model on high-resource languages to include the information in both parent and child models, as well as the initially trained model that only contains the lexicon features and word embeddings of the parent model instead of the child languages feature [39]. Additionally, Cross-Document Coreference Annotation Tool (CDCAT), a new multi-language open-source manual annotation tool for cross-document entity and event Coreference, can handle different input/output formats, pre-processing functions, languages, and annotation systems. This new tool allows annotators to label a reference relation with only two mouse clicks. Best practice analyses reveal that annotators can reach an annotation speed of 0.025 coreference relations per second on a corpus with a coreference density of 0.076 coreference relations per word [38]. Finally, refs. [40,41] illustrates the Clarification of research design, research methods, and methodology: A guide for public administration researchers and practitioners, and tabular Comparing and contrasting research methods and methodology concepts.

To sum up, based on our literature review, it can be stated that the design area of research has not yet developed a theory that can standardize the area. Previous studies have focused mainly on research directions. Moreover, previous studies have demonstrated diverse methodologies and a wide range of topics. Moreover, previous studies have not presented a single study that comprehensively identifies or draws conclusions for research directions in this area. Thus, in this paper, there was the first recognized attempt under the obligation to acknowledge domain regions through text analysis using keywords from design studies. The sections immediately following describe the research methodology and data analysis.

3. Research Methodology

This research paper pursued three research questions that enhanced our experience and knowledge of the design research discipline. Given below are the research questions:

RQ1: What are the major design research topics observed in the dataset?

RQ2: What changes in design studies were observed during the sample period from January 2007 to March 2019?

RQ3: What are the vital design research topics that determine the direction of future research?

Many keywords were used in the study, including articles related to design and research topics. We used a set of published keywords along with the article's abstract, year of publication, and other information about the keywords, such as indexed keywords. The most famous studies available in the field, ranked by the index of the (ISI Collection) Web of Science website, were used in the study. Those journals' titles were used that comprised the word 'design'. The primary criteria for selecting the journals was the strong relation of design discipline to ICT, sciences, education, ergonomics, engineering, technology, and service/product design and development. Based on that, some journals were excluded for two reasons: first, not having been indexed by the Web of Science (ISI-core collection database) and/or considered as an Emerging Source Citation Index (ESCI), such as 'she Ji: The Journal of design, economics, and Innovation'. However, some journals were indexed in the web of science (ISI-core collection), as they had some relation to design, such as 'Innovation and Management Review'. However, it was excluded based on the research team's evaluation criteria. Second, some journals were excluded that did not cover key topics, such as journals: design and culture, design for culture, design for health, and journal of design history.

On the other hand, some publications (i.e., editorial board, introduction, reviews, articles, and other sources) were published under the mentioned journals (See Table 1). Roughly were excluded for not having the keywords that serve the research goal and/or for not aligning with the paper topic (i.e., design discipline). Therefore, these publications were omitted based on the research team's opinion and judgment criterion. We specifically selected each journal because we wanted to assess trends in more specific areas. Additionally, by extension, this would have represented changes occurring in a broad spectrum of fields. Figure 1 illustrates the research methodology used for the review of existing work.

Table 1. Journal list and summary of articles and keywords ranged from 2007–2019.

Code	Journal Name	Total Articles	Total Keywords
1	Research in engineering design	271	1315
2	International Journal of technology and design education	441	2185
3	Design studies	390	1798
4	Design journal	1152	5271
5	Co-design-International journal of co-creation in design and the arts	186	955
6	Journal of Engineering design	275	1288
7	International journal of design	252	1218
8	Journal of Engineering design and technology	231	1255
9	Ergonomics in design	81	677
10	International journal of art and design education	274	1524

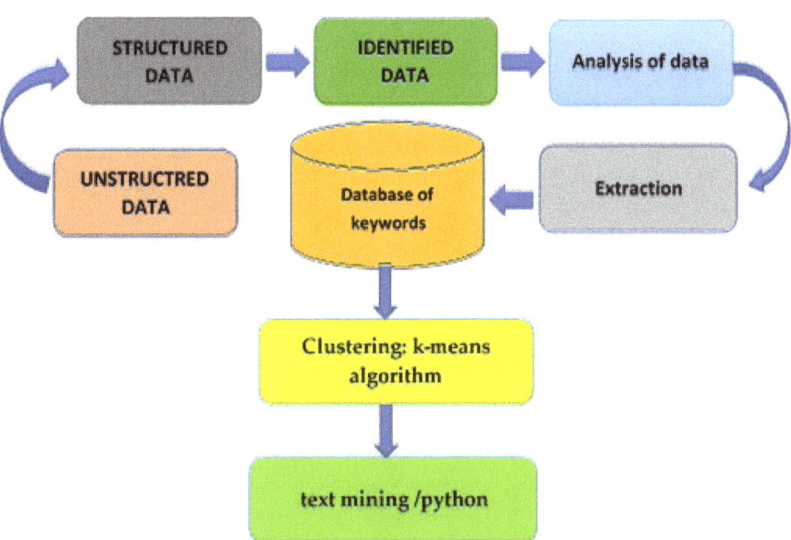

Figure 1. Research methodology used for the review of existing work.

We used the research published in the journals listed in Table 1 with the corresponding study and publication years. The data covered the years 2007 through March 2019. This research report uses 3553 research articles from ten journals and 17,486 keywords. The research titles, publication year, names, and issue numbers were also added to the data collected. We also included publications from each author's website by harvesting data mining techniques from the data set (structured and unstructured), where the keywords were designated under abstract and separated by a comma or semicolon. The research data were entered into an excel sheet (CSV) file for analysis because this is a Python language-acceptable file format. We created a Python script that extracts knowledge intelligently, automatically, consistently, and reliably from HTML and XML files to compile pertinent and important data. The data patterns that were employed to achieve the intended result were found by a smart correlation engine that was programmed. The results of the experiment demonstrated that a programmed script can mine data repeatedly at the identical levels of accuracy as a human but at highly efficient manner with privilege of ease to convert (e.g., HTML (input) to CSV (output) file format), operate, collect, and associate data.

4. Data Analysis and Discussion

In the following two parts, we will describe the two analysis directions. Using the descriptive analysis, we could relate our literature review and gain a better understanding of the domains. This allowed us to move on to the next step, which involved employing text mining techniques.

4.1. Descriptive Analysis

The research dataset inserted into Microsoft Excel was managed and used to perform a cluster and frequency analysis. In the beginning, we considered the distribution of publications per year, as shown in Figure 3. Research in design fields attracted and flourished in the ultimate few years, which appeared normal due to the vogue of the design domain and technological improvement. Furthermore, a few of the selected set of journals/publications were founded between 2007 and 2011 (See Figure 2), which brought an essential decrease in the number of keywords' frequencies (See Table 2). The next step of the analysis was to produce an initial keyword distribution, where the frequency of top/popular keywords was expected (See Table 2). Unsurprisingly, the design showed the top keyword with the highest frequency among all keywords. It seemed like the desired result based on our selection of journals. Table 2 offers perceptions of other keywords that abundance the domain. The frequencies of the keywords are very different; the data limits the repetition of the keywords and explains the use of high-frequency associated keywords. Table 2 represents the keywords with the highest frequency. While Figure 3 shows the distribution of publications per year and leads to the publication distribution per journal. Keywords such as design education, design, creativity, co-design, design process, participatory design, innovation, and product design appeared as the top keywords with the highest frequency in the literature that attracted more research in the last few years. Furthermore, we found that the keywords, such as design thinking, technology education, design research, collaborative design, conceptual design, sustainability, and design cognition, drew more attention and attraction.

Table 2. The keywords with the highest frequency.

Keyword	Keyword	Keyword Count
0	Designeducation	185
1	design	181
2	Creativity	163
3	product design	122
4	co-design	117
5	Designprocess	115
6	Participtorydesign	108
7	Innovation	107
8	Designthinking	97
9	Technologyeducation	87
10	Designresearch	86

Table 2. *Cont.*

Keyword	Keyword	Keyword Count
11	Collaborativeresearch	79
12	Conceptualdesign	78
13	Sustainability	77
14	Designcognition	74
15	Designtheory	70
16	Servicedesign	69
17	Engineeringdesign	66
18	Industrialdesign	66
19	Designpractice	64
20	Interactiondesign	62
21	Collaboration	58
22	Designmethods	54
23	Designtools	49
24	Casestudy	48
25	Education	45
26	Aesthetics	44
27	Communication	44
28	Designactivity	42
29	Evaluation	42
30	Architecturaldesign	42
31	Socialinnovation	42
32	Productdevelopment	39
33	Designknowledge	37
34	Learning	36
35	Pedagogy	35
36	Technology	35
37	Arteducation	35
38	Protocolanalysis	34
39	Designmanegment	33
40	Researchmethods	33
41	Architecture	32
42	Usability	31
43	Participation	31
44	Healthcare	31
45	Designmethodology	30
46	user-centereddesign	30
47	Problemsolving	29
48	Simulation	28
49	Sustainabledesign	28

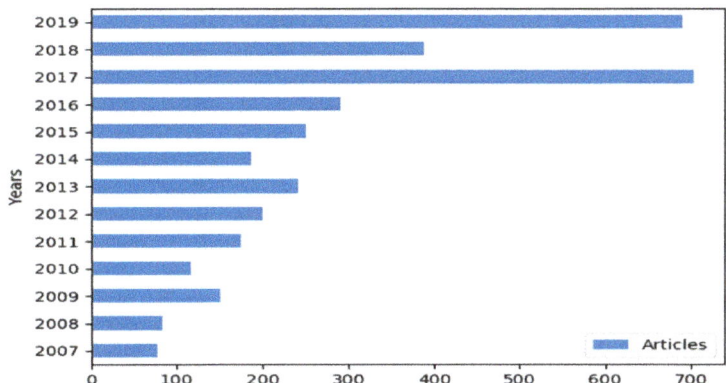

Figure 2. Distribution of publication per year.

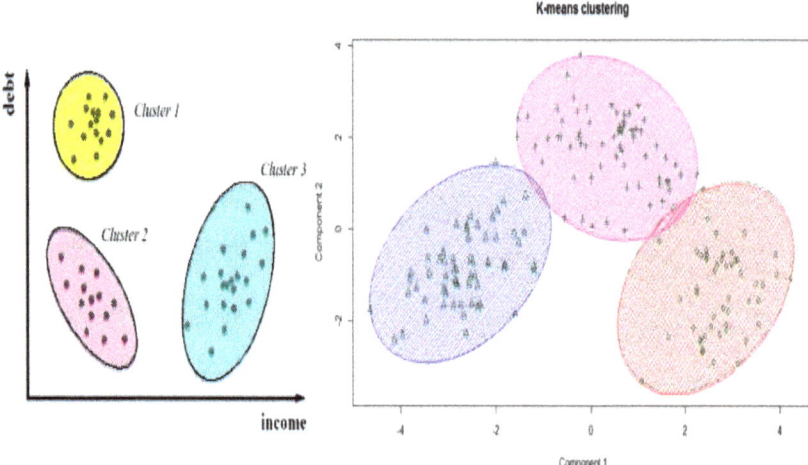

Figure 3. Clustering in more quantitative.

4.2. Text Mining Analysis (Clustering)

The document clustering text mining model was utilized to answer the study's research questions. Clustering is a collection of data reduction techniques used to group similar observations in a dataset so that observations in the same group are as similar as possible, and observations in different groups are as different as possible.

In this study, K-means was used, which is a cluster analysis method that groups observations by minimizing Euclidean distances between them. The difference between two observations on two variables (x and y) is plugged into the Pythagorean equation to solve for the shortest distance between the two points in Euclidean distances (length of the hypotenuse). Figure 3 illustrates clustering in more quantitative.

In this approach, clusters of keywords were created using the k-means clustering algorithm. Because it is practical, easy to use, and successful, the k-means method is frequently employed in clustering algorithms. This process does not need supervision, nor does it have predefined labels or classes. This process involves the formation of clusters determined by the similarity of keywords. A corpus summarization is provided by the clustering of algorithms that may be used to offer insight into what is contained in the corpus [42,43]. The "k" within the k-means clustering algorithms represents a predetermined number of clusters. The algorithm generates k random points as initial cluster centers. The algorithm then assigns each point to the nearest cluster center. A convergence criterion is then achieved by re-computing the new cluster centers until there is no more change occurring [44]. The method illustrates in Figure 4.

Text mining analysis can, therefore, be conducted using several tools. For instance, in this study, Python <www.python.org> was used to perform the text mining technique. Python is an open-source language that is commonly used for text processing. Moreover, it is popularly used because its packages are highly flexible [45]. NumPy, pandas, and sci-kit-learn python packages were used in performing k-means clustering. Besides, NLTK (the Natural Language Toolkit package) was also used to perform pre-processing tasks on the data [46]. For instance, a 'regular expression' in Python was used to convert the texts to lowercase and remove punctuation and numbers [45]. Figure 5 shows the distribution of publication per journal with number of articles in each.

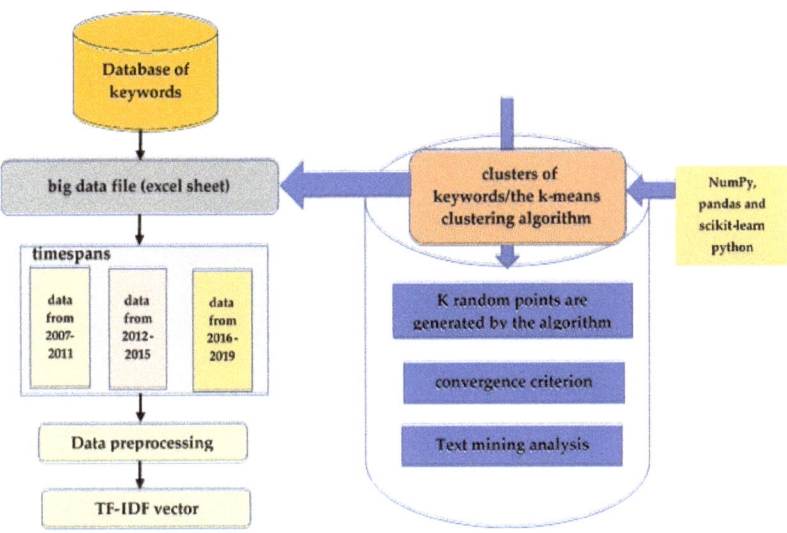

Figure 4. Flow diagram of the entire approach.

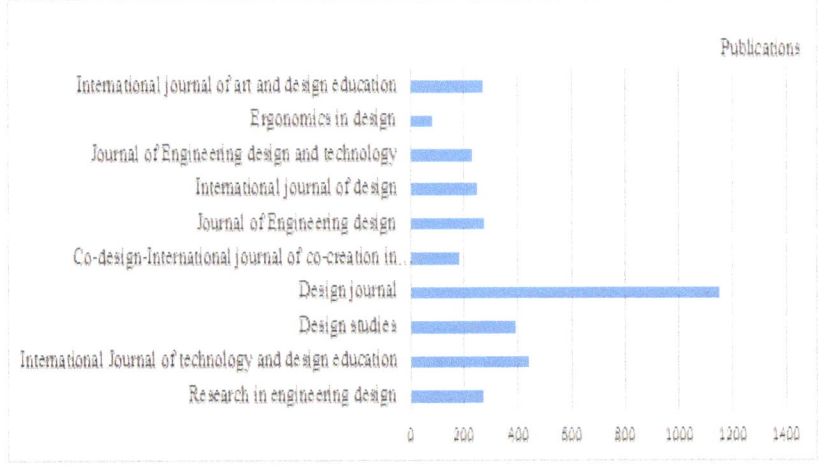

Figure 5. Distribution of publication per journal.

In order to classify the keywords into text mining models (i.e., clusters) using the k-means clustering method, we combined all articles' keywords into one big data file (excel sheet) and manipulated each article's keywords one by one as one document (i.e., 3553 documents). Thus, we imported the data into Python and divided the whole dataset into three different time-span (i.e., corpora) based on their related publication year (variable; See Figure 6). The first time span (corpus) comprised data from 2007 to 2011, and the second time-span comprised data from 2012–2015 and third time-span comprised data from 2016–2019. This division was essential to answering the research questions and analyzing the design of research disciplines for each corpus.

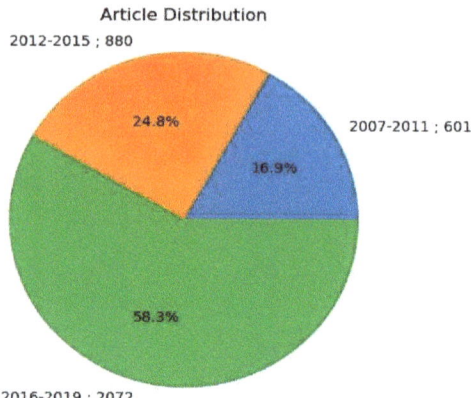

Figure 6. Research articles distribution according to three time spans.

4.3. Clustering Results

We changed the time span and uniformed all the keywords by setting lowercase letters to produce the expected results. Any other insignificant signs that include marks, signs, words, numbers, and full stops were removed from the clusters because they had no values in the analysis. We generated equations to manipulate the compound terms, for example, to have the design process as a single term as seen; this will help research and interpretations.

TF-IDF is a weighing schema commonly and widely used during text mining research [46]. This research involved the calculation of the TF-IDF vector for each document instead of using a simple term document frequency by keywords. TF is term frequency while IDF is the inverse of document frequency [47]. The frequency of a particular word in a document is counted using the term frequency. The IDF's value determines a word's importance in a document. Additionally, inverse document frequency is determined by taking the quotient of the number of documents containing the term (DF) and the total number of documents (N) and finding its logarithm (log(N/DF)). The IDF value represents the frequency at which a word appears in a document file. This value may increase when some documents contain specific words among other documents. In this regard, the most frequent words represent each cluster.

Nevertheless, in using the k-means cluster for this study, the K-means clustering algorithm was used in defining the number of clusters (k). The best numbers of clusters for this study were specified based on a trial and error approach [47]. This was done by comparing the values of k that were clustered against the value of k that is most applicable in each dataset. Ten clusters were used in this study. The research shown in Figure 6 is the general distribution of publications grouped by category of time-span. About 16.9 % of the publications were made between the time-span of 2007 to 2011. Additionally, during the period between 2012 and 2015, 24.8 % of the publications were made, while 58.3 % of the publications were made in the period between 2016 and 2019. The total number of keywords for every time span is shown in Figure 7. About 16.1% (2813) of the total keywords (17,486) related to all gathered publications fall from 2007 to 2011. On the other hand, 24.7% (4318) fell from 2012 to 2015, while 59.2% (10,355) fell from 2016 to 2019.

The frequencies of samples were decomposed for the same period, as shown in Table 3. The design research topic is essential, especially in designing the research topic by the keywords' distribution. Table 3 shows the keyword distribution with general terms, where the first time span (2007–2011) included very few keywords related to the design research discipline less than ten times. This research is limited in its coverage of the first time span for the selected papers' titles and related concepts to design topics. However, we provided a justification based on the frequency of keywords in this period compared to the frequency of total keywords, which were mentioned in the second and third time-spans.

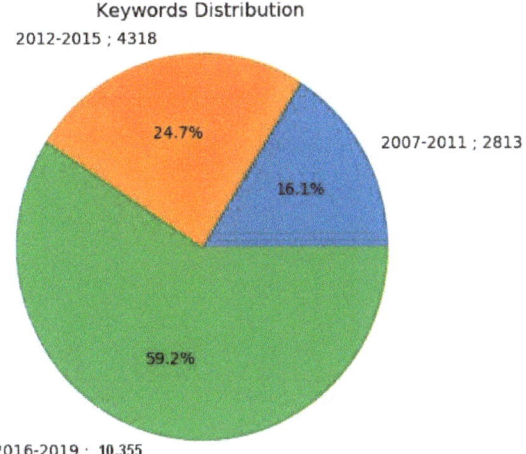

Figure 7. Research keywords distribution according to three-time spans.

Table 3. Sample of terms distribution by the three time-spans.

Term	2007–2011	2012–2015	2016–2019
0 creativity	40	48	68
1 product design	30	31	48
2 design process	27	31	49
3 design education	25	49	97
4 collaborative design	24	18	27
5 design	23	40	117
6 conceptual design	23	27	20
7 technology education	23	25	25
8 engineering design	21	19	15
9 innovation	18	24	30
10 design cognition	17	19	26
11 design theory	16	20	28
12 industrial design	16	32	12
13 communication	14	18	10
14 design practice	14	10	30
15 design management	0	17	18
16 problem solving	13	0	0
17 aesthetics	13	10	21

The results of this part of the research will be discussed based on the clustering method. Following the previous study, we reduced the number of concepts in each cluster to 10 and the number of clusters in each period to 10 conducted by Abu-Shanab and Harb [48]. We renamed each cluster for a better name based on the relationship and cluster associate information. Each cluster has been separated from the other, clearly using the unique words that best describe the cluster. The results have exposed each cluster according to the time differences, which directs future research. Some keywords closely related to the clusters were not included during the labeling of the clusters. Keywords such as technology, designs, technology, and architecture have forced us to verify the existing general keywords cautiously, which has helped the clustering process. We also came up with some restrictions to govern the blurrier of the clusters. The clusters have been estimated for a time-span of three, as shown in Figures 8–10. The conceptual variance represents the similarity between clusters as portrayed by the intelligent algorithm in the world of miscue [49–51]. Our discussion has been set on the rigorous list of keywords collected from very popular designs that are highly known, as seen in Table 2.

Human-centered design	Collaboration	Collaborative design	Design technology & education
Design-process collaborative-design Eng-design design-education design-theory design-practice conceptual-design interaction industrial-design design-methods	Design-methodology teamwork Communication problem-solving System participatory-design art empowerment Critical-design human-centered-design	Cases-study design-education creativity product-design interdisciplinary collaborative-design research methods methodology design-activity evaluation	Design-technology design-education professional-development design secondary-education designers art & design designing Eng-education

Design administration	Design development	Service/product design	Creativity
Marketing design-strategy product-development design-management styling creative-industries empowerment critical-design framing reflection	technology-education technological-literacy curriculum professional-development motivation gender problem-solving primary-education environmental-sustainability programing	Product-design industrial-design design-tools design-management product-personality perception culture user-behaviour interface-design collaborative-design	Creativity design conceptual-design design cognation evaluation problem-solving Eng-design protocol-analysis design-process design-tools

Generative tools	Design theories
Design creativity innovation technology pedagogy system risk learning collaboration idea generation	Design-techniques conceptual-design creative case-study prototypes evaluation innovation framing empowerment critical-design

Figure 8. The ten clusters for the time span 2007–2011.

Generative method	Collaboration 1	Design practice	Design process
Collaborative-design design-process conceptual-design implementing design-education communication design-practice design-cognition methodology built-environment distribute-design	Design participatory pedagogy innovation design-education implementing creativity technology collaboration architecture	Communication engineering interaction-design conceptual-design architecture-design optimization design-knowledge distribute-design design-education design-practice	Protocol-analysis design-cognition design-activity creativity design-process design-behaviour conceptual-design design-precedents architecture-design design-strategy

Design thinking	Design education	Design technology & education	Usability design
Change-propagation Eng-management Eng-change design-matrix iteration change designer-use product-platform sustainability functional-modeling	Technology-education technology-knowledge teacher-education gender design-process evaluation development design-methodology secondary-education research	Design-education creativity design-process architecture-design design-research design-studies assessment design-methods built-environment Eng-design	product-design design-activity usability creativity aesthetics product-development affordance conceptual-design universal-design perception

Co-innovation	Design theories 1
Creativity innovation design-theory ,Eng-design conceptual-design participatory-design design-process case-study design-thinking art-education	co-design design-tools system-design case-study user-behavior design-process user-behavior idea-generation practice design-methods

Figure 9. The ten clusters for the time-span 2012–2015.

The previous results regarding the clustering step exposed a few research directions to carry on, where some terms appeared in the three time-spans. The following research directions existed in the three periods:

- *Co-creation:* for instance, that work is related to design thinking, innovation, creativity, design process, and design.
- *Co-innovation:* increasing the number in design research fields is a hot topic, and it seems very motivating as it appeared in three periods with a greater concern on collaborative design.
- *Ethical design:* offer new insights/knowledge about the design process within design research.
- *Social practice design:* it is essential to associate terms that focus on its adoption and other elements affecting the area—research related to participatory design, collaboration, sustainability, design innovation, and articulating design.

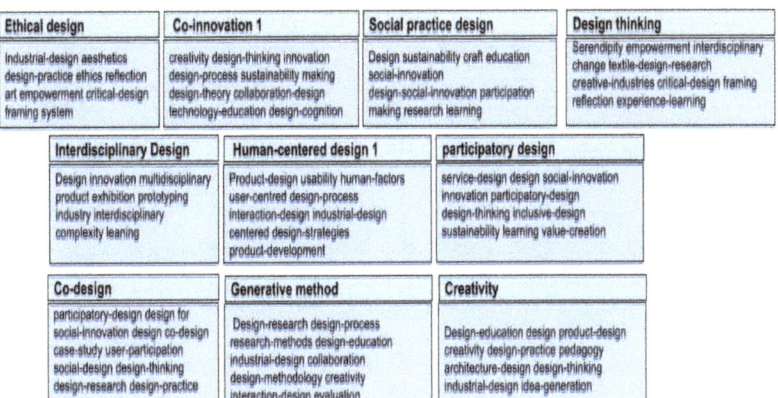

Figure 10. The ten clusters for the time-span 2016–2019.

On the other hand, research areas/topics that began gaining popularity later, particularly during the last period (based on word frequencies), were related to design, creativity, education, research, co-design, design process, and participatory design. Identifying the relevance of examining clusters is best explained by analyzing keywords is important. The selection of keywords by the author had issues of significance, whereby it was not consistent. The limitation of keywords would have been the best if it had been concentrated on. Our results were based on the author's arguments in a three-time period. We decided to contrite on the last two periods to bypass the limitations. (From 2012–2019), although this was likely to divest our analysis of depth over time. On the other hand, splitting the data range into last two periods (time-spans) would lead to the same limitation.

4.4. Word Frequency Distribution

A word frequency distribution was used depending on the period with the study of Abu-Shanab and Abu-Baker [52]. Abu-Shanab and Abu-Baker [52] estimated the frequencies of all famous words within the clusters, after which they were summated into major concepts. Their research paid attention to mobile phone purchases and use by applying mixed methods and new methodologies that aided us in this research study. In addition, the estimations that were used also focused on three periods. The data shown in Appendix A was generated using a clustering tool. The clustering tool was used to create the data provided in Table 3. The magnitude was assigned to the frequency regarding the total size of frequencies, after which it was compared with other terms. This would help the readers recognize the popular terms within the data. The list of a popular terms produced by the clustering process was taken and summated manually into logical terms as shown in Table 4. Frequency distribution depends on a sample of the dataset. Text analysis was the basis of determining the frequencies and clustering words in this research.

A summation of keywords followed this step into more general dimensions (See Figures 8–10). Figures 8–10 across the period were drawn using the research directions that interest the researchers. Furthermore, we summed the new set of clusters into ten major dimensions according to each period (See Figures 8–10). The following trend can be seen based on this kind of analysis (i.e., text analysis). On the one hand, we experienced the thriving direction of some clusters such as design, co-design, creativity, innovation, design-thinking, participatory design, sustainability, design education, and design research.

Table 4. General terms and their corresponding frequencies.

Terms	2007–2011	2012–2015	2016–2019	Trend Lines	General Term
Service design	9	9	43		
Design tools	9	11	24		
Design research	9	16	54		
Participatory design	9	18	59		Co-design method and approach
Design methodology	8	8	0		
Collaboration	8	14	32		
Participation	0	0	17		
Design graphic	7	0	0		
Usability design	0	0	17		
Emotion	7	0	0		Anthropomorphic design
Perception	7	8	0		
Interface design	8	0	0		
Philosophy of design	7	8	0		
Design fiction	0	0	21		Assumptions, foundations and implications of design
Technology design	7	0	19		
Design strategy	7	7	0		
Sustainability design	8	10	51		Eco-design strategy
User participation	7	0	0		
User-centered design	0	0	17		Co-innovation
Co-innovation	0	3	23		
Product experience	7	0	0		
Product development	0	0	10		Co-production
Design management	0	17	18		
Ethical design	0	6	19		
Inclusive design	0	0	8		
Speculative design	0	0	17		Social-practice design
Social design	0	0	16		
Social practice design	0	2	21		

On the other hand, we observed diminishing interest in the design strategy, perception, epistemology, philosophy of design, and pedagogy. This was unexpected considering the related literature research. Most of the terms/topics listed in Table 4 appeared to be very motivating though some of them faded in the first period (2007–2011). However, the terms/topics in the last period appeared interesting for the researchers from 2016 to 2019. It is necessary to reveal the logic behind our classification approach, where terms (see Appendix A) such as 'design strategy' might open an argument: is it a design-related issue or any design discipline? Similarly, do aesthetics only belong to usability/user experience or might they fit in a graphic design domain is also a question. Thus, these terms and others will open debates leading to enriching the topic and figures the strength of design research theories and methodologies.

5. Conclusions

The study aimed to explore the research directions with the design research topic. The study journals selected were of higher quality, congregated different keywords from different articles, and were used in the analysis. Ten journals were chosen for 3553 research articles and 17,486 keywords. This big dataset, a rich sample of keywords, was analyzed to conclude the design research's main directions. New terms/trends were investigated as results in the design domain, attracting researchers, practitioners, and journal editorial boards. It was found that topics like co-innovation, ethical design, design thinking, co-design, creativity, social practice design, and generative methods/tools have been attracting more research. On the other hand, researchers persisted in pursuing topics such as collaborative design, human-centered design, interdisciplinary design, design education, participatory design, design practice, collaborative design, design development, collaboration, design theories, design administration, and service/product design areas. Finally, researchers and/or practitioners' pursuit of a framework as guidelines to study the design research has faded. The design research area is guided by design theories (for researchers' issues), design methodologies (for researchers, managerial, and/or administrative matters), and design methods/tools (for researchers' and practitioners' issues). A term distribution and analysis were founded based on the dataset and trend analysis (See Appendix A). The results identified ten main clusters/categories in each period, with a few overlapping among them during different periods (See Figures 8–10) that govern research in other design areas. The first period (2007–2011) focused on topics like collaboration, human-centered design, collaborative design, design development, design administration, design technology and education, service/product design, creativity, generative tools, and design theories. The second period (2012–2015) focused on productive method, collaboration 1, design practice, design process, design thinking, design education, design technology, usability design, co-innovation 1, and design theories 1. The last period (2016–2019) focused on ethical design, co-innovation 1, social practice design, design thinking 1, interdisciplinary design, human-centered design 1, participatory design, co-design, creativity 1, and generative method 1.

5.1. Contributions

This research study utilized one of the most extensive samples of publications (i.e., papers). Prior research studies relied on the qualitative method and piece-by-piece assessment and had a tiny sample size (i.e., small sample size). A total of 17,486 words from design journals were used in this research report. The key categories examined and presented in this paper could determine what fields are thriving and degrading. In this study, the sample dataset underwent a quantitative analysis. A quantitative analysis was conducted to prevent author bias when analyzing research and how we look at and analyze the data collected. Future scholars might examine and cluster the information acquired in this research study (data available in Appendix A can be used manually). Each researcher will have a unique perspective and thoughts on the subject domains. Finally, the work is the first attempt to use text mining to examine research directions in design research. Additionally, this research study provides perceptions/observations concerning new dimensions critical in the design and associated areas.

Importantly, we start classifying text as easily as possible using pre-trained BERT models. However, we found that BERT has many parameters and requires high computational resources, which are not available in our lab research. Training a model takes a lot of time and money. For future work, we will combine text mining with another existing embedding model called GloVe to accelerate the training speed of the model.

5.2. Limitations

This research paper was limited by the total number of journals used (web of science (ISI-core collection database) for data gathering. This limitation calls for a more thorough research or in-depth research projects using a more efficient approach. Design research topics are not only decisively published within the list of journals (design research is also published in chapters' books and at proceedings' conferences) used in this research paper (See Table 2). Furthermore, some journals (i.e., The Design Journal and Design Issues) were excluded due to the research team's criterion, even when they considered them significant in the design discipline. They could have led to some compelling results. In addition, the accessibility of data (i.e., keywords fetching) within each time span is considered another restriction, as the first time-span (2007–2011) comprised fewer articles than the second and third time-spans. This research paper declares this limitation important but contributes by providing an initial insight into the design research area.

Another limitation we faced in this research study was our judgment about the clusters/categories built (manual clustering as we categorized each 10 clusters into main categories based on authors' experience, knowledge, and previous studies in design research). The types (See Figures 8–10) built are significant for future design research. Research studies [53,54] found that the design domain is derived from four dimensions based on design aspects. Those dimensions included composition, performance, experience, and communication. The measurements might be considered vague when observing the results of this research study. Therefore, we summarize that the fragmented nature of the design areas among different disciplines and the various topics that shape it (i.e., industrial, ergonomics, engineering, design and technology, ICT, and design and arts) prevent theory conceptualization.

Supplementary Materials: The following supporting information can be downloaded at: https://www.mdpi.com/article/10.3390/electronics11233930/s1.

Author Contributions: Conceptualization, M.N.; A.L. and U.T.; methodology, M.N.; software, H.L.; validation, M.N.; A.L.; H.L. and U.T.; formal analysis, A.L. and H.L.; investigation, R.A.Z.; L.A. and A.H.G.; data curation, M.N. and U.T.; writing—original draft preparation, M.N.; A.L.; H.L. and U.T.; writing—review and editing, M.N. and L.A.; visualization, R.A.Z.; L.A. and A.H.G.; supervision, M.N.; funding acquisition, A.H.G. All authors have read and agreed to the published version of the manuscript.

Funding: This research received no internal/external funding.

Data Availability Statement: The Dataset was uploaded within supplementary files via system.

Conflicts of Interest: The Authors declare that there is no conflict of interest.

Appendix A. The Most Popular Terms

Term	2007–2011	2012–2015	2016–2019
creativity	47	48	68
product design	35	39	48
design process	31	35	49
design education	30	52	97
collaborative design	29	23	27
design	24	40	117
conceptual design	26	32	20
collaborative design	23	25	25
technology education	26	25	15
engineering design	29	30	48
innovation	17	19	26
design cognition	19	23	28
design theory	16	32	12
industrial design	16	18	12
communication	14	10	30
design practice	0	17	18
problem solving	13	0	0
aesthetics	13	10	21
interaction design	13	13	21
product development	12	10	0
case study	12	18	0
design methods	11	15	23
architectural design	11	15	0
evaluation	11	12	16
design activity	11	17	0
creative design	10	0	0
teamwork	10	3	0
service design	9	9	43
technological literacy	9	0	0
research methods	9	10	10
design tools	9	11	24
design research	9	16	54
participatory design	9	18	59
design methodology	8	8	0
collaboration	8	14	32
curriculum	8	9	0
sustainability design	8	10	51
interface design	8	0	0
learning	7	0	18
technology	7	0	19
architecture	7	0	0
culture	7	0	0
design strategy	7	7	0
graphic design	7	0	0
emotion	7	0	0
perception	7	8	0
philosophy of design	7	8	0
user participation	7	0	0
product experience	7	0	0
healthcare	0	0	25
interdisciplinary	0	0	21
craft	0	0	22
design fiction	0	0	21
circular economy	0	0	20
design management	0	17	18

Appendix A. *Cont.*

Term	2007–2011	2012–2015	2016–2019
usability design	0	0	17
user-centered design	0	0	17
speculative design	0	0	17
participation	0	0	17
social design	0	0	16
decision making	0	0	16
product development	0	0	10
inclusive design	0	0	8
epistemology	0	0	8
art education	0	11	16
empathy	0	0	16
pedagogy	0	0	16
epistemology	0	0	8
co-innovation	0	3	23
ethical design	0	6	19
social practice design	0	2	21

Appendix B. List of Abbreviations

Abbreviation	Description
CAD	computer-aided design
ICT	Information and Communication Technology
IT	Information technology
MDO	Multidisciplinary Design Optimization
AM	Additive manufacturing
ABSA	The aspect-based sentiment analysis
MTMVN	multitask Multiview network
SOTA	Most State-Of-The-Art
NMT	Neural Machine Translation
LRLs	Low-Resource Languages
TL	Transfer Learning
CDCAT	Cross-Document Coreference Annotation Tool
ESCI	Emerging Source Citation Index
CSV	excel sheet
HTML	Hypertext Markup Language
XML	extensible markup language
TF-IDF	term frequency-inverse document frequency

References

1. Gemser, G.; de Bont, C. Design-Related and Design-Focused Research: A Study of Publication Patterns in Design Journals. *She Ji* **2016**, *2*, 46–58. [CrossRef]
2. Cooper, R. Editorial: Moving design forward. *Des. J.* **2008**, *11*, 5–7. [CrossRef]
3. Atkinson, P. The Design Journal and the Meaning of Design. *Des. J.* **2017**, *20*, 1–4. [CrossRef]
4. Cooper, R. Design Research: Past, Present and Future. *Des. J.* **2017**, *20*, 5–11. [CrossRef]
5. Giacomin, J. What is Design for Meaning? *J. Des. Bus. Soc.* **2017**, *3*, 167–190. [CrossRef] [PubMed]
6. Cooper, R. Design Research Comes of Age. *Des. J.* **1997**, *1* (Suppl. 1), 1. [CrossRef]
7. Ralph, P.; Wand, Y. A proposal for a formal definition of the design concept. In *Design Requirements Engineering: A Ten-Year Perspective*; Lecture Notes in Business Information Processing; Springer: Berlin/Heidelberg, Germany, 2009; Volume 14, pp. 103–136. [CrossRef]
8. Cross, N. Developing design as a discipline. *J. Eng. Des.* **2018**, *29*, 691–708. [CrossRef]
9. Overkamp, T.; Blomkvist, J.; Rodrigues, V.; Arvola, M.; Holmlid, S. Resource Integration as a Perspective on Value in Interaction Design. In Proceedings of the 32nd International BCS Human Computer Interaction Conference, Belfast, UK, 4–6 July 2018.
10. Jain, A.K. Data clustering: 50 years beyond K-means. *Pattern Recognit. Lett.* **2010**, *31*, 651–666. [CrossRef]
11. Cross, N. Designerly ways of knowing Journal Item. *Des. Stud.* **1982**, *3*, 221–227. [CrossRef]

12. Christensen, B.T.; Ball, L.J. Building a discipline: Indicators of expansion, integration and consolidation in design research across four decades. *Des. Stud.* **2019**, *65*, 18–34. [CrossRef]
13. Liedtka, J. Perspective: Linking Design Thinking with Innovation Outcomes through Cognitive Bias Reduction. *J. Prod. Innov. Manag.* **2015**, *32*, 925–938. [CrossRef]
14. Bremner, C.; Rodgers, P. Design Without Discipline. *Des. Issues* **2013**, *29*, 4–13. [CrossRef]
15. Cash, P.J. Developing theory-driven design research. *Des. Stud.* **2018**, *56*, 84–119. [CrossRef]
16. Dorst, K. The core of design thinking and its application. *Des. Stud.* **2011**, *32*, 521–532. [CrossRef]
17. Brown, T. *Change by Design: How Design Thinking Transforms Organizations and Inspires Innovation*; HarperCollins Publishers: New York, NY, USA, 2009.
18. Chamberlain, P.; Bonsiepe, G.; Cross, N.; Keller, I.; Frens, J.; Buchanan, R.; Schneider, B. *Design Research Now: Essays and Selected Projects*; Walter de Gruyter: Berlin, Germany, 2012.
19. Grudin, J. Interface: An evolving concept. *Commun. ACM* **1993**, *36*, 110–119. [CrossRef]
20. Hirtz, J.; Stone, R.B.; McAdams, D.A.; Szykman, S.; Wood, K.L. A functional basis for engineering design: Reconciling and evolving previous efforts. *Res. Eng. Des.* **2002**, *13*, 65–82. [CrossRef]
21. Johnson, C. Strategic planning for post-disaster temporary housing. *Disasters* **2007**, *31*, 435–458. [CrossRef]
22. Chai, K.H.; Xiao, X. Understanding design research: A bibliometric analysis of Design Studies (1996–2010). *Des. Stud.* **2012**, *33*, 24–43. [CrossRef]
23. Riaz, M.; Breaux, T.; Williams, L. How have we evaluated software pattern application? A systematic mapping study of research design practices. *Inf. Softw. Technol.* **2015**, *65*, 14–38. [CrossRef]
24. Chakrabarti, A. Towards a taxonomy of design research areas. In *The future of Design Methodology*; Springer: London, UK, 2011; pp. 249–259. [CrossRef]
25. Caussade, S.; de Dios Ortúzar, J.; Rizzi, L.I.; Hensher, D.A. Assessing the influence of design dimensions on stated choice experiment estimates. *Transp. Res. Part B Methodol.* **2005**, *39*, 621–640. [CrossRef]
26. Fan, Z.; Ge, Y. The Influence of Techno ethics on Industrial Design. *MATEC Web Conf.* **2018**, *167*, 01008. [CrossRef]
27. Hernández, R.J.; Cooper, R.; Tether, B.; Murphy, E. Design, the language of innovation: A review of the design studies literature. *She Ji J. Des. Econ. Innov.* **2018**, *4*, 249–274. [CrossRef]
28. Lee, D.; Lee, H. Mapping the Characteristics of Design Research in Social Sciences. *Arch. Des. Res.* **2019**, *32*, 39–51. [CrossRef]
29. Nusir, M.; Tariq, U.; Ahanger, T.A. Engaging Diverse Stakeholders in Interdisciplinary Co-Design Project for Better Service Design. *J. Cases Inf. Technol. (JCIT)* **2021**, *23*, 1–29. [CrossRef]
30. Bentley, R.A. Random Drift Versus Selection in Academic Vocabulary: An Evolutionary Analysis of Published Keywords. 2008. Available online: https://www.ncbi.nlm.nih.gov/pmc/articles/PMC2518107/ (accessed on 13 March 2019).
31. Evans, M. Design Thinking: Understanding How Designers Think and Work by Nigel Cross. *Des. J.* **2012**, *15*, 141–143. [CrossRef]
32. Wang, L.H.; Wang, Q.; Zhang, X.; Cai, W.; Sun, X. A bibliometric analysis of anaerobic digestion for methane research during the period 1994–2011. *J. Mater. Cycles Waste Manag.* **2013**, *15*, 1–8. [CrossRef]
33. Yao, X.; Moon, S.K.; Bi, G. Multidisciplinary design optimization to identify additive manufacturing resources in customized product development. *J. Comput. Des. Eng.* **2017**, *4*, 131–142. [CrossRef]
34. Nie, B.; Sun, S. Using text mining techniques to identify research trends: A case study of design research. *Appl. Sci.* **2017**, *7*, 401. [CrossRef]
35. Andreasen, M.M. 45 Years with design methodology. *J. Eng. Des.* **2011**, *22*, 293–332. [CrossRef]
36. Johnson, J.; Cook, M. Policy Design: A New Area of Design Research and Practice. In *Complex Systems Design and Management*; Springer: Cham, Switzerland, 2014; pp. 51–62. [CrossRef]
37. Kavousi, S.; Miller, P.A.; Alexander, P.A. Modeling metacognition in design thinking and design making. *Int. J. Technol. Des. Educ.* **2020**, *30*, 709–735. [CrossRef]
38. Lloyd, P. From Design Methods to Future-Focused Thinking: 50 years of design research. *Des. Stud.* **2017**, *48*, A1–A8. [CrossRef]
39. Yong, B.; Yang, Y. A multitask multiview neural network for end-to-end aspect-based sentiment analysis. *Big Data Min. Anal.* **2021**, *4*, 195–207. [CrossRef]
40. Maimaiti, M.; Liu, Y.; Luan, H.; Sun, M. Enriching the transfer learning with pre-trained lexicon embedding for low-resource neural machine translation. *Tsinghua Sci. Technol.* **2022**, *27*, 150–163. [CrossRef]
41. Xu, Y.; Xia, B.; Wan, Y.; Zhang, F.; Xu, J.; Ning, H. CDCAT: A multi-language cross-document entity and event coreference annotation tool. *Tsinghua Sci. Technol.* **2022**, *27*, 589–598. [CrossRef]
42. Shen, L.; Liu, Q.; Chen, G.; Ji, S. Text-based price recommendation system for online rental houses. *Big Data Min. Anal.* **2020**, *3*, 143–152. [CrossRef]
43. Sawsan, A.; Jaradat, R. Clarification of research design, research methods, and research methodology: A guide for public administration researchers and practitioners. *Teach. Public Adm.* **2018**, *36*, 237–258.–258. [CrossRef]
44. Hicks, B. The language of collaborative engineering projects. In Proceedings of the 19th International Conference on Engineering Design (ICED13), Seoul, Korea, 19–22 August 2013; pp. 321–330. [CrossRef]
45. Aggarwal, C.C.; Zhai, C.X. Aggarwal, C.C.; Zhai, C.X. A survey of text clustering algorithms. In *Mining Text Data*; Springer US.: Boston, MA, USA, 2012; pp. 77–128. [CrossRef]

46. Bekkerman, R.; El-Yaniv, R.; Winter, Y.; Tishby, N. On feature distributional clustering for text categorization. In Proceedings of the 24th Annual International ACM SIGIR Conference on Research and Development in Information Retrieval, New Orleans, LA, USA, 9–13 September 2001; pp. 146–153. [CrossRef]
47. Abu-Shanab, E.; Harb, Y. E-government research insights: Text mining analysis. *Electron. Commer. Res. Appl.* **2019**, *38*, 100892. [CrossRef]
48. Bird, S.; Klein, E.; Loper, E. Natural Language Processing with Python. 2009. Available online: https://books.google.com.au/books/about/Natural_Language_Processing_with_Python.html?id=KGIbfiiP1i4C&source=kp_book_description&redir_esc=y (accessed on 19 March 2020).
49. Cielen, D.; Meysman, A.; Ali, M. Introducing Data Science: Big Data, Machine Learning, and More, Using Python Tools. 2016. Available online: https://dl.acm.org/citation.cfm?id=3051941 (accessed on 19 March 2020).
50. Haddi, E.; Liu, X.; Shi, Y. The role of text pre-processing in sentiment analysis. *Procedia Comput. Sci.* **2013**, *17*, 26–32. [CrossRef]
51. Pham, D.T.; Dimov, S.S.; Nguyen, C.D. Selection of K in K-means clustering. *Proc. Inst. Mech. Eng. Part C J. Mech. Eng. Sci.* **2005**, *219*, 103–119. [CrossRef]
52. Abu-Shanab, E.A.; Abu-Baker, A.N. Using and buying mobile phones in Jordan: Implications for future research and the Development of New Methodology. *Technol. Soc.* **2014**, *38*, 103–110. [CrossRef]
53. Salton, G.; Wong, A.; Yang, C.S. A Vector Space Model for Automatic Indexing. *Commun. ACM* **1975**, *18*, 613–620. [CrossRef]
54. Haug, A. Four dimensions of product designs. *J. Des. Res.* **2015**, *13*, 20–35. [CrossRef]

 *electronics*

Article

A Robust Chronic Kidney Disease Classifier Using Machine Learning

Debabrata Swain [1], **Utsav Mehta** [1], **Ayush Bhatt** [1], **Hardeep Patel** [1], **Kevin Patel** [1], **Devanshu Mehta** [1], **Biswaranjan Acharya** [2,*], **Vassilis C. Gerogiannis** [3,*], **Andreas Kanavos** [4,*] and **Stella Manika** [5]

1   Computer Science and Engineering Department, Pandit Deendayal Energy University, Gandhinagar 382007, India
2   Department of Computer Engineering-AI, Marwadi University, Rajkot 360003, India
3   Department of Digital Systems, University of Thessaly, 41500 Larissa, Greece
4   Department of Informatics, Ionian University, 49100 Corfu, Greece
5   Department of Planning and Regional Development, University of Thessaly, 38334 Volos, Greece
*   Correspondence: biswaranjan.acharya@marwadieducation.edu.in (B.A.); vgerogian@uth.gr (V.C.G.); akanavos@ionio.gr (A.K.)

Citation: Swain, D.; Mehta, U.; Bhatt, A.; Patel, H.; Patel, K.; Mehta, D.; Acharya, B.; Gerogiannis, V.C.; Kanavos, A.; Manika, S. A Robust Chronic Kidney Disease Classifier Using Machine Learning. *Electronics* **2023**, *12*, 212. https://doi.org/10.3390/electronics12010212

Academic Editors: Amir H. Gandomi, Fang Chen and Laith Abualigah

Received: 5 November 2022
Revised: 21 December 2022
Accepted: 26 December 2022
Published: 1 January 2023

Abstract: Clinical support systems are affected by the issue of high variance in terms of chronic disorder prognosis. This uncertainty is one of the principal causes for the demise of large populations around the world suffering from some fatal diseases such as chronic kidney disease (CKD). Due to this reason, the diagnosis of this disease is of great concern for healthcare systems. In such a case, machine learning can be used as an effective tool to reduce the randomness in clinical decision making. Conventional methods for the detection of chronic kidney disease are not always accurate because of their high degree of dependency on several sets of biological attributes. Machine learning is the process of training a machine using a vast collection of historical data for the purpose of intelligent classification. This work aims at developing a machine-learning model that can use a publicly available data to forecast the occurrence of chronic kidney disease. A set of data preprocessing steps were performed on this dataset in order to construct a generic model. This set of steps includes the appropriate imputation of missing data points, along with the balancing of data using the SMOTE algorithm and the scaling of the features. A statistical technique, namely, the chi-squared test, is used for the extraction of the least-required set of adequate and highly correlated features to the output. For the model training, a stack of supervised-learning techniques is used for the development of a robust machine-learning model. Out of all the applied learning techniques, support vector machine (SVM) and random forest (RF) achieved the lowest false-negative rates and test accuracy, equal to 99.33% and 98.67%, respectively. However, SVM achieved better results than RF did when validated with 10-fold cross-validation.

Keywords: chronic kidney disease; data balancing; hyperparameter tuning; machine learning; SMOTE; supervised learning

1. Introduction

Kidneys are vital organs that keep track of salt, potassium, and caustic substances within the human body [1], and consist of 5 L of blood. If the kidneys cease to function normally, squanders form in the blood. As a result, this blood is converted into 9–10 L of a toxic fluid containing urea and creatinine in just 2–3 days. This condition is called chronic kidney disease (CKD). People possessing medical conditions such as diabetes, hypertension, cardiac disorder, or other kidney problems are more likely to have chronic kidney disease, while some kidney diseases are hereditary. Moreover, kidney disease becomes more likely as a person ages [2].

Individuals aged 65 or older (38.1%) are more prone to CKD than individuals in the ranges of 45–64 (12.4%) and 18–44 (6%) years are, and women are more prone to CKD

(14.3%) than men (12.4%) are [3]. According to the current medical statistics, CKD affects a stunning 10% of the world's population. In 2005, approximately 38 million deaths out of the 58 million total fatalities that occurred in that year were caused by CKD [4]. COVID-19 was found in 4.09% of CKD patients (193/4716 patients), but only in a percentage equal to 0.46% of the general population (5195/1,125,574). The crude mortality rate among COVID-19-positive CKD patients was 44.6% (86/193), compared to 4.7% (215/4523) in COVID-19-negative CKD patients [5]. When analyzing cases requiring renal replacement therapy (RRT), 55% of the patients had Stage 5 CKD, and 30% had Stage 3 CKD. In addition, 70% of patients who required RRT had a fatal outcome [6].

Healthcare practitioners employ two basic approaches for obtaining clear patient insights to detect kidney disease. Initially, blood and urine tests are used to determine if a person has CKD; a blood test can determine kidney function, also known as the glomerular filtration rate (GFR). If the GFR value equals 60, this indicates normal kidney function, while values between 15 and 60 mean the kidneys are substandard. Lastly, if the GFR value equals to 15 or less, this indicates kidney failure [2]. The second approach, the urinalysis test, looks for albumin that can flow into the urine if the kidneys are not properly working.

The significance of early diagnosis is very high for reducing the mortality rate in CKD patients. A late diagnosis of this condition often leads to renal failure, which provokes the need for dialysis or kidney transplantation [7]. Because of the growing number of CKD patients, a paucity of specialized physicians has led to high costs of diagnosis and treatment. Particularly in developing countries, computer-assisted systems for diagnostics are needed to assist physicians and radiologists in making diagnostic judgments [8].

In such a situation, for the early and efficient prognosis of the disease, computer-aided diagnosis can play a crucial part. Machine learning (ML), which is a subdomain of artificial intelligence (AI), can be used for the adept identification of an ailment. These systems are aimed to aid clinical decision makers in performing more accurate disease classification. This work proposes a refined CKD identification ML model trained using the UCI CKD dataset and supervised-learning techniques SVM and RF. For enhancing the model's scalability, several steps, such as missing-value imputation, data balancing and feature scaling, were employed [9]. The chi-squared technique was also used for the feature selection methodology. In addition to this, ML-based performance boosting methods such as hyperparameter tuning were also used to tune the model using the best possible set of parameters. The efficiency of the proposed work in terms of the testing accuracy was compared with that of various other studies.

The rest of the paper is organized as follows. The related work and the novelty of our work are introduced in Section 2. Section 3 overviews the basic concepts, methods, algorithms, and used dataset that were utilized in this paper. Section 4 presents the research results, while Section 5 depicts the comparison between the proposed framework and others from the literature. Lastly, Section 6 outlines the conclusions and draws directions for future work.

2. Related Work

Different methods and techniques for the problem of chronic kidney disease classification have been proposed and employed in the literature. The proposed research takes into account the existing literature, and further contributes towards enhancing the currently achievable results in the field of chronic kidney disease prediction.

An ML-based disease classification system using the UCI CKD dataset was employed in [10]. Out of all implemented algorithms, random forest achieved the highest accuracy value. This study, however, did not consider outliers while imputing the missing numerical values. The model was also trained on imbalanced data, and no feature selection was performed. Other drawbacks are the absence of hyperparameter tuning and the fact that the model was not cross-validated. In [8], a set of ML algorithms for the development of the CKD classifier was implemented. Random forest achieved the best accuracy. However, no outlier considered imputation, and no data balancing and hyperparameter tuning were performed. In addition, the efficiency of the proposed model was not cross-validated.

The authors in [11] implemented a method based on both machine learning and deep learning. Specifically, out of all the implemented machine-learning algorithms, the SVM model had the highest accuracy. The imputation of the missing values, i.e., the outliers, was not considered in that study. However, this work utilized all the features present in the dataset in terms of the ML model training. Furthermore, another ML-based CKD classifier was developed in [12]. Again, the SVM model showed the highest testing set accuracy. As above, the imputation was implemented without considering the presence of outliers. Data balancing was not performed, while this work uses 12 features for building and training the ML model. Moreover, hyperparameter tuning to improve the model accuracy was not performed.

A healthcare support system based on machine learning for the prognosis of the CKD was introduced in [13]. The decision tree (DT) algorithm showed the highest accuracy. However, an inconsistency lay with the imputation of the missing data that was performed without considering the presence of outliers; in addition, no data balancing was performed. This study uses the correlation-based feature selection (CFS) method for feature selection. This study developed the proposed model with the use of 15 features; however, again, no hyperparameter tuning was performed. Lastly, machine-learning and deep-learning techniques were employed for the construction of an ailment classifier in [14]. The highest accuracy was achieved by the random forest algorithm. Similarly, the imputation was implemented without considering outliers in the numerical features, and the training was utilized on the imbalanced dataset. Hyperparameter tuning was not performed while training the model, and the developed models were not cross-validated.

After investigating the contributions of different researchers for the prediction of CKD in the literature, the following research gaps were identified:

(i)   None of the literature papers considered the presence of outliers in the numerical features during the data preprocessing phase. Due to this, the imputed values in such features are prone to deviating from the overall central tendency.

(ii)   The majority of the literature trained their models on imbalanced data, which lead to a biased model.

(iii)   The majority of the literature did not perform hyperparameter tuning to boost the model's efficacy.

(iv)   Most of the literature did not consider a feature selection method to identify the most relevant and optimal number of features. Hence, in this case, the models were fed with a set of extraneous features. Economically, this increases the cost of the medical examination of this renal ailment.

(v)   This work focuses on the cost-efficient and accurate medical examination of CKD while using fewer than 10 features for the model training and classification of the condition.

3. Methodology

A step-by-step and rather meticulous description of the methodology employed in this work is outlined in the following section.

3.1. Proposed System

An accurate system for the identification of chronic kidney disease using a robust model is proposed in this work. An ML-based approach was utilized for the development of an effective and accurate prediction model. Figure 1 illustrates a schematic representation that depicts the different stages of the proposed system.

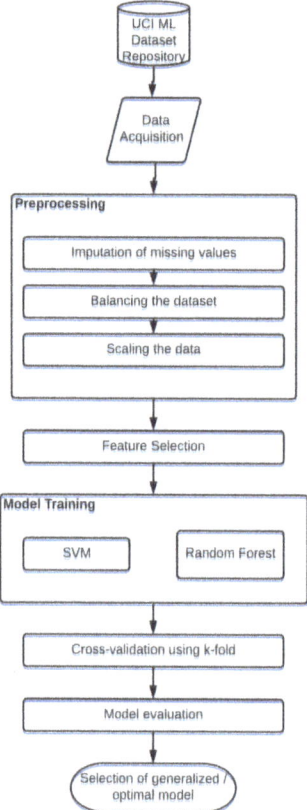

Figure 1. Block diagram of the proposed system.

3.2. Dataset

The dataset used for performing the model training in this work was acquired from the UCI ML repository [15]. This repository is one of the most reliable and used dataset sources for researching and implementing machine-learning algorithms. There are 400 records and 25 features in this particular collection, including class attributes such as CKD and NOTCKD, indicating the status of chronic kidney disease in the patient. This dataset includes 14 categorical and 11 numerical features. This dataset had a considerable number of missing values, with only 158 records having no missing values. There was a significant imbalance between the presence of 250 CKD (62.5%) and 150 NOTCKD (37.5%) observations. Table 1 displays the descriptions and essential information of the features.

3.3. Data Preprocessing

The CKD dataset comprises outliers and missing data that need to be cleaned up during the preprocessing stage. There was also an imbalance in the dataset that caused a bias in the model. The preprocessing stage consists of the estimation and imputation of missing values, noise removal such as outliers, and dataset balancing [16]. To perform the preprocessing steps, the categorical features in the dataset were initially replaced with dummy values such as 0 and 1 using a label-encoding technique.

The dataset contained several missing values, with only 158 patients' records contained no missing values. In the preprocessing stage, these missing data were mainly imputed using two central tendency values. The missing values in the numerical features with no outliers were imputed using the mean ($\bar{x}$) of the respective column. In the case of numerical features with outliers, the central tendency mode (*Mo*) was used for the imputation of the missing values, as imputation with x̄ in such features deviates the imputed value from the average feature value range due to the presence of the outlier [17]. For all the missing values in the categorical features, *Mo* was used for the imputation.

Table 1. Attribute descriptions.

Attributes	Information
Age	Discrete integer values
Blood pressure (BP)	Discrete integer values
Specific gravity (SG)	Discrete integer values
Albumin (AL)	Nominal values (0, 1, 2, 3, 4, 5)
Sugar (SU)	Nominal values (0, 1, 2, 3, 4, 5)
Red blood cells (RBC)	Nominal values (normal, abnormal)
Pus cell (PC)	Nominal values (normal, abnormal)
Pus cell clumps (PCC)	Nominal values (present, not present)
Bacteria (BA)	Nominal values (present, not present)
Blood glucose (BGR)	Numerical values in mg/dL
Blood urea (BU)	Numerical values in mg/dL
Serum creatinine (SC)	Numerical values
Sodium (SOD)	Numerical values in mEq/L
Potassium (POT)	Numerical values in mEq/L
Hemoglobin (HEMO)	Numerical values in gms
Packed cell volume (PCV)	Numerical values
White blood cell count (WC)	Discrete integer values
Red blood cell count (RC)	Numeric values
Hypertension (HTN)	Nominal values (yes, bo)
Diabetes mellitus (DM)	Nominal values (yes, no)
Coronary artery disease (CAD)	Nominal values (yes, no)
Appetite (APPET)	Nominal values (good, poor)
Pedal edema (PED)	Nominal values (yes, no)
Anemia (ANE)	Nominal values (yes, no)
Classification (CLASS)	Nominal Values (CKD, not CKD)

Following imputation, the data were balanced. The dataset consisted of 250 instances of patients with this disorder, and 150 instances of patients not having the disorder, as depicted in Figure 2; this type of distribution caused the bias in the model. Hence, balancing the dataset was performed in the preprocessing stage.

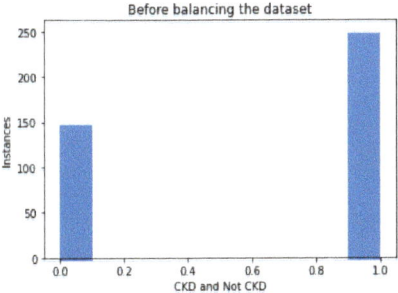

Figure 2. Instances before balancing.

The balancing of the dataset was performed with the use of an oversampling method. Rather than the random generation of data points in terms of balancing, a SMOTE-based oversampling algorithm was employed in this work [18]; the SMOTE algorithm workflow is illustrated in Figure 3. To be more specific, a random sample from the minority class was initially selected, and *k* nearest neighbors were identified. Then, the vector between the selected data point and the neighbor was identified. This vector was multiplied by any random number from 0 to 1. Lastly, after we had added this vector to the current data point, the synthetic data point was obtained.

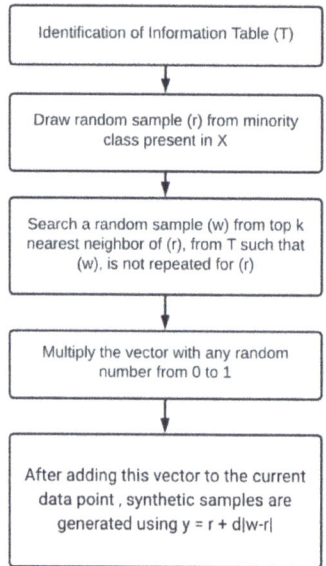

Figure 3. SMOTE algorithm workflow.

Figure 4 illustrates a bar diagram that depicts the instances of CKD and NOTCKD in the dataset after the balancing phase using the SMOTE algorithm.

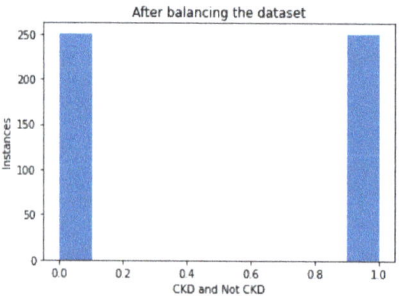

Figure 4. Instances after balancing.

After balancing the dataset, the next step was to remove noise such as outliers present in the dataset. For this purpose, feature scaling was employed, which was implemented with the use of MinMaxScaler [19].

3.4. Feature Selection

Each trained machine-learning classifier requires feature selection, since the results may be impacted if extraneous features are used while training the model [20].

The correlation of independent features with the target class is determined using the chi-squared feature selection approach [21]. With its robustness in handling categorical data and its property of making no assumptions in the distribution of the data, the chi-squared test was chosen for the purpose of feature selection in this work. Additionally, in this test, the target class and each independent feature's chi-squared value were computed.

Features with better chi-squared scores were selected for the prediction because model prediction could thus be enhanced. This test is based on hypothesis testing, and the null hypothesis states that the features are independent of one another. The chi-squared score was calculated with the use of Equation (1):

$$\chi_f^2 = \sum \frac{(O_i - E_i)^2}{E_i} \qquad (1)$$

where f denotes degrees of freedom, O denotes the observed values, and E denotes the expected values.

For the null hypothesis to be rejected, a high chi-squared score is required. Therefore, a high chi-squared value denotes a feature with great sustainability. The top 9 features based on the chi-squared test along with their chi-squared scores are shown in Table 2.

Table 2. Selected features and their chi-squared scores.

Feature	Chi-Squared Score
Specific gravity	28.524025
Albumin	76.082337
Sugar	33.677092
Pus cell clumps	42.000000
Hypertension	144.042405
Diabetes mellitus	137.000000
Coronary artery disease	34.000000
Pedel edema	76.000000
Anemia	60.000000

Figure 5 illustrates the bar graph plot of the chi-squared values of all the features presented in the dataset. We noticed higher values of albumin, diabetes mellitus, coronary artery disease, pedel edema, and anemia, as identified from the corresponding dataset.

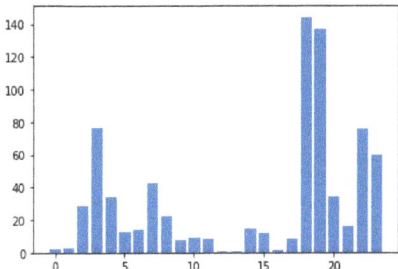

Figure 5. Chi-squared value plot.

3.5. Training and Test Split

The preprocessed dataset containing the selected features was split for model training and evaluation into two parts: training and testing. The training set contained 70% of the records in the preprocessed dataset, whereas the testing set contained 30% of the records. Furthermore, the total number of training samples used was 350.

3.6. Model Training

During the model training phase, the two most efficient machine-learning classifiers, namely support vector machine (SVM) and random forest (RF), were trained using the preprocessed and cleaned dataset. During model training, the hyperparameters for the two algorithms were tuned to boost the performance.

3.6.1. Hyperparameter Tuning

Hyperparameters (HPs) are the set of parameters used to define the model's design and architecture [22]. For an accurate model design, different arrangements of HPs were investigated while preparing the model, and the best arrangement was chosen to characterize the model design. This method of boosting the model accuracy is referred to as hyperparameter tuning (HPT). To find the optimal model design, a search is performed through the various possible sets of HPs.

In this work, regarding HPT, the method of GridSearchCV was implemented in order to find the optimal values of the selected HP values. The workflow of GridSearchCV for the selection of HPs is illustrated in Figure 6.

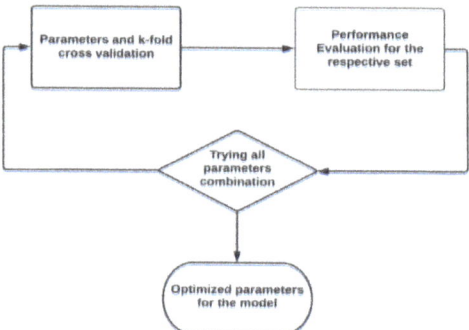

Figure 6. Workflow of GridSearchCV.

3.6.2. Support Vector Machine

The SVM is a widely used and adopted supervised ML algorithm utilized for problems such as classification [23]. The SVM works with the generation of an optimal line known as a hyperplane. The function of this hyperplane is to segregate a given number of dimensions into more than one. As a result, whenever a new data point is to be evaluated, it can be assigned to the most appropriate category. The SVM chooses the point along with a vector representing the extremes for the generation of hyperplanes. These extremes are referred to as support vectors, which is why this algorithm is referred to as SVM [24].

Furthermore, the SVM can be characterized by two HPs, i.e., C and Kernel [23]. The C parameter penalizes a misclassified point in a dataset. A lower value of C implies a low penalty for misclassification, showing that a decision boundary with a relatively higher margin is chosen at the cost of a greater number of wrong classifications.

On the other hand, Kernel is a measure of similarity. This resemblance implies a degree of closeness. Common values of Kernel HP are linear and rbf. Specifically, the values chosen by GridSearchCV were {C: 14, Kernel: rbf}.

rbf stands for radial basis function, and due to its resemblance to the Gaussian distribution, it is among the most commonly utilized types of kernelization. The similarity or degree of proximity between two points, x_1 and x_2, is calculated using the RBF Kernel function. This Kernel's mathematical representation is presented in Equation (2).

$$k(x_1, x_2) = exp(-\frac{||x_1 - x_2||^2}{2\sigma^2})$$ (2)

where σ denotes variance, and $||x_1 - x_2||$ is the Euclidean distance between two points, x_1 and x_2.

3.6.3. Random Forest

The RF constitutes an ensemble method that resembles the closest neighbor predictor in several ways [25]. The divide-and-conquer strategy of ensembles is employed to boost performance. This follows the concept of combining several weak learners to form a robust learner. In the case of RF, the DT algorithm acts as a weak learner that is to be aggregated, and repeatedly divides the dataset using a criterion that optimizes the separation of the data, thus producing a structure resembling a tree. The predictions of unknown inputs after training are calculated using Equation (3) [26].

$$f' = \frac{1}{B} \sum_{b=1}^{B} f_b(x') \tag{3}$$

where B is the optimal number of trees.

The uncertainty σ of the prediction is depicted in Equation (4).

$$\sigma = \sqrt{\frac{\sum_{b=1}^{B}(f_b(x') - f')^2}{B - 1}} \tag{4}$$

HPs that can be used to define the random forest start with a criterion. This parameter is used to estimate the grade of the split. The information gain to be performed for this parameter is channelized using either *entropy* or *gini*.

min_samples_leaf signifies the minimal sample size that must be present in the leaf node after splitting the node, while *min_samples_split* stands for the number of observations required for splitting it. Another important HP is the number of estimators (*n_estimators*), which signifies how dense the random forest is. Moreover, it depicts the number of trees that are to be used to construct the random forest.

The next vital HP in RF is the number of jobs (*n_jobs*), which indicates the restrictions on using the processor, if any. A value that equals −1 indicates the presence of no restrictions on the use of the processor, whereas a value equaling 1 shows that only one processor is to be used.

Random state is a numerical parameter representing the random combination of the training and test split. The values chosen by GridSearchCV were {*criterion*: *gini*, *min_samples_leaf*: 1, *min_samples_split*: 3, *n_estimators*: 16, *n_jobs*: 1, *random_state*: 123}.

4. Results

To establish the effectiveness of the proposed models, the different performance parameters of accuracy, confusion matrix, precision, recall, F1 score, Cohen's kappa coefficient, ROC curve, and cross-validation score were utilized as shown in Tables 3–6 and Figures 7 and 8 [27]. Classifier accuracy is the ratio of successfully identified cases to the total number of instances [28]. Recall signifies the model's efficacy in terms of identification of positive samples, and precision signifies the model's efficacy in identifying the quality of positive cases detected by the classifier [29,30]. The model's effectiveness in terms of both recall and precision is measured by their calculated geometric mean, known as the F1 score. The macro average is the mean of scores, and the weighted average uses the added weight of the count to the scores. The support is the count of records belonging to a specific class in the test dataset. The log loss value is the score of the cross-entropy of the error, and Cohen's kappa coefficient is a measure of the inter-rating.

The PR curve is a plot drawn between true positives and false positives, used to gauge a classifier's sensitivity [29]. The area under the curve (AUC) ranges from 0 to 1 [31]. The higher the AUC score is, i.e., closer to 1, the higher the model's efficacy is. The testing set accuracy of SVM and RF is 99.33% and 98.67%, respectively.

The trained model's generalization capability can be validated using the 10-fold cross validation score. SVM and RF showed the same cross-validation score, equal to 98%. However, in terms of test accuracy and recall score, SVM was more robust than RF. The 10-fold cross-validation of SVM and RF is represented in Figure 8.

Electronics **2023**, *12*, 212

Table 3. Classification report of the trained models, selected features, and their chi-squared scores.

	Support Vector Machine				Random Forest			
	Precision	Recall	F1 Score	Support	Precision	Recall	F1 Score	Support
CKD	0.99	1.00	0.99	76	0.97	1.00	0.99	76
NOT-CKD	1.00	0.99	0.99	74	1.00	0.97	0.99	74
Macro avg	0.99	0.99	0.99	150	0.99	0.99	0.99	150
Weighted avg	0.99	0.99	0.99	150	0.99	0.99	0.99	150

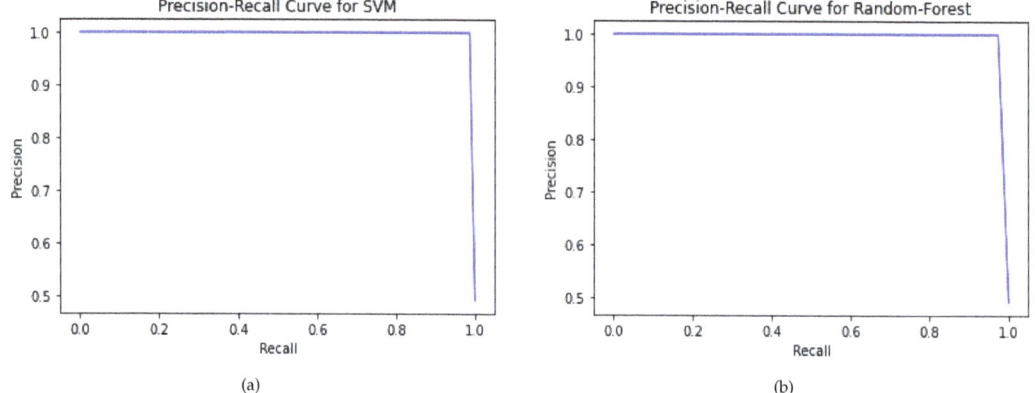

(a)   (b)

Figure 7. Precision and recall curves for (**a**) support vector machine and (**b**) random forest.

Table 4. Confusion matrix for the trained models.

	Support Vector Machine		Random Forest	
	Positive	Negative	Positive	Negative
Positive	76	0	76	0
Negative	1	73	2	72

Table 5. AUC-ROC, log loss value, and Cohen's kappa coefficient.

	Support Vector Machine	Random Forest
AUC-ROC	0.9932	0.9864
Log loss value	0.2303	0.4605
Cohen's kappa	0.9867	0.9733

Table 6. Foldwise score of the trained models.

Support Vector Machine		Random Forest	
Folds	Accuracy (%)	Folds	Accuracy (%)
2	98	2	96.9
3	98	3	97.7
4	98	4	97.7
5	98	5	97.7
6	98	6	97.4
7	98	7	98
8	98	8	97.4
9	98	9	98
10	97.8	10	98

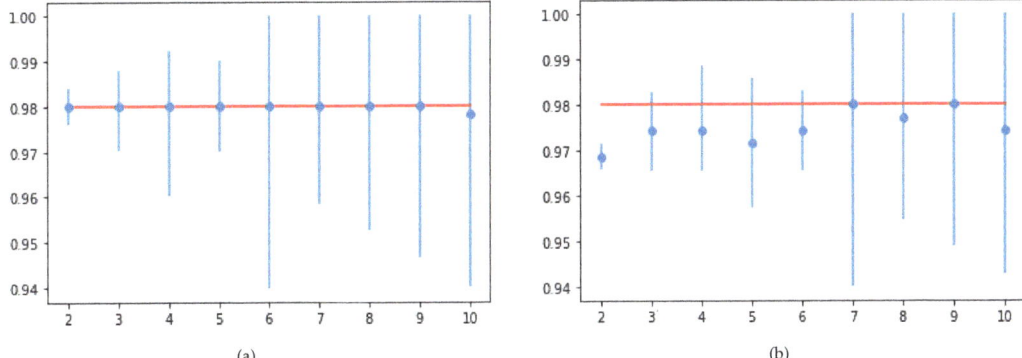

(a) (b)

Figure 8. Plot for foldwise score: (**a**) support vector machine; (**b**) random forest.

5. Comparative Analysis

The comparative analysis presented in Table 7 presents the accuracy achieved in various studies by various authors for CKD classification. The proposed model in our study showed great efficacy in terms of CKD classification with a test accuracy value equal to 99.33% in SVM, and *k*-fold cross validation score equal to 98% [32]. This generalized result compared to that of other works is attributed to several methodologies adopted in this work, such as appropriate data imputation, data balancing, feature scaling, chi-squared-based feature selection, and HPT using GridSearchCV.

Initially, the appropriate data imputation was performed while taking into consideration the outliers present in the numerical features. For the class of numerical features containing outliers, the imputation was performed using the *Mo* (mode) of the respective feature. None of the other corresponding related works considered the outliers that were present in the dataset during the time of imputation.

Second, a major performed step was data balancing with the use of the SMOTE algorithm. The majority of the works listed in the table trained their models on imbalanced data, thus causing a bias in the model. Third, a set of 9 highly correlated features were extracted using the chi-squared score.

A major part of the listed works did not consider feature selection, leading to feeding the classifier with extraneous and irrelevant features. Additionally, the accuracy boosting practice of HPT was performed to find the set of optimal values for the model using GridSearchCV. Lastly, the model's generalization test was performed using 10-fold cross validation, showing a promising score equal to 98%.

Table 7. Comparative analysis of the various studies.

Reference Number	Method	Accuracy (%)
Senan et al. [8]	Random forest	100
Revathy et al. [10]	Random forest	99.16
Chittora et al. [11]	Support vector machine	98.46
Reshma et al. [12]	Support vector machine	96
Cahyani et al. [13]	C4.5 (decision tree)	97.5
Shankar et al. [14]	Random forest	99
Proposed model–SVM		99.33

6. Conclusions and Future Work

A thorough investigation of the performance of various methods regarding chronic kidney disease (CKD) identification was initially performed in this work. Following this investigation, appropriate data preprocessing steps were performed to handle flaws in the CKD dataset such as missing values, imbalanced data, and the presence of outliers; then, an effective SVM model was created by tuning the hyperparameters. The nine most important features for improving the accuracy and other performance parameters were selected. When the model was evaluated on the testing set containing 150 records, it showed promising results, with just 0.67% false negative rates. This method can have real-time application for the accurate diagnosis of the fatal renal condition of chronic kidney disease. Early diagnosis can be performed with the help of this application, eventually leading to a reduction in the mortality rate.

The main novelty of the proposed paper lies with the features used for identification. On the one hand, highly advanced and expensive tests for CKD detection are difficult in rural areas, and on the other hand, the medical examination of the features used in this work is generally available even in rural area's pathology laboratories.

Diagnoses based on MRI and CT scan methods are not always accurate, incur high costs, and are time-consuming. The proposed method had a low false-positive rate and zero false negatives. A diagnosis using the proposed method needs fewer inputs, which reduces the test cost and prediction time. Hence, for rural areas, diagnosis using the proposed method is more feasible as compared to that with conventional MRI and CT scan methods.

Lastly, a possible future scope lies with the achievement of similar or even higher accuracy values with fewer features with the aim to reduce the cost of medical diagnosis even more. For the same purpose of feature selection, rather than classical. statistical methods, hybrid feature selection techniques can also be employed to extract a more general and appropriate set of features. This work can only predict the absence or the presence of the disease. Hence, a more intense dataset can be employed to predict the severity stage of the disease of any patient.

Author Contributions: Conceptualization, D.S., U.M., A.B., H.P., K.P., D.M. and B.A.; methodology, D.S., U.M., A.B., H.P., K.P., D.M. and B.A.; writing—original draft, D.S., U.M., A.B., H.P., K.P., D.M., B.A., V.C.G. and A.K.; writing—review and editing, D.S., U.M., A.B., H.P., K.P., D.M., B.A., V.C.G., A.K. and S.M.; supervision: B.A., V.C.G. and A.K.; project administration: B.A., V.C.G. and A.K. All authors have read and agreed to the published version of the manuscript.

Funding: This research received no external funding.

Data Availability Statement: Not applicable.

Conflicts of Interest: The authors declare no conflict of interest.

References

1. National Kidney Foundation Inc. How Your Kidneys Work. Available online: https://www.kidney.org/kidneydisease/howkidneyswrk (accessed on 11 December 2022).
2. National Institute of Diabetes and Digestive and Kidney Diseases (NIDDK). Chronic Kidzney Disease (CKD). Available online: https://www.niddk.nih.gov/health-information/kidney-disease/chronic-kidney-disease-ckd (accessed on 11 December 2022).
3. Centers for Disease Control and Prevention. Chronic Kidney Disease in the United States, 2021. Available online: https://www.cdc.gov/kidneydisease/publications-resources/CKD-national-facts.html (accessed on 11 December 2022).
4. Levey, A.S.; Atkins, R.; Coresh, J.; Cohen, E.P.; Collins, A.J.; Eckardt, K.U.; Nahas, M.E.; Jaber, B.L.; M.Jadoul.; Levin, A.; et al. Chronic Kidney Disease as a Global Public Health Problem: Approaches and Initiatives—A Position Statement from Kidney Disease Improving Global Outcomes. *Kidney Int.* **2007**, *72*, 247–259. [CrossRef] [PubMed]
5. Gibertoni, D.; Reno, C.; Rucci, P.; Fantini, M.P.; Buscaroli, A.; Mosconi, G.; Rigotti, A.; Giudicissi, A.; Mambelli, E.; Righini, M.; et al. COVID-19 Incidence and Mortality in Non-Dialysis Chronic Kidney Disease Patients. *PLoS ONE* **2021**, *16*, e0254525. [CrossRef] [PubMed]
6. Pawar, N.; Tiwari, V.; Gupta, A.; Bhargava, V.; Malik, M.; Gupta, A.; Bhalla, A.K.; Rana, D.S. COVID-19 in CKD Patients: Report from India. *Indian J. Nephrol.* **2021**, *31*, 524.
7. Garcia, G.G.; Harden, P.; Chapman, J. The Global Role of Kidney Transplantation. *Kidney Blood Press. Res.* **2012**, *35*, 299–304. [CrossRef] [PubMed]
8. Senan, E.M.; Al-Adhaileh, M.H.; Alsaade, F.W.; Aldhyani, T.H.H.; Alqarni, A.A.; Alsharif, N.; Uddin, I.; Alahmadi, A.H.; Jadhav, M.E.; Alzahrani, M.Y. Diagnosis of Chronic Kidney Disease Using Effective Classification Algorithms and Recursive Feature Elimination Techniques. *J. Healthc. Eng.* **2021**, *2021*, 1004767. [CrossRef]
9. Das, D.; Nayak, M.; Pani, S.K. Missing Value Imputation—A Review. *Int. J. Comput. Sci. Eng.* **2019**, *7*, 548–558. [CrossRef]

10. Revathy, S.; Bharathi, B.; Jeyanthi, P.; Ramesh, M. Chronic Kidney Disease Prediction Using Machine Learning Models. *Int. J. Eng. Adv. Technol.* **2019**, *9*, 6364–6367. [CrossRef]
11. Chittora, P.; Chaurasia, S.; Chakrabarti, P.; Kumawat, G.; Chakrabarti, T.; Leonowicz, Z.; Jasiński, M.; Jasinski, L.; Gono, R.; Jasinska, E.; et al. Prediction of Chronic Kidney Disease—A Machine Learning Perspective. *IEEE Access* **2021**, *9*, 17312–17334. [CrossRef]
12. Reshma, S.; Shaji, S.; Ajina, S.R.; Priya, S.R.V.; Janisha, A. Chronic Kidney Disease Prediction using Machine Learning. *Int. J. Eng. Res. Technol.* **2020**, *9*, 548–558. [CrossRef]
13. Cahyani, N.; Muslim, M.A. Increasing Accuracy of C4.5 Algorithm by Applying Discretization and Correlation-based Feature Selection for Chronic Kidney Disease Diagnosis. *J. Telecommun.* **2020**, *12*, 25–32.
14. Shankar, S.; Verma, S.; Elavarthy, S.; Kiran, T.; Ghuli, P. Analysis and Prediction of Chronic Kidney Disease. *Int. Res. J. Eng. Technol.* **2020**, *7*, 4536–4541.
15. UCI Machine Learning Repository. Chronic Kidney Disease Dataset. Available online: https://archive.ics.uci.edu/ml/datasets/chronic_kidney_disease (accessed on 11 December 2022).
16. Kotsiantis, S.; Kanellopoulos, D.; Pintelas, P. Handling Imbalanced Datasets: A Review. *GESTS Int. Trans. Comput. Sci. Eng.* **2006**, *30*, 25–36.
17. Audu, A.; Danbaba, A.; Ahmad, S.K.; Musa, N.; Shehu, A.; Ndatsu, A.M.; Joseph, A.O. On The Efficiency of Almost Unbiased Mean Imputation When Population Mean of Auxiliary Variable is Unknown. *Asian J. Probab. Stat.* **2021**, *15*, 235–250. [CrossRef]
18. Chawla, N.V.; Bowyer, K.W.; Hall, L.O.; Kegelmeyer, W.P. SMOTE: Synthetic Minority Over-sampling Technique. *J. Artif. Intell. Res.* **2002**, *16*, 321–357. [CrossRef]
19. Jain, Y.K.; Bhandare, S.K. Min Max Normalization Based Data Perturbation Method for Privacy Protection. *Int. J. Comput. Commun. Technol.* **2011**, *2*, 45–50. [CrossRef]
20. Guyon, I.; Elisseeff, A. An Introduction to Variable and Feature Selection. *J. Mach. Learn. Res.* **2003**, *3*, 1157–1182.
21. Cai, L.J.; Lv, S.; Shi, K.B. Application of an Improved CHI Feature Selection Algorithm. *Discret. Dyn. Nat. Soc.* **2021**, *2021*, 9963382. [CrossRef]
22. Elgeldawi, E.; Sayed, A.; Galal, A.R.; Zaki, A.M. Hyperparameter Tuning for Machine Learning Algorithms Used for Arabic Sentiment Analysis. *Informatics* **2021**, *8*, 79. [CrossRef]
23. Zhang, Y. Support Vector Machine Classification Algorithm and Its Application. In *International Conference on Information Computing and Applications*; Springer: Berlin/Heidelberg, Germany, 2012; Volume 308, pp. 179–186.
24. Swain, D.; Pani, S.K.; Swain, D. Diagnosis of Coronary Artery Disease using 1-D Convolutional Neural Network. *Int. J. Recent Technol. Eng.* **2019**, *8*.
25. Biau, G. Analysis of a Random Forests Model. *J. Mach. Learn. Res.* **2012**, *13*, 1063–1095.
26. Duan, H.; Liu, X. Lower C Limits in Support Vector Machines with Radial Basis Function Kernels. In Proceedings of the International Symposium on Information Technologies in Medicine and Education, Hokkaido, Japan, 3–5 August 2012; Volume 2, pp. 768–771.
27. Liu, Y.; Zhou, Y.; Wen, S.; Tang, C. A Strategy on Selecting Performance Metrics for Classifier Evaluation. *Int. J. Mob. Comput. Multimed. Commun.* **2014**, *6*, 20–35. [CrossRef]
28. Nishat, M.M.; Faisal, F.; Dip, R.R.; Nasrullah, S.M.; Ahsan, R.; Shikder, F.; Asif, M.A.; Hoque, M.A. A Comprehensive Analysis on Detecting Chronic Kidney Disease by Employing Machine Learning Algorithms. *EAI Endorsed Trans. Pervasive Health Technol.* **2021**, *7*, e1. [CrossRef]
29. Swain, D.; Pani, S.K.; Swain, D. A Metaphoric Investigation on Prediction of Heart Disease using Machine Learning. In Proceedings of the 2018 International Conference on Advanced Computation and Telecommunication (ICACAT), Bhopal, India, 28–29 December 2018; pp. 1–6.
30. Swain, D.; Pani, S.K.; Swain, D. An Efficient System for the Prediction of Coronary Artery Disease using Dense Neural Network with Hyper Parameter Tuning. *Int. J. Innov. Technol. Explor. Eng.* **2019**, *8*, 689–695.
31. Swain, D.; Bijawe, S.S.; Akolkar, P.P.; Shinde, A.; Mahajani, M.V. Diabetic Retinopathy using Image Processing and Deep Learning. *Int. J. Comput. Sci. Math.* **2021**, *14*, 397–409. [CrossRef]
32. Darapureddy, N.; Karatapu, N.; Battula, T.K. Research of Machine Learning Algorithms using K-Fold Cross Validation. *Int. J. Eng. Adv. Technol.* **2021**, *8*, 215–218.

 *electronics*

Editorial

Big Data Analytics Using Artificial Intelligence

Amir H. Gandomi [1,2,*], **Fang Chen** [3] **and Laith Abualigah** [4,5,6,7,8,9,*]

1   Faculty of Engineering & Information Technology, University of Technology Sydney, 15 Broadway, Ultimo, NSW 2007, Australia
2   University Research and Innovation Center (EKIK), Óbuda University, 1034 Budapest, Hungary
3   Data Science Institute, University of Technology Sydney, Ultimo, NSW 2007, Australia
4   Computer Science Department, Prince Hussein Bin Abdullah Faculty for Information Technology, Al Al-Bayt University, Mafraq 25113, Jordan
5   Hourani Center for Applied Scientific Research, Al-Ahliyya Amman University, Amman 19328, Jordan
6   Center for Engineering Application & Technology Solutions, Ho Chi Minh City Open University, Ho Chi Minh 700000, Vietnam
7   Faculty of Information Technology, Middle East University, Amman 11831, Jordan
8   Applied Science Research Center, Applied Science Private University, Amman 11931, Jordan
9   School of Computer Sciences, Universiti Sains Malaysia, Pulau Pinang 11800, Malaysia
*   Correspondence: gandomi@uts.edu.au (A.H.G.); aligah.2020@gmail.com (L.A.)

1. Introduction

Data analytics using artificial intelligence is the process of leveraging advanced AI techniques to extract insights and knowledge from large and complex datasets [1]. This involves utilizing machine learning algorithms, deep learning models, and natural language processing techniques to uncover patterns and relationships within big data that can inform decision making and drive innovation. The goal of big data analytics using AI is to automate data analysis and make the process faster, more accurate, and more scalable, enabling organizations to harness the full potential of their data and gain a competitive advantage.

2. The Present Issue

This Special Issue consists of fourteen articles covering different aspects of machine learning and artificial intelligence.

This study focuses on creating a machine learning model that can predict the likelihood of chronic kidney disease using publicly available data [2]. The data underwent several preprocessing steps, including the imputation of missing values, balancing through the SMOTE algorithm, and scaling of features. The chi-squared test was utilized to select the most relevant and highly correlated features. The machine learning model was built using a combination of supervised learning techniques, with support vector machine (SVM) and random forest (RF) achieving the lowest false-negative rate and highest test accuracy of 99.33% and 98.67%, respectively. SVM was found to perform better than RF upon validation through 10-fold cross-validation.

This study represents the first attempt to examine selected design research publications using a sophisticated method called "text mining" [3]. This method generates results based on the presence of specific research terms (i.e., keywords), which provides a more reliable outcome compared to other approaches that rely on contextual information or authors' perspectives. The primary objective of this research is to increase awareness and understanding of design research, and to identify potential future research directions by addressing gaps in the literature. Based on the literature review, it can be concluded that the field of design research still lacks a unifying theory. Text mining, with its features, enhances the validity and generalizability of the results compared to other methods in the literature. The text mining technique was applied to collect data from 3553 articles from 10 journals, utilizing 17,487 keywords. This research explores new topics in the field of

Citation: Gandomi, A.H.; Chen, F.; Abualigah, L. Big Data Analytics Using Artificial Intelligence. *Electronics* **2023**, *12*, 957. https://doi.org/10.3390/electronics12040957

Received: 6 February 2023
Accepted: 10 February 2023
Published: 15 February 2023

design concepts, drawing the attention of researchers, practitioners, and journal editorial boards. The key categories analyzed and presented in this paper provide insights into the growth and decline in various fields in the domain of design.

This paper presents a novel deep learning approach for detecting student emotions [4]. The main objective of the study is to explore the relationship between teaching practices and student learning, based on emotional impact. The system uses facial recognition algorithms to gather information from online platforms and image classification techniques to identify the emotions of students and teachers. Two deep learning models are compared for their performance, and the results show promising outcomes, as discussed in the Experimental Results section. The proposed system is validated using an online course with students, and the results indicate that the technique operates effectively. Various deep learning techniques are applied for emotional analysis, including transfer learning for a pre-trained deep neural network, which increases the accuracy of the emotion classification stage. The results of the experiment demonstrate that the proposed method is promising, as discussed in the Experimental Results section.

This paper proposes a deep learning solution for detecting masks worn in public to prevent the spread of coronavirus [5]. The system, designed for real-time use with a webcam, utilizes an ensemble method for high accuracy and improved detection speed. Transfer learning on pre-trained models and rigorous testing on objective data resulted in a dependable and cost-effective solution. The findings indicate the effectiveness of the solution in real-world settings, contributing to pandemic control. Compared to existing methods, the proposed solution achieves improved accuracy and performance metrics, such as specificity, precision, recall, and F measure, in three-class outputs. A careful balance is maintained between the number of parameters and processing time.

This study proposes a deep learning method for the classification and analysis of scientific literature using convolutional neural networks (CNNs) [6]. The research is divided into three dimensions, publication features, author features, and content features, with explicit and implicit features forming a set of scientometric terms. The CNN model uses weighted scientometric term vectors to achieve dual-label classification of literature based on its content and methods. The study showcases the effectiveness of the proposed model through an application example from data science and analytics literature, with results showing improved precision, recognition, and F1 score compared to other machine learning classification methods. The proposed scientometric classification model also exhibits higher accuracy than deep learning classification using only explicit and dominant features. This study offers a guide for fine-grained classification of scientific literature and provides insight into its practical application.

This research aims to help science students identify butterfly species without causing harm to the insects during analysis [7]. The study employs transfer learning with neural network models to classify butterfly species based on images. The dataset consists of 10,035 images of 75 butterfly species and 15 unusual species were selected for the study, with various orientations, photography angles, lengths, and backgrounds. The imbalanced class distribution in the dataset resulted in overfitting, which was addressed with data augmentation. Transfer learning was applied using several convolutional neural network architectures, including VGG16, VGG19, MobileNet, Xception, ResNet50, and InceptionV3. The models were evaluated based on precision, recall, F measure, and accuracy. The results showed that the InceptionV3 architecture provided an accuracy of 94.66%, which was superior to all other architectures. This work proposes a new approach for identifying glaucoma from fundus images using a deep belief network (DBN), optimized by the elephant-herding optimization (EHO) algorithm [8]. The system is designed to be tested on various datasets, which can help to improve the accuracy of glaucoma diagnosis.

This paper examines 66 machine learning models using a two-stage evaluation process [9]. The evaluation was performed on a real-world dataset of European credit card frauds and used stratified K-fold cross-validation. Out of 330 evaluation metrics, the All K-Nearest Neighbors (AllKNN) undersampling technique with CatBoost (AllKNN–CatBoost) was found to be the best model, achieving an AUC of 97.94%, recall of 95.91%, and F1 score of 87.40%. The AllKNN–CatBoost model was compared to relevant studies and was found to outperform previous models.

This research presents a hybrid data analytics framework that combines convolutional neural networks and bidirectional long short-term memory (CNN-BiLSTM) to examine the effect of merging news events and sentiment analysis with financial data on stock trend prediction [10]. Two real-world case studies were conducted using data from the Dubai Financial Market between 1 January 2020 and 1 December 2021, in the real estate and communications sectors. The results demonstrate that incorporating news events and sentiment analysis with financial data improves the accuracy of stock trend prediction. The CNN–BiLSTM model achieved an improvement of 11.6% in the real estate sector and 25.6% in communications compared to benchmarked machine learning models.

This study introduces a four-layer model and proposes a hybrid imputation method (HIMP) for filling in multi-pattern missing data, including non-random, random, and completely random patterns [11]. HIMP starts by imputing non-random missing data patterns and then dividing the resulting dataset into two datasets with random and completely random missing data patterns. Next, different imputation methods are applied to each dataset based on the missing data pattern. The final dataset is created by merging the best imputed datasets from random and completely random patterns. The effectiveness of HIMP was evaluated using a real dataset named IRDia that had all three missing data patterns. HIMP was compared to other methods using accuracy, precision, recall, and F1 score with different classifiers, and the results showed that HIMP outperformed other methods in imputing multi-pattern missing values.

This paper presents a new Whale Optimization Algorithm (EWOA) to solve Optimal Power Flow (OPF) problems, with the aim of improving exploration capability and maintaining a balance between exploration and exploitation [12]. The movement strategy of whales in the EWOA is improved through the introduction of two new techniques: (1) encircling the target using Levy motion and (2) searching for the target using Brownian motion, which work in conjunction with the traditional bubble-net attacking method. To evaluate the performance of EWOA-OPF, it is compared with six well-known optimization algorithms in solving both single- and multi-objective OPF problems under system constraints. The comparison results show that the EWOA-OPF outperforms the other algorithms and provides better solutions for both single- and multi-objective OPF problems.

In this review, the authors examine the advancements and applications of the Harris Hawk Optimizer (HHO), a robust optimization technique that has gained popularity in recent years [13]. Through experiments conducted on the Congress on Evolutionary Computation (CEC2005) and CEC2017, HHO is compared to nine other state-of-the-art algorithms, showing its efficacy and effectiveness. The paper provides a comprehensive overview of HHO and delves into future directions and areas for further investigation of new variants of the algorithm and its widespread use.

This paper provides a comprehensive overview of effective communication techniques for space exploration of ground, aerial, and underwater vehicles [14]. The study not only summarizes the challenges faced in trajectory planning, space exploration, optimization, and other areas, but also highlights the future directions for research. Aiming to fill the gap in the literature for those interested in path planning, this paper includes optimization strategies for terrestrial, underwater, and airborne applications. The study covers numerical, bio-inspired, and hybrid methodologies for each dimension discussed. The goal of this paper is to establish a centralized platform for publishing research on autonomous vehicles on land and their trajectory optimizations, airborne vehicles, and underwater vehicles.

This review looks at the drawbacks of traditional TB diagnostic methods and provides a comprehensive overview of various machine learning algorithms and their use in TB diagnosis [15]. It also examines the integration of deep learning techniques with other systems, such as neuro-fuzzy logic, genetic algorithms, and artificial immune systems.

Finally, the review highlights several cutting-edge tools, such as CAD4TB, Lunit INSIGHT, qXR, and InferRead DR Chest, which are shaping the future of AI-assisted TB diagnosis.

3. Future Directions

The future of Big Data Analytics using Artificial Intelligence is expected to follow several key directions, including:

- Real-time analytics: the increasing demand for real-time insights and decision making will drive the development of AI-powered big data analytics platforms that can process large volumes of data in near real time.
- Edge analytics: with the proliferation of IoT devices, there will be a growing need for edge analytics, where data are analyzed and processed at the source, reducing the need for data to be transferred to centralized data centers.
- Explainable AI: as AI-powered analytics become more widespread, there will be a growing need for explainable AI, where the reasoning behind AI-generated insights and predictions is made transparent and understandable.
- Integration with other technologies: the integration of AI-powered big data analytics with other technologies, such as cloud computing, blockchain, and quantum computing, will enable organizations to take full advantage of the potential of big data.
- Personalized analytics: the development of AI algorithms that can tailor insights and predictions to specific individuals and organizations will drive the growth of personalized analytics, making big data analytics even more accessible and relevant.

These are some of the key directions that the future of big data analytics using AI is expected to take, enabling organizations to leverage the full potential of their data and drive innovation and growth.

Author Contributions: Conceptualization, A.H.G., F.C. and L.A.; formal analysis, A.H.G., F.C. and L.A.; writing—original draft preparation, A.H.G., F.C. and L.A.; writing—review and editing, A.H.G., F.C. and L.A.; supervision, A.H.G., F.C. and L.A.; project administration, A.H.G., F.C. and L.A. All authors have read and agreed to the published version of the manuscript.

Funding: This research received no external funding.

Data Availability Statement: Not Applicable.

Acknowledgments: I would like to express my gratitude to all the researchers who submitted articles for this Special Issue and made outstanding contributions. My appreciation goes to the reviewers as well, who played a crucial role in evaluating the manuscripts and offering insightful suggestions to enhance the quality of the contributions. I recognize the editorial board of *Electronics* for granting me the opportunity to guest edit this Special Issue. Lastly, I am grateful to the *Electronics* Editorial Office staff for their dedication in maintaining a rigorous peer-review process and ensuring timely publication.

Conflicts of Interest: The authors declare no conflict of interest.

References

1. Gandomi, A.H.; Chen, F.; Abualigah, L. Machine Learning Technologies for Big Data Analytics. *Electronics* **2022**, *11*, 421. [CrossRef]
2. Swain, D.; Mehta, U.; Bhatt, A.; Patel, H.; Patel, K.; Mehta, D.; Acharya, B.; Gerogiannis, V.C.; Kanavos, A.; Manika, S. A Robust Chronic Kidney Disease Classifier Using Machine Learning. *Electronics* **2023**, *12*, 212. [CrossRef]
3. Nusir, M.; Louati, A.; Louati, H.; Tariq, U.; Abu Zitar, R.; Abualigah, L.; Gandomi, A.H. Design Research Insights on Text Mining Analysis: Establishing the Most Used and Trends in Keywords of Design Research Journals. *Electronics* **2022**, *11*, 3930. [CrossRef]
4. AlZu'bi, S.; Abu Zitar, R.; Hawashin, B.; Abu Shanab, S.; Zraiqat, A.; Mughaid, A.; Almotairi, K.H.; Abualigah, L. A Novel Deep Learning Technique for Detecting Emotional Impact in Online Education. *Electronics* **2022**, *11*, 2964. [CrossRef]
5. Ai, M.A.S.; Shanmugam, A.; Muthusamy, S.; Viswanathan, C.; Panchal, H.; Krishnamoorthy, M.; Elminaam, D.S.A.; Orban, R. Real-Time Facemask Detection for Preventing COVID-19 Spread Using Transfer Learning Based Deep Neural Network. *Electronics* **2022**, *11*, 2250. [CrossRef]
6. Daradkeh, M.; Abualigah, L.; Atalla, S.; Mansoor, W. Scientometric Analysis and Classification of Research Using Convolutional Neural Networks: A Case Study in Data Science and Analytics. *Electronics* **2022**, *11*, 2066. [CrossRef]

7. Fathimathul Rajeena, P.P.; Orban, R.; Vadivel, K.S.; Subramanian, M.; Muthusamy, S.; Elminaam, D.S.A.; Nabil, A.; Abualigah, L.; Ahmadi, M.; Ali, M.A. A novel method for the classification of butterfly species using pre-trained CNN models. *Electronics* **2022**, *11*, 2016. [CrossRef]

8. Ali, M.A.S.; Balasubramanian, K.; Krishnamoorthy, G.D.; Muthusamy, S.; Pandiyan, S.; Panchal, H.; Mann, S.; Thangaraj, K.; El-Attar, N.E.; Abualigah, L.; et al. Classification of Glaucoma Based on Elephant-Herding Optimization Algorithm and Deep Belief Network. *Electronics* **2022**, *11*, 1763. [CrossRef]

9. Alfaiz, N.S.; Fati, S.M. Enhanced Credit Card Fraud Detection Model Using Machine Learning. *Electronics* **2022**, *11*, 662. [CrossRef]

10. Daradkeh, M.K. A Hybrid Data Analytics Framework with Sentiment Convergence and Multi-Feature Fusion for Stock Trend Prediction. *Electronics* **2022**, *11*, 250. [CrossRef]

11. Nadimi-Shahraki, M.H.; Mohammadi, S.; Zamani, H.; Gandomi, M.; Gandomi, A.H. A Hybrid Imputation Method for Multi-Pattern Missing Data: A Case Study on Type II Diabetes Diagnosis. *Electronics* **2021**, *10*, 3167. [CrossRef]

12. Nadimi-Shahraki, M.H.; Taghian, S.; Mirjalili, S.; Abualigah, L.; Elaziz, M.A.; Oliva, D. EWOA-OPF: Effective Whale Optimization Algorithm to Solve Optimal Power Flow Problem. *Electronics* **2021**, *10*, 2975. [CrossRef]

13. Hussien, A.G.; Abualigah, L.; Abu Zitar, R.; Hashim, F.A.; Amin, M.; Saber, A.; Almotairi, K.H.; Gandomi, A.H. Recent Advances in Harris Hawks Optimization: A Comparative Study and Applications. *Electronics* **2022**, *11*, 1919. [CrossRef]

14. Mir, I.; Gul, F.; Mir, S.; Khan, M.A.; Saeed, N.; Abualigah, L.; Abuhaija, B.; Gandomi, A.H. A Survey of Trajectory Planning Techniques for Autonomous Systems. *Electronics* **2022**, *11*, 2801. [CrossRef]

15. Singh, M.; Pujar, G.V.; Kumar, S.A.; Bhagyalalitha, M.; Akshatha, H.S.; Abuhaija, B.; Alsoud, A.R.; Abualigah, L.; Beeraka, N.M.; Gandomi, A.H. Evolution of Machine Learning in Tuberculosis Diagnosis: A Review of Deep Learning-Based Medical Applications. *Electronics* **2022**, *11*, 2634. [CrossRef]

MDPI

St. Alban-Anlage 66

4052 Basel

Switzerland

www.mdpi.com

Electronics Editorial Office

E-mail: electronics@mdpi.com

www.mdpi.com/journal/electronics